The New Model Army

ON REFERENCE

To my mother and father

The New Model Army
in England, Ireland and Scotland, 1645–1653

Ian Gentles

BLACKWELL
Oxford UK & Cambridge USA

First published 1992
Reprinted 1994

Blackwell Publishers
108 Cowley Road, Oxford, OX4 1JF, UK

238 Main Street
Cambridge, Massachusetts 02142, USA

British Library Cataloguing in Publication Data
A CIP catalogue record for this book is available from the British Library.

Library of Congress Cataloging-in-Publication Data
Gentles, I. J.
The new model army in England, Ireland and Scotland, 1645–1653 /
Ian Gentles.
p.   cm.
Includes bibliographical references and index.
ISBN 0–631–15869–3   0–631–19347–2 (pbk.)
1. Great Britain – History – Puritan Revolution, 1642–1660.
2. Great Britain – History, Military – 17th century.   3. Great
Britain. Army – History – 17th century.   I. Title.
DA405.G46   1992
941.06'2–dc20   90–28320   CIP

Typeset in 10 on 12 pt Sabon
by Graphicraft Typesetters Ltd., Hong Kong

Contents

Contents

Maps

Illustrations

Preface

This is the fourth book about the army of Sir Thomas Fairfax and Oliver Cromwell to appear in the twentieth century. In 1902 C. H. Firth published *Cromwell's Army*. This valuable study anatomized the army's pay, feeding and equipment, as well as its conduct of sieges and use of artillery. But it gave no connected account of the army's experience on the battlefield, nor of its lengthy involvement in the high politics of the revolutionary era. Nor did Firth attend to the army's relations with the civilian population, though he did include valuable chapters on discipline and religion. In collaboration with Godfrey Davies, Firth also published posthumously the *Regimental History of Cromwell's Army* (2 vols, Clarendon Press, Oxford, 1940). Apart from the occasional error it provides a reliable detailed history of each New Model regiment and its successor in the 1650s. All the regiments' military exploits are separately chronicled, and almost every officer of the rank of captain or higher is identified. While a mine of information for scholars, it is in truth a dismal book, since it says nothing about the history of the army as a whole. Significantly it has never been reprinted, in contrast to *Cromwell's Army*, which has had four editions, the most recent, in 1962, with a fine bibliographical introduction by Paul Hardacre.

In 1979 Mark Kishlansky produced *The Rise of the New Model Army*. Vigorously revisionist in approach, it flatly denies that there was much distinctive about the army. Kishlansky's historical method is to exclude evidence that does not originate in the years about which he writes (1645–7). Besides telling the story of the army and its early career, he seeks to refashion our understanding of the politics of the civil war. The Self-Denying Ordinance and the New Model Army, he argues, were the final product of consensus politics, and the army gained no radical consciousness until the spring of 1647. The Levellers exercised little influence in the army's councils, while the soldiers' chief concern was to vindicate its honour, indemnify its members against legal reprisals at the hands of civilians, and secure its back pay. Religion played a minor explanatory role in the army's political history.

In writing my own book I have benefited greatly from the ground-breaking work of C. H. Firth and the close analysis of Kishlansky. Aside from offering fresh interpretations at certain points, I have had a different goal from that of either previous author. I have set out to write a connected account of the army's military and political career from the time of its founding to the summoning of Barebone's Parliament in July 1653. At the same time I have probed deeper than Firth was able to do into recruitment, pay, provisioning and discipline, as well as the role of religion in shaping its peculiar identity. I have also investigated the army's relations with civilian society. Whether I have succeeded in capturing the complex, many-faceted character of the army is for the reader to decide.

Over the decade which it took to write this book I have incurred many debts of gratitude which it is a pleasure to acknowledge. Austin Woolrych has been a wonderful mentor and friend; he has read almost every word of the manuscript, offered many valuable criticisms, and helped me to avoid a number of pitfalls. John Morrill has also read much of the book, argued with me about it, and given much stimulating criticism. He and his wife Frances have furnished excellent hospitality during many visits to Cambridge. My tutor Ian Roy has shared freely his enormous erudition about the military history of the interregnum.

Others who have read various chapters and offered constructive criticism include Gerald Aylmer, Blair Worden, Keith Wrightson, Bob Tittler, Paul Christianson, Clive Holmes, Paul Hardacre, Barbara Donagan, Barbara Taft, Ronald Hutton, Murray Tolmie and John Adamson. Derek Massarella and Henry Reece have generously shared with me their detailed knowledge of army affairs from 1647 to 1660. The members of the English History Research Group in Toronto have cheerfully allowed me to inflict on them first drafts of several chapters, and have retaliated with a good deal of searching, though always friendly, criticism. I am especially grateful to John Beattie, David Levine, Michael Finlayson, Doug Hay, Nicholas Rogers, Jeanette Neeson, Donna Andrew, Sarah Mendelson, Jim Alsop and John Morgan. Of course, none of this army of amiable critics is responsible for any errors which remain.

The scope of the book could not have attained its present breadth had it not been for Stephen Porter. In him I was fortunate to find the best research assistant that anyone could ask for.

I am grateful to the trustees of His Grace, the Duke of Northumberland for kind permission to quote from the MSS at Alnwick Castle, to the trustees of Dr Williams's Library for permission to quote from Thomas

Juxon's Diary, and to Mrs J. Mary D. Foster for permission to quote from William Clarke's account book in the Library of the Thoresby Society.

The staffs of the Public Record Office, the British Library, the Institute of Historical Research, Dr Williams's Library, the House of Lords Record Office, the Bodleian Library, the Cambridge University Library and a host of local record offices and repositories were uniformly courteous and efficient in helping me to locate the books and manuscripts I needed for my research. Everyone who has had the pleasure of working on the pamphlet and manuscript collections of the army's secretary William Clarke will know why I make special mention of Lesley Le Claire, the librarian of Worcester College. For her hospitality, endless patience and many lively conversations about the civil war I am most grateful. I am also indebted to Frances McDonald for help with William Clarke's shorthand. The maps were drawn by Carolyn King of the Department of Cartography, York University. The staff of the Research Office, Glendon College, handled a great quantity of typing. I also owe a great debt of gratitude to the editorial staff of Basil Blackwell, in particular to John Davey, Virginia Murphy, Jan Chamier, Graham Eyre and Ginny Stroud-Lewis.

The Social Sciences and Humanities Research Council of Canada provided several grants which enabled me to travel to England. Glendon College generously allowed me sabbatical and research leave during which much of the book was written. If there is a scholar's paradise on earth it is the Huntington Library in San Marino, California. I thank the trustees for permitting me to experience that paradise through a research fellowship in the winter of 1988.

My family have been patient and understanding during the years it took to complete this book. I am especially thankful to my wife, Sandy, for never losing faith, as well to Stephen and Peter for their not always unwelcome interruptions. My parents have given of themselves in more ways than they can know. In love and gratitude I dedicate this book to them.

Note Spelling has been modernised, while dates are old style, except that the year is taken to begin on 1 January.

Map 1 The principal battles in Great Britain and Ireland, 1645–53

1

The Founding of the New Model Army

God seems not to favour the great officers. Certainly we are ill served by them.[1]

Throughout the autumn and winter of 1644–5 parliament supporters were sunk in a slough of despond as they wrestled with the problem of how to restore lost momentum to their war against the king. But little over a year later their new army would carry all before it with a breathtaking roll call of victories, culminating in the surrender of the king's forces in all parts of the kingdom. How did this astonishing turn in the wheel of parliamentary fortunes come about? At the time men attributed it to divine providence smiling upon the efforts of humble soldiers.[2] Parliament's enemies took a more jaundiced view, blaming the incompetence or stupidity of their own commanders.[3]

The first historian of the English Revolution, the Earl of Clarendon, saw the foundation of the New Model Army as a great alteration in parliament's war effort. Hatched by Vane and Cromwell, and promoted by their Independent followers, the scheme's objective was to purge the lukewarm leadership of Essex and Manchester. Those who disagreed with the scheme were increasingly driven into the peace-party camp. While attributing the New Model's success principally to the folly and faction of the king's counsellors, Clarendon recognized the discipline of Cromwell's cavalry as a telling factor, but he did not address the question of how this discipline was achieved.[4]

In the nineteenth century Cromwell's first editor, Thomas Carlyle, asserted that the New Model Army marked the start of 'an entirely new epoch' in parliament's affairs, but he did not explain his assertion.[5] Half a century later S. R. Gardiner noted that the new army's success had more than a little to do with its superior numbers and provisioning; yet he also regarded it as an army very different from its predecessors. Not only was it a united force dedicated to parliament's interest, it was infected with religious zeal and a desire for liberty of conscience; in short it was pervaded by a revolutionary spirit.[6] More judiciously, Gardiner's pupil C. H. Firth pointed out that at its founding the New Model was composed of men from the three existing armies, as well as a large number of infantry conscripts. In its early months the army was plagued with desertion, while religious zealots were a small minority, and chaplains few in number. Only in 1647, two years after its founding, were the zealots able to take decisive control of the army and mould it into an instrument of godliness.[7] Writing several decades after Firth, W. C. Abbott, Cromwell's second editor, echoed the view first propounded by Gardiner, that the New Model was essentially 'Cromwell's' army. At its core were the Ironsides. This double regiment, recruited, drilled and equipped by Oliver himself, was the yeast that leavened the whole lump. It was they who imparted to their more apathetic brethren the discipline and fervour for which they had already made themselves famous. With Cromwell at its head the New Model cavalry became 'the most formidable body of fighting men in the British Isles, if not indeed in Europe or the world.' A leader superior to Prince Rupert, Cromwell was as great an innovator in the sphere of cavalry tactics as Gustavus Adolphus was in artillery.[8]

More recently Christopher Hill, in words reminiscent of Carlyle, has stated that 'there had never been anything like the New Model Army before.' Socially representative of the English people, the army was characterized by freedom of organization and discussion, and was 'a hothouse of political ideas.'[9] In contrast to Hill, Mark Kishlansky in *The Rise of the New Model Army* offers a thoroughly revisionist interpretation. He vigorously rejects the notion that there was anything distinctive, much less unique, about the new army. It was founded on conservative military principles, and its appearance marked the last triumph of consensus politics in the history of the Long Parliament. In composition, form and finance it differed little from its predecessors. It functioned much like the armies it replaced, and was plagued with the familiar problems of under-recruitment, desertion, absenteeism and pay arrears. Religion was of minor political importance in an army characterized by 'secular domination'. Radical religion was unconnected with the radical political activity of 1647; nor was there any link between the religious convictions of a zealous minority and the army's morale and success in battle.[10] Kishlansky's revisionism has been immensely stimulating, but some of his boldest interpretations have been greeted with scepticism.[11]

In chapters 1–4 I undertake a fresh scrutiny of the events and human motivations that together produced the new army; review its experiences in battle; and attempt to lay bare the relationship between the army's morale or *esprit de corps* and its religion. This, I hope, will help to clarify, if it does not resolve, the debate that continues to animate historians.

The Quarrel between Cromwell, Manchester and Essex

The desperate state of parliament's war against the king had arisen very suddenly. In the summer of 1644, parliament, with the help of the Scots, had delivered a stunning defeat to the king's forces at Marston Moor. Almost before the smoke had cleared from the battlefield, however, things began to go wrong, as the generals proved unable to follow up the victory. By the autumn it seemed as if the war effort against the king had become completely unravelled. After his humiliation at Cropredy Bridge, Sir William Waller's army had disintegrated, and he had retired to London; the Earl of Essex had been compelled to surrender at Lostwithiel; and in October the Earl of Manchester had failed to stop the relief of Donnington Castle by a royalist force half the size of his own. This dismal record of failure had its natural consequence: discord and discontent within the armies, in parliament, and in London, as people cast about for someone to blame. Wide cracks disfigured the fragile façade of parliamentary unity. The fissures appeared along the lines that had already been laid down the previous winter (1643–4): the tensions between Scots and English, presbyterians and sectaries, war group and peace group.[12] These tensions, which pitted Oliver Cromwell and his friends against the Earl of Manchester and his Scottish major-general, Lawrence Crawford, were of long standing. In the summer of 1641, for example, Cromwell and Manchester had clashed bitterly over the drainage of the Somersham fen;[13] and in February 1644, it was alleged, Cromwell had circulated a petition in the Eastern Association army calling for the expulsion of all who were not 'Brownists or of such like sects'. When some officers refused to sign the petition they were subjected to intimidation.[14]

A strict adherent of the Solemn League and Covenant, Crawford suspended Lieutenant William Packer, who had expounded Baptist views. Cromwell rose eloquently to Packer's defence, but Manchester backed Crawford, who from that time onward gathered around him the presbyterian officers whom Cromwell had aggrieved, or who sought to escape his domination.[15] The victory of the parliamentary armies at Marston Moor, which might have been expected to soften the discord, only hardened it. As the Scots commissioner Robert Baillie reported, the Independents cried up Oliver Cromwell as the hero of the battle, causing fierce resentment among the Scots at the neglect of General Alexander Leslie's contribution.[16] During the succeeding months the split in Manchester's army broadened to a gaping chasm. Its chief cause was Manchester's sudden, perplexing loss of appetite for fighting the king. Paradoxically his altered attitude may have been due to the result at Marston Moor, which for the first time opened up the prospect of total victory.[17] The moderate earl, who had hoped all along for a negotiated peace that would preserve parliament and extinguish the incipient flames of social revolution, was appalled. Moreover, he was acutely conscious of the unpredictable dangers of the battlefield. Thus his famous statement to the council of war before Donnington Castle: 'if we beat the king ninety-nine times he would be king still, and his posterity; and we subjects still. But if he beat us once we should be hanged and our posterity undone.'[18]

Manchester's growing caution manifested itself in a deliberate policy of inactivity.[19] To vent their frustration against their idle commander-in-chief, Cromwell and his allies launched a purge against their foes. Officers unacceptable to the tolerationists were cashiered, though the attempt to drive out Major-General Crawford foundered on Manchester's resistance.[20] Cromwell now rapidly became disenchanted with the earl as well as his major-general of foot.

After the combined armies of Manchester, Essex and Waller failed to crush the numerically far inferior royalist army at the second battle of Newbury, or to engage the king at Donnington Castle, the Committee of Both Kingdoms expressed bitter disappointment, while public opinion in London blamed Manchester, Crawford and Balfour.[21]

With the end of the fighting season the parliamentary commanders were now free to carry on their quarrel by other means. In the Commons Cromwell and Waller launched an attack on Manchester's military conduct, aiming to secure his removal as commander-in-chief of the Eastern Association. On 25 November 1644 the house spent a good part of the day hearing Cromwell's allegations. They were referred to the Committee for the Army chaired by Zouch Tate for further examination and a speedy report back to the house.[22] In the Lords seven days later Manchester delivered an equally forceful indictment of Cromwell's military record, at the same time raising the alarm against Cromwell's religious and political radicalism.[23] Acknowledging that the trend of public opinion was running heavily against him, he denied being 'a discountenancer of honest and godly men'. Always, he maintained, he had shown respect even to those with whom he disagreed; the intolerant one was Cromwell,

> for his expressions were sometimes against the nobility, that he hoped to live to see never a noble man in England, and he loved such better than others because they did not love lords. He hath further expressed himself with contempt of the Assembly of Divines, to whom I pay a reverence, as to the most learned and godly convention that hath been this many ages, yet these he

termed persecutors. And that they persecuted honester men then themselves. His animosity against the Scottish nation ... was such as he told me, that ... he could as soon draw his sword against them as against any in the king's army. And he grew so pressing for his designs as he told me that he would not deny but that he desired to have none in my army but such as were of the Independent judgement, giving me this reason: that in case there should be propositions for peace or any conclusion of a peace such as might not stand with those ends that honest men should aim at, this army might prevent such a mischief.[24]

Denzil Holles's report to the Commons on 4 December of Manchester's counter-charge to Cromwell's accusations provoked a long debate which resulted in the creation of a large committee chaired by John Lisle to investigate the allegations and consider whether a breach of privilege had been committed.[25]

In London it was clearly understood that the quarrel was about more than military competence and obedience. It was perceived to have sprung from the antagonism between the win-the-war and peace groups, and to have been made more bitter by religious difference.[26] In the weeks following Cromwell's and Manchester's mutual accusations a fierce conflict raged behind the scenes between the two factions. As early as 25 November it was known that a remodelling of the armies was planned. The general awareness of this fact explains the intense jockeying for position that marked the days leading up to the introduction of the Self-Denying Ordinance.[27] The quarrel between Manchester and Cromwell was common knowledge; what was less well known was that Cromwell had an even more dangerous enemy in the Earl of Essex.

One night around the beginning of December Essex summoned to his house in the Strand the Scots commissioners, and MPs Denzil Holles, Sir Philip Stapleton, Sir John Meyrick, Bulstrode Whitelocke and John Maynard. The meeting marks an important shift in political alignment in the Long Parliament. The Scots, hitherto supporters of the war faction in parliament, had by now decisively switched their support to the peace party. The middle group was at the same time in a process of disintegration, with some of its members gravitating to the war, others to the peace faction. During the ensuing months the war faction would come to be known as the Independents, while the peace party would acquire the label 'presbyterian'. It should be borne in mind that most MPs did not identify themselves with any political grouping.[28] The purpose of the meeting at Essex's house was to frame a plan to bring down Oliver Cromwell by having him indicted as an incendiary.[29] Holles and Stapleton were keen to launch an action at once. Whitelocke, an admirer of Essex, was asked for his advice on the legal practicality of the scheme. Sidestepping the question,

Whitelocke urged tactical caution. When it came to political manoeuvre no one was more adroit than Oliver Cromwell, 'a gentleman of quick and subtle parts'.[30] Furthermore, because of his numerous friends in both houses, he was not someone to be trifled with. John Maynard echoed Whitelocke's views. The Scots commissioners, impressed by these men's judicious approach, drew back.[31]

In the Committee for the Army Cromwell and his friends pulled out all the stops in their campaign to convict Manchester of military incompetence, unwillingness to fight the king, and contempt of parliament. Nathaniel Rich, Valentine Wauton, Thomas Hammond, Sir William Waller, Sir Arthur Hesilrige, John Pickering, Henry Ireton, Edward Whalley and John Disbrowe joined the chorus which denounced the earl's dilatoriness.[32] To their enemies their intentions were crystal clear: a 'high and mighty plot of the Independent party to have gotten an army for themself under Cromwell.'[33]

The Self-Denying Ordinance

The combination of the armies' indifferent record since the summer of 1644, and their officers' incorrigible tendency to fracture along political and religious lines provided compelling reasons for establishing a new military dispensation. Men whose overriding motive was to win the war against the king came to grasp the advantages of wiping the slate clean. At the same time those whose orientation was more ideological, whose agenda more hidden, saw that great political gains could be made by a thorough shaking-up of the existing leadership and structure.[34]

On 9 December members crowded into the House of Commons to hear Zouch Tate, a presbyterian supporter of the war party, report from the Committee for the Army that the chief causes of division were 'pride and covetousness'. Following a long debate, the house moved into committee of the whole, 'where there was a general silence for a good space of time, many looking upon one another to see who would break the ice, and speak first in so tender and so sharp a point.' Then Oliver Cromwell rose to his feet. With a show of magnanimity he admitted that he had been guilty of oversights, along with the other commanders on the battlefield. However, the time had come for all to put aside their private interests for the public good. Being deliberately vague, he suggested 'that if the army be not put into another method, and the war more vigorously prosecuted, the people can bear the war no longer, and will enforce you to a dishonourable peace.' Another speaker echoed his argument, asserting that more damaging than financial exhaustion and the wasted state of the country was the divided leadership of parliament's armies.[35] The stage had been set for Tate to introduce his resolution, seconded by the war-party spokesman, Sir Henry Vane junior,

> that during the time of this war, no member of either house shall have or execute any office or command, military or civil, granted or conferred by both or either of the Houses of Parliament or any authority derived from both or either of the houses, and that an ordinance be brought in accordingly.[36]

On the same day it was decided to hold a public fast, evidently to generate support for the new measure. The fast was kept by both houses in Lincoln's Inn Chapel, to which only parliamentarians were admitted.[37]

The eight members nominated to bring in the ordinance embodying the resolution reflect the slight preponderance of the war-party–middle-group alliance at this juncture: Oliver St John, John Glyn, John Crewe, William Pierrepont, John Maynard, Robert Reynolds, William Ellis and John Lisle.[38] But the resolution had appeal for peace advocates as well. It defused their criticism that too many people in parliament were profiting from the war, and therefore had a vested interest in its continuation. In October the Committee of Privileges had been asked to investigate the employments of MPs. Two weeks later a committee dominated by the peace party was called upon to inquire into the offices bestowed on all members of both houses. In one way the concept of self-denial might be seen as a ploy by the peace group to embarrass the militants. By alleging that MPs were profiting from the war they had cast serious doubt on the motives of those who called for a more vigorous military effort.[39]

Nevertheless, war-party members were surprised when the Commons actually approved the principle of self-denial.[40] The opposition had been caught off guard. 'As yet it seems a dream', Robert Baillie confided to one of his correspondents, 'and the bottom of it is not understood.'[41] Several London newsbook editors congratulated the MPs on their statesmanship and impartiality in giving up their commands in order to achieve reconciliation and put an end to accusations of self-interested behaviour.[42] In London however there was a clear awareness of the political implications of the proposed ordinance. On the day that Tate introduced his resolution the citizens awoke to find a broadside attacking Manchester and Essex scattered about the streets. Both were accused of being on the king's side. 'One [Essex?] hath made use of rogues, cutpurses, players, peddlers and tinkers to forward a Reformation, and the other [Manchester?] hath culled out all the honestest youth in the Kingdom to keep them from actions, or for slaughter.'[43]

Three days later a petition was presented from the City congratulating the Commons for their vote of 9 December. Henry Walker, the editor of

Perfect Occurrences, felt constrained to assure his readers that the petition had been submitted not by Brownists or Anabaptists, 'but honest, able, godly and conscientious men, such as are ready to venture their estates, lives and all they have, in defence of the parliament.'[44] In the same vein the editor of the *Kingdomes Weekly Intelligencer* referred to the popular objection that '… your Anabaptists and Brownists shall now command.' In reply he pointed out that Cromwell was to be excluded along with the others, and had already announced his willingness to resign.[45] The fact that editors felt called upon to make such statements suggests a widespread perception that the ordinance was a radical manoeuvre. From another newsbook we have the names of the twenty-four commanders who stood to lose their commissions under the ordinance. Seven were peers; the rest commoners. Well under half of them – Ferdinando Lord Fairfax, Sir William Waller, Sir William Brereton, Oliver Cromwell, Valentine Wauton, William Purefoy, Sir Arthur Hesilrige, Isaac Pennington, John Ven, and Anthony Stapley – were either war-party or middle-group supporters in 1644–5, or men who would become known as Independents or revolutionaries in 1647–8. Four of the lords to be eliminated would enter their dissents to the list of officers approved in March. A fifth – the Earl of Warwick – opposed it but failed to enter his dissent. A sixth peer – Lord Robartes – was an Essex supporter.[46] Not too much significance needs to be attached to the fact that war-party and middle-group supporters suffered less from the Self-Denying Ordinance than supporters of the peace group. We cannot know how many of the latter became adherents to the peace group *because* of their exclusion. On the other hand it may be significant that while only two of the moderate or peace-party commanders would be reappointed after the passage of the New Model Ordinance (Jephson and Middleton), at least five of the war-party commanders (Brereton, Cromwell, Purefoy, Hesilrige and Wauton) would find their way back into the army.[47]

The question of which faction would gain or lose by the passage of the ordinance cannot have escaped the attention of parliamentarians. After being read a second time it was moved into committee of the whole, where it was debated at length. The debate was then adjourned to 17 December, when it ran into heavy weather. Turbulence was stirred up by a proposal to exempt the Earl of Essex from the provisions of the ordinance. There was also apparently considerable sentiment for exempting Warwick as Lord High Admiral of the navy, but it was not formulated. After a long debate that lasted till almost seven o'clock, the house divided, with Essex's supporters, led by Holles and Stapleton, mustering 93 votes against 100 for the war party, whose tellers were Vane and Sir John Evelyn. It needs to be stressed that at the time both journalists and politicians saw the principal target of the Self-Denying Ordinance as not Manchester, but the Earl of

Essex. The Commons divided over whether to keep Essex, but they were silent about Manchester. Bulstrode Whitelocke, always alert to other people's hidden agendas, believed that the ordinance 'was set on by that party who contrived the outing of the lord-general.'[48]

On 19 December two further amendments were debated. Without dissent the house agreed to exempt lords lieutenant, deputy lieutenants, keepers of the rolls, justices of the peace, and commissioners of oyer and terminer and gaol delivery. But it rejected the other amendment, which would have required all officers and officials to take the Solemn League and Covenant and submit to the government and discipline of the Church as laid down by parliament. The first amendment was an evident attempt to make the bill more palatable to the Lords and to conservative localists. The latter amendment, which would be revived by the Lords, illustrates the continuing split over religion. The whole bill was then debated until late at night, when, in the words of an embittered Bulstrode Whitelocke, 'envy and self ends prevailing', it passed.[49]

The bill was not, however, expected to clear the Lords.[50] It was carried there on 21 December by William Pierrepont, but not given its first reading till three days later, after Sir Robert Pye had been sent up to urge its passage.[51] Not much progress was made during the remaining days of the year. When pressure was applied by the lower house the peers reacted by urging that they hurry up with the consideration of the Earl of Manchester's accusations against Cromwell.[52] The Commons majority kept up counterpressure by ordering the revival of the investigation of the debacle at Donnington Castle and by emphasizing that the ordinance was necessary in order to put the armies in a fighting posture and compel the king to negotiate seriously at Uxbridge.[53]

The peers meanwhile had shunted the 'Great Ordinance' aside until 3 January, by which time they had come to a firm decision not to pass it.[54] Straightforwardly they announced their alarm at the great changes being suggested. Not only would the purge of leaders introduce confusion and disarray into the existing forces; it would also be an offence to the Scots, who had not been consulted. Although a minority of war-party lords led by Saye and Sele supported the bill, the majority interpreted it as an insult to their own honour. It treated them 'worse ... than any free subject', since it excluded them all without exception, whereas only those commoners who were MPs were excluded. Moreover an MP could choose to resign his seat in parliament, in order to take up an office or military command, whereas the peers had no such choice. The ordinance also flew in the face of centuries of practice, whereby the peerage had always taken the lead in defending the liberties of England. Finally, the ordinance impugned their contribution to the present struggle.[55]

Instantly the Commons appointed a committee dominated by war-party and middle-group members to answer the peers' objections. They also professed indignation at the peers' procedural irregularity in not sending back the ordinance so that alterations could be considered.[56] On 13 January the whole house, led by Speaker William Lenthall, trooped up to the Lords to present these arguments for the passage of the ordinance.[57] Unimpressed by this show of determination, the Lords' majority shot back that they saw no need to return the ordinance for amendment, since they objected to its whole substance.[58]

The Creation of the New Model

Seeing that the bill's prospects were now hopeless, the war party in the Commons at once began implementing their second plan, which involved a protracted outflanking manoeuvre against the Lords' refusal to sanction a purge of the existing armies' leadership. The manoeuvre consisted in setting up a new southern army with new commanders. The three existing armies would be bled of their officers and men in order to fill up the new one. They would likewise be denied funding, as all new revenues would be devoted to the new force. Finally demoralised and in a state of imminent disintegration, the remnants of the existing armies would be transferred to the new force. If the Lords refused to step aside gracefully, they would have the rug ruthlessly pulled from beneath their feet.

Whether this strategy was consciously formulated in advance cannot be proven from surviving sources. That it was the strategy actually implemented between January and April 1645 can be clearly demonstrated. Having failed initially to reconstruct their forces from the top down, the Commons resolved on 11 January to work from the bottom up. A new army would be constituted, numbering 6000 horse (later increased to 6600), 1000 dragoons and 14,400 foot.[59] Two days later the financing of the new army was mapped out. A monthly assessment of approximately £45,000 was laid on the seventeen counties of East Anglia, the Midlands and the south-east. The scheme for a new army originated in the Committee of Both Kingdoms, where the war party was dominant.[60] Indeed, the idea of unifying the three armies of Essex, Manchester and Waller, and placing them under collective leadership, had been adumbrated as early as the previous October, perhaps on the initiative of Oliver St John.[61]

With the outline of the new army sketched out, a three-man committee of moderates was appointed to draft the ordinance.[62] To impress upon the upper house the seriousness with which they regarded the project the Commons leaders let it be known that they would not allow the Uxbridge treaty to go forward until the armies had been remodelled.[63] At the same time they retaliated against the peers' obstructionism by resurrecting the Cromwell–Manchester quarrel.[64]

Having decided the size of the new army, and taken steps to finance it, the Commons war party now set about the sensitive task of choosing its commanders. At least one observer recognized the naming of officers for the ploy that it was: a circumventing of the Lords' rejection of the Self-Denying Ordinance. By naming new officers, none of whom was a member of either house, the Commons achieved their end 'as well as if the said ordinance were passed.'[65] Who would replace Essex as commander-in-chief? As early as the middle of December 1644 Lord Wharton had expressed to Ferdinando Lord Fairfax his admiration for his son Sir Thomas, in whom he had a meritorious successor as commander of the Northern Army, should Ferdinando be compelled to resign by the passage of the Self-Denying Ordinance.[66] Could it be that already in the back of Wharton's mind was the thought that Ferdinando's son might be suitable for an even more honourable appointment in the southern army? Four weeks later the war-party MP James Chaloner wrote to Lord Fairfax to tell him that his son was the most likely candidate for the generalship of the cavalry in the new army.[67] On 21 January 1645 the question of naming Sir Thomas Fairfax commander-in-chief came before the house. The vote was a clear trial of strength between war and peace parties, with the tellers for the ayes being Vane and Cromwell. The tellers for the noes were the same two men who had tried to exempt Essex from the provisions of the Self-Denying Ordinance in December – Holles and Stapleton. This time the peace party could only muster 69 votes, but the number who voted for Fairfax was almost identical (at 101), to the number who had voted against Essex a month earlier.[68] While Fairfax would later become known as a moderate presbyterian, at the beginning of 1645 he was perceived as a friend of the war party. That this was an accurate perception is suggested by the names of his and his father's principal correspondents on political affairs in this period: the Earl of Northumberland, Lord Wharton, James Chaloner, Thomas Widdrington and John Lambart.[69]

The Commons then proceeded to name Philip Skippon as major-general of the new army, and also the colonels of the twelve foot and eleven horse regiments as well as the regiment of dragoons. The names, which included men of widely differing political and religious positions, as well as a handful of Scots, were adopted without division, although later there would be fierce debate as to whether Nathaniel Rich ought to be a colonel. As a sop to Essex's supporters the victorious war party ordered Zouch Tate's Committee for the Army to propose some way of honouring and remunerating the ailing lord general 'as a testimony to posterity and an acknowledgement of the great and faithful services he has done to the parliament and kingdom.' The same reward was voted for Sir William Balfour.[70]

After several long sessions chaired by war-party member John Lisle in the committee of the whole, the Commons passed the ordinance for a new army under the command of Sir Thomas Fairfax on 28 January.[71] Lisle then went up to the Lords and urged their speedy concurrence.[72] Subsequently, MPs trekked almost daily across to the upper chamber to pressure the peers into passing the ordinance. War-party MP William Purefoy went on the 29th, followed by Sir Christopher Yelverton of the middle group, on the 31st, and Sir Anthony Irby, who straddled the peace party and middle group, on 1 February, and the middle-group Recorder of London, John Glyn, on the 3rd.[73] Pointed reference was made to military necessity: the king's army was at that very moment drawing into a body.[74] The majority in the Lords however, showed their sympathies to be with the peace party, as they stalled consideration of the bill until 4 February.[75] More important to them apparently was the identification and arrest of John Dillingham, editor of the *Parliament Scout* and a close acquaintance of Oliver Cromwell, for a supposedly defamatory attack on Essex.[76] Finally on 4 February they addressed the ordinance for a New Model Army. After lengthy debate several sweeping changes were adopted to make the ordinance more palatable to the peace group. In the first place all officers should be nominated by both houses of parliament rather than the commander-in-chief. Secondly, all officers and soldiers should take the Solemn League and Covenant and submit to the form of church government to be voted by parliament. Thirdly, all present lords lieutenant should be members of the county committees created under the ordinance. Finally, the arrears of the weekly assessment in the Eastern Association should be levied, notwithstanding the expiration of the ordinances under which they were imposed.[77]

Meanwhile political opinion was making itself felt on the issue of a new army. On 31 January Kentish petitioners supporting the Self-Denying Ordinance were received with every mark of courtesy by the Commons, who referred their petition to a large committee.[78] Five days later an opposing petition signed by thirty-five members of the seven county committees of the Eastern Association arrived at the House of Lords. The committee members expressed their 'sad apprehension' that the proposed alterations would destroy their association. Doubting that soldiers would be willing to serve under 'unknown' commanders, they requested permission to continue conscripting men for local service, and paying them out of the revenues in the county where they were enlisted. The Lords referred the letter to the Commons, with a request for answers to the objections raised by the Eastern Association.[79]

Whether these diametrically opposed petitions were genuine expressions of county opinion, or whether they were orchestrated from the centre, they both showed an awareness that great changes were implied in the move to remodel parliament's armies.[80]

The Commons fell to debating the Lords' amendments as soon as they arrived. On the crucial question of Fairfax's right to appoint his own officers the war party wanted to reject the Lords' amendment out of hand. However, after a five-hour debate a compromise was accepted. The modified wording allowed Fairfax to appoint his officers in the first instance but required him to submit his nominations to both houses for their approval. For this reasonable compromise Stapleton and Reynolds were able to muster 82 votes to Cromwell and Sir John Evelyn's 63.[81] The next day the Commons debated the Lords' amendments for almost twelve hours, in the end passing all of them except the requirement that the common soldiers submit to the form of church government laid down by parliament – this for the common-sense reason that, if it passed, anyone wanting to evade military service would only have to refuse the oath.[82] On 11 February an all-day joint conference was held between Lords and Commons to thrash out their differences.[83] On the 12th, despite the appearance at their door of a delegation led by war-party MP Sir Henry Mildmay, beseeching them to dispatch the amended ordinance, the Lords put off further debate until the 13th.[84]

Against a background of mounting anxiety over the imminent collapse of the parliamentary forces the Commons exploited the sense of near-panic welling up among parliament's most dedicated supporters to force the Lords' compliance.[85] At the end of January 'robberies, ravishings and innumerable wicked actions' by parliamentary soldiers were alleged in Bedfordshire, Buckinghamshire and Sussex. Two weeks later the news arrived in London that Sir William Waller had surrendered the outworks of Weymouth to his royalist besiegers.[86] It may be wondered whether the Commons majority was deliberately allowing the existing forces to deteriorate in order to oblige the Lords to sanction the creation of the New Model for lack of any alternative. We know that this fear had been already expressed by the members of the Eastern Association.[87] When Sir John Evelyn went to the peers to desire their urgent attention to the amended ordinance he too hinted broadly that the Commons might use its coercive power of the purse. Action was necessary, 'because there are no monies to be raised for the supply of the forces without the passing of that ordinance.'[88] In other words, the Commons intended to starve the three existing armies out of existence by the simple expedient of denying them funds. There would be only one army allowed to operate in the south – the New

Model – and the Lords would have to choose between it and no army at all. A self-denying ordinance was no longer necessary: the same end would be achieved by other means.

While putting on a show of political muscle for the peers' benefit, the House of Commons in fact remained bitterly split. On the question of displacing officers who refused to swear the Solemn League and Covenant as the Lords demanded, the lower house divided along party lines. After a long debate the Commons agreed to administer the Covenant to the officers, but not to discharge those who refused. The Lords' proviso was rejected by a margin of 60 to 44.[89] The three men sent to explain the Commons' reasons for rejecting their provision were all at that time in favour of vigorously prosecuting the war.[90] In their conference with the peers the next day the three representatives professed to be 'of the same mind as their Lordships' regarding the Covenant, but regarded it as 'inconvenient to disable them when at this time many officers refuse to obey the commands of parliament.'[91] The soldiers defying parliament's authority belonged to the Earl of Essex and Major-General Crawford. On the other hand, Cromwell's troops were reported to be keen to get on with the war and to have no qualms about accepting the authority of Sir William Waller, the most senior officer then in the field. Yet it was Cromwell's officers who might be expected to balk at the Covenant.[92] As the news filtered back to London of the imminent breakdown of negotiations with the king at Uxbridge, the war party pressed its case all the more strongly. At length the Lords swallowed their objections to the ordinance for remodelling the army, and it passed into law.[93]

The final wording of the ordinance revealed that the peace party in the Lords had sacrificed its insistence that existing officers who refused the Covenant 'be displaced and made incapable to have any charge or command.' But the majority in the lower house had had to accept the less harsh requirement that for the future no one would be commissioned an officer unless he had taken the Covenant.[94] Both sides had given way.

The ordinance for raising and maintaining of forces under the command of Sir Thomas Fairfax called for the creation forthwith of an army of twenty-four regiments – eleven of horse, one of dragoons, twelve of foot – containing a total of 22,000 men. The post of commander of the cavalry was left unfilled. A monthly assessment, ranging from £8059 15s. for London and Middlesex to £184 for Rutland, was imposed on the seventeen counties under parliamentary control. The total assessment came to £53, 436. It was to be levied on all inhabitants according to the true value of their estates. Committees were nominated for each county to bring in the money. This was the substance of the ordinance – setting out the army's size and how it was to be financed. At the end came the six 'provisos' or amendments adopted to appease the Lords. The first proviso gave the counties of the Southern Association – Sussex, Surrey and Kent – permission to raise assessment arrears due for the period prior to 1 February 1644 to pay for their forces. The second stipulated that Fairfax was to nominate his officers out of parliament's existing forces, with the approval of both houses of parliament. This proviso may have been aimed at minimizing the number of officers who would lose their jobs as a result of the new modelling of the army, and perhaps at heading off any move to commission untried radicals. The third proviso required all officers to take the Covenant, while the fourth required private soldiers to take it as well, but left the time and manner of their taking it discreetly vague. The fifth proviso made every lord lieutenant who had not been disabled from sitting in the House of Lords an *ex officio* member of his county's committee for the administration of the ordinance. Finally, the monies due upon the weekly assessments for the Eastern Association were still to be collected notwithstanding the expiration of the ordinances under which they were levied. The first and sixth provisos give a hint of the ruthless tactics that had been planned by the war party in the Commons to bring the Lords to heel. Defiantly they had circumvented the Lords' refusal to pass the Self-Denying Ordinance. Ignoring the peers' expressed views, they had gone ahead to create a new army under fresh leadership. Funding had been cut off from the existing armies, and the resulting disorder in these forces was exploited to drive home the argument for the reorganization of the southern forces. The commanders of the existing armies saw themselves unceremoniously stripped of men to command. All that the peace-party peers had been able to salvage was the right to collect arrears of assessment by the Southern and Eastern Associations, and the right of the lords lieutenant to sit on the committees for their respective counties to collect the assessment for the new army.[95]

Once the ordinance had been passed, the Commons sped ahead with their plans to raise men and money.[96] Thomas Fairfax was brought to London, where he was ushered into the House of Commons by four war-party MPs: Sir Thomas Widdrington, Colonel Alexander Rigby, Sir Arthur Hesilrige and Sir Peter Wentworth. Refusing the chair proferred him, he stood bareheaded as Speaker Lenthall commended him for his valour and experience. Warming to his theme, Lenthall went on to state that parliament was now giving Fairfax 'the greatest trust and confidence ... as was ever put in the hands of a subject', namely, 'the command of a very great army'. After his reception by the Commons the new general paid a courtesy visit to the Earl of Essex, the man he had just supplanted.[97]

Initially the troops in the Earl of Essex's cavalry regiments refused to march under new commanders. 'This new model causeth a great alteration', wrote Peregrine Pelham to the mayor of Hull; 'there are great distractions in our army.'[98] In an effort to appease the malcontents the Commons passed an order to pay £4000 to Essex's army and £2000 for Sir William Waller's forces, out of the excise receipts. An ordinance was also passed to levy an assessment of £21,000 a month for the Scots army in the north.[99]

Meanwhile disorder had spread to Manchester's army, where Captain Taylor, a man unfriendly to Independency, led a mutiny against Colonel Montagu.[100] Even Cromwell's Ironsides proved troublesome to Sir William Waller at the siege of Weymouth.[101]

The Choosing of Officers

With efforts going ahead on all fronts to put the new army into the field by the spring, the Commons now turned their attention to Sir Thomas Fairfax's list of officers. Contrary to what they would say later, the Commons scrutinized Fairfax's nominations closely, and subjected at least eight (4 per cent of the total) to heated debate.[102] The war party suffered a sharp reproof when Nathaniel Rich, an ally of Oliver Cromwell, was replaced by Sir Robert Pye junior, son of a prominent peace-party MP.[103]

As soon as the three-day debate was finished, Sir William Strickland was appointed to take the officer list to the upper house. Two days later, on 5 March, John Lisle was sent to ask their lordships to pass down the names of the officers piecemeal as they approved them, so that regimental recruitment could commence immediately. The following day Sir Christopher Yelverton performed the same errand. A large committee was meanwhile appointed to confer with the London Common Council for a loan of £80,000 to launch the army. The Lords yielded to the Commons' pressure to the extent of approving six 'safe' regiments – the two belonging to Sir Thomas Fairfax, those of the future presbyterian Richard Graves, the Dutch colonel Bartholomew Vermuyden, and Philip Skippon, and Ralph Weldon's regiment of Kentish foot.[104] In sum, fifty officers – just over a quarter of the list – were approved almost immediately. But then the Lords dug in their heels and refused to be rushed. Over the next four days they subjected the remaining three quarters of the names to microscopic scrutiny. The fruit of their deliberations was a demand for fifty-seven changes among the 143 officers distributed in the eighteen remaining regiments.[105] The proposed changes are summarized in the tables 1.1–1.5.

The large number of alterations attempted in Manchester's regiments reflects both the size of his army's contribution to the New Model, and the advanced state of politicization already existing among his officers. From the tables it can be seen that the Lords attempted to alter close to one third

Table 1.1 The Lords' response to Fairfax's officer list

Accepted	136
Proposed transfers	5
Proposed demotions and expulsions	52
Total	193

Note. There were a total of 198 commissions to be filled, but Fairfax and Skippon each had three, while Ingoldsby's regiment had only nine, instead of ten. Thus only 193 names were sent to the upper house.

Table 1.2 Nominations accepted by the Lords

Rank	Foot	Cavalry and dragoons	Total
General	2		2
Colonel/lieutenant-colonel	15	10	25
Major	6	6	12
Captain	61	36	97
Total	84	52	136

Table 1.3 Changes demanded by the Lords in Fairfax's regiments

Previous army	Foot	Horse	Dragoons	Total
Manchester's	22	11	–	33
Essex's	14	4	–	18
Waller's	–	4	–	4
New	–	–	2	2
Total	36	19	2	57

Table 1.4 Officers whom the Lords proposed to expel or demote

Radical or Independent	
Evidence before 10 March 1645	11
Evidence after 10 March 1645	24
Moderate or presbyterian	
Evidence before 10 March 1645	–
Evidence after 10 March 1645	1
Unknown	16
Total	52

Note. In addition the Lords proposed five transfers between regiments, for a total of 57 proposed changes.

Table 1.5   Officers whom the Lords attempted to insert or to assign higher rank

Radical or Independent	
Evidence before 10 March 1645	–
Evidence after 10 March 1645	1
Moderate, presbyterian, Essex's kinsmen or protégés	
Evidence before 10 March 1645	12
Evidence after 10 March 1645	8
Scots[a]	9
Unknown	19
Total	49

[a] Two additional Scots are included in the category of presbyterian and Essex protégés before 10 March 1645.

of Fairfax's nominations, tampering rather more with the foot than with the horse and dragoons. Evidence about the political and religious leanings of those whom the Lords wished to demote or expel has been easier to come by than evidence about those whom they wished to introduce or to promote. It has also been easier to turn up evidence from 1647 and later, when the army became thoroughly politicized, than from the period before the Lords attempted their changes. Standing by itself, evidence of later political behaviour would be of little value. However, in this instance the later evidence points in the same direction as the evidence for 1644–5. Overwhelmingly, the officers of whom the Lords disapproved were radicals or Independents, or would later show themselves to be such, while those whom the Lords wished to promote, or to introduce into the army, were moderates, presbyterians, or protégés or kinsmen of the Earl of Essex.

Thus there are strong grounds for concluding that many if not most of the fifty-seven proposed changes were politically or religiously motivated. Some of them were doubtless prompted by considerations of seniority or a desire to preserve the integrity of regiments. Yet at least three of the changes plainly violated the principle of seniority. Moreover, the fact that the Lords tried to boost the rank of at least four Scottish officers – Abercromby, Blyth, Sterling and Strahan – reinforces the impression that the principle of seniority was not uppermost in their minds. Another of the Lords' alterations would have rudely shattered the integrity of Rainborowe's regiment by the introduction of a Scottish colonel (Ogleby).

In light of the fierce and protracted struggle over the officer list between factions in both houses, Kishlansky's thesis that the New Model was the last achievement of consensus decision-making is unpersuasive.[106] The peers of course did not admit that any of their proposed changes were politically motivated. When they sent down their alterations they explained their radical surgery in terms of the need to replace 'young and little experienced commanders' with 'able and experienced men'.[107] If this explanation is to be taken at face value, the question arises of why, when better qualified men were available, Fairfax and the Commons had sanctioned the appointment of young and inexperienced officers. If the Lords' motivation was non-political, what does that imply about the motivation of Fairfax and the Commons? Yet, as Kishlansky has demonstrated, there is strong circumstantial evidence that Fairfax had striven to achieve a measure of religious and political balance in his list.[108] Robert Temple has observed that the success of Fairfax and his parliamentary allies in finally getting their list accepted meant 'not that moderates were purged from the New Model, but that *radicals were not purged.*'[109] It is also clear that considerations of patronage and kinship, as well as politics and religion, were at work on both sides. Significantly, the partisans of the new army interpreted the peers' proposed changes as nothing less than obstructionism. As Peregrine Pelham commented, Fairfax's list had been 'much obstructed in the lords' house'.[110] Thomas Juxon believed that the peers, alienated by their exclusion from all commands in the new army, had formed an alliance with the Scots and the peace party in the Commons to alter the list, putting out 'not only Independents but such as were good, and putting in most vile persons of both nations, by which appears ... how little they regard the good of the nation, their peerage being their great idol.'[111]

At this juncture the war party devised a 'subtle ruse' to exert additional pressure on the upper house. They went to the London Common Council and prevailed on the City magistrates to make their £80,000 loan for the launching of the New Model conditional upon there being no tampering with Fairfax's list.[112] Victory did not come immediately however, and the struggle had to be conducted on more than one front. On 13 March 1645 the Commons resolved to adhere to the list as they had sent it up to the Lords and named a powerful nine-man delegation led by Sir Henry Vane junior and Oliver St John to prepare reasons for not altering the list, and to present them to the Lords at a joint conference.[113] This conference lasted an entire day but at the end of it the Lords were still unbending.[114] A day later, however, they yielded some ground by waiving their right to nominate replacements for Fairfax's nominees, insisting only on their right to veto appointments of which they disapproved.[115] This compromise was unacceptable to the Commons, however, and the deadlock continued. The Commons committee to negotiate with the Lords developed more muscle with the addition of four members – Sir Arthur Hesilrige, John Glyn, Samuel Browne and Sir Peter Wentworth.[116] At the same time the Lords were bluntly told that if they refused to approve of what was 'for the apparent good of the kingdom' the Commons would go ahead without them.[117] Allowing each house to alter the list 'must make the difference endless'; moreover, the consequent delay would give the king the advantage of earlier recruitment of his forces. Finally, all of Fairfax's nominees had commissions in the existing armies, which ought to be testimony enough to their competence. Taking their cue from the Commons' message, the war party in the Lords moved to pass the list 'as presented by Sir Thomas Fairfax to the House of Commons and brought up by the House of Commons to this House.' There must have been some lords who were aware of the disingenuousness of this motion, given that the Commons had already taken the liberty of altering several of the names on Fairfax's original list.[118]

Those for and against the motion were equally divided, which prompted Lord Saye and Sele to tender the proxy of the Earl of Mulgrave in favour of the motion. But an objection was raised, so a search was ordered to see if the proxy could be allowed. The search delayed the decision for another day, but on 18 March, having heard the clerk's report, the Lords allowed Mulgrave's proxy to stand.[119] At this point Essex pulled Lord Clanricarde's proxy from his pocket, but Saye successfully challenged Clanricarde's right to vote, on the grounds that he was a Roman Catholic.[120] Thus the list passed by the narrowest of margins, and only because one of the two proxies entered was ruled ineligible. The old military leadership remained alienated and unreconciled. Excluded from the command of the new army, which had been acknowledged already as 'the chief visible strength upon which we are to rely for the safety of the parliament and kingdom,'[121] four of these excluded men – Essex, Manchester, Denbigh and Stamford – were among the ten who bitterly recorded their dissents.[122] It is fitting that the man whose proxy enabled Fairfax's list finally to squeeze through was his own grandfather. The next week, as if to reward Mulgrave for his crucial contribution, the House of Commons voted him financial compensation for the losses that he and his son, Lord Sheffield, had sustained as a result of the war.[123]

Attempting to display magnanimity in victory, the Commons resolved, as soon as the Lords capitulated, to frame a declaration expressing their desire to preserved good relations with the upper house. The effectiveness of this effort to patch up the frayed relations between the two houses is doubtful, for on the same day they moved to reintroduce the Self-Denying Ordinance.

The following week the ordinance was read twice and sent to a large committee before the third reading. Notably absent from all committees having to do with the New Model was Denzil Holles, implacable enemy of the war party, and chief spokesman of the Essex party in the Commons. A day later the ordinance to secure the £80,000 loan for launching the New Model was also read twice and committed. Without waiting for the Lords' concurrence, the Commons pressed on the same day, voting £7000 out of the £80,000 for a fortnight's pay to those who enlisted voluntarily in the army. The following day, perhaps anxious about the constitutionality of what they had done, they sent Sir Henry Mildmay to acquaint the peers with the necessity of speedily passing the ordinance, 'otherwise no money can be had for the immediate and present service.' By now the heart had gone out of the Lords' resistance. They yielded to the Commons' importunities, passing the bill without a division the same day, and naming ten of their number to serve on the committee to administer the ordinance.[124]

It took some days or weeks for the full political significance of the creation of the new army to sink into people's consciousness. In the first place it was gradually realized that the exclusion or resignation of Scottish officers from the new army considerably diminished that nation's role in English affairs. It was said that over 300 officers who had formerly served with parliament left the service.[125] The Scots commissioners wrote to the Speaker of the Commons urging that the officers who had been displaced be paid their arrears so that they could return home and serve their country. They singled out twelve leading officers for particular recommendation: some of them had been offered commissions by Fairfax but had declined to serve – Lieutenant-General John Middleton, Major-General Lawrence Crawford, Major-General James Holborne, Colonel Harry Barclay and Major Ennis. Others had been unsuccessfully promoted by the Lords to replace Fairfax's nominees – Colonel (or Major) Sterling, Colonel Mill, Lieutenant-Colonel Hunter and Major Wray.[126]

Fairfax's Commission

The Lords had not yet completely abandoned the political struggle. At the end of March 1645 a fierce and protracted argument flared up over the wording of Sir Thomas Fairfax's commission. At issue was the question of whether he should be required, as every previous commander had been, to preserve the safety of the king's person. On 24 March, Robert Scawen reported from the Committee of the Army an ordinance limiting this requirement and also giving Fairfax authority over all forts, castles, towns and garrisons in the territory under his control.[127] Entitled 'an ordinance for giving more power to Sir Thomas Fairfax', it was passed the same day and sent to the Lords. Four days later the Lords returned it with extensive changes. The Commons then appointed a committee of eight, all war-party men, under the chairmanship of Sir John Evelyn, to prepare reasons for not accepting the amendments concerning forts and garrisons, and the obligation to preserve the king's safety. Against the clause on the safety of the king's person, two reasons were adduced. The first, which denied that the king was in fact defending 'the true protestant religion', was struck out, perhaps because it was too blunt. The second reason, which merely suggested that the Lords' proviso would give the king too much of a military advantage, was adopted. On garrisons and forts, the Lords had demanded that Fairfax's authority only apply in regions adjacent to his field of operations. Evelyn's committee answered that the word 'adjacent' was open to dispute and warned the Lords that their fear of granting Fairfax too much power could end by destroying the army.[128]

The Lords proved to be as sharply divided on Fairfax's commission as they had been on his officer list. They voted 10 to 9 to maintain the clause preserving the king's person, but then Lord Saye and Sele tendered Mulgrave's proxy, thereby making the votes equal and causing the motion to fail. The peers then voted by a clear majority to keep the clause giving Fairfax authority only over *adjacent* garrisons; however, eight peers entered their dissents to this decision. All eight had also supported Fairfax's officer list. They deplored 'the great prejudice and hazard it may be to the safety of the parliament and kingdom if, by insisting upon the said alteration, there be any delay in the passing of the said ordinance.'[129]

Two days later the motion to keep the clause preserving the king's person was again introduced, but the result was identical: Mulgrave's proxy produced a tied vote which meant that the motion failed. At that point the Commons stepped up the pressure to pass the ordinance without further change. Lenthall vacated the chair so that any MP who desired could accompany John Lisle to present a message that he and Oliver St John had prepared. In substance it declared that letters had arrived that very morning revealing 'that the army is in mutiny and disorder and they know not who to obey: and until this ordinance be passed Sir Thomas Fairfax has no power to do anything.'[130] Any misfortune that arose from this delay would not be the Commons' fault. Unmoved by Lisle and St John's bluster, the Lords reconvened in the afternoon, one stronger than they had been in the morning.[131] The resolution to preserve the king's person was brought in a third time. Thanks to their additional recruit the peace party carried the resolution 11 to 9, which rendered Mulgrave's proxy useless. None the less, all nine opposing peers insisted on entering their dissents in the *Journal*.[132]

The following day the Lords began to wilt under the pressure. While the Earl of Denbigh submitted a list of reasons defending the additional clauses that the Lords wanted in Fairfax's commission, Essex announced that he was resigning his commission 'so there will be no obstacle for the passing of the clause concerning the forts and garrisons to be put into the command of Sir Thomas Fairfax.' He was shortly followed by Manchester and Denbigh, the three of them 'having opposed the others [i.e. the war party] to the last.'[133] Those not privy to Essex's decision were shocked by his announcement. He had previously assured Sabran that he would never surrender his commission, and the French ambassador feared that his arrest was now imminent.[134] The Lords then withdrew their opposition to Fairfax's unrestricted authority over forts and garrisons. They also immediately voted, for the fourth time in four days, on the additional clause on the king's safety. Again it was upheld, and again a conference with the Commons had to be convened to try to resolve the conflict. By now wearied with the hectoring of militant MPs, they agreed, the fifth time around, to omit the additional clause.[135]

The next day, 2 April, Essex delivered up his commission. Unconvincingly he stated that he had wanted to resign after the action of Gloucester but had been overruled by others. In a more sardonic vein he expressed the hope that his resignation 'may prove as good an expedient to the present distempers as some will have it believed.'[136]

Essex and his supporters had resigned their commissions in order to spare themselves the humiliation of dismissal. For almost four months they had fought tenaciously against a purge of the army command, but events had swept them along. Parliament's parlous military situation and the gathering strength of those who wanted outright victory over the king rather than a compromise peace overwhelmed them. And so they had been forced to yield one point after another. While they staved off the Self-Denying Ordinance, the war-party majority in the Commons and the Committee of Both Kingdoms had gone ahead to build a new army out of the wreckage of the old ones. A monthly assessment had been approved, to commence on 1 February. An immediate transfusion of funds had been supplied in the form of an £80,000 loan from the City of London. To this the Lords had been compelled to assent, salvaging from the defeat of Essex's party a guarantee that all money collected under previous ordinances for the old armies would be paid first, before the repayment of the £80,000 loan was begun.[137] Sir Thomas Fairfax, a man of known radical connections, who was regarded with suspicion by many, was imposed as the war party's choice for commander-in-chief.[138] It is unlikely that we shall ever know precisely who advised Fairfax on his selections for higher officers. But the Lords found almost 30 per cent of them unsatisfactory. Once again, however, the mounting belligerence of the militants forced them to back down. Finally, they had been deeply disturbed by the terms of Fairfax's commission, which deleted the requirement that he protect the person of the king. Essex's party fought even harder over this issue than they had over Fairfax's nominations. The ordinance that was whisked through three readings in a single morning in the lower house was blocked for days in the upper house. Extra votes were rounded up to make it impossible for Saye and Sele to invoke Mulgrave's proxy. The principle at stake was of the highest importance: was parliament waging war on papists, Irishmen and wicked counsellors who had misled the king, or was it waging war on Charles himself? The deletion of the clause obliging Fairfax to protect the person of the king represented the abandonment of the fiction that they were fighting the king's evil counsellors, and the first step towards the conversion of a civil war into a revolution.

The Self-Denying Ordinance (Revised Version)

Having retreated with a modicum of decorum, Essex's party lifted their veto of the Self-Denying Ordinance, which was read a second time and committed on 2 April 1645. The following day it passed its third and final reading. In its amended form the ordinance was significantly different from the resolution passed by the Commons at the beginning of December. Instead of making parliamentarians incapable of executing any office or command for the duration of the war, it now simply dismissed them with forty days' notice. This change, because it was integral to the final text rather than being tacked on as a proviso, very likely originated in the Commons, perhaps as early as mid-December 1644. On the other hand, the changes for which the Lords were responsible had less far-reaching implications. Lords lieutenant, deputy lieutenants, keepers of the rolls, justices of the peace, and commissioners of oyer and terminer and gaol delivery were all exempted from the ordinance's provisions. Also protected were those who had enjoyed royal office before 1640 but were displaced by the king and later restored to their offices by parliamentary authority.[139] Ironically, the Lords retrieved their civilian appointments, whereas what had offended them most about the Self-Denying Ordinance was its robbing the nobility of their historic military function in the state. Having lost the main bone of contention, they were only able to pick up some rather insignificant crumbs.

The totality of the collapse of lordly opposition is seen in their participation in a joint committee named on 8 April 1645 to recommend what to do with MPs who had been displaced by the Self-Denying Ordinance. At first the peers appointed a balanced committee of twelve on which the supporters of the New Model had a slight edge over the members of Essex's party. Later in the day, however, all of Essex's supporters withdrew from the committee, which was reduced to only five members from the upper house, every one of whom had been a consistent supporter of the New Model Army.[140] The problem of what to do with unemployed officers in general, not just with displaced MPs, occupied a great deal of people's attention. When it became known that many redundant officers were volunteering as common soldiers, the Commons drafted a letter to Fairfax asking for their names so that they could be taken into special consideration.[141] A few days later Fairfax submitted to the Committee of Both Kingdoms a list of the officers whom he did not intend to employ. They in turn forwarded the list to the Committee of the West so that they could select whom they needed. The committee also urged the House of Commons to set aside £4000 to pay the arrears of officers from Essex's and Manchester's armies who were not to be employed in the New Model.[142]

The Return of Oliver Cromwell

The Lords' resentment against the New Model flared up yet again over the question of continuing Oliver Cromwell's commission as a cavalry commander. The grace period allowed under the Self-Denying Ordinance came to an end on 13 May 1645. At the end of April the Committee of Both Kingdoms had decided that Cromwell and Major-General Richard Browne, since they were both in active service, would be continued in their commands until further notice.[143] A few days later the Commons extended Cromwell's commission by another forty days. The Lords concurred, but not before members of Essex's party had spoken sharply against it as a breach of the ordinance, and a revelation of the war party's intentions to use the ordinance to remove their enemies but retain their friends.[144]

When had Cromwell formed his intention to carry on in active military service? Had he planned it all along? Was there a specific moment between December 1644 and June 1645 when he decided that he would try to remain in the army? Or did he simply succumb to the popular demand that he be made lieutenant-general of the cavalry, for the good reason that he was supremely qualified for the position? Why had the post of lieutenant-general been left conspicuously vacant, ever since 21 January? Many scholars have puzzled over these questions, and it must be acknowledged that the evidence does not permit definitive answers. Cromwell may have decided to seek the command of the New Model cavalry at the point when the ordinance was converted from one which barred the members of both houses from wartime service to one which merely discharged them while not prohibiting their reappointment. From the text it appears that this change was part of the original second version of the ordinance formulated in the Commons. Had it also been part of the bill that was introduced in mid-December? No copy of the defeated bill has been found; therefore we cannot be certain. But we do know that the wording which left the door open to the reappointment of parliamentarians was integral to the text of the ordinance passed on 3 April.

Two months before that date Cromwell had been active in the Committee of Both Kingdoms, making plans for the new army establishment.[145] Then for three months he was on the battlefield, making himself indispensable to the parliamentary war effort. At the end of February he left for the west to join Waller in resisting the royalists who were threatening Melcombe and Weymouth. In contrast to Waller, who responded to the Self-Denying Ordinance by resigning immediately, Cromwell stayed on, mustering all the forces he could collect in order to prevent a junction of the royalists between Oxford and Worcester. Though he failed to surprise Northampton's horse at Islip, he managed to take the strongly fortified post of Bletchingdon House without firing a shot.[146] Encouraged by this success, he proceeded to beat up the country around Oxford, further disrupting Charles's communications with Worcester. Though thwarted in his attempt to take the garrison of Faringdon, he was given an additional 4000 men (bringing his total force to about 5500) to block up Oxford while Fairfax journeyed with the main army to relieve Taunton. As he performed this service he continued helping to organize the new forces. By early May he was co-ordinating a march on Oxford with Major-General Browne. He now commanded five horse and six foot regiments, reportedly totalling 7000 men. At Fairfax's request the houses extended his commission by another forty days.[147]

No opportunity for battle presented itself over the next few weeks, but on the 26th, fearing an attack on the eastern counties, the Committee of Both Kingdoms ordered him to fortify the Isle of Ely. By early June he had assembled 3000 horse in the eastern counties.[148]

The shock engendered by the storm and sack of Leicester on 31 May unexpectedly enhanced Cromwell's prospects. This sudden reverse produced dismay bordering on panic in the capital, prompting the City authorities to frame a petition extremely critical of the conduct of the war. Pointing to various signs of feeble resolution on the part of the strategists in London, they called for an end to warfare conducted by remote control, firm orders to the Scots army to move southward, a vigorous campaign to meet the recruitment targets of the New Model, a speedy engagement with the enemy, and the appointment of Cromwell as commander of the Eastern Association. The Lords did not thank the City for its petition, but it had a powerful influence, and steps were taken to implement most of its demands during the ensuing fortnight.[149]

In a separate and apparently unco-ordinated petition, Fairfax, his council of war and the parliamentary commissioners wrote to both houses six days before the battle of Naseby, requesting Cromwell's appointment not as head of the Eastern Association, but as lieutenant-general of cavalry in the New Model.[150] The Lords did not answer this petition either. The Commons on the other hand wrote giving Fairfax the asked-for permission. The general at once sent a message to Cromwell at Ely telling him of his appointment and ordering him to join the main army without delay.[151] Evidently judging that the Lords were unalterably opposed to Cromwell's nomination as lieutenant-general, the Commons significantly chose to ignore the requirement that military appointments be approved by both houses. However, the stunning victory at Naseby, Cromwell's contribution to which could not be denied, transformed the political situation. The war party pressed home the advantage created by Naseby to make Cromwell's appointment permanent. But the Lords repudiated the proffered ordinance and substituted one of their own, allowing the appointment for three months only.[152]

The insistence by the upper house that the appointment be only temporary confirms the continuing antagonism of Essex's supporters towards Cromwell, as well as their recovered dominance of the House of Lords. Essex's antagonism was of long standing, as Cromwell knew. Whatever his ambitions, he also knew that any reappointment would require the approval of the upper chamber, where Essex and Manchester were dominant. Consequently we may conclude that he had probably been sincere when he spoke for the principle of self-denial in December 1644. His own resignation would not have been too high a price to pay for the elimination of a bagful of aristocratic and other enemies. Yet with the advent of the spring fighting season his desire to be militarily active was rekindled, and he did everything he could to stave off the day of his final dismissal. Only the unforeseen victory at Naseby on 14 June was powerful enough to override the Lords' continuing opposition, and secure for him the commission that by now he fiercely coveted.

2

Recruitment, Provisioning and Pay

A new army had been formed. The old aristocratic leaders had been purged; three armies had been merged into one; a new officer list had been approved. Now the hard practical work began. Money, arms, clothing and provisions had to be amassed to put this army into the field. Men had to be rounded up to fill the vacancies in the infantry and dragoon regiments. Parliament's success in meeting the challenges of money, recruitment and supply would, in no small measure, be responsible for Fairfax's unbroken chain of victories in the year to come.

Revenue

Since 1643 parliament had collected a weekly, then a monthly, assessment to help pay for its war against the king. For a time the excise, first introduced in 1643, was intended to provide most of parliament's revenue for its war treasury, and indeed it remained the single most fruitful revenue source throughout 1644.[1] From 1645, however, the monthly assessment replaced the excise as the foundation of army finance. The accounts of the treasurers at war show that £5,228,873 of the total revenue of £7,621,149 taken in from February 1645 to the end of December 1651 came from the assessment. The next greatest source was delinquents' fines (£680,396), followed by the sale of crown-fee farm rents (£417,397) and excise receipts (£372,158).[2]

Totalling £53,436 each month, the assessment was levied on the seventeen counties under parliament's control. The bulk – over two thirds – of the assessment was laid on the eastern and home counties: London and Middlesex (£8060), Norfolk (£7436), Suffolk (£7070), Kent (£7070) and Essex (6750).[3] To ensure that the population understood the new initiative that had been launched, 2000 copies of the ordinance were printed for circulation throughout the seventeen counties.[4] At first the assessment was authorized for only ten months, but when that time had elapsed and the war was still not over it was extended another six months, and then a further four months, which took it up to October 1646.[5] In the end 87 per cent of the gross amount due on these twenty months' assessment was actually collected, a strikingly high return by the standards of the time.[6]

The pay of the army was expected to total about £45,000 a month, leaving a balance of over £8000 to be spent on arms, ammunition and supplies. Since the men were expected to feed and clothe themselves out of their wages, this balance should have been enough to cover the army's other expenses. The main problems with the assessment were that it was slow to reach the treasurers at war in Guildhall. Impatient to have the new army operational, the Commons had already told the war treasurers to advance Fairfax £8000 from the City's £80,000 loan so that among other things he could provide two weeks' pay to those who enlisted in the army voluntarily.[7]

Parliamentary officials were plagued with problems over the assessment from its inception. In May 1645 a letter was sent to several counties hectoring them about their overdue payments, which were vital to the siege of Oxford. A direct consequence of the money shortage was a shortage of recruits, 'a great disservice to the public'.[8] At no time during its twenty-month history was the first monthly assessment adequate to finance the army. Apart from people's understandable reluctance after two and a half years of war to have their tax burden increased, there was the additional reluctance of county officials to see money go to Westminster when there were so many urgent calls for it locally. Thus the Eastern Association counties continued to maintain substantial forces after the New Model's creation, and had to be admonished in September 1645 against diverting assessment revenue to their support.[9]

A more common hindrance to the smooth flow of assessment money was the military practice of free quarter. Colonel Edward King complained that, after paying £2800 a month for a year, Lincolnshire was still a prey to the exactions of Colonel Rossiter's regiment, which was based there. Elsewhere it was not the New Model but local regiments or garrisons, starved for money, who had recourse to free quarter. To the inhabitants it mattered little whether the unwelcome attentions came from local or New Model troops. The experience was the same: they paid twice. The Somerset Committee drew parliament's attention to the fact that the clubmen were reactivating themselves because of this double exaction, while the Dorset Committee spoke feelingly about their similar experience of the oppressions of local forces against the civilian population:

> We do assure you that we are reduced to that Egyptian pressure, as to make brick without straw, our weekly assessments being expired, our fifth and twentieth parts exhausted, and our sequestrations come to so low an ebb as will no way do our work.

With yet another assessment looming up for the Irish expedition, they professed to be in a state of unrelieved despair.[10] Such eloquence needs to be taken with a grain of salt, however. One of the self-perceived duties of county committees was to ward off fresh exactions by means of heart-rending protestations of their utter inability to bear existing ones.

The New Model Army was first obliged formally to resort to free quarter in September 1645.[11] In that month assessment revenue was so deficient that £50,000 had to be borrowed against future excise receipts.[12] By October a further £40,000 had to be raised, this time in the form of a loan repayable out of future excise receipts collected in London, Westminster and the adjacent area.[13] The fact that the capital was singled out to bear this burden may have reflected its extraordinarily poor showing in assessment remittances.[14] Further sums of £30,000 and £84,847 were charged against the excise in December 1645 and March 1646 respectively.[15] Finally, £2000 out of a royalist composition fine was diverted to the army's pressing needs in the autumn of 1645.[16] Thus during the first fifteen months of the army's existence over £200,000 or about 25 per cent of the £801,540 budgeted revenue from the monthly assessment came from sources not originally planned for.[17]

After the expiry of the assessment on 1 October 1646 it was not renewed until 25 March 1647. At that time the monthly rate was increased to £60,000, but for the first time it was spread over all the counties of England and Wales. Notwithstanding the lighter burden on each county, tax resistance had become more obstinate. By December 1647 not a penny of the new assessment had been received during its nine months of operation.[18] Nor had there been any money for the army out of the excise after November 1646. The revenue from other sources was negligible.[19] Despite the theoretical evaporation of revenue after the autumn of 1646, arrears from the first twenty months' assessment continued to trickle into the war treasury in Guildhall for many months afterwards. Moreover, the Committee of the Army ordered extraordinary payments in November and December 1646, so that the army did not experience financial crisis until the spring of 1647.[20] With few expenses other than weekly wages, the army paradoxically enjoyed at least as good financial treatment during its three quarters of a year of idleness as it had during its militarily active year and a quarter.

It is no surprise that revenue from the source which was meant to be the sole financial support for the army proved inadequate. Nor is it remarkable that parliament resorted to *ad hoc* measures to keep the army paid and equipped. Governments at all times have taken money where they could find it to keep their war machines functioning. What is striking is that the monthly assessment was good for four fifths of the army's needs, and that, supplemented by the excise, it was more than adequate to the task of reducing the royalist foe.

Recruitment

Immediately after the ordinance for a monthly assessment was in place, the Commons set about raising men for the new army. A large committee under the chairmanship of Robert Scawen, soon to be known as the Committee for (or of) the Army, was appointed and instructed to organize the recruiting effort.[21] By 25 February 1645 an impressment bill was sent to the Lords. Three days later it became law. The responsibility for conscripting men was laid on the shoulders of the London Militia Committee, the deputy lieutenants and county committees as directed by parliament, the Committee of Both Kingdoms, and Sir Thomas Fairfax. The long list of people and occupations exempt from impressment made it clear that it was the poor who were being targeted. Any man, or the son of any man, rated at £5 in goods or £3 in lands could not be pressed. Only those between the ages of eighteen and sixty-five were liable to impressment, while all clergymen, scholars, students at law or university, esquires' sons, MPs or peers, mariners, watermen, fishermen and tax officials were exempt.[22]

Two weeks later, with the officer list only partially approved, Fairfax was authorized to take all the soldiers and officers of the rank of lieutenant and lower that he wanted from the armies of Essex, Manchester and Waller. What was startling was that this ordinance ignored the fact that the three existing armies had not been formally ended, the Self-Denying Ordinance had not been passed, and the three commanders still held their commissions. Yet their armies were being cannibalized to furnish regiments for Fairfax.[23] The recruitment of regiments already approved by both houses went ahead without delay. In addition the remaining regiments of Essex's infantry were to be condensed into three more regiments, a delicate task that was entrusted to Major-General Philip Skippon. Given the previous rebelliousness of these regiments there was more than a little anxiety that the prospect of reorganization would only inflame them more. As it happened, the guarantee of two weeks' pay for reduced officers, and new clothes and weapons for the rank and file, as well as the considerable diplomatic finesse of Skippon, allowed the transition to be effected without incident. Skippon's success with these regiments, potentially the most volatile in the old armies, set an example to the others, so that in a short time the balance of Essex's army was merged into the New Model.[24] Regiments from the other two armies were also absorbed smoothly, so that the quota of 6600 horse troopers was easily met, little further recruitment of cavalry being necessary. Service in Fairfax's cavalry was so attractive that numbers of redundant officers from the old armies signed on as private troopers in the new army.[25] With 3048 men from Essex's infantry, 3578 from Manchester's and 600 from Waller's the strength of the new army's foot stood at 7226 exclusive of officers.[26] There remained 7174 infantry besides a new regiment of 1000 dragoons still to be raised.

For many reasons service in the infantry was far less attractive than service in the cavalry. Impressment was therefore a costly and arduous business. Not only did the recruits have to be clothed and fed; they had to be closely guarded until their escorts delivered them to the assembly point at Reading. The expenses of county officials, high collectors and local militia had to be reimbursed. In order to meet the target of just over 7000 men the Committee of Both Kingdoms assigned quotas to London and the ten south-eastern counties between Norfolk and Sussex. The same counties as were obliged to raise most of the money for the new army also had to raise most of its manpower. The London region was told to raise 2500 men, while the four counties of Norfolk, Suffolk, Essex and Kent were instructed to bring in a thousand each.[27] Chaplains were not forgotten, and the Assembly of Divines was asked to supply Fairfax with the names of 'godly and learned ministers' whom he could approach to staff his army.[28] The parliamentary authorities evidently believed, however, that London, Westminster and the suburbs, with their great reserves of population, would be the most fertile soil from which to harvest pressed men.[29] In the event they would be strangely disappointed. Conscripts came in slowly, and from nowhere more slowly than the City.[30] By the middle of April the second batch of recruits, 470 in number, arrived from Kent. Accompanied by guards, they were transported up the Thames in boats to Windsor, where they were handed over to the army.[31] While the Kentish recruits mutinied and attempted to escape, some of their counterparts from Hertfordshire perpetrated robberies and other felonies on their march through the county. Two of them were convicted and one was hanged. A few days later the Lords ratified an ordinance prescribing the death penalty for any conscript who deserted his colours.[32]

Despite parliament's best efforts Fairfax was always short of foot soldiers during the year and a quarter of active fighting. His authority to impress men had to be continually extended until the summer of 1646.[33] Not only were the counties sluggish in meeting their quotas, but the army's strength was continually bled by desertions, which meant that over the period of a year almost two men had to be conscripted for every one that was retained. Conscripting infantry in 1645–6 was like ladling water into a leaky bucket. During the weeks leading up to Naseby, for example, conscripts, having received their shilling of 'pressed money' did 'daily run away'. Alarmed by the problem, parliament took the drastic step of delegating to county committees the authority to inflict the death penalty upon deserters.[34]

Immediately after Naseby there was a massive haemorrhaging of the army's numbers as thousands of men left in search of a safe hiding place for the booty they had seized in battle.[35] Parliament responded vigorously to the depletion of its forces by sending MPs and officers into their native counties to communicate the urgent need to raise new men and punish deserters.[36] Following the capture of Bristol in September 1645 the army's numbers again diminished. Demoralized by harsh weather, shortages of pay, food and clothing, and the absence of many of their officers who had retreated to the comfort of London, the foot fell to only 8000 men, though the horse were maintained at nearly full strength.[38] By April 1646 the winter recruiting campaign had restored the army's strength to about 17,000.[38]

Why did the foot desert in such large numbers? Apart from the hardship of being a low-paid common soldier on active duty – carrying a 60-pound load and often sleeping under the open sky – there is the undoubted fact that few foot soldiers understood or cared about the reasons for fighting against the king. Drawn from the lowest ranks of society, many having no fixed address, they found it easy to desert because they were next to impossible to trace once they had fled.[39] Colonel John Venn reflected the frustration caused by the low quality of conscripted men when he wrote to parliament in April 1646 from Northampton, where he had gone to collect 2400 recruits from the Midlands. That figure would have been larger, but almost half the men from Lincolnshire had run away. Venn observed that this high attrition rate was attributable to the fact that 'most countries press the scum of all their inhabitants, the king's soldiers, men taken out of prison, tinkers, pedlars and vagrants that have no dwelling, and such of whom no account can be given. It is no marvel if such run away.' If the next batch of recruits proved no better, Venn declared, he would rather go and face the enemy than shepherd such men to their destination.[40] Venn's complaint was echoed by the normally effusive *Moderate Intelligencer*, which damned the new conscripts as 'the vilest rogues and cowards that ever breathed.' Their roguery extended to defiant expressions of royalism.

Having arrived at Woodstock, they swore that if Fairfax were there they would kill him and raise the siege of the town for the king.[42] We may interpret this incident as an expression of men's alienation from the cause to which they were unwillingly attached rather than signifying any real warmth for Charles I. However, it is interesting to recall that there were already in the army a substantial number of men who had previously fought on the king's side. After Naseby 102 royalist prisoners took the Covenant and were admitted to the army.[43] After Torrington 200 royalists signed on, with several score more trickling in later.[44] As Lord Hopton's army disintegrated at the end of February, between 300 and 400 men changed sides, while a further 1000 declared their willingness to serve parliament in Ireland.[45]

Besides royalists the New Model also welcomed west-country clubmen to its ranks. Initially more hostile to parliament than to the king, these professed neutralists were won over by the favourable contrast between the conduct of the New Model and that of the royalists. A few days after the storming of Bristol their numbers were reported by Fairfax as 2000 and 1500 from Somerset and Gloucestershire respectively. Nothing is heard of the clubmen recruits after September 1645, so their presence may have been temporary. Some may have formed part of the garrison that Fairfax left in Bristol when he moved on to the west.[46]

An unforeseen and unauthorized source of recruits was the deserters from Colonel Edward Massey's Western Brigade. As early as April 1645 Massey complained that his troops were leaving him because he was unable to horse, clothe and arm them properly. Every day they ran to places of better entertainment.[47] Massey's losses to the New Model had not abated several months later, leading the House of Lords to move that Fairfax be forbidden to receive deserters from the Western Brigade. Refusal by the Commons to sanction this instruction meant that the practice continued unchecked.[48]

Ex-royalists, clubmen and deserters from other parliamentary forces never composed more than a small fraction of the New Model foot. The great bulk were pressed men drawn from the south-east in 1645 and from the south-east and west in 1646. Raw force was needed to get them to serve under the parliamentary standard, and their patent unwillingness to be enlisted made it very expensive to round them up. Recruitment accounts from various counties show local officials spending between £2 and £2 10s. per man.[49] Each conscript had to be closely guarded until he was handed over to the military authorities. The ratio of guards to conscripts ranged from a maximum of two to one to a minimum of one to two.[50] Conscription was a labour-intensive business. In addition the men had to be clothed, and to soften the bitterness of military servitude each one was given a shilling of 'pressed money'. They had, as well, to be fed, and when they were transported by water there were additional costs of boat hire. Even when they had been handed over to the army the direct costs of conscription did not cease, for, once the army had left Reading in May 1645, recruits had to be escorted to the front where they could finally be assimilated and subjected to regimental discipline. In July 1645 Colonel Thomas Rainborowe and fifteen lieutenants, captains and majors were given a budget of £1000 to deliver 1457 recruits to the army. Thanks to Rainborowe's scrupulous efficiency the task was accomplished for less than half that sum, and the unused balance returned to the treasury.[51] Recruitment records from London show that officials concentrated their efforts in the poor and suburban parishes – St Giles Cripplegate, Clerkenwell, St Martin-in-the-Fields, Finsbury, St Clement Danes and the Savoy.[52] These records, though incomplete, lend support to the claim of Westminster, Southwark and the Tower Hamlets in 1646 to have raised twice as many recruits for the New Model as the City.[53]

The second and third waves of recruitment, in the summer and autumn of 1645, were a great disappointment, partly because of the growing lack of cooperation from London, and partly because the Eastern Association counties had been given the additional responsibility of raising 2000 troops to shadow the king's forces so that they could not break through to London.[54] Accordingly, in 1646 Fairfax was authorized to recruit men where he was, in the west. The counties newly brought under parliamentary control, from Hampshire to the Devon border and as far north as Gloucestershire, were also given specific recruitment quotas.[55]

We can now review the results of the recruitment campaigns and their impact upon the fluctuating strength of the New Model Army during the year of fighting from April 1645 to April 1646. Between February and April 1645: 7226 infantry, and most of the complement of 6600 cavalry were voluntarily recruited from the now-defunct armies of Essex, Manchester and Waller.[56] This left 7174 foot and a regiment of 1000 dragoons still to be raised. Accordingly, a target of 8460 was set for London and the ten southeastern counties. Every pressed man was to be supplied with a suit of clothes, including a red coat faced with blue, and the county committees were authorized to deduct the costs of impressment from the first monthly assessment levied for the new army.[57]

The Committee of the Army, the general staff and county officials worked together rapidly to meet this quota. By 23 April 1645 the army's strength was reported to be 15,000. At the muster four days later it had reached 19,000–20,000.[58] A few days later the dragoon regiment stood at over 400 men, and the army's total strength at between 20,000 and 21,000.[59] Included in this total were the New Model regiments commanded by Oliver

Cromwell and Major-General Richard Browne near Oxford. Cromwell had been on the march and recruiting actively for over three months. His brigade now numbered 7000 men, distributed among six regiments of horse and six of foot. Nine of these twelve regiments, or about 5000 men, belonged to the New Model. It was a curious fact that the man who had no commission in the new army was in command of over a third of its regiments in the field.[60]

After Fairfax had departed to relieve Taunton at the beginning of May, 2000 more troops arrived at Reading, and at least a further 2000 flowed in at the end of May. These figures yield a total of between 24,000 and 25,000 two weeks before the battle of Naseby. Only half that number were under Fairfax's immediate command. A brigade of 4000 had been dispatched north under Colonel Bartholomew Vermuyden to assist the Scots; perhaps 5000 were under Oliver Cromwell and a small force of perhaps 500 had been stationed at Boarstall, Oxfordshire. Although combat and sickness had as yet claimed few casualties, heavy attrition had already been experienced from men running away. The gruelling 78-mile march to Witchampton, near Taunton, and the slower march back to Oxfordshire (79 miles in thirteen days) seems to have resulted in a loss of at least 3000 infantry.[61] Around the beginning of June Cromwell's brigade was divided between the Isle of Ely, where Cromwell himself led a force of 3000–4000 to protect the eastern counties, and Oxford, where the remainder under Major-General Browne kept watch on the king's headquarters.[62] With the arrival of Cromwell's troops on 6 June and Vermuyden's on the 8th, the New Model reached a strength of a least 20,000, made up as follows.

At Taunton	4,000
Under Cromwell	3,000+
Under Vermuyden	2,500
At Boarstall	500
Under Fairfax	10,000
Total[63]	20,000+

At Naseby the New Model Army was augmented by 1000 horse in Colonel John Fiennes's regiment, and a regiment of probably 500 from the Eastern Association.[64] This yields a figure of 17,000 on the battlefield, substantially higher than previous estimates of the size of the parliamentary army.[65] Yet even if we accept this higher figure we cannot avoid the inference that the army had already lost about 4000 of the men it had recruited in the previous two months. It was to lose a similar number after Naseby. Six days after the battle the Committee of Both Kingdoms sent urgent letters to the Eastern Association counties demanding that they meet their quotas in order to bring the army up to strength.[66] At the end of the month the Committee of Both Kingdoms ordered a second major recruitment campaign in London and eleven south-eastern counties. The target was set at 4050 men, implying that the New Model was this much under strength. It was said that weakness of numbers prevented the immediate assault by the army on Oxford which Parliament desired.[67] In fact the army's deficiency was substantially more than 4050, for at the beginning of July Fairfax was in command of only 10,000 troops apart from the 4000 still at Taunton.[68] How is this catastrophic drop in numbers to be explained? The dead and wounded at Naseby amounted to around 500. When this figure is subtracted there still remain 6500 men to be accounted for.[69] Observers at the time agreed that a large number of men – both horse and foot – had departed the army in order to find safe storage for the booty they had taken on the battlefield. No figures were cited for the number of deserters, but Fairfax, never a man given to hyperbole, declared to the House of Lords that both his horse and foot had been weakened, the latter by at least 50 per cent. Complaining that the associated counties did nothing to stanch the flow of deserters, he urged parliament to take speedy action to restore the army's strength.[70] The situation did not change before the end of July, when similar figures were again broadcast: a shortfall of 6000 foot and 1400 horse. It was confidently expected that the second recruitment campaign would make good this lack, but the army commanders were to be bitterly disappointed. It is not known how many horse were raised, but the foot came to scarcely 2000, including over 100 cavaliers. Even this modest number shrank to 1300 during the journey from Reading to Sherborne in Dorset.[71]

In the autumn of 1645 a third recruitment campaign was launched with a combined target of 500 horse, 500 dragoons and 5489 foot. Tacitly recognizing the likelihood that this target would not be met, the Commons gave Fairfax permission to do what he had begun to do already: recruit from the local region around Bristol.[72] Again it may be inferred that the New Model was only slightly over two thirds of its intended strength.[73] Responsibility for finding the 1000 horse and dragoons was laid on the London Militia Committee, which was told to collect from eligible householders either a horse and rider, or £12. This is the one time we hear of coercion being applied to raise mounted troops for the army. It took only a few days to assemble this force, but indecisiveness by the Committee of Both Kingdoms resulted in another month's delay before the troops were sent to Fairfax.[74] By that time the Committee of the Army had tabulated the totals of infantry conscripts from the third recruitment campaign. Only 2080, or 38 per cent of the target had been collected. While most counties had realized over half their quota, the overall proportion was dragged down by London's failure to bring in more than fifty-seven of the 1469 that had been asked of it.[75] Desperate for more foot, Fairfax had meanwhile taken on 3500 clubmen from Somerset and Gloucestershire at Bristol,[76] but the presence of these men in the army seems to have been ephemeral.

The third press had produced an infusion of over 3000 men in October 1645. Yet the idleness of the autumn months, the wet weather and disease, food scarcities throughout the south-west, and delays in sending money and clothing to the army meant that this gain was completely wiped out by December.[77] The principal reason again was desertion. In an effort to deal with the problem the Commons ordered the committees of Hampshire and Wiltshire to seize runaway soldiers and send them back to the army.[78] Muscle was added to the effort by an ordinance empowering county committees, deputy lieutenants and militia officers to try deserters and whip or hang them.[79]

In January 1646 the New Model's fourth and final recruitment campaign of the first civil war was launched. Seventeen counties were now included. To the traditional sources in the east and south-east were added the five newly subdued counties stretching in an arc from Hampshire to the Devon border and up to Gloucestershire. The individual quotas added up to 8800, implying that the army was at its lowest ebb since its launching almost a year before. More than half this total was assigned to the recently absorbed counties.[80] Fairfax was also given the personal authority to grant commissions to gentlemen in the west to raise troops for his army.[81] About 50 per cent of the quota appears to have been met by the beginning of March, but within a few weeks half the pressed men had made good their escape. Thanks to an additional contribution of 1300 men from Warwickshire and Lincolnshire, and the arrival of 300–400 men from Hopton's army, the New Model attained a strength of 17,000 by April 1646. With these numbers Fairfax was confident that he could launch the final strike against the royalist heartland of Oxfordshire, Worcestershire and south Wales.[82]

The strength of the army (see table 2.1) does not always reflect the results of these official recruitment campaigns, since other counties also contributed, royalist soldiers switched sides on at least three occasions, and the army had some success in recruiting locally, most notably when Hugh Peters persuaded the clubmen of Somerset and Gloucestershire to throw support behind the New Model at Bristol. The figures for the army's strength at a particular date, while based on a sifting of official records, newsbook reports and other contemporary sources, should be regarded as only approximate.

The picture that emerges from this examination of the army's recruitment differs from the conventional one in several important respects. First, the gulf separating the horse and the foot was even wider than hitherto thought. The men of the cavalry were clearly the sons of yeomen and

Table 2.1 Numerical strength of Sir Thomas Fairfax's army, 1645–6

Recruitment campaign	Quota	Numbers raised	Strength of army	Date
1 April–May 1645	8,460	approx. 11,000	24,800[a]	End of May 1645
			20,000+	Eve of Naseby (10 June 1645)
			16,000	Beginning of July 1645
			13,800	End of July 1645
2 July 1645	4,050	1,300	15,100	15 August 1645
			18,600	15 September 1645
3 September–October 1645	5,489	2,080	?	
			14,000	December 1645
			13,400	January 1646
4 January–April 1646	8,800	approx. 3,400	17,000	End of April 1646

[a] This total includes 13,800 who had already volunteered from the older armies of Essex, Manchester and Waller.

craftsmen – at the lower end of the scale of 'middling sort of people.' While most of them could not afford to equip themselves with a horse and weapons, they thought for themselves to the extent of wishing to serve voluntarily under the parliamentary standard. The foot, by contrast, were drawn from the lowest ranks of society. They were the 'scum', as one official called them in a moment of exasperation, men who, once clothed and given their shilling of 'pressed money', wanted nothing more than to run away. Two were pressed for every one who eventually arrived at the front. Few of them had any political opinions, for, if they were not there under protest, they were royalists who switched sides for the sake of a new suit of clothes and regular pay. While the number of horse remained fairly stable between roughly 5000 and 6500, the foot and dragoons underwent violent fluctuations in numbers, from 18,000 to 7000, owing to massive desertions.[83] The men who stamped the New Model with a distinctive character were therefore a tight group numbering about 5000 horse and 7000 foot. For the rest, membership in the army was no more than a revolving door through which they exited almost as quickly as they entered. By the summer of 1646 the number of men who had served, however briefly, in Thomas Fairfax's army, must have been well over 30,000. If we add to this total those who were conscripted but ran away before seeing active service, we reach 40,000 as the total number of men who were recruited, in a period of only twelve months, to serve in the New Model. By a strange irony, great victories such as those at Naseby and Bristol brought no numerical strengthening of the army, but seem to have accelerated the already-worrying attrition rate. Thus it can be appreciated that parliament's experience in raising troops was not different in kind from that of the king. Both sides ran into the same resistance, and both suffered constant haemorrhaging of their numbers, which meant chronic shortages of foot soldiers. The most that can be said about the difference between the two armies in terms of recruitment is that the royalist army, with its inferior financing, divided leadership and mounting tally of defeats, suffered these problems even more acutely than the army of Fairfax.[84]

Arms, Clothing and Food

The gigantic task of outfitting the new army began as soon as the officer list was completed, the monthly assessment scheme put in place and the loan from London arranged. A committee of six MPs was named to contract for arms, ammunition, clothing and other equipment needed for the summer campaign.[85] Contracts were let almost immediately, and by early April supplies began pouring into the army stores at Reading.

The system of provisioning was administered efficiently and, by delivering *matériel* to the army when it was needed, was instrumental in achieving the victories of 1645. Based on prompt payment in cash, this new centralized system soon supplanted other schemes for equipping the army. The maids of Norwich had once raised enough money to outfit a troop of horse under Captain Swallow, but locally initiated voluntary charity had proven itself unequal to the task of maintaining a large field army. Relics of the earlier voluntaristic approach occasionally reappeared, as when a Commons committee drafted a letter to gentlemen in several counties asking them to bring in whatever provisions they could for Fairfax's army, with a promise of future reimbursement; or when a call went out at the end of the year for old clothes and shoes to help tide the army over the bitter winter.[86] Neither of these initiatives bore much fruit, and the results were insignificant beside the tremendous volume of supplies that was raised and paid for in London with tax revenues.

About 200 suppliers, virtually all of them based in or near London, were given contracts.[87] Once they had fulfilled their side of the bargain the Committee for the Army issued a warrant to the treasurers at war for payment. The revenues from the London loan, the monthly assessment, and – when these fell short – delinquents' compositions and the excise, were always adequate to ensure prompt payment of these suppliers. Thus members of the Cutlers Company contracted on 31 March 1645 to supply 9200 swords and belts. The cutlers met the terms of their contract and were paid in full within sixteen days.[88] Again, Daniel Judd contracted to supply 20 tons of English match on 4 October 1645. He made two deliveries and was paid in two instalments, the second on 23 December.[89] Likewise, thirteen shoemakers signed contracts on 24 February 1646 to deliver 8000 pairs of shoes 'of good neat leather'. They evidently made good on their contracts, since precisely four weeks later they were issued warrants for payment in full.[90] These contracts, of which examples could be multiplied endlessly, vividly illustrate the economic power of the metropolis to feed the army's voracious appetite for clothing, equipment, weapons and ammunition. Equally, the Army Committee's supply warrants impressively demonstrate parliament's ability to summon the vast financial resources needed to pay these suppliers promptly. These records also document the favoured position enjoyed by the New Model. While Fairfax's men represented well under half the fighting forces at Parliament's disposal in 1645, they were given far more than all the rest put together. The Scots army, the Northern Association army, Massey's Western Brigade and the numerous provincial garrisons were all penalized by this favouritism.

With the membership of the Committee of the Army reflecting the ascendancy of the war party in parliament it is not surprising to find that a number of the suppliers were men of the same political hue. Thomas Andrewes, a linen draper and future Commonwealth lord mayor, supplied $4\frac{1}{2}$ tons of Flemish match. A consortium of cloth merchants – Stephen Estwick, Thomas Player, Maurice Gething, Tempest Milner and John Pocock – furnished several thousand coats, breeches and pairs of stockings. Except for Pocock, the members of this consortium are known to have been active in City government and in the London trained bands. The cutler Alexander Normington, a political Independent in 1647, supplied swords to the New Model in 1646. The future regicide Colonel Owen Rowe, who was to dominate the Common Council from 1649 onwards, supplied 1000 suits of armour and 1000 pikes. Thomas Prince, Leveller and cheesemonger, was one of a group of three who sold almost 900 cwt of cheese. Two officers in the army itself also acted as suppliers: Thomas Hammond, lieutenant-general of the ordnance, brought in 526 reconditioned muskets, for which he received £270, while Captain Christopher Mercer furnished ten drums for Colonel Okey's regiment of dragoons. The political attitudes of most of the suppliers are unknown, and indeed they may well not have had any. At least some of them, however, were unsympathetic to the war or even crypto-royalist in their leanings. Colonel Lawrence Bromfield, who in 1647 emerged as a militant presbyterian, hostile to the army, had sold it 1500 swords and belts in 1645 and 1646. Charles I's gunfounder, John Browne, was evidently the only man to whom parliament could turn for ordnance. Based in Kent, at London's southern edge, he was prevented by geography from helping the king. Always regarded with suspicion, he was at least once accused of trying to sabotage Fairfax's army by underfilling orders.[91]

All these suppliers, including the forementioned radicals, were paid promptly,[92] and undoubtedly prospered out of the war. But there were no scandals connected with the provisioning of the army; not even any allegations of profiteering. The Committee for the army drove good or even hard bargains, as is evidenced by the prices it negotiated.

A great volume of supplies left London for the army during the first twelve months of its existence. In value they amounted to £116,823. The supplying of the army was done mainly in three waves: in April and May 1645, when it was launched; in late June and July, when it was re-equipped after Naseby; and in January–March 1646, when extensive preparations were undertaken for the campaign which never materialized. The first wave is self-explanatory; the second wave, after Naseby, is explained by the continuing effort to bring the army up to its targeted strength of 22,000 and to replace the large number of deserters. In July 1645 there were several thousand new men to be outfitted. The third wave, in early 1646, resulted from the palpable suffering caused by nasty weather and deprivation after the siege of Bristol the previous September. Fairfax and his London friends, who included several newsbook editors, had publicized their suffering effectively. The message was not lost upon Robert Scawen, the able chairman of the Committee of the Army. In December he had brought down a report on the condition of the army, calling for a massive refit in preparation for the spring campaign. As adopted by the commons, the report set targets for various kinds of clothing, arms and munitions. Several of the most important targets – including those for swords and suits of clothing – were impressively met over the next three months.[93]

These financial records tell us much about the operation of a seventeenth-century army. They show, for example, how much better the cavalry was treated than the dragoons, and how much better the dragoons were treated than the infantry. Dragoon horses were lighter, weaker and cheaper than those of the cavalry. The wide range in seventeenth-century horse prices is comparable to the range in car prices today. At one end of the scale a dragoon horse could be had for as little as £2. At the other end, Major Thomas Harrison, who always loved quality in his apparel and equipment, was allowed £50 to buy himself two horses.[94]

Everyone in the rank and file, whether horse trooper or foot soldier, had the same quality of sword, but dragoon muskets, even though they were shorter barrelled, cost 20 to 30 per cent more than the matchlock muskets supplied to the foot. Some dragooners carried carbines, which were also more expensive than infantry muskets. Cavalry troopers sat in saddles that were more substantial, fancier and twice as costly as the saddles provided for their comrades in the dragoons. Pistols, which were highly prized, and upon which a great deal of money was lavished, seem to have been given only to the cavalry. They doubtless contributed to a trooper's sense of well-being, but inflicted little damage upon the enemy.

A great deal of money was spent on firearms in general. Pistols, muskets and carbines cost more than pikes and halberds, and many more of them were bought. Virtually everyone seems to have carried a sword, which was still probably the most effective hand weapon, but musketeers outnumbered pikemen by two to one, or more.

Powder, match, shot and shells consumed a considerable amount of money, but the New Model is known to have purchased no more than three pieces of artillery during its first year. The small attention paid to ordnance does not reflect a failure to appreciate its importance, but rather the fact that a good deal of ordnance had been inherited from the three armies that went out of existence in 1645. A clue to the size of the artillery train is contained in the report of the army's marching formation in the spring of 1645. The carriages and the main body of the train marched in the middle of the army, flanked by troops of horse on all sides. In addition, four pieces of ordnance were drawn between each of the twenty-four regiments.[95] Ordnance was not used to great effect on the battlefield, but it came into its own during the manifold sieges that began in July 1645. Fairfax's preference for lightning assaults against royalist castles and fortified towns was made practical by the gigantic haul of ordnance at Naseby (much of it having been previously captured by the royalists from Essex at Lostwithiel). Over a century before on the continent, the new cannon had sounded the death knell for the stone walls of medieval cities. The same sentence was now executed in England as one castle and city wall after another collapsed into rubble at the shock of the New Model artillery. Even though its effectiveness was well appreciated, artillery was still not fully exploited in the sieges of 1645–6. Poor road conditions and the sometime unavailability of transport for heavy guns meant that they could not always be brought into play.

The supply warrants reveal that the Commons directive to county committees to ensure that all recruits were provided with a coat, breeches, shirt, pair of stockings, pair of shoes and knapsack, costing not more than 24s. in all, was not observed.[96] It was the army itself, not the county committees, that clothed most men, and thanks to its ability to make volume purchases it managed to do it for less than 25s. per man. It is also clear that few cavalry troopers or dragoons brought their own horses. The only troop in the army known to have furnished all its own horses belonged to Captain Ralph Knight of Sir Robert Pye's regiment. Its members also brought their own arms, and in return were paid a shilling a day more than the normal trooper's rate of 2s.[97] Some Londoners, in order to avoid conscription or other exactions, paid for a trooper and a horse at £12 a time, but for the most part men volunteered as troopers and then were outfitted. Those who came from the armies of Essex, Manchester and Waller brought their horses with them, so that only 280 horses had to be bought before the battle of Naseby.[98] During the next ten months several thousand horses were taken from the enemy – most notably at Naseby, where 2000 were taken, and at the surrender of Hopton's army in Cornwall, when 2500 more were acquired.[99] Nevertheless the demand for troop horses was insatiable, so that the treasurers at war had to pay for no fewer than 2318 troop horses in the New Model's first year. Most of them were bought in the summer of 1645.

The creation of the New Model was also marked by the introduction of the British army's distinctive uniform for over two centuries: the redcoat. It was faced with blue, the colour of Sir Thomas Fairfax, while the breeches were grey.[100]

In addition to being clothed and transported to the army's assembly point at Reading, the new troops were fed until the time they received their first wages. The most elementary staples – cheese and hard biscuit – were purchased centrally. Almost 90,000 lbs of Suffolk and other cheeses and 1503 cwt of biscuit were distributed during the first two months. After that the men were on their own. Like most contemporary European armies they procured a good 90 per cent of their consumption locally.[101] They were expected to buy food out of their wages, and the cavalry were also responsible for feeding their horses. So long as the army was regularly paid the commissariat did not have to worry about feeding and lodging the soldiers, since this was arranged privately between each man and the householder who quartered him. Sympathetic journalists made much of the soldiers' relatively good record in paying for what they took, and indeed it appears that the favourable impression created in the western counties was instrumental in neutralizing the clubmen or even bringing them over to the parliamentary side. The 'free enterprise' system of feeding the army provided stimulation to local markets, and, once it was known that the soldiers could be trusted to pay for what they needed, farmers were only too happy to sell. Thus at Bristol in August and September, Devon in January, and Oxfordshire in May 1646, local economies were quickened by the infusion of money from soldiers' pockets.[102]

But, if the army stayed too long in one place or if the caravan bearing the month's pay was delayed, a regional economy would be devastated. The region near Crediton, Devon, in February 1646, where a large part of the army had been stationed for several weeks, became 'miserably exhausted and ruined' with hardly any food or fodder to be had, despite the fact that the soldiers could pay cash for them.[103] Given the relative immobility of food supplies and the very high cost of inland transport in the seventeenth century, an army that did not keep on the move became an insupportable burden on the district where it was stationed.

Lack of pay merely complicated a problem that was continually on the verge of getting completely out of hand. At the time of Naseby, for example, the newly recruited army descended like clouds of locusts on the defenceless countryside of Northamptonshire and Warwickshire. For four months from April to July the army was being relatively well paid: thirteen out of seventeen weeks for the foot, and nine or ten out of seventeen for the horse.[104] Yet, if the householders of both counties can be believed, Fairfax's men seized mammoth quantities of sheep, lambs, pigs, calves, butter, cheese, bacon, beer, wheat, barley, peas, oats, meal and malt. Bored with their spartan diet of cheese and biscuit, the soldiers were ravenous for meat on the eve of battle. Their horses were no less hungry: between 7000 and 8000 of them consumed whole meadows and pastures, some freshly seeded. The loss of grass was a leading complaint, heard over and over again. The insistent need for fodder in pre-mechanized armies is demonstrated by the oft-repeated cry that valuable pasture had been devoured or trampled. Horses needed to be shod as well as fed, and horseshoes are a further item for which compensation was frequently demanded. Another expense borne locally arose from the New Model's habit of commandeering wagons for short distances.

No article in the agrarian inventory was exempt from the soldiers' grasping fingers. In addition to foodstuffs, claims were submitted for clothing – shoes, shirts, gloves and stockings; for bedding and linen; for fuel – coal, turf and firewood; and for miscellaneous items – straw, a brass pot, a bottle, money and a Bible. Besides using up some families' entire hoard of firewood in a few nights, the soldiers cut down trees and quartered without payment on unwilling householders. The taking of free quarter – so potent a source of animosity between soldier and civilian – was more the rule than the exception in the spring of 1645. The parish of Kineton alone claimed compensation amounting to over £27 19s. 4d. for quartering and the loss of property when Colonel Rich's regiment stopped for three nights. A year later the inhabitants of the village of Stretton under Fosse said wearily, 'we have been charged so often with so many for free quarter, that we cannot make any certainty thereof, but estimate the cost to be above £30.'[105]

These accounts, preserved in the army's own records, belie the publicists' boast that it behaved honourably towards its civilian hosts at all times. Military conduct towards civilians seems to have improved after Naseby, however. The two and a half months leading up to that climactic encounter were a period of administrative chaos, as officers tried to cope with an infantry a good half of whose members were raw undisciplined conscripts. Over the succeeding months Fairfax and his staff knocked the army into shape by punishing harshly those who took from civilians without paying. Consequently, far fewer claims were submitted for the southern and western counties where the New Model sojourned between July 1645 and June 1646. When money ran short, as it often did, soldiers were more inclined to tighten their belts than risk punishment for seizing food for which they could not pay. It was said that one of the causes of the widespread sickness in the army in the late autumn of 1645, apart from poor accommodation and lack of warm clothing, was the inability to pay for bread. This reduced the soldiers to living off 'fruit and roots', a demoralizing experience to men not inspired with the modern enthusiasm for such ingredients in the human diet.[106]

As soon as it became apparent that the war was won, taxpayers and parliament both slackened in their efforts to keep the army well provisioned and paid. From the late spring of 1646 to the autumn of that year, the army's financial position steadily deteriorated. Ironically, at the very moment when a pro-army newsbook boasted that the soldiers besieging Oxfordshire paid in ready money for everything that they consumed, Fairfax published a severe proclamation throughout the army against taking free quarter.

> I do strictly charge and order all officers and soldiers ... to discharge their quarters according to the several rates expressed in an ordinance of parliament; *viz.*, 4d. a night hay, 2d. a night grass, 4d. a peck oats, 6d. a peck peas and beans and also 8d. a day for every trooper or horseman, 7d. a day for every dragooner and 6d. a day for every foot soldier, pioneer, waggoner or carter, not commissioned.[107]

But in the next breath the policy was vitiated by a proviso that unpaid soldiers who were unable to pay full value were to give tickets, signed by their commanding officer, for what they received in the way of board and lodging.

The improvement in the army's conduct during the ten months after Naseby in no way diminishes the truth of the statement that the New Model fundamentally lived off the countryside where it was located. If about £117,000 was disbursed centrally for supplies, many times that value was taken locally. Some supplies were paid for at the time; some were taken in return for certificates promising future payment, and some were unceremoniously seized. The only type of supplies that were not picked up locally was weapons and ammunition. Otherwise the region supplied the army with what it needed: food and lodging, spades and shovels, transport for its equipment, horses and occasionally also clothing. In mitigation of the New Model's record in taking free quarter and supplies, we may note that the royalist forces were even more outrageous and undisciplined in their behaviour.[108]

Pay

Once men had been recruited into the army, clothed and equipped, the major continuing expense was their daily wage, ranging from 8d. for a foot soldier, 1s. 6d. for a dragoon and 2s. for a cavalry trooper, to 30s. a day for a colonel and £10 for the commander-in-chief. Officers who were paid between 5s. and 10s. a day had one third of it withheld, or 'respited upon the public faith', while those paid above 10s. a day had half of it withheld. Even the cavalry trooper saw a quarter of his pay deducted in forced savings.[109] Private soldiers were expected to feed and clothe themselves out of their wages, while the cavalry troopers were also responsible for feeding their horses.

In theory the system of paying the troops was both rational and highly centralized. Regiments were mustered every four to six weeks. On the basis of the number recorded present at the muster, a warrant for one week's or for two or four weeks' pay for the foot or dragoon company or horse regiment in question was drawn up, signed by Fairfax and dispatched to the Treasurers at War. Roughly once a month a shipment of money would leave London for the army in its several locations. Delivering the money was a major operation involving wagons, teams of horses and guards. In the modern era of paper, plastic and even less tangible instruments of exchange, we need to be reminded of the sheer weight of silver currency. Twenty-five chests were required to carry less than a month's pay to the army in Dorset in August 1645. The cargo was shipped overland and by sea, the leg from Poole to Sherborne requiring twenty-two horses in four teams, and eight drivers. The transportation alone cost over £16.[110] Protecting the money *en route* was an additional cost which does not appear in the accounts, since the guards were supplied by the army itself. So long as the royalists remained a real threat, the monthly train of money had to be heavily guarded. In October 1645 the pay sent to the west was conveyed by no fewer than 500 horse and 1000 dragoons.[111] Even while money passed through friendly territory it would normally be guarded by several dozen local or New Model troops.[112]

Once the money had reached the army it would be paid out to the officers on the basis of the mustered strength of their companies or regiments. An officer's signature on the back of his unit's pay warrant constituted the treasurers at war's receipt. The officers would then look after distributing the money among their men. The virtual absence of any complaints against New Model officers for withholding money from their troops suggests that this final stage in the payment process was carried out fairly.[113] As table 2.2 demonstrates, the army was paid quite regularly for the first year of its existence.

Over the twenty-seven months from April 1645 to June 1647 the foot received pay for approximately eighty-nine weeks, or 76 per cent of the period as a whole. The horse, whose pay allowed them a standard of living slightly higher than mere subsistence, were deliberately paid less constantly, their total pay coming to sixty-eight weeks, or 58 per cent of the full period.[114] Officers of horse and foot saw half their pay 'respited' in enforced savings. A surprising finding of this survey is how well the army was paid in late 1646 and early 1647. By then Oxford had capitulated, the military conflict was over except for a few isolated garrisons in the west, and civilian dissatisfaction was mounting at the continued existence of an expensively idle army. Yet during the six months ending in April 1647 both horse and foot received virtually full pay.[115]

Nevertheless, short-term delays in the delivery of money to the army could produce enormous problems. After the summer of 1645 pay was frequently between one month and three months late reaching the soldiers. Tardiness of this magnitude can only have accelerated the rate of desertion. Thus we read that at the beginning of October 1645 the army was sad and discouraged for want of pay.[116] The failure of money to arrive turned the soldiers' minds to mutiny, and some were heard to mutter that they would wheel around and go to London for their money if it did not come to them.[117] The crisis in the autumn of 1645 was tied to a blockage in the receipts from the monthly assessment. The best parliament could offer in the short term were piecemeal expedients. Bread, cheese and biscuit to the value of £1000 were ordered to be sent down. Part of a £2000 composition fine was earmarked to provide shoes and stockings for the infantry.[118] The payment dates for these items show that the shoes and stockings were sent almost immediately, while the food shipment took rather longer to organize.[119] In addition, officers dug into their own pockets to ensure that their men did not starve. Meanwhile the army exploited its London connections to gain the maximum publicity in the capital. An effective lobbyist for the cause was Ferdinando Lord Fairfax, Sir Thomas's father, who had moved to London earlier that year. Letters from the general to his father outlining the army's needs were quickly brought to the attention of MPs and newsbook writers.[120] Hugh Peters also deployed his considerable talents for oratory and political influence to keep the New Model at the top of parliament's list of priorities. Journalists co-operated eagerly, printing poignant descriptions of the barrenness of the countryside and the nakedness of the soldier, and writing editorials on the folly of pinching pennies at so crucial a juncture in the struggle against the king. Guilty feelings were shrewdly stirred up amongst well-fed Londoners for living safe, warm and comfortable lives while shivering soldiers fell sick for want of clothing and scavenged for 'fruit and roots' because lack of money denied them the luxury of bread.[121]

What this survey shows is that the New Model Army was paid with remarkable regularity for more than two years. While not discounting the suffering that was experienced when money was delayed even by a few weeks, it must be recognized that the New Model was better cared for than other contemporary armies or than the ones it had replaced. This is why men fled from Massey's brigade to the New Model despite the Lords' attempts to stem the flow. It explains why royalist soldiers signed on for the New Model with such alacrity. It also illuminates the soldiers' statement in June 1647 that their pre-New Model arrears were much greater than what they had accumulated since 1645.[122] The total arrears owing to all the forces of parliament by early 1647 was about £3 million. But half that sum at least

Table 2.2 Pattern of pay of Fairfax's army, April 1645–June 1647

Month	Foot and artillery		Horse and dragoons	
	No. of weeks paid	Reference: SP28/	No. of weeks paid	Reference: SP28/
1645				
April	4	29	2	29
May	3	30	2	30
June	4	30	3–5	30, 31
July	2	31	2	31
August	3–4	31	2	31
September	0	—	0	—
October	4	32	3	32
November	1	33	1	33
December	7	33	3	33
1646				
January	0[a]	—	2	36
February	2	36	2	36
March	2	37	2	37
April	5[b]	37	1	37
May	4	38	6	38
June	8[c]	38–9	3	38

July	0	–	3	39
August	10	39	4	39
September	0	–	0[d]	40
October	0	–	0	–
November	6	41	4	41
December	6	41	4	41
1647				
January	4	44	4	44
February	4	44	4	44
March	3	45	3	45
April	3	45	3	45
May	0	–	0	–
June	4	46	4	46

[a] The artillery were issued warrants for four weeks' pay (vol. 36, fo. 106). It may be that the foot regiments also received four weeks' pay, but that the warrants are missing.

[b] In April the foot regiments received unequal treatment, a fact which is difficult to discern because of the disorganized state of volume 37. Three regiments received two weeks' pay; two received four weeks'; three received six weeks'; one received eight weeks'; one received nine weeks', and one received eleven weeks'. A total of sixty weeks' pay was distributed, or an average of five weeks' per regiment.

[c] Some warrants were dated 1–2 July (vol. 39).

[d] A few cavalry troops received four weeks' pay, as did a number of troop commanders (vol. 40, fos 252–85).

was owed to non-New Model forces. Of the roughly £1½ million owed to the New Model soldiers, three fifths was for pre-New Model service. Moreover, close to half the post-1644 arrears were owed to officers. Of the remainder, almost all belonged to the cavalry troopers who were on three quarters pay. The back pay of the New Model foot for service since April 1645 was almost negligible. Fairfax's infantry had not had to rely on free quarter except rarely, or in defiance of military orders. Free quarter had been the unhappy recourse of the much worse-paid local and garrison forces. Most noteworthy of all, the New Model was paid punctually and in full during the four months before it became politically active in March 1647. The threat of disbandment, and the political motivation behind that threat, as well as other grievances, must thus be given much greater prominence than the question of arrears in understanding the upheavals of 1647.

3

Victory in Battle, 1645–6

Militarily the New Model Army had an untidy beginning. Foot regiments formerly belonging to the Earl of Essex were in a state of mutiny and seemed indisposed to accept Fairfax's authority. Colonel Dalbeir, with his eight troops of horse, stood aloof, apparently ready to join the king at Oxford.[1] Sir Michael Livesey also led his regiment in a mutiny against the new dispensation, and was at once replaced by Henry Ireton.[2] A number of other officers, instead of joining their troops at Windsor, where mobilization was taking place, wasted their time in 'idleness and prophaneness' in London, scandalizing citizens with their drunken brawling.[3] Fairfax, whose health was fragile at the best of times, succumbed to a fever just before he was to advance the army from Windsor to Reading.[4] The key post of lieutenant-general of cavalry remained unfilled throughout April and May 1645.

More seriously, Fairfax and his commanders found their freedom of manoeuvre hobbled by the Committee of Both Kingdoms, which continued to direct military strategy from London. Prominent on the committee were the peers, several of whom had just lost their commands by the Self-Denying Ordinance. As soon as the army had reached a strength of about 10,000 the committee ordered Fairfax, against his better judgement, to relieve the garrison of Taunton, Somerset, where the besieging forces under the royalist general Lord Goring were tightening their grip. Obediently Fairfax set out for the west at the beginning of May. At Blandford, Dorset, seven days later he was greeted with fresh instructions to turn around and make for Oxford, which was now thought vulnerable to attack since the king had withdrawn from the garrison there to take his forces into the field. Colonel Weldon was left at Taunton with a brigade of 5000 horse and foot and a few days later succeeded in raising the siege. Fairfax thought it pointless to surround Oxford while the king was in the field, but he obeyed orders.[5] Not only was the Committee of Both Kingdoms strategically inept, but it was incapable of ensuring that Fairfax got the provisions he needed; so he sat idle before the fortifications for fifteen days.[6] The reason for this attention to Oxford was Saye and Sele's conviction, based on information from Lord Savile, that the governor of Oxford was ready to betray the city to parliament. The hope was illusory. Meanwhile, the Scots complained bitterly of the New Model's immobility at the same time as they were expected to bear the brunt of the king's field offensive.[8]

Interestingly, Fairfax found the Scots an ally in his campaign to get out from under the irksome rule of the armchair strategists in London.[9] But it took a major disaster to bring the Committee of Both Kingdoms to its senses. In its restless shifting of pieces over the chessboard of southern England, it had inadvertently created a vacuum at the centre.[10] In late May the New Model forces were distributed between Taunton (5000), Oxford (10,000) and the north, where Vermuyden had been dispatched with 2500 troops to help the Scots engage the king. Cromwell had been sent to the Isle of Ely to prevent an incursion into East Anglia. The whole strategy began to unravel when the Scots, feeling betrayed and worried about the menace of Montrose at home, declined to meet the king's main army and faded back towards Westmorland. Their unauthorized withdrawal forced Brereton to abandon the siege of Chester. At this moment the king, had he desired, could have assaulted the heavily invested stronghold of Chester, but instead he circled back to fill the vacuum at the centre. On 31 May he stormed and brutally sacked Leicester without a finger being raised against him. A week later, only five days before the decisive battle of the civil war, the Committee of Both Kingdoms acknowledged the futility of directing field operations and gave Fairfax the free hand he had sought.[11]

Thus by the beginning of June, thanks to political infighting, poor strategy and administrative delay, parliament's fortunes had dipped to their lowest point since 1643. Objectively however, the king's position was even more perilous. Cromwell's daring movements in April, when he had beaten up the countryside to the west of Oxford, had disrupted the passage of the royalist artillery train to Hereford. By impounding all the draught horses in the region he had made it temporarily impossible for Prince Maurice to remove the heavy guns from Oxford for several days and stymied Charles's plan for an early opening to the campaign.[12] If Fairfax had been straitjacketed by the Committee of Both Kingdoms, Charles had been distracted by irreconcilable divisions within his council. Isolated from his supporters in the west and the north, Charles had command of fewer than 9000 troops, while Fairfax's ranks continued to swell by the day.

At this juncture the London Common Council raised the issue which no one else had been bold enough to mention publicly: the status of Oliver Cromwell, whose resignation under the terms of the Self-Denying Ordinance was imminent.[13] Encouraged by this evidence of Cromwell's good standing in London, Fairfax's council of war wrote urging that Cromwell be nominated to the vacant lieutenant-generalship of the cavalry. The Commons, though not the Lords, gave speedy assent to this request[14] a mere four days before battle was joined at Naseby. By the time Cromwell rode into the New Model lines with 600 of the horse and dragoons that he had recruited in the Eastern Association, that climactic event was only a day away.[15]

Naseby

That the battle occurred at all was thanks to Charles's indecision about whether to link up with Goring in the south-west, meet Langdale in the north, or launch an attack on the Eastern Association. When he found himself in proximity to Fairfax's army he listened to Rupert, whose contempt for the New Model was so great that no flicker of doubt troubled him as to his ability to conquer a force nearly twice as large as his own. Yet Charles might still have postponed the day of battle had he received Goring's letter promising to overrun Taunton, and then hasten to the king's aid within three weeks.[16]

On 14 June 1645 Fairfax disposed of eleven horse regiments more or less at full strength, a regiment of dragoons, eight regiments of foot, and 200 lifeguards as well as a similar number of firelocks. As we have seen in chapter 2, his total strength cannot have been less than 15,000 and was probably closer to 17,000, not counting officers. Charles had less than three fifths that number.[17] The parliamentary generals also chose their ground well. In the early morning of 14 June, the armies faced each other on two low hills just north of Naseby. Finding that the king's army to the north-west had the advantage of the wind blowing out of the west, Fairfax shifted to the left so that two armies now faced each other on a north–south axis (see map 2). Fairfax then withdrew his troops 100 paces behind the brow of the hill in order to conceal their disposition from the king. This manoeuvre may also have prompted Charles to think that Fairfax was fleeing. In addition to facing an uphill charge to meet the parliamentarians, Charles's cavalry would have to wade through low wet ground in the middle, slowing them down considerably. Fairfax's cavalry was augmented by Colonel John Fiennes's regiment and the regiment brought by Cromwell from the Eastern Association. Five and a half regiments were arranged, two deep, on the left, under the command of Henry Ireton, who had been made commissary-general that morning. With five and a half regiments plus the lifeguard, the right wing under Cromwell was a trifle heavier. This preponderance was

Plate 1   Sir Thomas Fairfax, Captain-General of the New Model Army

(The British Library: Thomason Collection)

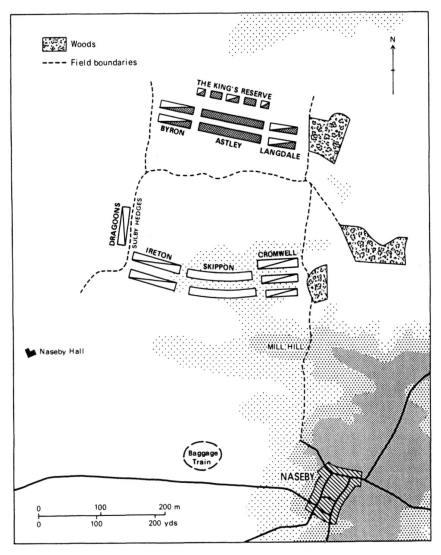

Map 2 The battle of Naseby, 14 June 1645

entirely due to the arrival of Rossiter's regiment from Lincolnshire just after the battle was joined. Of greater significance was the fact that it was drawn up three lines deep instead of the more usual two. The left wing's slight deficiency in numbers was more than compensated by stationing Okey's crack regiment of dragoons behind the hedges on the far left, at right angles to the line of battle. From there they would be able to distract the king's advancing horse by pouring musket fire across their flank. At a later stage in the battle, the dragoons' intervention would be decisive. Between the two wings of cavalry were the eight foot regiments, drawn up in two lines, with a 'forlorn hope' of 300 musketeers ahead of the front line.[18] The battleline was a mile in breadth. A mile back, just west of Naseby, was the baggage and artillery train guarded by firelocks. Overall, it was a simple order of battle, as Peter Young points out, apart from the 'one touch of tactical subtlety' – the placement of the dragoons. The lack of a brigade structure meant that orders had to be transmitted in cumbersome fashion from the general officers to each regimental commander in turn.[19]

Jockeying for position had begun at three o'clock in the morning. Around ten the cannon on both sides began to play, but the exchange lasted less than an hour, since the parliamentary commanders wanted to use the daylight hours for fighting. While ordnance might be crucial in sieges, the conventional wisdom of the time held that it scarcely affected the outcome of a battlefield confrontation.

In a scant two hours the battle was over. Around eleven o'clock Rupert advanced with his cavalry against the left wing under Ireton, who tried to gain the upper hand by charging down the hill to meet him. The charge was ragged, however, with part of the line holding back, and part of it pushing so deeply into the enemy's ranks that it came up against the reserve and was routed. Some of the horse stumbled into shallow waterholes and ditches. Ireton in his inexperience allowed himself to become distracted. Seeing the infantry in trouble, he ordered the detachment nearest him to force their way through and rescue them. While preoccupied with this diversion his own horse was shot under him and he himself was run through the thigh with a pike and struck in the face with a halberd. Taken prisoner, he was out of action until the tide turned. One regiment – Butler's on the far left – was saved from the general rout of Ireton's wing by musket fire from the dragoons in the hedges.

Having scattered nearly half the New Model cavalry and left it headless, Rupert ought to have seen the trouble that Langdale's cavalry was in on the other side of the field. Instead he tried to capture the artillery train on the outskirts of Naseby and met with unexpectedly fierce resistance from Thomas Hammond's seasoned men.

At the same time as Ireton was being ignominiously captured, Cromwell on the right wing led a successful charge against Langdale's horse. The whole of Langdale's wing was pushed back, leaving the flank of the royalist infantry exposed to cavalry attack. But the parliamentary foot under Skippon was in even direr straits. The enemy had rolled back the front line, except for Fairfax's own foot regiment, until they fell behind the reserves. The reserves, however, under Colonels Rainborowe, Pride and Robert Hammond, did not retreat but halted the royalist advance before all was lost. Like the left wing the centre was by now also leaderless, though the wounded Skippon insisted on remaining on the field. Far more seriously hurt than Ireton, Skippon required almost a year of convalescence before he was again well enough for active service. He cannot have been very effective that morning in directing the the middle. It was now about noon and the New Model had lost two of its field generals, only Fairfax, Cromwell and Thomas Hammond remaining. By a co-ordinated effort they managed to save the day. Seeing the distress of the left wing and the middle, Fairfax and Cromwell wheeled about. With a detachment of horse Cromwell crossed the field and attempted to rally Ireton's fragmented divisions. He and Fairfax, who was now bareheaded, having lost his helmet, then charged from opposite sides into the main body of the king's infantry in order to bring relief to their own beleaguered regiments. The manoeuvre worked. Having restored order to the parliamentary line, Fairfax then prepared to lead a second charge against the king's left wing of horse, which had regrouped and been augmented by Rupert's divisions, now back on the field. This meant waiting until the parliamentary foot recovered the quarter mile they had lost at the beginning of the battle. As soon as the horse and foot were abreast, and the horse arranged again in two wings, the whole army advanced once more under Fairfax's direction. This time the general was careful to ensure that the horse did not leave the flanks of the infantry exposed by too impetuous a charge. Sighting the monolithic approach of the New Model and overawed by its crushing superiority of numbers, the remnant of the king's army now turned tail and fled. Cromwell directed the pursuit of these demoralized forces for 13 or 14 miles, almost to the gates of Leicester.

Contemporary narratives of the battle of Naseby are not perfectly clear about the chronological order of events, and there are small differences of detail, but one thing that is evident, especially from the accounts that appeared within the first two days, is the central role of Sir Thomas Fairfax. Cromwell's arrival on the day before gave a fillip to the soldiers' morale. It was he who had suggested moving the army west to the higher ground of Mill Hill. It was he who arranged the cavalry, making his own right wing three lines deep. It should be noted, however, that this formation may have been an improvisation to accommodate the arrival of Rossiter's regiment after the battle was under way. It was Cromwell who led the first successful charge by the right wing. But when his friend Ireton, whom he had entrusted with the leadership of the left wing, faltered and fell, Cromwell raced to rescue him and reinspire his shattered regiments. Fairfax then saved the infantry from complete collapse by his own qualities of courage and leadership. At most times a quiet and even sickly man, Fairfax's personality was transformed on the battlefield. In the words of one eyewitness, his courage and determination 'did so animate the soldiers as is hardly to be expressed. Sir, had you seen him and how his spirit was raised, it would have made an impression on you never to be obliterated.'[20] Fairfax did not hesitate to expose himself to personal hazard by wading into the thick of the battle at critical moments. More important was his capacity to keep his head amidst the terrible confusion, flux and panic of an actual battle. Cromwell chose the ground, set the troops in order and decisively broke Langdale's horse. Fairfax, thirteen years his junior, but with the benefit of several years of continental and northern battlefield experience, directed troop movements and responded to the unpredictable fluidity, the overwhelming rush of events, that were compressed into the two hours when the outcome of the English civil war was decided. 'He was to and again in the front, carrying orders, bringing on divisions in the midst of dangers, with gallant bravery and routed that enemy.'[21] In the opinion of the army's secretary, John Rushworth, at all times a shrewd observer of events, what 'made our horse so terrible to them was the thickness of our reserves and their orderly and timely coming on, not one failing to come on in time.'[22] After the first charge it was Fairfax who directed the remaining charges by the right wing, Cromwell being preoccupied with filling the gap left by Ireton's capture. Fairfax synchronized the advance of horse and foot, and saw to the 'timely coming on' of the reserves. To him belongs major credit for the victory of Naseby. [23]

The price of the victory, measured in human lives, was relatively cheap. Fairfax lost 150 men, none higher in rank than a captain, while the king lost about 1000. Charles was also deprived of 4000 of his foot, who were taken prisoner, 2000 horses, his entire artillery and baggage train, and his file of secret letters. Soon-to-be-published excerpts from these letters would do irreparable damage to the king's credibility as a negotiator. The disaster was rendered less than total, however, by the fact that the royalist cavalry had got away virtually intact.[24] The ugliest episode of the day was the massacre of over 100 defenceless women by the victorious soldiers. Parliamentarian accounts referred to them as whores and Irishwomen 'of cruel countenance', but Rushworth conceded that many of them were in reality soldiers' wives. [25]

The South-Western Campaign (see map 3)

Not pausing to rest or observe the sabbath, Fairfax advanced his army the next day to within a mile of Leicester, whence the King's remaining forces fled westward in dismay. On the Tuesday following, the earlier loss of the town was easily reversed without a shot being fired, the mere threat of an assault sufficing to induce Lord Hastings to cede the garrison. Fairfax now turned his mind again to Taunton, the key to the west. He wrote to parliament asking authorization to follow up his victory. A Commons motion to restore to the Committee of Both Kingdoms its old power to direct the army's movements was easily blocked, and Fairfax was given the green light to march and relieve Taunton.[26] The Committee of Both Kingdoms also endorsed Fairfax's strategy, confining itself to suggesting that he co-ordinate his movements closely with the Scots, and letting him know that Massey was also marching from the opposite direction towards Taunton with 2200 horse and dragoons. There was still an inclination to besiege Oxford, but the shortfall in recruitment combined with serious loss of numbers from desertion ruled out that option.[27]

The clubmen

Without delay Fairfax now bent his steps towards Taunton. When at the beginning of July 1645 he crossed the county boundary into Dorset, he came for the first time against a group of clubmen. Over the next three months relations with this protest movement, recently sprung up in the south and west of England, were to play an important part in his strategic calculations. Although many groups were lumped together under the same name, the clubmen by their very nature were not a homogeneous movement. They represented a regionally organized resistance to the ravages of civil war. Their leadership, their policies and their tactics were all unco-ordinated. What united them was an outraged reaction to plundering by undisciplined troops, and an earnest yearning for peace. Their numbers easily exceeded those of the royalist and parliamentary forces in their region and for a few months they posed a real threat to the armies of both sides. On at least one occasion they proved themselves almost a match for the cream of the New Model cavalry. Fairfax was right to approach them with the utmost care.

There was no uncertainty in his mind however, about his ultimate intention towards those clubmen who obstructed his way – it was to crush them.

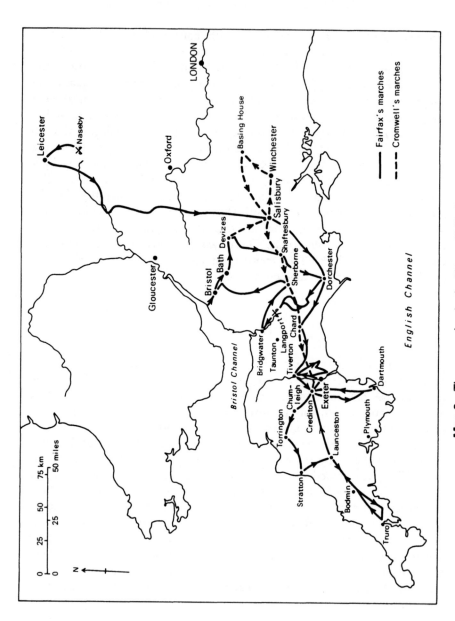

Map 3 The campaign in the West, 1645–6

Until that objective was practicable, however, he made it his business to parley courteously with them and gather as much information as he could about their internal organization and strength.[28]

Early in July at Dorchester, Fairfax met with one of the leaders of the Dorset–Wiltshire clubmen, Robert Hollis, who showed him their articles of association. The clubmen wanted passes to travel through his lines and deliver petitions to king and parliament. Judging them to be more royalist than neutralist, Fairfax refused their request. He then wrote to the Committee of Both Kingdoms stating flatly that he could not continue his westward march unless his rear were protected by the dispatch of two more regiments. It would be the job of these regiments, with the help of Colonel Edmund Ludlowe, sheriff of Wiltshire, to stop the clubmen from mobilizing.[29] After his sweeping victory over Goring's army at Langport on 10 July, Fairfax encountered a much friendlier reception from the mid-Somerset clubmen led by Humphrey Willis. They confiscated the royalists' horses and arms, and took some of the fleeing soldiers prisoner.[30] Over the next ten days until the storm of Bridgwater, clubmen blocked the roads to Bristol with their musketeers, preventing Goring from escaping to join Prince Rupert's garrison.[31] They also joined the siege of Bridgwater, where they were assigned to help Massey's forces on the opposite side of the river Parrett.[32] Preserving the appearance of neutrality, they did not take part in the actual attack on the town, but, when the royalist infantry came fleeing down the hedge-lined roads, they stopped them, disarmed them and ordered them home.[33] After Bridgwater, clubmen from Somerset, Wiltshire and Devon slid more and more rapidly into the parliamentary camp. This shift of allegiances did not spring solely from a desire to be seen on the winning side. The parliamentary commissioners who accompanied the army were convinced that the high standard of conduct observed by the army and its prompt payment for food and lodgings had been instrumental in winning the hearts and minds of the clubmen: 'Thousands have laid down their arms merely upon the attention of the soldiers' carriage, which worketh upon them more than laws will.'[34] The power of the New Model Army, combined with its excellent conduct, enabled the 'submerged parliamentarianism' of many west-country clubmen to rise to the surface.[35]

The Dorset clubmen, however, as well as some from Wiltshire and the Somerset border, continued to hold out against Fairfax and parliament even after Bridgwater. Egged on by the royalist garrison at Sherborne, fifty-one of their leaders convened a meeting at Shaftesbury to plan the raising of Fairfax's siege of Sherborne. Before any plans could be concerted, though, Fairfax dispatched two of his best cavalry regiments – Fleetwood's and Whalley's – to the scene. They surprised the leaders in the midst of their deliberations and brought them before the general, who shipped them to

London in the company of other royalist prisoners. This ruthless decapitation of the movement had its inevitable repercussion: a few days later 2000 or more armed men of Dorset gathered at Hambledon Hill, near Blandford, to demand the release of their leaders. Fairfax set Cromwell with 1000 horse against them before they could be reinforced from Wiltshire. At first Cromwell tried to disperse them with words, but when these proved futile he sent Captain-Lieutenant Gladman at the head of Fairfax's own troop of horse to discharge them. But the clubmen did not budge, presenting a wall of pikes and halberds that the horse could not penetrate. Cromwell then ordered his own troop of horse against them under Captain Berry, but Berry too was beaten back. Finally Major Disbrowe led another troop of horse around a ledge of the hill and surprised them from the rear. Only after this third charge by troops of Ironsides were the Dorset clubmen routed.[36]

The capture of Bridgwater and Sherborne removed centres of active encouragement for royalist-leaning clubmen in the Dorset and Somerset border region, while repeated outrages by Goring farther west would cause the country there to rise up against him. The slaughter of twenty clubmen in Devon towards the end of August was both a symptom and a cause of that country's alienation from the cavaliers.[37] Though the disaffected clubmen in the west were now quiescent, Fairfax still believed that he had to deal with Rupert at Bristol before marching into Devon, because he feared an attack on his army's rear by Rupert, perhaps assisted by Goring and 'the malignant incensed club-men of Dorsetshire'.[38] On the advice of the parliamentary commissioner John Ashe, Fairfax ordered Sir John Horner, sheriff of Somerset, 'to raise the power of the country'. Horner's call was heeded with alacrity, so that by the end of August country men were flocking to be listed and armed. A large force of clubmen assisted operations against the fort at Portishead on the Bristol Channel, which surrendered on 28 August.[39] A few days later Sheriff Horner's effort produced a great meeting of 4000–5000 horse and foot on the hills near Chewton Mendip. The country men were greeted by Ashe and a delegation of officers headed by Cromwell. Fairfax's chaplain, Hugh Peters, was invited to preach on horseback, which he did twice. Next day 2000 men appeared to assist with the siege, all, according to Peters, because of his preaching.[40] Another 1500 arrived from Gloucestershire.[41] While they did not play a prominent role at the storming of Bristol, the clubmen helped materially. They fell on Bedminster, one of the outposts, and struck terror into the defenders, who soon surrendered.[42]

By the time Fairfax was ready to enter Devon in mid-October the clubmen had already prepared the way for him by declaring for parliament and killing the governor of Barnstaple, Sir Leven Ashley. This was presum-

Plate 2 Hugh Peters, Chaplain to the Artillery Train

(Source: *Cromwelliana*)

ably in revenge for Goring's massacre of clubmen in August, but was also partly a shrewd realignment to make sure they were on the winning side. When Fairfax sat down before Exeter in late October he was assisted by a contingent of clubmen under the command of Colonel Popham. Finally, in Cornwall in March 1646 the country people near St Columb helped him in blocking up the passes to hinder the king's forces from escaping.[43]

From beginning to end Fairfax's handling of the clubmen was a diplomatic and military triumph. Initially he had been gravely disturbed by the appearance of this destabilizing force at the very moment when he was on the verge of complete victory over the cavaliers. He approached the clubmen cautiously and made every effort to collect as much information as he could about their internal structure, policies, personnel and agenda. His early impression was that they were merely royalists in the guise of neutralist, peace-seeking provincials. Waiting for the right moment to pounce, he laboured to win the respect of the civilian population by a combination of strict discipline and prompt payment for supplies. Disenchantment with the king and his lieutenants, together with a conviction that decisive victory by one side or the other would bring relief to their war-ravaged region, drew the west-country clubmen more and more rapidly to back the New Model. Only the Dorset clubmen remained stubborn in their fidelity to the royalists, but a calculated show of force was enough to destroy them as a military threat. From that point (August 1645) until the end of the first civil war the next spring, the west-country clubmen remained loyal to Fairfax, not only because they detested marauding cavaliers, but also because they were convinced that total victory by the New Model held out the best promise of lifting the curse of civil war from their counties. Not until a year later would they come to the bitter realization that their new masters were hardly better than the old.

The summer campaign

In the wake of Naseby the Committee of Both Kingdoms had adopted a minute that the enemy should be vigorously prosecuted in the field.[44] Fairfax scarcely needed this advice. After resecuring Leicester for parliament and sending 4000 prisoners of war to London under the escort of Nathaniel Fiennes's regiment, he wheeled around to take on the second most important royalist army, led by Goring. He covered the 136 miles from Leicester to the Somerset border in fifteen days.[45] Until he reached Marlborough, Wiltshire, Fairfax left open the option of pursuing the king into Herefordshire, but with the Commons' support and with the check upon the authority of the Committee of Both Kingdoms reaffirmed, he headed for Taunton again.[46] From the opposite direction Massey approached with a brigade of 2200 horse and dragoons. Goring's army was said to number 10,000, equally divided between horse and foot.[47] Notwithstanding the great haul of treasure, artillery and secret papers at Naseby, the New Model was in some distress as it moved west, because of thinness of numbers, scarcity of arms, and lack of horses. [48]

Langport

On 5 July 1645, as he was pushing through Crewkerne, Fairfax made his first contact with the enemy. The day before, Goring had abandoned his siege of Taunton and fallen back to Langport, where the rivers Yeo and Parrett protected him against surprise attack. Expecting strong re-inforcements from Wales, Goring was playing for time: Fairfax's task was to engage with him as speedily as possible. Parties of horse were sent out to capture the passes at Petherton, Ilchester, Load-Bridge and Yeovil. The broken bridges were quickly repaired, and the parliamentarian horse poured across them. Goring was now desperate, as the combined forces of Fairfax and Massey, more than double his own, encircled him. On Tuesday the 8th he attempted to distract the parliamentarians with a feint towards Taunton. Perhaps he hoped that the garrison, relieved after so long a siege, would let down its guard. In the event the cavalry that he sent under Lieutenant-General Charles Porter were themselves surprised. As soon as Fairfax learnt of the enemy's approach towards Taunton he dispatched Massey's brigade, reinforced with regiments of New Model horse and dragoons. On the 9th they came upon Porter's men relaxing by a stream, their horses at grass in the meadow, the men bathing, drinking or strolling along the riverbank. Massey pounced upon them unawares, took 500 prisoners, and chased the rest back towards Langport. By nightfall Goring had decided to retreat to Bridgwater and sent his heavy guns there in advance of his main force. On the morning of the 10th he drew up his army on a hill outside Langport, and prepared to block the enemy's advance against what he intended to be a gradual, orderly withdrawal. The dis-astrous encounter with Massey the day before had paid at least one divi-dend. Massey and Fairfax were now 12 miles apart and separated by three rivers, with no way of coming together again before a battle was joined. Goring had chosen his ground well. At the bottom of the hill upon which he stood was a small stream that Fairfax's men had to ford. Though the day was hot and dry, recent rains had swollen the stream so that when the soldiers crossed it they were belly-high in water. From the ford a narrow hedged lane ascended the hill towards Goring's position. He stationed a strong force of musketeers among the hedges that both traversed the fields and lined the lane leading up to his position. At this point Goring had no intention of fighting; he believed his position so impregnable that he would be able to maintain it until his baggage train had reached Bridgwater.

For his part, Fairfax had at the most 2000 cavalry troopers at his disposal on that morning (the others were with Massey). Even then he could employ only a fraction of that small number, since the lane was not wide enough for more than two horse to ride abreast. Against Goring's tactical cleverness Fairfax had three telling advantages: intelligence, firepower and morale. From scouts and local inhabitants he learned that Goring was without his baggage and artillery. Fairfax knew therefore that his opponent had already opted for a retreat. Until that moment Fairfax and his council of war had been baffled by a foe who had made such skilful use of the terrain. But they were now emboldened to strike. Fairfax and Cromwell drew up their 10,000 men in battle formation on the other side of the valley.

Their second advantage was that they were in possession of all the New Model's heavy guns. These soon silenced the royalists' two remaining small cannon, and 'made the other side of the hill so hot' that Goring pulled his cavalry back, leaving the musketeers who populated the hedges devoid of support. After fifty or sixty cannonades Fairfax sent Colonel Rainborowe and 1500 musketeers splashing across the stream. 'With admirable re-solution' they advanced up the lane from hedge to hedge until the entire passage was theirs. It was now about midday under a blazing July sun. Sensing that the moment was ripe, Fairfax sent two troops of horse (a mere 200 men) galloping up the lane led by Major Christopher Bethell. Given the demoralized state of his enemy, Fairfax could not be accused of foolhardiness, but it was an audacious manoeuvre none the less, and one which tested the mettle of his cavalry. When they reached the top of the hill they charged straight at the front ranks of Goring's cavalry brigade, who outnumbered them perhaps six or eight to one. For a few minutes there was a hectic struggle at swordpoint, but then Major Disbrowe appeared with another detachment of horse. Colonel Rainborowe's musketeers were by now also upon the scene and the dispirited royalists began to scatter. The chaplain Richard Baxter watched fascinated from the safety of the opposite hill while panic spread through the royalist ranks. As the cavalier army crumbled, Baxter heard Major Thomas Harrison, who was standing nearby, 'with a loud voice break forth into the praises of God with fluent expressions as if he had been in a rapture.' Bethell and Disbrowe wanted to pursue the terrified cavaliers, but Fairfax ordered them to wait until reinforcements came up lest the enemy regroup, face about and charge them with superior numbers. The discipline of soldiers was such that they instantly halted their pursuit. The full body of Fairfax's horse – seven regiments in all – then advanced to within 2 miles of Bridgwater, taking about 1400 prisoners, 2000 horses, 4000 arms, two cannon and three wagonloads of ammunition. As at Naseby, the human cost of this stunning victory was not high: about 300 royalists, and a tenth that number of parliamentarians were killed. 'To see this,' exclaimed Cromwell, 'is it not to see the face of God!' Fairfax had triumphantly achieved his objective of engaging Goring before he could be strengthened by the Welsh reinforcements under Grenville and Prince Charles. The events of the past month had been decisive. At Naseby Fairfax had struck the king a mortal blow. 'Then swinging round to face the only other army in the field he lunged at Goring.' The war had been effectively won in less than four weeks.[49]

Bridgwater

On 11 July 1645 neither Fairfax nor his adversaries were aware that the war had been won. Ahead of them lay eleven more months of sieges, pitched battles, cold, hunger, sickness and anxiety. Many strongholds were still in royalist hands, including Bristol, the second port in the realm, and the main distribution centre for the king's weaponry, ammunition and materials. There was also continuing worry about the clubmen.

Bridgwater was a formidable stronghold. Connected by river to the Bristol Channel, it could be supplied by sea, and was a barrier to communication with the west. The 15-foot-thick walls of the town were plentifully studded with cannon and barbed with forts. Surrounding them was a tidal ditch 10 yards wide and up to 10 feet deep. Behind the walls were 1800 well-armed soldiers, and a high castle. To keep its options open, the council of war ordered that preparations be made to storm the fortress. Every foot soldier was told to cut a faggot and fasten it onto his musket or pike to help get across the ditch. Lieutenant-General Thomas Hammond, 'a gentleman of approved fidelity and of a most dextrous and ripe invention', supervised the construction of eight movable bridges 30–40 feet in length. After several days it was concluded that a storm was the least disagreeable of the alternatives. To leave without reducing it would be to repeat the error that had brought the Earl of Essex to disaster at Lostwithiel: advancing west with an unconquered enemy in the rear.

The army finally resolved to storm Bridgwater in the early morning of Monday 22 July. On the day before, Hugh Peters and Edward Bowles preached in the morning and afternoon respectively. The troops were then drawn into the field, at which time Peters addressed an additional warlike exhortation to the forlorn hope who were to lead the storm. According to the preacher's own reckoning, 'it took great place in their hearts.'[50] A brigade of six regiments (of which four were from the New Model) was stationed on the west side of the town under Massey's command. At two o'clock in the morning the assault began, led by Lieutenant-Colonel Hewson, the Westminster shoemaker, on the north-east side. Massey, being unprepared, did not participate in the assault on his side, but only gave the enemy a 'hot alarm'. Hewson's men quickly crossed the bridges that they had thrown across the moat, clambered over the walls in the teeth of furious musket fire, beat the defenders from their cannon and then turned the cannon against them, and let down the drawbridge. As soon as the cavalry had entered, many of the enemy surrendered, but the others retreated across the river in the western half of the town, raising the drawbridge behind them. They then fired grenades and slugs of hot iron into the district that they had vacated. Buildings caught fire, so that by daybreak most of the eastern half of the town was a smouldering ruin.

The governor, Sir Edmund Wyndham, still refused to yield, although Fairfax granted a pause of two hours for women and children to leave the town. The New Model cannon then opened fire, starting a huge conflagration which, fanned by a strong wind, raced through the remainder of the town. Again Massey's forces failed to join the battle, a source of evident annoyance to those on Fairfax's side. The lack of co-ordination did not matter, however. Surrounded by terrified townspeople crying, 'mercy, for the Lord's sake', Wyndham could only capitulate. Vast quantities of arms and ammunition, forty-four pieces of ordnance, and 1000 prisoners fell to parliament, as well as a fabulous haul of plate, jewels and tapestries. After giving up their arms 2000 men were allowed to march away.

The strategic significance of Bridgwater was almost greater than that of Langport. With parliament now controlling a string of garrisons – Bridgwater, Langport, Taunton and Lyme – from the Bristol to the English Channel, the retreating royalists were quarantined in Devon and Cornwall, and denied any contact with their allies in Bristol, the west Midlands and Wales. Yet in the wake of this triumph the first cracks appeared in the façade of parliamentary unity. An army writer pointedly drew attention to Massey's failure to fall on when the agreed signal for the storm was given. The failure occurred not once but on two separate occasions. The army was displeased since it was widely believed that the town could have been taken in one fell swoop had Massey played his part, while London presbyterians were discomfited at the poor showing of their political ally.[51]

Bath and Sherborne

Fairfax, ever prudent, was none the less worried about royalist garrisons in his rear: Bath, Sherborne and Bristol. It troubled him that the Dorset and Wiltshire clubmen continued to take direction from Sir Lewis Dyve, governor of Sherborne. The council of war by contrast thought it more important to keep driving Goring farther west before he could regroup his shattered forces. Fairfax, however, overruled them, and marched the army to Wells, halfway between Bath and Sherborne. From Wells he dispatched a brigade to Sherborne and a party of horse and dragoons to Bath. The latter town was taken on Tuesday 29 July without firing a shot, thanks to the ingenuity and bravado of some of Okey's dragoons. Creeping on their bellies across the bridge to the town gate, they seized the ends of the guards' muskets, which were sticking through the holes of the grate. Then they shouted at the defenders to accept quarter. In a panic the guards dropped their guns and ran to safety within the town. Okey's men then blew open the gate, and the town was quickly yielded.[52]

Fairfax now gathered all but two of his regiments together for the approach to Sherborne, which he knew would be harder to penetrate. Because the long-awaited money and ammunition had still not arrived and the number of recruits brought from Reading by Pye and Sheffield was meagre,[53] he proceeded cautiously. The expertise of the Mendip miners was exploited to prepare approaches to the fortification. While this work continued the soldiers and their civilian helpers had to dodge flaming faggots and deadly sniper fire from one of the castle towers. Two captains were killed and several more wounded.[54] A shipment of treasure and ordnance arrived on 11 August, but there was still no new ammunition. Nevertheless, the great guns began firing on the morning of 14 August and by the evening had smashed a large opening in the middle of the 12-foot-thick wall. That the cannonade lasted a full seven hours was due to another piece of bravado on the part of some of the common soldiers. With an incentive of 6d. for every piece recovered, they stole up to the walls of the town to retrieve the shot that had issued from their own guns. Not only did they fetch back 200 cannon-, demi-cannon- and culverin-shot, but some of them had the audacity to climb the walls and throw stones at the enemy within. Others managed to pull the wool out of the sacks that lay on top of the wall.[55] Yet, even after his wall had been breached, Dyve three times scornfully rejected the summons to surrender. By 15 August the mining of the wall was complete, but before it could be exploded the soldiers drove the defenders from the fortifications, by leaping over the walls and forcing them to take refuge in the castle while Fairfax's men overran the town. When two of the castle towers also fell into the attackers' hands, the royalists hung out the white flag, threw down their arms and cried for quarter. Once inside the castle Fairfax's soldiers gave themselves over to an uncontrolled orgy of looting. In the officers' view the men were justified by parliament's failure to send the promised bonus of 10s. for storming Bridgwater. The town, however, itself was left untouched. On the morrow, which was market day, the soldiers offered the goods they had seized to the country people who had come to town.[56] The capture and destruction of Sherborne ended the threat from the disaffected clubmen of the Wiltshire, Dorset and Somerset border.

Bristol

At the next council of the war the question was whether to proceed west or to attack Bristol, which had been ignominiously lost by Nathaniel Fiennes in 1643. This time Fairfax had no trouble winning the officers to his point of view. In favour of marching west it was argued that the sooner Goring was crushed and the miseries of Devon and Cornwall relieved the better. Also, it would be wise to give Bristol a wide berth, since the city was reported to be suffering 100 deaths a week from the plague. Those who advocated dealing with Bristol first pointed out that Rupert's ability to put 3000 men in the field, and the prospect of fresh recruits from Wales and the Midlands posed a threat to the army's rear. Besides, Bristol was the king's chief port and his principal magazine. Its loss would deal a fatal blow to his hope of recovery.

After it was agreed to make Bristol the priority, a day of fasting was appointed. Led by Dell and Peters on 29 August 1645, the spiritual exercise was directed at winning divine blessing upon the endeavour. The council of war then met again, and resolved to 'punish the vices of the army'. The sense of urgency was heightened by news of Montrose's victory against the Scots and the approach of Charles and Goring in the direction of Somerset. Distressing too was criticism emanating from London.[57] Those hostile to the army believed that it was frittering away valuable time during which the royalists would be able to regroup and concentrate their forces. In the days before and after the siege, army spokesmen – Peters, Fairfax, Cromwell, Rushworth and Montagu – would reiterate their conviction that the siege and storm of Bristol was necessary precisely in order to prevent a conjunction of the king's, Goring's and Rupert's forces.[58]

Given the strategic importance of Bristol and its massive fortifications, the forces which Rupert disposed of were embarrassingly slender. Indeed, they were wholly inadequate to defend the city's 3-mile perimeter. Though well supplied with ordnance, ammunition and victuals, his men were demoralized. The regular soldiers, decimated by the plague and bled by desertion, had shrunk to about 3500 by the day of the battle.[59] Because the city lay in a hollow, outworks over a mile in length had been built on the north-west side across the top of a hill several hundred yards away from the city wall. Studded with six or seven forts and redoubts, as well as numerous redans, the fortifications bristled with heavy cannon. The much shorter perimeter (less than half a mile) on the south side of the Avon was also secure, with high thick walls. The eastern perimeter on the other hand was weak – the $1\frac{1}{4}$-mile wall from Prior's Hill Fort to the Avon being a mere 5 feet high.

Fairfax's position was plainly stronger. While theoretically threatened by the approach of royalist forces from the north and the west, he did not need to worry. Goring had made moves on 25 August to come and raise the siege, but his way from Devon was blocked by Massey's brigade stationed at Taunton.[60] The Scots had abandoned the siege of Hereford and on 4 September the king triumphantly re-entered that city. Yet his army only numbered about 3000 weary cavalry, and he was being watched by a formidable brigade under Poynts and Rossiter. For his assault Fairfax could call upon 9000–10,000 horse and foot.[61] Apart from the 4000–5000 New Model troops at his disposal there were as many as 5000 country men who had joined him outside the walls of the city – close to 3000 from Somerset, and 2000 from Gloucestershire.[62] In addition the vice-admiral of the navy, Captain Moulton, sent ships to blockade the Bristol Channel.[63] Once Portishead had been taken by the Somerset clubmen, the ships moved up the Severn, ready to join the assault from positions on the river.[64] When they arrived the tide was low, and the seamen were thrown into the assault on Prior's Hill Fort to good effect.[65]

Besides overwhelming superiority of numbers, Fairfax had the benefit of high morale. On 3 September the rank and file were assembled and asked whether they wanted to storm the place. They shouted yes, and to cement their enthusiasm for the task Fairfax ordered the immediate payment of 6s. per man, in partial satisfaction of the promise that had been made at Bridgwater.[66]

At the end of August it had been agreed to invest Bristol, but whether it was to be by a long blockade, a meticulous siege involving arduous trench work and mining, or a lightning assault had been left open. On 2 September all the colonels were summoned to a council of war to resolve the issue. It took several days before a storm was agreed upon, the decisive factor apparently being Rupert's recalcitrance.[67] The colonels were then given a day to draw up the plan of attack. On 4 September, as the New Model artillery began thundering against Prior's Hill Fort, Fairfax had written a long letter inviting Rupert to surrender. He assured the prince of parliament's moderation and denied harbouring any animus against the institution of monarchy. They were fighting

> to maintain the rights of the crown and kingdom jointly; a principal part whereof is, that the king, in supreme acts is not to be advised by men of whom the law takes no notice, but by his parliament, the great counsel of the kingdom, in whom (as much as man is capable of) he hears all his people as it were

at once advising him, and in which multitude of counsellors lies his safety, and his people's interest.[68]

Rupert was denied permission to send to the king for his instructions.[69] By now Fairfax's soldiers were fairly dancing with impatience for the attack, but he insisted on seeing the negotiation through to the end. Rupert's next offer was to yield up the city provided he and all his army could march away fully armed. Fairfax had no intention of letting the prince join Charles with his army intact; so, after the impasse had lasted another two days, he ordered the assault to begin at 1 a.m. on Wednesday 10 September.

Despite his overwhelming advantage of numbers, Fairfax knew that the assault would be far harder than at Bridgwater, Bath or Sherborne. The artillery had been active since 4 September, but no breach had been effected. The walls would have to be surmounted by sheer bravery. Everything depended upon the conscripted foot. Until they got inside the city and opened one of its gates the horse could do nothing.

The storm was terrible to behold. Protected by darkness and with the advantage of surprise, Montagu and Pickering overran Langford's gate on the east side, quickly followed by Major Disbrowe and a large body of horse. At this initial encounter no fewer than twenty-two cannon fell into the attackers' hands. Rupert's horse, dismayed by the suddenness and ferocity of the attack, soon retreated to the main fort on the other side of the city. Meanwhile, Weldon's brigade had fared considerably worse on the strongly fortified south side. The main difficulty was that the walls were higher than anticipated. The great thirty-rung ladders did not reach to the top, and the men who tried to scale them were thrown back with 100 losses. Among the dead were Lieutenant-Colonel Dursey, Major Philip Cromwell (Oliver's kinsman) and Major Christopher Bethell, who succumbed several weeks later to his wounds.

The most heroic exploit of the day took place at Prior's Hill Fort. Besides musket fire, Colonel Rainborowe's men had to contend with four cannon pouring round- and case-shot upon them as they struggled to scale the walls. For three hours the battle raged. The men faced the same obstacle as Weldon's brigade: their ladders were not tall enough. Undaunted, a few men made it to the top while others crept in at the portholes. They were led by Captain Lagoe of Pride's regiment, who was the first man to lay hold on the enemy's colours. Lieutenant-Colonel Bowen and a party of Rainborowe's regiment made it onto the palisades, where they struggled for two hours 'at push of pike' but could not force their way into the fort. Finally Colonel Hammond got over the low wall on the eastern side, and stormed the fort from the inward-facing side. Captain Thomas Ireton with a small party from Rich's horse regiment stood between Rupert's cavalry on the hill along the inside of the eastern line and Hammond's foot. Thus protected they were able to storm the fort from inside the lines while Lagoe's men kept the enemy busy on the opposite side. By this co-ordinated effort both regiments made good the capture of Prior's Hill Fort.[70] Even though only one third of the line had now been lost, the cavaliers saw that the end was near, and in despair began setting fire to the city. A short time later Rupert sent word that he would surrender.

It had been the infantry's day. Nothing was heard about Cromwell, and little about the cavalry's role, except for the protection they offered Hammond's regiment at the critical moment when it attacked Prior's Hill Fort from inside the line. The parliamentary commissioners witnessing the assault paid tribute to the care of its preparation and the courage of its execution.[71] Six days of bombardment had failed to dent the walls, with the result that artillery played less of a role at Bristol then at any other siege in 1645–6. In the end the army abandoned the attempt to smash the walls and simply jumped over them. It was a tactic which required lightning speed and tremendous daring. The New Model infantry, so shaky at Naseby, had come of age. Their ranks sifted by desertion and disease, and hardened by the experience of several sieges, the men at Bristol had shown extraordinary courage in hurling themselves against a nearly impregnable fortress.

The strategic significance of the capture of Bristol was lost on no one. In yielding the country's second port Charles gave up the main centre for both the manufacture and import of ordnance. The verdict of the royalist secretary at war was that the city's loss was 'the loss of all our magazines and warlike provisions, and so by consequence in very short time of South Wales, the West, and all other places in the kingdom.'[72] Charles's abrupt dismissal of Rupert was a measure of royalist despair.[73] The fall of Bristol also had far-ranging political repercussions in London. It instantly rehabilitated the reputation of Nathaniel Fiennes, who had been disgraced two years earlier for having surrendered the city to Rupert. In an access of contrition the House of Commons recognized that Fiennes had faced even greater difficulties than Rupert, and immediately voted to restore him to his seat in parliament.[74] The longer-term consequence was a widening of the breach between Independents and presbyterians in London. For the army Bristol was a euphoric highpoint. Welded together by the thrilling experience of shared danger and total victory, the army momentarily breathed the spirit of unity uncontaminated by backbiting. It was perhaps the last time that such unalloyed exaltation occurred. In this mood Cromwell climaxed his letter to the Speaker of the Commons with an appeal for liberty of conscience:

Presbyterians, Independents, all have here the same spirit of faith and prayer, the same presence and answer; they agree here, have no names of difference; pity it is it should be otherwise anywhere. All that believe have the real unity, which is most glorious, because inward and spiritual, in the body and to the head. For being united in forms, commonly called uniformity, every Christian will, for peace sake, study and do as far as conscience will permit. And for brethren, in things of the mind, we look for no compulsion, but that of light and reason.[75]

In thanking Cromwell, Speaker Lenthall rejoiced at the unity of which the lieutenant-general had spoken, but when his letter was printed the passage about religion was omitted.[76] Cromwell's friends in the house retaliated by leaking the suppressed portion, which was then anonymously printed and scattered up and down the streets on the night of 21 September.[77] Informed opinion on both sides in the capital was highly sensitized to the political implications of the army's lengthening string of victories.

Basing

Losing no time after the reduction of Bristol, Fairfax moved to pick off as many remaining strongholds as he could in the weeks before the winter doldrums made further campaigning all but impossible. At a council of war it was agreed that the main army would march west, first relieving Plymouth, while brigades would be sent into Gloucestershire, Wiltshire and Hampshire to subdue the garrisons that were still in royalist hands. Fairfax stuck to his western strategy over the next half-year until every garrison had capitulated. It was a strategy from which the Committee of Both Kingdoms and sundry critics of the army in London frequently tried to distract him. Fairfax, however, was protected from their interference by the majority in the Commons as well as strong administrative support from the Committee for the Army and the treasurers at war. The Commons voted on 17 October that Fairfax and Cromwell were to 'be left free to dispose of their forces in such manner as they shall think most advantageous for the commonwealth in relation to the affairs of the west.' Ten days later Fairfax's power was further enhanced when he was given authority over any commander-in-chief to be appointed in the future. The only fly in the ointment was the Lords' failure to ratify this Commons decision. The lower house's tangible esteem for Fairfax was manifested in the shape of a large diamond worth £800 and horses worth £1000 which were presented to him in November and January respectively.[78] With these material signs of support Fairfax felt more confident about ignoring the Committee of Both Kingdoms' vexing requests.

The brigades under Rainborowe and Cromwell had little difficulty in accomplishing their objectives. Rainborowe and his three foot regiments quickly made themselves masters of the outworks and the church at Berkeley Castle on the road from Bristol to Gloucester. When Sir Charles Lucas saw the formidable cannon being trained upon the all-too-vulnerable castle walls, he threw up his hands and bargained for terms.[79] At Devizes on the road to London a few salvoes from Cromwell's cannon and mortar pieces persuaded the royalists of the wisdom of a parley. Lacock House, a much smaller outpost, was easily overrun by Colonel Pickering with three regiments.[80] Next Cromwell ventured even farther from the main army to take in two more strongholds. At the beginning of November Winchester became the nineteenth garrison to be overrun by the New Model since June, opening up a large free-trade area to the south and west of London. In his report of parliament Hugh Peters waxed eloquent on the benefits this had brought. Inns were now filled with guests, and the satisfying hum of economic activity could be heard once again throughout the region.[81]

The twentieth garrison to fall was Basing, seat of the Catholic Marquess of Winchester. Since August it had undergone its third siege. The local parliamentary gentry, after twice failing to overrun this stubborn royalist outpost, had concluded that a more scientific approach was needed. They were able to secure the services of Colonel John Dalbeir, 'a cunning engineer' from Holland, at whose disposal they placed 900 men.[82] Impatient to see the job finished, Cromwell arrived on 8 October with three foot regiments and a complete train of artillery. While Dalbeir watched the north side, Cromwell subjected the south side to withering fire from his heavy guns. Five days later he had blown two gaping holes in the wall, but the defenders still refused to yield. As the parliamentarians prepared to storm on the morning of the 14th, Cromwell spent the night on his knees, praying and meditating upon the psalmist's denunciation of idolaters. He had in reality encountered fiercer resistance at Basing than at almost any other garrison. Though they knew they were doomed, the defenders disputed every wall and gate. The New Model foot advanced shouting, 'Down with papists', and Cromwell allowed his men to put a large number of the house's occupants to the sword even as they cried for mercy. The slain included a young woman who had provoked the soldiers' fury with her sharp tongue.[83] Other women were treated 'somewhat coarsely' meaning that they were stripped of some of their clothes. The soldiers were also given free rein to pillage the house for a day. Afterwards they held a market to dispose of unportable items. Basing House had been stocked to hold out for years, so that the price of wheat collapsed temporarily when its whole supply was suddenly offered for sale.[84] On a small scale the bloody conquest of Basing House prefigured the much bloodier victories in Ireland in 1649. As at Drogheda, quarter was denied not just because the garrison had refused to surrender, but because it was Catholic. Had Fairfax rather than Cromwell been the commanding officer, the outcome might have been different, both at Basing and in Ireland.

Tiverton

At army headquarters Fairfax, in consultation with the council of war, had decided to take Tiverton before advancing on Exeter and Plymouth. Like Basing it was regarded as a popish enclave, but its real importance was strategic: situated in a pass, it had the potential to annoy the army from behind. At a time when the enemy was trying to break through with 2000 horse and link up with the king at Oxford, it was essential that parliament's forces, not the king's, should control this pass. Although Massey's and Weldon's brigades overran the town on 16 October, the governor, Sir Gilbert Talbot, confident in the strength of the castle, determined to hold out, hoping for relief from Exeter.

After the morning sermon on 19 October the officers met again to discuss how the storm should be executed. While they conferred, the ordnance kept up intense fire against the outworks and the castle walls. One round of shot happened to hit the chain of the drawbridge, snapping it in two. The soldiers could scarcely believe their eyes as the bridge came crashing down before them. Without waiting for orders they raced across it, entered the fortifications, and took possession of the churchyard. Fairfax had already ordered that anyone taken alive should be spared, and so quarter was given to the terrified enemy. The contrast between Fairfax's mildness and Cromwell's ruthlessness at Basing could not have been plainer.[85]

It was now near the end of October, and the weather was becoming more wretched by the day. The roads leading to Exeter were impassable because of deep mud which wore out horses and broke the carriages bearing the army's artillery. Over the next three months the morale of both cavalry and infantry reached its nadir. During their enforced idleness not a few men fell sick and died. Many of them had arrived from London on 11 October, but, in the words of one newswriter, an army is like 'sandy ground, on which there is no sooner one shower fallen, but immediately it is ready to receive another, that it may fully satisfy the toil and expectation of the seedsman.'[86] After paying for their quarters and shoeing their horses, the men were again penniless. Living sometimes fifteen or twenty in a room, with no fresh straw, dining off roots and shivering from the lack of shoes and clothing, some fell to quarrelling while others perished. In early December, half the infantry were reported ill and Colonel Pickering had died of sickness, while other officers retreated to London.[87] At the beginning of January the troops' misery was exacerbated by the bitter cold around Exeter. Snow covered the ground, making it treacherously slippery to horses. The officers kept a day of humiliation to seek the counsel of heaven. The answer came back that they should advance westward. At the moment when spirits were at their blackest, the diligence of Robert Scawen and the Committee for the Army suddenly bore fruit: a shipment of stockings and shoes arrived for the infantry.[88]

As if it were not enough that his army was cold, hungry and wasted by disease, Fairfax had to cope with renewed demands from the Committee of Both Kingdoms to divert forces to the Midlands. In London the army's critics condemned its apparent indolence. Without appreciating the reasons for its reduced level of activity, the Committee of Both Kingdoms felt justified in demanding the release of several regiments. Fairfax, who was himself quite sick, wrote back wearily that he could if need be, spare 7000 or 8000 troops for service in the Midlands. In doing so he gave a confusing signal. His letter to the Lords made it clear that he did not believe he could spare these troops if he was to execute his western strategy; he would however do as parliament (not the Committee of Both Kingdoms) ordered. This was interpreted by some MPs and newsbook writers to mean that he was *proposing* to send troops to the Midlands.[89] To his dismay the Commons reversed its earlier support for his unfettered right to make strategic decisions and backed the committee's demand for horse and dragoons to be sent into the Midlands. Although the Commons appeared to restore Fairfax's autonomy four days later, on 25 November, he was constrained to draw some of his forces out of the west. Rainborowe's foot regiment was brought to full strength and sent to Abingdon. Ireton and Whalley were sent into Buckinghamshire with their horse regiments to stop royalist incursions and tighten the noose around Oxford. A few days later Major Disbrowe was sent with another horse regiment – probably Fairfax's own – to assist Whalley in this design. Fairfax finally composed a polite note of protest against the continual bleeding of his army. To his relief, the Committee of Both Kingdoms refrained from making further requests.[90]

Dartmouth

The arrival of shoes and stockings had cheered Fairfax's men tremendously. Though the rest of their clothes were in tatters, they were impatient to be on the march against the enemy once more.[91] One of their goals was to avenge the setback at Powderham Castle the previous month. Captain Richard Deane, comptroller of the ordnance, had led a party of foot and dragoons across the river Exe to seize the castle, which was one of the outer defences of Exeter. However, the castle had been reinforced in anticipation of an attack, so they had to be content with occupying an adjacent church. The day following (15 December) they found themselves assaulted by a force almost four times their number. The attackers threw in many hand grenades, but were unable to shake the occupants. After three hours they withdrew, leaving their dead and dragging their wounded, whose mute testimony was the bloodstained snow outside the church. The beleaguered men were then able to make good their retreat from the church where they had shivered for two days, while the soldiers in the castle looked on but did nothing.[92]

The army arrived at Dartmouth on 12 January 1646. Owing to the deep mud on the roads, the carriages of the artillery train had been left behind, and limited quantities of ammunition had been loaded onto horseback. His summons to surrender rejected, Fairfax prepared for a storm, 'for we find more loss of men by lingering sieges than sudden storms.' At the general's request Captain Batten stationed a squadron of ships to prevent enemy ships from getting in or out of the harbour. Scaling ladders were commandeered in the district and lots were drawn to determine which men should lead the assault.

In the morning and evening of Sunday the 18th, Peters and Dell stirred up the soldiers with their eloquence.[93] Late that night the assault began. Though artillery support was completely lacking John Rushworth declared, 'I never saw men fall on more cheerfully or merrily.' After the royalists had discharged their 100 cannon, the advance party of attackers got under the guns, took possession, turned them around and pointed them at their enemy. By this 'strange and unparalleled undertaking', Fairfax's forces made themselves masters of the town. The next day the governor surrendered the castle in exchange for quarter. About 120 of the 800 prisoners taken in the storm were Cornishmen. Fairfax released them with 2s. each to pay their expenses home. This generous act soon paid handsome dividends. The returning soldiers spread a good report about the New Model, contradicting the horror stories previously disseminated by royalist commanders. When Fairfax arrived in the county a month later, his public-relations work had already been done for him by these returning enemy soldiers.

The unqualified triumph (only two men died in the storm) temporarily silenced the London critics who had questioned the siege of Dartmouth as a distraction from the more important objective, Exeter. By capturing Dartmouth Fairfax had hindered both the royalist relief of Exeter and the enemy's whole recruitment effort in the west. Plymouth had been relieved, while the remains of Goring's and Grenville's army had been driven into Cornwall. Here was further proof if any were needed, of the wisdom of leaving military strategy to men in the field. Hugh Peters, while in London, made the further observation that the army was animated by a spirit of unity and action. 'Here', he boasted, 'men grow religious and more spiritual thriving than in any place of the kingdom.' In a punning lampoon against the disputatious presbyterian clergy of the capital, he challenged them to help with the Herculean labour of evangelizing the countryside.[94]

Torrington

The combination of severe hardship and sweeping success put Fairfax in a defiant mood towards the never-ending demands of the Committee of Both Kingdoms. He ignored their request to send a regiment to bolster the Roundhead gentry of Wiltshire. To underline his own necessities he ordered Colonel Overton's regiment back from Corfe Castle, where they had been sent at the committee's request. Even more boldly, he pulled Skippon's foot regiment out of Bristol and ordered it to join him in Devon. Skippon, as newly appointed governor of Bristol, was too loyal to question his superior officer's order, but he did write plaintively to parliament urging that he now had barely 700 soldiers to man the second port in England. Alarmed, the Lords exhorted the Commons to reverse Fairfax's order withdrawing Skippon's regiment, but the request was rebuffed.[95] A thousand of Skippon's seasoned infantry were worth at least twice that number of new recruits to Fairfax. When 3000 men of Devon volunteered to serve under him he selected a third of them and sent the rest home.[96] This flocking of men to his standard was only one of many manifestations of rapidly collapsing royalist resistance.[97] Every sign seemed propitious for the long-awaited strike against Exeter.

But to Fairfax's dismay the assault had to be postponed once again. Word had reached him of a menacing build-up of forces to the north and east. With their concern for keeping the royalist forces in Oxford and Chester separate, the Committee of Both Kingdoms had left the area to the south of Oxford too weakly protected. As a consequence 1500 royalist horse had descended from their headquarters at Oxford to occupy Dunster Castle in Somerset. Simultaneously a large force of horse and foot, estimated to number 9000, had marched out of Cornwall to relieve Exeter. By 8 February they lay to the north between Barnstaple and Torrington. Goring had left for France, supposedly to raise forces there, and the royalist army in the west was now in the capable hands of Sir Ralph Hopton. If his army were able to link up with the Oxford horse contingent and join forces with the beleaguered garrison in Exeter, the New Model's position would suddenly be in jeopardy.

To confront this peril Fairfax met with his council of war and decided to leave Sir Hardress Waller in charge of the siege (Exeter being now completely surrounded) while he took five horse regiments, seven of foot and half the regiment of dragoons north towards Torrington. Hopton's forces, which had been rumoured to number 10,000, turned out to be barely half that many, making the two sides about equal.[98] On Monday 17 February the army drew up in battle formation 5 miles south of Torrington and advanced towards the town through narrow lanes lined with dense hedges. An advance guard of dragoons, sent to penetrate the enemy's defences, inadvertently triggered a full-scale attack. Before anyone realized what was happening, half the army was engaged and the rest of the soldiers were demanding to join in. Seeing their determination, Fairfax on the spot reversed the decision to do battle the next morning, and gave the command to fall on, with only moonlight to show the way, and lacking the advantage of surprise. At first the fight was not easy. Hopton's infantry fought tenaciously. Before the barricades could be scaled royalists had to be routed at push of pike and butt end of musket, from thirteen different hedges. 'For indeed every hedge was [as] it were a bulwark to the enemy; so strong are the hedges in these parts.'[99] The assault had started in earnest at eight o'clock. After two hours of hand-to-hand fighting Fairfax's foot surmounted the barricades and cleared the way for the horse to enter. A body of Hopton's horse which had been stationed behind the infantry to give it support turned tail and galloped down the long street sloping westwards towards the river Torridge. Their flight prompted the collapse of further resistance by the foot, who dropped their arms and fled in every direction. The invading horse actually found their entry hampered by the muskets strewn about the streets. So sudden was the reversal that Hopton had to leave his dinner uneaten on the table. By eleven o'clock a large number of prisoners had been rounded up and lodged in the church where Hopton had kept his magazine. At that moment the eighty barrels of gunpowder were blown up by one of the royalists, killing about 200 prisoners and sending hot metal and debris flying all over the town. 'Hell itself could not make a more hideous sulphur.'[100] Great webs of lead from the church windows fell thickly near where Fairfax stood, killing a horse next to him but leaving the general himself unscathed.[101]

Casualties were unexpectedly heavy on the parliamentary side: twenty slain and 100 wounded. Once again, as at Bath, Bristol and Tiverton, the New Model rank and file showed great daring and resourcefulness, and a willingness to seize the initiative from their officers. Strategically the victory was overshadowed only by Naseby and Langport. Langport had destroyed the last formidable body of horse in the west; Torrington had scattered the last remaining body of infantry. With the fall of Chester at about the same time there now remained only one major fortress in royalist hands: the king's headquarters at Oxford; and only one royalist force of any size in the field: the prince's 5000 horse and 1000 foot in Cornwall.

Cornwall

In the flush of victory Fairfax and his secretary Rushworth exploited their enhanced prestige to spell out for parliament's benefit their strategy for subduing Cornwall. Forces which had hitherto patrolled the district between Oxford and Chester should now be disposed southward so as to prevent any incursions from Oxford into the west. To this end Whalley's brigade should be quartered near Newbury to keep watch on Oxford from the south. This advice was followed.[102] Despite the devastating defeat suffered by Hopton, Fairfax was still apprehensive about Cornwall, as a great reserve of royalist manpower, and he took seriously the danger of a French landing on the south coast.[103]

The council of war met again on 21 February and decided, rather than storm Exeter or Barnstaple, to disperse the remaining forces under the Prince of Wales. Steps were taken to bottle up the cavaliers on the west side of the river Tamar and prevent them from breaking through in the direction of Oxford.[104] Enemy morale was undermined by again releasing Cornish prisoners and putting 2s. in their pockets. A double agent was sent into Cornwall to inform the population of 'the good condition of our army and the desperate condition of theirs by the defeat given to them at Torrington.'[105] Hugh Peters rode into his native county to convince his compatriots of the benevolence of the invading force.[106]

Fairfax's careful advance work was triumphantly rewarded when he entered the county. Launceston and Bodmin surrendered with little resistance. Hopton's efforts at recruitment collapsed as people lost their fear of the New Model. Happy to encounter soldiers who paid for what they needed, the inhabitants reopened their markets and felt the vitalizing stimulus of the army's presence in the local economy. People said they were glad to see the end of Goring's crew. The gentry changed sides.[107] Royalist prisoners said they were glad to be captured. Plainly the end was near.[108] By the beginning of March, the utter demoralization of Hopton's forces was highlighted by the astounding exploits of the New Model. Four troopers rounded up forty-two musketeers near Bodmin without firing a shot. Six troopers captured a sizable convoy consisting of four wagons of match, powder, bullet and muskets. On 4 March the Prince of Wales virtually abandoned the struggle by retiring to the Scilly Isles.[109]

The treaty eventually concluded between Fairfax and Hopton was a model of civilized humanitarianism, which also showed careful respect for the differences in social degree of the men who were being demobilized.[110] The army leaders were understandably proud of their accomplishment. With well under 10,000 men, including a body of cavalry that was actually smaller than Hopton's, they had pushed the enemy through cragged country into a narrow neck of land until no escape was possible. They had projected parliament's power almost 200 miles from London into the royalist heartland. In subduing Cornwall they had cut the source of a hitherto inexhaustible supply of recruits to the king's army. All this had been done amidst the bitterest of winters. With the defeat of Astley at Stow-on-the-Wold the following week, the king no longer had any armies in the field. A few secondary garrisons in Wales and the west midlands had yet to be reduced, but Fairfax's only remaining major task was to invest Oxford.[111]

Oxford

In celebration of this year of victories parliament ordered a day of Thanksgiving on 2 April 1646, the anniversary of the New Model's taking to the field, and invited Hugh Peters to preach before it. In his sermon the 'strenuous puritan' exalted the New Model soldiers, 'the very off-scourings of the world' who had nevertheless delivered the nation from bondage and brought the blessings of prosperity and peace. He counted it a privilege to be a member of such an army. The challenge now belonged to the politicians to erect a just social order characterized by decent care for the sick and the poor, and an improved legal system – the laws in English, the courts decentralized, imprisonment for debt abolished. If they were doubtful that such an order could be brought into being, they had only to gaze upon New England, 'where in seven years I never saw beggar, nor heard an oath, nor looked upon a drunkard.'[112]

When Peters was delivering his sermon Sir John Berkeley had just signalled his desire to negotiate the surrender of Exeter. Not waiting for the conclusion of the treaty Fairfax immediately dispatched his remaining horse regiments, containing only 3000 troopers, to Oxford to strengthen the siege there.[113] Robert Hammond became the new governor of Exeter.[114] The surrenders of Barnstaple and Dunster followed swiftly upon the heels of the cathedral city's. Local forces were left in charge of these garrisons, and also sent to block up Pendennis and St Michael's Mount in Cornwall, which continued to hold out.[115]

Now that the army's military role was winding down, Cromwell returned to his seat in the Commons. As he passed through Westminster Hall, his colleagues stared at him with awe.[116] Charles I meanwhile slipped out of Oxford in disguise, leaving to its governor, Sir Thomas Glemham, the distasteful job of yielding the garrison. A few days later the king surrendered himself to the Scots army near Newark, having previously satisfied himself about the Scots' disenchantment with both the New Model Army and the House of Commons.

In the meantime, the defenders of Oxford made unexpectedly high demands for its surrender. To allow for the eventuality that a storm might be necessary, Captain Hooper, the English engineer, was brought in to supervise the digging of trenches and mines. In addition, the New Model's heavy guns were dragged from Reading. Cromwell returned from Westminster to help, as did Bulstrode Whitelocke, eager to be on hand for the final scene of the drama that had been unfolding since the previous spring. At Oxford, to his immense gratification, he was treated with every mark of respect, included in the deliberations of the 'select council' of the army (composed of Fairfax, Ireton, Cromwell, Lambart and Fleetwood), asked his opinion, and invited to be the council's secretary.[117] Another familiar figure who rejoined the army at that time was Philip Skippon, finally restored to health following his long convalescence after Naseby. His duties as governor of Bristol had been light, permitting him to spend a large part of his time at nearby Bath. During his first appearance at the general rendezvous of 1 May he was greated with 'much joy and acclamations' by the foot.[118] At the end of May, Colonel Graves also returned to Fairfax's headquarters, having spent most of the preceding year near Chester, where he been dangerously wounded.[119] All the chief actors were thus back on stage for the *dénouement* of the southern campaign. There was a momentary rush of excitement when the garrison remained obdurate, and artillery fire was briefly exchanged,[120] but on 15 June word came from the king that all his strongholds were to surrender.[121]

Glemham handed over the city to Fairfax on 24 June. Hoping to conquer peacefully and so spare Oxford's intellectual and aesthetic treasures, the general had consented to terms so generous that they earned him harsh words in London.[122] He guaranteed that the city would not be vandalized nor its citizens plundered. No one whose estates had been sequestered would have to pay more than two years' revenue to get them back; the defenders could go wherever they liked in England or beyond the seas, and they could conduct their exit with dignity: 'colours flying, trumpets sounding, drums beating, matches lighted at both ends, bullet in their mouths, and every soldier to have twelve charges of powder.'[123]

The army's opening and closing actions of the war had been at Oxford. The symmetry was fitting. Fairfax, his work accomplished, now took a long vacation at Bath to nurse his kidney stone and repair his ruined health. In November he rode to London and a hero's welcome. The City militia and many citizens turned out to greet him; there was a formal welcome from parliament, and two days later several peers arrived in their coaches at his house in Queen Street. The Earl of Manchester delivered a short speech of thanks, following which the Speaker of the Commons, William Lenthall, gave a longer and more effusive address, comparing Fairfax with Julius Caesar and declaring his exploits 'nothing else but the *Magnalia Dei*'.[124] Three days later, not wishing to appear remiss, the mayor and aldermen of the City arrived in a train of coaches to pay their own homage. These expressions of delight and gratitude were short-lived, soon to be overtaken by resentment at the expense of the army and impatience with its religious diversity.

The *annus mirabilis* was over: what lay ahead was a much more treacherous and complicated war that would be fought with petitions, pamphlets and intrigue. The army's political education was shortly to begin.

4

The Importance of Religion

You will easily discern a thread of divinity running through the whole proceeding of this army.... Their actions have been nothing else but a copy of the wisdom, power and providence and love of God put forth in men.[1]

[The officers] were better Christians than soldiers and wiser in faith than in fighting, and could believe in a victory sooner than contrive it; and yet I think they were as wise in the way of the soldiery as the little time and experience they had could make them.... Many of them with their soldiery, were much in prayer and reading scripture, an exercise that soldiers till of late have used but little and thus [they] went on and prospered.... Men conquer better as they are saints, than soldiers; and in the countries where they came they left something of God as well as of Caesar behind them, something of piety as well as pay.[2]

Without doubt the New Model enjoyed markedly higher morale than most armies in the seventeenth century. High morale contributed to, and was in turn enhanced by, the army's victories on the battlefield. Our task in this chapter is to explore how religious convictions and practice affected the army's spirit and conduct. The first step will be to determine the extent to which the army was religious. We know that at most times there were in the army several chaplains who preached often, that there were days of humiliation involving prayers and fasting, and that scripture study was encouraged. Were these religious observances meaningful to those who participated in them? Did they affect the soldiers' conduct? Or were they largely formal, conventional, and devoid of military or political significance?

The Negative Evidence

Recruitment

There is sufficient evidence of religious indifference and scepticism to raise doubts about the genuineness of the army's official religious professions. In the first place we know that a high proportion of the soldiers (over a third) joined because they were conscripted.[3] Once in the army they were all too ready to desert – after the battle of Naseby for example, or when bad weather, diseases and shortages made conditions miserable in the army. Morale sank so low in the autumn of 1645 that fighting broke out in the ranks, and some of Oliver Cromwell's own troopers died, their killers 'glorying in that they had butchered some of Cromwell's bastards'.[4] Plainly the quality of most pressed men left much to be desired. The editor of the *Moderate Intelligencer*, normally a keen booster of the army, did not hesitate to describe a recent batch of conscripts in April 1646 as 'the vilest rogues and cowards that ever breathed.'[5] Their demoralizing example encouraged some men to try to escape. A few of the new recruits evidently showed more affection for the king than for Fairfax, whom they swore to kill if he came near them.[6]

Nor is this the only reference to royalism in the New Model Army. On a number of occasions defeated and captured royalist soldiers happily took up service with their enemy, by whom they were just as happily received.[7] It is doubtful if such men, who may have numbered in the thousands, were notable for their godliness.

Religious scepticism

Another fact that must give us pause is the existence of extremist ideas bordering on scepticism and unbelief. Agnosticism towards the central tenets of Christianity was an intellectual luxury few men could afford to indulge under battle conditions. Once the fighting had stopped, however, many of the soldiers, radicalized by their experience of war, and enjoying leisure that permitted them to discuss radical ideas with their comrades, strayed farther and farther from orthodox puritanism. But it has to be recognized that most of the evidence of unbelief and heterodoxy comes from critics hostile to the army and will not bear too much weight. In 1645 and 1646 for example, evidence of unbelief was eagerly collected and purveyed to shocked readers by Thomas Edwardes. One alleged incident involved a blasphemous parody of the sacrament of baptism, in which soldiers took a horse into a parish church, filled the baptismal font with urine, and then poured it over the hapless animal while reciting the service from the Book of Common Prayer.[8] In 1646 Captain Paul Hobson was said to have preached that Christians were liberated from the moral law and that the saints were equal in perfection to Christ. Another officer, a surgeon, was reported to have repudiated the moral law, the sabbath, the sacraments, the authority of the Bible and the need for forgiveness. Some soldiers and officers were apparently anti-Trinitarian, rejecting the divinity of Christ, and scoffed at prayer. Still others reasoned that every spirit was God, that hell did not exist, or that God was as much in hell as in heaven. Whole troops were said to deny the resurrection of the dead, while others flouted the sabbath by playing football on College Green.

The persistent strain of hysteria in Edwardes' writing is a warning against literal acceptance of these charges.[10] Nevertheless, the type of behaviour that he ascribes to some of the soldiers is also delineated in other, less inflammatory texts. At a somewhat higher intellectual level there was the attack on the London presbyterian clergy published on the eve of the king's execution in January 1649. The anonymous author declared himself a soldier, but we cannot be sure of the claim. Rationalist, sardonic and bitterly anti-clerical, he did not include a trace of religious apologetics in his offhand justification of the army's purge of parliament and trial of the king.[11] Coming as it did from a hostile pen or from an anonymous pamphlet, this evidence of atheistic attitudes is admittedly slight. More worrying to the higher officers however, was the growing attraction to the rank and file of radical antinomianism. According to this doctrine, Christ's dispensation entailed the abolition of the Mosaic law of the Old Testament, and its replacement by free grace. The liberty of the sons and daughters of Christ meant that sin had been abolished; consequently, nothing that a follower of Christ did could be viewed as unlawful. According to Thomas Edwardes, these doctrines had been actively canvassed in the army in 1646 and perhaps earlier. By 1649, it was alleged, radical theory was being turned into practice. Extreme antinomians were exuberantly throwing off all external restraints upon individual liberty of action – not only traditional moral guidelines, but the Bible and the clergy as well.[12] The results were sometimes shocking, and in the 1650s people listened with delicious horror to reports of Ranter meetings, where, it was said, adherents drank freely, smoked, swore, took off their clothes and practised 'community of wives' – meaning group sex. As Colin Davis has shown, virtually all of these reports came from the yellow press, and there was in truth 'no core, no sect, no mass movement of Ranters.' Yet in the early 1650s there was, in McGregor's words, a 'climate of opinion' and 'a loosely coordinated campaign' to overthrow all ecclesiastical authority and deny the reality of sin.[13]

Radical antinomians were often sceptics as well as cultural rebels.

Denying the authority of scripture, they also did not hesitate to reject the authority and hence the divinity of Christ. If a soldier asserted such views publicly he violated the first article of the army's Laws and Ordinances of War.[14] By September 1649 the officers were so worried by the phenomenon that they kept a day of humiliation to combat the 'atheism and profaneness' which had crept into the army.[15] Yet profaneness only seemed to spread. In June 1650 two troopers in Rich's regiment were punished and cashiered for keeping company with Ranters, and having in their possession 'several scandalous songs, and other prophane and mutinous books and papers.'[16] Later the same summer a dragoon was punished in Scotland for blasphemy and 'a ranting humour brought on by too much drink.'[17] That autumn Thomas Margetts wrote from Whitehall that 'abundance of those they call ranters are in several parts.' One soldier had to endure the exceptionally harsh punishment of riding the wooden horse at St Paul's Cathedral with two muskets strapped to each heel, while another was given thirty lashes, for expressing ranting opinions.[18] Around the same time Captain William Covell of Fairfax's horse regiment was cashiered for denying the divinity of Christ and holding that 'sin was no sin'. Lieutenant-Colonel Henry Bowen lost his commission too for being 'an absolute atheist' and 'a blasphemer'.[19] Cornet Underwood, formerly of Cromwell's horse regiment, reportedly confessed when he was dying in the spring of 1651 to 'the damnable delusions of God's being all things', in other words to pantheism. Another man was cashiered during the same period for holding dangerous opinions, 'as that God was reason, &c.'[20] A year later clergy and citizens from Newcastle upon Tyne wrote to Cromwell complaining of the heretical activities of former captain Robert Everard, and his lieutenant-colonel John Mason, said to be guilty of arminianism, socinianism and 'that cursed doctrine that so much pulls down God and sets up man.'[21]

With the passage of time the army experienced a greater and greater fracturing of the spiritual unity it had briefly known on the battlefield. Such a devout and sensitive observer as Colonel John Jones was depressed by the endless arid debates over inessentials such as infant baptism, as well as the growth of religious subjectivism which rejected prayer, a transcendent God and the reality of sin. The end of it all, thought Jones, was 'a fearful spiritual Babel'.[22] This decline in orthodox religious belief was also witnessed by Captain Hugh Prichard in a letter he wrote to the Welsh puritan Morgan Llwyd in December 1652. Everywhere he looked in south-eastern England he encountered anarchic and atheistic religious radicalism. 'In all places where we quarter', he wrote from Buckinghamshire, 'free willers and non sinners [antinomians] do abound in these countries, and have their meetings, but refuse to hear the most precious gospel preachers that is.

There is more ranters over all the country that slight all ordinances and abhors godly conversations than there is of sober-minded saints.'[23]

In the early 1650s the forces of religious heterodoxy seemed to be making alarming inroads into the army. Besides radical antinomians and other sceptics, there were substantial numbers of Fifth Monarchists, who believed that the return of Christ to rule the earth with his saints was imminent, and Quakers, who held that all religious truth was subjective, emanating from the holy spirit that dwelt within each individual.[24]

The Positive Evidence

Harmony and sweet union: personal piety

In the beginning, however, when the army was preoccupied with conquering the king on the battlefield, little was heard of debate or heresy and much of sweet unity and a passionate fervour that sometimes reached intoxicating heights. Indeed, the evidence for devoutness and piety in the New Model Army is at all times far more voluminous than that for irreligion. This piety extended from the highest to the lowest ranks.[25] The commander-in-chief, Sir Thomas Fairfax, exemplified it well. As Joshua Sprigge, the chaplain who chronicled the army's first year and a half, observed, Fairfax always liked to consult religious men first before embarking on any course of action, 'as if the best place he could find for counsel and action was there where God was; and he prospered accordingly, as if Providence would let him see, there is the best policy where there is the best piety.' Sprigge said Fairfax believed nothing was impossible for God or 'for man to do in God's strength, if they would up and be doing.'[26] That was why, despite constant ill health, he accomplished so much. That was also why Fairfax appointed Hugh Peters, 'the strenuous puritan', as chaplain to the army, and gave him so much latitude and responsibility in preaching, recruiting, negotiating with the enemy, and corresponding with parliament and the public. Peters signalled his gratitude in a letter to Fairfax, saluting him for his impartial love of both God and the saints, and declaring that one of his greatest joys had been to be a member of the army, and to witness God's presence in it and its commander. He hoped to meet Fairfax 'triumphing in heaven'.[27]

On several occasions Fairfax manifested an acute sense of God's special favour towards him and the army. When he besieged Bristol in the late summer of 1645 he found the whole region infested with plague. Many officers advised against attacking the city, but Fairfax brought them around to his view, declaring, 'as for the sickness, let us trust God with the army, who will be as ready to protect us, in the siege from infection as in the field from the bullet.' In the event, according to Sprigge, only one soldier in the whole army succumbed to the plague.[28] While Sprigge and Peters are not objective witnesses to Fairfax's faith, the mere fact that he appointed such men points to his own sympathy with their outlook. Furthermore, Fairfax showed a lively awareness of God's personal favour in private as well as public utterances. When he stormed Torrington the defeated royalists' last act was to blow up their powder magazine of eighty barrels in the town church. The explosion killed 200 men, mostly royalist prisoners, and sent 'timber, stones, and sheets of lead, showering down as hail on all parts of the town.' To his father he confided, 'I must acknowledge God's great mercy to me, and some others that stood where great webs of lead fell thickest, yet, praised be God, no man hurt.... I could not but mention this as one of the strange accidents that I have seen, and as a great providence in preservation of some.'[29]

There were many successes that confirmed Fairfax's opinion of God's active and intimate involvement in his life. But he also found 'God a sure rock of defence' in times of hardship, as when the army was cold, sick and hungry. Though himself suffering a succession of complaints – rheumatism, the stone and 'a benumbing coldness in my head, legs and arms' – he told his father, 'it hath pleased the Lord to help me through much extremities, and I trust He will lay no more on me than He will enable me to bear. The mercies I have received ought to stop all complaints in His service.'[30]

The major-general of the infantry, Philip Skippon, was like Fairfax a man of few words. But like his commander-in-chief he had an unquestioning confidence in God's favour which he was able to communicate to the rank and file. In 1642 at Turnham Green he exhorted the troops with the words, 'Come, my honest brave boys, pray heartily and fight heartily and God will bless us.'[31] More loquacious in print, Skippon published three books of devotion addressed to his fellow soldiers, and at the end of the interregnum left a lengthy will that breathed an elaborate puritan piety.[32]

The lieutenant-general of the cavalry, Oliver Cromwell, is renowned for his colossal, exuberant religious zeal. His habit of wearing his spiritual heart on his sleeve has caused many to doubt his sincerity, and in his own day he was regularly accused of hypocrisy. But his private letters are of a piece with his public statements, and testify to his sincerity. Writing to his daughter Bridget shortly after her marriage to Henry Ireton, Oliver's comrade-in-arms, he urged on her the joy of being a religious seeker:

> Who ever tasted that graciousness of His, and could go less in desire, and less in pressing after full enjoyment? Dear Heart, press on; let not husband, let not anything cool thy affections after Christ. I hope he will be an occasion to

inflame them. That which is best worthy of love in thy husband is that of the image of Christ he bears.[33]

With Thomas Fairfax, Cromwell shared the misery of periodic bouts of ill health. His reaction to sickness was similar to Fairfax's but articulated in a baroque diction appropriate to his more flamboyant theology. In the late winter of 1647 he wrote to Fairfax after an illness that by his own account nearly killed him,

> I received in myself the sentence of death, that I might learn to trust in him that raiseth from the dead, and have no confidence in the flesh. It's a blessed thing to die daily, for what is there in this world to be accounted of. The best men according to the flesh, and things, are lighter than vanity. I find this only good, to love the Lord and his poor despised people, to do for them, and to be ready to suffer with them: and he that is found worthy of this hath obtained great favour from the Lord; and he that is established in this shall (being conformed to Christ and the rest of the Body) participate in the glory of a Resurrection which will answer all.[34]

These letters to his daughter and to Fairfax give us a glimpse of the personal, private side of Cromwell's religion, and they establish his sincerity. More important for our purposes, though, is the public, political face of his religion. Its chief ingredients are threefold: the sovereignty of conscience, the continual looking to providence as a warrant for action, and the belief in an imminent millennium which renders moral reformation urgent.[35] In his observances and his dispatches Cromwell manifests the Calvinist belief in a ceaselessly active God, a God of battles who in his overarching cosmic strategy as well as his attention to the smallest details, helps those who are on his side. Thus on the eve of the assault on Basing House, seat of the Marquess of Winchester, royalist stronghold and 'nest of idolatrous papists', we see Cromwell on his knees most of the night, praying and reading scripture. He is strengthened according to Hugh Peters by the scriptural text 'They that make [idols] are like unto them, so is every one that trusteth in them' (Psalm 115:8). After the house was overrun he wrote to the Speaker of the Commons, 'God exceedingly abounds in His goodness to us, and will not be weary until righteousness and peace meet and that He hath brought forth a glorious work for the happiness of this poor kingdom.'[36] During this period there was never any doubt in Cromwell's mind that he understood perfectly the mind and the plans of God. Trumpeting the crushing victory at Naseby, he told the Speaker, 'Sir, this is none other but the hand of God; and to Him alone belongs the glory.'[37] A month later, after the equally decisive victory at Langport, he demanded of a member of parliament, 'to see this, is it not to see the face of God!'[38] The victory at Bristol two months after that was, beyond the shadow of a doubt, 'none other than the work of

God. He must be a very atheist that doth not acknowledge it.' He went on to expound one of his favourite themes: the efficacy of aggressive, combative prayer in achieving results:

> Sir, they that have been employed in this service know that faith and prayer obtained this city for you. I do not say ours only, but of the people of God with you and all England over, who have wrestled with God for a blessing in this very thing.[39]

This unashamed religious exaltation was more frequently expressed by officers than by men of lower rank.[40] The officers were the religious vanguard who set their stamp on the army. The rank and file were a much more mixed bag. While a critical observer acknowledged that there were plenty of godly men, there were also 'many as ungodly as ever I saw'.[41] A more sympathetic observer, William Dell the chaplain, recalled 'the spirit of prayer' that he had often witnessed among the rank and file. On occasion he had accidentally overheard troopers praying 'with that faith and familiarity with God that have stood wondering at the grace'.[42] Captain John Hodgson recorded a similar experience on the eve of the battle of Dunbar. As he rode through the darkness he passed near a cornet who was praying aloud. Involuntarily Hodgson stopped to listen, finding the man 'exceedingly carried on in the duty. I met with so much of God in it, as I was satisfied deliverance was at hand.'[43] This habit of praying aloud extemporaneously won for the New Model a reputation among London sectaries as 'the praying army'.[44] Even a witness as unfriendly as the Earl of Southampton was compelled to acknowledge the 'sober and religious' quality of the army.[45] Soldiers customarily carried Bibles in their breast pockets, and Ambrose Barnes asserted that many had their faith confirmed when these Bibles shielded them from enemy bullets.[46]

Sermons often drew large crowds, with the soldiers straining to hear what the preachers said. On a Sunday in May 1646, for example, William Dell and William Sedgewick preached in the morning and afternoon, while John Saltmarsh preached a day later. Each of these sermons was two hours long, yet they were well attended, many soldiers climbing the trees in the orchard before Fairfax's tent in order to hear better.[47] Naturally, the chaplains who accompanied the army on its marches played a key part in stirring up the fervour of the rank and file. They encouraged the conviction that the events the soldiers had witnessed were holy history, part of God's own plan for their country. Appointed by the army commanders, chaplains such as Hugh Peters and William Dell were powerful personalities in their own right, who did much more than simply echo the views of Fairfax and Cromwell. By their eloquence they greatly strengthened the conviction that the army was an almost passive instrument in the hands of the Almighty.[48]

Peters – preacher, recruiter, pamphleteer, war correspondent, negotiator and reporter to parliament – loved to describe to anyone who would listen the 'pieces of God's providence' he had witnessed in the army. The taking of Dartmouth in January 1646 was a notable example. Even though the army was sickly, the weather violent, and the men ill-clothed, they were drawn mysteriously to attempt the royalist stronghold. To their astonishment the enemy fled in panic, six of Colonel Okey's dragoons, in one instance, driving off 500 of their cavalry. There was also the celebrated miraculous draught of fishes near Dartmouth. For seven weeks before the New Model's approach no fish had been caught along the coast. 'But now there was so many mullets taken as comfortably supplied our army, which continueth to this time.' The fortress itself was taken with the loss of only two men. 'The Lord hath scattered them like chaff before the wind; they fly when none pursues them; they are broken, and divided in their counsels.' By the end of the summer of 1646 Peters professed his readiness to die, having seen the wondrous works of God in the army's unbroken string of victories. Both he and Dell were also immensely proud of the superior standard of conduct, which was, in their view, the natural concomitant of the intense spirituality that pervaded not only the officer corps, but even the lowest ranks. It was Peters' claim that, whereas in most armies men emerged coarser and more brutal from the experience of war, 'here men grow religious, and more spiritual thriving, than in any place of the kingdom.'[49]

William Dell corroborated this high estimate of the army's virtues. In June 1646 he listed six of its salient characteristics. Most remarkable perhaps was the army's faith, which gave it tremendous power. Bristol, for example, 'was conquered by faith more than by force; it was conquered in the hearts of the godly by faith, before ever they stretched forth a hand against it; and they went not so much to storm it as to take it, in the assurance of faith.' Faith explained why small handfuls of New Model soldiers were able to put much larger numbers of royalists to flight. Next he remarked on the special sense of the presence of God in the army. It was because of this awareness of God in their midst, Dell was convinced, that 'our enemies have perished (not by our valour, and weapons, and strength), but at the rebuke of his countenance.' The last characteristic that Dell thought noteworthy was the army's faithfulness to the state. Unlike other armies it had not shirked battle, but had been continually active, even through the winter, when most seventeenth-century armies took a holiday from fighting. It had travelled long distances in all sorts of weather in order to bring the war to a speedy close.[50]

The chaplains were not merely expressing their professional point of view. They were articulating the army's own interpretation of what it had done. As Mark Kishlansky and Anne Laurence have shown, the chaplains did not play a primary role in shaping the religious character of the army. Chaplains were appointed personally by their colonels, and, while they were not mouthpieces for the higher officers, they tended to reflect their views. The chaplains were also representative of the religious pluralism of the army. Well-educated men, they were always in short supply, though the number known to have served between 1645 and 1651 is, at forty-three, higher than used to be thought. No more than four of them were presbyterian in 1645, and this number had shrunk to zero before 1649.[51] The chaplains' main function was not to convert men but to persuade them of the righteousness of fighting against their fellow Englishmen. Thus at Edgehill in 1642 they 'rode up and down the army, through the thickest dangers, and in much personal hazard, most faithfully and courageously exhorting and encouraging the soldiers to fight valiantly, and not to fly, but now if ever to stand to it, and to fight for their religion, laws and Christian liberties.'[52] Although many chaplains left after Edgehill, those who remained probably continued to play this hortatory role. We know that at Naseby, for example, Hugh Peters 'rode from rank to rank with a Bible in one hand and a pistol in the other exhorting the men to do their duty.'[53]

Some officers took if anything a keener interest in their men's spiritual welfare than the chaplains did. John Pickering, whose early death in November 1645 was much lamented, is a prime example of an evangelizing colonel. An admiring journalist enthused that, 'instead of drinking, swearing, roaring, carding, dicing and drabbing, he spent that little time he had to spare in the study of scriptures and exercising to his regiment, labouring to distill good discipline by his counsel, as he did valour by his practice.'[54]

In addition to sermons the chaplains and officers devised an elaborate programme of religious exercises to occupy the army when it was not fighting. Except when obliged by military necessity the army observed the sabbath as a day of rest and prayer. On that day, as well as after major battles, the soldiers would 'exercise their minds' in Bible study.[55] The discussion of scripture and the sharing of religious experience could bind soldiers more tightly together. In 1647 for example, a soldier from Hewson's regiment, writing of 'the manifest presence of God' among them, exclaimed, 'the sweet union we had with God doth endear us together in love.'[56]

Visual iconography was also deployed to remind the soldiers of the godly character of their mission. The mottoes on parliamentary standards, for example, were mostly religious in their subject matter, while the usual theme of the royalist standards was loyalty to the king. Major-General Skippon's motto read, 'Pray and fight. May Jehovah help us, and help us he will'; Captain (later Colonel) Graves's, 'For the Protestants'; Ludlowe's, 'The Word of God'; and Sheffield's, 'With God as our guide, there is no need to despair'.[57] The London volunteers bore a standard depicting a sword and Bible.[58] Passwords in battle reinforced the providential consciousness: 'God our strength' at Naseby, 'God with us' at Dartmouth, 'Emmanuel' at Torrington, and 'The Lord of Hosts' at Dunbar and Worcester.[59]

Fasting and 'humiliation' were other techniques used to raise consciousness for the trials ahead. Fasting was used frequently. At Bristol it was combined with sermons and a resolution by the Council of War 'to punish the vices in the army' in the hope of pleasing God. A day of humiliation was held a few months later to discover if the Lord wanted the army to advance on the enemy in Devon.[60] Days of humiliation and fasting continued to be a favoured activity of the high command long after the emotional high points of the first civil war were behind them. In 1649 and 1650 all the garrisons in England were urged to join with headquarters in such exercises to prepare for the invasions of Ireland and Scotland. When, in August 1650, the army was racked by plague in Munster, Ireton imposed an eight-day fast spread over a three-week period to entreat the Lord 'to remove the heavy judgement of pestilence in our quarters'. In late 1652, when there was growing anxiety about the troubles with Holland and the failure of the Rump to enact the army's political programme, fasts, prayers and days of humiliation were laid on again.[61] Indeed, the jaundiced writer of *Mercurius Militaris* noted that all the officers' political mischief was 'ever done after fasting and prayer.'[62]

That these calls for spiritual humiliation evoked a committed response throughout the army is amply demonstrated by the struggles many garrisons undertook to secure civilian co-operation in their prayers for military success. In Poole, Exeter and Taunton opposition from clergy and civilians frustrated the soldiers' efforts to make these days universally observed. Other garrisons, however, such as Nantwich, Canterbury, Pendennis and St Mawes, concentrated on their own spiritual improvement, and wrote back to headquarters in perfervid language. 'Where [the Lamb's] strength is engaged and his warriors' hearts steeled by faith on him, what can they not do or suffer! ... no weapons can prosper against him,' exulted Nantwich. Having prayed and fasted, Canterbury was unequivocal: 'Our God hath crowned you with successes, hath made you as fire to the wood, and as a torch in the midst of the sheaf of your and our enemies.' The men of Pendennis reminded their comrades that their success was assured, 'your crown being cast down at the feet of the Lamb, through whose blood the saints both overcome, and are more than conquerors, all things conspiring and working together for their good.' That these were not perfunctory responses is suggested both by the vividness of the language and by the differences in each garrison's response.[63]

It is worth emphasizing that what the soldiers said in private paralleled what they said in public. We have already seen what Fairfax and Cromwell wrote to members of their own families about their religious beliefs. Other examples can be drawn from the writings of lesser officers. Captain Stephen Winthrop, son of the governor of Massachusetts, wrote to his brother that 'God hath done great things here in England, Scotland and Ireland.... Powers fall down apace, and not any persecuting spirit either in nation or person doth stand when discovered.'[64] Captain Nathaniel Barton wrote to his friend Major Thomas Saunders, who was trying to leave Colonel Gell's service and join the New Model in the spring of 1646, 'I make no question ... but our good God will settle you there where at length you shall do him the best service and have for greater comfort.... The Lord be with you, and in due time give you the desires of your soul that do relate to his glory, his church's good and your own comfort.'[65] Colonel Edward Harley, a member of the presbyterian minority that was driven out of the army in 1647, wrote for his own benefit 'A catalogue of some of these many mercies my God hath vouchsafed unto me.' Though chastened by misfortune and disappointment, he preserved a tone of pious and humble gratitude throughout.[66]

Those who stuck with Cromwell normally managed to preserve a more triumphalist tone in their letters. Thus at the beginning of 1648 army secretary William Clarke, while uneasy that political pressure was forcing the army to reduce its strength almost by half, was fortified by his personal faith, which he expressed in a letter to his friend Lieutenant-Colonel John Rede, governor of Poole:

> I fear we go to support a rotten structure which God will have fall. He's happy that can escape crushing if once the pillars break. Lay then a foundation of peace and comfort in the bosom of Christ, which will keep us safe and secure in storms and calms.[67]

Officers such as Colonels Hewson and Whalley manifested a crude arrogance in their self-assurance that God backed the parliamentary conquests of Ireland and Scotland.[68]

The regicide Colonel John Jones had a similar faith in divine providence, but expressed it with greater sensitivity. Though he did well out of the interregnum, Jones was continually troubled by the divisions and quarrels that afflicted the saints. But to Morgan Llwyd he confided,

> This comfort remains firm, that although we are weak, dark, deformed and peevish, we steadfastly believe, that we are completely strong, wise, beautiful and meek in the Lord Jesus, who is our sun, our shield, and our life, our light, our strength, and rock, from whom we are hewn.[69]

Most remarkable of all is the message addressed to their fellow soldiers in Wallingford garrison by about thirty London officers and separatist clergy in July 1649. The incandescent fervour suffusing the whole letter may have had something to do with the imminent invasion of Ireland, but there is no mention of that or any other political concern. Lamenting that their neglect of duty had caused 'the glory of Christ [to be] eclipsed', they had attempted to rectify matters by coming together 'to seek the face of God'. Acknowledging their failure in 'provoking one another to love and to good works, of pouring out our souls together before the Lord and of that care and watchfulness over each other's souls as became those who had received God', they prayed that as a result of their joint religious exercises they would all become 'burning and shining lights in our generation, to the stopping of the mouths of our enemies, the cheering of the upright in heart, and above all, the glorifying of our father which is in heaven.'[70] It was no cynical heart that penned these lines.

Professions of humility

Intense piety was frequently accompanied by exaggerated humility and self-abasement. Man was reduced in order the make God seem all the greater. Paradoxically self-abasement grew with the army's worldly success. The more powerful it became the more it insisted on its weakness and humility. At Naseby, asserted Cromwell, God had given the victory to 'a company of poor, ignorant men'. Why? 'Because God would by things that are not, bring to naught things that are.'[71] Some of the officers were mere 'babes and sucklings', said Hugh Peters, alluding to Colonel Montagu, who was only twenty years old. The storming of Bridgwater had been led by Lieutenant-Colonel Hewson, a shoemaker. 'Thus God gets glory by things despised, and not by humane great ones.'[72] Army spokesmen did not mind admitting that some of the officers were better Christians than soldiers, for, as Oliver Cromwell was convinced, 'he that prays and preaches best will fight best.'[73] When Fairfax crossed intellectual swords with Lord Hopton in Cornwall early in 1646 his argument was rigorously Calvinist. He acknowledged that divine favour did not spring from any merit on the part of the army, 'but from his own free grace and goodness towards his people.'[74] In December 1648, when the army was poised for its most daring stroke of all, Colonel Mackworth mused that 'God who comforteth the abject and loves to turn the wisdom of carnal men into folly hath in part freed us from our former fears.'[75] It seems not to have crossed Mackworth's mind that at that juncture the abject ones were the king, and the recently expelled and imprisoned MPs, not the all-powerful army. Still, the unconscious irony of

Mackworth's words gives a clue to the psychology of self-abasement. The more the army swelled in power, the more it mythologized its own weakness. Sometimes this meant fudging the facts, as when Joshua Sprigge, in a rare lapse from accuracy, said that the two sides were equal in number at Naseby.[76] Similarly, in an immensely flattering sermon preached to the army on the eve of its departure for Ireland in 1649, John Maudit likened the purge of a few hundred Levellers from the ranks to the action of Gideon in the Old Testament. In order to enhance God's glory he had reduced his army from 32,000 to 300 men, with whom he conquered the much larger army of the Midianites (Judges 7). Counselling the officers that 'out of weakness [they would be] made strong', Maudit exhorted them to 'be contented to endure persecution for Christ's sake', for 'God is doing his greatest work when he takes to him the weakest means.' He chooses 'the poor contemptible ones of the world that are rich in faith ... to bring his great designs about.'[77]

Whether the army had ever been poor and contemptible, in 1649 it was the master of England. Yet it was flattering to be told not to trust the arm of flesh, not to be daunted by persecution, and to visualize oneself as the underdog. Never mind that the army commanded overwhelming superiority of manpower and resources. It gave soldiers greater confidence to think of themselves as God's humble servants. Their morale was paradoxically enhanced by the thought that the victory was his alone, not theirs. Success in the 'arm of flesh' only reinforced the myth, as when the officers referred to their subjugation of the three kingdoms, sealed at Worcester, as 'the poor endeavours of his servants', or when, after the taking of Ross in October 1649, Cromwell referred to his comrades and himself as 'a company of poor worthless creatures'.[78]

Evangelism and lay preaching

Besides the dimension of personal piety, puritan zeal also possessed an outward, dynamic, proselytizing thrust. This outwardness is exemplified most strikingly in the phenomenon of lay preaching practised by officers and common soldiers alike. Before the New Model took to the field Colonel Pickering had already caused an uproar in his regiment by exercising his gifts of religious oratory. As a consequence parliament quickly passed an ordinance banning lay preaching and issued strict orders to Fairfax to see it enforced in the army.[79]

The practice however was irrepressible. In June 1645 Pickering's was noted as one of the seven 'chiefest praying and preaching regiments in the army'.[80] Just before the battle of Naseby two infantry captains, Richard

Beaumont and Paul Hobson, arrived at Newport Pagnell garrison, where they took up residence and prayed and preached to the soldiers. The governor, Sir Samuel Luke, grew impatient with their activities, which he found 'irregular and contrary' to the rules laid down by the Westminster Assembly of Divines. Consequently he had them escorted back to Colonel Fleetwood. Far from being disturbed by their men's illegal activities, both Fairfax and Fleetwood wrote to Luke underlining their displeasure at the discourtesy he had shown them. Fairfax ordered the two officers who had roughly handled the preaching captains to be cashiered, and his order was obeyed. Fleetwood warned Luke that 'to disturb a saint, Christ takes it as done to himself', and told him to respect liberty of conscience in the future.[81]

In the end, lay preaching ineluctably implies the principle of liberty of conscience. For that reason alone it was anathema to presbyterian clergy like Thomas Edwardes. His *Gangraena* is full of horrified accounts of officers and common soldiers interrupting sermons, usurping pulpits, and boldly claiming equality with the clergy. There was the redoubtable Paul Hobson, who attracted Edwardes' special ire because he travelled up and down the country sermonizing, an activity at which he seems to have spent more time than he did in fighting.[82] In February 1646 six or seven of Colonel Whalley's troopers preached in private houses in Wellingborough, Northamptonshire, and had a violent clash with the minister of the town.[83]

During the summer of 1646, with royalism defeated, soldiers and officers took advantage of their spare time to invade pulpits throughout southern England. In Exeter officers preached frequently at the castle, the guildhall and in private houses. In Ravensden, Bedfordshire, a private soldier preached against infant baptism, against tithes, and for universal grace. In the Isle of Ely Captain Kendall preached against humane learning and the universities. Another captain preached, sometimes twice on Sundays, in Auster, Warwickshire. More soldiers preached in Berkshire, Warwickshire and Oxfordshire on the theme of Antichrist, the necessity of rebaptism, the untrustworthiness of the Bible, and the black frog of Revelation.[84] In Buckinghamshire in January 1647 preaching by the trooper and future agitator Jeremy Ives provoked a brawl with local inhabitants in which some soldiers were dangerously wounded. Around the same time lay preaching caused serious friction in Northamptonshire, prompting Fairfax to order his soldiers to keep out of pulpits and to refrain from disturbing ordained ministers while they were preaching. In Somerset in August 1652 when the minister of Wookey fell sick, a soldier named Daniel Lewes took over the pulpit and began preaching on Psalm 106. Some indignant people then barged into the church, and with 'railing language' asked Lewes for his commission. Finally they tried to drown him out by ringing the bell.[85]

Sometimes extemporaneous prayer could turn into a form of lay preaching, as when the lieutenant-colonel who was deputy-governor of Edinburgh met with the town magistrates of Musselburgh in May 1652 and 'prayed very near an hour so sweetly, that it won much upon them.'[86]

What gave even greater offence was the soldiers' usurpation of pulpits in Oxford, ancient centre of learning, and headquarters of the royalist forces. Clergy and scholars found it repugnant to be lectured on their profession by rude unlettered soldiers. These men preached daily in Christ Church, '(one of the greatest colleges in Oxford) in a kind of gallery, where the soldier stands that preaches, many sitting on the stairs, others standing below.' Colonel Hewson, the Westminster shoemaker, took some of his men to Aston Church, a few miles outside the city, where twice in one day he openly defied the ordinance against lay preaching. In the second sermon he proved that the hapless incumbent minister was an Antichrist, by the thirteen marks of a false prophet. The previous Sunday Hewson had been with his major, Daniel Axtell, at Wallington Church, where they elbowed out the incumbent and took turns preaching in the morning and afternoon.[87]

The soldiers' intervention in the religious and intellectual life of Oxford was formalized in a public disputation between several officers and six presbyterian ministers in November 1646. The conference, which lasted from three in the afternoon till nine at night, was dedicated to resolving whether only the ordained could be permitted to preach. A leading participant was Colonel Hewson, 'a most categorical disputant, yet so rude ... we wondered [at] so much true logic and false English.' Many other 'gifted officers' also took part, as well as the chaplain William Erbery. A hostile reporter noted that the proceedings were chaired by the deputy governor of Oxford, Captain John Grimes, a carpenter. The question at issue was not resolved, so the clergy were invited to return the following Thursday, which they failed to do. Unabashed, the officers then threw out a public challenge to the university as a whole to prove that their calling was from Christ.[88]

Apart from the argument that they had an intrinsic moral right to exercise their 'gifts' for religious oratory, the soldiers justified lay preaching on two grounds. First, there had never been enough qualified chaplains in the army. Hungry for spiritual nourishment, the soldiers had therefore taken on the job of preaching to one another. Both W[illiam] G[offe] and Lieutenant Edmund Chillenden penned eloquent apologies for the right of the humblest soldier to act as a channel of divine revelation.[89] Second, as Marshal-General Richard Laurence pointed out, the country people were in desperate need of having the gospel preached to them. Who were better equipped than the soldiers to rise to this challenge and combat presbyterian clergy, who were nothing but agents of Antichrist?[90]

The volume and range of religious activities engaged in by the New Model Army – private and corporate prayer, fasting, reading and expounding of scripture, alternately listening to and delivering sermons – show that there was in the army a great store of spiritual and intellectual energy. This energy was expressed in the vocabularies of both Calvinistic puritanism and libertarian antinomianism. We must now examine whether this fund of energy made any practical difference to the army's military and political activities.

Religion's Practical Consequences

Morale

Egalitarianism

The phenomenon of a godly army had its practical consequence in high morale. This condition was first noted in the summer of 1645 and it continued through the bad months of early 1646, when disease, dismal weather, and shortages of money and supplies might have been expected to promote discontent or unhappiness. Soon after the army's founding, newsbook commentators remarked on the sense of unity, fellowship and love that they observed amongst all ranks. This harmony existed even though the army contained presbyterians, Independents and sectaries, and it manifested itself in an elevated standard of conduct. 'Instead of drinking, gaming, plundering,' exclaimed the *Moderate Intelligencer*, 'they pray and discourse.'[91] Hugh Peters exulted that he had not seen more love among men than he found in the New Model.[92] Reporting on the storming of Bristol, Oliver Cromwell adduced this fraternal feeling amongst the soldiers to make a political point about religious toleration.[93] The feeling of fellowship and unity was enhanced by the spiritual egalitarianism implicit in the preaching of Dell, Saltmarsh and Peters. If it was true that God was no respecter of persons, that works were useless to salvation, that grace was available to all, and that Christ judged by the heart rather than outward show, then all were of equal importance. During the Putney debates Henry Ireton asserted that the Holy Spirit is 'the only searcher of hearts' who can reveal to a man 'the error of his own ways and … the workings of his own heart.'[94] Indeed, the very creation of the General Council of the Army in 1647 and the Reading and Putney debates of that year are emblematic of the religious conviction that even the humblest individual has immeasurable value in the eyes of God. For several months the rank and file, through their elected agitators, were on a nearly equal footing with the higher officers in the task of making policy for the army.

The commanders were not unaware of the practical benefits of spiritual egalitarianism in welding men into an effective fighting unit. During the first month after the army took to the field Fairfax decided that every foot regiment should take turns marching at the head. At first the men of his own foot regiment balked at giving up the prestige status normally reserved to the commander-in-chief's regiment; so Fairfax, rather than discipline them, alighted from his horse and marched on foot with them for 2 miles. From that day onward his regiment took its turn with the others in bringing up the rear. This small act made a deep impression on the soldiers.[95]

Egalitarianism was also expressed and morale fortified by the frequent willingness of officers to share the risks of battle on an equal basis with their men. Thus Major John Disbrowe led Fairfax's horse regiment up Hambleton Hill in an assault against the clubmen. At the dangerous assault on Bridgwater the forlorn hope of foot was led by Lieutenant-Colonel Hewson. Once they had got over the outworks and let down the drawbridge the forlorn hope of horse streamed into the town, with Captain John Reynolds at their head. Major Bethell was shot in the hand while taking his troops through the narrow pass below Langport. Similar bravery at Bristol cost him his life. Captain Thomas Ireton led the horse in attacking the line at Bristol. In the same battle Captain Lagoe of the infantry scrambled up a ladder at Prior's Hill Fort, and was the first man to lay hold on the enemy's colours. At Berkeley Castle, Colonel Herbert led his men in a daring assault on the heavily fortified stronghold, narrowly escaping death when he was shot through the hat.[96] Perhaps not too much should be made of these examples; there were after all many cavalier officers of equal bravery who betrayed little godliness. Yet it may be significant that, with the possible exception of Herbert, all the officers cited above were men of piety.

Extraordinary displays of courage are an unfailing means to weld together officers and men. Another means was shared financial hardship. It was widely believed that many of the higher officers had depleted their own fortunes in order to promote parliament's war effort. Cromwell, for example, was reported to have made great personal sacrifices, while Fairfax forewent his pay as a colonel.[97] Other officers reached into their own pockets to help their men when pay fell seriously into arrears.[98] This practical concern for the material welfare was encouraged by the spiritual egalitarianism that the army chaplains preached.

'The sweetness, union and love that is amongst the saints'[99] was most intensely experienced at the regimental and garrison level. Some units formed themselves into 'gathered churches' or voluntary associations for religious worship. Cromwell's regiment of Ironsides did so early in the war,[100] as did Sir William Brereton's regiment in the north.[101] In a broad sense William Dell regarded the whole New Model in 1646 as a gathered church, after its bonding experience of battle over the previous twelve months.[102] Smaller units within the army also saw themselves through the same prism. Each of the troops of Colonel Whalley's regiment, for example, acted as a gathered church when they were stationed in Nottinghamshire and Derbyshire in the 1650s.[103] By 1649 the officers at headquarters in Whitehall had also come together as a church and sought to transmit their practices to the garrisons. The responses from many garrisons in 1649 and 1650 to the appeals issued from headquarters suggest that the model was widely imitated.[104] In Dublin Colonel John Jones was zealous in promoting religious observance in the garrison, and preached regularly. As he said to a friend, 'the communion and fellowship of saints ... is one of the most principal parts of the saints' privileges and enjoyment.'[105]

The other side of the coin of egalitarianism, fellowship, unity and love was a sense of separateness from the rest of society. At Putney Lieutenant-Colonel William Goffe admonished his fellow officers and agitators that their ways should not be 'such as the world hath walked in'.[106] In July 1651 the English council of officers in Ireland wrote to their counterparts in Scotland,

> let us ... live and walk as becomes a people ... under such high and choice dispensations of mercy as we are, ... that our conversation may tell the world we are not of it, but are strangers and pilgrims here, travelling through it towards our own country and city, whose maker and builder is God.[107]

The soldiers were under no illusion that their vision was shared by the majority of English people. Their sense of alienation from what they considered the corrupt, ungodly mass of society was felt more acutely after 1648 but it had never been wholly absent. There were enough references in the Bible to the faithful remnant, to many being called but few chosen, to reassure the soldiers that their unpopularity with men was a sign of their favour with God. Opposition and conflict were to be expected as part of God's plan, and opponents were dismissed as 'those that support the Beast and oppose the advancement of the kingdom of our Lord Jesus Christ.'[108] Internal spiritual solidarity combined with alienation from the bulk of the population also explains the army's aggressive behaviour in suppressing traditional religious observances, enforcing the reformation of manners, and protecting like-minded sectarian congregations.[109]

Courage, discipline and personal conduct

The conviction that they belonged to an army bathed in the rays of providential favour, that they were fighting 'the warfare of heaven', 'overcoming evil by doing good', that God was exceedingly bountiful in his goodness towards them, had a liberating effect throughout the army which led to many acts of exceptional courage and improvisation.[110] As we have seen, when the army was besieging Bath, men from one of the more religious regiments (Okey's) crept on their bellies to the town gates, and seized on the small end of the defenders' muskets which were sticking through the iron grate. So terrified were the defenders that they dropped their muskets and fled. Okey's men took possession of the gate and the bridge, and the town was quickly overrun. Two weeks later at Sherborne Castle, while the army's great guns were firing, soldiers stole up to the fortress and retrieved bullets from under the very walls. When Bristol was stormed the following month the most heavily fortified position was Prior's Hill Fort, which held out for two hours after the rest of the city had fallen. The army's scaling ladders turned out to be too short, but, instead of holding back, some of Lieutenant-Colonel Pride's men clambered up and wriggled through the portholes below the top of the wall. At the siege of Tiverton a stray cannon shot fortuitously broke the chain of the drawbridge, which came crashing down. Instantly appreciating this stroke of fortune, a band of common soldiers, without waiting for orders, streamed over the bridge and possessed themselves of the churchyard. Their display of daring so overwhelmed the defenders that they abandoned their positions and 'cried out in a lamentable manner for quarter'.[111] By the late winter of 1646 royalists had become convinced of the invincibility of the New Model, and a great fright overtook them whenever they came into contact with their enemy.[112]

There is no doubt that an accumulation of successes bred steadily increasing self-confidence in the army. But in an organization saturated with religious thinking success confirmed a providentialist outlook, while providentialism contributed to success. The process was circular. But providentialism was more than a just the smug attribution of success to divine favour. Risk-taking was also involved. When, for example, in the spring of 1649 there were bitter differences over which regiments should be sent to Ireland, conflict was resolved by scrapping the list previously drawn up by headquarters staff and drawing lots. This signified that the officers were turning the decision over to God, and each one was accepting the chance that he would be selected for a dangerous and unpalatable mission.[113]

That the army's high morale was not due solely to its military success is suggested by the strict code of personal conduct that was successfully imposed during at least the first year and a half of its existence. For three months after the army's founding, Fairfax employed harsh measures to knock it into shape. Deserters, mutineers and plunderers were shot.[114] Then, with the most serious threats to the army's integrity regulated, Fairfax took aim at lesser sins: swearing, drunkenness and whoring. In most armies this kind of conduct is regarded with indulgence, but in the New Model, next to desertion, the crime most often punished was blasphemy. A man unfortunate enough to be convicted had his tongue pulled out of his mouth with surgeon's pincers and bored through with a hot iron. The speech impediment he was left with was a permanent reminder to him and his comrades of the gravity of taking the Lord's name in vain.[115] Officers were occasionally cashiered for quarrelling and falsifying their musters; drunkards were made to ride the wooden horse with their head strapped to their heels, and with papers pinned to their hats describing their crime. This punishment, together with running the gauntlet, were also inflicted for other misdemeanours. Both these punishments, besides being painful, contained a significant element of humiliation. To be fully effective they depended on the approval and active support of the rank and file. Corporal punishment, which was the most common punishment in the eighteenth-century army, seems to have been reserved for sexual transgressions. Whores who contaminated the army with their presence were whipped and sent on their way, while men guilty of fornication and adultery were treated in the same manner.[116]

Because the army was well paid, fed and clothed by the standards of the day, the harsh code of discipline was accepted and even internalized. So effective was the code that for at least two years it was possible for pro-army journalists to boast without fear of contradiction of the troops' admirable conduct. 'A general reformation is passed through the soldiery', enthused Henry Walker, 'no oaths nor cursing, no drunkenness, nor quarrelling but love, unanimity is amongst them. I have been in the army an eye witness of their admirable carriages; none daring to take the worth of a penny but what they pay for.'[117] To the intellectually simple it was self-evident that God delighted in the army's good behaviour. His delight meant his blessing and his blessing meant victory in battle.[118]

Ruthlessness

Success added to a providentialist world view banished self-doubt. As victory piled upon victory, the army became imbued with a holy ruthlessness. This phenomenon is comprehensible to a twentieth-century mind if we think of the even greater ruthlessness of revolutionaries inspired by the secular providentialism of Marxism – Leninism, which saw victory as inevitable and justified any act which hastened that victory.

After Naseby one journalist labelled the army as the instrument that would destroy Antichrist root and branch.[119] The army was glad enough to wear this label. Civilian opposition merely fed the conviction that the army was the divinely chosen weapon to combat Antichrist. By the autumn of 1648, fortified by inflammatory preaching and scriptural texts, the army identified Antichrist in the person of Charles I, 'that man of blood', the 'man against whom God hath witnessed'. Propelled by this conviction they rode roughshod over the majority of the English people to bring the king to his public trial and execution.[120]

Over the following two years this ruthlessness was displayed in the army's relations with Scotland and Ireland. Writing to the garrisons to gird themselves for the war against Scotland, the officers at headquarters called the army 'a rod of iron in Christ's hand to dash his enemies in pieces.'[121] But it is in the army's actions in Ireland that the full dimensions of its holy ruthlessness were displayed. Early in the revolution a few feeble voices had objected to the proposed conquest of Ireland on the ground that the cause of the Irish was just.[122] However, the great majority in the army agreed that the Irish were barbarous wretches; they were 'that cursed people' who had brought catastrophe upon themselves by defying God's will. Thanks to the survival of his letterbooks, we have a more complete view of the attitude of Colonel John Jones to Ireland than that of any other officer, but there is every reason for thinking that he was representative of commanders such as Cromwell, Ireton, Hewson and Ludlowe. The Irish people were seen as treacherous and cowardly because they had no trust in God. Repeated plagues and crop failures in the early 1650s demonstrated God's displeasure with them. Although he wept for 'poor bleeding Ireland', Jones had not a shred of sympathy for the native inhabitants. His solution was to wipe the slate clean and strive for 'the framing or forming of a commonwealth out of a corrupt rude mass, the dividing of the country amongst the servants of the lord, who have passed through the Red Sea, and endured hardship in the wilderness.' As the representative of England – 'a great nation and a wise and understanding people' – Jones knew he had the right to impose his policies upon Ireland, a nation 'guided and governed by corrupt, carnal, selfish interests'.[123]

The civilian communities

The army's ruthlessness was practised off the battlefield as well as on. Animated by a militant faith, and having an apocalyptic, millenarian vision of England's political destiny,[124] the leaders, and some of the rank and file, saw it as part of their mission to tear down the idols of Antichrist and bring about a reformation of manners through the suppression of immoral behaviour. While recognizing that no one could be brought by force of arms to share their faith, they did not hesitate to use their power to protect civilian separatist congregations from the hostility of local populations.

Iconoclasm

The aspect of the New Model's impact upon English society that endures most vividly to this day in the popular memory is its iconoclasm – the destruction of stained glass, religious statuary, stone altars, altar rails, rood screens, brasses, crosses, vestments, prayerbooks, organs and printed music. To most people this orgy of destructiveness was an incomprehensible outrage, but to the soldiers it was a necessary purging of the relics of popish superstition, justified by the biblical injunction against the making of graven images. A word of caution is required about the extent of army responsibility for the destruction of religious art and architecture. Much iconoclasm had in fact occurred a century earlier under Thomas Cromwell or during the reigns of Edward VI and Elizabeth.[125] Most revolutionary iconoclasm took place during the opening years, from 1642 to 1644. When iconoclasm was not the work of an 'enraged rabble' it was frequently undertaken by local officials – the mayors and aldermen of towns, for example – or the Earl of Manchester's remarkable agent in the Eastern Association, William Dowsing.[126]

But there remains a sizable amount of soldierly iconoclasm, which was more than just the carrying-out of parliament's orders, or the supplying of protection to civilian iconoclasts. Most of the evidence comes from hostile sources, and it is clearly exaggerated as well as repetitive. The familiar tale of parliamentary soldiers who obscenely baptized a horse or a pig or a calf, whether at Lostwithiel or Yaxley or Lichfield, is repeated in several royalist accounts.[127] Desecration seems to have horrified royalist commentators more than iconoclasm: soldiers stabling horses in the nave of St Paul's Cathedral and other places, setting hounds to hunt cats in the aisles of Lichfield, resorting to other churches to 'ease nature', using stone altars as chopping blocks for meat, dressing up in priests' or bishops' vestments, and brazenly smoking, drinking and swearing inside the sacred space of churches.[128]

Most military attention appears to have been focused on cathedrals. Soldiers were responsible for extensive destruction in Canterbury, Rochester, Winchester, Peterborough, Lincoln, Worcester, Chichester, Lichfield, Exeter, Salisbury and Gloucester cathedrals and in Westminster Abbey.[129] York Minster, on the other hand, managed to preserve the biggest collection of medieval stained glass in Europe thanks to Thomas Fairfax's guarantee that none of the city's churches would suffer desecration.[130]

The building that suffered most from the violent hands of soldiers appears to be have been St Paul's Cathedral. Money raised for repairs just before the civil war was seized, while scaffolding erected around the tower was given to Colonel Jephson's regiment in partial satisfaction of its arrears of pay. On striking the scaffolding, the soldiers brought down part of the south transept with its roof. The portico of the cathedral was let out for shops, and its carving 'broken down with axes and hammers'. In December 1648 soldiers were lodged in the cathedral; to keep warm they tore the carved wainscotting from the walls and lit bonfires on the floor. During the interregnum the nave was used to stable horses belonging to the cavalry.[131]

Besides these cathedrals a few dozen parish churches dotted over most parts of the country suffered from the iconoclastic attentions of parliamentary soldiers. Acton and Chiswick parish churches in Middlesex were defaced; altar rails were burned at Wendover, Buckinghamshire; and Christchurch and St Mary Redcliffe, Bristol, were vandalized, even to the extent of burning Bibles.[132] However, given that there were more than 9000 parish churches in England, the spoliation of fewer than thirty by parliamentary soldiers does not qualify as an orgy of destruction.

Enforcement of the reformation of manners

Soldiers were also in the forefront of the campaign to correct those social practices that offended puritan sensibilities. From the establishment of the republic in 1649 they went about aggressively to eradicate stage plays, cock-fighting, morris dancing, maypoles, alehouses and horse-racing. Some of their activities would qualify as enlightened by late twentieth-century standards – for example, their suppression of cock-fighting, bear- and bull-baiting, and prize fencing. Also, there is the creditable example of Lieutenant-Colonel Paul Hobson, who seems to have blocked the efforts of the Scottish witch-finder in Newcastle in 1650.[133] The army's attitude to popular festive culture was also on occasion coloured by strategic considerations. It was well known, for example, that the Kentish insurrection of 1648 was organized under cover of horse races, wrestlings and maypoles.[134] But the army also believed in the reformation of manners for its own sake. It took seriously the Rump Parliament's abolition of Christmas and other 'popish' festivals, such as Ascension Day. In London soldiers attempted to tear down the holly with which festive citizens had decorated the streets, and to compel shopkeepers to open on Christmas Day. On Thursday 3 May 1649 Colonel Philip Twisleton's troopers rode into Worcester, where Ascension Day was being observed. When they quarrelled with some of the inhabitants, the mayor intervened, 'until at last it grew hot, one of the horses were killed, and the inhabitants beat the soldiers out of town.'[135] One holy day however had to be upheld – the sabbath. Both work and play on Sunday were suppressed. Notably active in sabbath enforcement was Colonel Pride, who made his will felt in Chester, Manchester, Liverpool and London.[136] Major-General Robert Lilburne had market day in Durham and Yorkshire changed from Monday to Tuesday so that preparations would not profane the Lord's Day.[137]

Protection of the godly

Far more important to the soldiers than iconoclasm and the enforcement of the reformation of manners was the eradication of what they regarded as popish or Laudian worship, and its replacement by acceptably puritan forms. The campaign to refashion the religious practices of Englishmen gathered momentum after the war had been won. First there was the negative work. Disaffected clergy had to be silenced, and use of the Book of Common Prayer stopped. One technique of discrediting hostile clergy was to publicize their peccadilloes. Thus in Exeter a minister was reportedly put into the stocks for being drunk, while in Devizes another was dragged from the pulpit on the same pretext.[138] In Newark and London we find soldiers invading churches to block the use of the Prayer Book. But in Newark, if we can believe the royalist account, 'the resolute and religious dames of the town fell upon [the soldiers], beat them forth of the church, and afterwards performed their devotion in despite of the cowards.'[139] Conservative clergymen were often the focus of military wrath, for the good reason that they were the ones who rallied popular resistance to the revolution. They tangled with Colonel Pride, for example, in Lancashire on the issue of the 1649 Engagement oath, and they also condemned the Engagement from the pulpit in Chester.[140] Another bone of contention was the day of thanksgiving proclaimed by parliament after the army's victories at Dunbar and Worcester. Ministers from Somerset fled into Devon in October 1650 rather than give thanks for the victory over the Scots, while the preacher at Taunton delivered a thinly veiled attack on the government. He was publicly rebuked by the governor of the castle for his sermon.[141] In Exeter, thanks to 'froward ministers', only a few people observed the day of thanksgiving in 1650, while the rest of the population had to be restrained from working. Both parish churches and cathedral had been shut and the ministers had disappeared. Only after the importation of new ministers was the day celebrated at all. Facing chronic disaffection from the clergy, the city's godly finally prevailed upon the government to expel two ministers, while extra soldiers came up from Plymouth to 'encourage' a more enthusiastic response.[142] In Northampton it was a similar story. The minister had locked the church, and the thanksgiving service could not begin until Captain Mercer had wrested the keys from the hands of an unwilling churchwarden.[143] Elsewhere, strong-willed officers like Major Hobson in Newcastle and Colonel Whichcote in Windsor took matters into their own hands and fired unsatisfactory ministers.[144] Eventually the harassment of conservative clergy and congregations became so resented that in April 1653 Cromwell's committee of officers in Whitehall commanded the soldiers to refrain from disturbing 'any ministers or people peaceably met together in any public places to worship God.'[145]

In all these struggles with civilians the army exhibited an acute awareness of its religious function. To godly officers there was no question but that the army 'hath been a shelter to honest people that had otherwise been hammered to dust.' Equally, many Independent and sectarian congregations were only too conscious that the army was a prop to their survival.[146]

This is not to say that godly officers were always strong enough to withstand the fury of conservatives. Colonel John Rede, governor of Poole from 1647, for example, so annoyed the magistrates of the town by his alleged support of 'exorbitant Levellers and ranters', that they exerted unremitting pressure at Westminster to have him removed. In time he was replaced by the former governor, whose views were much more palatable to the local rulers.[147]

An even more bitter struggle erupted in Hull, but there the city fathers encountered in Colonel Robert Overton, the governor, a man who was more than their match. Having opposed Overton's appointment in the first place, they resisted taking the Engagement from the end of 1649, while 'malignant' ministers preached against it from the pulpit. The city fathers strove to have the garrison disbanded, but its strategic importance foreclosed that option. With not more than four sympathetic men on the aldermanic bench, the town's godly looked for relief to the 'faithful and confiding officers and soldiers' whom Overton had installed.

The split between garrison and corporation become even more pronounced during the second half of 1650, when John Canne arrived as chaplain to the garrison. A leader of the Brownists in Amsterdam in the 1630s and 1640s, Canne was regarded as 'a grand heretic on an ancient standing' by Hull's orthodox clergy. Reluctantly the corporation agreed to his preaching in the chancel of the high church twice during the week. Before long the officers were demanding that he preach on Sundays as well. To accommodate the regular services in the main body of the church at the same time as Canne preached in the chancel, Overton, with the backing of the Council of State, erected a brick wall between the chancel and the nave.[148] This church-splitting wall was the architectural metaphor for the religious incomprehension and hostility that separated the two factions in the city.

Parliamentary soldiers also played an influential role in the religious life of Bristol. In the 1650s the city became a stronghold for Quakers. Their growth in numbers would not have been possible without the active encouragement and protection of highly placed officers in the garrison. At the end of the civil wars the conservative city corporation had been purged of its most disaffected elements, giving the signal for the emergence of a radical preacher, Dennis Hollister, much favoured by Colonels Thomas Harrison and Adrian Scrope, the latter becoming a member of his congregation. Members of the garrison were responsible for preventing John Wells, an orthodox London minister, from preaching and for bringing radical preachers like Morgan Llwyd and William Erbery to Bristol. On one occasion Llwyd and Erbery invaded the church of one of the leading conservative ministers of the city, Ralph Farmer, and, in Farmer's words, 'abused the people with their delusions'. Whenever the government leaned towards the disbandment of Bristol garrison, Hollister's congregation mobilized petitions to London arguing for the garrison's continuance on the ground that the majority of the city were 'malignants and ill affected'. It cannot have escaped the government's notice that the religious radicals relied heavily upon the soldiers for personal protection. At any rate, between 1652 and 1654 all moves to disband the garrison were blocked. When in 1654 elections were held to the first protectoral parliament the contest, in Colonel Scrope's eyes, pitted the 'godly' against the 'enemies of God'. To his distress, God's enemies won, with both radical candidates, George Bishop and Colonel John Haggett, going down to defeat.

At the end of 1654 a group of Quakers descended on Bristol in an evangelizing mission from the north. Before long Hollister and Bishop, who was also a radical preacher well connected with the army leadership, threw in their lot with them, as did the deputy governors, Captains Henry Beale and Richard Watson, the commanders of the fort and castle respectively. As the Quakers' numbers grew, their meetings could no longer be accommodated in private houses; accordingly, at the invitation of the two captains they met both in the castle and the fort, 'whither many hundred resorted out of city and country.' Whenever Quakers wished to preach in the countryside they were provided with an armed escort through the city. The fondness of the soldiers for the Quakers is not surprising if we bear in mind that a significant number of Quakers were themselves former soldiers. Many Bristol citizens, however, were repelled by the Quakers' extravagant spirituality and their disruptive practices – such as their refusal to show respect to their social superiors, and their invasion of churches to dispute with the conservative clergy. In December 1654 a 'rude multitude' which included many apprentices attacked two prominent Quakers in the street. At the instigation of the garrison three ringleaders of this assault were brought to trial. But their interrogation was the occasion for another crowd to assemble, and a second riot erupted during which the parliamentary soldiers were taunted for their protection of Quakers. Five days later, on Christmas, several hundred people attacked a Quaker in his own home but were again dispersed by the soldiers. There was a large measure of truth in Ralph Farmer's bitter accusation that the Quakers flourished in Bristol only because they were 'upheld, countenanced, maintained and propagated...by the strength and power of these soldiers.'

The days of military protection were numbered, however. Disturbed at the depth of religious and political dissension in the city, and feeling militarily secure in the region, the government in 1655 ordered the disgarrisoning of Bristol. From then on the Quakers had to fend for themselves.[149]

Not all soldiers showed Quakers the same sympathy as they enjoyed in Bristol. In parts of the west country they ran into hostile officers who mocked them and threw them into gaol. Major John Blackmore instructed Devon constables to enforce the order for the apprehension of all travelling Quakers who distributed printed matter or disturbed ministers in their congregations, and Major Thomas Saunders was instrumental in having several of them arrested. Some sympathetic officers tried to make life easier for the Quakers. When a number were being tormented in Launceston Gaol, Colonel Robert Bennett put in a kind word for them, and Captain William Braddon fruitlessly offered £100 as surety for their good behaviour. On another occasion soldiers rescued Quakers from an angry crowd in Plymouth. Major-General John Disbrowe came personally to Launceston to investigate why the Quakers had been imprisoned. He sacked the gaoler who had mistreated them and ordered their release on the understanding they would leave Launceston and return home. Even though they balked at this condition, Bennett and Braddon had them released anyway. Almost at once the freed men locked horns with local officials and landed in gaol again. A second time they refused to leave town, but now Major-General Disbrowe did not come to their rescue. Presiding at their trial was Colonel Bennett, who finally lost patience at their refusal to remove their hats in court, and sent them back to prison.[150]

Elsewhere in England the religious activities of the army were less conflict-ridden, but no less valued by the godly. In Newcastle, Colonel Robert Lilburne, the governor, and his deputy, Captain Paul Hobson, helped found the first Baptist congregations on Tyneside.[151] In London, a radical preacher whose sermon was disturbed by presbyterian and royalist hecklers found relief when cavalry troops came and drove them out.[152] In Chester, the 'honest party' testified to the encouragement that the arrival of Colonel Barkstead's forces had given them in their struggle with the city's clergy, all but one of whom were 'Scottified presbyterians'.[153] In Manchester, Major-General Harrison fought the conservative clergy by importing a radical preacher, the celebrated Morgan Llwyd, who invaded the pulpit of the leading disaffected minister and 'preached unto them things of Christ most sweetly.'[154]

In some districts the soldiers found that they had to be less aggressive. When the peripatetic haberdasher Captain Paul Hobson returned to his native county of Buckinghamshire he was refused admittance to the church in Wycombe, so he preached to his proselytes in a garden. One of his themes was the evils of tobacco, 'And in derision thereof he told them he would show them the best way of taking it, and having a pipe filled he lighted it, and then put the little end into the fundament of his horse.'[155] Likewise, Colonel Whalley's troopers in Nottingham were denied access to the town's churches for their religious exercises, disaffected clergy denouncing them as 'the greatest plague that ever befell this town.' As a consequence of their ostracism the soldiers had little religious influence on the townspeople, and were compelled to huddle in a small room at an inn for their prayer meetings. At nearby Newark and Worksop, however, other troops of the same regiment found the people 'very loving' to them, even though they conducted religious exercises similar to those of their comrades in Nottingham.[156]

To sum up, we have seen that the religious energy with which the army was imbued made a palpable difference to its fortunes on the battlefield and its relations with civilians. Religion produced high morale, even in the midst of disease, bad weather and hardship. Spiritual equality was demonstrated in the officers' willingness to share risks with their men and in the solidarity that was frequently manifested amongst them. Solidarity based on a shared conviction of righteousness produced many feats of extraordinary courage which in turn hastened the collapse of enemy morale. Religion also caused large numbers of ordinary soldiers to internalize a singularly exacting code of personal discipline. During its early years at least the New Model engaged in less drunkenness, swearing and exploitation of civilians than other armies of early-modern Europe. Equally, its religiously grounded self-confidence made it ruthless. From 1648 onward most opponents, whether king, royalists or Irishmen were regarded as agents of Antichrist, against whom almost any measure was justified. The army's conviction of its own righteousness led it as well to interfere with civilian society – demolishing the visible signs of popish superstition, enforcing the puritan reformation of manners, and fostering separatist congregations in towns and cities throughout England and Ireland. Few of these were the activities of a normal army; they are directly traceable to the New Model's peculiar religious stamp.

The Experience of Defeat

God hath indeed of late humbled us with many ill successes, which I acknowledge as a very certain evidence of his just judgement against us for our personal crimes. Yet give me leave to say, your present prosperity cannot be so certain an evidence of his being altogether pleased with you.[157]

... the providence of God (which is so often pleaded in justification of your ways) is no safe rule to walk by, especially in such acts as the Word of God condemns. God doth not approve the practice of whatsoever his providence doth permit.[158]

I am assured it was done by the wise disposing hand of God, without whose providence not a sparrow falls to the ground, much less the blood of any of his precious saints and faithful witnesses.... Yet so it is that the Lord is pleased for the present to make them the tail, who before were the head, and that they should bow down that their enemies may go over them.[159]

The providentialist view of history is good for morale when things are going well. When success turns to failure, however, it is a harsh doctrine. If God had willed the countless illustrious victories of the army, as well as the political revolution that the army imposed on the three kingdoms, did he also will the reversal of that revolution in 1660? Justification by success logically implies condemnation by defeat, but few members of the revolutionary army could bring themselves to accept that God had condemned their life's work when he brought Charles II back to the throne.

Many, it is true, were reduced to silence by the Restoration. Others found solace in a personal, quietistic religion that henceforth ignored politics. But some remained defiant to the end, and went down with colours flying. A few were able to persuade themselves that what had happened was only a temporary setback, a sojourn in the wilderness, after which the saints would surely reach the promised land. Hardly any could bring themselves to say, 'We were wrong; we misinterpreted God's will.'

Belief in providence is perfectly able to accommodate secondary setbacks and reverses, especially those of a personal nature. Colonel John Jones lost seven of his eight children, as well as his wife. Harrison buried his first child just after the king's execution, and the other two over the next four years. Cromwell also lost children, and with Fairfax was frequently a prey to sickness. Disappointment and suffering of this kind were familiar to everyone in the seventeenth century, and were regarded by puritan soldiers as part of a chastening process by which they were spiritually strengthened. Fairfax was confident that he would not be burdened with more sickness than he would be able to bear. Cromwell thought that illness taught him not to rely on the 'arm of flesh'.[160]

It was also possible for men functioning within this mental framework to deal with temporary setbacks of a military or political nature. When in the late summer of 1645 the Scots' affairs were going badly, the higher officers in the New Model wrote to commiserate with them on their reverses. There was no hint in the letter that God was punishing the Scots for anything they had done wrong. It was just that his ways were mysterious and his 'secret ends' unfathomable. The English officers assured their comrades that they would not slacken in their prayers, 'and to wrestle with God, for one blessing of God upon both nations.'[161] A year or so later, when the New Model was beginning to feel the heat of civilian wrath at its continued existence, there was again no thought that God too might be angry with the army; merely that his ways were hidden for the moment. 'But this is our comfort,' confided Cromwell to his commander-in-chief, 'God is in heaven, and He doth what pleaseth Him; His and only His counsel shall stand, whatever the designs of men, and the fury of the people be.'[162]

By 1651 Henry Ireton, then Lord Deputy of Ireland, did not shrink from the thought that adversity, in the form of their setback at Clonmel and the 'heavy stroke of the pestilence upon all our garrisons' was God's way of bringing the army back to dependence on himself.[163] Later still, when it was clear that the reign of Christ had not yet begun in England, many officers were prepared to entertain the possibility that God was indeed chastening them. The letter from headquarters to the garrisons in January 1653 acknowledged that recent setbacks, particularly in the war against the Dutch, had prompted them to seek the Lord and to humble themselves before him, in an attempt to discern what wrongdoings on their part had made God 'withdraw his presence from us'. These divine chastisements and the officers' spiritual exercises led directly to several concrete proposals for political reform.[164] In the crisis of 1659–60, however, the imminent prospect of total political defeat paralysed any similar constructive response. Despairingly Major-General Fleetwood concluded that 'the Lord had blasted them and spit in their faces.'[165]

Fleetwood's cry from the heart was one of very few such responses to defeat. Others retreated into silence or sought consolation in religious pietism. Several of the regicides who did not live long enough to take in the enormity of their failure responded heroically.[166] Fortified by their providentialist faith, they went unshaken to their deaths, convinced that the triumph of royalism had only temporarily postponed their millenarian expectations. 'Where is your good old cause?' jeered a bystander when Harrison was on his way to his execution at Charing Cross. Smiling, he answered, 'Here it is', clapping his hand over his heart, 'and I am going to seal it with my blood.'[167] At his trial he had articulated a complete confidence in the righteousness of his cause:

The finger of God hath been amongst us of late years in the deliverance of his people from their oppressors, and in bringing to judgement those that were guilty of the precious blood of the dear servants of the Lord.... Be not discouraged by reason of the cloud that now is upon you; for the Son will shine and God will give a testimony unto what he hath been a-doing in a short time.[168]

But how could God have sanctioned both 1649 and 1660? How could he sacrifice his own servants even if others had let down the cause? Did these hard questions arising from the experience of crushing political defeat effectively destroy the providentialist interpretation of history? For many doubtless they did, but at least one participant in the events of the revolutionary decades kept his allegiance to it. Writing more than two decades after the Restoration, Lieutenant-General Edmund Ludlowe was still able to interpret that event as only a temporary setback for the saints. Preserving his Calvinistic conviction of God's ceaseless involvement in the minutest of human affairs, Ludlowe had the intellectual consistency to attribute the changes of 1660 to the 'immediate hand of God'. Along with other radicals Ludlowe was critical of the ambition and avarice of some of the higher officers, and he deplored the army's lack of unity. The nation in general was also to blame for its unreadiness to profit from 'that glorious work which he seemed to be doing for them by the means of some of his poor people.' None the less the return of Charles II and the humiliation of the saints represented only a temporary detour into the wilderness. It was impossible that evil should triumph permanently, and the present sufferings were only a preparation for the next opportunity that God would put into their hands. Ludlowe did not shrink from acknowledging the full measure of the defeat of the Good Old Cause, but the dignity and the optimism of his response are worthy of comparison with Milton's in *Samson Agonistes*.[169]

Historians have long debated the reasons for the stunning military success of the New Model, coming in the wake of so many disasters endured by the parliamentary armies between 1642 and 1645. There is no gainsaying that the army owed more than a little of its success to the fact that it was relatively well financed, clothed, provisioned and armed. It also enjoyed excellent leadership free of interference by parliamentary committees remote from the scene of action. The military weakness of the adversary, and blunders by the king and his advisers were also major factors. But to complete the picture we must also acknowledge the role of ideas. If ideas are the steam that drives the locomotive of history, then the ideas that powered the army may be grouped under the heading of Calvinistic puritanism, and to a lesser extent, libertarian antinomianism. These creeds enabled the soldiers to overcome their anxiety about their social origins, and their fear about challenging their anointed king. They liberated them psychologically, transformed them into men of iron, endowed them with a holy ruthlessness, and furnished them with the invincible belief that in turning their own society upside-down and exporting their revolution to Ireland and Scotland they were performing the will of God. When in 1660 the edifice they had constructed came crashing about their ears, some responded heroically and went with undiminished faith to their deaths. Others interpreted the catastrophe as only an epiphenomenon of history, God having imposed upon his saints a temporary detour into the wilderness. Such was the force of religious ideology in the New Model Army.

5

The Army and the People

Civil war brought the armies of king and parliament into prolonged contact with the non-combatant population. Uneasy at the best of times, relations between soldiers and civilians deteriorated steadily as the wars ground on. Discipline grew more ragged, military appetites more voracious and political differences more unbridgeable. Early in the war a *modus vivendi* had been negotiated in many counties, either through the medium of neutrality pacts, or thanks to the active resistance of clubmen. In a number of towns an occupying garrison discovered techniques of peaceful coexistence with its citizen hosts. But in general the passage of time witnessed a steady deepening of resentment against heavier and heavier military exactions. When the war was at its hottest, with field armies cutting a swathe throughout the countryside, there was little that neutralists and clubmen could do to escape its depredations. No soldier relished sleeping under the stars or even in a tent, so innkeepers and householders were usually required to provide a roof over their heads. Since armies were frequently behind in their pay, their reluctant hosts had to furnish meals as well. Soldiers were condemned for their luxurious taste for poultry 'boiled in butter and white wine' according to one journalist.[1] If food was not promptly forthcoming, soldiers were more than ready to fend for themselves, confiscating grain and hay, and rounding up livestock and slaughtering it. Some took up poaching, even acquiring packs of hounds for the purpose.[2] If the army was short of horses, the soldiers merely seized them wherever they were to be found.

When fighting died down in 1646 the non-combatant population was even more reluctant to support large standing forces, even though there was no political settlement. Troops found it increasingly necessary to collect the requisite money to pay and feed themselves. Wartime exactions meant that many tenants could not afford to pay their rents in full, and landlords' revenues may have shrunk by a third.[3] Idle soldiers were also prone to turn into sexual predators, leaving, as William Prynne angrily put it, 'not a few great bellies and bastards on the inhabitants' and countries' charge.'[4] The army's parasitism towards civilian society could not but generate friction; friction not infrequently flared into violence, and in the long run military – civilian relations became frozen in implacable hostility.

The Indemnity Ordinance

By the spring of 1647 Fairfax's soldiers were obsessed with worry about what fate awaited them after they laid down their arms. Already alarming stories were circulating of soldiers being prosecuted and imprisoned on charges of trespass, assault, debt, theft, burglary and even murder. Existing ordinances which guaranteed legal immunity for acts committed while under military orders had made little difference, because no machinery had been created to enforce them. Now, with disbandment imminent, the soldiers feared that the stream of lawsuits against them would become a torrent. The men of Rich's regiment spoke for all their comrades with their pointed observation, 'after our disbanding we have no security to free us from the inveterate malice not of private but of public enemies who gladly would have sheathed their swords in our bowels.'[5]

A vital ingredient in parliament's appeasement package for the mutinous army was therefore a comprehensive indemnity ordinance, which on 21 May 1647 erected a quasi-judicial tribunal to protect everyone, not just soldiers, from prosecution for acts done by authority of parliament. Seventy-nine peers and commoners were constituted a powerful, Independent-dominated committee to hear petitions, grant indemnity and award costs.[6] On 7 June the ordinance was amended to guarantee soldiers explicit protection for all acts committed 'while ... in arms for the service of parliament'. At the end of the year the committee was empowered to hear petitions from soldiers whose masters or companies were refusing to readmit them to their apprenticeship or allow them to deduct their period of military service from that apprenticeship. At the outbreak of the second civil war a glaring loophole in the earlier legislation was plugged with the guarantee of indemnity to people who would commit illegal acts in the parliament's service at any time in the future.[7] The expense and inconvenience of having to come to London to testify was remedied in 1649 by allowing justices of the peace to take evidence from the parties to a suit and forward it to Westminster for judgement. In April 1652 the Indemnity Committee was dissolved and its powers transferred to the Committee for Compounding. Cases continued to be heard until 1655.[8]

In the first year or so of its life the committee operated with efficiency and despatch. The volume of cases was high; only two or three hearings were usually needed to resolve each one, and the time from petition to judgement was rarely longer than two or three weeks. A high proportion of the petitioners were soldiers. As time wore on, however, the committee's deliberations became slower and slower, and the proportion of civilian cases grew. The sluggishness of the committee's deliberations seems to have been a function partly of the great volume of business, which never diminished, and partly of the growing skill of the defendants at exploiting the possibilities for obstruction and delay. To many cases there *was* no formal conclusion, while in numerous others the committee found itself obliged to issue repeated orders to people to obey its injunctions. Undoubtedly many cases were never concluded because an appeal for indemnity was enough to persuade people to drop their judicial prosecutions. On the other hand, the ever-increasing number of hearings that were required to dispose of one case leaves the distinct impression that by the 1650s the committee was succumbing to procedural sclerosis.

During the eight years when indemnity hearings were held, there were over 1100 suits involving soldiers. With this total we may safely assume that soldiers were the object of several thousand judicial prosecutions between 1645 and 1655. They were harassed not only in quarter sessions, town courts and assizes up and down the country, but also in the central courts: King's Bench, Exchequer, Chancery and Common Pleas.[9] Not a few were unfortunate enough to find themselves behind bars, usually in one of the country's many debtors' prisons: the Wood Street Compter (London), the Southwark Compter, and the Marshalsea; but also in Newgate, King's Bench, and Clerkenwell prisons, and in various town gaols.[10] Once the Indemnity Committee had set to work and proven its effectiveness a large proportion of these suits must have been dropped. Other suits must have been dismissed when judges had the Indemnity Ordinance read out to them.[11] The 1116 cases known to have reached the indemnity commissioners represent therefore only a small fraction of the legal onslaught with which the parliamentary soldiers had to contend. These were barely a third of the committee's business, the other two thirds being concerned largely with the sequestration of royalist property, tithes, the excise tax, the assessment, and quarrels between ejected and intruded clergy, and their respective supporters.

With one or two exceptions the nature of the cases heard by the indemnity commissioners did not change much over time. The first case involving opprobrious words was not heard until late June 1648, by which time much of the army had become highly politicized.[12] In the 1650s there were relatively fewer cases to do with quarters or personal violence, and relatively more to do with debt. This shift reflected the change in the character of the army from a fighting to a largely garrison force. Another change that is noticeable over time is the commissioners' growing tendency to rule against the soldiers. The first dismissal of a military petition did not occur until the commissioners had been sitting for almost three quarters of a year.[13] After 1649, by contrast, the commissioners were more and more willing to dismiss a petition if they suspected that the debt or quarrel in question was essentially a private one.

It has been possible to determine the place of origin of over four fifths of the military cases (see table 5.1). Not surprisingly the areas outside the main theatres of war generated comparatively few cases. None has been identified from Northumberland or Durham; Kent, Surrey and Sussex provided only thirty-nine incidents, while Norfolk, Suffolk and Essex furnished forty-nine. The counties slightly farther west – Derbyshire, Buckinghamshire, Berkshire and Oxfordshire – produced higher figures. The three places of highest incidence were Yorkshire (84), Gloucestershire and Bristol (67) and London (77). London's total is explicable largely in terms of disputes between masters and apprentices over the right to deduct military service from the term of apprenticeship, while Yorkshire's position at the top of the table is a reflection both of its size and of its being the scene of much military strife.[14]

Gloucestershire's high total is doubtless owing to the fact that it was disputed territory for most of the first civil war, that it was well garrisoned, and that the pressure on Gloucester itself provoked exceptional bitterness between the parliamentary garrison and the population of the surrounding region. What the figures point to is that the Indemnity Ordinance was most needed in the parts of the country where the war was hotly contested, and where royalist disaffection ran deepest – Yorkshire, the west Midlands and Wales.

The Indemnity Committee and Due Process

The soldiers were right to allege that they had been in mortal danger from the law. The central courts at Westminster had continued to sit throughout the war, while quarter sessions and assizes were under way again by 1646. From then on soldiers were frequently arrested, imprisoned, tried, and occasionally sentenced to death for acts that they had carried out under military orders. Despite the fact that the parliamentary army had achieved virtually complete victory by the spring of 1646, numerous soldiers, including at least one lieutenant-colonel (John Jackson), petitioned for indemnity between 1647 and 1650 *from prison*.[15] Several soldiers were charged with felonies, usually on account of having seized goods, and thus were in jeopardy of hanging.[16] At least one soldier was under sentence of death at the

Table 5.1　The distribution of military indemnity cases by region, June 1647 to November 1655

	No.	Percentage of total known cases
West Midlands	221	24.2
East Midlands	123	13.5
South-west	119	13.0
North	108	11.8
London and Middlesex	99	10.8
South	85	9.3
East	80	8.7
Wales and Monmouthshire	39	4.3
South-east	39	4.3
Scotland	1	0.1
Unknown	202	
Total	1116	100.0

Regions

West Midlands	Cheshire, Shropshire, Herefordshire, Gloucestershire and Bristol, Worcestershire, Warwickshire, Staffordshire
East Midlands	Rutland, Lincolnshire, Derbyshire, Nottinghamshire, Leicestershire, Northamptonshire
South-west	Cornwall, Devon, Somerset, Dorset, Wiltshire
North	Cumberland, Northumberland, Westmorland, Durham, Yorkshire, Lancashire
East	Norfolk, Suffolk, Essex, Hertfordshire, Bedfordshire, Cambridgeshire, Huntingdonshire
South	Berkshire, Buckinghamshire, Oxfordshire, Hampshire
South-east	Kent, Surrey, Sussex

time of his petition.[17] Nor was it just the rank and file who found themselves enmeshed in the coils of the law. A surprising number of knights, such as Sir Thomas Honywood, Sir Edward Baynton MP, Sir John Gell, Sir Edward Hungerford, Sir Robert Pye and Sir Thomas Middleton, had to resort to the Indemnity Committee for protection.[18] While none of the general officers of the army appeared as suppliants, no fewer than thirty-three colonels did, including such distinguished men as John Barkstead, Edward King, Robert Hammond, Thomas Ceely, Alexander Popham and Anthony Rous.[19]

Barkstead was sued for falsely imprisoning a local inhabitant while he had been governor of Reading. The case was raised twice before the committee, but there was never a hearing at which Barkstead and the defendant presented their arguments. This suggests that petitioning was sufficient to persuade the local man to drop his suit against one of the leading parliamentary grandees.[20]

A denizen of the Isle of Wight who had been imprisoned by Colonel Hammond for disturbing the peace retaliated by obtaining a writ of outlawry against the colonel upon an action of false imprisonment. According to Hammond, the inhabitant had been guilty of 'several deboisht and riotous actions'. The committee granted him indemnity and awarded £19 costs against the defendant.[21]

Sir Robert Pye, who had been colonel of horse in the New Model Army, later found himself sued for a horse which he had commandeered after the fall of Reading. Social and military eminence were of no avail to him, as his goods were taken, and his tenants and servants forced to give bonds. After dealing with the case on five separate occasions the committee had still not decided whether to indemnify the hapless ex-colonel.[22] Unsurprisingly, most higher officers won their cases, but Colonel Howell Gwyn did so only after a lengthy appeal,[23] while the petition of Captain George Hutchinson, brother of the governor of Nottingham, was actually dismissed.[24] More than the fact of powerful men appealing for indemnity, it was the scrupulous legalism of the committee itself that shows the anxiety of the new regime to establish a reputation for lawful procedures. A soldier seeking shelter under the ordinance had to produce written authority for what he had done in the form of a warrant or order from a superior officer, a parliamentary official or a county committee.[25] The committee also paid close attention to the testimony of defendants, and did not invariably accept soldiers' allegations that their adversaries were malignant. Two soldiers who had robbed a Cumberland man of a belt and two silk petticoats in 1648 were not indemnified, because the committee found that they had not acted on orders and there was no proof that the goods belonged to the enemy.[26] In over a fifth of the cases where a final judgement was rendered (seventy-seven out of 362), the petitioner – i.e. the soldier – lost. There are also fifty-three cases for which petitions survive but for which no corresponding entry in the order books could be found. They were probably all summarily dismissed.[27] Thus, while the evidence in the Indemnity Papers is certainly biased in the soldiers' favour, the fact that it was carefully sifted by the commissioners, and often repudiated by them, enhances the credibility of the evidence which *was* admitted.[28]

The Persistence of Royalist Antagonism

The Indemnity Papers also suggest that, at least until the late 1640s, royalist disaffection in England was both pervasive and powerful. Time and again one reads of parliamentary soldiers being abused as 'roundhead rogues', 'parliament dogs' and 'parliament whores'. Indeed it is surprising how often passions were inflamed on either side by insulting political language. Parliamentary soldiers sometimes made unflattering references to the queen. Such references seem to have been so familiar an ingredient of their speech that when one soldier referred to the queen's army as 'a member of the Romish whore' he was construed as having cast aspersions upon Henrietta Maria and clapped into Norwich Gaol.[29] Another soldier endured long and hard imprisonment in Newgate, London, after the first civil war 'for certain words falsely pretended to be spoken against the queen.'[30]

Often in these exchanges the antagonists did not stop at words. John Cox, another Londoner, appealed against William Stephens, who had had him imprisoned on a charge of breaking into his house in Spitalfields and feloniously removing two muskets and a sword. The previous July Coxe had arrested a certain Thomas White. But as soon as he had been taken into custody William Stephens, the constable of Spitalfields, got together a crowd of people and

> with force and by strong hands rescued the said White. Then seeing the writ and hearing it to be in the name of the keepers of the Liberty of England by authority of Parliament, uttering these words: 'You and the Parliament are all rogues, for we will keep our liberty for Charles the second, for we will not obey any such rogues' power as they are', meaning this present parliament.

Coxe resorted for help to Colonel Nathaniel Rich, whose horse regiment was quartered nearby. He dispatched troopers under Captain Elsmore to apprehend the seditious constable. Arriving at Stephens' house the soldiers discovered that he had gone into hiding, but were able to remove the arms he had left behind. Coxe neither entered Stephens' house nor removed the arms, yet it was he who ended up in Newgate, where he spent three weeks in irons. The Indemnity Committee ordered his release and awarded him £15 damages, but left it up to him to recover the money. So in January 1653 he returned to Stephens' house, accompanied by a constable and a gentleman. When those within refused to open the door, Coxe began to read out the Indemnity Commissioners' warrant in public. This was too much for Stephens' wife, who burst from the house

> with a great stick in her hand and ran and struck John Coxe under the elbow and called him rogue and kicked him [in] the [privy] members, and swore that she would run a knife in his guts and spoke a great many more words to that effect and never left striking at him in despite of all the men that were there, and they could all hardly keep her from doing him a further mischief and threatened to [ar]rest him and said she would make him [sorry?] for ever coming on her ground.[31]

We do not know if Coxe ever obtained redress for his humiliating injuries at the hands of Mrs Stephens, but it is interesting that a fiercely royalist constable in Spitalfields was able to vent his seditious views with impunity, at a time when the Commonwealth government was at the height of its political power.

In another London case a soldier was travelling in the vicinity of the metropolis in the spring of 1648 when he met a royalist who quarrelled with him, abusing him as a 'parliament dog' and other unflattering things. Blows were exchanged, and the soldier seems to have been worsted when the royalist bit off a joint of his finger. Later, when the soldier came to London, the royalist sent him a rude letter, seeking to reopen the quarrel. They met in Drury Lane, the royalist this time calling him a 'roundhead rogue'. But the soldier avenged himself by administering a beating, for which he was then sued for battery, and against which suit he appealed for indemnity.[32]

From several parts of the country we find evidence of local officials doing what they could to aid royalists. Ralph Moreton, marshal under Major Joseph Rigby, was a zealous hunter of popish delinquents. He boasted of having arrested a Jesuit priest and refused a bribe to allow him to escape. He also confiscated weapons from another popish delinquent, and arrested four others. The delinquents had now combined with a sympathetic justice of the peace to have Moreton indicted at the Lancaster assizes merely for having done his military duty.[33]

Another instance of royalist local officials comes from Kent at the time of the parliamentary sweep through that county in the spring of 1648. A trooper had confiscated a royalist gunman's horse and sold it to a fellow soldier. The royalist then complained to Justice Swallow, who ordered the horse returned and the soldiers charged with a felony. Even though one of them produced a letter from General Fairfax ordering his release, they were kept in gaol. The indemnity commissioners instructed the justice to free the men and the royalist to pay them damages for having 'most maliciously and unjustly prosecuted' them. Continued recalcitrance led to an order for the royalist's arrest on a charge of contempt.[34]

In Devon the justices brought down a judgement of trespass and ordered the arrest of Robert Cheeke for searching the house of a man suspected of harbouring delinquents.[35] They likewise ruled against Colonel John Coppleston, who took money from an Exeter mercer when recruiting a troop of horse. Coppleston was unable to repay the mercer because he himself had not been paid for his military service, yet while he was away fighting, the mercer sued him for the money and obtained a verdict against him. When he returned from the wars he was arrested and gaoled pending repayment of the money. A sympathetic gaoler who permitted him a degree of personal liberty was 'violently prosecuted [on] an action of escape'.[36]

The town of Andover, Hampshire, lived up to its royalist reputation by its treatment of a parliamentarian captain. While on his way to London on the business of the Committee for the Advance of Money, Captain John Ash found himself violently attacked upon Salisbury Plain by three men hostile to parliament. Supposing that the local authorities would give him redress against this flagrant insult he had the men apprehended and brought before the bailiff of Andover. Far from vindicating the captain, however, the bailiff combined with the town clerk to let them escape, and imprisoned Ash instead. Eventually Captain Ash was indemnified but the three men who assaulted him apparently went unpunished.[37] Then a few days later the captain found himself in trouble with civilian authorities a second time. Having apprehended several 'malignants' in Somerset, he was faced with a warrant from the deputy lieutenants of that county, and again had to resort to the Indemnity commissioners to halt proceedings against him.[38]

Early in the civil war, Captain Anthony Beckwith, an officer under Colonel Charles Fairfax, clashed with a truculent royalist in Beverley, Yorkshire. Words led to blows, and it was only after being subjected to a severe drubbing by the royalist that Beckwith was rescued by some of his own soldiers, who managed to inflict a few blows themselves. As a consequence the captain found himself prosecuted in King's Bench, declared an outlaw, required to post special bail, and sued for battery. As the parliamentary justices in King's Bench were at that time striving to establish a reputation for strict impartiality, it fell to the indemnity commissioners to rescue the captain from this criminal action.[39]

King's Bench is known to have given a receptive hearing to royalists in at least two other suits against parliamentary officers. Edward Nevitt, who was stopped while travelling without a pass or warrant between the royalist garrisons of Newark and York, was imprisoned by Sir Edward Rhodes, the commander at Beverley, until he testified his affection to parliament. Once freed he successfully sued Sir Edward for false imprisonment.[40] A certain John Griffith was arrested, armed, on his way from the royalist garrison of Sheffield. Yet the soldier who arrested him was subsequently hailed before the King's Bench to answer an action for outlawry for assault and wrongful imprisonment.[41]

It is remarkable how often royalists exploited traditional legal channels to win back property of which they had been deprived by the Long Parliament or its agents. During the second civil war a parliamentary soldier took from a royalist soldier, as a lawful prize, a box containing money and plate worth £70, which he then delivered to the Devon County Committee. For this act he had to be indemnified from prosecution.[42] Another royalist whose estate had been sequestered sued his tenant, Captain William Pease, for the rent that he had paid to parliament.[43] Similar were the difficulties in which Colonel Thomas Ceely found himself the same year when he disposed of debts owing to two delinquents. They retaliated by suing the colonel and sealing leases of ejectment upon his lands.[44] Lieutenant-Colonel Gilbert Gerrard also had to appeal against prosecution for a debt of £50 which he had paid to the Cheshire Committee on the grounds that his creditor was a delinquent.[45]

Rooted antagonism towards the parliamentary army extended to frequent defiance of the Indemnity Committee itself.[46] Having lost the war on the battlefield, royalists continued to fight it by judicial means. In King's Bench, in the assizes and at quarter sessions they found many co-operative officials.

Types of Indemnity Cases

A striking feature of the Indemnity Committee's records is the paucity of cases involving the original New Model regiments. Only forty-nine have been positively identified. Even if the true number is twice as high, it is doubtful if the New Model's share reached 10 per cent of the total. There were in addition a small number of cases pertaining to soldiers in non-New Model field regiments after the Kent and Essex campaigns of 1648, the Scottish campaign of 1650, and the battle of Worcester in 1651. Soldiers attached to local or garrison forces figure far more prominently in the committee's deliberations than the members of the field army who had fought for and won the privilege of indemnity in the first place. The latter were more often than not strangers, unknown in the county where they performed their illegal acts. They were also on the move, making it very difficult to pin a legal action on them. Understandably it was local men, in daily contact with the civilian population adjacent to their garrison, who stood a strong chance of ending up in court for seizing livestock, confiscating hay, or assaulting a landlord. But, in any event, provincial troops seem to have committed more murders and outrages than the New Model forces. The Kentish gentry were not the only ones who feared 'lest poor England be overwhelmed in the Red Sea of subdivisions.' Massey's brigade in the west, for example, gained special notoriety for its menacing behaviour in the spring and summer of 1646.[47]

The seizure of livestock and provisions

By far the commonest source of contention, accounting for nearly a third of the military cases, was horses (see table 5.2). England's horse population had grown rapidly since 1500, as more and more people took to riding

Table 5.2 Types of military cases brought to the Indemnity Committee
1647–55

	No.	Percentage of cases
Horses	341	30.6
Goods, provisions, livestock, weapons	246	22.0
Quarters, money, debts, arrears	190	17.0
Apprenticeship	103	9.2
Assault, battery	50	4.5
Trespass	40	3.6
Arrest, imprisonment	33	3.0
Taxation	22	2.0
Words	14	1.3
Homicide	9	0.8
Burglary	7	0.6
Military discipline	4	0.3
Miscellaneous	36	3.2
Unspecified	21	1.9
Total	1116	100.0

them, but the civil war produced an insatiable demand for horses, to serve
both as mounts and as draft animals, and prices rose accordingly.[48] Besides
their value, horses possessed the added attraction of being portable and easy
to remove; moreover, a soldier had the legal right to capture one as a prize
from the enemy. On the other hand, hundreds of people tried to recover
their horses, especially when soldiers subsequently disposed of them to
third parties who happened to be civilians. The loss of horses entailed
extreme hardship for the rural population, so there was much conflict over
them. Yet one wonders at the confidence with which men identified – as
much as four years after the event – the horses of which they had been
deprived.

The second category is one that would be expected to arise from military
operations: the commandeering of cattle, hay, food and clothing, and the
interception of weapons, money and wine on their way to enemy quarters.

In the third category, most of the cases having to do with debts, money
and quarters stemmed from parliament's failure to pay its forces promptly
or in full. While the financial circumstances of the parliamentary soldiers
were superior to those of the royalists, they too were frequently compelled
to live off the civilians in whose town or region they were stationed. A
soldier being sued for debt could usually argue with impeccable logic that
he would be only too pleased to settle his account as soon as parliament
gave him his arrears. The taking of free quarter, which was the direct conse-

quence of pay falling behind, provoked some of the most heated conflicts between soldiers and civilians – suits over assault and battery, and obscene or seditious words. Off the battlefield, however, the amount of physical violence seems to have been quite low. In the newsbooks and the Clarke Papers cases with a sexual dimension were negligible in number. I have not come across a single allegation of rape against Fairfax's or Cromwell's soldiers between 1645 and 1653. All the sources agree that attacks upon women by parliamentary soldiers were extraordinarily infrequent. Indeed, we are more likely to read of enraged women attacking soldiers.

The invasion of houses

Livestock, provisions and money may have been the most frequent occasion for dispute, but what aroused the deepest emotions was the invasion of people's homes. When in September 1647 a parliamentary captain entered the house of a suspected royalist near Bideford, Devon, and confiscated the weapons he found there, the infuriated victim fomented a riot which 'engaged the whole town'.[49] When Cornet Morris Price was sent to arrest the royalist soldier Richard Longwell, he broke into Longwell's home in the dead of night in order to have the advantage of surprise. The indignant royalist retaliated by preferring an indictment of burglary and robbery at the Shrewsbury Assizes in autumn 1647.[50] At the Gloucestershire assizes in 1648 a soldier was actually convicted of trespass for having searched a house for a royalist soldier.[51] When Sir John Gell was disturbed by noise coming from a house near his quarters in Derby he sent one of his soldiers to put a stop to it. However, the 'tumult', which seems to have been nothing more than a noisy party, was difficult to suppress. The revellers defied the soldier's order to leave, and so Sir John had to go and expel them himself. For this act the soldier, but not Sir John, was convicted of assault and battery.[52]

In Berkshire, Captain Henry Beale was ordered to arrest two suspected delinquents, Francis Fells, a New Windsor weaver, and his son, in November 1642. Beale went with some soldiers to Fells's house, but the door was barred and they were greeted with menacing words from the other side. Beale blasted open the lock with his pistol, injuring Fells in the process. The soldiers then hauled the son off to gaol, leaving the injured father lying in the house. Fortunately we also have Fells's side of the story. According to him Beale came pretending to search for venison. Terrified by the soldiers' hostile manner – swords drawn and pistols cocked – Fells asked for their warrant for invading his house, but they failed to produce any. His daughter, who had recently given birth, screamed for him to shut the door, which was no sooner done than Beale shot him twice in the thigh.

Fells later appealed to Colonel Venn, the governor of Windsor, who sent a surgeon to dress the wound. One bullet remained embedded in his body, however, preventing him from practising his trade. The Earl of Essex gave Fells a warrant to arrest Captain Beale on a charge of assault, but the captain ran away, and was only located late in 1647, when he petitioned for indemnity. Fells begged the Indemnity Committee, on grounds of his lameness and poverty, not to compel him to travel to London to attend its hearings. Beale, however, was able to win the case when he produced a deposition from Colonel Venn corroborating his version of the incident.[53]

The commonest reason for entering houses was to quarter soldiers, a practice which directly violated the Petition of Right. Yet shortage of funds left parliament with no other recourse. Not only inn- and alehouse-keepers, but also householders, were required, sometimes for long periods, to furnish a bed and meals to garrison, local or field-army troops. In theory quarters were paid for, as the civilian host was given a ticket certifying that he had entertained soldiers for a certain period, and that he would be repaid. Reimbursement, however, was slow in coming, and for many unwilling hosts it did not come at all. At times, as in London in 1648 and Worcester in 1651, the exaction of free quarter was used as a means of coaxing a recalcitrant or impoverished population into paying its back taxes. Despite the cries of anguish from a despairing citizenry, the method usually worked.[54]

Everyone resented having to board soldiers. People in Cambridgeshire were typical in their fear that they would be 'utterly undone' by the large-scale quartering of the New Model Army during the crisis of June 1647; the town of Linton was unusual only in its resistance to accepting soldiers in the first place. In 1646 the county committee had ordered eleven soldiers to be quartered on those householders who were behind in their taxes. Led by John Bitten, 'a turbulent spirit', they blankly refused, and prosecuted the constable who tried to carry out the committee's orders.[55]

Parliament's laggardliness in honouring its debts from free quarter led a great many frustrated civilians to try to recover their money directly by suing the hapless soldiers who had been imposed on them. Sometimes a soldier might even find himself in debtors' prison for having failed to repay civilian hospitality. The plea that he could only pay his creditor after parliament paid him was usually sufficient for the indemnity commissioners, even if it did not impress the courts.[56]

But civilians were angered by more than just having to provide free beds and meals; they hated the invasion of their privacy. That seems to explain why in 1644 a householder of Nantwich, Cheshire, refused to accept two of Sir William Brereton's soldiers who had been assigned to him by the quartermaster-general of the garrison. 'It being evening, and the weather very cold', however, 'and the soldiers having had a weary march', they came back to the house and broke down two doors before they were finally given a bed for the night. The quartermaster-general later had to face an action at the Cheshire assizes for assault and burglary, against which he was indemnified in August 1648.[57]

Insults were often traded between soldiers and people on these occasions, pointing to the tensions that were never far from the surface as a result of the practice of free quarter.[58] The experience of Captain Thomas French in Warwickshire illustrates how the pettiest incidents could flare into violent and protracted quarrels. One night Captain French asked Elizabeth Wright, a servant of the house where he was quartered, to get his bed ready for him. When she went to open the door of his room she could not find her bunch of keys, so she turned on French, and in the presence of others averred that this was the second time French had stolen them since he had been living in the house. 'The petitioner desiring her in a fair way to forbear the charging of him with any such thing she again repeated the same words before the same company that the petitioner stole the said keys.' A few minutes later she found the keys where she had mislaid them. Now beside himself with fury at the servant woman's affront to his honour, French struck her with his sheathed sword. Mrs Wright complained against him to a justice in Warwick and, according to French, obtained 'satisfaction, with which she seemed contented'. Since that time, however, her husband had continued to molest and prosecute him in several courts upon an action of battery. Eventually, in May 1648, he was indemnified.[59]

One dispute over the quartering of soldiers was complicated by the presence of the plague. In 1646 Barnstaple, Devon, was so grievously afflicted that 'scarce ten houses ... (where any inhabitant remained) were free from it.' Wroth Rogers, the governor of the garrison, prevailed upon the mayor, John Downe, to establish a pesthouse outside the town, so that the garrison would be less endangered by the infection. Two houses were found; one was empty, while the soldiers expelled a poor tenant from the other. By the employment of 'a skilful surgeon' and other measures they managed to free Barnstaple of the plague, yet the mayor then found himself the target of five separate suits initiated by one of the anti-parliamentarian householders, merely for carrying out the wishes of Colonel Rogers. But after it had obtained reports from the Devon justices the Indemnity Committee concluded that the mayor had previously agreed to compensate the landlords of the two houses and was therefore not eligible for indemnity.[60] Soldiers were also frequently accused of spreading the plague, typhus and smallpox in the regions through which they moved.[61]

Money, taxes and debt

Wishing to preserve good relations with the local population, garrison forces often wrote IOUs when they confiscated a horse, a cheese, a load of hay, or a bale of cloth. When no money came from parliament, they were unable to honour these IOUs. Inevitably they fell prey to legal actions. In July 1647, for example, fifteen officers petitioned parliament that they were 'in hourly danger' of being arrested for debt because they could not obtain their arrears.[62] The Indemnity Committee dealt with many such instances and, unless it was persuaded that the case was one of private indebtedness, granted protection to the military petitioner.[63] A less edifying spectacle about which we read in the newsbooks (rather than the Indemnity Papers) was the frequent eruption of pub brawls between soldiers and civilians. Rather than political differences it was normally the soldiers' reluctance to pay for their drink that prompted these flare-ups.[64]

Money can also be seen as the root cause of most of the friction that occurred when soldiers were employed in a police function. Sometimes they had to arrest parliament's enemies, but oftener they were called upon to help with the collection of taxes, enforce sequestration orders, or direct the payment of tithes to newly appointed ministers. Thus we read of Captain Peter Backhouse, who, at the direction of the Committee of Stafford, went with his troop to gather assessments for the maintenance of the forces at Lichfield Close. A man who was arrested for refusing to pay subsequently brought a counter-action of false imprisonment against Backhouse.[65] In Gloucestershire the county committee sent out several soldiers to distrain livestock from the lands of Lady Finch, who was behind in her tax payments. The livestock were then sold, but later repossessed by Lady Finch's tenants following a successful legal action. In the end the soldiers were vindicated and the purchaser presumably got back the cattle for which he had paid.[66] An even more distinguished tax resister was the Earl of Middlesex, who compounded his offence by refusing to take the Engagement. The Gloucestershire Committee ordered his cattle seized; the earl appealed to the Indemnity Committee; but the soldiers who had taken the cattle were upheld.[67] The menace of forcible collection of back taxes often threw people into a panic. Bristol Common Council sought to spare the city the rough attention of soldiers by promising Fairfax to make personal approaches to those delinquent citizens who were behind in their assessments.[68]

Sometimes taxes were so fiercely resented by the population that the effort to collect them provoked riots resulting in injury and death. Captain Daniel Prescott ran into violent opposition when he tried to collect the excise tax from the inhabitants and saltmen of Droitwich, Worcestershire. As he was preparing for bed after his first day in the town in September 1649, he heard an uproar outside his window, with shouts of 'Fall on, burn the house.' He flew downstairs and mounted his horse, but the rioters 'shot at him, threw stones, knocked him off his horse', and pursued him crying, 'Kill them, kill the rogues, fire the house.' The captain and his friends eventually drove the rioters back to the saltworks; serious injuries were inflicted on both sides, and one rioter was killed. The Worcestershire justices committed Prescott to gaol for being an accomplice to the killing. A grand jury then indicted him, denied bail, and was preparing to proceed against him before the Indemnity Committee had had a chance to hear his appeal. The assize proceedings were only halted in the nick of time.[69] But it was not just soldiers who were victims in these struggles over the collection of money, as we can see from the high-handed tactics of Colonel Edward King in Lincolnshire. There a certain William Turner had bought a parcel of wool from Richard White, for which they had agreed a price of £133 2s. Colonel King, however, seized White as a malignant and ordered Turner to pay the money to him, which he did. In 1649 he faced a suit by White for the money, but was sheltered by the Indemnity Committee.[70]

Law enforcement

With the cessation of armed conflict in 1646 and 1648 the soldiers were required to assume many police functions. Often their job was to enforce the orders of unpopular parliamentary committees. Nicholas Colborne, a soldier in Hertfordshire, was called upon by his local sequestration committee to put John Gilpin in possession of the vicarage house and glebe in Aldenham. But a group of inhabitants led by Susan Hoare forcibly blocked the order and sued Colborne for trespass.[71] In October 1646 the Lancashire Committee ordered its marshal, Lieutenant Rowland Gascoigne, to remove an obstreperous petitioner from its midst. Force was necessary to get the man out of the room, but he counter-attacked with an action of false imprisonment and battery, which was only halted by the Indemnity Committee.[72]

The policing function was sometimes broadened to include the control of urban crowds, a branch of military science still in its infancy in Europe. In the summer of 1643, for example, a group of women from Surrey had demonstrated their hostility to the civil war by marching with a petition to parliament, white ribbons fluttering from 'their hats and arms and other parts of their bodies'. Their demonstration erupted in a riot in which several people were wounded or killed. When the trained bands of Southwark arrived on the scene, Lieutenant Robert Firth waded into the crowd with his men and arrested a number of the women. The incensed husbands of two of the women launched actions in both Exchequer and the Surrey assizes, causing Firth to be arrested. In imminent jeopardy of a conviction for unlawful imprisonment, he was saved only by the quick action of the Indemnity Committee, which awarded him double damages.[73]

In Norwich, a military intervention to control an unruly royalist crowd at the height of the second civil war brought in its train a terrible toll of death and destruction. Led by a group of apprentices who had adopted the password 'for God and King Charles', the crowd attacked the houses of the leading puritan aldermen and the sheriff. The authorities appealed for help to Colonel Charles Fleetwood's horse regiment stationed at nearby East Dereham. One and a half troops were dispatched to the scene, but their arrival and attempted dispersal of the crowd served to inflame it all the more. Cursing the soldiers as 'roundheadly rogues and whores', they broke into the committee house, where the city's magazine was stored, and began removing quantities of arms and breaking open the eighty barrels of gunpowder. The powder was accidentally ignited, producing a tremendous explosion in which over forty people were killed and countless more injured. That all the casualties were royalist was widely interpreted as an indication of God's allegiance to the Roundhead cause.[74]

Property Destruction

Soldiers were resented as consumers of the nation's agricultural and industrial production; and as the protectors of an unpopular regime. They were also viewed as the destroyers of the nation's capital wealth through their activities of fortification and siege. Overall, royalists appear to have destroyed more property than their enemies. But who was responsible mattered less than the fact of destruction, which was bitterly resented wherever it occurred. Damage was caused by both attackers and defenders. Offensive damage could be punitive in aim – either to break the morale of the civilian population or to enforce the collection of money and supplies. At other times its goal was to breach a town's defences. More of this offensive destruction was recorded by royalist forces, but there were a few celebrated instances attributable to parliament. In 1645 and 1646 parts of Bridgwater and Worcester were ignited by firing heated shot and grenades over their walls. In neither place was damage very extensive, however, as it was found to be easier to extinguish fires than to start them. At Great Torrington, Devon, in February 1646 the New Model ordnance may have scored a direct hit when the church, which had been used as a magazine, blew up, damaging many of the surrounding houses. Parliamentarian forces also conducted raids against towns in royalist-controlled regions, sometimes to intimidate the civilian population, sometimes to exact tribute. In 1643 £300 was prised from the purses of the people of Whitchurch, Shropshire, under the threat of worse plunder if the money was not forthcoming. The following year William Waller's troops embarked on a similar raid against Pershore, Worcestershire, but were thwarted. Another raid, both punitive and plundering in intent, was conducted against Blandford Forum, Dorset the same year.

Even more destruction, however, was caused by the defenders of towns than by their besiegers. The restoration and erection of fortifications resulted in much initial damage, but not nearly as much as the damage precipitated by the clearance of land beyond the defences. The razing of buildings, cutting of timber and uprooting of hedges was undertaken to frustrate enemy attempts to approach the defences undetected. Demolishing all visual obstacles also provided an unrestricted field of fire for defenders and deprived a besieging force of accommodation and materials. But it also inflicted great suffering upon the local population. Suburban householders lost their homes and sometimes their belongings as well. Landlords lost both their capital and the income that their capital had generated. Stephen Porter has estimated that the razing of buildings, as well as their destruction by fire between 1642 and 1646 and in 1648, may have equalled the destruction wrought by accidental fires in all the other years of the seventeenth century. This destruction left an enduring legacy. Towns were deprived of the goods and services provided by their suburbs: the goods produced by tradesmen – tanners, brewers and the like – who worked there, and the accommodation for travellers furnished by inns. As if that were not enough, there was the crisis generated by the displaced persons who crowded through the town's gates seeking shelter with friends and relatives, or in hastily erected temporary buildings. A poor and occasionally lawless element, their presence created a tremendous problem of poor relief, increased the danger of accidental fire and the likelihood of infectious disease, and heightened people's fears of a breakdown of public order. Understandably civic authorities resisted the destruction of their suburbs, and this resistance had to be dealt with by garrison commanders. We know of intense conflict in Chester, Nottingham, Taunton, Gloucester, Carlisle, Bristol, Coventry and Shrewsbury over the destruction of these cities' suburbs. Colonel John Hutchinson, for example, had many clashes with the Nottingham Committee over the amount of destruction that he believed to be necessary. In Gloucester in the summer of 1643 Colonel Edward Massey reduced many inhabitants to despair by burning down 241 houses, valued at over £22,000. This grievous loss followed hard on the heels of two decades of economic recession and almost dealt a death blow to the city's fortunes. Indeed, major rebuilding of the suburbs did not take place until the eighteenth century. Less serious was the blow to Coventry, which lost under 100 houses, valued at £3485 and housing less than 10 per cent of the 7000 inhabitants of the town.

Demolition was not limited to houses. Churches and almshouses fell under the wrecker's hammer as well. St Owen's Church, just outside Gloucester's south gate; the parish church of Oswestry, which had the misfortune to have been built outside the walls; St Mary's Church, Malmesbury, and the Charterhouse at Hull: these are the non-domestic suburban buildings about whose demolition we are certain. There are a few instances where a town or village some distance from a garrison town also suffered destruction. In the autumn of 1644, for example, parliamentary soldiers from Lyme Regis inflicted a devastating blow upon Axminster, 5 miles away, when they destroyed 200 houses there.

It was suburban destruction that was most sweeping in the misery it brought to people's lives, but sometimes it happened within the walls as well. The renovation of Cambridge Castle's defences involved pulling down fifteen families' dwellings. At Nottingham the royalists plunged Colonel Hutchinson into a dilemma when during their brief occupation of the town they mounted a cannon in the tower of St Nicholas' Church. From their vantage point in the church tower they were able to fire into the castle yard; accordingly, after regaining the town, Hutchinson had the church demolished. It requires little imagination to appreciate the angry despair to which these acts of military destruction, not perpetrated in the heat of battle but carried out after deliberate strategic calculation, reduced their helpless victims.[75] Overwhelmingly then, the evidence of the Indemnity Papers, newsbooks, pamplets and letters shows that relations between the parliamentary armies and the English people were characterized by discord and animosity. Conflict arose from the seizure of movable property, the invasion of people's homes, the forcible collection of heavy taxes, the policing of individuals and crowds who threatened the government's security, and the destruction of landed property. But conflict was also embedded in the fundamental issues of the war. What should be the character of the national church? Ought England to be a monarchy or a republic?

Indeed, as we have seen in chapter four, much of the antipathy was partly or wholly ideological in content. Time and again we hear the enraged voices of people venting their anger against the soldiers who are about to topple the monarchy or have recently done so. In every part of the country we observe soldiers acting upon their religious convictions by destroying the visible symbols of popery and prelacy. We hear of them suppressing the Book of Common Prayer, and combating their bitterest enemies, the conservative, presbyterian, 'Scottified' clergy. We see them enforcing sabbatarianism. Above all we witness them protecting and nurturing radical separatist congregations against a largely hostile population. Civilians hated the parliamentary soldiers not only because they had introduced violence into their communities; not only because they were a crushing economic burden; but also because they were the aggressive propagators of a new and disturbing set of political and religious ideas.

6

The Political Wars 1646–8 (I): From the King's Surrender to the Assault on Parliament

The Growth of Hostility to the Army

The army's military success contributed to mounting apprehension about its religious and political role once the fighting was over. The strife surrounding its creation, together with the reputation for religious radicalism of many officers, had not been forgotten even during its palmiest days. As early as the autumn of 1645 friendly newsbook editors were openly describing the New Model as 'the Independent army'.[1] The Scottish writer David Buchanan accused army Independents of expelling all who disagreed with them.[2] In January 1646 there was conflict between Lords and Commons over the ordinance to continue two institutions indispensable to the New Model's survival, the Committee for the Army and the treasurers at war. The obstinacy of the Commons majority indicated that they continued to regard the New Model as 'their' army, just as they had at the beginning of 1645.[3]

In early 1646 the London presbyterian minister Thomas Edwardes voiced the fears of many in the first two volumes of *Gangraena*, his scurrilous catalogue of the heretical beliefs and activities of religious separatists. Although he would save his systematic treatment of the army's heresies for the third volume, which appeared in December, from the outset Edwardes made no secret of his animosity towards the New Model. Most alarming to Edwardes was the action of a group of soldiers who had brazenly disrupted his sermon in Christ Church, Newgate, one Sunday in April 1646. This traumatic experience convinced him that, for all their talk about liberty of conscience, the soldiers would show no toleration to their religious enemies should they ever come to power.[4] The first two volumes of *Gangraena* both articulated and accelerated the deepening distrust between the army and political and religious conservatives. In March 1646 an anonymous Independent writer upbraided the City for its rigid insistence on compulsory presbyterianism. If they were to succeed in imposing their views upon the nation, 'the army (that hath recovered you out of a most languishing estate) will instantly be scattered, if not dissolved.'[5] City conservatives' fears of religious radicalism were given political expression in the Remonstrance addressed by London officials to parliament in May. Calling for an end to religious toleration in order to check the growth of sectarianism and schism in the metropolis, they spoke warmly of the Scottish army's contribution to the war, but were silent about the achievements of Fairfax's army. Another sign of the City's growing wariness towards the army was the demand that London resume the control of its own militia that it had exercised at the beginning of the war.[6]

As one observer would later declare, the Remonstrance of May 1646 'bred the first scab' on relations between London and the army.[7] 'Is this the reward ... our preservers must expect?' inquired another, 'To be disarmed and rooted out as sect[arie]s?'[8] The soldiers themselves, Edwardes averred, railed against the City and the Westminster Assembly of Divines on account of the Remonstrance. Hugh Peters added fuel to the fire with his anti-City preaching. So incensed were the soldiers that some of them said they would just as happily march against the City as against the cavaliers.[9] Of Thomas Edwardes' taste for scurrility there is no doubt; but radical ideas and practices were in fact common currency in the army. In March 1646 an anonymous *Late Letter from Sir Thomas Fairfax's Army Now in Truro* had been published with an engraving of the victorious general, at the bottom of which appeared an axe cleaving through a crown.[10] Any political or religious conservative into whose hands this engraving fell would have had ample reason to be worried. A large measure of the blame for the army's radicalism was heaped on the shoulders of Hugh Peters and his London friends. Not only had the chaplain favoured sectaries in his own dealings, charged one City pamphleteer, but urban Independents had tried to stir up the army to petition parliament, 'whilst the sword is in their hands'.[11]

In July 1646 the House of Lords, now dominated by the Earl of Essex's faction,[12] responded to the City's Remonstrance and to pressure from the Scots, by ordering the imposition of the Covenant throughout the army, and the enforcement of the ban on lay preaching. The Commons, under the leadership of Hesilrige and Evelyn, sidestepped the issue, thereby preventing the Lords' motion from becoming law. Essex's faction did not give up easily, however. Fortified by the transfer of Mulgrave's proxy from Saye to Essex, they returned to the attack in August, with a demand that 'such persons may be in command of the forces in this kingdom as shall pursue the end of the Covenant.' Again the Commons stonewalled, and so in

Plate 3   Sir Thomas Fairfax, the scourge of monarchy (1646)

(The Bodleian Library, Oxford)

retaliation the Lords refused to pass the legislation for the continuance of the Committee of the Army and the treasurers at war.[13] At one point during the summer of 1646 the party of Holles and Stapleton nearly won the upper hand over the army's friends. Pretending the necessity of relieving Ireland, as Edmund Ludlowe saw it, they moved that four foot and two horse regiments from Fairfax's army should be sent to that kingdom forthwith. The motion was lost by only one vote.[14]

While negotiations with the king dragged on inconclusively at Newcastle, the chief political question at Westminster during the autumn of 1646 was how parliament should set about shedding its financial burdens. Since the armies were the heaviest drain on the treasury, the issue boiled down to which forces should be disbanded first, and how far disbandment should be carried. Nightmarish accounts from the north concerning the behaviour of the Scots soldiers[15] persuaded the majority that they must be sent packing as soon as possible.

At the same time the party of Holles and Stapleton endured a severe setback in the death of the Earl of Essex after a hunting accident in Windsor Forest in September. His funeral was celebrated a month later with the extravagant pomp appropriate for parliament's first general. Almost without exception his official mourners were prominent presbyterians. They included only three officers from the New Model Army, and even these three had held commissions under his command. Colonels Thomas Sheffield and Richard Graves were both staunch presbyterians, while Major-General Philip Skippon was regarded at the time as a moderate presbyterian. Notably absent from the official mourning party were Thomas Fairfax, Oliver Cromwell and Henry Ireton.[16]

The Disbandment of Massey's Brigade

Before Essex was even interred, the life of the Western Brigade, which he had so often promoted and defended, was also brought to an end. Friction between the brigade and the New Model went back as far as the summer of 1645, when Massey and his supporters believed themselves slighted by the official failure to appreciate their role at the siege of Taunton and the battle of Langport.[17] Massey's sense of grievance was sharpened when, after the capture of Bristol in September 1645, Skippon was made governor of that western city, without having to acknowledge Massey's authority in the region.[18] As governor Skippon assumed powers of martial law and diverted revenue from Gloucestershire to his garrison. The jealousy between the two men spilled over into the House of Lords, where Essex and his friends joined the fray on Massey's side.[19] They lost the first skirmish but returned to the attack with an ambitious scheme for the virtual reconstruction of the Western Brigade, and its transformation into a self-sufficient army capable of acting as a counterweight to the New Model.[20] Promotion of the scheme coincided with Massey's arrival in London in early 1646, but despite some weeks of intense lobbying it came to nothing.[21]

This failure led to the demise of the Western Brigade. For all the efforts of Massey, Essex, Holles and Stapleton, the superior discipline of the New Model proved to be the telling factor in the Commons' decision to preserve it at the expense of the Western Brigade.[22] Fairfax and Ireton, bolstered by two regiments of horse, were appointed to supervise the disbandment, a task which they accomplished without bloodshed.[23] This was remarkable, since the Lords had issued a countermanding order, declaring that forces raised by both houses could only be dissolved by order of both.[24] Fairfax, however, juggled his contradictory instructions, blandly telling the peers that he had completed the disbandment by the time their instructions had officially come to his notice. The peers were furious. When the general returned to London the following month, six of them dissented from the motion to attend his arrival, as a way of venting their displeasure at his co-operation in the Commons' usurpation of their authority.[25] Ultimately the survival of the New Model and the destruction of the Western Brigade was due to the superior strength of the parliamentary group led by Lord Saye and Hesilrige, in relation to the group led by Essex and Holles. Presbyterian weakness throughout the summer and autumn of 1646 meant that provincial forces were steadily broken up while the New Model remained intact.[26]

As with most political victories, the triumph of the Independents over the party of Essex and Holles was not a clean one. Before long London was swarming with reformadoes from Massey's brigade. With their wives they besieged parliament, shouting insults at MPs and peers alike, and demanding their back pay.[27] They continued to hang around the capital, making a nuisance of themselves, for many months to come.[28] Their annoying presence was to be a continuing reminder of what many regarded as a disgraceful Independent manoeuvre, while their willingness to throw their weight behind the planned presbyterian counter-revolution of June–July 1647 would help to make that scheme a frightening reality.

The Departure of the Scots

Another strategic objective of the parliamentary Independents was to get the Scots army out of England. Its realization would reduce the drain on the treasury, spare the northern counties further barbarities at the hands of their unwelcome visitors, and diminish the pressure for England to adopt the Scottish brand of church government. The party of Holles and Stapleton was understandably less enthusiastic about the disappearance of the military arm of its friends the Scots commissioners, but so great was the popular longing to see the last of the Scots that it dared not oppose their departure. One stumbling block remained, however: the Scots were reluctant to leave before a hefty proportion of the money owing them had been paid. The City of London was approached for a loan, but it demanded both the bishops' lands and the excise tax as collateral. At first the Lords balked at abolishing the bishops, but at length they gave in under pressure, and the ordinance was passed on 9 October 1646. Another ordinance was immediately approved to raise a loan of £200,000 on the security of the bishops' lands and the excise. Those who had lent money to parliament on the public faith could, by advancing the same sum again, receive a new bill for twice the original sum plus interest, and have first crack at the bishops' lands when they came onto the market. This was the device known as doubling, a fiscal innovation that would be used repeatedly in the sale of confiscated lands throughout the interregnum. It was a sensational success. People scrambled to double their previously worthless bills, and it took barely eight days to raise the money needed to get the Scots out of the kingdom.[29] By 11 February 1647 the money had been paid to the Scots, who then handed Charles over to the care of Colonel Graves and quit English soil, and Charles was on his way south to his palace at Holdenby. Skippon won kudos for the finesse with which he handled these sensitive transactions.[30]

The Attempt to Disband the New Model

Paradoxically, the parliamentary presbyterians, who had viewed the departure of the Scots with misgivings, were to profit enormously from it. No longer hampered by their identification with an unpopular military force, they could now devote their whole effort to getting rid of the New Model. The exit of the Scots army removed at a stroke the last remaining reason for keeping the New Model in existence. This transformation of the political scene at Westminster had already been foreshadowed by political events in London. In September 1646, when the mayoralty fell vacant, the high presbyterians on the aldermanic bench had united behind the presbyterian neo-royalist Sir John Gayre, overcoming the resistance of the Independents, who were in disarray.[31] Little over a month later members of the Common Council were expressing alarm at the spread of sectarianism, which was linked with the continued existence of the New Model. Moreover, faced with the prospect of a miserable winter brought on by the poor harvest that autumn,[32] Londoners searched for any means of lightening their financial burdens. While praising the New Model for its many victories, the magistrates added,

> there are some officers and many common soldiers of that army who either have never taken the Covenant or are disaffected to the church government held forth by parliament.... The pulpits of divers godly ministers are often usurped by preaching soldiers and others who infect their flock and all places where they come, with strange and dangerous errors.... What security or settlement can be expected, while they are masters of such a power ...?[33]

Disbanding the army would not only curb sectarianism and save money, but also enable parliament to attend to 'gasping, dying Ireland'. The petition said just what the Lords wanted to hear. They voted it their 'hearty thanks' and ordered it printed. The Commons by contrast returned no thanks and postponed consideration of the petition's demands.[34] MPs such as Sir John Evelyn and Bulstrode Whitelocke had already reproved the City petitioners for raising divisions and provoking tumults.[35] But within days there was a political turnabout that made manifest the sea change in public opinion which had occurred since the previous year. The king in captivity was no longer a menace, and had begun attracting ever more sympathy for his plight. The growing number of reports of religious outrages committed by New Model soldiers contributed to popular disenchantment with the army.[36] Equally, the burdens of the assessment and the excise made most people welcome any solution that promised financial relief. The day after the London petition was presented to parliament, the City elections were held. Common-councillors who had opposed the petition went down to defeat, making for a council of an almost exclusively presbyterian stamp.[37]

The new Common Council maintained a continuous lobby at the Commons chamber. Deputies and councillors from two wards were sent each day on a rotating basis to keep pressure on the MPs until they relented and took up the business of the City's petition.[38] Heartened by this dramatic turn of events, the Lords decided to intimidate the religious radicals by directing Fairfax to investigate and report how many officers and men had not yet taken the Covenant.[39] The Lords also kept up their obstruction of the Commons' October ordinances renewing the mandate of the Committee for the Army and extending the assessment for the army's pay by another six months. Eventually, on 4 March 1647, when it was clear to all that the Commons majority no longer supported the ordinances, the Lords rejected them outright.[40]

The imminent departure of the Scots, combined with the presbyterian triumph in London, and the City lobby at Westminster beginning in late December 1646, revived the spirits of the political presbyterians in the Commons too. By a large margin they persuaded the house to debate the City petition.[41] The publication of the third part of Edwardes' *Gangraena* at the end of December, with its comprehensive catalogue of sacrilegious acts and heretical preaching by New Model soldiers, confirmed the worst suspicions of many. Joshua Sprigge's *Anglia Rediviva*, which came out the following month, full of praise for the exploits and the piety of the New Model, fell upon deaf ears because its message was one that the majority did not wish to hear.[42]

Aware of their unpopularity at Westminster, in parish pulpits and among the tax-paying population, both the high command and the rank and file took counter-measures against the growing threat to their survival. In the autumn the New Model had been quartered chiefly in the counties of Oxford, Northampton, Hertford, Warwick, Huntingdon, Leicester and Buckingham.[43] Immediately after the Common Council election two cavalry regiments were moved to quarters in Surrey. Their purpose, the French ambassador thought, was to frighten the City.[44] Neither the army nor its supporters acknowledged these troop movements, but the City was alive with talk of them in early January 1647. One pro-army editor tried to dismiss the reports as the product of groundless jealousy.[45] In any case a petition of London citizens to the Common Council on 25 January called for 'removal of that part of the army presently quartered near the City', denouncing the soldiers for their 'mutinous and menacing words'.[46] In frustration Richard Laurance, marshal-general of the horse, lashed out at the presbyterians as representatives of Antichrist.[47]

At Westminster, however, the army's supporters were in disarray. In early February the Commons chamber echoed with 'complaints and cavils' against officers and men who held 'erroneous and schismatical opinions' and had the effrontery to preach 'not being learned nor ordained'.[48] Now that the kingdom was almost empty of Scots soldiers, political moderates gravitated towards Holles and Stapleton with their programme of disbandment and lower taxes.[49]

Accentuating the Independents' political demoralization was the dangerous illness to which Cromwell succumbed at the beginning of February.[50] There were still, however, two major impediments to the New Model's demise. One was the large deficit parliament had run up by its failure to maintain 'constant pay'. Many New Model soldiers also held pre-1645 arrears certificates that were at least equal to the sums they had accumulated since that date, and they expected parliament to honour all its debts.[51]

The second impediment to disbandment was that, as the larger of the two remaining armies (the other being Poynts's northern army, numbering less than 10,000 men), the New Model would be difficult to discipline should it decide to resist parliament's orders. This thought had already occurred to the members of the peace party, but they had reckoned that they could get away with meting out the same treatment as had been given to Massey's brigade. William Strode had bragged indiscreetly to a colonel of the Somerset militia, 'they had already an army in and about London of forty thousand at command, with which he said "We will destroy them all, for Sir Thomas Fairfax will be deceived, for part of his army will join with us, and besides the Scots are very honest men and will come to assist us." '[52] The peace party's blunder was to think that a coalition of unrelated military forces could stare down the New Model if it came to a head-on clash.

Lacking foreknowledge of the New Model's indestructibility, the parliamentary majority opted to cut through its financial dilemma by ordering the disbandment of most of the army before settling its debt to the soldiers. On 18 February, after an exhausting all-day debate, the Commons resolved that apart from garrison forces only 5400 horse and a thousand dragoons would be kept up in England. The New Model foot would either go to Ireland or be dissolved.[53] The previous day a motion to delay disbandment had been lost by only two votes.[54] An attempt to have garrison and county forces dissolved before the New Model was also overridden.[55] The parliamentary majority steeled themselves with the knowledge that they would win favour with the population if not the army. In Smithfield there was an excise riot; from Suffolk and Essex came anti-army petitions; in the capital fast- and humiliation-day sermons were preached against the army for infecting the nation with heresy.[56] Reassured by a message that the king was safely in the hands of two horse regiments, and five dragoon troops, all led by political presbyterians, the parliamentary majority now threw caution to the winds.[57] Fairfax himself only escaped by a margin of 159 to 147 votes being replaced as commander-in-chief by the undistinguished presbyterian colonel Richard Graves.[58] Irrepressibly, the presbyterians sought to eliminate Fairfax another way by carrying a motion that in future no member of the Commons should hold a military commission. Moreover, there would no longer be any exceptions to the rule that officers had to swear the presbyterian Covenant. Fairfax and Colonel Nathaniel Rich had recently stood as candidates at Cirencester, and would have been returned as MPs had cavaliers not prevented the poll from being taken. Besides these two, Cromwell, Ireton, Rainborowe, Harrison and Fleetwood would now have to choose between resigning their seats and resigning their commissions.[59]

The anticipated extinction of the New Model widened the political fissures within the City. At the beginning of March a group of young men and apprentices questioned whether the army should be disbanded before parliament's enemies had been completely subdued.[60] Simultaneously the presbyterian-led Common Council and the opposition radical Independents – soon to be known as Levellers – submitted rival petitions. The magistrates urged parliament to disband the army and 'stop the malicious tongues of sectaries'. They also asked parliament to surrender to them the power to nominate the London militia, and complained that the soldiers were circulating among themselves 'a most dangerous and seditious petition', while the army as a body was drawing nearer the city.[61] The radical Petition of Many Thousands represented minority opinion in the City, notwithstanding its title, although it probably attracted considerable support in the suburbs.[62] Its thirteen points mapped out the Leveller programme for the next two years and, in an oblique reference to army disbandment, also exhorted parliament not to 'lay by that strength, which (under God) hath hitherto made you powerful to all good works.'[63] In another publication the City radicals were more explicit in their opposition to army disbandment, describing the New Model as 'a refuge pillar for the oppressed and distressed commons of England.'[64] As one of the enemies of the radicals taunted them, 'In plain English you are loath to see this army by subdivisions enfeebled, upon whose strength you rely for support, wherein you think there are many props of your extravagancy: You fancy yourselves wings out of their feathers, and therefore unwillingly see any quill drop.' The radicals, he charged, had deceived themselves, for the bulk of the army was uninterested in their programme.[65]

An anonymous statement from a group of private soldiers demonstrated that, while political awareness was well advanced in the army, its priorities were different from those of the London radicals. For these soldiers religion came first: the extirpation of ungodliness and the preservation of the gospel. The liberty of the subject came second, and the privileges of parliament third. With reluctance (so they said), they mentioned 'this our just and lawful service in which we have served them, which we do tender in respect of our liberties ten thousand times more than all our arrears.' They would be content with their wages, 'having our brethren the Scots', they added sardonically, 'for an example in that particular.'[66] In March 1647 the radical Independent party of London saw clearly the importance of the New Model Army for its political survival. The army for its part was already politicized, but had not yet thought of an alliance with its civilian supporters. A variety of petitions drafted by the rank and file had been circulating in the army during that climactic month. Because some of them trespassed too obviously onto political territory, 'beyond the proper concernments of soldiers', the officers gathered them together, deleted the offending passages, and boiled them down to a single document of five points:

1 a parliamentary ordinance, 'to which the royal assent may be desired', indemnifying them from prosecution for all acts of war;
2 the auditing and payment of arrears before disbandment;
3 no conscription for service outside the kingdom of those who had joined the army voluntarily, and no cavalry to be conscripted into the infantry;
4 fair compensation for maimed soldiers and the families of the slain;
5 regular pay until disbandment.[67]

These demands would be the ground bass of all army statements for the remainder of the year. Political events along the way would lead to new grievances and fresh demands, but these were embellishments. Fundamentally what stirred the soldiers' fear and anger from the spring of 1647 until the second civil war were indemnity, pay and conscription.[68]

When, on the day that the petition was promulgated, a deputation from the presbyterian-dominated Derby House Committee for Irish Affairs went to meet the officers at their Saffron Walden headquarters, they were startled to be confronted with a demand for answers to four questions before there could be any enlistment for the Irish expedition.

1 What regiments were to be kept up in England?
2 Who was to command the army in Ireland?
3 How would the soldiers who went to Ireland be paid, fed and clothed?
4 How would the soldiers be satisfied regarding arrears of pay and indemnity?

The forty-four officers present did not endorse all four questions unanimously. Twelve of them, including Colonels Butler, Harley, Fortescue and Rich, opposed the first question. Six of them also dissented from the second question. Except for Colonel Rich, Captain Awdeley and Captain Young, these dissenters would form the core of the presbyterian faction which left the army at the end of May.[69]

The Declaration of Dislike, and Irish Recruitment

By the end of March 1647 the army was pervaded by a deep sense of paranoia in respect of its erstwhile friends. The religious excitement found among all ranks fed this paranoia by spreading the belief that only the army and a remnant of the civilian population continued to follow God's ways. The army was painfully conscious that the country was divided between friend and foe, and that the foes greatly outnumbered the friends. In this sense it was already thoroughly politicized.[70] Yet it was far from being in a state of mutiny. The only regiment which had come close to open defiance was Rich's in Norfolk, where angry mutterings were heard about economic and military grievances.[71] Tactful handling of the army, and serious attention to its grievances over pay and indemnity would have achieved the goal for which Holles and Stapleton aimed. As it happened, they were incapable of tact and unwilling to offer the soldiers a fair deal.

When Waller, Clotworthy and Salwey reported the soldiers' concerns to the Commons the immediate response of the presbyterian leaders was to order Fairfax to suppress the petition circulating in the army.[72] Two days later, on the 29th, they were alarmed to hear that soldiers were still being pressured into signing it. Nevertheless, an anonymous correspondent of the presbyterian colonel Edward Harley believed that, if parliament provided money and called Major-General Skippon down from Newcastle to promote the Irish service, 'they might do what they please with the army.'[73] Another correspondent had written to Colonel Rossiter, also a presbyterian, informing him that the petition had been brought to his regiment from Lieutenant Griffith Lloyd of Fleetwood's regiment and Lieutenant John Byfield of Cromwell's regiment. The whole effort was said to be co-ordinated by Thomas Hammond, lieutenant-general of the artillery, Colonel Robert Hammond, Commissary-General Henry Ireton, Colonel Robert Lilburne and Lieutenant-Colonel Mark Grime.[74]

Too late to undo the damage wrought by these anonymous letters, Fairfax wrote to the Commons Speaker, reluctantly complying with the order to suppress the petition, and sending its organizers to Westminster to explain themselves.[75] The presbyterian leaders privately sent for Skippon, believing he would be an effective salesman for the Irish expedition.[76] Publicly they exploded with rage at the army's disobedience. Late in the evening of Monday 29 March Holles left the chamber and hurriedly scribbled the text of a motion accusing those who persisted in promoting the petition of 'tending to put the army into a distemper and mutiny, to put conditions upon the parliament, and obstruct the relief of Ireland', and threatening that if they continued their illegal activity they would be 'looked upon and proceeded against as enemies to the state and disturbers of the public place.' The provocative motion passed in a thin house.[77]

Holles's Declaration of Dislike, as it came to be known, was his crossing of the Rubicon. It opened between the presbyterian party and the army a chasm of distrust that no subsequent concessions could breach. A royalist commentator characterized the presbyterian leaders as 'cocksure' and questioned their wisdom in provoking an undefeated body of 21,000 armed men.[78] Holles evidently thought he could minimize the danger by segregating those willing to enlist for the Irish service from those who declined it. An active campaign was now launched to divide the army by offering back pay to those who quit, and a month's pay in advance to those who volunteered for Ireland. Officers who signed up were offered their respited pay in rebels' lands instead of nearly worthless public-faith bills.[79] Commissioners were sent to drum up business for Ireland, but it was a political miscalculation, compounded by naming for the task a preponderance of well-known presbyterians.[80] Nor were matters improved by the announcement of the expedition's commanders. At first Sir William Waller was designated general of foot and Edward Massey as general of horse. However, Waller recognized his unacceptability to the soldiers, and bowed out in favour of Skippon in the second week of April.[81] At first Skippon tried to beg off, citing his age and infirmities, but the presbyterians, counting heavily on his popularity with the soldiers, pressured him into accepting the appointment as a patriotic duty.[82] With the announcement that the horse regiments to be retained in England would be commanded by men of the same stripe as Waller and Massey, the soldiers realized that they were soon to be deprived of their trusted commanders in both kingdoms.[83] In Captain Edward Wogan's words, the army remaining in England 'was to be all presbyterians'.[84]

The systematic hostility of the Holles-Stapleton party from the end of March onward transmuted the army's already sharp political consciousness into revolutionary militancy. The Declaration of Dislike instantly became a new grievance added to the top of the list that had been compiled a month earlier. To be called enemies of the state was an attack on soldiers' honour. To be denied the right of petition was a restriction they refused to accept. Rather than submit passively to gagging they issued a 'vindication' of their conduct.[85] A group of radicals within the army also published an anonymous attack on the Essex petitioners[86] as deluded men who had forgotten the irreproachable behaviour of the regiments stationed in their county, and had allowed themselves to be made the dupes of 'a treacherous party of corrupt members in both Houses and covetous ambitious clergy.' But the radicals' greatest scorn was reserved for Colonels Harley and Rossiter on account of their aspersions in the House of Commons, which had led to the Declaration of Dislike. The pamphlet was circulated in the army, and also distributed to some of the Essex clergy by William Style, a London leather-seller and captain in Lambart's foot regiment.[87] A reference to the imprisonment of Major Alexander Tulidah, allegedly for nothing more than speaking the truth to the parliamentary presbyterians, showed that the army radicals were now in open sympathy with their counterparts in the City.[88] Tulidah had been arrested for promoting the March Petition of Many Thousands, but was later discharged on bail. A member of neither the New Model nor the London militia, his military background is obscure, though he is known to have been one of the pallbearers at the funeral of the religiously radical Major Christopher Bethell in October 1645. Evidently a continental soldier, he had by July 1647 been appointed adjutant-general of the New Model horse, a post which he held for only a few months.[89]

So great was the resentment of the eight horse regiments stationed in the Eastern Association that they pressed their superior officers to draw them all to a rendezvous so that they could draft a document vindicating their conduct. At headquarters Fairfax, who with Thomas Hammond was the only general officer on the spot, did his best to keep the army under control.[90] While he could suppress public, official expressions of animosity to presbyterian politicians and clergy, he could not divert the accelerating radicalization of all ranks. By the middle of April men in Ireton's regiment in Suffolk were not stickling to call their foes tyrants, and some of them were heard quoting John Lilburne's writings as 'statute law'.[91] At the same time the soldiers began exploring the possibility of making common cause with civilian sympathizers. In the countryside they strove to win favour by their exemplary behaviour.[92] Through Gilbert Mabbott, a radical attached to the army's clerical staff at Fairfax's house in Queen Street, Westminster, they kept themselves informed of developments in the capital.[93]

Meanwhile, the party of Holles and Stapleton, unperturbed by this radical ferment, pressed ahead with the Irish expedition. The extent of their commitment to this project is shown by their willingness to offer royalist estates as security for the £200,000 loan they sought from the City.[94] The peace party dispatched the Earl of Pembroke to tell the City magistrates that army disbandment could not go ahead without the loan. Disbandment was an urgent priority, not least of all because, he alleged, there were 7000 cavaliers in the New Model who sought to restore the king to his throne.[95] To army militants Pembroke's allegation was just another unscrupulous attempt to besmirch the New Model's reputation. Indignantly they added a further grievance to their list: those who had scandalized the army by accusing it of royalism should be officially repudiated and the army vindicated.[96]

For all the bluster of the militants, there was something in what Pembroke had said. We have already seen how royalist infantry flocked to join Fairfax's army after almost every victory in 1645 and 1646.[97] Likewise, in the spring of 1647, there are clues that lend weight to Pembroke's apparently wild accusation. It was reported to Speaker Lenthall that on 7 April an officer had laid a petition before the king entreating him to allow himself to be escorted to the head of the army, 'who would restore him to his honour, crown and dignity.'[98] Two weeks later, a letter from Suffolk claimed that the soldiers there and in Norfolk 'sing one note; namely that they have fought all this time to bring the king to London; and to London they will bring the king.'[99] According to another report at about the same time many soldiers were crying, 'Viva the king.' In Norfolk some of them beat up a presbyterian constable and his friends for refusing to drink the king's health.[100] At the beginning of May some of the infantry stationed in Cambridgeshire scandalized their officers by threatening to go to Holdenby and fetch the king.[101] The following month one of Hyde's correspondents told him that 3000 foot in the New Model used the Book of Common Prayer.[102] In London it was widely believed that Charles was encouraging overtures from the army. Indeed, it was supposed that their confidence of the king's support was partly what made the soldiers so peremptory.[103]

The evidence of army royalism, so persistent, and emanating from so many sources, cannot be dismissed as merely a malicious attempt to blacken the New Model's reputation. A strain of royalist sentiment was present in the spring of 1647, though it was subordinate to the dominant theme of resentment over material grievances.[104] What cannot be gainsaid is that there was in all ranks less resentment of the king than of the parliamentary peace party. In light of this evidence, the army's seizure of the king in June takes on a more ambiguous significance. There were doubtless many among the rank and file who hoped that Cornet Joyce's act was just the first step towards the restoration of the king. Given the sometimes concealed royalism of segments of the rank and file, it is more understandable why the higher officers were so marked in their friendliness towards Charles during the summer of 1647. Moreover, the widespread public perception that they were about to restore him to power did a lot to take the wind out of the sails of the presbyterian counter-revolution during those same months.

Regardless of their feelings about the king, both soldiers and officers became progressively more disenchanted with the prospect of going to Ireland. A combination of blunders by the Holles – Stapleton party and diligent political education by army militants at length turned all but a handful of the rank and file against the Irish service. But among the officers there had at first been much uncertainty and division about whether to volunteer. Colonel Robert Hammond, for example, was involved in serious negotiations with the Derby House Committee early in March. If parliament had been willing to meet a number of his conditions, including appointment as governor of Dublin, he would have been more than willing to take a contingent there.[105] Skippon too, despite his wounds and his age, was in April willing to lead the infantry to Ireland. Colonel Nathaniel Rich was another senior officer sympathetic to the Irish service, as were Captains Lewis Awdeley and Arthur Young.[106] Within a few weeks all these men had repudiated it. In addition, at least one other officer, Major George Sedascue, who publicly supported parliament's recruitment for Ireland, subsequently underwent a change of heart and was readmitted to the army.[107] On the other hand twenty-nine officers of the rank of captain or higher had signified by the end of March that they were willing to lead men across the Irish Sea, and to recruit for that purpose within the army.[108] Among the rank and file there were many who would have enrolled had they been given an assurance that the money owed for previous service would be paid before they left England. Their enthusiasm would have been all the greater if they could have been accompanied by their familiar commanders. Skippon was widely respected, but he had not seen much action after being wounded at Naseby. Give us 'Fairfax and Cromwell and we all go', the men shouted to the parliamentary commissioners in mid-April.[109] Instead they were offered Massey and Skippon.

On 15 April the parliamentary commissioners came to dine at Fairfax's quarters. After the meal they expressed their unease at the reports of resistance to Irish recruitment, and pulled out a draft declaration for him to sign. It threatened punishment to anyone who obstructed the service. Fairfax, who was loth to see the army any more divided than it was, answered evasively.[110] But he did not discourage the efforts of the handful of officers who were enthusiastic to recruit for Ireland. Rather, he instructed those who signed up to march with their officers to Bridgnorth, Shropshire. On the 17th Fairfax convoked the officers to consider the request of the Derby House Committee. Those in attendance, numbering over a hundred, chose a high-level committee to represent their views. Their nominees were the two Hammonds, Colonel John Lambart, who had just arrived from the north, Colonel Lilburne, Colonel Rich and Colonel Hewson, who had just returned from Ireland. They all pledged to promote the Irish service, even if they did not go themselves, but asked parliament to answer the propositions they had submitted after their meeting on 21 March.[111] In the event most officers remained idle. The high-pressure methods of the few who sought to round up recruits for Ireland were neutralized by those who strove to head off the army's imminent dissolution. By 19 April at least nine of the twenty-nine who had originally committed themselves to Ireland withdrew.[112] From this point not more than half-a-dozen cavalry officers continued to express any interest in the Irish service.

Hoping to strengthen the incentive for recruitment, the parliamentary commissioners advised parliament to begin disbandment, so that those who did not wish to return to civilian life would be compelled to sign on for Ireland.[113] A few days later they reported that substantial headway had been made in nine of the foot regiments, four of the horse regiments, the general's lifeguard and Okey's dragoons. The commissioners were guilty of wild optimism, for, while officers from fifty companies and eight troops had indeed engaged, there was no assurance that their men would follow them. Plans were formulated to march the recruits away from the army to quarters in Staffordshire, Northamptonshire, Bedfordshire, Worcestershire, Somerset and Gloucestershire.[114]

In the event, very few of these recruits materialized. Lieutenant-Colonel Kempson persuaded four companies to come by marching away with the regimental colours and pay, intimating that if the men did not stick with him they would not be paid. He showed lack of judgement by carrying out this manoeuvre while Colonel Lilburne was reading Fairfax's message to the other half of the regiment. At the same rendezvous Edward Massey attempted to stimulate enlistment by misinforming the men that Colonel Herbert was already on the march with his regiment towards Cheshire.[115] When he heard what was happening, Lilburne tore after the departing companies. Overtaking them, he aimed a stinging rebuke at Kempson. 'Fellow soldiers, I am sorry you are marching up and down in such weather as this. You may thank your lieutenant-colonel for it.' An officer beside him added, 'they delude you as ignorant men to go for Ireland. No godly man would desire you to go for that affair.' Once reassured that they would be paid regardless of whether they volunteered or not, the men abandoned Kempson and followed Lilburne back to camp.[116]

The efforts of Captain Howard in Fleetwood's regiment were likewise abortive.[117] In Hammond's regiment Captains Stratton and O'Hara tried getting their men drunk before bringing out the enlistment papers. In this fashion they drew off nearly two companies. Their success was probably short-lived, however, in light of the fierce opposition of the commanding officer, Major Robert Saunders. 'Mark my words,' he barked at one of the ensigns, 'all godly men, and those that carry themselves civilly shall be put out of their places after they come into Ireland, and other men put in their room.'[118] By the beginning of May the pro-parliamentary officers were experiencing rapidly diminishing success in their recruitment for Ireland. The officers at headquarters in Saffron Walden were said to be unanimous that they would see Englishmen's liberties and privileges settled before venturing abroad. Their preference was to 'suffer with the godly party here than go away and leave them to the mercy of their adversaries.'[119] Skippon laboured in vain to turn the officers around. When he convened a meeting in Walden Church there were 150 foot officers present, but only thirty from the cavalry bothered to turn up.[120] In an impassioned appeal he laid his reputation and popularity on the line. The officers were discomfited by his transparent piety and emotionalism. Robert Hammond tried to ease the embarrassment by explaining that their reluctance to serve did not reflect in any way on the major-general's honour and gallantry. The other parliamentary commissioners then asked the officers what grievances were causing them to hold back. Circumspectly they answered that they must first consult their regiments.[121] But they did not mask their bitterness against the Declaration of Dislike or their indignation against the current allegations that the army was infected with royalism.[122] The near-unanimity of the higher officers was partly the result of the stiff resistance of the lower officers and rank and file. For example, the continuing efforts of Lieutenant-Colonel Kempson to win over Robert Lilburne's regiment were sabotaged by one of the ensigns, Francis Nicholls. He took it upon himself to promise the men three weeks' pay if they would resist Kempson's blandishments. He also circulated the banned petition, and warned that those who signed up for Ireland would not have a penny until they were on board ship. He also made a baseless promise that Lilburne's regiment would continue to be kept up in England.[123] When word reached him of Nicholls' activities, the regiment's major, Francis Dormer, an ally of Kempson, took quick action. Nicholls was arrested, his pockets were searched, and he was sent to London without Fairfax's knowledge.[124]

The cavalry were also industriously engaged in propagandizing the foot against the Irish service. In one incident two troopers from Cromwell's regiment accosted another of Lilburne's ensigns. They inquired 'how the foot stood affected to the horse', and appealed to them on the basis of the lowest common denominator: arrears of pay. On 17 April the same ensign encountered a party of horse riding towards Newmarket, while he marched with his own men to their regimental rendezvous at Bury St Edmunds. As they passed, the horse cried out to the foot, 'Fellow soldiers, now stand all for your arrears.'[125]

This negative lobbying by the rank and file and junior officers meant a meagre harvest of recruits for Ireland. On 23 April the parliamentary commissioners reported that 115 officers were ready to serve in that kingdom. Almost all of them were infantry, as were the rank and file, who numbered at a generous estimate no more than a thousand.[126] The respected Sir Hardress Waller, the man designated by Fairfax to lead the New Model infantry contingent for Ireland, gave up the assignment. Accordingly, at the end of April the contingent was led to Reading and from thence west into Gloucestershire, by men of lesser stature: Colonels Herbert and O'Connelly, and Lieutenant-Colonel Kempson and Adjutant-General Gray. Short of officers and supplies, their morale was poor, and they found themselves 'in a distracted and broken posture'.[127] As we have seen, Colonel Lilburne did not have much difficulty retrieving four companies of his regiment from this dispirited crew. Major Gooday was able to muster about half his company, but none of the expected recruits materialized from either Hewson's or Fleetwood's regiments.[128] Captain Thomas's efforts to coerce Waller's regiment with threats that those who declined would be forced to 'follow like dogs' were equally barren.[129] The Derby House Committee tacitly recognized that its recruitment campaign in the New Model was in ruins by turning to provincial forces to make up the deficit.[130]

What held the New Model together in the face of presbyterian efforts to dismember it and in spite of the uncertainty of some of its officers was the extraordinary solidarity of the rank and file.[131] Their dismay over parliamentary mistreatment and civilian hostility never caused them to lose sight of the importance of sticking together. Forbidden to petition at the end of March, they turned to their commander-in-chief for succour. It did not take long for the majority of the officers to reciprocate this movement for unity, with the result that between April and November 1647 there was close collaboration between the leaders and the led. Growing evidence of presbyterian preparations to intimidate them only served to knit soldiers and officers more tightly together.

The Purging of the London Militia and the Rise of the Agitators

Since December 1646 the City had been claiming back the power to nominate the members of its militia committee. This issue had been a source of dissension since 1643, when parliament had first wrested the power of nomination from the City's hands. Another aspect of the conflict was the desire of the City's conservative oligarchy to absorb the suburban militias of Southwark, Westminster and the Tower Hamlets into their jurisdiction. The suburbs, with their more lower-class, radical population, resisted the hegemonic attempts of the City.[132] But in April 1647 the party of Holles and Stapleton, now firmly in control of the House of Commons, granted the City's request. This concession had been an indispensable precondition of the £200,000 loan from the City for the Irish expedition.[133] At once the City magistrates drew up a slate devoid of radical Independents. The radical Independent remnant fought so bitterly against their expulsion from the militia committee that one of their number, Alderman Stephen Estwick, was violently ejected from the meeting that approved the new nominations.[134] Parliament then ratified the City's slate and surrendered the power to make appointments in the future.[135] The new committee at once set about dismissing Independent militia officers and replacing them with men trusted by the presbyterian regime.[136] The significance of this revolution in City affairs was not lost upon army radicals, although they did not publicly denounce it until the beginning of July.[137] When their demand for reinstatement of the ousted committee members was granted on 22 July it became the proximate cause of the presbyterian crowd's assault on parliament four days later.

Signs that the groundwork was being laid for a presbyterian counter-revolution raised the soldiers' anxiety to a new pitch. The eight cavalry regiments quartered in East Anglia drew together, elected two representatives or 'commissioners' each, and addressed an impassioned letter to Fairfax. They now found themselves, they said, face to face with enemies far more dangerous than any they had fought on the battlefield. 'Like foxes [they] lurk in their dens, and cannot be dealt withall, though discovered, being protected by those who are entrusted with the government of the kingdom.' The way the Irish expedition was being organized, with inferior talent promoted ahead of such commanders as Fairfax and Cromwell, showed it to be nothing else than 'a design to ruin and break this army in pieces'. The soldiers responsible for this appeal were more sensitive than anyone to 'the bleeding condition of Ireland, crying aloud for a brotherly assistance', but they refused to go there until their own grievances had been redressed, and 'the just rights and liberties of the subjects maintained.'[138]

Hard on the heels of this appeal to their commander came a second apology, much grimmer and more menacing. The officers were exhorted to 'stand fast in your integrity', for any who did not would be 'marked with a brand of infamy forever, as a traitor to his country and an enemy to his army.' In addition to the standard material grievances the petitioners presented a demand for that the army's honour to be vindicated, 'and justice done upon the fomenters' of the Declaration of Dislike. They also reminded Fairfax that their reason for taking up arms had been so that 'the meanest subject should fully enjoy his right, liberty and proprieties in all things.'[139]

At this point the officers' thinking was nearly congruent with that of the soldiers. In their own petition published around the same time they also declared that they had fought for 'the removal of every yoke from the people's necks'. While they did not call for justice against the framers of the Declaration of Dislike, they took the bolder step of addressing their petition not to Fairfax, but to parliament. Openly defying the recent prohibition against petitions from the army, a high-level delegation consisting of Colonels Okey and Hewson, Lieutenant-Colonels Reade and Pride, Major Wroth Rogers and Captains Reynolds and Goffe laid it before the Commons on 27 April.[140] Instead of hearing the Vindication, however, the Commons chose to summon three other officers to appear before them: Colonel Lilburne for turning his men against the Irish service; and Captain William Style and Major Robert Saunders for handing out copies of *A New Found Stratagem*. They also threw Ensign Nicholls in prison. Pressing their current advantage against the parliamentary Independents, the Holles-led majority voted that disbanded troops should receive only six weeks' pay – less than £70,000 of the close to £3 million that was due to all the armies.[141]

The officers' Vindication finally rose to the top of the Commons' agenda late in the day on 30 April. Yet discussion of it was sidetracked by Skippon, who handed the Speaker the copy of the soldiers' *Apologie* given him by three troopers the previous day. At this point Cromwell and Fairfax admitted possessing copies as well, and handed them in with Skippon's. The men who had presented the *Apologie* to Fairfax two days before were at the door. Along with the other thirteen signatories they had labelled themselves 'commissioners' for their regiments. Before long they would become known as agitators or adjutators, and less frequently as agents.[142] At the time the word 'agitator' had none of its modern pejorative ring, and meant simply one who had been empowered to act on behalf of others. The sixteen 'commissioners' had evidently been chosen by their regiments when their officers had summoned them to a rendezvous to hear the terms for the Irish service. The presence of the officers hints at their approval, if not supervision, of this novel form of rank-and-file representation.[143] The action of the eight cavalry regiments was quickly emulated throughout the army. By early May Herbert's, Harley's and Fairfax's foot regiments had chosen eleven, twenty and seven agitators respectively.[144] By then it was becoming the practice to select two agitators from each troop or company. In June, when the officers put themselves at the head of the army revolt, it was decided to formalize the system by balancing the soldier agitators with an equal number of officers from each regiment. Together with the general officers present at army headquarters, they formed the General Council of the Army which began meeting in July and was dissolved in January 1648.[145] Nothing is known about most of the soldier agitators beyond their names, and they quickly sank back into the obscurity from which they had briefly emerged in the spring of 1647. Their civilian occupations were probably no more exalted than that of William Allen, a feltmaker from Southwark.[146] While they were men of humble origins, several of them would impress their superiors enough by their talents to win rapid promotion. Edward Sexby, perhaps the most active, and certainly one of the most radical, was rewarded with the rank of captain.[147] Thomas Sheppard became cornet to William Cecil's troop, while William Allen rose to be adjutant-general of horse in Ireland.[148] Consolation Fox became a lieutenant and then evidently captain-lieutenant to Colonel Ingoldsby.[149] Many of the officer agitators were also honoured with promotions. Captains John Reynolds and James Berry, who were early leaders of the agitators, both became colonels.[150] Among other promotions, William Knowles, Robert Kirkby, Josiah Mullineux and John Peck became captains, Thomas Bayly a lieutenant, William Russell a cornet and Timothy Thornbury a quartermaster. Most of these promotions occurred after the purge of presbyterian officers in May and June.[151]

As we have seen, debate on the officers' Vindication was interrupted by the first official notice of the agitators' activity. After hearing Skippon's information the house called in the three troopers so that they could be questioned directly. They testified that their officers had drawn the eight regiments of horse to separate rendezvous, where they heard the letter read. Although it had been approved unanimously, the three troopers could not or would not say who had drafted it, but offered their opinion that few officers were involved. When the MPs tried to elicit the meaning of phrases like 'some that had tasted of sovereignty had degenerated into tyrants', they insisted that all questions be submitted in writing to the regiments, who would answer them collectively.[152] Denzil Holles and his followers were enraged by what they took to be the impudence of these three men, and called for their punishment. Reflecting later upon these events, Holles thought that parliament should have had the courage to hang one of the three as a warning to the army. Had it done so it could have avoided a good deal of future mischief. But parliament was divided. When the presbyterians moved to have the three agitators committed, the MP for Newcastle stood up and said 'he would have them committed indeed, but it should be to the best inn of the town, and good sack and sugar provided.' This ridiculous suggestion, snorted the humourless Holles, was 'a bold and insolent scorn put upon the parliament'.[153] His view was evidently not shared by moderate MPs. The Commons majority refrained from punishing the agitators, and contented themselves with directing the military MPs – Skippon, Cromwell, Ireton and Fleetwood – to go down to their regiments and quieten the distemper.[154] The next day Fairfax issued an order to all officers to repair to their commands within twenty-four hours.[155] Holles would later accuse the grandees of having deliberately stayed away from their regiments so that the rebellion could flare unchecked,[156] but there is no evidence to support this contention. Both Fairfax and Cromwell had been ill between February and April, while Skippon, Sir Hardress Waller and Hewson were occupied in the north and in Ireland. It was nothing out of the ordinary for higher officers, whether presbyterian or Independent, to seek the comforts of London when the army was inactive.[157]

Obeying Fairfax's order, the officers returned to find their regiments in a state of near-hysteria. On 26 April the four horse regiments stationed in Norfolk had met together to promote their March petition. The meeting almost turned into an insurrection, but a group of officers led by Major Huntington was able to persuade the soldiers instead to appoint an officer and man from each troop to meet and continue discussing the matter.[158] In Essex on Sunday 2 May the general officers at headquarters returned from the afternoon sermon to meet a panicky Lieutenant-Colonel Jubbes of Hewson's regiment. He had just received intelligence that the Essex trained bands were preparing to attack and disarm them that night. In self-defence the regiment had crowded into a church with their arms. When no attack materialized, Hewson's men sheepishly filed out of the church the next day, conceding that it had been a false alarm.[159] The army was painfully aware of local antagonism. Not only had a second Essex petition called for its disbandment; the same demand was made by the counties of the Eastern Association at the beginning of May.[160] From London came reports of Pembroke's inflammatory speech about the army being inseminated with royalism, and the purge of radicals from the City militia committee.[161] Small wonder that some of the fiery spirits began to propose extreme measures. Among the papers collected by army secretary William Clarke is a draft 'Heads of demands made to the parliament' which reflects the unmistakable influence of Leveller thinking on parliamentary and electoral matters. Calling for a reform of election abuses, it advocates annual elections, and closes with a ringing assertion of the sovereignty of the people, 'princes being but the kingdom's great servants, entrusted for their weal, not for their woe.'[162] To have published these demands would have been to embrace a revolutionary strategy by claiming the right to speak for the English people and to sit in judgement over parliament. John Lilburne threw his weight behind such a strategy, and sometime in May began pressing the soldiers to adopt his personal struggle as their own.[163]

But, whatever impression some people had gained, Lilburne's word was far from being statute law throughout the army. The agitator leadership correctly judged that the time was not ripe to take an openly revolutionary line. Publicly they followed Rushworth's advice to 'demand nothing but what is relating to them as soldiers', while they assured their friends in the Northern Army that they only wanted what parliament had promised them and the 'known laws of the nation allow us to enjoy'.[164] At the same time they quietly prepared for the day when they would throw down the gauntlet before parliament. They moved for the creation of a representative body to administer the army's business. They prepared a team of writers at Oxford and army headquarters to draft pamphlets for an army press 'to satisfy and undeceive the people'. They sent envoys to forge links with non-New Model forces and 'well-affected friends' throughout the kingdom. They took steps to prevent the seizure of the king by those hostile to the army. Anticipating a hostile attempt to remove the king from the army's control, they put him under more vigilant surveillance. They launched a spirited campaign to dissuade the general officers from quitting the army before the crisis was over.[165]

Not unaware of the dangerous state of the army, the party of Holles and Stapleton took what they were sure would be effective measures to keep it under control. The order to the higher officers to return to their charges was one precaution. Another was to vote large chunks of money to the higher officers: £1000 to Skippon, and the promise of land worth £5000 and £2500 a year to Fairfax and Cromwell respectively.[166] Skippon did what he could to oblige his parliamentary masters. As we have seen, however, he was unable to wring from his fellow officers anything more definite than a commitment to consult their regiments.[167]

The men were ready to be consulted. Regimental committees were set up with representation from every troop and company. The meetings were convened at Bury, well away from army headquarters, the foot soldiers reportedly contributing 4d. each to defray the costs. These regimental meetings were not placid affairs. Reports reached London of 'high discontents' amid cries for 'vindication and reparations'.[168] The papers that emerged from the meetings revealed that tempers were indeed running high. Lambart's men cried out for vengeance against presbyterian ministers like Thomas Edwardes and Christopher Love for their efforts to render the army 'odious to the kingdom'. Fairfax's infantry wanted the laws translated from 'an unknown tongue' into English. The regiment was in fact bitterly divided. Those led by its lieutenant-colonel, Thomas Jackson, reaffirmed their willingness to go to Ireland, and said that the main thing on their minds was an indemnity ordinance. The dissenters were led by Captain Francis White.[169] Sir Hardress Waller's regiment used 'scurrilous language' against parliament to voice its demand for liberty of conscience. The men of Fairfax's horse regiment objected to the Covenant, complaining 'that some who have declared themselves enemies to this present parliament are in part become our judges.' Calling for the repeal of the Declaration of Dislike, they also demanded the punishment of its framers. Clearly many soldiers harboured a deep sense of wrong at the public's failure to honour the risks they had undergone. The men of Rich's regiment alluded to 'the scarlet dye of our valiant fellow-soldiers' blood.' They went on in this extravagant vein to contrast their sacrifice to 'the inveterate malice' of their present enemies, 'who gladly would have sheathed their swords in our bowels.'[170]

From the regimental papers it was evident that, while publicly the soldiers declared that they accounted their honour 'more dear to us than anything in the world besides',[171] privately they feared for their safety. What obsessed them about the Declaration of Dislike was the thought that, if they disbanded with it unexpunged from the record, they would be completely vulnerable to criminal prosecution as 'enemies to the state'.[172] Minimal grievances, or none at all, were reported from the regiments that had been consulted by presbyterian commanders.[173] On Saturday 15 May the officers met at Saffron Walden Church to hear the regimental reports. Tempers flared when Sheffield and other presbyterian officers questioned the officers' right to canvass their regiments' grievances without informing them fully of parliament's latest offers. Lambart rounded on the presbyterians, scornfully accusing them of speaking only for themselves, since they had in effect already closed their minds by volunteering for Ireland before the consultative process began. Ruthlessly pressing his point, Lambart averred that men who had refrained from endorsing the army's March petition had now cut themselves off from their fellow soldiers.[174] After all the reports had been aired, a committee composed of Colonels Whalley, Hammond, Rich, Lambart, Ingoldsby, Okey and Hewson, and Majors Disbrowe and Cowell, was instructed to summarize the reports for presentation to Skippon and the other commissioners.[175] The committee did its work promptly and had the statement ready by the next day. In the few hours it spent on its task it cannot have sifted carefully through all the papers. What it seems to have done is to adopt the paper from Rich's regiment with slight modification.[176] By this means it sidestepped the inflammatory expressions and esoteric demands of some regiments, confining itself to 'what pertains unto them as soldiers'.[177] Condescendingly and somewhat disingenuously it explained to the parliamentary commissioners that the regimental papers had been 'confused and full of tautologies, impertinences and weaknesses answerable to the soldiers' dialect.'[178]

The committee had done its job well. The eleven grievances it selected for presentation to the parliamentary commissioners were limited to army matters. All extremist language had been excluded, as well as any demand that did not strictly pertain to the army. The longstanding bread-and-butter concerns were at the core of the committee's brief: arrears, free quarter, indemnity, compensation for the wounded and the families of the slain, and conscription. Parliament's high-handedness in arresting Ensign Nicholls was resented. The less tangible question of the army's reputation or honour also loomed large.[179] The Declaration of Dislike still stood as 'a memorandum of infamy upon us to posterity'. The allegation by Pembroke and others of royalism in the New Model was almost as galling. This and the calumnies of Thomas Edwardes and others had rendered the army odious to the kingdom. Although several regiments had called for the impeachment of the army's enemies, the higher officers contented themselves with requesting that they be required to furnish 'judicial proof' of their accusations.[180] But honour obsessed the soldiers less than simple raw fear of what would happen to them if they were disbanded while the Declaration of Dislike was still on the books, and the calumnies of their enemies unrefuted. Pervading the committee's eleven grievances was a down-to-earth practicality.

At the meeting with the parliamentary commissioners on 16 May fierce conflict erupted between the majority who backed the committee's report and those who favoured obedience to parliament. At one point Colonels Whalley and Sheffield nearly came to blows.[181] The antagonism had now become so rooted that the two sides could no longer live together within the same army. The weaker would have to give way to the stronger or be driven out. In vain Skippon tried to mediate the heated clashes, which he found 'a very great pressure to my spirit'.[182] The more pragmatic Cromwell admonished his fellow officers that disobedience to parliament could only end in confusion and disaster for the army.[183]

Parliament's commissioners – Cromwell, Ireton, Skippon and Fleetwood – dutifully reported that they had communicated parliament's concessions to the officers and sent them back to their regiments. Pointedly, however, they added that they had found the army 'under a deep sense of some sufferings, and the common soldiers much unsettled.' While awaiting further instructions the four commissioners decided to stay with the army and do their best to keep the soldiers in order.[184] Fairfax himself arrived at Saffron Walden on 20 May. In spite of his illness, he had been harshly criticized for being in London while the army was 'in a distemper'.[185] By the time he reached headquarters Cromwell had already returned to the house, where he warned the presbyterians that the soldiers would no longer restrict themselves to purely military concerns, but were becoming involved in larger, political issues. The officers, he said, no longer had control over their men, who were ready to desert them if crossed.[186]

Word of the disunity and discontent aroused alarm in London. Rumours were rife of a presbyterian plan to organize a loyal army in the capital to overawe the New Model if it refused to disband.[187] The soldiers for their part took the precaution of strengthening the guard on the magazine at Oxford.[188] From London Edward Sexby wrote instructing his fellow agitators to approach the officers for money to buy a printing press for the army. The press was duly purchased.[189]

It was still not too late to quench the flames of rebellion in the army. The revocation of the Declaration of Dislike, an act indemnifying the soldiers for acts committed while in arms, and a more generous settlement of arrears would have been sufficient to pacify the bulk of the soldiery. At that juncture however, the political loss of face entailed in repealing the Declaration of Dislike was unacceptable to the presbyterian leadership. An indemnity ordinance had already been introduced in the house, and would be passed in early June.[190] To the soldiers it was unsatisfactory on two counts: (1) there was no provision for the king to sign it and thereby guarantee the soldiers that there would be no reprisals after he was re-enthroned; (2) the ordinance only indemnified soldiers for illegal acts committed under conditions of war ('*in tempore et loco belli*'), whereas many offences, including those of indebtedness, had occurred after the end of active fighting. Of all the grievances arrears would have been the easiest to satisfy. Granted, parliament could not soon have found the nearly £3 million it owed its forces in the spring of 1647; yet for the purpose of disbanding the New Model a fraction of that sum would have sufficed. Fairfax's own foot regiment, one of the most militant in the army, stated at the beginning of June that it would have been content with an initial instalment of four months' pay. Four months' pay for the whole New Model would have equalled about £180,000.[192] The City had already lent £200,000 for the dual purpose of launching the Irish expedition and paying the New Model six weeks' arrears. There is little doubt that it would have been willing to add a little over £100,000 more to be rid of the force it so feared and mistrusted.[193] Around this time Bellièvre, the French ambassador, commented that, if the army unrest went unchecked and led to the overthrow of the English monarchy, it would be largely because 'the presbyterians fail [ed] to act generously in the present circumstance.'[194] It was a just comment.

In mid-May however, the presbyterians were in no mood to deal generously with the army. On the 18th the king's reply to the revised Newcastle Propositions was read at Westminster and at once accepted by both presbyterian leaders and Scots commissioners as a basis for reconciliation. The prospect of coming to terms with the king spurred their determination to dismantle the army.[195] On 21 May concessions were made regarding the soldiers' lesser grievances: conscription for overseas service, compensation for the wounded and the families of the slain, and the allowance for time in uniform to count towards a man's apprenticeship. But there was no indication when these concessions would take the shape of ordinances.[196] An indemnity ordinance was also passed in the Lords,[197] but its terms were still regarded as unsatisfactory. The demand to repeal the Declaration of Dislike was ignored, while the army's hero, Ensign Nicholls, remained in custody.[198]

At about the same time the soldiers received a fresh jolt in the form of a letter to the king from his chief negotiator, John Ashburnham, which Captain Abbott intercepted at Holdenby. Counselling Charles not to come to terms with the army, Ashburnham observed that, with peace on the continent almost concluded, the king could expect the assistance of 40,000 or 50,000 men 'from beyond the seas'.[199] If royalists were plotting to renew the war, reasoned the agitators, why was parliament so eager to disarm? Why too was it so implacably hostile to those who sought social reform? The rejection of the third Independent petition and its burning by the common hangman drove agitators and London radicals into each others' arms.[200] A thrill of horror rippled through presbyterian circles at the testimony of a Buckinghamshire hawker that he had heard of 'a design of Independents to make head against parliament while the army is in discontent; [and] that some who within this fortnight were in their judgement against this way of proceeding, are now for it.'[201] So deep was the suspicion between the army and the parliamentary majority that, when on 18 May they learnt of the house's intention to vote full arrears for the rank and file, the agitators interpreted it as a move to drive a wedge between soldiers and officers.[202]

The agitators had good reason to be suspicious, for the party of Holles and Stapleton, fearing an imminent revolution by a conjunction of radical Independents, Levellers and army firebrands, had now embarked on counter-revolutionary measures. Orders were issued for the magazine at Oxford to be removed to the Tower of London. Massey was sent to secure the garrison at Gloucester, and Pye to take charge of his regiment at Holdenby.[203] Richard Graves, the king's keeper, was summoned to London for consultation on 22 May and returned to his post the same day.[204] Reportedly he had complained that he felt himself 'besieged by some of the army', and so the parliamentary leadership concluded that they should remove the king from this dangerous situation.[205]

The fateful day for the presbyterians was 25 May, when they forced through the Commons a motion for the immediate disbandment of the New Model foot, commencing with Fairfax's own regiment. £40,000 was set aside to cover the two months' arrears that had been promised a week earlier, but at the same time £12,000 was allotted to the London trained bands, now under firm presbyterian control.[206] The presbyterians were confident that the various measures they had taken had so riven the New Model with dissension that it was no longer capable of offering united resistance to disbandment. Cleverly – or so they believed – they had divided volunteers for Ireland from those who declined; officers from men, and foot from horse.[207] Major-General Sedenham Poynts was dispatched from London to York, with instructions to draw up his army in readiness to crush Fairfax's.[208] The Earl of Dunfermline was sent to France, allegedly to per-suade Henrietta Maria to send the Prince of Wales into Scotland to unite the presbyterian and royalist forces there.[209] Men who left the New Model to volunteer for the Irish expedition were quartered in strategic locations. Most of the foot soldiers were sent to Worcestershire, where they were joined with other forces to make up four regiments under presbyterian commanders,[210] but on 6 June they were ordered to advance to Reading.[211] The cavalry and dragoons who split off from the New Model numbered about 400 men. In order to utilize them, an ordinance was adopted authorizing the City to raise its own cavalry. By this means the 400 troopers were incorporated into the trained bands and quartered close to the City.[212] All the troops that left the New Model and were being marshalled for the expected showdown with their erstwhile comrades-in-arms were rewarded with immediate and generous payments.[213] In early June a committee of safety was set up to recruit and organize forces from the counties.[214] Colonel John Birch's regiment in Windsor Castle was brought up to strength, moved to Herefordshire and told to await further instructions. Colonel Thornton was sent to rally the forces in the Isle of Ely.[215] In London the task of mustering the large number of reformadoes was entrusted to Colonel Dalbeir.[216]

On paper the presbyterian strategy for vanquishing the New Model was impressive; yet by August it was in ruins, and those who framed it had fled. How are we to account for the presbyterian collapse? Its causes were two-fold and closely linked. First, the New Model presented a united front against disbandment; secondly, in the face of this unity many elements in the presbyterian coalition wavered and then capitulated before superior force.

Hopes of splitting the horse from the foot, and officers from men, were dashed by the army's tenacity in sticking together against presbyterian enticements. From the agitators came a call for an immediate rendezvous of the army in order to resist piecemeal disbandment. Officers who favoured obedience to parliament had by now either left the army or found themselves rudely driven out by their men.[217] But the great majority of officers opted to stay with their men, hoping that if they rode the back of the mutiny they would have a better chance of reining in its worst excesses. The number of senior regimental officers of the rank of captain- lieutenant and above who left the army in May and June 1647 was fifty-seven. This represents just over a quarter (25.8 per cent) of the officers of those ranks in the New Model at the time.[218] If we look at the officer class as a whole, the percentage who left shrinks much smaller. According to army records, in the spring of 1647 there were 2320 officers of all ranks.[219] The number who volunteered and/or left the army by June is not known with exactitude, but the highest figure cited at the time was 167, or 7 per cent of the total.[220] The percentage of rank and file who left was even less. The 800 or so who separated from their comrades represented little more than 4 per cent of the soldiery.[221]

Overall then, the army showed remarkable solidarity in resisting parliament's efforts to pit one man against another. Nevertheless, the qualitative impact of these departures was considerable. Eight colonels, two lieutenant-colonels and seven majors were replaced. The cost of restoring unity to the army was the elimination of political presbyterians like Colonels Pye, Graves, Butler, Sheffield and Rossiter in the cavalry, and Harley, Herbert and Fortescue in the infantry. The fifty-seven senior officers who quit could have been counted upon to act as a brake against the more radical demands of the agitators – for a march on London, for example. Equally significant, the men who stepped into their places – individuals such as Harrison, Pride, Tomlinson, Goffe and John Cobbett – were on the whole less socially distinguished and more politically militant than their predecessors.

When the parliamentary order for disbandment reached the army the Council of War ordered the regiments to contract their quarters for a general rendezvous. Fairfax shifted headquarters from Saffron Walden to the agitators' meeting place at Bury St Edmunds.[222] As they explained to the the House of Lords, given that the soldiers were determined to meet together anyway, it was better to yield to their insistence than to have an illegal and therefore far more dangerous meeting occur.[223] In the meantime Rainborowe's regiment marched from Hampshire to Oxford to secure the magazine against parliament's attempts to remove it to London, and the money sent for disbanding Ingoldsby's and Fairfax's regiments was seized.[224] Because Fairfax had again fallen ill,[225] a committee of officers composed of Ireton, Colonels Lilburne, Okey, Rich and Harrison and

Lieutenant-Colonel Jackson was appointed by the Council of War to draft a document for his approval.[226]

The Seizure of the King

The most decisive of all the army's moves to avoid extinction was its taking of Charles I into custody. By the end of May 1647 officers and agitators had become unshakably convinced of a presbyterian plot to transfer the king to Scotland.[227] The motive they ascribed to their foes was to make Charles the leader of the coalition of forces being constructed for military action against the New Model. Already the agitators had been meditating counter-action to remove him from the hands of the parliamentary commissioners and the presbyterian colonel Richard Graves.[228] Fairfax was politically too moderate and too ill in any case to encourage so brazen a step. But Cromwell had recovered from his illness and knew the full dimensions of the menace facing the army. To his house in Drury Lane there now trailed an assortment of sectaries and officers. Frugally entertained by Mrs Cromwell with small beer, bread and butter, they laid bare to the lieutenant-general their fear of the presbyterians and their ideas for the army's salvation. At one of these encounters in the garden at Drury Lane, on the night of 31 May, Cromwell approved the plan by Cornet George Joyce of Fairfax's horse regiment to march to Holdenby and replace the guards under Graves with troops whose loyalty to the army could be counted upon.[229]

Joyce and the agitators had already put together a force of 1000 horse, many drawn, it was said, from the very regiments of the presbyterian colonels Pye, Rossiter and Graves that guarded the king.[230] Alerted by Chillenden to presbyterian plans to transfer the magazine from Oxford to the Tower of London, they had ridden to Oxford on the 29th, where they secured the train of artillery with its store of powder and ammunition. The day after, Joyce gave orders to part of his force to advance towards Holdenby before he rode up to London.[231] On 1 June, armed with Cromwell's blessing, Joyce caught up with them, and they all proceeded to the royal manor of Holdenby to block the anticipated removal of the king by Graves and the parliamentary commissioners. Night had fallen before they reached the manor house, but the reluctance of Graves's men to resist their comrades-in-arms gave the colonel and a handful of loyal officers no choice but to quit the grounds. The four parliamentary commissioners also bowed to superior force, though unlike Graves they did not flee.

Joyce had accomplished his mission without a hitch. But he was still very nervous. He could not quell a suspicion that Graves would soon come back with reinforcements to wrest the king from his hands.[232] So at 8 a.m. on 3 June he wrote an urgent letter to London asking for further instructions.[233] Who was the intended recipient of Joyce's letter? It bore the name of no addressee, but according to the MP Laurence Whitacre Joyce had directed 'that it should be delivered to Lieutenant-General Cromwell, or in his absence to Sir Arthur Hesilrige or Colonel Fleetwood.'[234] Who answered the letter we do not know, but there can have been little time for Cromwell to deal with it. By the afternoon of the 3rd he was in imminent personal danger, since all London now knew what Joyce had done. That night Holles's party resolved to arrest Cromwell when he came to the House of Commons the next day. Anticipating their intention, the 'subtle fox'[235] opted to take refuge with the New Model. Before sunrise on the 4th he had set out in the company of Hugh Peters for army headquarters, now at Newmarket. By now Joyce had decided that he could not wait for Cromwell's instructions, even assuming there were any. More and more jittery about the prospect of being counterattacked by a superior force, he took matters into his own hands, doubtless spurred on by the soldiers around him. Late in the evening of the 3rd he resolved to transport the king and his servants to a safer location. It was after ten o'clock, and Charles was in bed, but Joyce insisted on breaking into his chamber and telling him that he must leave Holdenby early the next morning.

At daybreak Charles signalled his acquiescence but demanded to know by what authority Joyce acted. By the authority of 'the soldiery of the army', the cornet replied. The king was unsatisfied and pressed to know if he had anything in writing from Sir Thomas Fairfax. Joyce evaded the question, but the king would not be put off. 'I pray Mr Joyce, deal ingeniously with me, and tell me what commission you have?' 'Here is my commission', answered the cornet. 'Where?' asked the king. 'Behind me' (pointing to the mounted soldiers). At which the king smiled and said 'it is as fair a commission, and as well written as he had seen a commission in his life; and a company of handsome proper gentlemen as he had seen a great while.'[236]

Having elicited the nature of Joyce's authority, Charles next enquired where they were going. The cornet did not appear to have a fixed idea, but at length deferred to the king's suggestion that they go to Newmarket because 'its air did very well agree with him.'[237] Was it the superior air or the fact that the army rendezvous was about to be held at Newmarket that prompted Charles's choice? Whatever the reason Fairfax would take pains to keep the king well out of sight on that risky occasion.[238]

Once he learnt what Joyce had done Fairfax dispatched Edward Whalley with his regiment to take the king back to Holdenby. When the two parties met the situation was potentially explosive. Conflict was avoided when Charles intervened to say that he had no desire to return to Holdenby, but wanted to press on to Newmarket. Joyce went ahead, and after he arrived Fairfax relieved him of his charge, putting the more reliable Whalley at the head of the king's guards. Writing to the House of Lords, he assured them 'as in the presence of God ... that his remove of His Majesty from Holdenby was without any design, knowledge or privity thereof on our parts; and a thing altogether unexpected to us.'[239] In the king's presence the general officers likewise swore that Joyce had acted 'without their privity, knowledge or consent.'[240] Joyce and Cromwell would later exchange heated words over their respective responsibilities for what had happened at Holdenby, with Cromwell calling the cornet a rascal for insinuating that he was only carrying out Cromwell's instructions.[241]

Was Cromwell a liar? Are we to believe that the agitators acted alone, without the sanction of their superior officers? Neither royalists, presbyterians nor radicals could credit such a notion.[242] If we mark closely the wording of the grandees' disclaimer, we can see how it may be reconciled with the suspicions of everyone around them. It is almost certain that Cromwell and other higher officers did indeed give orders to secure the king at Holdenby and prevent his *removal* by hostile forces. In effect they decided to furnish the king with new guards. But they had not sanctioned his forcible *removal* to army headquarters. That decision had been negotiated by Joyce and the king alone. Thus, by remaining silent on the question of who authorized the *seizure* of the king, and merely denying that they had authorized his *removal* from Holdenby, the grandees stayed just on the right side of the truth.[243]

But what of the larger question: who at this critical moment was in control of the army? Were the feet giving orders to the head, to use a seventeenth-century metaphor, or did the head still have charge over the body military? Though Fairfax's memoirs would later claim that he was the helpless puppet of political activists between 1647 and 1649, the claim is exaggerated.[244] It is true that at the time he wrote to the Commons Speaker, 'I am forced to yield to something out of order, to keep the army from disorder, or worse inconveniences.'[245] But he chose not to join the 167 other officers who quit the army. By staying on as commander-in-chief, he implicitly endorsed what the agitators had done.

This is not to gainsay that there was plenty of conflict between agitators and grandees during the summer and autumn of 1647. But the arguments over whether to invade London, how to treat with the king and whether to impose a constitutional settlement on England masked a basic harmony of purpose to which the conflicts were only a secondary theme. All agreed that the army must stay united, that its grievances must be satisfied and that there ought to be an honourable peace with the king.

The agitators may have forced the pace of events until 4 June, but on the

5th the grandees, perhaps led by Ireton, moved for the creation of a council of the army consisting of four representatives from each regiment – two officers and two soldiers plus the fifteen or more officers of the general staff. In this, the first formal experiment in representative government, it was shrewdly prearranged that the officers should have a permanent majority over the rank and file.

In contrast to the instinctive drawing-together of all ranks was the discord and lack of confidence displayed by the constituent members of the presbyterian coalition. Basic disunity caused the coalition to pursue contradictory policies of confrontation and conciliation.[246] The policies worked at cross-purposes and fatally weakened the struggle against the New Model, which, after it had excluded presbyterians from its ranks, hewed to a consistent policy of self-defence. The inability of Holles and Stapleton to inspire confidence in their followers was what initially led men on the fringe such as Philip Skippon to waver, and Whitelocke to withdraw his support.[247] Two of the parliamentary commissioners to the army, Lords Nottingham and De La Warr, decided to work for a reconciliation between the two bodies, warning that to levy troops in London and encourage desertion from the New Model would likely 'beget some disorder'.[248]

Some of the presbyterians' closest friends displayed the same lack of faith in their leadership.[249] During the month of June the City magistrates too began to waver, for the good reason that the trained bands refused to obey their new presbyterian officers. Even the mayor and sheriffs' command to turn out 'upon pain of death' could not make them budge. Boys jeered the drummers in the streets, while shopkeepers ignored the order to shut their shops.[250] Only in Westminster did any substantial numbers answer the mayor's summons, but by the afternoon they had all returned home. The timorousness of the trained bands is not surprising when it is recalled that they had seen no active service since before the foundation of the New Model. Indeed, the last time they had even been mustered was for the Earl of Essex's funeral the previous autumn.[251] They knew they were no match for Fairfax's battle-scarred veterans.

In the face of popular rejection of the presbyterian strategy of confrontation, the Common Council altered its tactics and named a committee of three to reside with the army and work for a rapprochement.[252] Once at Fairfax's headquarters these men gained insight into the army's grievances and described them sympathetically to the Common Council. Their well-meaning diplomacy further undermined presbyterian strategy.[253]

The hope of aid from the Northern Army under Poynts was dashed by the timely action of the agitators. Emissaries from the New Model persuaded the northern soldiers to flout Poynts's commands and throw in their lot with their comrades in the south. Early in July militants from his own army arrested him at his house in York and brought him to Fairfax's headquarters in Reading to answer the charge of fomenting a new war.[254] Unenthusiastic about court-martialling higher officers, Fairfax released Poynts, but later sent John Lambart to replace him as commander in the north.[255]

Two other members of the hoped-for presbyterian coalition, the king and the Scots, also turned into broken reeds. In the spring, cavaliers in London had volunteered their help to overthrow the New Model. But, shortly after he was taken into Joyce's custody, Charles, impressed by the liberal treatment and expressions of friendliness he received, ordered his supporters to cease their co-operation with the presbyterians. This royalist about-face was instrumental in convincing the City to stop supplying money for the mustering of a counter-revolutionary force.[256] Waller and Massey had each written to the Marquess of Argyle inviting him to bring a Scottish army into England, but he refused to commit himself.[257] The Estates did indeed meet several times in Edinburgh to debate such a scheme, but by 12 July all they could agree upon was that anyone who wanted to invade England was welcome to do so on his own.[258] By then the moment had passed when assistance from Scotland could have made a material difference to the presbyterians.

Once the king was lost the parliamentary majority displayed their want of confidence in the presbyterian leadership by switching to a policy of appeasement towards the army. Sitting until 2 a.m. on the night of 8–9 June, the Commons erased the 29 March Declaration of Dislike from their journal, and the Lords grudgingly followed suit a few days later.[259] On 7 June an unqualified ordinance of indemnity for all offences committed by soldiers while in the service of parliament became law.[260]

The Solemn Engagement at Newmarket

But it was too late for appeasement to work. Concessions that would have quieted the army in March or April were now greeted with scepticism. At this juncture the soldiers, content no longer to press for satisfaction of their material demands, were crying for vengeance on those who had plotted their destruction, and for fundamental changes in England's constitution. Their confidence was only increased by the intoxicating experience of unity during the general rendezvous near Newmarket on 4–5 June. Once the dissenting officers had been 'hooted off the field',[261] the men listened attentively to 'An Humble Representation of the Dissatisfactions of the Armie', which had been inspired if not written by the agitators. In addition to rehearsing the familiar grievances that had been accumulated over the past four months, it excoriated parliament for failing to revoke the Declaration of Dislike or punish its authors.[262] Relieved that most of the higher officers had thrown in their lot with them, the soldiers greeted Sir Thomas Fairfax with rapturous joy. He paid them the compliment of visiting each regiment in turn, hoping thereby to keep the extremists under control. The thirteen regiments present – six of horse and seven of foot – cannot have numbered over 10,000 men, but it was a full day's work to address each of them. Not until nightfall was Fairfax able to snatch a short rest in Kentford village.[263] Cromwell arrived in Newmarket that same evening, and was present for the second day's transactions, which were to have far more momentous consequences than those of the first. By the terms of the Solemn Engagement officers and soldiers entered into a military covenant that they would 'cheerfully and readily disband' only when the grievances specified the previous day had been redressed. The soldiers' safety and that of the freeborn people of England in general would have to be guaranteed by a watertight provision of indemnity, and also by the displacement from power of those who had abused the army and endangered the kingdom. The judgement as to whether these conditions had been met would be made by a council consisting of the general officers and four representatives from each regiment: two commissioned officers and two soldiers. The general would be responsible for calling this body together.

The Solemn Engagement ended with a disavowal of any wish to overthrow the presbyterian form of church government or establish 'licentiousness in religion under pretence of liberty of conscience'. But the authors did not disguise their desire to 'promote such an establishment of common and equal right and freedom to the whole, as all might equally partake of.'

The document was probably drafted by Ireton, but it must also have been cleared by the agitators before being presented to the army as a whole. By instituting a general council, the officers assimilated the agitators into the army's command structure. As we have noted, the composition of the council gave the officers a permanent majority over the rank and file.[264] Moreover, the general's power to convene the council or not to convene it, as he saw fit, meant that it would remain firmly under Fairfax's control, or of those who advised him. Neither of these provisions seems to have bothered the agitators at the time, for they doubtless viewed the achievement of unity between officers and men as of far greater importance. Later the Levellers would argue that the Solemn Engagement had dissolved the existing power structure of the army and vested supreme authority in the General Council. In 1649, as we shall see, disaffected radicals would maintain that the Newmarket covenant required that the rank and file through their agitators assent to any scheme to disband or divide the army. In the heady days of

1647, however, the spirit of trust within the army prevented anyone from raising such tendentious points.[265] The document referred to 'two commission officers, and two soldiers to be chosen for each regiment.' Is it safe to assume that the agitators were elected by the rank and file, or did the officers play a role in the selections?[266] We know that the army had thrown up agitators several weeks before they were formally recognized by the Solemn Engagement. They first appear, a jumble of officers and men, in a letter to Fairfax on 25 April.[267] A week later two representatives from each of seven horse regiments, calling themselves 'commissioners', attached their names to the *Apologie of the Common Souldiers*. Over succeeding weeks more and more regiments selected agitators or 'adjutators', as they were also called. At least three regiments, and probably more, selected one or two agitators from each troop or company.[268] Thus there were up to twenty agitators per regiment. In the north the seven regiments under Colonel-General Poynts 'elected' two agitators each in early July.[269] John Lilburne later maintained that the agitators were 'chosen by common consent from amongst themselves'.[270] According to another radical source the Council of the Army was constituted not by the general, but 'in a parliamentary way by the soldiers' free election.'[271] It seems plausible that each regiment may have had a mini-council of agitators, numbering up to twelve in a horse regiment and up to twenty in a foot regiment. This mini-council may have elected the two men to represent the regiment in the General Council of the Army. I have not come across any evidence that the officers supervised this process or selected the agitators themselves.[272]

In the autumn new 'agents' would emerge from five of the cavalry regiments to promote *The Case of the Armie Truly Stated*. By November the number of regiments claiming to have new agents had swelled to ten, in addition to the general's lifeguard. Some regiments showed only one new agent, but Twisleton's boasted six – evidently one for each troop. The status of these new representatives was dubious. They seem not to have been elected by the soldiers they purported to represent, but to have been self-appointed.[273] They were repudiated by their regiments, and were not heard of again after the Ware mutiny.

Between June and November, however, there was close co-operation and unity of purpose between officers and agitators. Thanks to the survival of William Clarke's account book of disbursements from the army's contingency fund, we now know that the agitators' activities after the Newmarket rendezvous were approved of and even directed by the general staff. The agitators made trips all over the country to explain and garner support for the army's defiance of parliament – to London, Kent, Wales, Hereford, Bristol and the north. Because of the size of the Northern Army, and its value as a buffer against a Scottish invasion, the agitators invested much effort into winning it over. They downplayed their material grievances, proclaiming instead their goal as

> the glory of God, the just preservation of the king's person, the just privileges of parliament, the redeeming of the lives and liberties of the free people of England from tyranny, oppression and injustice, the maintenance of just laws, and the necessary support and defence of this kingdom, together with the free and impartial distribution of justice to all.[274]

The agitators' political work in the north reached its climax when they arrested Colonel Poynts and brought him before Fairfax. They also arranged for the printing of army pamphlets, and bought a printing press. All their expenses were paid for by army headquarters. A few key agitators, such as Edward Sexby, William Allen, Richard Kingdome, Cornet George Joyce, Lieutenant Edmund Chillenden and Captain Edmund Rolphe, were issued substantial sums of money. Rolphe, for example, who seems to have been a paymaster to the agitators, received £150 in two instalments. A payment of £30 to the agitators who arrested Colonel Poynts and brought him south shows that this action was approved by headquarters. The first recorded payment to an agitator was made on 10 June. During the next five months they received over £1000 for their expenses. The grandees' temporary harmony of purpose with both civilian and military radicals is further suggested by the £2 paid to Ensign Nicholls in compensation for his imprisonment, the £19 12s. paid to Major Tulidah for his arrears, and the £10 paid to John Lilburne on 7 August, perhaps in the vain hope of discouraging him from making further wounding comments about the grandees.[275]

The Impeachment of the Eleven Members

By July, Lilburne and Overton were complaining that the new arrangements had sapped the agitators' authority, but, as Woolrych has observed, the documents the agitators themselves published around that time conveyed no sense that they were being abused or cold-shouldered.[276] They collaborated closely, for example, in drawing up and presenting to the House of Commons, on 6 July, the articles of impeachment against the Eleven Members. It was at their behest that the army had formally demanded impeachment proceedings around 8 June.[277] Six days later the army lodged a brief indictment of the Eleven Members with the parliamentary commissioners at St Albans. The MPs were charged with having endeavoured to overthrow the rights and liberties of the subject, foment hostility against the army in parliament, divide the army against itself, raise another army to embroil the kingdom in a new war, and encourage reformadoes to intimidate the members of the House of Commons.[278] A showdown between army and parliament was averted by the flight of the

Eleven on 27 June, and both sides heaved a sigh of relief.[279] On the eve of the submission of the impeachment to parliament the Council of War appointed seventeen officers and four agitators to meet with the lawyers and approve the text of the impeachment. On 6 July six senior officers, led by Colonel Scrope, and six agitators, of whom Edward Sexby and Henry Gittings were from the ranks, submitted the charge to the House of Commons.[280] It was a formidable document, containing twenty-five articles and running to over thirty folio pages in a contemporary manuscript.[281] Many of the articles were of minor importance, and would almost certainly have been thrown out had the impeachment ever come to a trial before the Lords. Nevertheless, the core of the document was an indictment of the presbyterian leadership for having plotted a counter-revolution against the army and its Independent friends in the House of Commons. There were four key ingredients in this counter-revolutionary plot. First, the presbyterian leaders had manipulated the House of Commons, after many members had left for the night, into adopting a resolution condemning the army's petitioners as 'enemies to the state'. Secondly, they had invited the Scots and other foreign forces into the kingdom to aid their designs. Aiming to restore the king on their own terms, they had recently advised his wife to send the Prince of Wales into Scotland to head the army that was being assembled there. Thirdly, they had ordered forces that had supposedly been recruited for Ireland back from Worcestershire to Reading 'with an evil intent to beget a new war in England.' Fourthly, they had purged several 'eminent and faithful men' from the London militia. They had also harassed the Leveller petitioners in London, imprisoning two leaders, Nicholas Tew and Major Alexander Tulidah.

To avoid handling this hot potato, the Commons postponed debate until the 8th. The twelve from the army patiently turned up on that day, only to witness the shelving of the impeachment again 'by reason of other business'. Finally on the 10th the Commons grasped the nettle, but after a full day's debate came to no conclusion.[282] On the 12th, however, they voted it 'a charge', and commanded the accused to give their answer by the following week.[283] To no one's surprise the Eleven Members remained silent, and in the rush of events during the climacteric summer of 1647 the impeachment never again came before the House.

The Presbyterian Counter-revolution and Preparations to Invade London

We return now to the army and to Cambridgeshire, where Fairfax summoned another general rendezvous on 10 June, this time at Triploe Heath, not far from Cambridge. The purpose of the assembly was to hear the latest response from parliament, and the soldiers were instructed to be 'silent and civil' while the commissioners spoke. An officer of Fairfax's horse regiment asked that its answer might be returned by the officers and agitators whom it had elected, and when the soldiers were consulted they unanimously endorsed this suggested mode of consultation. Other regiments, however, instantly demonstrated their dissatisfaction with parliament's offer, and according to one account hooted the commissioners off the field.[284]

Taking their cue from the bluntly expressed militancy of the troops, the army leaders advanced their headquarters to St Albans, a mere 20 miles from London. At the army's approach both parliament and City had second thoughts about their previous belligerence. But simultaneously they were being pulled in the opposite direction by the intransigent members of the Derby House Committee and the turbulent reformadoes who daily besieged parliament.[285] Efforts were made to bring the Scots army into England, while the troops quartered in Worcestershire were told that they would be employed 'in a new war', and the reformadoes in the metropolis were mobilized. The few precious cavalry who had left the New Model were stationed in various defensive positions on the outskirts of London. On 6 June, Colonel Massey had ridden through the streets of London in his coach, exhorting the citizens to defend themselves against the madmen of the army, and that night double guards were posted and the portcullis of every gate was slammed down.[286] At times it seemed that the right hand did not know what the left was doing. Parliament, as we have seen, had adopted several motions to appease the army, and the London Common Council added its weight to the peace effort.[287] At the same time, however, the City magistrates sought and received permission to raise their own cavalry.[288] War preparations in the capital were co-ordinated by parliament's Committee of Safety and the London Militia Committee.[289] Yet the inhabitants had less and less stomach for battle the closer the army approached.[290]

In theory the army's chief demands of the previous month had been met. The soldiers would be paid in full; their safety against prosecution had been guaranteed; and the army's honour had been vindicated. The contradictory signals from the capital, however, prompted the soldiers not to lay down their arms, but to continue raising the stakes. No longer concerned about their honour, they still feared for their safety, and for the liberty of all Englishmen, so long as Holles's party controlled the apparatus of government.[291]

On 14 June, without formally involving the agitators, Fairfax and his Council of War announced an about-face in army policy. Whereas on the 10th they had assured the City that they sought 'no alteration of the civil government', they now unveiled a full-dress political programme. Their justification for so doing was that 'we were not a mere mercenary army hired to serve any arbitrary power of a state, but called forth and conjured by the several declarations of parliament to the defence of our own and the people's just rights and liberties.'[292] In the name of the people they called for a purge of all delinquent and corrupt members of parliament, a fixed limit on the life of future parliaments, an end to the king's arbitrary power of dissolution, the right of petition, and a public accounting for the vast sums levied during the war. Tacked on at the end was a request for some 'provision for tender consciences'.[293] The most likely author of the *Declaration or Representation* was Commissary-General Henry Ireton. It embodied the minimal programme that would satisfy the agitators, who had now begun to clamour for a march on London to pull the Eleven Members out by the ears, and return the militia to Independent hands. Parliament did not publicly acknowledge these political demands, but on 16 June voted a month's pay for the army. The money found its way into the men's pockets a few days later, enabling the officers to keep the lid on rank-and-file discontent for a little bit longer.[294] Nevertheless, continuing reports of a hostile military build-up kept the army in a state of high tension. Not only were cavalry and dragoons being stationed around London,[295] but Holles and Stapleton were apparently organizing the reformadoes, who still swirled about the Commons in menacing fashion.[296] In response Colonel Rainborowe and Major Disbrowe were deployed at Windsor with two regiments of foot and 200 cavalry respectively.[297] Windsor Castle was occupied, as was the blockhouse at Tilbury, while additional detachments were stationed at Kingston upon Thames and in Kent.[298] The army's quarters were drawn closer together, and Major Twisleton was ordered to bring Rossiter's regiment down from Lincolnshire.[299] The presbyterian Colonel Birch was arrested before he could get to his garrison at Hereford. Though they soon released him, his agitators kept possession of his brother the major, as well as Hereford Castle and the money in it.[300] Leaving the king at Royston, Fairfax moved his headquarters in an arc around London, from St Albans to Berkhamsted, and then to Uxbridge, a mere 15 miles west of the houses of parliament, on 25 June.[301] Several foot regiments took up positions considerably closer than that.[302] Matching these military manoeuvres was the army's harsh public voice. The *Remonstrance of the Representations of the Army*[303] added to the familiar agenda demands for liberty of conscience, for reform of the judiciary and 'that the glory of God may be exalted'. Two days later it complained that the reformadoes were still out of control and demanded their suppression, the dismissal of the troops that had recently left the New Model, and the expulsion of the Eleven Members from the Commons. It also flatly rejected parliament's command to bring the king to Richmond, alleging that this would simply put him within reach of those who were plotting against the kingdom.[304]

These words and actions brought home to the moderates in parliament and City that the army meant business. The month leading up to 26 July was consequently a period of adroit conflict management by both sides.[305] The clear message that the City did not wish to fight, combined with the army's presence almost on London's doorstep, persuaded the Eleven Members that it was time to quit the parliamentary arena.[306] Hard on the heels of their departure the Commons ordered that no soldier should leave the army without Fairfax's permission, thus signalling that the attempt to split the army was at an end. They also adopted without division a resolution 'that they do own this army as their army; and will make provision for their maintenance, and will take order, that, so soon as money can be conveniently raised, they shall be paid up equally with those that have left the army.'[307] Favourably impressed by the withdrawal of the Eleven, as well as by parliament's gestures of appeasement, the army expressed its confidence that its remaining demands would soon be met.[308] It also agreed to suspend proceedings against the Eleven until the 'greater and more general matters of the kingdom' had been settled.[309] As a tangible sign of appreciation, Fairfax removed his headquarters from Uxbridge to High Wycombe and then to Reading, 36 miles west of London.[310] In spite of the army's submission of the articles of impeachment against the Eleven Members on 6 July, and the persistence of reports of political turbulence in the capital, the movement for reconciliation appeared to gather momentum with the Commons' order for the disbandment of the four infantry regiments whose stationing near Worcester had been such an offence to the New Model.[311]

On 16 July, using as a pretext the mutiny of the Northern Army against Colonel Poynts, Fairfax wrote to the Commons Speaker asking that all the land forces in England be unified under one command. The Commons responded with alacrity, making Fairfax supreme commander, responsible both for the security of England and for the conquest of Ireland.[312] This gesture decisively laid to rest the army's nightmare of the previous three months, in which the northern regiments, the various garrison and provincial troops and the soldiers who had left the New Model were welded into a counter-force to crush it. Fairfax now seemed to be at the height of his influence.[313] At this juncture, from the army's perspective, only London still lay in enemy hands. What to do about the capital was the immediate occasion for the assembling of the Council of the Army for its first meeting on 16 July.

The Reading Debates

The agitators had made their demand for a march on London the chief item on the agenda. They were convinced that, the farther away they were from the capital, the slacker parliament became in its efforts to meet their demands. At the same time the high presbyterians continued to enlist men to oppose the army. An immediate march was needed

1   to expel the eleven impeached Members from the House;
2   to restore the London militia to Independent hands;
3   to obtain a declaration against the inviting-in of foreign forces;
4   to release John Lilburne and other radicals from prison; and
5   to secure army pay on a basis equal with those who had deserted it.[314]

Although the Representation was signed only by three officer agitators – Major Abbott, Captain John Clarke and Captain Rolphe – there is little doubt that it enjoyed the support of the agitators as a whole.[315]

To a man the senior officers argued against an immediate march on London. For Ireton it looked too much like picking a quarrel just when parliament had satisfied most of the army's demands. Cromwell counselled patience, exhorting the agitators not to 'quarrell with every dog in the street that barks at us.'

But on the agitators' side patience was in short supply. They argued that parliament had made its concessions precisely because the army had approached London at the end of June. If they expected their proposals for a settlement to be taken seriously, they must be ready to use force to back them up. In vain Cromwell tried to convince them that the army's over-riding priority should be unity. To them it seemed that his idea of unity boiled down to agreeing with the grandees. His eloquence also failed to persuade them of the futility of coercion. 'That [which] you have by force, I look upon it as nothing', he declared with unconscious irony.

Radical officers such as Lieutenant Scotten and Cornet Spencer kept up the attack, urging that the army must not disappoint its friends in London. They were particularly incensed at the continued imprisonment of Lilburne, Overton, Tew and others. Cromwell shot back that they should be more concerned with the good of the kingdom than with pleasing the London Levellers. 'That's the question, what's for their good, not what pleases them', he declared, giving voice to an impeccably puritan principle.

The Heads of the Proposals

The next day (17 July), hoping to convince the agitators of the genuineness of their efforts to reach a settlement, the higher officers introduced the draft of the Heads of the Proposals. This document had been Ireton's main pre-occupation since the completion of the impeachment of the Eleven Members at the beginning of the month. To the frustration of the parliamentary commissioners, negotiations were stalled while Ireton and Lambart worked on 'the foundation of a treaty, or rather a whole map of every particular to be treated upon.'[316] As he sketched out his 'whole map' Ireton was in daily contact with Lord Wharton, one of the commissioners at headquarters. Another peer, Lord Saye, was also closely consulted. Communication with high-ranking friends in London was maintained through three army intermediaries stationed there: Dr William Stane, the commissary-general of musters, Major Leonard Watson, the scoutmaster-general, and Colonel Nathaniel Rich.[317] On 14 July the Council of War spent the whole day discussing the Heads of the Proposals. More at issue than the substance of the draft treaty was the question of whether it should be published before the London militia and the kingdom as a whole were in 'safe and confiding hands.' Having cleared the Council of War, the Heads went on the 17th to the Council of the Army. William Clarke's notes for that day are only fragmentary, but we know that it was the first opportunity the agitators had had to hear Ireton's draft. Speaking for his comrades, William Allen asked for more time to assess them, since 'we are most of us but young statesmen.' Showing no inclination to ram through his proposals without proper debate, Ireton agreed that a committee of twelve officers and twelve agitators should scrutinize the Proposals and report back to the Council of the Army.[318]

The terms of the Heads of the Proposals represented at once the most generous and the most radical settlement that Charles was ever offered.[319] Compared to the Newcastle Propositions of twelve months earlier, they treated him handsomely. Parliament was to control the armed forces for ten years instead of twenty. Instead of nominating the chief officers of state and judges in perpetuity, it was to do so for only ten years. In religion there was to be a broad liberty of conscience. Bishops, rather than being abolished outright, would merely lose their coercive power. The Book of Common Prayer would be allowed to continue in use, so long as it was not made compulsory. The tolerant character of the church envisioned by Ireton and his colleagues was underlined by the provision for the abolition of tithes.[320] The penalties for royalists would have been much less harsh, and a maximum of five only would have been excepted from pardon. Everyone else, including of course parliament's soldiers, would have had the benefit of an act of oblivion for all illegal acts done in prosecution of the war.

The army's document went far beyond the Newcastle Propositions in its suggestions for refashioning the English polity. Parliaments were to become biennial, and the existing one was to be dissolved within a year at the latest. Each parliament would sit for no fewer than 120 and no more than 240 days. Seats would be redistributed strictly according to taxation. In addition there was a long string of social reforms that was probably added by the committee of officers and agitators established on 17 July.[321] The burdens of

Plate 4 Commissary-General Henry Ireton

(Reproduced by courtesy of The National Portrait Gallery, London)

the common people were to be lightened by the abolition of the hated excise, the forest laws, trade monopolies and imprisonment for debt. Tax rates were to be equalized. The people were also to enjoy the right of petition and the right not to incriminate themselves in criminal trials. Finally, all public debts, including the army's arrears, were to be paid off. These social reforms almost certainly reflected the influence of the Levellers, William Walwyn in particular, on army thinking.[322]

Before being published the Heads of the Proposals were shown to the king and his advisers on about 23 July. The officers' awareness of the pervasive popular longing for the return of the king to his capital made it imperative to show him that the army could effect his return on terms more attractive than those being offered by parliament. Their agent in this delicate mission was Robert Huntington, major of Oliver Cromwell's regiment.[323] Believing that the army could not subsist without him, Charles rebuffed Huntington, confident that he would soon be back with better terms. As it happened, the counter-revolutionary assault on parliament on 26 July lent greater urgency to the army's quest for rapprochement with the king. If it could have escorted both him and the fugitive members back to Westminster, the popular rejoicing would have stopped the attempted presbyterian *coup d'état* in its tracks. There can be no doubt that the senior officers were passionately eager to come to a binding agreement with Charles before the army embarked on its trek to the capital.[324] To Berkeley they had confided that if the king came to terms with them they would force parliament to ratify the agreement, even if it meant purging the opposition.[325]

Consequently, on about the 28th a delegation composed of Ireton, Rainborowe, Hammond and Rich rode to the king's residence at Woburn, and spent three hours in negotiation with him. Unfortunately, the ill-judged hostility of all his advisers except Berkeley encouraged Charles to entertain the army emissaries with 'sharp and bitter language'. 'You cannot be without me', he informed them; 'you will fall to ruin if I do not sustain you.' Rainborowe, who had little regard for the king in any case, took this outburst as his cue to walk out of the conference. Returning to the army he retailed the news of the king's appalling treatment of its delegation.[326]

The king's obstinacy and the upheavals in London would delay publication of the Heads of the Proposals until August. On 31 July the members of both houses who had fled the disorders in London encountered senior army officers at Syon House, the Earl of Northumberland's Middlesex residence. There the Heads of the Proposals received a final going-over. The following day the Council of War adopted them, and on 2 August they were printed as the army's own programme for the settlement of the kingdom.[327]

The Assault on Parliament, 26 July 1647

Meanwhile, disillusioned by the king's arrogance, the senior officers digested the unpalatable truth that they would have to march to London unfortified by the most highly prized piece in the political chess game that was now being played out. London had in any case now erupted with counter-revolutionary violence. This had been brought about by the convergence of several forces:

1   popular frustration at the failure of parliament to reach a settlement with the king that preserved his honour and rights;
2   high-presbyterian despair over the army's apparently imminent success at coming to terms with him; and
3   civic indignation at the loss of control over the London trained bands.

Although Fairfax had been created commander-in-chief of all parliament's land forces, for the moment he was not able to exploit his expanded authority to bring the London trained bands under control. Since 4 May they had been in the hands of men loyal to Holles. In their overweening ambition the new London Militia Committee had also purged the Southwark and Tower Hamlets militias.[328] Snubbing the conciliatory policy of the parliamentary commissioners and the City's own emissaries, they had also joined forces with the parliamentary Committee of Safety, to continue preparing for a confrontation with the New Model.[329] But the agitators were alert to the menace of high presbyterianism, and had been pressing since the middle of June, if not before, to have the purge of the London Militia Committee reversed.[330] The issue had been debated at Reading on 16 July, and was to be the paramount cause of the invasion of London.[331] On 22 July, however, the need for a march on the capital seemingly disappeared when the Commons voted to return the London militia to the Independents who had controlled it before 4 May.[332] Seeing that the presbyterian counter-revolution was in ruins, the committee members sympathetic to Holles salvaged what they could from the wreckage of their scheme by hurriedly voting money for their friends.[333] The day before the Commons vote there had been a meeting of royalist and conservative citizens in Skinners' Hall, at which a 'Petition and Solemn Engagement' was adopted asking for the king to be brought to London 'without the nearer approach of the army'.[334] The following evening a crowd of between 2000 and 3000 reformadoes met in St James's Field, resolving to throw their weight behind the campaign for the restoration of the king.[335] The news that the Commons had voted to restore the old militia committee threw

Plate 5 The General Council of the Army in Session, from the title page of the *Army Book of Declarations*

(The British Library: Thomason E409/25)

these men into a frenzy of despair as they realized that their vision of a settlement with the king and the disbandment of the New Model had been irretrievably smashed. Fruitlessly they petitioned the Common Council to have the presbyterian militia committee restored, for it was not in that body's power to grant the request. On the night of Saturday the 24th they pressured the council into taking their petition to the House of Commons, but by the time they arrived the Commons had already adjourned.[336] In rage and frustration they went back to the city, where they found the Independent-dominated militia committee transacting business in Guildhall. Spoiling for a fight, some young members of the crowd invaded their meeting place and drove them out, threatening to 'hang their guts about their ears' if they caught them meeting together again.[337]

As soon as parliament resumed sitting on Monday the 26th, both houses were besieged by an angry crowd demanding the return of the militia to the May committee. When the Lords rebuffed a delegation of aldermen, these magistrates came out and addressed the crowd, saying they had done what they could, and that it now rested with them to play their parts.[338] Most of them then departed, except for James Bunce, an extreme presbyterian, and some clergy who stayed behind in the Palace Yard to egg on the rioters. In his on-the-spot direction of the day's events Bunce, a leather-seller in Gracechurch Street and a captain in the City's Red Regiment,[339] was joined by a small group of presbyterian clergy, militia officers and common-councilmen.[340]

First the crowd invaded the Lords' chamber crying for Manchester's blood. He had already fled, so they forced the remaining peers to recall their former resolution on the militia and repeal their declaration against the City petition. The peers then hurriedly adjourned, to be saluted with a loud cry of 'a king, a king, no government without a king' as they exited from their chamber.[341]

Around two o'clock the crowd turned its attention to the lower house. The Commons gave the same unyielding answer that the Lords had at first returned, and held out for five long hours, at one point drawing their own swords to repel invaders.[342] Scoutmaster Watson, the army's go-between with the Saye, Vane and St John group, was seized and carried into the City.[343] Finally the apprentices grew bolder and broke into the House of Commons. Keeping their hats on as a mark of contempt, they ordered the MPs to pass the same resolution as the Lords. By eight o'clock the Commons too had capitulated. No one was allowed to leave until they had resolved that the king should immediately be brought to London. The MPs were encouraged in their work by shouts of 'Vote, vote' from their captors.[344]

Was the rape of parliament on 26 July a spontaneous eruption by the 'rude multitude', a 'sudden tumultuary thing of idle people without design', as Holles later averred?[345] Or was it the culmination of deeply laid plans carefully orchestrated by the leading members of the presbyterian party, including Holles himself? Recent historians have given different answers to this question,[346] but there can be little doubt that the City magistrates and presbyterian clergy were heavily involved.[347] There is also ample evidence of involvement by MPs. Sir William Waller dined with the lord mayor three days before the tumult, and two of the apprentices consulted with Waller about their petition before they presented it.[348] Two witnesses to the events of 26 July later testified before the Lords that the rioters had professed to be 'advised by a member of the House of Commons'.[349] Lisle and Scot also claimed to have seen members of the household of Recorder Glyn fortify the crowd by passing bottles of refreshment through the windows to them.[350] In a draft letter to a member of the king's court at the beginning of August, Sir John Maynard rejoiced at the assault on parliament, outlined the financial and military steps being taken to repel the expected invasion of London by the New Model, and urged the king to ally himself with the Eleven Members, who were his friends, rather than with the army, whose proposals came from his greatest enemies, Saye, St John and Vane.[351] It is also known that at the very time when the crowd was swirling around the parliament house, five of the Eleven were sitting only a stone's-throw away in the Bell tavern in King Street. According to Holles they had met there to divide up the legal costs connected with their impeachment, and the news of the hubbub at Westminster Hall came to them as a complete surprise.[352] Holles's explanation strains credulity; nevertheless it seems more likely that the MPs sought to ride the crest of this second counter-revolutionary wave than that they generated it themselves. The crowd's primary motivation was to reverse parliament's decision on the London Militia Committee. The Eleven were more alarmed by the news that the army and the group led by Saye, Vane and St John were on the brink of reaching an agreement with the king.[353] The prospect of a political settlement engineered by the Independents may have stirred them to resume their leadership of the counter-revolution that they had recently abandoned. The insurgents after all were pursuing the same programme as the Eleven, and there was an out-side chance that properly led they might succeed.[354] By the 29th it was clear to Bulstrode Whitelocke that Holles and his cronies were in the saddle once again, directing the resistance to the New Model.[355]

Yet the presbyterian counter-revolution had already been crushed, and the impeached MPs were not oblivious to this fact. The Scots had failed to make good on their promises; the Northern Army had rallied behind the agitators and kicked out Poynts; the London trained bands had proved a broken reed; and moderates in parliament and the City had quailed at the prospect of a head-on collision with their undefeated army. That is why Holles and the other ten had asked on 20 July for permission to leave the country. The reactionary violence of 26 July was a last desperate fling by men who should have known better.

7

The Political Wars 1646–8 (II): From the Occupation of London to the Second Civil War

The Occupation of London, 5–7 August 1647

The crowd's assault on parliament vindicated the agitators' insistent call for a march on London. Overnight, revolutionary theory was converted into practice. The army's hand was immensely strengthened by the co-operation of its parliamentary allies. In the capital Arthur Hesilrige and Oliver St John played a central role in rounding up sympathetic MPs and convincing them to take refuge with the army. The toughest nut they had to crack was the Commons Speaker, William Lenthall, who would evidently have preferred to sit out the crisis without taking sides.[1] In the end, both Speakers, as well as fifty-seven MPs and eight peers, made the pilgrimage to Fairfax's head-quarters.[2] In Westminster the remaining MPs reassembled on 30 July with a mace borrowed from the City.[3] They elected a new Speaker, as did the Lords, and readmitted the Eleven Members.[4] Warning the army to keep at least 30 miles away from London, they revived the Committee of Public Safety, adding to its membership Massey, Sir William Waller and, curiously, Colonel Nathaniel Rich. Waller and Massey were also added to the reconstituted London Militia Committee.[5] Finally, overriding the order of 17 July, the Commons voted that Fairfax's authority as commander-in-chief did not extend to the London trained bands.[6] The City had already been organizing its militia and welcomed the opportunity to act in concert with parliament to resist the army. Hoping to broaden their base of support, the militia committee offered the command of the trained bands to Major-General Skippon, but when he temporized they handed it to the more reliable Edward Massey.[7] The ex-New Model cavalry under Colonels Pye and Graves was ordered to draw closer to the City.[8] Reformadoes were added to the counter-revolutionary army as fast as they could be enlisted. Horses were commandeered and seamen recruited.[9] On the monthly fast day (28 July) Thomas Edwardes and other presbyterian clergy strove to whip up their congregations' zeal to raise arms and face down the New Model.[10] Three days later all the City clergy were instructed to follow suit.[11] According to another report, militia officers were issued secret commissions to 'force, kill, slay and destroy', in order to hold off the New Model.[12]

But none of this frenetic activity produced lasting results, and presbyterian bravado soon wilted in the face of the army's determined response. On the 28th Fairfax sent the City commissioners packing, publicly accused the aldermen of complicity in the mob assault on parliament, and announced that the army would shortly march on the capital in order to restore parliament's freedom.[13] His hand was strengthened by the fact that these actions appeared less as an invasion of London than as a response to the fugitive MPs' request to be escorted back to their seats. Had the king at the same time been willing to endorse the Heads of the Proposals, the army would have been able to bask in the adulation of the populace. Lacking the concordat they had so assiduously sought, they exhorted the king at least to dissociate himself from the tumult of 26 July. Always believing that time was on his side, Charles delayed giving an answer until 3 August, when it was almost too late to be of material use, and even then his condemnation of the tumult was lukewarm. In both the content and timing of his statement he left the impression that he only repudiated the presbyterian counter-revolutionaries after they could no longer do him any good. Nevertheless, the publication of his statement in London on 4 August can only have further discouraged resistance to the New Model.[14] As far as the City was concerned, Fairfax did not disguise the main reason for invading, which was to restore the Independent-dominated militia committee.[15]

In the final analysis the army did not have to worry about its failure to win over the king. It still had the bigger battalions, and its confidence swelled as messages of support streamed into headquarters. There had been petitions from Norfolk, Suffolk, Essex, Buckinghamshire, Hertfordshire, Hampshire and Glamorgan in June and early July.[16] Fresh petitions now arrived from the county committees of Hertford and Devon, while Colonel Blunt made it known that Fairfax could count on the support of the county forces in Kent.[17] A group of apprentices from the City implored the army to be 'our deliverers out of the jaws of inevitable slavery'.[18] More significant was the dismay shown by the suburbs at the City's reckless defiance of the army. Both Southwark and the Tower Hamlets made it known that they wished to have no part of the City's activities.[19]

By the beginning of August presbyterian euphoria at having bent parliament to its will had evaporated, and the City was gripped with a terrible fear. Those who could fled the apprehended massacre.[20] They had good reason to feel frightened. Within days Fairfax had drawn together his scattered regiments and put the army into an offensive posture. Every military move by the London Militia Committee and the parliamentary Committee of Public Safety was swiftly checkmated. Major Disbrowe with a party of horse intercepted those of Pye and Graves at Deptford and 'basely butchered' seven. The forts at Tilbury and the blockhouse at Townshend were seized, and 2000 troops stationed there.[21] By 2 August army headquarters were at Colnbrook, near Windsor. Emboldened by the army's approach, the Independent faction in the City brought a petition for peace before the Common Council meeting at Guildhall. They were joined by a delegation from Southwark, who also announced their opposition to the City's hostile gestures, and their determination to look after their own defence. These demonstrations infuriated the hardliners. When they heard about the petitioners Poynts and Massey, who were with their troops in the Artillery Garden, rode down to Guildhall

> and with their swords drawn fell upon the naked [i.e. unarmed] men whom they slashed and cut barbarously, and killed some outright, and followed them up and down the streets cutting them. And at last the horsemen came into Cheapside with their swords drawn crying out for King Charles.[22]

Whatever satisfaction Poynts and Massey derived from hacking at defenceless petitioners, they had no success in rallying the citizens against the army. Almost none of the auxiliaries or apprentices turned up for guard duty; of the 10,000 seamen promised by Trinity House only 300 materialized; the inhabitants of the Tower Hamlets refused to obey the City's orders, and their officers laid down their arms. On the night of 2 August a nervous crowd thronged about Guildhall hungry for news about the New Model's approach. If a scout brought hopeful intelligence – that the army had halted, for example – they plucked up their spirits, shouting, 'One and all, one and all.' But if the news was bad they quickly changed their minds and cried, 'Treat, treat.' By the end of the night they had prevailed upon the Common Council to write a letter of submission to Fairfax.[23]

On the morning of 3 August the army staged a show of strength at Hounslow Heath, just over 10 miles west of the city. Besides some 15,000 troops of the New Model, about 100 MPs and fourteen peers were in attendance. Accompanied by Fairfax the Speakers and members of both houses reviewed the assembled ranks, a mile and a half in length. As they rode past each regiment, the soldiers flung their hats into the air shouting, 'Lords and Commons and a free parliament!'[24] That night, recognizing that the game was up, Massey and Poynts quit the City for Holland. Pye and Prynne followed soon after.[25]

The occupation of London was a bloodless operation. Early in the morning of 4 August an advance party of 4000 horse and foot led by Colonel Rainborowe penetrated Southwark, where they were welcomed by Colonel John Hardwick of the borough's trained bands. For several days this militia had stood guard at the foot of London Bridge, blocking access to the City, but permitting anyone who wanted to leave to do so. In this manner a considerable number of radical citizens were enabled to stream out of London and flock to the army. The trained bands, however, were forbidden to come across the bridge. Southwark's refusal to co-operate with the City was the immediate cause of the military collapse of resistance to the New Model.[26] When 2000 horse arrived later the same day to possess the City, the portcullis was at first lowered against them. However, they had only to bring two guns into position to make the defenders give up. The guards at all the other gates, lines and forts around the City had already abandoned their positions. London was occupied without a blow or shot being exchanged.[27] The next day five additional regiments of foot and horse were distributed throughout the forts encircling the City.[28]

With London and the environs now secure, Fairfax was free to escort the Speakers and members of both houses back to Westminster. The soldiers of four regiments and the general's lifeguard decked their hats with laurel leaves, and church bells pealed as the triumphal procession wound its way through the city streets to the Palace of Westminster.[29] Pride of place was reserved for the timorous Commons Speaker, William Lenthall. Following the main body of soldiers was a throng of civilian well-wishers from the radical Independent party of London. Next came Hugh Peters and another divine (perhaps William Dell). Then a group of coaches rolled by bearing the army's aristocratic supporters: Northumberland, Salisbury, Manchester, Saye, Kent and Denbigh. Taking up the rear was a regiment of horse.[30]

The final scene in the drama was played out on Saturday 7 August, when the army gathered all available forces for a prolonged walk through the City. Besides the lifeguard and train of artillery, twenty regiments – ten of foot, one of dragoons and nine of horse – assembled in Hyde Park. Accompanied by flying colours and the music of trumpets and drums, they marched to Cheapside in the City's heart.[31] Since London had been secured three days before, the purpose of this exercise was entirely propagandistic. From Cheapside the soldiers fanned out and tramped through every street from eleven in the morning until eight at night. All observers agreed on their exemplary conduct. They neither made an offensive gesture nor stole so much as an apple during their entire sojourn. With them was the train of artillery consisting of twenty pieces of ordnance. There were also eighty wagons for provisions and a number of carts into which the men had piled their arms. Thomas Juxon, a major in the trained bands and a seasoned judge of soldiers, esteemed them able-bodied men, especially the cavalry, most of whom were under the age of forty.[32] There was no disagreement about the army's excellent deportment while it was in the City. What was less widely commented upon, and which has been also missed by most historians, was the enthusiasm with which many citizens greeted the troops:

> Yea, and the common people through the whole City filling the streets, as the general and army thus passed along, admiring and applauding with the highest panegyrics that their greedily-gazing eyes could manifest (like so many sottish and dull Issachar's asses).[33]

At the end of the day, satisfied that his troops had made the desired impression, Fairfax marched them across London Bridge, whence they dispersed to quarters in Kent and Surrey.[34]

The army had won its war with the City and parliament. Winning the peace was to prove considerably more difficult. The senior officers soon realized that, instead of solving problems, power only multiplied them. True, there were a few agreeable perquisites. Both houses of parliament resolved that Thursday 12 August would be observed as a day of thanksgiving for the army's political intervention. More concretely, they appointed Fairfax constable of the Tower of London.[35] The general immediately named two politically reliable City officers, Colonel Robert Tichborne and Lieutenant-Colonel William Shambrooke, as lieutenant of the Tower and lieutenant-colonel of the Tower Guards respectively.[36] An economic consequence of handing control of the Tower to the New Model was a flight of gold, as a number of merchants shipped their bullion to what they thought was the safer haven of Holland. Trade also slackened in the months to come.[37] Despite its show of economic non-confidence, the City exerted itself to get on the army's good side politically by inviting Fairfax and his officers to a banquet. However, the magistrates were coldly rebuffed. By contrast the Earl of Manchester's invitation to Fairfax to dine at his house in Chelsea with several other peers, presumably of the Saye – Wharton group, was accepted.[38]

The more fiery spirits in the army cried for vengeance against its political enemies, and demanded to know why it had not been exacted immediately. True, Recorder Glyn and Sir John Maynard had been consigned to the Tower, and seven peers had been turned over to Black Rod.[39] Other enemies of the army had made the grandees' work easier by obligingly taking flight. But most of the impeached Eleven Members continued to attend the house. It was evidently thanks to their assiduous efforts that the Commons were able to frustrate the army's will for a full two weeks after the occupation of London.[40] In this respect the Commons diverged sharply from the peers, who, without seven peace-party supporters, lost no time passing an ordinance declaring all of parliament's proceedings since 26 July null and void.[41] They also returned the London Militia Committee to the control of the Independents who had been ousted on 4 May, established a committee to investigate the violence against parliament, and voted a gratuity of one month's pay to all non-commissioned officers and private soldiers.[42] In the Commons the presbyterians mustered enough strength to defeat by a margin of 2 the motion annulling the votes since 26 July. They also defeated by 34 votes the resolution implying approval of the army's proceedings. On the 13th the Lords informed them that the presbyterian militia committee which had been restored on 26 July was continuing to sit. This was a flagrant challenge to the New Model; nevertheless the Commons declined to endorse the Lords' declaration that the militia committee was sitting 'without authority'. On the 19th they defeated for the fifth time the ordinance from the Lords pronouncing the legislation of 26 July to 6 August null and void.[43]

The agitators were by now boiling with indignation at the Commons' insolent assertion of independence. Already, On 5 August, they had demanded the expulsion of MPs who had continued to sit after 26 July. Nine days later they had published their demand and were distributing it in London.[44] The higher officers, however, quailed at the thought of laying violent hands directly on parliament. Instead they composed a Remonstrance requesting that the Commons itself should inflict condign punishment on those who had continued to sit between 26 July and 6 August. On 20 August, the day after he dined with Fairfax, Manchester wrote approving the Remonstrance, and thanking the army for having preserved parliament's honour and freedom.[45] The friendly majority in the Lords must have been aware of the show of force that the army had devised to back up its words. On the day after the motion nullifying the votes of 26 July to 6 August was defeated for the fifth time – which was also the day that the Remonstrance was tabled – Major John Disbrowe drew up 1000 cavalry in Hyde Park, scarcely a mile away from parliament. Simultaneously the New Model guards around both houses were doubled. According to one report the soldiers 'openly threatened at the door, to pull out all the Members by head and shoulders that sat and voted in the Speaker's absence, if they presumed to intrude themselves or but enter into the House.' There was a concerted turn-out of military MPs who made 'high and menacing speeches which daunted many'.[46] This calculated and limited show of force had its intended effect. The Commons finally declared the votes passed between 26 July and 6 August void without a division, after an attempt to amend the resolution had been defeated by 112 to 85. They also voted a month's pay for the army.[47] Seeing that the tide had turned in the army's favour, Fairfax chose this moment to issue instructions to Cromwell to procure if he could an order for the release of Lilburne and Overton.[48] However, the progressivism of the Saye – Wharton group did not extend to supporting the Leveller leader who had insulted them so often in print; consequently Lilburne remained technically in custody, though he was allowed to go abroad pretty much when he pleased.[49] The remaining MPs of the Eleven took the hint delivered by the troops in Hyde Park, and withdrew from parliament on the 21st.[50]

Having brought the Commons around, the army now turned its attention to the City of London. Presbyterian ringleaders who had not already fled or gone into hiding were rounded up. Charged with high treason, the royalist mayor, John Gayre, and three high-ranking aldermen, Langham, Adams and Bunce, were thrown in the Tower. Two militia colonels and a captain were voted guilty of high misdemeanours, while an assortment of lesser officers, citizens, ministers and apprentices were ordered to stand trial for treason in the court of King's Bench.[51] Not content to gut the City of its presbyterian leadership, the army also imposed its own nominee for lord mayor, John Warner, who was sworn in at the end of September. The presbyterian lieutenant of the Tower, Francis West, had already been supplanted by Colonel Robert Tichborne. The Tower Guards were now replaced by Colonel Pride's infantry regiment until a fresh regiment of trustworthy citizens could be recruited.[52] Finally, and vitally important, the purged Independents returned to their seats on the London Militia Committee. As a reward for their support of the army, Southwark and Westminster were cut free from the London committee's jurisdiction and given their own militia committees.[53]

The most dramatic measure of all was the destruction of the lines of communication. This 11-mile ring of forts and earthworks, erected at immense cost in human labour in 1643, was the visual metaphor of the City's military self-sufficiency. To demonstrate to the citizens their military impotence the army insisted that these defences be dismantled. Londoners were understandably loath to undo their own work, but with the army's help the demolition was accomplished before the end of September.[54]

The only issue over which urban recalcitrance remained unbroken was taxation. The City's accumulated debt of £64,337 on the monthly assessment was greater than that owed by any county, and prompted the Committee for the Army to demand immediate payment of £50,000. Despite the threat of 'tumult or outrages' monied men refused to loosen their purses; indeed, London was able to avoid paying anything to the army for almost two and a half years – from the summer of 1646 until the end of 1648.[55] The citizens' refusal to pay was shortsighted, for it constantly aggravated their relations with the army, and strengthened the hand of radicals within the ranks.

The New Agitators

Once they had realized most of their objectives in London and at Westminster, the higher officers had tactfully withdrawn from the metropolis, and established headquarters at Putney, 5 miles upstream from Westminster. This suburban parish was far enough from the capital to avoid direct confrontation with the City and parliament, yet close enough to allow the army to react quickly to any crisis. The agitators made their headquarters on the other side of the Thames, at nearby Hammersmith.[56] The army's nearness to the City made it more susceptible than ever to radical infiltration and propaganda. We have seen that the radical Independents, as the Levellers were first known, had evinced a lively interest in the army as early as March 1647.[57] By June the peers did not shrink from publicly accusing some of the prisoners in the Tower – chief among them John Lilburne – of fomenting the distempers in the army.[58] In early July the agitators reciprocated the Levellers' affection by protesting against the burning of their petitions by the common hangman.[59] From August to November the army in turn was the object of an intense lobbying effort mounted by Richard Overton, John Wildman, John Lilburne and other Leveller leaders.[60] Their strategy was facilitated by the swelling of the army's numbers in August, which allowed radicals from the metropolis to enlist for the purpose of influencing the army's political agenda.[61]

It is plausible to suppose that the new recruits threw their weight behind the campaign being waged by radical officers for the promotion of like-minded soldiers. The forum where promotions were discussed was the Committee of General Officers. This body had been created by Fairfax in August to ease his own administrative burden. Its composition tells us whom Fairfax regarded as his most important officers: Cromwell, Thomas Hammond, Henry Ireton, Thomas Rainborowe, Charles Fleetwood, Robert Hammond, Sir Hardress Waller, Nathaniel Rich, William Stane, Scoutmaster-General Leonard Watson, Quartermaster-General Thomas Ireton and Adjutant-General Richard Deane.[62] The committee's quorum was only three, but it had to include at least one of the eight field officers.[63]

The committee occupied itself with a variety of administrative tasks such as the reorganization of the Northern Army under Lambart, the manning of the Tower of London, and the reduction of troop strength in garrisons across the country.[64] But the core of its work was recommending men for promotion. Two of its number obtained promotions for themselves: Quartermaster-General Ireton became governor of Landguard and Harwich Fort, Essex, and Adjutant-General Deane got himself the colonelcy of Rainborowe's regiment.[65] The extent of radical influence is seen in the recommendations that Cornet Joyce should fill a vacant captaincy in Fleetwood's regiment, that Captain Reynolds should become governor of Weymouth and Melcombe Fort, Dorset, that John Wildman should be made governor of Poole and Brownsea Castle, and that Major Alexander Tulidah should be commissioned governor of Hereford Castle.[66] From the fact that none of these recommendations was acted upon we may infer that Fairfax vetoed them all.[67] There was more political manoeuvring surrounding Thomas Rainborowe's quest to become vice-admiral of the navy. Cromwell and the leading Independents tried to block the appointment, but Rainborowe temporarily triumphed after a violent quarrel in which he warned Cromwell that he would have the appointment even if it cost one of them his life.[68]

In the early summer the agitators had co-operated fully with the senior officers, but now some of them were taking the bit between their teeth. Apart from promoting the personal cause of John Lilburne and raising embarrassing questions as to why he remained formally in captivity, they campaigned for a group of Southwark radicals who had been imprisoned for uttering words against the king, and continued to press for the expulsion of all the MPs who had continued to sit after the London crowd's assault on parliament on 26 July.[69] The chronic irregularity of pay made the army fertile ground for the insemination of radical ideas. A month's pay had been received in August, but in September there was nothing.[70] John Lilburne exploited the army's unhappiness by turning the volume a notch louder in his denunciations of the grandees, who he said should be trusted 'no further than you can throw an ox'. This was by now a familiar refrain, but in September he was casting about for new scapegoats on whom to vent his frustrated rage. William Allen, one of the agitators of Cromwell's regiment, was unjustly attacked as a lackey of Oliver, while the soldiers were exhorted not to let their representatives remain in office too long, 'for standing waters though never so pure at first, in time putrifies.'[71] None the less, Cromwell braved Lilburne's choleric temper when he paid him a personal visit in the Tower in the hope of effecting a reconciliation. He as much as offered him a release from the Tower and a place in the army if he would cease his attacks on the grandees. Lilburne turned down the offer, thereby condemning himself to an indefinite future of imprisonment. After the interview was over the two men joined the lieutenant of the Tower, Colonel Tichborne, for dinner.[72]

By the end of September the mounting dissatisfaction in five horse regiments had led to the emergence of new agitators, or agents as they were commonly known. Lilburne's exhortations had borne fruit, and he continued to exercise a great influence over these men as they met frequently with the London Levellers during the autumn.[73] Over the next few weeks six more regiments, including the dragoons and two foot regiments (Waller's and Lilburne's), in addition to the lifeguard, threw up new agents. Their numbers ranged from one in Okey's, Waller's and Harrison's, to as many as twenty-three in Twisleton's regiment. At least five of them – William Symons, John Wood, John Dover (or Dober), Edward Sexby and Joseph Aleyn – are known to have served as agitators during the previous months, but most of them were otherwise unknown.[74] By 1 November, when they published the Agreement of the People, the new agents claimed the support of nine horse and seven foot regiments.[75]

Soon after their appearance the new agents were involved in a variety of political actions. Two of them rode north to Lambart's regiment in Yorkshire and persuaded it to choose new representatives 'for that the officers had broken their engagements.'[76] The new agents' larger political objectives included the suppression of Cromwell and his faction, and the dissolution of parliament, because, as Sir Lewis Dyve reported, they were convinced that it would set up a Scottish brand of presbyterianism.[77] But with their seemingly limitless energy and zeal they also took on a number of peripheral issues.[78]

Rather than staying with their regiments the new agents assembled in London, so that they could keep in constant touch with the civilian Levellers. In their more heady moments they dreamt of organizing a convention or parliament of agitators both military and civilian, with representatives from every county.[79] Ireton's regiment found civilians willing to represent Hampshire, and also attempted to organize the western garrisons between Bristol and Southampton.[80]

What mandate did the new agents have from the regiments they claimed to represent? They were never recognized by the General Council of the Army, and did not displace the existing agitators. It is sometimes thought that they were not really elected, and represented no one except themselves. However, if the agents of Ireton's regiment can be believed, they had solid support from five of its six troops. Twisleton's regiment was also said to be unanimously behind the new agents.[81] When the men of Captain Cannon's troop in Whalley's regiment wrote to one agent (William Russell, 'cleric') ordering him to leave London and rejoin the other agitators at army headquarters, they declared that he had been acting 'contrary to our intentions *when we chose you*.'[82] The evidence is only fragmentary, but it seems that in some regiments at least the new agents had a mandate from the rank and file.

This foundation of popular support explains why the senior officers treated the political demands of the new agents with the utmost seriousness. Since early September they had been painfully aware of the army's deepening unpopularity among the civilian population, the rank and file's irritability over the lack of pay, and their own vulnerability after their dream of a settlement with the king had been dashed. By clinging to this dream until the moment when the king himself destroyed it,[83] they thereby handed their radical critics a stick with which to beat them. Believing that their main hope of preserving the army's political quiescence lay in keeping money flowing into the soldiers' pockets, they busied themselves with the pay question, which used up most of the time of four General Council meetings in late September and early October.[84] All the while, however, the army's malaise worsened. Towards the middle of October Hugh Peters published what every soldier knew to be true: morale had become flaccid; the regiments were plagued with division. 'We have prayed more, loved more, believed more than we do now', he pontificated.[85] This consciousness of the army's unpopularity was expressed by no one more vividly than the new agents themselves:

> The love and affection of the people to the army, which is an army's greatest strength, is decayed, cooled and near lost. It's already the common voice of the people, 'what good hath our new saviours done for us? What grievances have they procured to be redressed? Wherein is our condition bettered? Or how are we more free than before?'...So that many soldiers are ashamed of themselves, and fear that the people should rise to destroy them.[86]

The new agents and their Leveller mentors asserted that there was only one way for the army to rescue itself from the people's wrath: by embracing a thoroughgoing programme of social justice. Announcing that 'the great mansion house of this commonwealth ... [is] on fire', they proclaimed to Fairfax that in publishing *The Case of the Armie* they were obeying the dictates of divinity, nature and reason.[87]

The tract was a massive indictment of the senior officers, not only for having rendered the army odious to the people, but also for failing to care adequately for the wants of the rank and file, maimed soldiers, and the widows and orphans of the slain. This failure was traceable to their reluctance to bring a recalcitrant and corrupt parliament to heel. Worse, by sanctioning schemes for disbanding the artillery, dispersing regiments throughout England, and sending troops to Ireland before grievances had been satisfied, they had broken the sacred engagements of the army at Newmarket on 5 June. After the intoxicating June and July days they had systematically shut the agitators out of any real consultation about army affairs. They had also neglected the people's interest by failing to insist on the abolition of monopolies, tithes and the excise. Conspicuously, however, the agents did not mention the tax that was heavier than all the others, the monthly assessment, prime source of the army's pay.

Social justice necessarily awaited the political revolution that would sweep away the corrupt powers presently holding sway. Such a revolution would be grounded in the principle that 'all power is originally and essentially in the whole body of the people of this nation, and ... [that] their free choice or consent by the representors is the only original or foundation of all just government.' Ineluctably it would entail the dissolution of the present parliament, biennial elections, votes for 'all the freeborn' men of England except 'those that have or shall deprive themselves of that their freedom, either for some years, or wholly by delinquency', religious liberty and freedom from conscription.[88]

The principled and uncompromising tone of *The Case of the Armie Truly Stated* masked the fact that, in publishing it, the agents and their Leveller advisers had created two serious difficulties for themselves. First, they had laid themselves open to the charge of sowing further dissension within the army and the kingdom. In anticipation of this charge they protested that they were only performing their duty to God, and that their goal was nothing less than the welfare of country, parliament and army. The second difficulty was that the interests of the two groups for whom they claimed to speak – the common people and the army – were in one fundamental respect incompatible. The people craved relief from taxation and free quarter, but relief could only come after the army had been disbanded. The army by contrast could not live without the proceeds of heavy taxation, and was understandably alarmed at the prospect of its own demise. This problem was not openly acknowledged in *The Case of the Armie*, but the authors' awareness of it is implicit in their avoidance of any demand for the abolition of the monthly assessment, and their pretence that army pay could be financed out of the large sums previously paid to court parasites and out of the 'millions of money' frozen in the 'dead stocks' of some of the City guilds. As for the enormous sums owing for arrears of pay, they could be raised by selling the dean and chapter lands.[89] The notion of paying the army £45,000 a month out of sinecurists' salaries and the hidden capital of City companies is akin to the belief that the modern welfare state can be financed merely by soaking the rich. The incompatibility between the people's interests and those of the army was a dilemma that would plague the Levellers for the next two years and ultimately spell their doom.[90]

The new agents presented *The Case of the Armie Truly Stated* to Fairfax on Monday 18 October, and three days later it was considered by the General Council at its regular weekly meeting.[91] Samuel Pecke reported that the document was greeted with hostility, that the army was not divided, and that no more than 400 out of 21,000 soldiers saw the army's problems through the same optic as the new agents.[92] Events were to show how misleading this report was. Although the senior officers' first impulse was to punish the subalterns who they were sure had promoted the agitation, they thought better of it, and instead appointed a broadly representative committee of field officers, and officer and soldier agitators, to meet at Ireton's quarters and consider *The Case of the Armie*. Their mandate was not only to vindicate the army 'from the aspersions cast upon them by the said paper', but also to deal with the vexed bread-and-butter issues of money, free quarter, arrears and over-enlistment.[93] All cavalry troopers who had enlisted since the army's march through London on 6–7 August were to be expelled. The acknowledged reason for this decision was the fear of infiltration by subversive elements.[94]

By the time of the weekly meeting of the General Council on Thursday 28 October the higher officers had evidently decided that the agents and their proposals had to be treated with respect. No more was heard of the threat to punish the officers who had subverted the rank and file. Instead, the agents and their civilian supporters were invited to the General Council, and several days were given over to debating the Agreement of the People. As Cromwell later admitted to the House of Commons, he had been mistaken in thinking that if he permitted the Levellers free rein to propagandize the army 'their follies would vanish.' Instead they had spread to such an alarming extent that 'many honest officers' had been 'infected' by their proposals. The Levellers' success in promoting their ideas in the army was what had necessitated the debates at Putney in the first place.[95]

The Putney Debates

When the General Council of the Army assembled on 28 October to debate the challenge thrown down by the new agents there was a sense of foreboding among the officers. The existence of a Leveller caucus within the army's bosom pointed to the evaporation of unity which had occurred since September. In parliament a corresponding rift between 'royal' Independents and the emergent 'commonwealthsmen' led by Henry Marten undermined their hegemony over the presbyterians. The king for his part showed less interest in coming to an agreement with either parliament or army, and had already begun a dangerous flirtation with the Scots.[96]

The day before the General Council met, Robert Everard had brought to headquarters a reply to the council's objections and also the first version of the Agreement of the People. It had been approved that day at a meeting attended by the agents of the five regiments and other soldiers, and also by

Plate 6 Colonel Thomas Rainborowe

(*Cromwelliana*)

Wildman and 'divers country-gentlemen'. The primary author may have been William Walwyn.[97] Certainly its brevity and sophistication made it a more formidable document to contend with than the disorganized and intemperate *Case of the Armie Truly Stated*. It seems to have been hastily improvised, but it contained two concepts that were novel both in Leveller literature and English political thought. The first was the idea of a written constitution to be subscribed by all the freeborn men of England. Second was the concept of powers that were reserved to the people alone and could not be exercised by any government. As it turned out, the second was to prove more fruitful than the first.

The session of 28 October opened with Cromwell in the chair, since Fairfax was nursing another illness across the river at Turnham Green.[98] Edward Sexby, speaking on behalf of himself and Nicholas Lockyer, presented the delegates from the radical caucus. They consisted of two soldiers, one from Cromwell's and the other from Whalley's regiment, as well as two civilians, John Wildman and Maximilian Petty. The soldier from Cromwell's regiment, referred to in William Clarke's notes as 'buff-coat', was Robert Everard. The one from Whalley's, whom Clarke called 'Bedfordshire man', was one of the four new agents from that regiment: Matthew Wealey, William Russell, Richard Seale or William Sampson.[99]

Sexby came straight to the point. There was dissatisfaction in the army because 'we have laboured to please a king ... and we have gone to support an house which will prove rotten studs, I mean the parliament which consists of a company of rotten Members.' Because Cromwell and Ireton had been so servile towards king and parliament, 'your credits and reputation hath been much blasted.'[100] Speaking in his own and Ireton's defence, Cromwell avowed that as a soldier he had done nothing without the authority of the General Council of the Army. Any words in the House of Commons were spoken in his capacity as an MP and in no way implicated the army. For his part, Ireton denied having anything to do with a design to set up the king. On the other hand he would not make common cause with any group that sought the destruction of either parliament or king. After this skirmish Robert Everard laid the Agreement of the People before the council and the members heard it read out for the first time.[101] Besides the two revolutionary concepts noted above, the Agreement called for the redistribution of parliamentary constituencies according to the number of inhabitants. The present parliament should be dissolved before the end of September 1648. Subsequent parliaments should be elected biennially, and their power should be 'inferior only to theirs who choose them'. The document was silent about the other two branches of the existing system, the king and the House of Lords. Nor did it say anything about who should exercise executive authority between parliamentary sessions. It was also mute about the franchise. The new House of Commons would exercise unfettered sovereignty, except that it would have no compulsive power in religion, and no power to conscript men for the army. Nor would it be permitted to violate the principle of equality before the law.

After the reading was over Cromwell immediately jumped in with the comment that the Agreement would entail 'very great alterations' of the government of the kingdom. What was to prevent another group of individuals from concocting an equally radical scheme in a different direction? 'Would it not be utter confusion? Would it not make England like the Switzerland country, one canton of the Swiss against another, and one county against another?'[102] Having raised the spectre of anarchy Cromwell then made the most telling criticism possible against the Agreement. The root principle of the proposed constitution was the sovereignty of the people, but he doubted 'whether ... the people of this nation are prepared to receive and to go on along with it.' What would be the status, he might have added, of an Agreement which most people refused to sign? Unity was of paramount importance to Cromwell, but in the Agreement he saw only a recipe for division and conflict. There was another difficulty: since the previous June the army had issued many statements binding itself to perform certain actions on behalf of the nation. To what extent was the proposed constitution of the new agents consistent with the engagements that the army had already undertaken? Without a flicker of hesitation, Wildman rejoined that they should first consider the merit of the Agreement, and, if it was found to be just and honest, then the army's previous engagements should be reviewed in its light. No engagement could be binding if it was found to be unjust.

Ireton angrily retorted that it ill became one who had criticized the officers for neglecting the Engagement of 5 June to speak slightingly of the army's other engagements. If men can break their engagements whenever they believe them to be unjust then 'this is a principle that will take away all commonwealth[s].' Unlike some civilians, he added pointedly, soldiers were required to take their engagements seriously. Before they did anything else, therefore, Ireton believed it incumbent upon them to go over all the declarations they had issued, to see if any of them would be in conflict with the document of the new agents.

At this point Colonel Thomas Rainborowe joined the fray on the side of Wildman and Everard. A truculent figure, Rainborowe had quarrelled with Cromwell over whether the army should press parliament to treat with the king over the Heads of the Proposals.[103] Rainborowe was also fiercely resentful of the Committee of General Officers for transferring his regimental command to Richard Deane after his appointment as vice-admiral of the navy on 27 September. Having got this matter off his chest, Rainborowe plainly stated that they should not be afraid of the radicalism of the Agreement of the People. If they were convinced that it was just, then in conscience they were bound to carry it through, 'and I think at the last day it can never be answered to God that you did not do it.' What if it was 'a huge alteration' to the existing constitution? 'If writings be true there hath been many scufflings between the honest men of England and those that have tyrannized over them.' All of England's good laws had originated as innovations, and infringements on the power of king and lords.[104] Cromwell tried to mollify Rainborowe, who strictly speaking had no right to attend, by welcoming him and saying how glad he was that they should enjoy his company longer than anticipated. 'If I should not be kicked out', Rainborowe sourly replied.

Cromwell then acknowledged that it was a duty for men to break unrighteous engagements, but cautioned that they should always 'have the fear of God before our eyes' and do nothing 'in the power of a fleshly strength, but to lay this as the foundation of all our actions, to do that which is the will of God.' No matter how imperfectly he adhered to it, this was Cromwell's credo. He continued that the army's declarations were public commitments to the whole kingdom, and therefore could not be laid aside lightly. Exhorting his hearers to 'seek God together, and see if God will give us an uniting spirit,' he moved for a committee to review the army's engagements. The fact that the motion won the support of Captain Lewis Awdeley, one of the more radical officer agitators, suggests that Cromwell was not engaged in a diversionary tactic.[105]

The agent from Whalley's regiment professed ignorance of the army's engagements, but said he hoped that nothing in them diminished the people's rights. He added that the present system of kingly government posed more dangers than the changes proposed under the Agreement. Those who felt themselves precluded by previous engagements from supporting the Agreement should bow out and give free rein to the Agreement's supporters. Not surprisingly, this suggestion got nowhere.

Lieutenant-Colonel William Goffe, who was perhaps the most pious of all the officers, seized upon Cromwell's idea of collectively seeking God and pressed for it to be acted upon. Echoing Hugh Peters' words earlier in the month, he worried that 'God hath not been with us as formerly.' Let us not, he said, be ashamed to declare to the world that our ways are not its ways, 'but that we have had a dependency upon God, and that our desires are to follow God (though never so much to our disadvantage in the world) if God may have the glory by it.'[106]

Ireton seconded Goffe's motion with the reverent observation that the divine spirit was for each man the best instrument to search out the error of his own ways. Perhaps the exercise would lead to the renewal of unity in the army. It was agreed to set aside the following morning for prayer in Quartermaster-General Grosvenor's lodgings at Mr Chamberlaine's house. Wildman, however, was not satisfied. A delay of even two or three days might lose them the kingdom, for in that time the king and parliament could come to a settlement which left all of the people's grievances unredressed. Ireton, even though he had been momentarily transported by Goffe's reflections, could not resist the impulse to reopen the debate on engagements. With all the eloquence he could summon he stressed that a fundamental law of civil society was that

> covenants freely made, freely entered into, must be kept one with another.... When I hear men speak of laying aside all engagements to [consider only] that wild or vast notion of what in every man's conception is just or unjust, I am afraid and do tremble at the boundless and endless consequences of it.[107]

Cromwell uttered his concern lest the agents and their civilian friends come to the prayer meeting not to seek God, but only to instruct the General Council, because their minds were already made up. Conciliatory words were spoken by two agitators of Rich's regiment, Nicholas Lockyer and Captain John Merriman, as well as Robert Everard and Lieutenant Edmund Chillenden of Whalley's regiment. Cromwell at once softened and assured Everard that he and his colleagues were not 'wedded and glued to forms of government'. Indeed, he concurred with them 'that the foundation and supremacy is in the people, radically in them, and to be set down by them in their representations.'[108]

The last item of business transacted that day was the appointment of a committee of twelve officers and six agitators to review the Agreement in the light of the army's declarations and engagements of the past few months. There were enough men on the committee who could be counted on to see eye to eye with Cromwell and Ireton: Lieutenant-General Thomas Hammond, Colonel Rich, Adjutant-General Richard Deane, and Colonel Scrope. But there were also men of a more revolutionary cast: Colonels Rainborowe, Overton, Okey and Tichborne (the London alderman whom the army had just appointed lieutenant of the Tower) and Sir Hardress Waller. No officer agitators were included, but no one seems to have minded their omission.[109]

The meeting adjourned late, but many officers rose early the next morning to meet at Quartermaster-General Grosvenor's lodgings and call upon God.[110] There is no record of attendance, but we know that Rainborowe was absent, later explaining that 'the ill disposition of my body caused me to go to London last night.' However, we know that on Sunday the 31st Rainborowe visited Lilburne in the Tower, and during their two-hour conversation professed cordial friendship to Lilburne, hatred of Cromwell and esteem for the king.[111] William Clarke recorded only the tail-end of the prayer meeting, just prior to the arrival of Everard and the other agents. Captain John Clarke, the Baptist and future MP,[112] opined that the army had sinned in following too much the candle of reason instead of the light of God. Captain John Carter, a Buckinghamshire man[113] from Hewson's regiment, then led the group in prayer once more, after which Adjutant-General Richard Deane moved that they should all meet again at the same place for prayer on Monday the 1st from 8 to 11 a.m. Lieutenant-Colonel William Goffe then launched upon an elaborate disquisition based on Revelation 17–20, and Numbers 14. The Revelation texts had convinced him that the army was to be Christ's instrument in overthrowing the 'mystery of iniquity' represented by the 'kings of the earth' who had surrendered their power to the Beast (whom he took to be the Pope). Though masked in biblical language, his rejection of Cromwell's and Ireton's efforts to come to an accommodation with the king was unmistakable. Yet he would have pleased Cromwell by his insistence on the paramount need to avoid disunity.[114] He also distanced himself from the Levellers by his stress upon the the vital importance of correct timing, and his advocacy of waiting upon God before embarking upon revolutionary action.[115]

The prayer meeting had evidently elated the officers and produced a sense of harmony and fellow feeling. The arrival of Rainborowe and the agents who had not shared that experience rudely shattered the mood. It was nearly midday when the new agents, three or four in number, made their entrance. They stood uncomfortably near the door, while their spokesman, Robert Everard, thanked the officers for receiving them. Calling himself 'a poor man', with 'many impediments' in his speech, he averred that the kingdom faced 'sudden destruction' unless the army took speedy action. Cromwell invited the men to draw closer and join the group. Since the committee had had no chance to examine the Agreement and the army's engagements, he suggested an adjournment until nine or ten o'clock that night, to enable them to do so. This suggestion was immediately opposed by Rainborowe, who perhaps as a result of his meeting with Lilburne now pressed the urgency of coming to a quick decision. Pointing to the army's 164-page *Book of Declarations*,[116] which Cromwell had held up for all to see, he declared that if they spent ten days debating its contents they would still not come to an agreement. They should therefore move directly to consider the document submitted by the new agents. Captain Awdeley also swung behind the Levellers, arguing that 'idleness ... hath begot this rust, and this gangrene amongst us.'[117] Commissary Cowling made the pertinent point that, with the army growing daily more unpopular because of its reliance upon free quarter, a speedy decision was highly desirable. Speaking for both himself and Cromwell, Ireton exclaimed that, if he thought it was God's will that king, lords and all property should be destroyed, he would not flinch, but quietly submit. While he yielded to Rainborowe's request, he exhorted his hearers to be guided by the wisdom from above. Divine wisdom was 'pure, and then peaceable, and then gentle, and easy to be entreated', so they would know by the character of their deliberations whether or not they were actuated by it.[118]

At last the Agreement was read out. As soon as the clerk had finished Ireton pounced on the first article. Did electoral redistribution 'according to the number of inhabitants' not imply universal manhood suffrage? If so, was it not an overthrowing of England's fundamental law since time immemorial? Ireton had committed a tactical blunder,[119] and had also violated his own precept to pursue unity and conciliation before all else. Not only was the issue divisive; it was one that Ireton and Cromwell could not win. Confident of his audience, Rainborowe took up the challenge in words that still ring in our ears after three and a half centuries:

> Really I think that the poorest he that is in England hath a life to live as the greatest he; and therefore truly, sir, I think it's clear, that every man that is to live under a government ought first by his own consent to put himself under that government; and I do think that the poorest man in England is not at all bound in a strict sense to that government that he hath not had a voice to put himself under. And I ... doubt whether he was an Englishman or no that should doubt of these things.[120]

Ireton now had something to sink his teeth into. Denying that there was any natural right to vote, he expounded a doctrine of political rights for the propertied alone:

> No person hath a right to an interest or share in the disposing or determining of the affairs of the kingdom, and in choosing those that shall determine what laws we shall be ruled by here, ... that hath not a permanent fixed interest in this kingdom ... that is, the persons in whom all land lies, and those in corporations in whom all trading lies.[121]

A landowner and merchant franchise, according to Ireton, was a 'fundamental part of the civil constitution'. It was a narrow definition, which corresponded ill with electoral reality in England at that time. Not only was there often little attempt to prevent all adult males from voting in county elections; many boroughs also practised what amounted to a householder franchise.[122] Rainborowe would not budge. Twice he reiterated his conviction that 'every man born in England' ought to have a voice in elections. Since all were subject to the laws, all should have a say in framing them.[123]

Seemingly unaware of the silent disagreement of almost all who sat in the room with him, Ireton stubbornly stuck to his position that, while seats should be redistributed, the franchise should remain the same. Raising the spectre of communism, he warned that votes for the propertyless would inexorably lead to the abolition of property. Rainborowe scornfully repudiated Ireton's reasoning and asked him not to 'make the world believe that we are for anarchy'. Cromwell, seeing the cherished unity of the army quickly vanishing, pleaded with the two men not to be 'so hot one with another'. Rainborowe, with the help of the civilian Leveller Maximilian Petty, kept up the attack, but Ireton modified his earlier intransigence. He was not against enlarging the franchise, he maintained, just against enlarging it 'beyond all bounds'.[124] At last someone spoke up for Ireton's position. Colonel Nathaniel Rich, a well-born and well-married landowner from Essex, was one of the most conservative officers in the army. Speaking from the window sill where he sat,[125] he suggested the compromise of separate chambers ('Representatives'), one for the poor and another for the rich. He reminded his listeners of the disaster that had befallen ancient Rome on account of the democratic franchise. The poor had sold their votes to the richest man, who had then made himself their perpetual dictator.[126]

There followed an inconclusive argument between Ireton and Commissary Cowling over the history and significance of the 40s. franchise. Finally, John Wildman exploded with impatience. Contemptuous of Ireton's reverence for history, precedent and law, he dismissed them all as fabrications of William the Conqueror and his descendants. What had the revolution been for if not to overthrow the state of slavery under which England had groaned for six centuries? Had they not fought for the principle that 'all government is in the free consent of the people'?[127] After another long and largely irrelevant discourse by Ireton on the rights of foreigners, Colonel Rainborowe's brother William pithily observed that the chief end of government was to preserve persons as well as estates, for 'my person ... is more dear than my estate.'[128] Sexby, the only accredited agitator to speak that day, now passionately defended the interests of the private soldier who had borne the heat and burden of the day. Making no effort to conceal his bitterness against Ireton he asserted,

> There are many thousands of us soldiers that have ventured our lives; we have had little property in the kingdom as to our estates, yet we have had a birthright. But it seems now except a man hath a fixed estate in this kingdom, he hath no right in this kingdom. I wonder we were so much deceived. If we had not a right to the kingdom, we *were* mere mercenary soldiers.[129]

Furthermore, the poor, far from threatening anarchy as Ireton feared, 'have been the means of the preservation of this kingdom.' But Ireton would not give up. By his tenacity he wearied many of his audience. Colonel Rainborowe's sardonic comment, 'I see that it is impossible to have liberty but all property must be taken away', must have prompted a murmur of approval. Encouraged, he continued,

> I would fain know what the soldier hath fought for all this while? He hath fought to enslave himself, to give power to men of riches.... When these gentlemen fall out among themselves they shall press the poor scrubs to come and kill [one another for] them.[130]

As a flight of rhetoric it was impressive, if inaccurate. Ireton brought Rainborowe back to earth with the observation that they had not fought the civil war for manhood suffrage, but to put an end to royal absolutism. Hugh Peters tried to carve out a middle ground by suggesting the enlargement of the franchise to include all those who had assisted parliament against the king. Cromwell too searched for middle ground. While chiding Sexby for a speech 'that did savour so much of will', he proposed that most copyholders by inheritance[131] ought to have the vote. He added that he was prepared to resign his command if it would serve the army and the public interest. Cromwell's words only seemed to make matters worse, for Sexby returned to the attack angrier than before. If the propertyless were to be excluded from the political process, they should have been told so at the beginning of the war, for then fewer of them would have fought. It was now plain that Ireton's argumentativeness had hurt his cause. Whereas the framers of the Agreement had deliberately refrained from dealing with the franchise, Ireton had succeeded in turning it into the issue on which the radicals would not compromise. Fiercely Sexby maintained what in a cooler moment he must have known was untrue: the franchise 'was the ground that we took up arms [on], and it is the ground which we shall maintain.'[132] Captain Awdeley probably spoke for the majority when he scolded both sides for their intransigence and for causing a seemingly endless dispute. Stung into defending his motives, Cromwell for the first time revealed his complete agreement with Ireton's arguments, declaring that in all the debate he had heard no satisfactory answer to them. Again he proposed a committee to try to break the impasse.

Ireton now decided to backpedal in the hope of averting certain defeat. He pointed out that he had been among the first to press for the dissolution of the present parliament, for regular elections in the future, and for the redistribution of constituencies. Now he was even prepared to yield on the franchise question if that was the clear will of the army. All he asked was that a committee should first weigh his own argument in favour of limiting the vote to men 'not given up to the wills of others'.[133] In an attempt to build consensus, Colonel Rainborowe apologized for his heated expressions, but did not back down on his demand for an immediate vote on the Agreement's first article. Striving to foster the emergence of this consensus, Captain Edmund Rolphe, officer agitator and former apprentice to a London clothworker,[134] proposed a 'composure' on the franchise question that would eliminate servants and foreigners. Another officer agitator,[134] Lieutenant Edmund Chillenden, religious libertarian, lay preacher and former button-seller in Cannon Street,[135] backed Cromwell's proposal for a committee as the speediest way of breaking the impasse. Captain Clarke questioned Ireton's contention that universal suffrage necessarily entailed the destruction of property rights, since by natural law everyone had a right to his own property.[136] Sir Hardress Waller, a practical man who was always impatient with loquacity, said it was clear they would never agree on this issue, and therefore there was no point in continuing the debate. The people did not care what paper constitution the army adopted if they continued to 'eat and feed upon them' as at present.[137]

But Ireton, who had already done about a quarter of the speaking that day, could not restrain himself from intervening once more: 'I have a thing put into my heart which I cannot but speak.'[138] It turned out to be an emotional recapitulation of Rich's earlier point that nothing could be so prejudicial to political liberty as giving the vote to men dependent on the will of others for their livelihood. He had apparently failed to hear the offer of compromise which would have excluded precisely those groups of men. Maxilimian Petty hastened to reiterate the compromise that Rolphe had already put forward. Apprentices, servants and those taking alms would be excluded 'because they depend on the will of other men.' There can be little doubt that this was a fall-back position for the new agents and Levellers. They had been driven to adopt it by the force of Ireton's and Rich's arguments, which Cromwell and Lieutenant-Colonel Thomas Reade had now both supported. The impassioned words of Wildman, Sexby, Rainborowe and Petty[139] earlier in the debate are ample proof that the Levellers had not intended initially to confine the franchise to property owners and independent tradesmen.[140] Only in the debates on the second version of the Agreement, in late 1648 and early 1649, would the Levellers and officers fully grasp the unpleasant reality that anything approaching universal suffrage would produce a royalist parliament.

Just as a fragile consensus seemed to be taking shape Rainborowe yielded to his impatience by moving 'that the army might be called to a rendezvous, and things settled.' This raised a sore point, for it was an unmistakable reference to the criticism first made in *The Case of the Armie* against the grandees for dispersing the army throughout the country. During the summer and early autumn some regiments had been sent as far away as Wales and Yorkshire, while others had been distributed in an arc more than 100 miles in radius around London. This dispersion of forces had been executed for straightforward reasons: to guard against insurrection in the west and north, and to relieve the pressure on scarce food resources in the metropolis. But the radicals suspiciously interpreted it as a violation of the provision in the 5 June Engagement against dividing the army. A rendezvous would meet the new agents' criticism by physically drawing the army back together. It would also allow Rainborowe to obtain, through the mass acclamation of the soldiers, the endorsement of the Agreement which he now realized could not be secured from the General Council of the Army. However, no action was taken on Rainborowe's motion, probably because

Cromwell ruled him out of order with a reminder that the meeting's purpose was to compare the Agreement with the army's past engagements.[141]

Responding to both the menace of a general rendezvous and the misinterpretation of the Engagement not to suffer the army to be divided, Ireton launched into another long and rancorous speech. With undisguised contempt he explained why the dispersal of regiments to distant quarters did not divide the army in the sense intended by the Newmarket Engagement. If the army was divided now, it was because certain elements had cut themselves off from the General Council and set up a rival caucus.

Did Ireton mean that there was henceforth to be no division of opinion in the army, inquired Rainborowe sardonically? An unnamed agitator rebutted the charge that the new agents had fomented dissension in the army by their separate meetings. The soldiers, he said, had authorized them to meet apart because of their dissatisfaction with the grandees.[142] What was the cause for dissatisfaction, Ireton wondered aloud, when the reforms that would have been wrought by the Heads of the Proposals were similar in many ways to those of the Agreement? Where he could not go along with the new agents, however, was in their attitude to engagements. Judging by the Agreement they were blithely prepared to destroy the power of king and lords, unconcerned about the fact that the army was solemnly pledged to preserve both. Petty, who had attended the debate on the Heads of the Proposals, said bluntly that the king and lords had always been agents of tyranny, and why had people fought for seven years if not to free themselves from tyranny?

Wildman weighed in with an attack on the grandees' negotiations with the king. Unless the present constitution were changed, he said, the soldiers would be vulnerable to reprisals as soon as the king got back into power. Any act of indemnity he signed could be repudiated as having been extracted under duress. Since it was an act of parliament, it could also be repealed by any future parliament. The only way to make indemnity secure was to enshrine it in an Agreement of the People that no parliament could repeal. It had been a long day, and Ireton must by now have felt like a chained bear beset by snarling dogs. Finally, with one mighty effort he determined to demolish his tormentors. He first rounded on Wildman, author of *The Case of the Armie*, which did 'so abuse the general and General Council of the army' merely for having accepted the existence of the House of Lords, and for having treated the king as an adversary with whom they were obliged to negotiate. To say that they had preferred the king's rights before the people's was 'as unworthy and as unchristian an injury as ever was done [by any] to men that were in society with them, and merely equivocation.' To imagine that the soldiers would be more secure against future reprisals if they threw their weight behind the Agreement of the People was a pipedream. Even if everyone in the army supported it, it only amounted to the army giving itself indemnity. Unless the whole kingdom 'to a man' subscribed to it they would still be vulnerable. If the army tried to impose the Agreement upon the kingdom by the power of the sword, there would be no peace settlement but only 'the perpetuating of combustions'. Worn out by his exertions against the new agents and their proposals, he concluded,

> I could tell you many other particulars wherein there are divers gross injuries done to the general and General Council, and such a wrong as is not fit to be done among Christians, and so wrong, and so false that I cannot think that they have gone so far in it.[143]

Then, after a lame attempt by Wildman to deny that he had had a hand in drafting *The Case of the Armie*, the record of the day's debate inconclusively breaks off. According to two other sources, however, the meeting agreed before adjourning to extend the vote to 'all soldiers and others, if they be not servants or beggars.' There were only three votes against this motion.[144]

The meeting had also appointed a new committee of eighteen officers and agitators to review the army's declarations and the Agreement of the People to see if they could be harmonized. The committee included seven field officers, including Cromwell, Ireton and Rainborowe, and five officer agitators, including Major William Rainborowe, Captain John Clarke and Lieutenant Edmund Chillenden. There were six soldier agitators, of whom four were previously known, and two may have been new agents.[145] The committee got to work the next day and kept to its task during most of the following week. Its recommendations illustrated the substantial common ground that existed between the respective authors of the Heads of the Proposals and the Agreement of the People. It recommended that the present parliament should dissolve not later than 1 September 1648, that future parliaments should be elected biennially, and that they should meet for six months. Between parliamentary sessions the country would be governed by a council of state with delegated powers. The continuance of monarchy and House of Lords was tacitly assumed, though with drastically reduced powers. Constituencies were to be redistributed, but whether according to taxation or population was left to parliament to decide. The qualifications for voting were also left up to parliament, with the proviso that all who had fought for parliament before the battle of Naseby, or voluntarily contributed to the war effort, should be included, while all who had opposed parliament should be excluded until after the second biennial parliament.

Significantly the draft was silent about the Levellers' revolutionary concept of an unalterable constitution signed by the people. None the less, the almost equally revolutionary concept of powers reserved from parliament – religion, conscription, and indemnity for things said or done in the late war – was embraced. Parliament, in its threefold character of king, lords and commons, was implicitly accepted as the agency through which the settlement of the kingdom must be achieved, but the power of the commons in relation to the other two branches was enormously enhanced. Tithes were to be abolished and replaced by a land tax or a permanent endowment for the clergy.[146]

In the midst of the committee's deliberations there was another meeting of the full General Council on Monday 1 November. It was the last such meeting that William Clarke recorded. Fairfax was still indisposed, and so Cromwell presided again. He led off with an invitation to those present to testify what answers God had given them in their prayers the day before. Captain Francis Allen reported that he and other godly people had been told that they should take away the king's and lords' negative voice. The burden of Captain Carter's and Commissary Cowling's communications was the same, but was checked by the sceptical maverick Lieutenant-Colonel Henry Lilburne. Younger brother to the famous Leveller, and to the radical-leaning Colonel Robert Lilburne, in whose regiment he served, Henry would turn royalist by the second civil war and be killed at Tynemouth Castle, where he was governor.[147] Cromwell too was sceptical, if for different reasons. He could not understand these men's obsession with the royal veto. The army should confine itself to military matters. He could discern 'no visible presence of the people, either by subscriptions or number' in favour of the Agreement; besides, were not forms of government but 'dross and dung in comparison of Christ'? Responsibility for deciding what was fit for the kingdom rested with parliament, and there it should remain. Instead of inciting disobedience to the general by calling for unauthorized rendezvous, they should wait upon God until he revealed his will unmistakably to them.

But it was becoming increasingly evident that articulate opinion in the army was now profoundly hostile to the king, perhaps in light of the growing knowledge of his meetings with emissaries from the Scots. John Jubbs, a native of Norwich, Leveller sympathizer and lieutenant-colonel in Hewson's regiment, suggested obliquely that the king was 'guilty of all the bloodshed, vast expense of treasure and ruin that hath been occasioned by all the wars both of England and Ireland.'[148] Lieutenant-Colonel William Goffe, always respectful of Cromwell, diffidently revealed that 'a voice from heaven' had informed him that 'we have sinned against the Lord in tampering with his enemies.' Trooper Sexby shared none of Goffe's diffidence. Echoing the prophet Jeremiah, he thundered, 'We have gone about to heal Babylon when she would not. We have gone about to wash a blackamoor, to wash him white, which he will not.' Because of their attempts to please the king the army commanders were 'in a wilderness condition.'[149]

As he had done the day before, Cromwell reproved Sexby for being self-willed. He was much less sure than the trooper what the will of God was, but he knew that God was not the author of contradictions. He therefore tried to demarcate the common ground between the Levellers and the higher officers. They shared the objective of freeing the nation from oppression and slavery, and they both apprehended the danger from the king and lords. What divided them was the issue of whether monarchy and peerage should be torn down. It would be almost another year before Cromwell was convinced that this was necessary, but even now he did not rule it out. Yet, if it was God's will that the king should be destroyed, Cromwell was sure that he would find a way of doing it that would not involve the army in scandal or sin.[150]

Captain George Bishop, the future Quaker,[151] was about a year ahead of his time when he bluntly asserted that if the kingdom was now in a dying condition it was because of their efforts to preserve 'that man of blood' whom God had 'manifestly declared against'.[152] With unwonted tact Wildman reflected that it was difficult to know when a man spoke from God and when he did not. He was confident, however, that what promoted the people's safety could not be contrary to the mind of God. There then followed an inconclusive argument between him and Ireton over whether the king was obligated by his coronation oath to confirm those laws which the people chose. As they had over the franchise, Cromwell, and even more Ireton, showed poor tactical sense. Ireton's love of argument made it impossible for him to refrain from exploring the history and finer points of the royal veto, seemingly oblivious to the fact that virtually everyone in the meeting wanted it abolished once and for all. Yet it was Ireton himself who observed that parliament, by passing and enforcing laws without the king's consent for five years, had permanently emasculated his negative voice. If that is so, declared the exasperated Captain Awdeley, we are all agreed. They were debating a non-issue.

Ireton then read the proposals that the committee had drafted the previous evening, hopeful that they would win the council's speedy assent. The idea which had attracted the committee's support on Saturday night, that the king and lords should have a suspensive veto, had since been dropped. Now it was suggested that the king and lords would only be able to veto laws that affected them personally, and would retain the privilege of being judged by their peers. This very slender concession to the first two estates of the realm again generated much more heat than its significance justified. The next proposal, to model the succession of parliaments on the existing Triennial Act of 1641 rather than the Agreement of the People, turned into another bone of contention. It disappeared from the resolutions that were brought forward on 2 November. A third proposal, that MPs should have a minimum income of £20 a year, was also dropped because of its negative reception, as was a proposal to allow peers to be elected to the lower house. Rainborowe preferred to let them sit with the commons as they did in Scotland. Yet to Ireton it was self-evident that a permanent group of lords would wield disproportionate power amidst a body of men who were replaced every two years.[153]

Behind William Clarke's fragmentary record of this protracted debate one can sense the General Council's diminishing interest in the recondite historical and theoretical arguments of Ireton, Wildman and (occasionally) Cowling. One imagines the sigh of relief with which they approved a motion to adjourn till the morrow and allow the committee to proceed with its work. We have seen the surprising extent to which officers and agitators were able to agree, and how far the officers were willing to go in adopting Leveller ideas. At the end of the 2 November meeting, according to Rushworth, the General Council agreed to a number of points that were to be framed into a 'Declaration to be presented to parliament'. The present parliament was to be dissolved by 30 September 1648. Future parliaments would meet for six months every two years. Elections would be 'free to freemen', meaning presumably those who were not dependent on the will of others. Of the three branches of parliament the commons were to be supreme. The king, for example, would have no power to pardon those who had been condemned by the commons. There was to be electoral redistribution. The people were to enjoy liberty of conscience, there was to be no conscription, and indemnity for acts committed during the civil war was to be absolute, 'save only what shall be adjudged by the present House of Commons.'[154] The above points were referred back to the committee to be put in final form for approval on Friday 5 November.[155] Except for the crucial provision that the package be submitted to parliament, the Levellers had virtually won the General Council to their way of thinking. Cromwell and Ireton must have been deeply unhappy at the way the debate had gone.

While the Agreement of the People occupied most of the officers' time around the beginning of November, it should be borne in mind that attention was given to other matters as well. On 4 November the General Council addressed itself to the treaty with the king, and also formulated a number of suggestions for handling army arrears.[156] On 5 November, while Cromwell was attending the House of Commons, the General Council at Rainborowe's instigation agreed to write to parliament opposing any further addresses to the king. Chagrined at his inability to block the dispatch of the letter, Ireton stormed out of the meeting.[157] Meanwhile, outside the doors of the council meetings the Levellers and new agents campaigned unremittingly against the grandees. In a demogogic indictment of them for their hostility to the authors of *The Case of the Armie Truly*

Stated, Wildman demanded their punishment for 'private tampering' with the king, and Charles's impeachment 'as a man of blood'. He urged the agitators to be militant, and not to shrink from overthrowing their present commanders, for 'ye have men amongst you as fit to govern, as others to be removed, and with a word, ye can create new officers.'[158] Another anonymous tract from a clandestine press berated the grandees for failing to achieve anything worthwile on behalf of the army or the people:

> What one good deed have you done since your march through the City of London? Show us if you can; the people cry none.... Do but your duty, remove all oppressions, ease the country, ... and ... we'll warrant you hobnails and clouted shoes will give you hearty thanks and help and assist you.[159]

A few days later Lewis Dyve reported having heard from John Lilburne that the new agents were planning to purge parliament and arrest Cromwell and his faction of officers in the army.[160] The fact that Lilburne, though a prisoner in the Tower, was often seen walking abroad cannot have been reassuring to the grandees.[161]

By 3 November the printed version of the Agreement of the People was on the bookstalls in London, carrying its boast of 'the general approbation of the army'. Fifteen regiments, as well as the lifeguard, were claimed as supporters.[162] At this juncture the senior officers decided enough was enough. Faced with the reality that the Levellers had as good as captured the General Council, and were now summoning the soldiery to revolution, Cromwell and Ireton, doubtless with Fairfax's support, resolved to meet the menace head-on. They had lost the argument in the General Council; so they moved to cut off further debate and send the agitators back to their regiments, with no announced date of recall. They were fortified in their determination by the gathering unease in many regiments at the visible disintegration of the army. Hewson's regiment bluntly condemned the forces of division, which everyone understood to mean the new agents and their Leveller backers.[163] In the same week an unspecified number of regiments apparently petitioned Fairfax to discharge the agitators.[164] Accordingly, Cromwell went on the offensive at the 8 November meeting of the General Council. Even though the matter had been settled, he reopened the question of the franchise, charging that the Leveller position would lead to anarchy. Then, after an inconclusive exchange with Captain-Lieutenant Bray, who was not even a member of the council, Cromwell moved to send the representative officers and agitators back to their quarters. The motion passed without a recorded vote.[165]

Considering the behaviour of the council during the previous ten days, it is remarkable that the lieutenant-general was able to swing the majority behind his motion. Since William Clarke's minutes for that day are skeletal, we can only guess at the dynamics of the debate. Probably the argument that most swayed his listeners was the necessity of acting to curb the disunity that the debates had exacerbated. Cromwell may also have pointed out the increasingly ugly attacks on the king emanating from radical quarters.[166] We may also be sure that Fairfax, who was in the chair that day, threw his full weight behind Cromwell's motion. Fairfax's political power within the army was all the greater for being rarely exercised. The prestige of his support, together with his promise of a rendezvous of the army, was what probably won the day for Cromwell. The council members must also have been favourably inclined by the knowledge that Fairfax was vigorously prosecuting their material demands. He had just written to the Commons requesting six weeks' pay for the army at once, the raising of the monthly assessment from £60,000 to £100,000 to eliminate the need for free quarter, and the earmarking of the dean and chapter lands as well as the remaining bishops' lands for the army's arrears.[167] Before adjourning, the General Council nominated a committee to draft the text of a Remonstrance to be offered to the regiments for their approval. The eighteen-man committee included only two agitators, Allen and Lockyer, as well as two radical officers, Major William Rainborowe and Commissary Cowling. The others were all hard-nosed conservatives such as Cromwell, Ireton, Hewson and Stane, or moderates such as Tichborne, Captain Deane and Lieutenant-Colonel Cowell.[168]

Leveller Subversion and the Mutiny at Ware

The General Council met for the last time before the army's rendezvous on 9 November. It approved a follow-up letter to the Speaker explaining that it did not intend its previous one to be interpreted as opposing parliament's right to send propositions to the king. It was also announced that the rendezvous would be held on different days in three separate places. This displeased the Levellers, who had hoped to be able to orchestrate a mass demonstration in favour of the Agreement of the People. But there were practical reasons for three rendezvous besides the grandees' wish to thwart the Levellers. The regiments were widely dispersed, and it would have been awkward to summon them to a single meeting point. Moreover, daylight was very short in November, and this alone would have prevented Fairfax from addressing the eighteen regiments one by one as he wished.[169]

The General Council's final piece of business before it adjourned was the appointment of another committee, to make a summary of what the army stood committed to in the Solemn Engagement and its other declarations concerning the good of the kingdom, the people's liberties and the interests of the army. This done, they were then to consider how these commitments could be harmonized with *The Case of the Armie* and the Agreement of the People. Other committees had performed similar tasks previously, but the purpose of this one was to assist Fairfax in drawing up the engagement that he was to present to the regiments at the three rendezvous. Apart from the absence of almost all the soldier agitators, the committee was well balanced, including such radicals as the two Rainborowe brothers and John Wildman. Wildman's appointment represented the first and only time that a non-member was named to one of the General Council's committees.[170] This committee is known to have met twice before the army rendezvous. Colonel Harrison, whose regiment was not stationed near London,[171] had missed the Putney debates. He used the present opportunity to testify that it lay upon his spirit 'that the king was a man of blood' who ought to be prosecuted for his crimes.[172] It was not the first time this label had been applied to Charles, and it pointed to a budding conviction in some sectors of the army that he had by now forfeited his right to live. Whether or not there was an actual conspiracy to murder the king, Charles can be forgiven for fearing that his life was in peril. Politically the army appeared dangerously near to being out of control. Twenty-one radical officers had just written to parliament denouncing 'accommodation with perfidious enemies' and identifying the king as 'your capital enemy'.[173] The same day an anonymous informer had warned the king of a plot to kill him.[174] Another anonymous letter told him that eight or nine agitators had just met and discussed killing him.[175] Anxious about these reports, Cromwell wrote to the king's keeper at Hampton Court, Colonel Whalley, intimating his fears of 'some murderous design ... against His Majesty'.[176] Presumably with Cromwell's authorization, Whalley showed Charles the letter, intending to convince the king that the general officers were doing everything in their power to avert such a catastrophe. It was strongly suspected in some quarters that Cromwell had an ulterior motive for frightening Charles into flight, but the hypothesis that Cromwell willed his escape is quite implausible, as most historians have long agreed.[177] Charles quit Hampton Court on the evening of the 11th, and arrived on the morning of the 14th at Carisbrooke Castle, where he threw himself on the mercy of Colonel Hammond.[178]

Meanwhile, in the army and in London the political temperature continued to rise. The Commons' flat rejection of the army's request to have the dean and chapter lands as security for arrears exasperated the grandees and played into the hands of the Levellers.[179] Seething with excitement at the signs of polarization in the army, the Levellers convened large meetings with the new agents and friends such as Henry Marten at two taverns – the Mouth at Aldersgate and the Windmill near Coleman Street – and also at an unnamed meeting place in Mile End to the east of the City.[180] There they uttered imprecations against the king, and concerted efforts to muster civilian support for army militants at the first rendezvous at Ware. Among the craftsmen of London the most responsive to the Levellers' efforts were the weavers. On 13 November 150 of them met at the Mouth, where they agreed to mobilize the men of their craft to attend the rendezvous at Ware the following Monday.[181]

Within the army Leveller organizing went on at a frenetic pace. On 11 November the new agents scattered about the streets of London a printed address to all the soldiers, disclosing the bitter debates that had taken place in the General Council, warning the rank and file not to trust their officers, and demanding a general rendezvous for the army.[182] But in the end only three horse regiments and perhaps one of foot are known to have been won over. They were Harrison's, which arrived without permission at the Ware rendezvous, Ireton's, Twisleton's and Lilburne's.

Though stationed farther from the capital than some, Ireton's regiment was in close touch with the convention of agents at London. It 'well approved of' *The Case of the Armie* and 'heartily' wished for a general rendezvous. Willing to organize the garrisons of Southampton, Bristol, Weymouth, Exeter, Gloucester and others, it also reported the intriguing news that a meeting of constables of the hundreds had been convened for 10 November to elect representatives to a parliament of agitators that was planned to be held in London. Five of the regiment's six troops were reported to have signed the Agreement of the People on 8 November. On the same broadside was printed a letter from twenty-three agents of Twisleton's regiment at Cambridge announcing the private soldiers' solidarity with the London agents 'for the rights and privileges of the subject and the bringing to justice of all sorts of offenders.' This curious document carried no printer's name, and it remains a puzzle why the two regiments in question allowed details of their organizational work to be made public. Perhaps they believed that after their imminent victory over the officers there would be no further need for secrets.[183]

More disturbing than the incipient mutinies in Ireton's and Twisleton's regiments was the actual disobedience of Robert Lilburne's foot. Fairfax had ordered the regiment to Newcastle, but on November 23, when it had gone some way beyond Dunstable, Bedfordshire, agents arrived with copies of *The Case of the Armie* and implored the soldiers to march no farther, since according to the Solemn Engagement the army had pledged not to let itself be divided until its demands were met.[184] They or others who had infiltrated the regiment intimated that the king would soon join them at the army's rendezvous.[185] While the soldiers hesitated, the officers held a council of war and dispatched letters to headquarters. Attempting to continue the march, they found the men unwilling. Those from Bray's company arrived at his quarters at night demanding the company's standard, and when he refused to surrender it they entered his bedroom and seized it.

Other detachments from the regiment were strung out as far as North-amptonshire. Bray therefore moved north and, if his later account can be believed, attempted to rally his men to obedience at Olney. But they had already been won over by the agents, and resolved to join the rest of the regiment at Dunstable. Around this time Lieutenant-Colonel Henry Lilburne and Major Paul Hobson arrived with an order from Fairfax to resume their march to Newcastle at once. Rather than obey, the soldiers drove off all their officers except their quartermaster and Captain-Lieutenant Bray, who the other officers believed was in league with the rebels. Later eight officers would issue a statement accusing Bray of being a ring-leader of the mutiny. According to them he had consistently opposed Fairfax's order to the regiment to march to Newcastle, and had refused to communicate that order to his own company.[186] In a struggle with the men of Captain Tolhurst's company two soldiers lost their lives and the lieuten-ant his hand. Their behaviour now became more and more anarchic. Not content to get rid of their officers, they pursued them, swearing revenge and seizing their horses. Inflamed by cavaliers in their midst, some of them belligerently demanded to know 'if there were any roundheads' in every town where they stopped. By Sunday 14 November the entire regiment, minus most of its officers, was at Dunstable, and had resolved to appear at the rendezvous at Ware, over 20 miles away, the next day.[187]

On the morning of Monday 15 November the general officers rode to the first rendezvous at Ware, Hertfordshire, with a high sense of apprehension. Would the soldiers accept the Remonstrance they had prepared for them, or would they shout it down in favour of the Agreement of the People? What about the growing manifestations of royalist feeling among the infan-try? Considering the pamphleteering of previous weeks, the organizing activities of the new agents, their collaboration with urban radicals, and the numerous meetings in the City, Southwark and Mile End, the army commanders had good reason for worry.[188]

Before the generals made their appearance at Corkbush Field outside Ware, Colonel William Eyre (or Eyres) and Major Thomas Scot had already come and were preaching up the Agreement to the seven regiments that had been authorized to attend. Other men busily distributed copies of the document and collected signatures.[189] When Fairfax arrived a delegation headed by Colonel Rainborowe formally presented a petition urging the army to embrace the Agreement of the People and warning of 'the sad consequences of being divided and scattered before our native freedoms [are] settled and our arrears secured.'[190] Rainborowe was no longer formally a member of the army; nor was his regiment, presently under the command of Colonel Richard Deane, part of the Ware rendezvous. His presence therefore was highly irregular. Fairfax's answer is not recorded, and no punishment was meted out to Rainborowe, except that a few weeks later the Commons voted to bar him from taking up his command at sea.[191] Probably he was ordered to leave the field along with Major Thomas Scott, the recruiter MP for Aldborough, who was escorted back to Westminster by Lieutenant Chillenden. Colonel William Eyre, who was also unconnected with the New Model, was arrested, along with Captain-Lieutenant William Bray. The only other officer to be disciplined for his conduct that day was Major John Cobbett, an officer agitator from Skippon's regiment, which had also not been summoned to the rendezvous.[192] Other arrests included Jeremy Ives, an agitator from Waller's regiment, and three London agents: Samuel Chidley, William Larner and Captain Taylor (perhaps from the Southwark trained bands).[193] John Lilburne and Richard Overton were also there, but avoided arrest by remaining at Ware waiting for the insurrection that never happened. They apparently shared their disappointment that day with Captain William Style of Lambart's regiment.[194]

The most dangerous moment of the day occurred when Colonel Thomas Harrison's regiment appeared on the field uninvited and without their officers. Evidently led by Joseph Aleyn, the new agent for the regiment, they bore copies of the Agreement pinned to their hats with the slogan 'England's Freedoms, Soldiers' Rights' written on the outside.[195] But the men's defiance collapsed when Fairfax issued a severe reproof and Cromwell tried to rip the papers from their hats. Seeing that none of the other seven regiments was ready to join them in mutiny, they removed the offending papers and swore to obey the general's commands.[196] Fairfax then began the review, pausing before each regiment to have his Remonstrance read aloud and subscribed. In it he blamed the army's distempers on the new agents, who had taken it upon themselves to be 'guided by divers private persons that are not of the army.' They had divided the New Model and brought about 'the dissolution of all that order, combination and government which is the essence of an army.' If these 'abuses and disorders' were not stopped Fairfax threatened to resign his commission. He then outlined the higher officers' platform for the army and the kingdom. For the army:

1 constant pay;
2 the stating of accounts and security for arrears;
3 an improved indemnity ordinance, with commissioners to reside in every county instead of just London;
4 provision for maimed soldiers, widows and orphans;
5 no conscription;
6 cancellation of apprenticeships for soldiers on active service.

For the kingdom:

1   a time limit for the present parliament;
2   future parliaments to meet and dissolve at prearranged times and sit for fixed periods;
3   provision also for the freedom and equality of elections.[197]

While the Levellers had been roundly denounced in the preamble to the Remonstrance, it is clear that they had influenced its content regarding conscription and elections. For most soldiers the Remonstrance was all they wanted. As Wildman ruefully recalled a month later, many regiments signified their approbation by crying, 'For the king and Sir Thomas, for the king and Sir Thomas.'[198]

When Fairfax's review was well under way, Lilburne's regiment suddenly made its appearance on the field. On the march all day from Dunstable, it cannot have arrived before the late afternoon. The regiment had been in a state of mutiny for two-and-a-half weeks, with Captain-Lieutenant Bray being the only officer to stick by the men. He was now arrested. The men defiantly wore the white Agreement in their hats 'as if they had been going to engage with an enemy.'[199] Colonel Thomas Pride's major, George Gregson, whose regiment was probably stationed nearby, turned to the unruly mass of soldiers and exhorted them to submit to discipline. Bartholomew Symonds, a soldier, took offence at Gregson's intervention, and shouted 'that the major was against the king.' Others took Symonds' words as a cue to begin stoning the unfortunate officer, who suffered a broken head. In December Symonds would be condemned to death but later reprieved for having instigated this violent incident.[200] Fairfax and his attendant officers rode up to Lilburne's regiment last, after reviewing all the others on the field. He ordered them to remove the papers from their hats. When at first they refused, some officers waded into the ranks and grabbed the offending papers with their own hands. According to a royalist newswriter Cromwell himself led the offensive, charging into the regiment with sword drawn and breathing fire against the mutineers. His display of courage and ruthlessness was enough to cow most of the soldiers, and the papers disappeared.[201] With order restored Fairfax determined to punish the men who had led a mutiny for over half a month. Eight or nine ringleaders were rounded up, court-martialled on the spot, found guilty and condemned to die. Having reduced them to abject fear, Fairfax then pardoned all but three. These men cast lots for their lives, and the unlucky one, Richard Arnold, was shot by the other two at the head of the regiment. In addition, an unspecified number of mutineers was held in custody for future trial.[202]

Two days after Ware the second army rendezvous took place, on Ruislip Heath near Watford. Only two full regiments were present – Sir Hardress Waller's and Lambart's – as well as three troops of Okey's dragoons. The

occasion was unmarred by any show of discontent, both regiments submitting papers promising unquestioning obedience to Fairfax's commands.[203]
The third and final rendezvous was held near Kingston, Surrey, on 18
November. In attendance were Cromwell's, Ireton's and Whalley's horse
regiments, Fairfax's lifeguard, and the foot regiments of Deane, Barkstead,
Overton and Hewson. Again harmony prevailed.[204] Already the officers and
men of Whalley's troop had dissociated themselves from the new agents,
cancelled their pretended authority and commanded them to return to their
posts in the army.[205] All eight regiments presented an address to Fairfax
pledging their loyalty to him and their 'most obedient loyalty to His
Majesty', but conspicuously failing to mention parliament. Repudiating the
convention of new agents that had met with 'the obnoxious party' (the
Levellers) near Mile End, they condemned them for introducing disorder
and disunity into the army.[206]

Over the three days seventeen and a third regiments[207] had been
reviewed, and all had solidly endorsed Fairfax's Remonstrance. Five
days later most of the officers of Robert Lilburne's regiment signed an
unqualified pledge of loyalty to the general. They took the opportunity to
point out that the recent trouble could have been avoided had the army's
legitimate grievances been attended to.[208] Just over a week later a similar
declaration of loyalty came from Colonel Scrope's regiment in Somerset,
which had not attended any of the rendezvous.[209]

In light of the rapid restoration of order in the army, are we right to conclude that the Levellers commanded less allegiance than they and others
had thought, or that indeed the threat of radical subversion had been a mir-
age?[210] This is certainly what some of the grandees and newswriters would
have liked the public to believe. On the other hand it is perhaps significant
that among the eight regiments excluded from the three rendezvous were
some of the most turbulent in the army. Besides Harrison's and Lilburne's,
who came uninvited to Ware, there was Ingoldsby's in Oxford and Scrope's
in Somerset, both of which would mutiny at the Levellers' instigation in
1649. Finally, there was Twisleton's regiment at Cambridge, which had
given a warm reception to *The Case of the Armie*, and had elected two new
agents from each troop.[211] The quiescence of Ireton's and Whalley's
regiments at Kingston has two probable explanations. While both had been
heavily implicated in the activities of the new agents, they must have
recognized that the failure of the hoped-for insurrection at Ware made
further defiance futile. The soldiers of the two regiments were doubtless
also subjected to an intensive barrage of propaganda by their officers
immediately before the 18 November rendezvous. Significantly, however,
both regiments would be turbulent and mutinous in 1649.

While perhaps only five regiments had been extensively radicalized in the autumn of 1647, it should not be overlooked that the officer class as a whole had shown itself to be disturbingly susceptible to Leveller arguments. To their surprise the conservative higher officers had found themselves a beleaguered minority during the Putney debates, and Ireton's long-winded eloquence had if anything trimmed that minority smaller over the course of ten days.

The City Levellers also continued to be troublesome. In spite of their devastating defeat at Ware they had boldly approached the Commons, whom they qualified as 'the supreme authority of England', demanding to know why they were accounted 'the off-scouring of the land' when their chief objective was to exalt the power of the lower house. They urged it to debate the Agreement of the People and to investigate the army's punishment of Colonel Eyre, Captain-Lieutenant Bray and Private Arnold. The petitioners' only reward was to see their five leaders committed to prison during the pleasure of the house.[212] During the debate on this petition Cromwell rose in the house to explain why he had come to the conclusion that the Levellers had to be suppressed. In the beginning he had permitted them to propagandize the army, confident that 'their follies would vanish.' But when he saw the success they had with the soldiers he changed his mind. He had supported a more equal representative merely because 'many honest officers' wanted it. Much more worrying was their acceptance of the Leveller demand to give the propertyless the vote. It was 'this drive at a levelling and parity' that made him determined to set his face against them.[213] Implicit in Cromwell's speech was a recognition of the gravity of the Leveller threat to take political control of the army, and a contradiction of the earlier glib assertion that no more than 400 men supported the Agreement.

Reconciliation and Restructuring

After the three rendezvous and the imprisonment of the London Levellers the senior officers strove to consolidate their position, first by vigorously prosecuting the army's material grievances, and second by attempting to conciliate the alienated radicals within the ranks.

They had already demonstrated their anger with London for dragging its feet on assessment payments, by ordering Colonel Hewson to quarter his regiment on City householders.[214] Fairfax informed the Committee of the Army of what he was doing, and the chairman, Robert Scawen, immediately alerted the Commons. Alarmed at the prospect of a fresh crisis in City – army relations, the Commons instructed Cromwell to halt Hewson's advance towards London. Simultaneously it sent a joint committee including the three London MPs and the Earls of Northumberland and Pembroke to treat with the City magistrates for the payment of their assessments. As a result of this intense activity the crisis was averted for the time being. Colonel Hewson's regiment drew up in Hyde Park, the City sent a delegation to Fairfax at Windsor, promising to do better with its overdue payments, and as a sign of goodwill the Merchant Adventurers offered a £10,000 loan to tide the army over.[215] The Commons spent the better part of 26 November in committee of the whole trying with little success to find a way of paying the army.[216] It was generally agreed that the best way to stem the inflation of state indebtedness to the army was to shed excess strength. Over the next month parliament genuinely came to grips with the problem of army finance for the first time since 1645. That it did so was chiefly attributable to insistent pressure from army headquarters. On 4 December the high command publicized the fact that it had tried but failed – owing to lack of money – to disband all the soldiers who had enlisted since the Newmarket Engagement the previous June. Faithful to parliament's wishes, Fairfax had issued orders to the officer commanding each regiment to discharge all soldiers who had enlisted since the army's occupation of Westminster on 6 August. However, he had insisted on providing them with a month's pay to cover their expenses home. Any soldier with previous service in a royalist army who had enlisted since the Engagement of 5 June was likewise to be dismissed.[217] This measure would, it was hoped, purge the army of both royalism and Levellerism at a stroke. Most of the politically oriented men who had flocked to the army's standard in the previous six months were infantry. Their numbers reportedly ranged between 3000 and 5000.[218] But when they arrived at Windsor for dismissal there was no cash on hand for them, so except for 'cavaliers or disorderly persons' they were all sent back to their regiments until parliament should provide the money.[219]

The next day Fairfax and his advisers sat down and composed a full-scale Representation of the army's demands. Colonels Sir Hardress Waller and Edward Whalley delivered it to parliament on 7 December. Focusing exclusively on bread-and-butter issues, the cool prose of this manifesto did not conceal the rage of the senior officers at parliament's dilatory approach to its financial needs. Since the end of the civil war parliament had been in control of the entire country, yet the soldier had been no better paid than when it had controlled only eighteen counties. After their one-day occupation of the capital four months had elapsed, during which the recent distempers within the army could have been averted by a timely attention to money. No longer petitioning, the officers now virtually ordered parliament to take the following steps: issue proper debentures to the soldiers *before* they disbanded; raise the monthly assessment from £60,000 to £100,000;

authorize the general or the Committee of the Army to nominate new members to county committees that neglected to collect their assessments; earmark two thirds of remaining delinquents' lands and compositions, as well as the dean and chapter lands, for the payment of military arrears; compel employers to deduct military service from the time of apprenticeships; and make adequate provision for maimed soldiers, widows and orphans.[220]

Parliament listened to what the officers were saying, and over the next few weeks passed an impressive volume of legislation that went a long way towards satisfying the demands of the 7 December Representation. Free quarter was formally abolished, and the arrears of the previous nine months' assessment were ordered to be paid up by 15 January 1648. Soldiers' arrears were secured on the excise, delinquents' compositions and estates, and the bishops's lands.[221] The request for the dean and chapter lands, however, was tacitly rejected. Soldiers' accounts were to be stated and debentures issued, with deductions for free quarter of 4d. a day for the foot soldier and 1s. a day for the horse trooper. All supernumerary forces were to be disbanded with two months' pay. The Indemnity Committee was given the task of enforcing the ordinances giving soldiers the right to deduct their military service from the term of their apprenticeship. Finally, justices of the peace were charged with doling out relief to maimed soldiers, widows, and orphans.[222] The Committee of the Army was directed to collect the monthly assessment aggressively, to use it first to disband supernumerary forces, and then to see that the army was regularly paid. The receipted warrants that survive from this period show that the new policy was strikingly successful. During the first six months of 1648 most regiments were paid in full, although by June it was taking several months before the warrants were actually honoured.[223]

In addition to taking much better care of army pay, the Committee of the Army was authorized to see that the streamlining of accounting procedures for military arrears that had been launched in June was carried through. The standard deductions for free quarter meant that soldiers no longer had to prove the value of the free quarter they had received before being issued arrears debentures.

It was now the job of army headquarters to uphold its part of the bargain by shaving 20,000 men off the military establishment. This difficult administrative exercise was postponed until January 1648, because the last three weeks of December were devoted to tidying up the discipline problems from the Ware mutiny, and rehabilitating army morale.

The catalyst of the army's internal reconciliation was Fairfax's personal chaplain, John Saltmarsh.[224] An austere, radical antinomian, he had quit the army on 26 November, apparently out of disgust with the policies of the higher officers.[225] A week later they had launched the court martial of the Ware mutineers. Corporal William Thompson was condemned to death, while six or seven privates from Robert Lilburne's regiment were sentenced to run the gauntlet. The privates were punished the next day, but Thompson's execution was put off until the conclusion of the trials of Captain-Lieutenant Bray and some of the other ringleaders. Bray's trial had commenced on the same day as the others', but he conducted himself so insolently that the Council of War adjourned the trial.[226] On the same day Saltmarsh had risen from his sickbed in Ilford, Essex, mounted his horse and set off on a 30-mile journey to Windsor. His purpose, as he told his wife, was to impart to the army a message that he had received from heaven. After getting lost in Windsor Forest during the night he finally arrived on Monday the 6th to find the General Council assembling. Fairfax was not there, but Saltmarsh told the others that 'he had formerly come to them as a lamb, but now in the spirit of a lion, to tell them [that] ... the Lord had now foresaken them and would not prosper them because they had forsaken him, their first principles, and imprisoned saints.' Later that day he met Fairfax, Cromwell and Ireton and gave them each the same message, keeping his hat on all the time. Cromwell was visibly moved by the pronouncements of this sepulchral figure, prompting the chaplain to declare that he was 'glad ... that there is some tenderness of heart in you.' On the 7th he left the army for the last time and returned to his home, where he died four days later. Stirred by his example, Henry Pinnell, chaplain to Hewson's regiment, added his own reproaches to Cromwell for failing to relieve the kingdom.[227]

There was no explicit acknowledgement from the army that Saltmarsh's mission effected a change of heart among the officers. However, he was a man who commanded enormous respect, and the fact that at the end of December the army authorized the radical printer Robert Ibbotson to publish the full account of his visit to headquarters is tacit acknowledgment of his impact on its deliberations.

Saltmarsh's denunciations did not prevent Bartholomew Symonds, the man who had stoned Major Gregson in the head at Ware, from being condemned to die at his court martial on 15 December. However, the sentence seems not to have been carried out. Another soldier, named Bell, was condemned to run the gauntlet twice for his role in the mutiny. Captain-Lieutenant Bray and Major John Cobbett were also tried that week, but no sentence was handed down. Captain-Lieutenant John Ingram of Fairfax's lifeguard questioned the Council of War's right to try Cobbett, and was himself cashiered.[228]

Cobbett, the son of a Northamptonshire gentleman, was a Middlesex resident whose two brothers, Ralph and Robert, were also infantry officers in the New Model. Like them he may also have been a London merchant. At the beginning of the war he had been lieutenant of foot in Essex's army. As officer agitator for Skippon's regiment, he became known for his radical views. In 1652 he bought crown land in Sussex, and at his death in 1657 left property worth £200 a year.[229] The exact offence for which he was tried is unknown, but on 20 December, having debated his case until midnight, the Council of War voted that he should be cashiered the army. Significantly however, the task of pronouncing sentence was left to the General Council.[230] This decision reflected a partial concession to the Leveller argument that soldiers should not be subjected to courts martial in peacetime, and that since the 5 June Engagement the General Council alone had the power to expel members from the army. The force of this concession was attenuated by the fact that the rank-and-file representatives were no longer participating in the General Council's deliberations.[231]

When the General Council met on 21 December, instead of pronouncing sentence against Cobbett it heard officers question whether the martial law then in force was not too strict for peacetime, and whether some of those in custody should not be freed.[232] Saltmarsh's words had evidently reached their mark. The first loosening of the logjam of reciprocal hostility was signalled when Major Francis White was readmitted to the General Council by unanimous vote after apologizing for his September statement that there was no power in the kingdom but the sword.[233] Rainborowe also made a full submission for his offence at the Ware rendezvous.[234] Profiting from the new spirit that was abroad, the senior officers appointed a prayer meeting for the morrow. The 'day of humiliation' lasted from nine in the morning till seven at night, and was observed with fasting and extemporaneous prayer. During the ten-hour marathon Cromwell, Ireton, Tichborne and Peters were among those who prayed 'fervently and pathetically'. A royalist correspondent cynically reported that the contributions of Cromwell and Ireton were 'such sweet music as the heavens *never before* knew.'[235] The declared aim of these exercises was to unite the army, and in this they were a resounding success. Rainborowe was readmitted, and a recommendation was made to parliament that he should take up his appointment as vice-admiral of the navy. The next day the court martial of Bray, Crossman and Joseph Aleyn was resumed. But, once they had made the gesture of acknowledging 'their rash and irregular proceedings' and promising to submit to army discipline in the future, the charge was dismissed and they were sent back to their regiments.[236]

Cromwell was not alone in appreciating the importance of unity to the preservation of the army's military and political strength. The king's flight from Hampton Court and the daily evidence of his efforts to forge a new alliance with the Scots against parliament and its army had convinced the senior officers that there was no longer any hope of a negotiated settlement with their adversary. From London they heard ever more disturbing reports of royalist preparations for a new insurrection in the volatile capital. Yet the great mass of the population was unconcerned with the threat of renewed civil war. Resentful of parliament's monthly assessment, and furious at the requirement to furnish free quarter to an idle army, nothing would appease them but a massive reduction in that army's numbers. For all their awareness that spring would almost certainly bring new strife, Fairfax and his colleagues knew they could not reverse their commitment to make drastic cuts in the payroll.

The Great Disbandment

The disbandment of January and February 1648 was conducted in such a way as to safeguard the military effectiveness and enhance the political unity of the army. It was done in three stages. First came the reduction of those field regiments which had not partaken of the reconciliation exercise at the end of December and were thought to be infected with presbyterianism. Second were those garrison and provincial troops which were both apolitical and unconnected with the New Model. Last came the selective dismissals from New Model regiments, mostly involving the elimination of known radicals.

The politically untrustworthy forces were based in Wales and the west, and included Kempson's, Eyre's, Herbert's, Gray's, Morgan's, Laugharne's and Mitton's foot regiments, and Birch's and Cooke's troops of horse. Most had been tainted by association with the abortive presbyterian counter-revolution of the previous summer. When ordered to disband they at first resisted and attempted to organize a general mutiny. But Fairfax's letter to the county committees of Worcester, Gloucester and Hereford ordering the arrest of soldiers who 'continue any longer in bodies together to the oppression or terror of the country' was sufficient to subdue all but Laugharne's.[237] Part of Sir William Constable's regiment was sent to replace Colonel Morgan's in Gloucester. There occurred a moment's anxiety when it seemed as if the occupants would not allow the new troops to enter the city, but, perhaps appeased by the prospect of receiving £1000 if they yielded peacefully, Morgan's men allowed the transfer to take place without incident.[238]

Another body of troops which no longer shared the army's political orientation were the gentlemen of Fairfax's lifeguard. Their captain-lieutenant, John Ingram, had already been cashiered for espousing the Leveller line in December. The remainder of the gentlemen, by contrast, cared chiefly about their back pay and were openly contemptuous of the religious radicalism dominant in the army. Most of them had apparently enlisted under the Earl of Essex at the beginning of the civil war.[239] By the beginning of February preparations had been made for the two months' pay, which the lifeguard duly received by 21 February.[240] A petition that they should receive debentures for their arrears, backed by 'visible security', was ignored, and they were ordered to assemble in St James's Fields for disbandment. At this their anger turned into open mutiny. Eight or ten of them seized the lifeguard's colours and carried them off. The next day, numbering close to a hundred, they descended on Fairfax at his house in Queen Street, Westminster, demanding that he pay them all their arrears. Voices rose on both sides, with Fairfax refusing to discuss arrears and taxing them with mutiny for their removal of the colours. They then stormed out of his house and headed for Whitehall and the Mews with the aim of stirring up Rich's horse and Barkstead's foot regiments to join them. Jeeringly they cried out to the men of these regiments, 'We shall be well paid for serving the state, we shall have liberty of conscience, and that's reward sufficient. What need ye ask for more?'[241] But Rich's and Barkstead's men were unmoved, and Fairfax quickly ordered the leaders of the mutiny arrested. This action brought about the collapse of the lifeguard's defiance. From that time until his resignation two years later, Fairfax's personal guard was furnished by regular troopers.

The second category of troops targeted for disbandment included the Northern Army and the occupants of most of the garrisons and castles of England and Wales. The motivation behind these disbandments was non-political, except that the provincial forces suffered treatment inferior to that enjoyed by the New Model regiments. Fairfax emptied dozens of fortresses from Northumberland to Cornwall, and dissolved all except five regiments of the Northern Army.[242] Unlike the more overtly political disbandments, these ones provoked little incident. Only the men of Plymouth garrison offered violent resistance, almost killing Colonel Fortescue in the process.[243]

Finally it was the turn of the New Model regiments. Initially the new establishment was to consist of just under 27,000 men distributed into twelve regiments of horse, fifteen of foot and one of dragoons. This number also included 200 men in the train of artillery and two companies of firelocks, numbering 100 each.[244] By the beginning of February, however, Fairfax had changed his mind. With the consent of the Commons,[245] he reduced the size of the establishment to about 24,000, but increased the number of regiments so as to accommodate more officers. Each cavalry troop and infantry company was reduced to eighty men. There would now be fourteen regiments of horse and seventeen of foot. Given the much higher pay scales of officers, even the elimination of 3000 common soldiers must have produced little net saving.[246]

The reasons for restructuring the army in this way were both administrative and political. It meant that none of the New Model regiments would have to be dissolved. All the officers who had proven their political reliability could be retained. The few essential non-New Model regiments and companies could also be absorbed.[247] About the middle of March army headquarters commenced the disbandment of nearly 4000 men from the original New Model regiments. A similar number who had enlisted since 6 August 1647 had already been sent home. Among this first group were London radicals who had flocked to the army's standard when it invaded the capital, hoping to participate in an authentic social revolution. The disbandment of March 1648 enabled the senior officers to weed out the remaining soldiers whom they suspected of radical sentiments or disaffection.

Which regiment experienced the most sweeping purge? It was Harrison's, whose men had turned up uninvited at Ware, hats defiantly garnished with the Agreement of the People and the Leveller motto 'England's Freedoms, Soldiers' Rights'. The senior officers had not forgotten this disobedience, and now cut the regiment by half.[248] Predictably, these drastic expulsions provoked a mutiny. Its details are obscure, but several men were brought to trial on 26 February, and three found guilty: Henry Gittings (one of the regiment's agitators), Thomas Latham and John Mallosse. The penalty was death, but Fairfax postponed the executions for a week, and they seem never to have been carried out.[249]

The other horse regiments were reduced by about 100 men each, and the reductions appear to have been effected without incident. It took until early May for the shedding of these supernumerary horse to be completed. [250] The dismissal of excess infantry was conducted with less formality. On 22 June 1648, at the height of the second civil war, 229 men and five non-commissioned officers of Fairfax's foot regiment were disbanded with two months' pay.[251] The records tell of no other foot regiment that was formally reduced in number. Could it be that in the other infantry regiments enough men simply melted away to render formal disbandment unnecessary?

In the early months of 1648, a gigantic reduction of the army's numbers, equal to almost 50 per cent of its strength, was carried through. The reduction was effected mainly at the expense of the provincial forces. Except for a few politically unreliable elements, the bulk of the original New Model regiments remained intact. It was an impressive administrative achievement, demonstrating to the people that parliament and army had heard their groans against heavy taxation and free quarter, and were determined to lighten the burden of both. Yet the issuing of two months' pay to 20,000 men, alongside the regular payment of the 24,000 continuing troops, could not have been accomplished without the ruthless work of the county committees in collecting the arrears of the previous nine months' assessment. Any who refused to pay underwent the disagreeable experience of having troops quartered upon them.[252]

By the spring of 1648 the military high command had reshaped the parliamentary army into a leaner, more politically homogeneous and less costly body of men. But there was to be no interval for this restructured force to catch its breath. Even as the last few thousand men were being demobilized, royalist insurrection was being fomented in the capital, and reports were arriving at headquarters that armed rebellion against the regime was imminent in the western border counties, Wales, the north, East Anglia, Kent and Essex.

8

The Second Civil War

Armed conflict broke out once again in May 1648, but the Second Civil War may be said to have begun on 11 November 1647, the day that Charles I fled from Hampton Court. As early as late October the king had secretly abandoned the settlement being crafted by the army grandees and their parliamentary allies, when he opened talks with the Scottish commissioners. The Earls of Lanark and Lauderdale had held out new hope of a military solution, this time with Scottish support, if Charles would allow them to rescue him and carry him to Berwick.[1] In the event Charles ended up at Carisbrooke Castle, under the nervous wardenship of Colonel Robert Hammond. As far as the officers were concerned, he had broken his parole. His flight prompted Cromwell and Ireton to jettison any further attempts at reconciliation with him, and to redirect their energies to unifying the army and turning it once more into an effective fighting instrument. Vexed by Leveller unrest on the one hand and Scottish–royalist conspiracy on the other, the grandees were in an ugly mood. Ireton was heard to say that he was ready to fight both king and parliament at once. On a visit to army headquarters at Windsor Castle, Charles's emissary Lord Berkeley got a frigid reception. Later the same night he learned from a member of the general staff – perhaps muster-master Dr William Stane[2] – that there was talk among the officers of bringing the monarch to trial. Cromwell was now freely admitting that his previous negotiations with Charles had been a blunder, which he blamed on 'the glory of this world [which] had so dazzled his eyes, [that] he could not discern clearly the great works that the Lord was doing.'[3] Army intelligence activities were stepped up with the aim of uncovering the schemes that the king and his new allies were concocting. We do not need to credit the fantastic story of Ireton and Cromwell dressing up as ordinary troopers and haunting the Boar Inn in London to intercept Charles's letters in order to accept that they kept a close watch on royal correspondence.[4]

The army's aristocratic allies, Saye and Wharton, played their part in showing that Charles was no longer bargaining in good faith. Four propositions were drafted and sent to the Commons, where they were turned into bills and sent back to the Lords for final passage on 14 December. The bills would have given parliament complete control of the armed forces for twenty years; annulled all the king's proclamations against parliament; cancelled peerages conferred since 20 May 1642; and granted parliament the right to adjourn itself to whatever place in England it pleased.[5] As soon as the Scots commissioners got wind of the Four Bills they denounced them. For his part Charles merely ignored them, and launched a campaign for a personal treaty in London.[6] In the coming months 'personal treaty with the king' were the code words by which the royalists knew one another, and attempted to bring moderate opinion to their side.

Bringing the king to London for a personal treaty with parliament was also the nub of the Engagement which Charles signed with the Scots shortly after rejecting the Four Bills. The fruit of two months' negotiations, the Engagement promised the king military aid as a reward for confirming presbyterianism for three years.[7]

Knowing what was up, the officers had acted promptly to neutralize the king both militarily and politically. Before Rainborowe had even made his formal apology, they got their friends in the Commons to move that he should take up his vice-admiralty in the Downs. It was crucial to have a trusted man in charge of the navy on the south coast to fend off any royalist attempt to rescue the king by sea. Initially the motion failed, but by Christmas Eve it was approved. In the Lords, however, Saye and Wharton had lost their majority, and the motion was turned back. Heedless of constitutional niceties, the Commons simply ordered Rainborowe to take command of the ships guarding the Solent.[8]

The officers were active on other fronts as well. In response to the revival of sympathy for the king in London and in parliament, Sir Henry Vane junior threatened fresh military interventions. As a large number of presbyterians left the house in disgust, Vane was able to obtain a majority vote against the City petition for the removal of the army farther from London.[9] Because of their perception of the City's growing political unreliability, the army shifted some regiments closer to the capital.[9] The grandees were extremely worried lest Charles escape from Carisbrooke Castle and become the rallying point of popular antagonism towards the army. The king's gaoler, Colonel Hammond, was less than wholly reliable. The previous spring he had shown interest in the Irish expedition, and by the summer he was disenchanted with the radical direction the army was taking. His appointment to the Isle of Wight in August had been intended to remove him from the eye of the political storm.[11] Cromwell himself went to the Isle of Wight to impress on Hammond the sudden gravity of his responsibility. Troop reinforcements soon followed. Upon his return to London Cromwell sent Colonel Constable and Lieutenant-Colonels Goffe and Salmon to stiffen Hammond's backbone.[12]

Meanwhile, on the floor of the House of Commons, Ireton and Cromwell spoke forcefully in favour of the Vote of No Addresses, which cut off further communication between parliament and the king. Ireton declared that, since the king had ceased to protect his people, they were no longer subject to him and could settle the kingdom without him. Cromwell denounced the king as a dissembler. According to a royalist report he underlined his *volte face* by citing scripture: 'Thou shalt not suffer an hypocrite to reign.'[13] For all the pressure exerted by the army, there was still substantial opposition, and the motion passed by only 140 to 92.[14] On the same day the Committee of Both Kingdoms was dissolved and replaced by a Committee of Safety, which soon came to be known as the Derby House Committee. Three places formerly occupied by presbyterians were filled by war-party men: Sir John Evelyn of Wiltshire, Nathaniel Fiennes and the Earl of Kent. The committee began functioning on 20 January, and quickly set about putting the country on a war footing.[15]

The Vote of No Addresses ran into heavy weather in the Lords, prompting another heavy-handed intervention by the officers. At a meeting of the General Council on 9 January they secured unanimous endorsation of the Vote of No Addresses, at the same time assuring the peers that they supported them in their just rights and in the prosecution of the common cause. Two days later seven colonels, led by Sir Hardress Waller, laid their declaration at the Commons' feet, and were thanked for their trouble.[16] On the 13th, however, a crowd crying 'For the king and no plunder' rioted over attempts to levy taxes for the army. The Commons majority responded to the disturbance by asking Fairfax for 2000 troops to protect parliament. Whether this measure was meant, as royalists alleged, to intimidate the Lords over the Vote of No Addresses is doubtful; none the less they did ratify the Vote on the 15th, with the Earls of Warwick and Manchester entering dissents. From their listening posts in the Mews and Whitehall the two trusted regiments – Colonel Rich's horse and Colonel Barkstead's foot – were able to maintain a close watch on parliamentary proceedings. In conjunction with Tichburne's reliable Tower regiment, they were also in a good position to keep the lid on seething urban unrest. Hewson's and Fairfax's foot regiments in Kent were also moved closer to London at about this time.

At the end of January the Scots commissions quit England, having completed, as they thought, arrangements for a co-ordinated raising in Kent and the Eastern Association, at the moment when their army should cross the border.[18] The next three months witnessed the organization of the provincial insurrections that together were to make up the second civil war. The first rumblings were heard in the capital. Two weeks before Christmas the officers were panicked by the report of a plot to seize the Tower of London and raise the City for the king.[19] Even if the plot was chimerical there was substance enough to the City's discontent. Royalist agitation and recruitment continued apace, so that by the end of the winter the political temperature in the metropolis had reached feverpoint. On the anniversary of Charles's coronation, 27 March, scores of bonfires were lit, coaches were stopped, their occupants obliged to drink the king's health, and an effigy of Colonel Hammond was dragged through the streets, drawn, quartered and burnt.[20]

The following week there occurred a much graver incident, which culminated in a violent attack on the army-nominated City magistrates. On Easter Sunday, 2 April, Mayor Warner ordered the trained bands to disperse a crowd of apprentices who were violating the sabbath by congregating in Finsbury Fields to play their customary game of tipcat. The Sunday after, an even larger crowd gathered with the same intent. This time the mayor sent a company of the Tower Hamlets militia under the radical Captain Gale, 'a tub preacher'. The apprentices soon overpowered these hapless soldiers, and then fanned out through the City and its suburbs calling on the inhabitants to join their insurrection. The main body, 3000 or 4000 strong, surged down Fleet Street, in the direction of Rich's and Barkstead's regimental barracks, shouting, 'Now for King Charles.' A detachment of horse rode out to meet the apprentices, and drove them back inside the City gates. Fairfax and his officers then passed an anxious night debating whether to throw the two regiments into the fray at once, or wait for reinforcements. At length they resolved, 'though they perish', to engage the rioters with their limited forces. In quelling the uprising the next day the army killed several apprentices and watermen, while Captain Merriman and his lieutenant were wounded. To guarantee that there would be no repetition of these alarming events, Tichborne's Tower regiment was quickly augmented by 400 foot and 100 horse, bringing it to over 1000 men.[21]

The Revolt of the Provinces

It proved easier to keep order in the metropolis than to extinguish the smouldering anger of the countryside. From one county after another the news was uniformly bad. The grievances were similar: the excise, the assessment, the tyranny of the county committee, the persistence of free quarter in defiance of the 24 December ordinance abolishing it, and the violation by

Westminster of the traditional rights of the county. Some historians have seen in these risings 'a widespread yearning for the good old days'. They have read significance into the fact that many of the appurtenances of traditional culture – Christmas celebrations, the drinking of healths, Sunday games, bonfires, maypoles and horse races – were called into service to organize resistance to a centralizing parliament and its hated army. They have construed the petitions that were organized as localist in their implications.[22]

More recently there has been a recognition that the second civil war was not just a localist revolt against central tyranny, although it was partly that. In an illuminating study, David Underdown has demonstrated how engagement with the forms of traditional culture was frequently a means of expressing royalist commitment. The ideological content of the second civil war has also been reasserted, since the king's restoration to his former power and dignity, and the re-establishment of the Church of England were seen as necessary objectives if the imagined harmony and stability of the past were ever to be recovered. On the parliamentary side, 'honest radicals' possessing a national consciousness continued to hold sway in Warwickshire, Somerset, Suffolk, Lancashire and elsewhere throughout 1648.[23]

After London the first report of open hostility came from Canterbury, which experienced a riot against the suppression of Christmas and the law requiring shops to stay open. When news arrived of Charles's attempt to escape from Carisbrooke Castle on the 29th, the cavaliers in the city openly declared their readiness to ally with the Scots and restore the king 'to his just rights'. Not until Sir Anthony Weldon arrived before the walls of Canterbury in early January with 3000 of the county trained bands did the rebels capitulate. Another uprising against the anti-Christmas ordinance occurred in Ipswich, and there were also pro-Christmas stirrings in London. As John Morrill has hinted, the more the puritans tried to abolish Christmas, the more certain their downfall became.[24]

Over the next six months the tempo of provincial protest quickened until the Derby House Committee, the Committee of the Army and the army commanders were sore pressed to maintain control of the country. Although military disbandment was being carried out with despatch in the hope of bringing fast relief to beleaguered county committees, it never seemed to be completed soon enough. Free quarter continued to be a huge grievance, exacerbated by the fact that the parliamentary ordinance of 24 December 1647 had in theory eliminated it.[25]

It is not immediately apparent why free quarter should have continued to be an urgent problem, since the Army Committee's records indicate that the field regiments were paid almost in full during the first half of 1648.[46] By May, it is true, some warrants were beginning to take several months to

Table 8.1 Pay issued to field regiments in 1648

	Horse and dragoons		Foot and artillery	
	No. of weeks	When received	No. of weeks	When received
January	4	February–May	4	January–May
February	4	February–March	4	February–March
March	4	March–April	4	March–April
April	4	April–May	4	April–May
May	4–10	May–November	4	May–August
June[a]	4	August–November	4	August–September
July[b]	0		0	
August[c]	4	August–September	4	August–September
September[d]	0		0	
October[e]	0		0	
November[f]	0		0	
December[g]	3–12	December–January	4–9	December–January

a Six horse and two foot regiments were not issued warrants in June.
b Three horse and four foot regiments received two to four weeks' pay.
c Seven horse and six foot regiments were not issued warrants.
d Six horse and seven foot regiments were issued warrants, typically for two to four weeks' pay, which they received for the most part between September and November.
e Three horse and six foot regiments received four weeks' pay.
f Five horse and two foot regiments received four weeks' pay.
g Six horse and five foot regiments were issued no warrants.

honour, while from June to November payment became very patchy. Not until December did the majority of regiments again receive a full four weeks' or more of pay (see table 8.1). The explanation may be that the regiments and local forces awaiting disbandment in the early months of 1648 extracted free quarter during the weeks before they were given two months' pay and sent home.

Whatever the facts of the matter, there was a widespread popular conviction that householders would never be rid of free-quartering soldiers until they were rid of the army itself. Reflecting this conviction, the Essex Grand Jury meeting at Chelmsford on 22 March adopted a petition for total disbandment and a personal treaty with the king. Although the county had previously been a pillar of parliamentary strength, the petition struck a responsive chord, and was brought to Westminster by 2000 men on 4 May. Failing to receive satisfaction, the grand jury met again a fortnight later to adopt an Engagement and Declaration. It militantly refused further tax payments and admissions of soldiers to the shire, and committed its adherents to defend King Charles and 'the known laws of this kingdom'.[27]

A serious disturbance erupted in Norwich on 23 April when soldiers came to fetch the city's mayor to Westminster to explain why he had permitted royalist festivities on the anniversary of Charles's coronation (27 March), and why he had sanctioned the election of malignant aldermen. A detachment from Fleetwood's regiment under Captain Richard Sankey attempted to disperse the turbulent crowd. In retaliation the crowd seized the city magazine and started to bring out gunpowder to use against the troopers. Whether deliberately or not, they set the magazine on fire, which ignited an explosion killing forty of their number, and perhaps three times as many bystanders. Order was restored with difficulty by nightfall.[28]

The next month it was neighbouring Suffolk that flared into revolt against the regime at Westminster. The pretext was a traditional May festivity. A crowd had gathered around a May bush or maypole in Bury St Edmunds when a troop of Fairfax's own cavalry regiment rode into town. To shouts of 'For God and King Charles' the crowd laid into the soldiers and chased them out of town. The political nature of their action was underlined when they shut the town gates, barricaded the streets, seized the magazine and attacked parliamentarians. Their numbers swelled to 600 armed men, and another 100 on horseback. Major Disbrowe threw five troops around the town to contain the revolt, and drove the rioters back when they sallied out. Luckily for Disbrowe there was a solid stratum of parliamentary support in Suffolk, and many of the county militia rallied to his side. Only with their help was he able at last to put down the rising. Royalism again went underground. Later in the month Sir Thomas Barnardiston anxiously informed the Lords that cavaliers were still active in the county. Some had migrated to Newmarket, where they congregated 'under pretence of horseracing'.[29]

Much more worrying news arrived from the west about the same time as the disturbances in East Anglia. There were royalist 'insolencies' in the city and county of Worcester. Plymouth mutinied against the imposition of Sir Hardress Waller as its governor. Exeter too was hostile, refusing to provide quarters for the soldiers or pay its assessment. Stunned by the depth of neutralist and cavalier sentiment he encountered, Waller marvelled that the western counties were not 'all in one flame'. The Commons were sufficiently impressed by the gravity of the situation to instruct him to withdraw his soldiers from Exeter for the time being. Colonel Alexander Popham was sent to neighbouring Somerset in an attempt to keep the royalist infection from spreading there.[30]

By the end of May there is a detectable sense of panic in the Derby House Committee minutes. In addition to major conflagrations in Wales, Kent and the northern border there were brushfires to be snuffed out in the counties of Nottingham, Lincoln, Huntingdon, Rutland, Leicester, Hertford, Cambridge, Sussex, Dorset, Hampshire, Surrey, Worcester and Warwick.[31]

Another element that contributed to parliamentary anxiety was the fact that as the crisis worsened the forces available to cope with it grew steadily fewer. The army general staff had been aware from the beginning of the army's vulnerability once it reduced its numbers by nearly half, but they also knew that disbandment was an absolute political necessity.[32] What no one could predict was how the supernumeraries would receive the news that they were no longer needed. In the event most of them took their two months' pay and went home with minimal grumbling. In Wales, however, there was trouble. As early as January it was known that Major-General Laugharne was unhappy with the terms of disbandment. One of his colonels, John Poyer, was more forthright about his grievance, vowing not to disband until more money was paid his men.[33] Poyer had good reason for fearing disbandment. As governor of Pembroke Castle he had antagonized many by his rough and ready methods and by his questionable financial dealings. Once out of power he would be all too vulnerable to his enemies' desire to even old scores. In desperation he turned to royalist agents, who gave him a ready welcome.[34] Laugharne, by contrast, played his cards more coolly. With a letter of support from Fairfax he and his men petitioned the Commons about their arrears and dissociated themselves from Poyer.[35] Doubtless hoping to preserve Laugharne's loyalty, the Committee of the Army issued him over £2500 in February and March.[36] Poyer exhibited no such talent for discretion. Turning increasingly to the bottle to stiffen his courage, he blurted out his royalist sympathies while defying parliament's orders to disband and yield up Pembroke Castle. On 24 March Fairfax ordered Colonels Horton, Rede, Fleming and Powell and Major-General Laugharne to bring Poyer to heel.[37] On that very day Laugharne, revealing his true colours, took a third of his regiment to join Poyer; together they chased Colonel Fleming out of Pembroke. They then swept through the county crying up the Book of Common Prayer, denouncing the imprisonment of the king, and demanding that he be brought to London for a personal treaty with parliament.[38] This unvarnished royalism evoked a passionate response in Wales. During April Poyer continued to gather strength.[39] Horton, meanwhile, conscious of the magnitude of Poyer's support, and commanding a brigade of only four under-strength regiments, approached Pembroke with caution.[40] The Derby House Committee was also apprehensive about Horton's capacity to subdue the Welsh revolt, and exhorted Fairfax to send reinforcements. With his army shrinking on every side, and threatened in Kent and East Anglia, the general was hard put to cater to Horton's needs. On 1 May he ordered Cromwell to march west with two horse and three foot regiments to bolster him.[41]

On 3 May Cromwell left London, reaching Gloucester on the morning of the 8th. There he reviewed his troops, which had swelled by now to 6500 well-armed horse and foot.[42] Forewarned of Cromwell's approach, the Welsh royalists decided that they must at all costs engage Horton before he was reinforced. Accordingly they fell upon him, 7000 strong, at St Fagans, just outside Cardiff. The royalists outnumbered Horton by about three to one, but they possessed only 500 cavalry, which they stationed in the rear to keep the infantry from turning tail. Although they fought stoutly they were no match for the New Model cavalry and dragoons.[43] The political fall-out from this battlefield verdict was almost instantaneous. Royalist spirits sank while presbyterians in the capital swung away from the king and towards the army.[44]

The Crisis within the Army, April–May 1648

Horton's victory also gave a needed fillip to army morale, which had been fragile for two months or more. Cromwell and Ireton had paid scant attention to military affairs before the end of April. While the great disbandment was proceeding, Cromwell had been wrapped up in parliamentary and City politics. On 1 February he was probably with Fairfax and 'some chief officers' when they were feasted by Robert Tichborne in the Tower of London. A few days later they dined with the mayor and some aldermen. According to Clement Walker, Cromwell was around this time labouring to forge an effective coalition with like-minded men in the City, the army and the two houses of parliament.[45] During the week leading up to 11 February he threw all his weight behind the Commons Declaration upholding the Vote of No Addresses, which passed only over bitter opposition.[46] According to some sources Cromwell was not afraid to voice implacable hostility to monarchical government at this time, but Ludlowe tells a different story. Some time that month he held a meeting at his house in King Street, Westminster, between army and parliamentary grandees on the one hand, and republicans on the other. The republican 'commonwealthsmen' forthrightly declared themselves against monarchy, but Cromwell and the grandees 'kept themselves in the clouds and would not declare their judgments.' After the meeting had gone on long enough for his taste, Oliver seized a cushion, flung it at Ludlowe's head, and then ran downstairs, 'but', Ludlowe relates with satisfaction, 'I overtook him with another, which made him hasten down faster than he desired.'[47]

As the clouds of war darkened, the coalition that Cromwell had so arduously knit together began to fall apart. Not only was England seething with turmoil, but MPs were increasingly jittery at the news of royalists flocking to Scotland to assist the military build-up there. Their nerves were not calmed at the news from Ireland that Lord Inchiquin had turned his coat and declared for the king. Nor were their tempers improved by Charles's unremitting effort to escape from his captivity at Carisbrooke. A number of members of the parliamentary war party now changed tack, and, in a bid to detach the king from his Scottish Engagement, urged that the Vote of No Addresses be cancelled and negotiations reopened.[48] Army thinking was shifting in a diametrically opposite direction to that which now prevailed in the capital. An excise man from Bedford sent a shiver of panic through the London Common Council when he related a conversation he had overheard on the night of 20 April at the Garter Inn in Windsor. In the next room were four officers from headquarters, including Quartermaster-General Grosvenor and Colonel Ewer. Convinced that the Scots would soon invade and that the City of London would throw its support behind them, one officer declared that they must disarm the City and extract £1 million in order to wage war on their enemies. He added that he had discussed the matter with Commissary-General Ireton. The excise man's testimony was also heard by both houses of parliament. The army's response was one of indignant denial, but, in light of the events of the next few weeks, I believe that the testimony furnishes a plausible glimpse of the discussions that were going on among the officers at headquarters.[49]

Among the rank and file radical ideology was being promoted once again. The reasons for the revived radical consciousness within four months of the dramatic reconciliation at headquarters in December 1647 are not clear, but may have had their seeds in the disgruntlement felt by many soldiers at the demobilization of many of their close friends. The royalist newswriter who estimated that seven or eight regiments were now backing the Leveller programme may have been exaggerating, but we do know that there was an unauthorized meeting of agitators from several horse regiments at St Albans, a known centre of political radicalism, on 24 April.[50] Rich's regiment sent a soldier from each troop to represent them. The main order of business was a petition to parliament embodying the Leveller Agreement of the People. A leading figure in this renewed agitation was Captain John Reynolds of Cromwell's regiment, who had also played a dominant role in the politics of the previous summer. The meeting had scarcely got under way when Captains Brown, Gladman and Packer of Fairfax's horse regiment arrived on the scene and broke it up. Some of the representatives were arrested, and at a court martial the same week Reynolds was sentenced to three months' imprisonment and cashiered. Despite the suppression of their meeting, the embittered radicals published their petition and a tract containing a slashing attack on Cromwell. The men of Rich's regiment also composed a petition to Fairfax demanding the release of their imprisoned comrades.[51]

Everything seemed to be going wrong for the army. Threatened by disunity within and mortal peril without, the officers resorted to the only remedy in which they had confidence: a prayer meeting. Amidst a mounting sense of crisis, they kept a solemn fast at Windsor on Thursday 27 April. Following an interruption on the 28th, when the court martials were held, the prayer meeting resumed in earnest on Saturday the 29th. For two days the officers pondered the causes of the 'sad dispensation' they witnessed on every side. There was no consensus; indeed some officers were inclined to lay down their arms in order to avoid a new war. They pointed to the example of Christ, who, when he had accomplished his work, willingly sacrificed his own life.

On the second day they met again in the morning, when 'many spoke from the word and prayed.' Then Cromwell 'did press very earnestly, on all there present, to a thorough consideration of our actions as an army, as well as our ways particularly, as private Christians, to see if any iniquity could be found in them ... that if possible we might ... remove the cause of such sad rebukes as were upon us.' The breakthrough came on the third day when Lieutenant-Colonel William Goffe rose to speak. Taking Proverbs 1:23ff. ('Turn you at my reproof ...') for his text,[52] he announced that all their mishaps were the fruit of not following the ways of of the Lord. Only by listening to God could they have peace of mind and freedom from fear. There ensued one of the most extraordinary scenes in the chronicles of any army. Goffe, who was almost universally respected among the officers, evidently spoke with such eloquence and intensity that everyone in the room was pierced to the heart. 'None was able to speak a word to each other for bitter weeping, partly in the sense and shame of our iniquities of unbelief, base fear of men, and carnal consultations, (as the fruit thereof) with our own wisdoms, and not with the word of the Lord.' Hard on the heels of this emotional catharsis came consensus. Without a murmur of dissent they agreed that they must go out and fight all enemies arrayed against them, 'with an humble confidence in the name of the Lord only, that we should destroy them.' They further agreed that it was their duty 'to call Charles Stuart, that man of blood, to an account for that blood he had shed, and mischief he had done ... against the Lord's cause and people in these poor nations.'[53]

The Renewal of Fighting

During the prayer meeting the Derby House Committee had sent Fairfax an urgent call to deliver more forces to south Wales. On the last day the news came through that Adjutant-General Fleming had been killed by Welsh royalists. As soon as the meeting broke up, the officers dispersed to fight royalist insurgency not only in Wales, but also in Cornwall, the north, Kent, Surrey and Essex. Four months would elapse before they met again under the same roof.[54]

With the army's resources sorely stretched in all parts of the country, royalists now redoubled their efforts to assault the capital. On 16 May a large contingent of armed men from Surrey, at least 3000 strong and well armed, arrived at Westminster to petition for a personal treaty with the king. A group of them invaded Westminster Hall, and either picked a quarrel or were provoked into one with the guards, one of whom they killed. Reinforcements were rushed in from Barkstead's and Rich's regiments, and in the ensuing mêlée five or six petitioners were killed and a great many wounded. Lieutenant-Colonel Cobbett went at once to the bar of the House of Commons to report on the episode, bleeding from the wounds that he had sustained.[55]

Despite the skirmish with the Surrey petitioners, Fairfax had no qualms about ordering the removal of Rich and Barkstead's regiments from London, because he knew that the City militia was now controlled by the politically reliable Skippon. With the commander of the New Model foot at its helm, the militia could be counted on to do the army's will. The Derby House Committee, however, was concerned about the public-relations impact of the withdrawal of troops, and on 19 May it asked Fairfax to leave Rich's cavalry in the Mews for the time being. A week later, the rising in Kent had assumed such menacing proportions that the Commons swallowed their earlier fears, and authorized the general to remove not only both New Model regiments, but Tichborne's Tower regiment of foot as well.[56]

Maidstone

More than the turmoil in London, it was the Kentish rising which obliged Fairfax to shelve his plan of marching north against the Scottish menace. After Horton's victory in Wales the royalists in Kent had decided to await the Scottish invasion before unleashing their rebellion. But they were pre-empted by the wave of indignation that swept the county when the trial of Christmas rioters opened at Canterbury on 10 May. As insurgents overran one town after another, a panicky Derby House Committee ordered Fairfax to send cavalry into the county. On the 22nd armed men rallied at Rochester, shut the city's gates and declared their support for the king. Thanks to the revolt of naval ships in the Downs, and the defection of many moderates from the parliamentary cause, the insurgents were successful in their key military objectives of seizing county magazines and coastal castles. The Commons tried to defuse the anger of the revolted ships by dispatching the Earl of Warwick to replace Rainborowe.[57] Behind the scenes meanwhile, Saye and Sele, acting for the Derby House Committee, concerted with Fairfax the military plan to crush the insurgency.[58] What gave Saye and the officers nightmares was the prospect that the royalist mobilization in Kent would be the springboard for an assault on London.[59] For that reason they did not flinch when Fairfax took the three London regiments, along with four others, and a few companies of Ingoldsby's, to a rendezvous on Blackheath. Tichborne was replaced as lieutenant of the Tower by the presbyterian Francis West, though parliament nullified the value of this sop to the City by emptying the Tower of all its arms and ammunition. They were transported up river to Windsor Castle, where they could be under the army's direct supervision.[60]

The combination of calculated concessions and a determined show of force had the desired effect of sowing disunity among the insurgents' ranks. As Everitt shows, a major source of division was the difference in outlook between the moderates of the county and the committed cavaliers, including several hundred London watermen and apprentices, who flocked to Kent from other parts of the kingdom. The fracturing of this fragile coalition was only avoided by the arrival of the Earl of Norwich, who was acclaimed as the insurgents' general at the end of May. The effect of Norwich's arrival proved to be more a papering-over of the cracks than a true healing of the conflict. Once Fairfax had held a rendezvous of his forces, about 4000 strong, on Blackheath, the more faint-hearted of the insurgents began to retreat to their homes, while the others fell back to Rochester.[61]

The same day (30 May) Fairfax advanced his army to Eltham and sent advance parties almost as far as Dartford to skirmish with the enemy. Pressing relentlessly ahead, he threw out one detachment to capture the bridge at Gravesend, and another under Major Gibbon to raise the siege of Dover Castle. With his main body of troops he approached Maidstone by a circuitous route. Hidden by thick woods of hazel, yew and whitebeam, he was able to keep the rebels in the dark as to his movements until, late in the evening of 31 May, the people of Maidstone discovered parliamentarian troops encamped 4 miles to the west. Fairfax continued to circle the town the next day, arriving before it at 7 p.m.[62]

The royalists had only 2000 soldiers in Maidstone. Fairfax had decided to attack the next morning, but his advance guard of dragoons, hearing the townsmen shout 'For God, King Charles and Kent', impetuously unleashed their assault at once, undeterred by a heavy downpour of rain. The parliamentarian onslaught was furious and violent, but to their surprise the veterans of the New Model ran into resolute resistance from the troops that had been raised scarcely ten days before. Pitched fighting began a mile outside the town, and it was two hours before the defenders were driven from hedge to hedge back inside. Once the attackers surmounted the barricades, they had to fight from street to street, for the royalists exacted a heavy price for every foot of ground they yielded up. One reason why the defenders of Maidstone fought so grimly may be that most of them were not countrymen, but 'seamen, apprentices, and ... commanders in the king's army'. In the narrow streets they used their cannon to deadly effect, cutting down thirty men, including Captain Price and Colonel Hewson's captain-lieutenant. Fairfax wisely held a large part of his brigade in reserve, pouring them in at critical junctures throughout the evening. He himself led his men through the greatest danger on horseback, despite suffering excruciating pain from gout. It was almost 1 a.m. by the time that the defenders were overpowered and the town was still.[63]

Maidstone was a critical victory for parliament. It was won partly by Fairfax's careful planning and personal valour, partly by the seasoned quality of his troops, Hewson's regiment in particular. Added to these considerations was the hard fact that Fairfax's force, small though it was, outnumbered the enemy by almost two to one. The royalists had put together an army of about 11,000 men in Kent, but they had scattered it into several towns: Maidstone, Canterbury, Sittingbourne, Sandwich and Dover. The next day, the majority opted to desert. Those who stuck with Norwich trudged over Rochester Bridge and, eluding their pursuers, got to Blackheath. By then their numbers did not exceed 3000.[64]

For all that Fairfax had won a sparkling triumph in Kent, there was now great anxiety at Derby House lest the City throw its support behind the royalists in their quest for a general rising of Surrey and Essex. All ferryboats across the Thames were stopped, while Skippon supervised the fortification of London Bridge. Thus blocked, Norwich spirited his remaining forces across the river into Essex. By morning 1500 of them had reached the opposite shore, some by swimming, others on horseback.[65]

The little band of rebels then began their trek to Chelmsford and Colchester, hoping that their friends in the county would be inspired to join them. The Essex royalists did indeed swing into action. Led by Lieutenant-Colonel Farr, they seized the members of the county committee as hostages. By the time Norwich reached Chelmsford the grand jury had pledged themselves 'to preserve and defend our royal king Charles, his kingly government; the subjects' liberty, and the known laws of this kingdom.'[66]

Fairfax dispatched Colonel Whalley with a small force into Essex to shadow Norwich. For the time being, however, the general stayed in Kent to complete the reduction of that county. On 5 June Colonel Rich, Colonel Livesey and Major Gibbon raised the siege of Dover Castle. The bulk of the rebel forces dispersed home or fled across the Downs to Canterbury, where they joined others under Sir Richard Hardres. Numbering no more than 1300 fighting men, the royalist remnant did not hold out for long against the pincer movement of Rich and Hewson from the south and Fairfax from the west. The few rebels still bent on resistance escaped towards Tonbridge, later lending their support to the planned rising in Sussex and Surrey.[67]

With Kent pacified, Essex now became the main scene of action. After ordering Ewer's and Scrope's regiments to assist Whalley in Essex, Fairfax himself prepared to cross over to the county at Gravesend. Barkstead's regiment would not be far behind. Not the most courageous of Fairfax's colonels, Whalley had already begun to panic, overestimating Norwich's strength first at 3000 and two days later at 5000 horse and foot. There were indeed no grounds for parliamentary complacency. Norwich *was* increasing in strength in Essex; half a dozen other counties in East Anglia and the Midlands were aflame with revolt; Poyer was keeping Cromwell and 8000 men pinned down at Pembroke; and unfriendly petitions were emanating from Sussex and Dorset. A further prospect that gave the Derby House Committee many anxious moments was that the revolted ships of the navy might spearhead an invasion of the Isle of Wight to rescue the king.[68]

The core of royalist strategy in June was to exploit insurgency in Essex as a means of regaining control of London. For the next two months the political and military situation in the metropolis was extremely unstable. The lieutenant of the Tower, as well as both sheriffs, were now high presbyterians. The imprisoned presbyterian aldermen and militia officers had been set free. Presbyterian royalist MPs such as Denzil Holles, William Waller and Edward Massey had crept back, the latter two to recruit actively for the royalist cause. Munition trains on their way to Fairfax's forces were attacked and overturned by royalist apprentices on 19 June. Thereafter military supply wagons had to give the City a wide berth on their trips to Essex. Nor, unlike in the first civil war, was London any longer a safe place to lodge royalist prisoners of war. A petition to bring King Charles to London received wide support, and on 7 August the Common Council went so far as to call the Scots 'our brethren' and to urge adoption of the programme recently expounded by the Prince of Wales. The chief reason why a royalist counter-revolution was not consummated in the capital in the summer of 1648 was that Major-General Skippon remained as commander of the trained bands with the added authority to recruit a regiment of cavalry. Skippon not only kept the City under control, he also strangled the flow of men and *matériel* to Norwich at Colchester.[69]

In spite of Fairfax's recent successes in Kent, therefore, it is hardly surprising that the minutes of the Derby House Committee reveal not a sense of inevitable victory, but one of barely controlled consternation.[70]

Because London could no longer be relied upon, parliament's resources were spread very thin. The looming danger south of the Thames, for example, compelled the withdrawal in early July of the guard of horse at Bow bridge. Skippon was also asked to send 100 of his newly raised cavalry to Kingston to help break up the royalist concentration there. The Hertfordshire militia and Michael Livesey were also enlisted to link up with small detachments from Rich's and Ireton's regiments. The Earl of Holland and the Duke of Buckingham, in Surrey, were striving to rally royalists from the southern counties. Their hope was to rendezvous with the Prince of Wales, who was daily expected to sail up the Thames. Together they would inspire the counter-revolution in the metropolis. But, before the Prince of Wales could arrive to help with this project, the fortune of battle shattered the second external attempt to rouse the capital for the king. Led by Sir Michael Livesey, parliament's motley force met and defeated the royalists at Kingston, killing Buckingham's son in the process.[71] Taken prisoner, Holland was incarcerated in Warwick Castle. In lodging him there, Fairfax was following the orders of the House of Commons, but the Lords took umbrage at the undignified treatment of a peer. The Earl of Manchester wrote to Fairfax ordering him to surrender Holland to the gentleman usher of the House of Lords, but Fairfax turned a deaf ear. Infuriated, the peers 'debated highly against the general, and moved to have his commission recalled.' In the end cooler heads prevailed, and the motion was not carried. At the root of this conflict was the fear in the Commons and the

Plate 7   Philip Skippon, Major-General of the Infantry

(The Bodleian Library, Oxford)

army that Holland's allies in the upper house would exercise their privileges as peers to release him. The peers in turn feared that Fairfax intended to try Holland according to martial law. In the end the dispute seems to have fizzled out, even though Fairfax remained in clear breach of the peers' privileges.[72]

The Siege of Colchester

Of all the theatres of war in 1648 it was Colchester that most consumed the energies of the Derby House Committee. So fearful were they of the danger posed by Norwich's 5000 hard-bitten men, a mere two days' march from

Sir Thomas Fairfax.

From a Miniature in the hands of Brian Fairfax, Esq.

G. Hulett del. & Sculp

Plate 8 Sir Thomas Fairfax

(British Library: Thomason Collection)

London, that never during the eleven-week siege did they dare suggest to Fairfax a storm of the town, even after its starving defenders had spent all their ammunition. Disenchantment with the parliamentary regime was less general in Essex than in Kent. On the other hand the Essex royalists, with their greater national consciousness, gave Norwich more effective help than did the more royalist but less nationally conscious counties of Kent and Surrey.

The rising in Essex had commenced with the March petition, submitted to parliament on 4 May and backed up with the 17 May Engagement of the grand jury and others to defend King Charles. On the day Norwich crossed into their county, Essex royalists were roused to action. Colonel Farr took 1000 members of the trained bands whom he had detached from their loyalty to parliament, and rounded up the members of the county committee at Chelmsford, holding them hostage until the end of the summer.[73]

A few days later Norwich met Sir Charles Lucas, the royalist general for the county. Together they marched to Chelmsford, where they were joined by Lord Capel, former commissioner of array for Hertfordshire; a soldier of fortune called Sir George Lisle; a Frenchman, Sir Bernard Gascoigne; and 'divers gentlemen of quality' from a number of counties. Shadowed at a safe distance by Whalley and 1000 cavalry, they made their way to Colchester, Lucas's native town. Whalley had no inclination to cross swords with an enemy who was 'like a snowball increasing'. Instead he made it his business to link up with Sir Thomas Honywood's 1200 Essex horse and foot, and to wait until Fairfax arrived with reinforcements. In his main strategic purpose, inhibiting an attack on London by Norwich, Whalley was successful.[74]

On the morning of Sunday 11 June, after hearing a sermon at Gravesend, Fairfax brought his brigade across the Thames at Tilbury Fort. Racked with gout, he nevertheless advanced with lightning speed, picking up Honywood and Whalley on the way, and pushing on to the outskirts of Colchester by the evening of the 12th. With the road to London now secured, the Derby House Committee fretted lest Norwich break out of Colchester and head north to join Langdale and the Scottish invaders. Their apprehension was well grounded, given Colchester's unsuitability for withstanding a siege.[75]

The town (see map 4) was oblong in shape, and its walls had only one salient bastion from which the defenders could fire on assailants in the flank. Moreover, the suburbs, which spread ribbon-like along the roads leading from the town, furnished cover to an assailant who approached near enough to make use of them. Yet there were disadvantages for the besieger as well. If he approached from the London side, as Fairfax did, he had to get past Lucas's house, which formed an excellent royalist outpost on high ground, a short distance beyond the south wall. The south wall

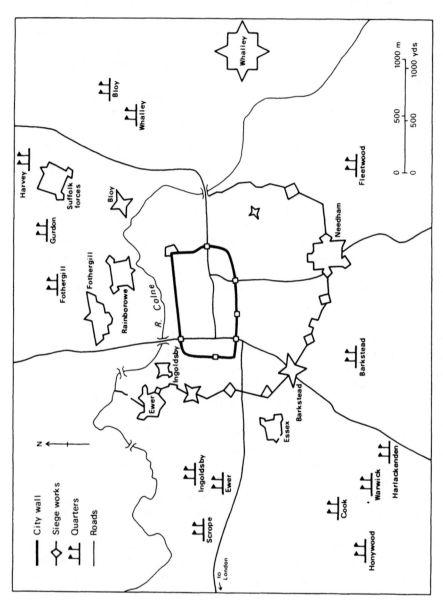

Map 4 The siege of Colchester, 13 July–26 August 1648

itself was commanded by a battery placed on the south-western angle in St Mary's churchyard.[76]

The royalists had not been greeted with unalloyed enthusiasm by the citizens of Colchester. Many clothworkers fled the town and threw in their lot with Fairfax. On Tuesday the 13th, the royalists paid the price for lax intelligence when they woke up to find the besiegers within musket shot of the suburbs. But Fairfax's summons to surrender was met with a characteristic piece of royalist bravado. Alluding to Fairfax's gout, Norwich asked the trumpeter to tell his master not to worry, for he 'would cure him of all diseases.' Lucas then hastily drew up the men in battle order across the London road, prepared to meet their enemy head-on. Fairfax hurled his troops at this target, expecting a decision as quick and telling as the one he had gained at Maidstone. To his dismay Barkstead's foot, who spearheaded the attack from the centre, were repulsed three times. Yet for a while it appeared that Fairfax's superior numbers might win the day, and the royalists were obliged to retreat inside the walls. As they entered the town, the parliamentary vanguard fell into a trap that Lucas had set for them. Taking advantage of their higher ground, the waiting royalist horse and foot charged from two directions and drove Barkstead's men back through the gate. The fighting lasted till midnight, almost eight hours. Royalist losses were between 150 and 500 men captured, wounded or killed, while Fairfax had lost perhaps 500 dead and wounded.[77]

Fairfax now had to face the disagreeable truth that Colchester would not be an easy nut to crack. Because an unsuccessful storm would place London in jeopardy, he had no recourse but to settle down for a long siege. His soldiers spent most of the next eleven weeks investing the town with a line of trenches and stockades punctuated with star-and square-shaped forts. The defenders for their part busily repaired the town's decaying walls and, where there was no wall, cast up ramparts and counterscarps. The perimeter of Fairfax's line stretched in a long semicircle within a stone's throw of the town walls, beginning and ending at the river Colne on the east and west sides of the town. Several fortified enclosures were erected for regiments stationed on both sides of the river, but the bulk of Fairfax's army made their quarters on open ground near the road to London, southwest of the town. If the defenders' main hardship was an ever-dwindling food supply, the besiegers were sorely tested by having to camp out of doors in the midst of an exceptionally cold and wet summer.[78]

Besides the regular foot regiments of Needham (Tower of London), Barkstead, Ingoldsby and Ewer, and the horse regiments of Fleetwood, Scrope, Whalley, Ireton and Fairfax, the parliamentary general profited from a major infusion of strength in the shape of county regiments from Essex (2000) and Suffolk (2400). His total numbers reached at least 9000 men. Midway through the siege his army was augmented by a further 1500 men recruited by Major-General Skippon in London. Norwich's forces, by contrast, had by now shrunk to 4000, of whom 600 were cavalry. If Rushworth is to be believed, scarcely 2500 of them were properly armed.[79]

The siege of Colchester is remembered as perhaps the bitterest episode of either civil war. Its sheer length was a major cause of the boundless contempt that each side expressed towards the other. Other contributing factors included the treatment of civilians, supposed violations of the rules of war, the misery induced by hunger and wet, and the strong ideological commitment on both sides. Fairfax's strategy was to make life as miserable as possible for the defenders, to undermine their morale and to turn the townsfolk against them. To this end he choked off the town's profitable trade with London, cut its water supply, prevented civilians from fleeing (thereby accelerating the depletion of the town's food stocks), but offered generous terms to any soldiers who would abandon their officers.[80]

By 19 August the royalists knew the game was up, and prepared themselves for surrender. During eleven weeks of stubborn resistance no one had come to their aid, except a trickle of apprentices, butchers, watermen and others from London. The news from Preston five days later was the last straw. Faced with mutiny the officers opted to accept Fairfax's stringent requirement that they surrender to mercy.[81]

The terms of surrender were signed on 27 August. When Rainborowe's soldiers entered the town they found a scene of desolation. Many houses had been reduced to ashes by the parliamentary bombardment; the inhabitants were sick and weak from malnourishment. Yet the town's humiliation was not over. In order to escape a sacking by the soldiers it had to pay a fine of £11,000.[82]

The soldiers were 'much troubled' at being forbidden to sack the town, but they had the satisfaction of seeing Lucas and Lisle shot to death. Norwich, Capel and Hastings, because they were peers, were turned over to the judgement of parliament.[83]

The executions of Lucas and Lisle have been the subject of historical controversy, Fairfax's severity at Colchester being contrasted with Cromwell's mildness after Preston. It has been suggested that the compassionate Fairfax was talked into countenancing the executions by the Iago-like figure of Ireton. There is no need to accept any of this speculation. Throughout his career, Fairfax did not shrink from severity when he thought it was called for. Two days before the surrender he wrote, 'justice must be done on such exemplary offenders who have embroiled the kingdom in a second bloody war.' In this instance the record shows that he enjoyed solid support from the Council of War. Parliament too betrayed no flicker of doubt as to the rightness of the executions; in fact it also ordered

Fairfax to court-martial Lieutenant-Colonel Farr for having seduced 1000 men of the Essex trained bands into joining the royalists. The justifications for the executions were twofold. First, according to the code of war at the time, officers who continued to hold an untenable position, thereby causing unnecessary bloodshed, forfeited their right to quarter. Second, an officer taken prisoner and then released broke his parole if he bore arms again against the enemy who had released him. This was the doctrine applied to Sir Charles Lucas, who had been taken prisoner at Marston Moor in 1644. Fairfax evidently wrote to him at the beginning of the siege pointing out that he had broken his parole and excepting him from mercy.[84]

When before the Council of War he protested that it was unheard-of for military prisoners to be killed in cold blood, Colonel Whalley reminded him that after the surrender of the parliamentary garrison of Wood-house in Wiltshire Sir Francis Dodington had had fourteen common soldiers hanged. Two private soldiers then chimed in with a recollection that struck nearer to home. At Stinchcombe, Gloucestershire, Lucas 'came in raging, ... swore a great oath', and ordered between twenty and forty of the garrison put to the sword in cold blood. This testimony put an end to the argument.[85]

The political legacy of Colchester was a deepened conviction on the part of most of the higher officers who had attended the siege that the king, as the ultimate author of the suffering and bloodshed that they and their comrades had undergone, must be brought to account for his crimes. Their abiding bitterness stemmed in part from the fact that Colchester had been a near thing. The town had become a rallying point for royalist diehards, Londoners in particular. The Prince of Wales had nearly succeeded in landing 2000 troops for Colchester's relief. The strategy of pinning down almost half of parliament's mobile forces had worked for nearly three months. Parliament's appreciation of the supreme importance of the siege is signalled by the fact that the Committee for the Army took up quarters at Colchester.[86] Thanks to the gritty perseverance of Norwich's men, the northern royalists and Scots invaders were handed a matchless opportunity. That they made so little of it is a tribute to their divided counsel and military incompetence.

Preston

We now turn our attention to the great conflict just concluded in the north. That it had been delayed so long was owing to difficulties on both sides. Lambart, with only 3000 fighting men at his disposal, had no choice but to play for time until Cromwell could be spared from Wales to bolster him.

The last of the Welsh rebels, who were holed up in Pembroke Castle, took an inconveniently long time to surrender. Cromwell had mustered 6500 horse and foot at Gloucester on 8 May, the day of Horton's stunning victory at St Fagans,[87] but there was still plenty of work for him in Wales. He dispatched part of his force under Colonel Ewer to Chepstow Castle, which had recently fallen to the royalists. It continued to hold out until 25 May, when Ewer succeeded in making a breach in its walls. Cromwell meanwhile had pushed on to Pembroke to confront the main royalist resistance in Wales. As soon as he heard that Chepstow had yielded, he sent Ewer's regiment and two troops of Colonel Thornhaugh's regiment to Coventry to assist Lambart in the north. This need to shore up the northern forces before Wales had been properly subdued almost certainly prolonged the task.[88]

On the last day of May, Overton's and part of Constable's foot regiments overran Tenby Castle. Horton was then able to bring these forces to Cromwell before Pembroke. The general now had about 8000 men under his command. Lacking artillery support, however, they were of little value in the face of the castle's massive stone walls. Inside were 2000 fighting men with three weeks' provisions to sustain them. It was all Cromwell could do to deflect the pressing demands of the Derby House Committee and Fairfax to dispatch more of his brigade to the north. By the end of June he had complied to the extent of parting with four troops of horse and two of dragoons.[89]

The key to toppling Poyer, however, was not men but artillery. The wet weather continued, and during one of the frequent storms the heavy guns making up the siege train were dumped in the mud at the mouth of the Severn. It took until 4 July to dig them out. On that day Cromwell swung into action and within the week Poyer had surrendered.[90]

The victory in Wales came none too soon, for the Duke of Hamilton had already been in England for three days at the head of 9000 men. He had been preceeded more than two months earlier by the English royalist Sir Marmaduke Langdale, who with only 100 troops had seized the fortress at Berwick. His companion Sir Philip Musgrave walked into Carlisle and took it over with only sixteen mounted men. At the beginning of June, Langdale scored another triumph when twenty of his men disguised themselves, got inside the mighty fortress at Pontefract, and wrested it from the parliamentary defenders.[91]

These surprise attacks jolted the friends of parliament into action in the north. Since Fairfax and Cromwell had their hands full in the south, they had to depend on their own resources. In Lancashire, Colonel Alexander Rigby set about mobilizing the county for parliament, and soon had 500 horse at his command. Similar efforts in Cheshire and Yorkshire bore fruit more slowly. In Durham, Sir Arthur Hesilrige watched events to the north of him, all the while trying to keep a tight grip on Newcastle. In vain he appealed to parliament to throw a naval blockade around Berwick. Langdale had annoyed his Scottish allies by rushing in before they were ready to invade, but the stirring welcome he received in every county except Lancashire seemed to vindicate his impetuosity. Hesilrige reported that many royalists and recently disbanded supernumeraries had flocked to Langdale's standard at Berwick, while those loyal to parliament had fled to Newcastle. Once they had consolidated their position in Cumberland and Westmorland, the royalists began probing Durham, Yorkshire and Lancashire. To the gloomy eye of Lambart's secretary, Thomas Margetts, it seemed that cavaliers outnumbered Roundheads twenty to one in the north-east. Hesilrige complained bitterly about Westminster's apparent lack of interest in what was happening in the north.[92]

Lambart meanwhile patiently proceeded to augment his numbers, at the same time playing a game of cat and mouse with the royalists. Though he only had 3000 troops he kept Langdale off-balance, and recaptured some small castles. As he awaited reinforcements from the south, he laid an excellent foundation for Cromwell's stunning successes in August. By 24 June he had added Colonel Ashton's 1500 Lancashire troops to his force, and from that time onward took the offensive more and more in his engagements with Langdale.[93]

On 8 July the Scottish invading army, 9000 or 10,000 strong,[94] crossed the border into England. Their project was doomed from the start. The Scottish-royalist alliance had brought together people who neither liked nor trusted one another. It was already several weeks too late to help the risings in England and Wales. The tardiness of the invasion was due to the bitter opposition of the Kirk, which had insisted that an alliance with Charles I would make a mockery of the Solemn League and Covenant. Prominent leaders such as Argyle, Loudon and Leslie would have nothing to do with the scheme, and so its command devolved upon a second-rate soldier, the Duke of Hamilton. His mediocrity fuelled dissension among his subordinates, and it was this that ultimately destroyed the army as an effective fighting force. Short of ammunition, artillery and money, the Scots army was reduced to plundering the English countryside to feed itself. Its outrageous conduct foreclosed any hope of garnering popular support for the invasion from the English population.[95]

Finally, the Scots were plagued throughout their adventure by 'constant rainy, stormy and tempestuous weather'. Torrential rains made the summer of 1648 the wettest in living memory. Rivers and streams that were easy to ford in normal years were turned into raging floods; roads became quagmires; match and powder were soaked; and life for the rank and file, shivering in their sodden clothes, was hellish. The English suffered from the weather too, but they at least were fighting on home ground.[96]

Once in England, Hamilton showed himself indecisive by his failure to engage Lambart, whom he vastly outnumbered. He also blundered by choosing to march west through Lancashire rather than east through Yorkshire. As we have seen, Lancashire was less royalist than any other northern county; furthermore, its many enclosures, hedges and ditches made it difficult terrain for cavalry. The more open country of Yorkshire might have given the cavalry, who were the pride of the Scottish army, scope for their talents. Because of the scarcity of forage, Hamilton was powerless to prevent the horse from enlarging their quarters and advancing ahead of the foot. At the climax of the struggle he found his main army strung out along a thin line more than 20 miles long. Thus dispersed, his troops were in no position to deliver a concentrated blow to their enemy when it was needed.[97]

Cromwell was now on the march to join Lambart. He had set out with 4200 men on 14 July, almost immediately after the fall of Pembroke Castle. Preceeding him were 1000 infantry that he had been able to spare from the siege of Pembroke. These had now arrived in the north, where they swelled Lambart's forces, as did a contingent of horse from Yorkshire. By the 27th Cromwell was at Warwick Castle, but already the thirty troops of horse (nearly 2400 men) that he had sent ahead had joined Lambart at Barnard Castle. This brought Lambart's numbers up to 9000, and Hamilton had now almost lost the chance to exploit his numerical superiority. He opted instead to stay at Kendal, thus allowing Lambart and Cromwell to combine forces with impunity.[98]

Cromwell did not hurry his men towards the north. As he passed through Leicester he stopped to augment them with green recruits from Nottinghamshire, Leicestershire and Derbyshire. His force now totalled 5000, but many of them were ill shod. Accordingly, when he reached Nottingham he stopped to collect the 2500 pairs of boots and stockings that had been shipped from Northampton and Coventry. Similarly, when he reached Doncaster on 8 August, he paused for three days until the artillery arrived from Hull. During that time he exchanged his new Midland levies for veterans whom he detached from the siege at Pontefract. At every step of the way we see Cromwell adhering to his usual policy of refusing to rush unprepared into battle.

On 13 August he rendezvoused with Lambart at Ripon. While waiting for his commander, Lambart had redeemed the time by sealing off Yorkshire from Scottish incursions, and taking up a position between Knaresborough and Leeds. Meanwhile, in the aftermath of Hamilton's decision to advance southward through Lancashire, Langdale returned to Settle, Yorkshire, where he marshalled his forces and directed them towards Preston, expecting to combine there with the Scots.[100]

It is hard to be sure of the exact size of Cromwell and Lambart's combined army. Cromwell informed the Speaker Lenthall that their strength was 8600, including 2100 from Lancashire, and this is the figure that has usually been accepted. In his *Memoirs*, John Hodgson estimated that they numbered between 8000 and 9000; yet Rushworth records a letter of 28 July from Lambart's quarters stating that the major-general's numbers had reached 9000, and that Cromwell had accumulated 5000. This yields a combined total of 14,000.[101] Perhaps the antagonists at Preston were more nearly equal than previously thought.

By 16 August Cromwell was marching, as Woolrych tells us, 'where the knotted muscles of the high Pennines relax into the pastoral slopes and fertile closes of the lower Ribble.' At a council of war that day he decided that their combined armies should fall on the enemy on the north side of the river Ribble. The less daring policy would have been to cross the Ribble and block Hamilton's way south as he left Preston. This would have allowed Hamilton the option of retreating to Scotland. By staying on the north side and falling on the enemy at Preston, Cromwell virtually ensured that there would be a decisive encounter (see map 5).[102]

Langdale and the Scots had no inkling of the peril they were in. Reports had reached Langdale that Cromwell was camped 3 miles east of him at Stonyhurst, but he had discounted them. Most of Hamilton's cavalry had advanced south to Wigan, leaving only a small rearguard to protect the infantry, which was strung out along a line 20 miles to their north. Langdale was 6 miles to the east of this line with his compact force of 3600.[103]

By the night of the 16th Langdale knew of Cromwell's proximity, and early on the morning of the 17th he began hurriedly to pull back towards Preston. Realizing that a battle could not be avoided, he took up a defensive position across the road leading to the town. The site was inhospitable to cavalry, as the road was waterlogged and lined on either side with enclosures and ditches.[104] Having perhaps three times Langdale's numbers at his disposal, Cromwell placed two of his crack horse regiments – Harrison's and his own – on the lane running through the middle of Langdale's position. Another horse regiment he kept in reserve. The two forward regiments were sandwiched between infantry: Reade's, Deane's and Pride's on the right, and Bright's and Thomas Fairfax's on the left. Colonel Ashton stayed back with the Lancashire regiments in reserve. The two layers of infantry were in turn hemmed in by horse regiments: Twisleton's and Thornhaugh's on the right and 'the remaining horse' on the left.[105]

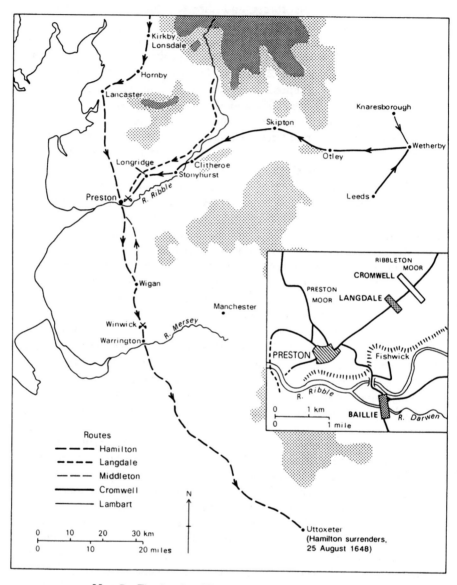

Map 5 The battle of Preston, 17 August 1648

Langdale now spurred his horse for Preston, where he met Hamilton and Callander with most of the Scottish foot drawn up. They had discounted the report about the nearness of Cromwell's army, had not recalled their horse from Wigan, and, astoundingly, were resolved to continue marching south with the foot. At the very moment the attack was beginning the Scottish foot were indeed tramping over the bridge across the Ribble.

By the time Langdale rode back to rejoin his troops Cromwell had sent a forlorn hope of 200 horse under Major Smithson, and 400 foot under Major Pownall and Captain Hodgson to probe the royalists' outer defences. When they came to a ditch one of Langdale's newly raised companies opened fire on them; but Hodgson could tell that they had already lost heart. 'They shot at the skies, which did so encourage our men, that they were willing to venture upon any attempt; ... and we came up to the hedge end, and the enemy, many of them threw down their arms, and run to their party, where was their stand of pikes.'[106] The playing out of this skirmish gave Cromwell time to bring up the whole army from Longridge, 4 miles off. The two sides were now engaged in a struggle that was to last from four to six hours. Given the cramped terrain, it was the infantry who bore the brunt of the fighting. On the right the Cromwellian cavalry worsted their opposite numbers after two charges. Having driven them from the field, they then wheeled around and rushed to the aid of the infantry on the left who were in danger of going under. The ground had now been contested tenaciously for two hours, and as Langdale later boasted, people 'never saw any foot fight better then mine did.' At the height of the battle, Hodgson relates, 'there was nothing but fire and smoke' and 'the bullets flew freely.' Seeing the trouble the left wing was in, Lambart ordered Hodgson to fetch the Lancashire reserves. Their contribution, along with the cavalry's, was decisive. Hodgson, a man of considerable personal courage, was awed by the bravery and resolution he saw around him, 'and how God hid from us the fears and dangers we were exposed to.'[107]

Most of Langdale's cavalry scattered northward in the direction of Lancaster, hoping to unite themselves with Monro's brigade, which had seen no action. Most of the infantry were taken prisoner. The great bulk of Hamilton's army, having sat immobile on the south side of the Ribble, were still unscathed. But they were profoundly demoralized by the news from Preston, and by the realization that their leaders' incompetence had prevented them from doing anything to avert the catastrophe.

Cromwell had rendered his next task easier by dividing the enemy in two. First he took the precaution of stationing a detachment of horse and dragoons with Ashton's Lancashire brigade at Whalley to block those to the south from retreating to join Monro. Then he proceeded to attack the 600 musketeers defending the bridge over the Ribble. They were easily swept back to the south side, and Cromwell prepared to press his advantage.[108]

The dispirited Hamilton now pulled his commanders together for a hurried council of war. They decided to retreat southwards to Middleton's cavalry, even though it meant abandoning their ammunition wagons, and shifting a shivering, hungry and exhausted body of infantry through mud-clogged lanes on a wet black night. During that night of horror almost half the infantry fell away. They also failed to make contact with Middleton, since he came north by a westerly route through Chorley, while Hamilton descended via the easterly road through Standish. As Middleton approached Preston he found himself face to face with a detachment of two or three regiments under Colonel Thornhaugh that Cromwell had dispatched to harass the rear of the retreating infantry. 'Pressing too boldly', Thornhaugh was run through the breast with a Scottish pike and perished. Cromwell had lost one of his best cavalry colonels, but Middleton's force was badly mauled, and left many dead along the roadside all the way to Wigan.[109]

Cromwell was now in hot pursuit with 5500 troops, and caught up with Hamilton at Winwick. There ensued a desperate struggle in the course of which 1000 Scots were slaughtered and several times as many taken prisoner.

Yet for all its losses Hamilton's army still outnumbered Cromwell's by about 1500. Such statistics were of little consequence, however, given the helpless and discouraged condition of the invaders. Following the disaster at Winwick, Callander persuaded Hamilton to abandon the foot so that the cavalry could either return to Scotland or make themselves useful to the English royalists. Accordingly, 4000 more captives, together with the bridge at Warrington, passed into Cromwell's hands.[110]

Cromwell was now burdened with almost 10,000 prisoners, and his men were almost as worn out as the cavalry they were pursuing. If only he had a thousand fresh horse, he was sure that he could make quick work of them, 'but truly we are so harassed and haggled out in this business, that we are not able to do more than walk an easy pace after them.' Confident of his ability to fight on two fronts, Oliver now divided his cavalry, dispatching Lambart southward to round up the remnant of Hamilton's force. He himself meanwhile turned northwards with eight regiments, including Ashton's four from Lancashire, to deal with Monro.[111]

Lambart's work was done for him mainly by the local county militias. After some indecisive meandering Hamilton had headed south for Uttoxeter, where he capitulated to the governor of Stratford, Colonel Stone, on 22 August.[112]

Despite the lengthy recriminations between English royalists and Scots

Engagers, the root causes of the debacle of Preston lay elsewhere.[113] First there was the fierce antagonism of the Kirk and key Scottish leaders towards the whole project. By the vehemence of their opposition they succeeded in hobbling the effort at mobilization, and they imposed a fatal delay on the timetable for the invasion. Second there was the failure of the inhabitants of the north of England to rally to the royalist standard. Their suspicion and hostility towards the Scots outweighed any desire they cherished to see Charles I recover his throne. Third was the strategic skill of Cromwell and Lambart, and the bravery of their men – New Model veterans and country troops alike. The commanders deployed their forces to best advantage by concentrating them at a single point, at the same time exploiting the geographical dividedness of their foes.

Cromwell's remaining tasks in the north amounted to a mopping-up operation. He hardly needed the instructions of the Derby House Committee to recapture Berwick and Carlisle. A trickier assignment was to extinguish the royalist base of operations north of the border. The collapse of the Engager army had been the signal for civil war to erupt in Scotland. Cromwell marched into the fray with five regiments of horse and a sizable contingent of foot. Once in Scotland he had to deal with Argyle, his supposed ally, who bent every effort to get him out of the country at the earliest possible date. Cromwell did not budge, however, until he had obtained the removal of all who had supported the Engagement. Then, leaving Argyle firmly in power, he set out for Pontefract to tidy up the remaining loose ends.[114] As it happened, the royalist defenders of Pontefract did not cede their stronghold for another five months. In that space of time a political revolution was consummated which rendered their resistance futile. It is to the scene of that revolution at Westminster that we now turn.

9

Revolution at Westminster, September 1648 to May 1649

... attending and acting the providence of God.[1]

The wet summer of 1648 was succeeded by an even wetter autumn. Disastrous harvests deepened the unease of the principal participants in the unfolding political crisis. Mirroring the opinion of most men, who craved nothing more than a permanent end to civil strife, parliament opted to resume talks with the twice-defeated king. This alarmed powerful figures within the army, who were at a loss to comprehend why the 'author of the late troubles' should be offered anything other than an imposed settlement. A fortnight or so before the negotiations with the king opened at Newport, Isle of Wight, Colonel Edmund Ludlowe, the Wiltshire MP, rode to Colchester to warn Fairfax of the peril that these negotiations represented for the army. Apart from the fact that Charles could never be trusted, those in parliament who were driving on the treaty intended nothing less than the destruction of the army. Fairfax gave an equivocal reply, so the republican colonel turned to Ireton, who he thought had influence with the commander-in-chief. The commissary-general agreed with Ludlowe's analysis, but disagreed with his tactics. Better to wait until king and parliament had made an agreement, he thought, before moving against them.[2]

Radical Agitation

In contrast with Fairfax, Ireton was no temporizer. The experiences of the previous year had left him disillusioned with the king and receptive to an alliance with radical forces in the City and the army. The autumn of 1648 would witness the forging of that alliance so ardently sought by the Levellers in 1647 but thwarted by the army high command. In the building of this alliance the key role was played by Ireton, with the counsel and approval of Cromwell, his father-in-law.

The Leveller 'large petition' of 11 September 1648 was the first salvo in the political battle whose culmination was the trial and execution of the king. Learning from their mistakes, the Levellers were much more solicitous of the army's interests than they had been in the spring of 1647. Besides the familiar social and economic programme, the petition urged regular pay for the army and indemnity for any illegal acts committed by the soldiers while in uniform. It also denounced the forthcoming negotiations with the king, and called for justice to be executed upon 'the capital authors of the late wars.'[3] Unsatisfied with the Commons' non-committal reception of their petition, the London Levellers returned to the fray two days later reinforced by a group of lower army officers, to complain of parliament's neglect of their proposals, and to urge that they be addressed before the beginning of the treaty with the king.[4] In the meantime Fairfax transferred his headquarters from Colchester to St Albans – significantly closer to London, as those apprehensive about the army's political intentions were quick to notice.[5] A few days later the army issued a statement of demands that was almost identical with the Leveller large petition.[6] The status of the document is uncertain, however. Produced by an anonymous printer it bore the initials of John Rushworth, and the claim that it had been 'sent from a great commander in the army, and desired to be printed and published in the name of the rest.' If the claim was true, the most likely of the 'great commanders' was Henry Ireton. The statement complained of the unchecked activity of London royalists in campaigning for a 'personal treaty' with the king, and in 'their continual, violent and pressing importunity at the parliament's doors.' Less than two months later the mask of anonymity would be torn off and the army's endorsement of Leveller demands would become official.

During that time Ireton's attitude shifted from near-despair to resolution. Towards the end of September he left army headquarters for Windsor, apparently to supervise the examination of the royalist prisoners of war.[7] At Windsor, reflecting unhappily on the imminent betrayal by parliament of everything that the army had fought for, and his inability to persuade Fairfax of the need for action, he handed in a long letter of resignation. The secretary at headquarters tersely noted that the resignation was 'not agreed unto', and indeed Ireton must have had a change of heart.[8] At the beginning of October he was reported to be of the opinion that it was 'high time' to 'clear the House again ... with a new purge of impeachment.'[9] To realize this goal Fairfax's mind had to be changed. Army militants appear to have combined with the Levellers to orchestrate an influx of petitions from regiments and garrisons throughout the country in favour of their programme. Whether Ireton threw his weight behind the campaign is impossible to say. Nevertheless, between 10 October and the adoption of the

Army Remonstrance on 18 November, nine petitions representing nine New Model regiments, the Northern Brigade, and 'several regiments' in the west of England were laid at Fairfax's door.[10] Five of the petitions explicitly supported the Leveller programme. Petitions continued to flow in after the adoption of the Remonstrance. Between 20 November and the end of December Fairfax received twenty-one more petitions from thirteen regiments, over twenty-five garrisons, the Northern Brigade and the county forces of Northumberland. Twelve of the petitions gave explicit support to the Leveller programme.[11] In all, thirty petitions are known to have reached army headquarters during the last three months of 1648: impressive testimony to the organizing ability of the army radicals and their London Leveller allies.

In vain Fairfax tried to damp the fires of political discontent by throwing himself into the campaign for satisfaction of the army's material demands – an end to free quarter, 'constant' pay, and a watertight act of indemnity for illegal acts committed during the civil wars. He laboured assiduously with Robert Scawen, who chaired the parliamentary Committee for the Army, to document the army's financial claims. Since the previous 15 January the arrears owing to the army had accumulated to £120,000, in addition to deductions for free quarter totalling about £60,000. As we have seen, the army had received regular pay for the first half of 1648, but then nothing for four of the succeeding six months.[13] When the Commons failed to act on Scawen's report, Fairfax wrote stressing the privation that the soldiers had undergone, and urging that the regiments be dispersed among various counties, to be paid directly by them in order to prevent the assessment money from sticking to too many hands before it reached the soldiers' pockets.[14] The house did nothing. At the end of the month Scawen and the parliamentary commissioners to the army proposed that, if Fairfax stopped the listing of new recruits to existing regiments, 3000 foot should be added to the establishment to man the garrisons of Berwick, Carlisle, Yarmouth, Rye, Carmarthen and Chepstow.[15] The house ordered the disbanding of newly raised forces but also vetoed the addition of 3000 soldiers to the establishment.[16] In mid-November Fairfax penned another eloquent appeal for parliamentary action on pay, but by then it was too late to deflate the swelling political and religious fervour of the troops. Many officers were convinced that the army was being deliberately starved of cash in order to throw it back on free quarter and render it even more unpopular with the civilian population.[17] The circle of moderates from whom Fairfax took counsel were becoming openly discredited. Chief among them was Dr William Stane, commissary-general of musters. Appointed to Fairfax's committee of officers in August 1647, he was also a go-between in the correspondence between the Saye – Northumberland group in the House of

Lords and the higher officers. Educated at Cambridge, he was accused of being deaf to the cries of the oppressed soldiers, and denounced as a 'sneak' and a 'quack' for advocating non-resistance to authority.[18] Other moderate or conservative officers close to Fairfax included two captains of his own regiment of horse, John Browne and John Gladman, as well as the judge-advocate of the army, Henry Whalley. Browne and Gladman were alleged to have reduced their men to 'Turkish slavery' by refusing to let them petition or exchange newspapers.[19] However, the voices of these spokesmen for moderation would soon be drowned out by the rising chorus favouring decisive action against parliament and City.[20] The organizers of the large petition of 11 September promised to 'live and die, and stand and fall' with the army, and to 'second them with their utmost power and might in their greatest straits and difficulties against all opposition whatsoever.'[21]

A letter-writing campaign preceeded the petitions of October and November, with the first two letters reaching Fairfax before the end of September. From Newcastle and Tynemouth, and another, unnamed northern garrison, and bearing the signatures of Majors Cobbett and Hobson, Captains Clarke and Hutton, and others, they warmly supported the Leveller petition of 11 September.[22] A bolder manifesto arrived from the same region a fortnight later. Entitled *The Declaration of the Armie ... to his Excellency the Lord Generall Fairfax*, it carried the names of Hobson and Clarke. Limited in scope, this letter only urged an end to the personal treaty with the king, and justice upon the army's enemies.[23] But, despite the formidable alliance between London radicals and army activists, and their relentless effort to bludgeon Fairfax into a change of mind, the higher councils of the army remained divided. On 18 October an anonymous military writer asserted that most of the army still wanted to see Charles back on the throne, and assured his readers that they would use their utmost endeavours to bring about this happy event, even though the regiments in the north were opposed.[24] Another pamphlet purporting to represent the army's views asserted more circumspectly that they would work for the king's restoration as soon as he yielded on religion.[25]

Nevertheless, most regiments were in a dangerous political condition by late October. Agitators had reappeared in at least two of them.[26] Numerous anonymous and unauthorized pamphlets were being published in the name of the army.[27] Often apocalyptic in tone and implacable in their hatred of the king, they witnessed to the fact that the army was nearly out of control. The fires of revolutionary sentiment were also stoked by pamphlets disseminated by civilian radicals in London and in various counties. From Oxfordshire came a call for innocent blood to be avenged.[28] An elitist London Leveller deplored the inconstancy of 'the rude multitude, having no good nor solid principles ... they being light as the dust in the drought of summer, are carried aloft, even with every small gale of wind, as well as by a great tempest, so that they are sometimes for the king, and sometimes for parliament, and sometimes for both.' The army represented the radicals' only hope for carrying through a genuine revolution.[29]

Their apocalyptic expectations were belied by the leisurely pace of negotiations at Newport, where the parliamentary peace party worked unremittingly for an accommodation with Charles. The army's sense of alienation was deepened by a number of hostile parliamentary actions. Besides the steps taken towards disbandment, the refusal to increase the establishment in order to man the newly captured garrisons, and the chronic failure to grapple with the army's financial crisis, there was the appointment of Anthony Nicholl, one of the Eleven Members impeached in 1647, to the mastership of the armouries in the Tower and at Greenwich.[30] Another slap in the face was the unexplained refusal to read a letter from Fairfax concerning the forces in Yorkshire.[31] Graver still was the Commons' repeated refusal to sanction the replacement of the London trained bands by 1000 of Fairfax's troops to guard parliament, even after this measure was recommended by Major-General Skippon.[32]

Paranoia about their false friends in London and Westminster caused some regiments to deteriorate into near-anarchy. Hewson's and Ewer's men vented their impatience at lack of pay by terrorizing the inhabitants of north Middlesex and St Albans.[33] Ireton's men brazenly disobeyed Fairfax's orders to disperse their quarters into three counties, and stuck together as one body in Sussex.[34] The regiment's temper was expressed in its indictment of Charles I: 'The King hath betrayed the trust reposed in him, and raised war against this nation to enslave it, violating his oaths and trampling underfoot our laws ... notwithstanding he is guilty of all the bloodshed in these intestine wars.'[35]

The Death of Colonel Rainborowe

Another event widened the gulf of mistrust still further: the killing of Thomas Rainborowe. At the end of September Fairfax had ordered Rainborowe and his regiment northward to assist in the siege of Pontefract.[36] His arrival at Doncaster was bitterly resented by the commander of the siege, Sir Henry Cholmley, who now found himself displaced by a junior colonel. He appealed to the House of Commons to override Fairfax's order, while the Yorkshire Committee chimed in with a letter of dismay at the prospect of having to find provisions for another 800 soldiers.[37] Fairfax too appealed to the House of Commons, which on the 24th October commanded Cholmley to obey his instructions.[38] Trying to spread the burden of his 800 soldiers, Rainborowe sent all but two of ten companies out of Doncaster into the surrounding countryside. He thereby prepared the way for his death. On the night of 29 October Rainborowe retired to bed leaving Captain-Lieutenant John Smith in charge of the guard. Smith, however, did not report for duty, being either indisposed (as he later maintained) or occupied in the local whorehouse (as the *Moderate* indignantly alleged). Royalist spies had already spotted Rainborowe's vulnerability. The previous evening twenty-two of them left Pontefract on horseback, unhindered by Cholmley's troops. When they reached the gates of Doncaster the next morning they told the sentry that they had been sent by Cromwell with a message for Rainborowe. Having gained admission to the city, they divided their forces, sending four men to Rainborowe's lodging. Their intention in seizing the colonel was to prevent him from taking over the siege, 'having as we thought a more easy enemy [Cholmley] to deal with.' Their mission was a success, though not in the manner they foresaw. Once they had surprised Rainborowe's guards, the other soldiers who were quartered in the house ran out the back door in their nightshirts. Only Rainborowe himself offered resistance. Seeing that he, his lieutenant and his sentinel were only held by four captors, he tore himself loose in the street, crying, 'Arms, arms!' No one answered his cry, however, and one of his royalist captors tried to drag him down by his waistcoat. In the struggle Rainborowe managed to seize his captor's sword, and his lieutenant got hold of a pistol, but the royalists overpowered them. Rainborowe was thrown to the ground and run through the throat, while his lieutenant was killed. A second time he broke free, brandishing his sword at his assailants, but was thrust through the body by another sword, and fell down dead. The royalist attackers then made their way back to Pontefract with impunity.[39]

Although Rainborowe's killing may have been unintentional, its repercussions were almost instantaneous. Parliamentarians and soldiers alike did not need to wait for Cromwell's report to know to their own satisfaction that this was the deliberate murder of one of the king's most outspoken antagonists. Sir Henry Cholmley was blamed for his slackness in so managing the siege that the enemy were allowed to come and go from the fortress as they pleased without ever being challenged.[40] From that moment onward most regimental petitions would contain a fresh demand: vengeance against Rainborowe's murderers.

The body of the fallen hero was brought to London a fortnight later. Entering the City by way of Islington, the funeral procession, consisting of women in fifty or sixty coaches, and men on horseback, numbering nearly 3000 in all, wound its way through Smithfield, past St Paul's Cathedral, along Cheapside, and out through the East End to Wapping, where he was buried beside his father. The crowd was impressively large, but not as large as the one that would attend the body of another Leveller hero, Robert Lockyer, the following April.[41]

The Remonstrance of the Army

In this volatile situation Fairfax summoned the Council of Officers on 7 November. Twenty officers assembled in the abbey church of St Alban for prayers and a sermon. They then turned to consider various regimental petitions, including a declaration from the agents of several regiments in the west that in prosecuting those who had started the recent war there should be no exemption for either king or subject. The next two days' debate focused on army pay. At the session on Friday the 10th a number of colonels said 'that they desire nothing more than to see this kingdom restored to a flourishing condition in peace and amity, and that the hearts of the king and people may be knit together in a threefold cord of love.'[42]

Evidently Ireton had not yet convinced Whalley and Hewson of the merit of his position. When someone – probably Ireton himself – presented an embryonic draft of what was to become the Remonstrance of the Army, no decision was taken.[43] The state of uncertainty in the army was exemplified by the communiqué issued from St Albans the day before Ireton submitted his draft Remonstrance. Addressing the citizens of London, the anonymous writer assured them that the army forswore any intention of obstructing the peace negotiations with the king, 'provided that we may be assured of security for the future, our arrears paid, the great burthen of the kingdom removed and taken off, religion settled, and the subject freed from all tyranny and oppression either from prince or representatives.'[44] Political lobbying was apparently done in the interim, for attendance at the next meeting rose dramatically to forty-eight, and included militant revolutionaries such as Colonels Harrison, Ewer, Pride and Tomlinson.[45]

The mood of militancy was enhanced by the Commons' vote on 14 November refusing Fairfax's request for 3000 additional troops to man the new garrisons under parliamentary control. On the 15th the Council of Officers began a three-day session at the Bull-head tavern in St Albans that culminated in the adoption of Ireton's Remonstrance calling for capital punishment on the king. In addition to a large turnout of militants Ireton was assisted by events in Westminster. On 15 November the peace party carried a motion 'that the king shall be settled in a condition of honour, freedom and safety, agreeable to the laws of the land.' This was precisely what crypto-royalist forces had pressed for the previous summer.[46] The expectation of imminent parliamentary surrender to the king brought almost all the non-militants to Ireton's way of thinking within the next two days.[47]

In London the Levellers had not been idle. At the beginning of the month the leaders had met with a group of 'gentleman Independents' at the Nag's Head tavern to discuss strategy. The Levellers were startled to learn that the Independents wanted the army to cut off the king's head and purge or dissolve parliament. Lilburne argued that the army could not be trusted to act in the people's interest. A second meeting was held at the same venue on 15 November. Agreement was secured on four points:

1   a constituent assembly made up of representatives from the army and the 'well-affected' in every county would be convoked to frame a new constitution;
2   the date of parliament's dissolution should be inserted in the constitution;
3   the army should endorse the new constitution or 'Agreement' in its forthcoming Remonstrance;
4   the demands of the Leveller 'great petition' of 11 September should be implemented.

Not least among the objections to the Leveller scheme was the impracticality of organizing a constituent assembly in the crisis situation of November 1648.

When the Levellers communicated their four points to the officers at St Albans they were sympathetically received. The first draft of the Remonstrance had already been approved, however, and to Lilburne's dismay it contained several anti-Leveller phrases. The Levellers and 'gentleman Independents' decided that they must speak with 'the steer-man himself', so they rode to Windsor, where Ireton was still in residence, and confronted him in the company of several officers at the Garter Inn. There was a loud argument over two issues: liberty of conscience, and whether parliament should have the power to punish where no visible law is transgressed. Ireton would not budge on either. The second point would become crucial if parliament proceeded to a trial of the king. Colonel Harrison, more sympathetic to the Levellers, explained the army's dilemma. If the Newport treaty was concluded, disbandment would come quickly on its heels, and the army's power would be at an end. The army therefore had to act now or perish. Lilburne shot back that the Levellers did not trust either parliament or the army. To break the impasse he proposed a committee of sixteen representing equally the four parties: Levellers, army, London Independents, and the 'honest party' in parliament. Because of the army's haste to get to London and purge the House of Commons, the committee did not accomplish much before December. [48]

The Leveller intervention had its desired impact. While the demand for the king's trial was not watered down, phrases directly offensive to the Levellers were removed; the 11 September petition was commended, and a new constitution based on an Agreement of the People was proposed. In the end only two officers, Captain William Cecil, son of the Earl of Salisbury, and Colonel Nathaniel Rich, are reported to have dissented from the Remonstrance, but according to Fairfax it was approved unanimously.[49]

On the very day that the Remonstrance was approved, Charles issued his final answer to the parliamentary commissioners at Newport. His sticking point was episcopacy. Willing to strip the bishops of most of their power and wealth, he insisted on preserving their name as well as their ancient pastoral function.[50]

The army's manifesto was laid before the House of Commons on Monday 20 November by a delegation of officers, with their spokesman, Colonel Isaac Ewer, asking the house to take it into 'speedy and serious consideration'. Advance copies had already been handed out to friendly MPs. During the four hours it took the clerk to read the 25,000 words of the Remonstrance they carefully watched the reactions of their more conservative colleagues.[51] As soon as the reading was finished, the radicals were on their feet moving a vote of thanks to the army, but conservatives like Prynne and Maynard were almost as quick to inveigh against the army's 'insolency'. At the end of the day the Remonstrance was laid aside for a week, evidently in the hope that the agreement with Charles would have been concluded by then. Stung by the Commons' refusal to accept their blueprint for settlement, the officers who had been hovering all day at the door pursued the hostile MPs down the stairs, threatening that if the Remonstrance was not 'debated out of hand ... the House might take what followed.'[52]

Why did the army's manifesto produce an irrevocable breach with parliament? Since the Remonstrance was the masterplan for the army's actions in the critical months of December 1648 and January 1649, and since it furnishes the chief theoretical justification for the *coup d'état*, it merits close attention.[53]

The Remonstrance opens with an appeal to the principle that the public safety is the highest law (*salus populi suprema lex*), as the army's justification for speaking out on political matters. It then reminds the MPs of their Vote of No Addresses, passed the previous January. This resolution had united the parliamentary side, enabling it to wage a successful war against the king's supporters. That the judgement of heaven was against the royalists was manifest 'in defeating with a small handful [Fairfax's army] the numerous parties they had thus engaged.' Why then had parliament provoked division among its own supporters, and given aid and comfort to the enemy by reopening negotiations when the king had been utterly defeated on the battlefield?

Instead of chasing the chimera of reconciliation with the king, parliament should be upholding the public interest. Concretely, the present political system should be replaced by a 'supreme council or parliament' elected frequently 'with as much equality as may be'. This supreme council should have exclusive responsiblity for 'making laws ... war or peace, the safety and welfare of the people, and all civil things whatsoever.' (p. 174). It would have the sole right to define the public interest, and call offenders to account, even if they had broken no existing law.

> And if they find the offence, though not particularly provided against by particular laws, yet against the general law of reason or nations and the vindication of the public interest to require justice; ... in such case no person whatsoever may be exempt from such account or punishment. (p. 175)

This power to create offences *ex post facto* aroused the violent objection of Lilburne and the Levellers. But to Ireton regicide was impossible without it. No king had ever before been tried by his subjects. To accuse the monarch of treason when the commonly accepted definition of that crime was 'compassing the death of the king' was a constitutional and logical absurdity. For a royal trial to have any shred of intellectual justification the supreme council had to have the retroactive power to declare certain acts punishable.

The king's great crime had been in breaking his covenant to protect the people's rights and liberties. By swallowing them into his own absolute will and power he had absolved the people from their convenant with him (p. 182).[54] More pointedly, if the king, having been defeated in his attempts to overthrow the public interest, should resume that struggle, causing bloodshed and desolation, 'we may justly say he is guilty of the highest treason against law among men ... and ... guilty of all the innocent blood spilt thereby.' (pp. 183–4). In such a case the wrath of God cannot be appeased unless judgement is executed against him.[55] Trying to reunite king and parliament is like trying to join 'light with darkness ... good with evil' (p. 187).

Those who think they can trust the king to keep his word are deluding themselves. As the Prince of Wales has declared, the king is in prison; consequently, as soon as he is back on the throne he can renounce his concessions as having been extracted under duress. In a startling acknowledgement of the king's popularity, the Remonstrance signals the danger of permitting him to return to London: 'The king comes in with the reputation among the people of having long graciously sought peace.' (p. 198). Even worse, should the re-enthroned king threaten a new war, the people 'will surely be more apt to join unanimously with him or let him have what he will, that there may be no war, than join with [Parliament] to maintain another war.' In summary, the king has committed treason against his people and must be brought to judgement for his crimes. Negotiating with such a tyrant is the utmost folly, because of both his untrustworthiness and his popularity.

One apparent obstacle to bringing the king to judgement remained: the Solemn League and Covenant, which obligated its adherents to preserve the king's person and authority. Ireton's answer was that, when this obligation conflicted with the higher duty to defend religion and the public interest, the former must yield to the latter. In any case, since the king was not a party to the Covenant, he could not claim benefit from it (p. 224).

While the Remonstrance clearly foresaw the king's condemnation, it did not call for the abolition of monarchy as such. In future the estates of the crown should be sequestered and replaced by a yearly revenue of £100,000. The Remonstrance ended by endorsing the Leveller petition of 11 September and underlining its call for parliament to set a date for its own dissolution, for equal distribution of seats according to population, and for annual or biennial elections. The franchise should be denied for 'a competent number of years' to all who had engaged against parliament. These points were to be embodied in 'a general contract or Agreement of the People'. Only those who subscribed to the Agreement would be eligible to benefit from it.[56] In noteworthy contrast to the Leveller scheme, the army's Remonstrance would have the new constitution provided by parliament, and *then* given further effect by an Agreement of the People.

Two features of the Remonstrance have gone generally unnoticed: (1) its frank admission of the king's popularity; and (2) the exclusive nature of the franchise under the Agreement of the People. As we shall see, the Agreement offered a practical solution to the dilemma of how to hold elections without ushering in a return of monarchical power.

Pride's Purge

Convinced that parliament had no intention of listening to their opinions, that a conclusion of the treaty was imminent, and that the king would shortly be summoned to London amidst popular acclamation, the officers took immediate steps to head off political catastrophe. Colonel Ewer was dispatched to the Isle of Wight with a complicated set of instructions. If the governor, Colonel Robert Hammond, was willing to arrest the king and carry out the desires of the Council of Officers, Ewer would allow him to remain at his post. But, if Hammond balked at arresting the king, Ewer was to escort him back to Windsor, leaving Charles in the custody of Major Edmund Rolphe, 'and such other honest officers as you find will be faithful and secret.'[57] The officers had been worried about Hammond for some weeks. At the beginning of November, Cromwell had written an uneasy, ingratiating letter to his friend 'Robin' exhorting him to 'be honest still'. He assured him that his friends had 'not dissembled their principles at all', while managing to envelop his own principles in a cloak of ambiguity. Do not be either afraid of the Levellers or too eager for peace, he advised his friend. 'We wait upon the Lord, who will teach us and lead us, whether to be doing or suffering.' Yet he made it clear that he disapproved of the Newport treaty, characterizing either it or the king as 'an accursed thing'.[58]

On 25 November, Cromwell wrote a second letter to Hammond, more tortured than the first. Hammond was evidently worried about Ireton's implicit argument that a minority was justified in coercing a majority if the minority were in the right.[59] Unconsciously ironic, Cromwell cautioned him to 'beware of men', and raised the question: could any good accrue to the people of God 'by this man against whom the Lord hath witnessed?'[60]

On this occasion Cromwell's persuasive powers were unequal to the task. When Hammond received letters from the army's secretary, John Rushworth, officially informing him of the Remonstrance, asking his assent to its contents, and ordering him to secure the king in Carisbrooke Castle, he forwarded them to the Commons Speaker, whom he continued to regard as the higher authority.[61] Despairing over the conflict of loyalties that he faced, he begged to be relieved of the governorship of the Isle of Wight. After sending the letter he was compelled to accompany Colonel Ewer to army headquarters at Windsor, leaving his three subordinates, Major Rolphe, Captain Hawes and Captain Boreman, in charge. He reminded them of the instruction against allowing anyone to remove the king from the Isle of Wight.[62] Only Major Rolphe, who earlier that summer had been accused of plotting the king's death, was enthusiastic about the army's actions.[63] Parliament attempted to counteract these moves by ordering the immediate disbandment of the 500 infantry recruited by the Council of Officers for the Isle of Wight, and the return of Hammond to his post.[64]

Since Ewer was occupied with arresting Hammond, the officers sent a second party led by another two trusty radicals, Lieutenant-Colonel Ralph Cobbett and Captain John Merriman, to remove Charles to Hurst Castle.[65] Charles asked Cobbett whether his instructions were from parliament or the general of the army. Significantly Cobbett told him they were from neither.[66] At this juncture it was clearly Ireton and his henchmen – not Fairfax – who were in control of the army's political strategy. Yet, despite his later denials, Fairfax continued to co-operate with the momentum of revolution. He was willing, for example, to sign the letter explaining the army's disobedience as a natural consequence of parliament's refusal to deal with the Remonstrance. Because of parliament's insulting behaviour in ignoring its seventy-page manifesto, the army was coming to London, 'attending and acting the providence of God for the gaining of such ends as we have proposed in our aforsaid Remonstrance.'[67]

By the end of the month the king was under heavy guard at Carisbrooke, and before long would be on his way to Hurst Castle and then Windsor. The army now turned to its second target: the House of Commons. Determined to extract a satisfactory response to the Remonstrance, the officers girded their loins for struggle. Initially they hoped that their parliamentary friends, in imitation of the events of July 1647, would flee from Westminster to army headquarters, giving the army a free hand to expel the recalcitrant majority. But their friends persuaded them to opt for a purge rather than a dissolution.[68] Lord Grey of Groby visited St Albans on 23 November, ostensibly to present a petition from Leicestershire in support of the Remonstrance, but more likely so that he could advise about the list of MPs slated for purging. The capital was alive with fears of the army's advance.[69]

On the 25th the army shifted its headquarters from St Albans to Windsor, where Ireton had been in residence since late September. While not situated appreciably closer to London than St Albans, Windsor had the advantage of possessing one of the strongest castles in England. Army headquarters was now on the edge of the Thames, perched atop a considerable arsenal. The castle was also a suitable prison for the king.

At once the officers wrote to every regiment, informing them of parliament's inaction over the Remonstrance, and suggesting a letter-writing campaign to reassure Fairfax of their support.[70] A high-level steering committee was set up 'to consider of such things as may be of concernment for the present affairs, and to make transaction thereof.' The militant character of this committee points to Ireton's control of the army's political strategy.[71]

The day following their arrival at Windsor Castle the officers convened a prayer meeting. As observers gradually came to realize, Fairfax's officers were never more politically dangerous than when they wrestled with the Almighty. During eight hours they 'sought God earnestly for a blessing upon their councils and to direct them in the way they should walk.' Chaplains were there in force: Hugh Peters as always, but Symonds and Knight as well. In addition, Lieutenant-Colonel Kelsey, who had first emerged as a political activist in the spring of 1647, 'prayed earnestly', along with several other officers unnamed.[72] In the course of this sabbath day of prayer the army's political worries kept breaking into the spiritual exercises. Uppermost in many minds was the question of whether they were right to challenge 'visible authority'. But, since the purpose of the day was 'only to wait upon God for his direction', the incipient debate was suppressed.[73]

Fortified by prayer, the officers returned to the debate on political strategy on Tuesday the 28th. There was no dissent to the proposition that they should advance on the capital and quarter in or about the City. Ireton, Constable, Harrison, Whalley and Hewson were appointed to compose a declaration explaining the reasons for the army's advance, while the first two plus Tomlinson, Barkstead, Kelsey and Packer were selected as the army's nominees to the committee of sixteen charged with drafting an Agreement of the People.[74]

One cannot but admire the defiant courage of the Commons majority during these days while the noose drew tighter around their necks. As the army approached Kensington, barely 2 miles away, tempers flared on the floor of the House. William Prynne moved, with misdirected anger, to strip Fairfax of his commission, while other MPs sought to order the army's withdrawal 40 miles from London.[75] Unyielding in its resolve, the army nevertheless strove to keep its political fences in as good repair as possible under the circumstances. The rank and file were ordered to be on their best behaviour, on pain of severe punishment.[76] Moderate MPs were courted in an effort to defuse their fears, and London was assured that the army had not 'the least thought of plunder or other wrong to your City'.[77]

On Thursday 30 November the Commons again refused to debate the Remonstrance. The same day the army published a lengthy denunciation of the parliamentary majority for rejecting the Remonstrance, continuing the treaty with Charles, and refusing to set a date for their own dissolution. It was heavily hinted that the army would perform that task for them, and see that they were supplanted by 'a more orderly and equal judicature of men in a just Representative according to our Remonstrance.' On the other hand, if the army only received an assurance that their suggested reforms would be implemented, they would lay down their arms. Failing such an assurance they would occupy London, 'there to follow Providence as God shall clear our way.'[78] The next morning the army mustered in Hyde Park. After being reviewed, the troops, numbering little over 7000, advanced to Westminster in the afternoon. The City was told that if it paid its £40,000 assessment arrears it could avoid having soldiers quartered within the walls.[79]

While the City trembled, the Commons majority continued their defiance. The Speaker wrote to Fairfax ordering him to rescind the instructions for Hammond to come to army headquarters and for the king to be secured at Carisbrooke. Fairfax wrote back ignoring this order and asking for an answer to the army's Remonstrance, but the request was again refused.[80] On 1 December he was ordered not to bring his army nearer to the City,[81] but this order too was overtaken by events. Hearing later in the day that the army was little over a mile away in Hyde Park, the House erupted into uproar. The sitting went on late into the night, but in the end the majority shrank from declaring that the army's approach was 'prejudicial to the freedom of parliament', and so adjourned.[82]

On Saturday the 2nd the regiments took up their positions in Westminster. Whitehall became army headquarters, protected by Colonel Hewson's foot regiment. Colonel Deane's men quartered in York House in the Strand, while Colonel Pride with his regiment and some companies belonging to Colonel Ingoldsby occupied St James's Palace and Lord Goring's house. Most of the horse quartered in a body at the Mews, near present-day Trafalgar Square. The remaining troops and companies were distributed on the outskirts and villages adjacent to the City. With the streets around Charing Cross so congested by soldiers, many gentlemen opted to quit their London houses for the country.[83] While Fairfax kept to his London house in Queen Street, a number of other officers and their parliamentary allies took up residence in Whitehall.

As late as 4 December the Council of Officers had still not decided exactly how it would deal with parliament. It continued to cherish an unrealistic hope that the House of Commons would purge itself of 'corrupt and apostasized members'. The army's friends were requested to separate themselves from the others. If they did this 'we shall own them and adhere to them, and be guided by them in their faithful prosecution of that trust.'[85] The army's friends, however, preferred a solution imposed from without. They did not have to wait long, for on the bitterly cold night of 30 November, amidst high winds and sheets of falling rain, the troops dispatched by Lieutenant-Colonel Saunders had arrived at Carisbrooke Castle. At 5 a.m. Charles was awakened by a loud knocking on his dressing-room door. Before he could get out of bed several officers rushed into his chamber and told him that they had orders to remove him to Hurst Castle. Three hours later the king and his party left for that destination.[86]

When the report reached Westminster of the king's removal, the Commons spent the whole of 4 December in acrimonious debate. It lasted well after a motion to bring in candles. In the end nothing was done except to approve a statement 'that the removal of the king out of the Isle of Wight was without the knowledge or consent of this House.' The members divided 136 to 102 over whether to include the word 'consent' in the motion.[87] Even though night had fallen, the house had yet to deal with the major item on the day's agenda: the king's answer to their propositions at the treaty of Newport. The king's answer had been before the house since the first of the month, and had aroused bitter controversy. On that day, one of the army's friends, Colonel Edmund Harvey, had denounced the king's offer of ninety-nine-year leases for the purchasers of bishops' lands.[88] There can have been no one in the house unaware of the fact that Harvey, purchaser of the palace and manor of Fulham, had one of the biggest stakes in the episcopal lands. Harvey's and many other officers' interest in these estates explains why the army echoed his criticism a few days later.[89]

Most MPs remained on the benches for a stormy all-night sitting that they knew would have the most far-reaching consequences. Not until eight o'clock on the morning of the 5th did the remaining members, crushed with fatigue, approve the resolution that the king's answer was 'a ground for the House to proceed upon, for the settlement of the peace of the kingdom.' The vote to put the question was carried by 129 votes to 83.[90]

The army reacted swiftly to this repudiation of its political programme. Anticipating the need for violence against parliament, the Council of Officers had already ordered more forces to move to London. The City's trained bands were relieved of their duty to guard the houses, and replaced by Colonel Rich's horse and Colonel Pride's foot regiments. Streets adjacent to parliament were patrolled by Fairfax's and Thomas Mauleverer's horse regiments, and Skippon's foot. In a futile attempt to appease the army's wrath the Commons appointed six of their number to go and explain their vote to the Council of Officers. At this point explanations were unwelcome, and the MPs were kept waiting for three hours before Fairfax informed them that the council was not in session, and that they should return the following day.[91]

What was to be done? The officers had still not finally made up their minds. Later the same day they had a 'full and free debate' with several of their parliamentary friends, Ireton still apparently pressing for the dissolution of parliament, but the MPs insisting on a purge. At length it was agreed to send a committee of three officers and three MPs into a private room to resolve the question. In order to preserve unity of action Ireton gave up his insistence on a dissolution, though later he could not overcome his contempt for the purged parliament as a 'mock power and a mock parliament'.[92] The committee of six agreed that the army should place troops in Westminster Hall, the Court of Requests and the lobby of the house, to prevent those inimical to the army from entering. The committee then analysed the Commons' membership and established the criteria for those to be arrested. They were twofold: (1) a vote that the king's answer to the Newport propositions was an acceptable basis for settlement; and (2) opposition to the August declaration labelling the Scots invaders as enemies, traitors and rebels. In all, between eighty and ninety MPs were marked out for arrest.[93] With these matters settled, Ireton went back to headquarters to inform Fairfax 'of the necessity of this extraordinary way of proceeding'.[94] Who were the six members of the committee that hammered out the details of the purge? Although Ludlowe does not specify, we can be sure that Ireton and he were both included. Harrison, who was at the centre of affairs during this period, was probably another, while Sir William Constable, the

most senior member of the Council of Officers' steering committee, may
have been the third officer.[95] The MPs apart from Ludlowe were very likely
Lord Grey of Groby, who stood at Pride's elbow the next morning to identify his colleagues, and Cornelius Holland.[96]

The regiments were on duty at seven o'clock on the morning of 6
December.[97] The City trained bands, who again reported for duty, were
sent packing by the men of Pride's and Rich's regiments. Standing in the
lobby of the House of Commons, Colonel Pride, assisted by one of the
doorkeepers and Lord Grey of Groby, arrested those MPs on the committee's list who were brave or unlucky enough to turn up that morning.
The soldiers then escorted them to the Queen's Court, the Court of Wards
and other rooms nearby, where they waited to learn what would become of
them. Forty-one MPs in all were seized that day, while many more, hearing
what was afoot, stayed away.[98] Although it was transparently obvious that
the army had committed violence against their house, the Commons
continued to sit instead of adjourning in protest. Several of them ra-
tionalized their conduct in terms of their duty to continue serving their
country.[99] At one point, to salvage their self-respect, they sent out the
sergeant-at-arms with a request that the imprisoned MPs attend the house.
The request was ignored. There were, however, behind-the-scenes efforts
by men of influence to free some of the prisoners. Two aristocratic
managers, Sir Benjamin Rudyerd and Nathaniel Fiennes – the one
associated with the Earl of Pembroke, the other the son of Lord Saye – were
released later in the day. It is perhaps significant too that Sir Michael
Oldisworth, Pembroke's patronage secretary and an active promoter of the
Newport treaty, was at no time marked out for arrest.[100]

Pierrepont and his colleagues meanwhile had obtained an audience with
Fairfax. His vague answer to their pointed questions is eloquent testimony
to his confused anguish at being thrust into the centre of affairs not of his
own making. The MPs asked for Fairfax's answer in writing; instead they
were favoured with a statement signed by John Rushworth and presented
by Colonel Whalley. The officers' demands were straightforward. The
Eleven Members whose impeachment was launched in June 1647 should be
forthwith brought to trial, and Major-General Richard Browne, sheriff of
London, should be added to their number on account of his role in inviting
the Scots to invade England last summer. An additional ninety or more MPs
who opposed the vote declaring the Scots enemies should be excluded from
the house. Those MPs who had opposed the revocation of the Vote of No
Addresses, the personal treaty with the king, and the vote of 5 December
accepting the king's answer to the Newport propositions should identify
themselves. Once these things had been done the officers hoped the house
would proceed to 'the execution of justice, to set a short period to your

own power, [and] to provide for a speedy succession of equal Representatives according to our late Remonstrance.'[101]

The Arrival of Cromwell

Later that day Oliver Cromwell arrived from the north, and took up residence in one of the king's bedrooms in Whitehall. About the purge his comment was that 'he had not been acquainted with this design; yet since it was
done, he was glad of it, and would endeavour to maintain it.'[102] This and
other enigmatic statements by Cromwell have given rise to differing
interpretations of his role in the events leading up to the trial and execution
of the king. Did he play a minor or leading part? When did he make up his
mind that the king must die? Why did he stay in the north during the critical months from September to November, when the most far-reaching
decisions were being taken at St Albans and Windsor? Did he remain a
middle-group man, or was he a convinced revolutionary all along?

The first thing to be noted is that Cromwell kept open his lines of
communication with both radicals and moderates. When Lilburne came
north in September he met with Cromwell. What was said at that meeting is
not known, but the two men stayed in touch throughout the autumn, and
Cromwell gave implicit support to the Leveller petition of 11 September. He
also advised on the negotiations over the Agreement of the People. His regiment was known as one which was especially receptive to Leveller agitation.[103] At the end of November he and the officers present at the siege of
Pontefract met with the parliamentary gentry of the four northern counties
and agreed upon a petition to parliament calling for justice upon delinquents.[104] In his letter to Colonel Robert Hammond on 6 November he
reassured him that he had not turned into a presbyterian, but was merely
attempting to come as close as possible to an accommodation with the non-
cavalierish Scots. Acknowledging what seems to have been Hammond's
own position, he allowed that a peaceful settlement was desirable, but
'peace is only good when we receive it out of our Father's hand.... War is
good when led to by our Father.'[105] Light is shed on these enigmatic words
by the answer Cromwell sent to Lilburne through Mr Hunt when Lilburne
had asked if Cromwell agreed that the sole end of the civil wars had been to
establish the people's rights and freedoms under a just government. Having
spoken to Mr Hunt, the Independents informed the Levellers at the Nag's
Head tavern that the army's desire was 'to cut off the king's head, ... and
force and thoroughly purge, if not dissolve the Parliament.'[106] Two weeks
later Cromwell wrote a covering letter to Fairfax commending his
regiment's petition to the general. The petition referred favourably to the

Leveller petition of 11 September, and demanded the restoration of the Vote of No Addresses 'until the king be acquitted of the charges therein.'[107] Cromwell underlined the strength of the petitioners' desires, saying, 'I find a very great sense in the officers of the regiments of the sufferings and the ruin of this poor kingdom, and in them all a very great zeal to have impartial justice done upon offenders; and I must confess, I do in all, from my heart, concur with them.'[108]

When the army presented its Remonstrance to the House of Commons on 20 November, Cromwell wrote to Hammond commending it, even if 'we could perhaps have wished the stay of it till after the [Newport] treaty.' The Council of Officers might have been over-hasty, but in the end could the people of God expect any good from 'this man against whom the Lord hath witnessed'?[109]

On 28 November, Fairfax wrote to Cromwell asking him to come to headquarters with all convenient speed so that he could help with 'the very great business now in agitation'.[110] Within a day or two Cromwell replied that he would come speedily; in fact he left almost immediately, arriving in Mansfield, Nottinghamshire, on 1 December.[111] Before his departure he had to ensure that his responsibilities in the north would be taken care of during his absence. Besides supervising the siege of Pontefract, one of the strongest castles in the kingdom, he was in charge of the garrisons at Berwick, Carlisle and Newcastle. Chief command of the north was transferred to Lambart, who had to bring regiments up to replace those Cromwell took south with him. When he left Pontefract he withdrew his own horse regiment, Fairfax's foot regiment, most of Okey's dragoons and most of Harrison's horse regiment 'and some others'. By the 5th he had probably reached Dunstable, Bedfordshire, where he left the bulk of his troops. He made the final leg of his trip with sixty cavalry troopers. In light of the numerous attacks on parliamentary leaders in the autumn of 1648, and with the killing of Rainborowe fresh in mind, sixty armed men would be the minimum lifeguard that could have ensured the lieutenant-general's safety.[112]

The accusation that Cromwell stayed in the north because his mind was not made up about purging parliament and trying the king, that he loitered after being commanded southward by Fairfax, and that he deliberately arrived in the capital after the dirty work had been done by his surrogates is therefore open to question.[113] He had taken part in the meeting of the army on the eve of the second civil war that had branded Charles as a 'Man of Blood', and despite his remoteness from the capital in the autumn of 1648 he continued to be known as Charles's greatest adversary.[114] In fact he was in the north not to indulge the luxury of indecision but to direct military operations in the last major theatre of the second civil war. The north was a challenging assignment, one that was not rendered any easier by the appalling weather of the autumn of 1648, nor by the failure of the essential heavy artillery from Hull to arrive at Pontefract before 6 November, nor by the tardy arrival of Major-General Lambart and his regiments from Scotland several days after that.[115] Equally important was the duty of organizing the north politically. His desire was to come south by the middle of November if not before,[116] but he could not do so before he had 'settle[d] counties and such officers as are and may prove true to [the army's] designs.'[117] That Cromwell took the duty seriously is evident from the stream of civilian and military petitions that flowed southward until the end of the year. While no correspondence between them survives, it is likely that Cromwell kept in close touch with his son-in-law Ireton concerning political developments at army headquarters and at Westminster. His statement on the evening of 6 December that he was not acquainted with the plans for Pride's Purge does not contradict this assumption. All along Ireton had hoped for a dissolution or a voluntary separation of the minority in the Commons from the 'corrupt' majority. Only when these hopes were irrevocably dashed on the morning of 5 December did the officers finally opt for the purge that their parliamentary friends had been proposing for over a week.[118]

Cromwell's political behaviour was of a piece before and after his arrival in London. If, as is likely, he supported the release of sixteen of the imprisoned MPs, it was not because he was a 'softliner' but because he recognized the importance of having as many MPs as possible backing the king's trial. The same motivation explains his lengthy interviews with Bulstrode Whitelocke and Sir Thomas Widdrington. He listened to them, not because he was unsure whether the king should die, but because the regime desperately needed respected lawyers to give a patina of legal rationality to its revolutionary acts. More significant than Cromwell's solemn pretence of 'join[ing] counsels for the public good' was his act of lolling on one of the king's rich beds during their second interview.[119] His deadly seriousness was manifested in his repeated and time-consuming efforts to extract from the Duke of Hamilton an admission that he had invaded England at the invitation of Charles himself. Such an admission would have furnished watertight evidence with which to convict Charles of treason against the English people. Although Cromwell paid several visits to Hamilton's cell in Windsor Castle, his efforts were in vain.[120]

The Agreement of the People and the Whitehall Debates

Between December and the end of January two great dramas were prepared for the political stage; one was thwarted, the other brought successfully to its climax. They were, respectively, the hammering-out of the new constitution known as the Agreement of the People, and the overthrow and decapitation of the king. Because of the army's intimate involvement, both dramas command our attention.

After Lilburne had secured the army's assent to a committee of sixteen to draft an Agreement of the People, little progress was made before Pride's Purge. But with the army in town it was easy for the four groups to assemble, and so several meetings were held at Whitehall. Even though the house was but a stone's throw away, the only MP to attend regularly was Henry Marten. It was not easy for the Levellers to bring Ireton to their way of thinking on two issues: liberty of conscience and the question of whether parliament had the right to punish where no law existed. It was 'a long and tedious tug', the meetings sometimes lasting through the night. Lilburne found Ireton 'very angry and lordly' in his attitude, and we may imagine what Ireton thought of his long-winded and conceited adversary. At the end of the week the draft was ready for submission to the Council of Officers. That it was only a draft is indicated by the fact that none of the committee of sixteen or their clerical supporters offered any objection when the officers proceeded to subject the Agreement to meticulous scrutiny.[121]

We may be grateful that they did not do so, and grateful also to William Clarke for preserving a record of these debates. Before the army secretary began keeping detailed notes on 14 December the officers had already met several times and approved most of the Agreement. The great stumbling block was religion. The debate on this subject lasted for five days, in addition to an indeterminate number of days spent on committee meetings, spread between 14 December and 13 January. At least 160 officers and civilians (including over thirty clerics) are known to have spoken, served on committees or attended the debates on the Agreement. All participants, including the recording secretary, seemed to share the conviction that they were taking part in deliberations of the greatest historical importance. They believed that they had been handed an unrepeatable opportunity to shape the political and spiritual destiny of their country.

The document on the table before them assumed the abolition of monarchy and House of Lords. It stipulated that the Long Parliament would dissolve on or before the last day of April 1649. Future parliaments or 'Representatives', as they were termed, would consist of 300 members chosen according to a radically redrawn electoral map reflecting current demographic realities. Electors would be male householders assessed for poor relief who were not royalists, servants or wage-earners, and who had signed the Agreement. An executive, or Council of State, appointed by the Representative and responsible to it, would govern in the intervals between biennial parliaments. The heart of the Agreement was the list of powers reserved by the people to themselves. The Representative would enjoy no power of compulsion in religion, no power to conscript for military service, no power to question people for their actions during the civil war, no power to violate the principle of equality before the law, and no power to punish where there was not an existing law. No member of the Representative would be permitted to handle public money. The Agreement also guaranteed freedom of commerce, jury trials and a maximum interest rate of 6 per cent per annum, and abolished the excise, imprisonment for debt, capital punishment (except for murder) and tithes.[122]

On 14 December in a room in Whitehall there occurred one of the finest debates on freedom of conscience ever recorded. Attended by forty-five members of the Council of Officers and twenty-three civilians, mostly radical clergy,[123] the debate produced classic statements of both the case for unfettered religious freedom and the case for the magistrate's exercising control in the interest of public peace and order. It produced unanswerable appeals to principle that were countered by equally unanswerable appeals to political reality. The fruit of the debate was victory for neither side, but a genuine compromise.[124]

The lower officers had already underlined their attachment to liberty of conscience in their published Articles and Proposals of 8 December, in which they had implored Fairfax not to permit the consciences of men to be cruelly shipwrecked.[125] On 14 December the faction of radical officers and their civilian supporters went on the offensive. So confident were they that they published in advance an unauthorized statement endorsing the whole Leveller programme and calling for 'a solemn contract upon these and the like principles [to] be drawn betwixt the people and their Representatives forever', and promising not to disband until this agenda had been realized.[126] Despite the procedural rule of alternating speakers on either side of the question, five speakers initially defended liberty of conscience with only two opposing it. John Goodwin, the radical Independent minister of St Stephen's Church, Coleman Street, declared categorically 'that God hath not invested any power in a civil magistrate in matters of religion' (p. 74). His ringing statement was echoed by Hewitt, Wildman, Lilburne and Colonel Deane. Only Colonels Hewson and Rich retorted weakly that, if the document did not explicitly give the magistrate a power over religion, one could assume that such power was thereby withheld from him (pp. 77–8).

It was left to Ireton to present a trenchant argument against absolute religious liberty. Gainsaying Wildman's statement that the civil wars had been about the nature of the magistrate's power, he asserted that the issue had been whether the king alone should exercise that power. If the only end that mattered was liberty, then there was no need for a commonwealth at all. But peace also mattered, so the question must be, what powers did the magistrate need in order to preserve civil peace? Ireton went on to insist that a measure of latitude should be left to the elected representatives when it came to judging what is necessary to maintain peace. We cannot spell out everything that they may or may not do. Ireton's final point was a telling one. If the Agreement was intended to embrace as many of the well-affected people as possible, it should contain no clause that would prevent such people from signing it. The reserve on religion, which denied all power to the magistrate, was such a clause (pp. 79–83).

Colonel Whalley drove home this last point by reminding his listeners that the reserve on religion had already been a stumbling block to many. If it had divided the army, think of how it would divide the kingdom. What was the sense in imposing liberty upon the people against their will?

> How can we term that an Agreement of the People which is neither an Agreement of the Major Part of the people, and truly for anything I can perceive ... not an agreement of the major part of the honest party of the kingdom? We have been necessitated to force the parliament, and I should be very unwilling we should force the people to an agreement. (p. 84)

Sir Hardress Waller and Hugh Peters also spoke up for moderation.

The pragmatism of Ireton and his supporters was brushed aside by Joshua Sprigge with a stirring appeal to principle. Sprigge had accompanied the army on the march through the south-west in 1645–6 and written the history of its successes from an unwavering providentialist perspective. For him there was a fundamental flaw in the Agreement: its failure to recognize explicitly the lordship of Jesus Christ. While he approved of enlarging 'the spiritual liberties of the saints', he wondered why there was such a rush to create a new constitution. The army should wait upon God until he showed them the way more clearly (pp. 84–7).

Captain John Clarke of Skippon's regiment attacked Sprigge's proposal for delay by insisting on the uniqueness of the historical moment in which they found themselves. They had been presented with an opportunity to effect fundamental change; they must not let it slip through their fingers, for the army had often during the past three years 'been a shelter to honest people that had otherwise been hammered to dust' (pp. 94–5).

Dr Parker expanded the religious argument with the claim that the laws of the Old Testament no longer applied under the dispensation of the New (pp. 100, 123–4). Goodwin and Wildman pushed the argument in a secularizing direction by stressing the difficulty of knowing God's will, or even of knowing whether there was a God (pp. 115–18, 120).

Ireton, who was at all times animated by the vision of a godly commonwealth, would have nothing to do with the implicit pluralism of the religious radicals. He took them to task for not basing their arguments upon scripture. While Christ had been uninterested in the question of political power, he had not thereby abrogated the function of the magistrate. It had been a duty to restrain sin in ancient times, and that duty continued in the present (pp. 112–14, 122, 128–30).

The more conservative higher officers were on the defensive throughout the debate, which, had it not been for Ireton's stubbornness, would have been over much sooner. Before the halfway point the Levellers' supporters shouted for the question to be called (p. 104). Shortly afterwards Fairfax, wearied by the loquacity of his colleagues, or perhaps feeling unwell, vacated the chair.[127]

Ireton's frequent and lengthy interventions show that he took the Agreement seriously. If the debate had been merely a sop to the radicals, a 'children's rattle' to distract them while the grandees got on with the more serious business of cutting off the king's head, it is hard to explain why the commissary-general expended so much time and intellectual energy trying to ensure that the Agreement said what he wanted it to say. The record shows the falsity of Lilburne's accusation that in debate Ireton behaved like 'an absolute king, if not an emperor, against whose will no man must dispute.'[128] Nevertheless, his stubbornness, and his refusal to allow the question to be called when the radical majority wanted it, paid off. Colonel Harrison's suggestion that a committee be created to study the reserve on religion and report back was adopted (p. 92).[129] A week later the committee recommended that the reserve on religion be replaced by an article spelling out the magistrate's power in religious matters. The motion that there should be no reserve on religion was carried 37 to 12 (p. 140). Instead, the revised version of the Agreement contained an article (no. 9) that reflected Ireton's thinking. It specified that Christianity would be 'held forth and recommended, as the public profession in this nation.' A ministry would be maintained out of the public treasury, not by tithes. Apart from papists and Anglicans, all who professed faith in Jesus Christ would be allowed to practise their religion freely. No one would be compelled to attend the state church, 'but only may be endeavoured to be won by sound doctrine, and the example of a good conversation.'[130] Article 9 of the Officers' Agreement, with its limited toleration and its loosely structured national church, foreshadowed the Cromwellian church of the 1650s. Only in its preservation of tithes would the Cromwellian church be different from Ireton's model.

Although the article on religion was debated over four days (8–11 January), there was less division on Ireton's compromise than there had been on the original reserve. William Erbury deplored the article's failure to provide toleration for the Jews, as well as its provision for a state church.

Captain George Joyce, who had been absent for the earlier debate, exploded the emerging consensus by denouncing the article in a speech of incandescent fervour. He exhorted his fellow officers to banish their fears and rededicate themselves as God's instruments. The army

> by belief [shall] remove mountains, [and do] such things as were never yet done by men on earth; and certainly if I mistake not, the spirit is now to break forth, so if it were not fear in us, we should not be disputing among ourselves. ... We should not so much endeavour to give away a power that God hath called us unto, or to contend about it, but to put that into your hearts which is in our hearts. (pp. 182–3)

Joyce spoke for the younger officers, disgusted with the caution of their seniors, unafraid of extreme solutions, and impatient to use the power that was in their hands. Colonel Harrison matched Joyce's apocalyptic rhetoric, but gently informed him of what had transpired during the debates of previous days (pp. 183–6). In the end Ireton's compromise article was inserted in place of the deleted reserve on religion.

Nothing else in the Agreement provoked as much debate as religion. The second reserve, prohibiting conscription, was debated and passed on 16 December. The original Leveller wording had been absolute in its prohibition.[131] Owing to the work of the committee of sixteen, a distinction was made between conscription for foreign and conscription for home service, with only the former now being prohibited.[132]

Two days later there appeared another anonymous pamphlet purporting to be from the army, summarizing the Agreement of the People, and pointedly referring to the scheduled date of the dissolution of the Long Parliament on 30 April 1649. Ignoring the fact that a compromise on religion was soon to be thrashed out by the committee meeting at Colonel Tichborne's house, it baldly affirmed that the Agreement would guarantee complete liberty of conscience. This pamphlet, which bore no printer's name, may testify to the sustained pressure of the lower officers to secure passage of the Agreement without modification. But alternatively it may have been a product of the Levellers. The impression it conveyed was that the Agreement was the army's own document.[133]

On 18 December there was again a large turnout – forty-nine officers as well as John Wildman and William Walwyn for the Levellers.[134] There was also a horrified royalist witness to the day's proceedings. The diarist John Evelyn, unable to restrain his curiosity about the debate that was currently the talk of the town, disguised himself and smuggled himself into the officers' meeting room. The draft Agreement lay before them in the form of a large scroll, with Ireton in the chair, Fairfax being absent that day. Evelyn was shocked to see such 'young, raw and ill-spoken men' debating constitutional law. He was convinced that the disrespectful, free-wheeling manner of the lower officers was nothing but 'disorder and irreverence', while Ireton was guilty of 'palpable cozenage' in the way he pushed the business on.[135]

Again the discussion centred on the heart of the Agreement: the reserved powers. The third reserve, that no one save royalists and those who had handled public money should be questioned for their actions in the civil wars, passed without dissent (p. 135). The fourth reserve, guaranteeing equality before the law and implicitly attacking the House of Lords, was 'laid aside'. Curiously, however, it would reappear when the officers brought the Agreement to the House of Commons on 20 January.[136] The fifth reserve, which was similar in content, was also set aside, and did not reappear in the final version presented to parliament.[137] Although none is recorded, there must have been intense debate on the sixth reserve:

> That the Representatives intermeddle not with the execution of Laws, nor give judgement upon any man's person or estate where no law hath been before provided; save only in calling to an account and punishing public officers for abusing or failing their trust.[138]

Ireton was evidently worried that this reserve might be used as a weapon to block the trial of the king, the qualifying phrase about punishing public officers notwithstanding. The motion to delete the sixth reserve was only narrowly defeated by 18 to 16. It was plainly a victory for the lower officers against their superiors. Lieutenant-General Hammond, Scoutmaster-General Rowe and all the colonels who voted supported Ireton, while all but a handful of officers of lesser rank opposed him.[139]

The morrow, 19 December, was kept as a day of humiliation, and on Thursday the 21st the Council reassembled to handle the thorny question of how to define the sovereign powers of the Representative, not including those that were explicitly reserved to the people. In a stunning confirmation of Leveller libertarianism the officers voted 27 to 17 that while the Representative should have 'highest and final judgment concerning all natural and civil things' it would not have any power over moral questions. Again, the higher officers were overwhelmed by their more numerous inferiors.[140] On the 26th the Council returned to the sixth reserve. Again it was upheld against the solid opposition of the commanders, by a margin of 22 to 14.[141]

Three days later the Council approved the final two reserves without dissent, and moved to consideration of the positive articles of the Agreement. The article empowering the Council of State to summon an emergency session of the Representative was amended to double the permitted length of the session from forty to eighty days.[142] Another article concerning public credit was amended so as to eliminate any obligation to royalist creditors.

The article against mutiny by the army was broadened to make it a capital offence for anyone to rebel against the Representative's authority.[143]

A high-powered ten-man committee was named to put the finishing touches on the Agreement before it was presented to parliament. The committee's composition was finely balanced, with four conservatives, four radicals and two moderates.[144] Besides making minor changes in the text of the Agreement it drafted 'the form of subscription for the officers of the army'. In it the officers were to declare the central articles and reserves 'fundamental to our common right, liberty and safety', and to promise to maintain them 'as God shall enable us'.[145]

On 6 January the termination of the present parliament was debated. The meeting witnessed the only occasion when Cromwell and Ireton are known to have disagreed publicly. Ireton argued that the date for parliament's dissolution should be the last day of April 1649, and that this stipulation should be included in the text of the Agreement. Cromwell opined that it would be more honourable to let parliament set the date for its own dissolution. Ireton's answer demonstrated the depth of his support for the Agreement. If parliament was permitted to dissolve itself without having adopted the Agreement, then parliaments would most likely continue to be elected in the old way. What he did not say, but which every one of his hearers must have understood, was that a parliament elected along the old lines would almost certainly be dominated by royalists. Conversely, if men were shown that the only way to get rid of the present parliament was through the Agreement of the People, they would be deterred from trying to sabotage that document. Ireton's reasoning showed that for him, if not for Cromwell, the Agreement was a key pillar of the political scenario that would follow the abolition of monarchy. He rightly perceived that the majority of the people were still royalist. Furthermore, he saw that only the Agreement could provide a bulwark strong enough to prevent the return of monarchy after the soldiers had laid down their arms.[146]

Indeed, it is only a slight exaggeration to say that the Agreement of the People, whether in the Levellers' or the officers' version, would have ushered in something more resembling a dictatorship of the godly than a golden age of democracy.[147] To be sure, electoral boundaries would have been redrawn on the principle of representation by population. The vote would have been extended to male householders. But it would have been withheld from all enemies of the regime. The Levellers would have denied it to all who refused to sign the Agreement. In the officers' version this requirement was relaxed, but in both versions the vote was denied for seven years to all who had supported the king in the civil wars, or who opposed the Agreement. The qualifications for election to the new Representative were much more stringent. Excluded from the first and second

Representatives were any who had aided the king, signed the London Engagement of the summer of 1647 calling for a personal treaty, petitioned for a truce with the Scots invaders in the summer of 1648, or offered any compliance with the rebels in the second civil war. Bearing in mind the massive support enjoyed by the royalists in 1648, we can appreciate that these provisions, combined with the exclusion of servants and wage-earners, would have disenfranchised much of the adult male population in England for several years and prevented all but a small minority from standing for election. While these facts have been overlooked by most historians, they were not missed at the time. Unfriendly critics attacked the Agreement for its restrictiveness,[148] while friends of the Levellers such as the editor of *The Moderate* recognized that the Agreement would initially disenfranchise a large segment of the people.[149]

That this point is not merely hypothetical is proved by the experience of London in its municipal elections of December 1648. In that month the Commons passed an ordinance excluding from the municipal franchise all who had signed the 1647 Engagement for a personal treaty with the king. The City protested that the ordinance would leave hardly anyone eligible to vote or hold office. The result of the Commons' refusal to back down was a revolution in London politics, and a Common Council led by radical militia officers.[150] There is reason to suppose that the Agreement would have effected an electoral upheaval of similar magnitude in the rest of the country. All but the 'well affected' or the 'godly' would have been excluded from political life until the new regime was securely on its feet.

In a published statement on 15 January the Army Council declared that they believed their version of the Agreement to contain 'the best and most hopeful foundations for the peace and future well government of this nation.' However, if the people were so blind as not be see the merit of their plan, they would consider their duty finished, 'and hope they shall be acquitted before God and good men, from the blame of any further troubles, distractions and miseries to the kingdom, which may arise through the neglect or rejection thereof.'

A delegation of officers led by Lieutenant-General Thomas Hammond brought the finished version of the Agreement, copied on parchment, to the Commons on Saturday 20 January 1649. After listening to Hammond, the Commons ordered the Agreement printed. The officers were commended for their 'good affections and serious representations', and promised that the Commons would consider the Agreement as soon as 'the present weighty and urgent affairs will permit.'[151] They never did, and the officers never reminded them of their promise. The contrast between the reaction of the officers to parliamentary indifference to the Remonstrance on the one hand and the Agreement on the other was striking. Why, if the officers were enraged by the dismissal of their Remonstrance, did they acquiesce in the similar treatment of the Agreement? The immediate reason may have been their preoccupation with the king's trial. More generally there was the undeniable reality that no one was passionately attached to the Agreement. Even the Levellers were less concerned with the structure of government than with decentralizing authority and liberalizing the laws. The Agreement evoked little public support from the quarters that might have been expected to enthuse over it. The gathered churches were more anxious to establish the reign of Christ than fashion a new constitution. As for the Rump, apart from an understandable reluctance to sign its own death warrant, many of its members were convinced by the unpopularity of the trial of Charles that the time was not ripe for radical alterations in the machinery of government. Nor was there any noticeable groundswell of support from the rank and file of the army. The most insistent pressure for the Agreement had come from the lower officers. Indeed, their repeated triumphs in the Council of Officers over Ireton and his supporters may have caused the latter to turn against the Agreement which hitherto they had taken so seriously. Whatever the explanation, the Agreement was pushed to the political sidelines, and soon forgotten by everyone except John Lilburne.[152]

The Trial of Charles I

From Pride's Purge onward the army kept a tight grip on parliament, the City of London and the king. The forty-one arrested MPs were initially imprisoned in the Queen's Court, the Court of Wards 'and other places'.[153] Later in the day Hugh Peters, wearing a sword in honour of the occasion, took a list of their names for Sir Thomas Fairfax, and returned after an interval, to announce that two of their number – Sir Benjamin Rudyerd and Nathaniel Fiennes – were released. Then, in a gesture of black humour, the remaining thirty-nine MPs were carted off in coaches to a nearby alehouse known as Hell. Denied food or bedding, they spent the night reading and singing psalms.[154]

The next morning they were brought to the king's lodgings in Whitehall for an audience with Fairfax. Underlining the members' utter dependence on their whim, or perhaps reflecting their own division, the officers kept them standing in an outer room for four hours, and finally dismissed them without an audience. They were then lodged in the two nearby inns, the Swan and the King's Head. As the MPs walked down Whitehall to the Strand, the soldiers on duty made a lane of muskets and pikes on either side, hurling insults as they passed.[155]

Many MPs, hearing of the violence committed against their house, stayed

Plate 9 New Palace Yard, Westminster

(Source: *Cromwelliana*)

O horrable Murder

But lo a Charg is drawne, a day is set
The silent Lamb is brought, the Wolves are met;
And where's the Slaughterhouse? Whitehall must be,
Lately his Palace, now his Calvarie
And now ye Senators, is this the thing
So oft declard. Is this your glorious King?
Religion vails her self; and mourns that she
Is forc'd to own such Horrid Villanie.

Plate 10 Charles I

(Source: *Cromwelliana*)

away that day and for many subsequent days. A remnant of forty or fifty continued to sit, however, attempting to salvage their self-respect, first by sending a message to their secluded colleagues ordering them to return, and then by demanding an explanation of the purge from Fairfax. Greatly embarrassed by events over which by now he had little control, the general temporized and refused to put anything in writing.[156] The 'fierce party'[157] meanwhile set about undoing the previous four months of parliament's work. The vote repealing the Vote of No Addresses was itself repealed, as was the resolution in favour of a personal treaty with the king. The Newport treaty was denounced as 'highly dishonourable' and 'destructive'. The vote of 5 December accepting the king's answer to the Newport propositions as a basis for settlement was also annulled. Finally, steps were taken to bring in the last six months' assessment for the army, now greatly in arrears. Having as they thought satisfied the army's agenda, the Commons then timidly attempted to reclaim their honour by sending a committee to Fairfax to know why their colleagues had been secluded.[158]

There were practical reasons, which the officers well understood, for trying to mitigate, if not reverse, the purge. The boycotting of the house by large numbers of moderate MPs meant that after a week attendance had dipped perilously close to the quorum of forty, and there were delays in beginning the sittings.[159] Accordingly, on 14 December, at the entreaty of the Speaker, Pride allowed a number of MPs to enter whom he had earlier excluded.[160] A few days later the house again asked Fairfax to explain the exclusion of MPs. Again he temporized, and asked them to stop sending such messages.[161] But on the same day he had sixteen of the imprisoned members brought to his lodgings. When they arrived they were kept waiting for two or three hours, until Ireton, Whalley and Rich emerged to tell them that Fairfax had fallen suddenly ill and could not see them. Again one suspects disagreement between Fairfax and the officers. Ireton, espying the irrepressible Prynne, who had managed to smuggle himself into the group, flew into a rage and ordered him back to confinement. For the rest, however, there was good news: they were free to go, provided they stayed out of trouble; otherwise 'it would be the worse for them.'[162] The release of imprisoned MPs was of a piece with the policy of extending olive branches to moderates. The significance of these conciliatory moves was not that the officers (other than Fairfax) had second thoughts about the course they had embarked upon, but rather that they saw the need to rally as much support as possible to their cause, and, where that was impossible, to neutralize opposition.

This explains why Cromwell devoted time to meetings with moderate MPs Bulstrode Whitelocke and Sir Thomas Widdrington. On three separate days in late December he had lengthy chats with the two men. On the third day (21 December), with Speaker Lenthall in tow, he asked them to draw up proposals for the settlement of the kingdom. Flattered by the attention lavished on them, Whitelocke and Widdrington complied with Oliver's request, and spent the whole of the 22 December fast day working on proposals that they expected would temper the militancy of the army, bring back the secluded MPs and settle the kingdom. They believed, as Oliver intended they should, that they were helping keep the army from falling into the hands of extremists. For him, on the other hand, the purpose of the exercise was to give them a feeling of importance and to keep them harmlessly busy while the army got on with eliminating the king. Nothing more was heard of Whitelocke's and Widdrington's proposals.[163] More important for Cromwell were his several meetings with the Duke of Hamilton at Windsor Castle, where Hamilton was imprisoned. The object of these visits was to extract from him a confession that he had been invited by the king himself to invade England the previous summer. Had Cromwell not already made up his mind about the king's trial, it is unlikely that he would have gone to all this trouble.[164]

The few peers who were amenable to persuasion were also cultivated. Not only were their clients, such as Rudyerd and Fiennes, released, but Michael Oldisworth, Pembroke's patronage secretary and an active promoter of the Newport treaty, was carefully omitted from the list of MPs to be imprisoned.[165] Pembroke was appointed constable of Windsor Castle, making him the king's titular gaoler. At the same time Pembroke, Denbigh, Mulgrave and Lord Grey of Warke visited Fairfax to assure him of their support of the army's position with respect to the House of Lords.[166] On 19 December the Earl of Denbigh led a delegation which included Pembroke, Salisbury and Northumberland to parley with the Council of Officers.[167] A day or two later Cromwell and Ireton visited Warwick, perhaps to discuss Denbigh's compromise scheme of preserving monarchy while stripping the king of his veto power.[168] When on 23 December the Earl of Middlesex dumped a full chamberpot onto the heads of some of Colonel Rich's troopers in Friday Street, he was brought before the Council of Officers but released with nothing more than a warning.[169]

All the time it was conciliating or neutralizing moderates, the army tightened its grip on the king and on its enemies in parliament and in the City. Hugh Peters' statement that the army would not prove so unreasonable as some men imagined may have been designed to lull the fears of moderates, or falsely to raise the hopes of royalists.[170] Certainly royalists welcomed any crumb of hope which fed their craving to believe that the army was divided, and that Cromwell in particular was working to save the king's life. It was mostly wishful thinking.[171] On 15 December the officers had Charles brought from Hurst Castle to Windsor. The purpose of Cromwell's visits to Windsor around this time may have included the overseeing of security arrangements for the royal prisoner. A committee of lower-ranking officers headed by Lieutenant-Colonel Venables was charged with the task of recommending within four days 'the best ways and grounds for the speedy bringing of the king to justice.'[172] Collectively, the officers took the greatest care over security measures designed to ensure that the king did not escape. Troops from Harrison's horse regiment, which had escorted the king to Windsor, were stationed at the castle under the reliable command of Colonel Tomlinson, Lieutenant-Colonel Cobbett, Captain Merriman and Captain Brayfield. The castle governor, Colonel Whichcote, besides his overall command of the garrison, had immediate responsibility for the foot guards in and about the rooms where the king and his servants were kept. Three officers were to be at the king's chamber at all times, of whom one was to be in the chamber, except when he was 'private at his devotion'. They were to read all letters addressed to him, and to be present at all his conversations. Cromwell alone among the officers is known to have opposed the latter instruction, perhaps because it inhibited last-minute negotiations for the king's abdication.[173]

On the very day that Hugh Peters was assuring whoever would listen that the army would not prove so unreasonable as men imagined, several regiments marched into London. Fairfax had previously stationed them in Westminster and the outskirts while waiting for the City to come up with £40,000 of back assessment. The Common Council had tried to appease the army with a hundred barrels of 'good strong beer' and two cartloads of the best bread, butter and cheese, but the officers no longer had patience for such gestures. Tired of seeing their men sleep on bare boards, they wheeled artillery into position at Blackfriars, while companies of foot occupied St Martin's Church near Ludgate, St Paul's Cathedral, Cheapside, Lombard Street and the heart of the City. Next, Colonels Deane and Hewson raided the treasuries at Goldsmiths', Weavers' and Haberdashers' Halls. Meanwhile, in St Paul's the men of Skippon's foot regiment warmed themselves at great fires on the cathedral floor, fuelled by carved timber, scaffolding and other materials which they found at hand. When the City implored Fairfax to remove the troops, he only escalated the army's demands: the troops would stay until every penny of London's assessment had been paid to the end of March 1649. Evidently enjoying his brief spell of good health, Fairfax sardonically informed the City fathers that the continued presence of his troops would facilitate the work of collection.[174]

Sensing the approach of the political climax to the struggles of the previous eight years, London presbyterian ministers held protest meetings at the beginning of January, accompanied by prayer and fasting. Alert to the power of these spiritual techniques, Cromwell, Ireton and Peters made it their business to go about the City visiting the ministers, trying to subdue them with threats of military force.[175] Prayer in fact rose in a crescendo on both sides. The soldiers were kept continually on their knees except when they were on duty. These exercises wrought them to a high pitch of tension and fortified them against the hatred of the urban population.[176] The rhetoric of Hugh Peters contributed to stiffening the soldiers' and officers' conviction of their own righteousness.[177]

While those MPs who promised good conduct were let go, others regarded as genuinely dangerous were put under closer confinement. Late in the afternoon of 12 December Sir William Waller, Major-General Edward Massey and Colonel Copley were removed from the King's Head in the Strand to St James's Palace, where they were joined by the sheriff of London, Major-General Richard Browne. The Londoner held chiefly responsible by the army for inviting the Scots to invade England the previous summer, Browne had been tracked down and arrested by a party of horse and foot led by the peripatetic George Joyce. When challenged with the illegality of his action, Joyce answered grandly, 'Do you think that I, who laid hands upon a king, fear to apprehend you, but his sheriff?' He then escorted his prey to Whitehall, and presented him to Fairfax.[178]

In early January the Council of Officers issued a a lengthy indictment of these five, and of William Prynne as a danger to the commonwealth. It laid at their feet the guilt for all the troubles of the past year and a half, from the effort to restore the king unconditionally in the summer of 1647, to the vote of 5 December 1648, which precipitated Pride's Purge.[179]

The army now felt confident enough to move against the king. The municipal elections of 21 December had produced a revolutionary Common Council dominated by radical militia officers who backed the army to the hilt and rapidly brought the financial obstructionism of the City to a halt.[180] The Commons had annulled all the repugnant votes of the previous year and resolved to renew the impeachment of the Eleven Members named by the army in June 1647.[181] Accordingly, a day or two before Christmas the army published its indictment of the king and called for his trial. He had, they charged, devoured the people's liberties, flouted parliament, and waged war against the kingdom, reducing it to a state of desolation. Consequently, 'this capital and grand offender and author of our troubles, the person of the king, ... is guilty of all the trouble, loss, hazard and expense of the blood and mischiefs that have happened by the late wars in this kingdom.'[182]

Marching in step with the army, the Commons voted at the same time to consider precisely 'how to proceed in a way of justice against the king and other capital offenders.' A large committee was appointed to look into the question. Besides Philip Skippon, Henry Marten and the normal array of radicals, Bulstrode Whitelocke and Thomas Widdrington were named, evidently because of their legal expertise. Cromwell was omitted.[183]

Since the king was to be tried, he had to be brought under heavy guard to the capital. Colonel Harrison, the man who had first labelled him 'that Man of Blood',[184] had ridden to Hurst Castle, to make arrangements for his removal to Windsor Castle. Charles was frightened that Harrison had come to the gloomy and out-of-the-way fortress to assassinate him, but Captain John Reynolds, a man of education and refinement, walked the grounds with him and subdued his fears.[185] On the morning of the 19th the king's party set out, encountering much popular acclaim along the way. The same evening at Farnham, Charles drew Harrison aside and expressed his fears of assassination. Harrison disavowed any such intention, but his words cannot have comforted the king. Declaring his hatred of 'all base and obscure undertakings', he assured Charles that whatever happened would be 'open and to the eyes of the world'. His only desire was 'that God may have the glory of all'.[186] The group resumed their journey on the 23rd, arriving at Windsor in drenching rain the same afternoon.[187]

While the king was being toasted by royalists in the taverns of Windsor, preparations were going ahead for his trial in Westminster. There was debate in both the army and the House of Commons over whether he should be executed or merely deposed; whether he should be replaced by one of his children, or whether there should be a king at all.[188] The Council of Officers gave precious time on two separate days to hearing and cross-examining a prophetess from Abingdon. According to Elizabeth Poole's vision the army could try, and even depose, the king, but they ought not to shed his blood. After listening respectfully to her presentation, several militant officers, among them Ireton, Colonel Richard Deane and Lieutenant-Colonel Kelsey, wanted to know how she could prove that her vision was from God. No one expressed open hostility or contempt towards this unusual woman, while senior officers like Harrison, Ireton and Rich made a point of showing her respect. It is an intriguing question who introduced her to the council. The most logical candidate would seem to be Colonel Rich, who, while deeply religious, took no part in bringing the king to the scaffold. Her views and her piety also corresponded exactly to those of Fairfax, but he does not seem to have attended either session where she spoke. Cromwell too was absent from both sessions.[189] Amongst the officers there was no vocal dissent to the proposition that they must be rid of Charles Stuart.

In the Commons meanwhile the debate had been launched the day after Christmas on whether to bring the king to trial for his life. Royalist wishful thinking came abruptly to an end when Cromwell rose to say that,

> if any man whatsoever had carried on this design of deposing the king and disinheriting his posterity, or if any man had yet such a design, he should be the greatest traitor and rebel in the world. But since the providence of God hath cast this upon us, I cannot but submit to providence, though I am not yet provided to give you my advice.[190]

Public business was suspended on the 27th for the monthly fast day. MPs and officers spent most of it in St Margaret's Church, Westminster. On this day too there appeared the first public sign that the debate over the king's fate had been finally settled in the army's inner councils. The Council of War ordered that Charles was no longer to be served on the knee at Windsor Castle, that all ceremonies of state were to be eliminated, and that the number of his attendants was to be reduced. On the 28th the charge against the king was read on the floor of the house. It was a comprehensive indictment, broadly similar to the one promulgated by the army four days before.[191]

The ordinance for erecting a High Court of Justice for the trial of the king was ready by the beginning of January, and sent to the Lords. The peers threw it out, as they did the Commons resolution that 'by the fundamental laws of this kingdom, it is treason in the king of England to levy war against the parliament and kingdom of England.' Hoping to make their obstruction insuperable, the Lords then adjourned for a week. The Commons retaliated by repassing their motions, and adding the statements that the people 'are, under God, the original of all just power', that the Commons, as representatives of the people, possess supreme power, and that whatever they decided had the force of law, even without the assent of king or lords.[192]

The efforts to ensure that the High Court would be broadly representative of the social and legal elite of England were a failure. None of the half-dozen peers named attended any of its sittings; nor did any of the lord chief justices. The business of the court was driven on by a combination of army officers and revolutionary MPs. Twenty-nine of the 135 commissioners were serving army officers;[193] but several of them would have a spotty attendance record and, when the time came, would decline to sign the death warrant. Fairfax, whose attendance would have been most highly prized, came only to the first meeting of the commissioners, on 8 January, but refused to sit down.[194] Skippon, although he was in London, attended few sittings, as did Colonels Lambart, Overton, Sidney, Tomlinson, Ingoldsby and Fenwick. Some had legitimate reasons for not being there. Tomlinson was preoccupied with guarding the king at St James's and Robert Cotton's house throughout the month of January. Overton, governor of the second-greatest arsenal in the kingdom, presumably found it advisable not to quit Hull. Sidney, governor of another important garrison – Dover – attended the court's planning meetings, but threw cold water on the proceedings with the dictum that the king could be tried by no court, and no one could be tried by this court. After being rebuked by Cromwell he retired to his father's house at Penshurst until it was all over. John Disbrowe, governor of Yarmouth, a garrison of minor strategic importance, could presumably have attended had he wished. The same was true of Ingoldsby at Oxford, though he did turn up to sign the death warrant.[195]

In the twelve days before the trial opened the commissioners were busy with a multitude of questions, great and small.[196] Given that Charles was to be found guilty, would he be sentenced to death or merely deposed? If condemned to die, where would the scaffold be erected; who would do the beheading; how would they prevent a riot or an attempt to rescue him on or before his execution day? While the commissioners grappled with these and other questions that had no precedent, their morale cannot have been improved by the chronic absence of nearly half their number.[197] A knot of men who had banished whatever doubts still troubled them kept the rest at their work and saw to it that they stuck to the agenda. Some of them were soldiers – Cromwell, Ireton and Colonel Harrison; some were MPs – Henry Marten, Thomas Scot, William Saye, John Lisle; and one was the redoubtable Hugh Peters, who, alternating between bouts of manic frenzy and melancholic sickness, dashed to and fro between Westminster and the City, inciting his colleagues and confuting his foes.[198]

On 13 January it was agreed that the trial would be held in Westminster Hall, the great medieval edifice next door to the House of Commons where Chancery and the common-law courts held their sittings. Colonel Francis Hacker and a company of guards would secure the king, while a large number of soldiers under Lieutenant-Colonel Axtell would be stationed between the king and the crowd to prevent a disturbance.

As the king's career approached its dénouement most royalists were paralysed with disbelief at what they saw. A few took up cudgels on his behalf. From abroad the ambassadors of France and the United Provinces, as well as the Scots commissioners, tried to save his life. Closer to home, the London presbyterian clergy demanded and got a meeting with the officers to dispute the legality of what they were doing. Several of them trudged to Fairfax's lodgings on the afternoon of Thursday 11 January.[199] The following week forty-seven of them publicly exhorted the army to search its heart and repent before it was too late.[200] The army's defenders made up for the smallness of their numbers by the forcefulness of their arguments. John Goodwin had set the tone at the beginning of the month with a vigorous address to the Council of War, buttressing the case for rebellion and prosecution of 'the warfare of heaven' with texts both scriptural and classical.[201] Cromwell, Ireton and Peters worked remorselessly to confound the opponents of regicide.[202] The recently elected radical Common Council of London, under the leadership of Colonel Robert Tichborne, also played a part in silencing the disaffected. On 15 January it dutifully framed a petition 'against all grand and capital actors in the late war against the parliament.'[203] There was also steady pressure from the forces outside London for the purged house and the Council of Officers not to falter in their resolve.[204] Besides taming their opponents, the grandees also had to curb the enthusiasm of those who wanted instant enactment of the full revolutionary agenda. Cromwell, conscious of the debt of gratitude he owed the Saye–Wharton group for past support, thought it inappropriate to abolish the House of Lords before the king had been disposed of. His preference was probably for an upper house with limited powers. He therefore blocked the radical attempt in mid-January to abolish the Lords, although he stood aside when the same objective was accomplished less than a month later.[205] Another step towards reducing distraction from secondary issues was taken with the release of William Prynne and most of the other imprisoned MPs during the week of 10 January.[206] After six weeks' seclusion these MPs were evidently no longer considered a serious threat to the realization of the revolutionaries' plans. Furthermore, their release removed a source of indignation against one violation of the law, leaving the grandees to get on with another more important one.

One group gave no cause for worry in January: the Levellers. From the early autumn until Christmas the grandees had taken pains to demonstrate their seriousness about the Leveller scheme for a new constitution. The finishing touches were now being applied to the officers' version of the Agreement of the People. In the meantime the radicals were reassured that the Agreement would soon be ready for public subscription. Key features such as the reserve against conscription were also leaked to the public via army pamphlets.[207] In addition, the grandees took action of a quite different nature to head off trouble from the Levellers. They piloted a bill through both houses to grant John Lilburne the £3000 that he had been claiming for almost a decade as damages for his sufferings at the hands of the Star Chamber. Because ready money was not to be had from the Treasury, Lilburne was instructed to recover his money from the sale of timber on the estates of royalist delinquents in his native county of Durham. Fearing that if he did not lay a hand on the revenue right away it would slip forever from his grasp; troubled too at the penury he had inflicted for so long on his wife and children; discouraged at the break-up of the Leveller party, and perhaps wishing neither to sanction nor to interfere with the execution of the king, Lilburne quit the capital, not to return until Charles had been beheaded.[208]

On the eve of Charles's trial the Lords found themselves marginalized; the presbyterian clergy were fuming but impotent; disaffected MPs had been neutralized and then conciliated; the Scots and foreign representatives were politely ignored; while the Levellers were quiescent and the royalists dumb with disbelief. There were still many details of the trial to be thrashed out. Ireton, Cromwell, Harrison and Peters met day and night, sometimes in the rooms near Westminster Hall, sometimes in taverns like the Star in Coleman Street, and occasionally in Ireton's lodgings in Windsor.[209] The last pre-trial meeting of the commissioners took place on 19 January. Following the usual prayers came an announcement that the king had just landed at the stairs on the river leading up to Sir Robert Cotton's house. As Cromwell watched him from the window it suddenly struck him that they had still not devised the answer they would give if Charles challenged their authority to try him. When he reminded his fellow commissioners of this omission they fell silent, except for Henry Marten. Always gifted with verbal facility, he improvised a formula that satisfied them all. They would inform the King that they acted 'in the name of the commons in parliament assembled, and all the good people of England.'[210]

The trial opened on Saturday 20 January. The mild wet weather of the previous autumn had by now given way to a bitter frost. The week of the trial would witness the freezing-over of the Thames, and a 'horrid tempest of winds' would sweep the metropolis.[211] Just before two o'clock, sixty-eight commissioners formed up in procession for their entry into Westminster Hall. Fairfax, who had boycotted the trial since the first meeting, resisted all attempts to get him to attend.[212] While twelve halberdiers went to fetch the king, the clerk, John Phelps, read the roll call of commissioners. The first name he pronounced was that of the army's commander-in-chief. 'He has more wit than to be here', shouted Lady Fairfax from behind her mask in one of the galleries.[213] Lieutenant-Colonel Daniel Axtell turned abruptly in her direction and commanded his men to shoot 'if they speak one word more'. One of the toughest officers in the army, Axtell had been put in charge of the red-coated foot guards on the floor of the hall. His men's muskets pointing at the gallery produced a sudden hush.[214]

Now the king appeared, tightly escorted by the halberdiers. At a signal from the president of the court, John Bradshaw, the prosecuting attorney, Solicitor John Cook, recited the charge. As King of England Charles had been 'trusted with a limited power to govern by, and according to, the laws of the land, and not otherwise.' Yet he had engineered 'a wicked design to erect and uphold in himself an unlimited and tyrannical power to rule according to his will, and to overthrow the rights and liberties of the people.' In prosecuting this design he had 'traitorously and maliciously levied war against the present parliament and the people therein repre-sented.' He was therefore worthy to be impeached as a 'tyrant, traitor and murderer, and a public and implacable enemy to the Commonwealth of England.'[215] When Charles stood up to answer the charge the great north gate swung open to admit the public. The noise of people flocking towards the bar drowned out his words for all except a few who sat close to him.[216] He answered with a question: by what *lawful* authority had he been sum-moned before them? Bradshaw only reiterated the substance of the charge and ordered the king to answer 'in the name of the people of England, of which you are *elected* king.' Charles pounced on this piece of novel constitutional theory. 'England was never an elective kingdom, but a her-editary kingdom for near these thousand years.' Moreover, 'I do stand more for the liberty of my people than any here that come to be my pretended judges.' Rattled by the king's unexpected eloquence, Bradshaw quickly brought the proceedings to a halt and ordered the prisoner removed. As if on cue, Axtell's soldiers cried 'Justice! Justice!' A few who were near the king sprinkled gunpowder on their palms, lit it, and blew it into his face.[217] Some spectators joined the cry for 'justice', but others shouted, 'God save the king!'

On the next day, Sunday, the commissioners fasted. Of the three preachers who addressed them, only one equivocally endorsed their course of action. Joshua Sprigge chose the text 'He that sheds blood, by man shall his blood be shed.' The second preacher, Mr Foxley, was more overtly doubtful, with the text 'Judge not that ye be not judged.' One wonders at the courage required of Sprigge and Foxley to challenge the policies of the officers. Who had selected them? Was it Fairfax? They were not alone in their doubts. Remarkably, only two clergymen had publicly declared their support for the army's conduct since the invasion of London in December. One was John Goodwin, the minister of the large Independent congre-gation at St Stephen's, Coleman Street. The other was Hugh Peters, the army's self-appointed emissary extraordinary. Taking Psalm 149 as his text – 'I will bind their kings in chains and their nobles in fetters of iron' – he made amends, as Gilbert Mabbott tersely put it, for the disturbing questions raised by his colleagues.[218]

On the afternoon of Monday the 22nd seventy commissioners assembled as the king was brought in for the second time. Again Charles refused to recognize the court's competence to try him, and again Bradshaw ordered him removed. The third public sitting of the court was held early in the afternoon of Tuesday 23 January. The proceedings were essentially a repetition of the previous day, with the king even more boldly repudiating the commissioners' competence to try him. Amidst the confusion that erupted as the king was hustled away, the court crier shouted out, 'God bless the kingdom of England', striving perhaps to drown out those shouting a shorter slogan: 'God bless the king.'[219]

At the end of this episode the commissioners went directly into secret session in the Painted Chamber to deal with their own crisis of self-confidence. In an effort to rally the waverers they decided to call witnesses against the king. The same night steps were taken to round up some of the court's notable absentees, chief among them Sir Thomas Fairfax. He was 'baited with fresh dogs ... to bring him into the hall on the morrow to countenance the business',[220] but could not be budged.

These days marked the nadir of Fairfax's public life. Having allowed himself to be pushed towards the precipice, he only stumbled back from it at the last moment. A soldier first and a politician second, he had none the less co-operated fully with the army's revolutionary acts until at least December. He was easily the most popular of all the officers, caring deeply for his men's welfare, working assiduously to keep them properly clothed, equipped and lodged, and writing countless letters demanding the pay that was due to them. He had not shrunk from putting himself at their head and chairing their revolutionary council from July to October 1647. Willingly he had led invasions of London, once in August 1647 and again in December 1648. While Cromwell and Ireton assumed a steadily higher political profile, Fairfax retained control of the army's appointments and promotions, on occasion vetoing proposed commissions for prominent radicals.[221] No friend to the Levellers, he had resisted the adoption of the November 1648 Remonstrance for as long as it was practical to do so, yet he made no attempt to block Pride's Purge. He drew the line, however, at trying his anointed sovereign. Allowing his name to stand as a commissioner for the trial was either a blunder or perhaps an agonized decision taken in the hope of saving the king. If Henry Vane and the chief justices could decline to serve, Fairfax could have declined as well. But his name appeared at the head of the list, and his attendance at the first meeting on 8 January, even though he had refused to sit down, decidedly enhanced the court's prestige. By failing to have his name removed from the list of commissioners he compromised his moral authority when the time came to ponder resistance to his colleagues' acts. Perhaps like many others he hoped that their threats to kill the king were only intended to intimidate him into unconditional surrender or abdication. Not until the first session in the Painted Chamber did the truth hit home that his colleagues were in deadly earnest. His consequent silent withdrawal signified the collapse of his per-

sonal influence among the officers. Torn between their overbearing determination, and his wife's as well as the presbyterian clergy's bitter hostility
to the trial, he resigned himself to political impotence.

On Wednesday the 24th the court had a closed session in the Painted
Chamber to hear a large quantity of mainly unremarkable testimony against
the king. The commissioners then resolved to sentence him to death. Ireton
and Harrison were part of the seven-man committee appointed to draw up
the sentence.[222]

At the next public sitting, in the afternoon of Saturday the 27th,
Bradshaw opened his remarks 'in the name of the people of England'. At
these words a masked lady in the gallery called out, 'Not half, not a quarter
of the people of England. Oliver Cromwell is a traitor.' Under Lieutenant-
Colonel Axtell's orders the guards turned their muskets in her direction. In
a few moments the commotion was over, and Lady Fairfax – for she it was –
had been hustled out. The care she had taken in disguising her identity
suggests that she had acted on her own rather than with her husband's
knowledge or encouragement.[223]

Once Bradshaw had completed his remarks, Charles was permitted to
speak. He had one request: prior to sentencing he wished to address the
Lords and Commons in the Painted Chamber. However, the commissioners
had decided in advance that such an appeal would be regarded as a stalling
tactic.

As Bradshaw began informing the king that the court would not countenance his request, he became aware of an embarrassing disturbance on the
tiered benches behind him. John Downes, a former royal servant, had
turned to the men beside him – Colonel Valentine Wauton and MP William
Cawley – and cried, 'Have we hearts of stone? Are we men?' In vain they
tried to silence him. Cromwell, sitting immediately below, turned around
and asked if he were himself. But Downes would not be suppressed, and
demanded an adjournment so that he could offer his reasons against the
sentence. Bradshaw was discomfited, but saw no way of overruling his
dissenting colleague. The commissioners accordingly filed into the Court of
Wards, which was adjacent to the south door of the hall. Cromwell was
furious at this unplanned disturbance. Summoning all the rage at his command, he demanded if Downes had forgotten that they were dealing with
the 'hardest hearted man that lives upon the earth'. It was 'not fit', he
stormed, 'that the court should be hindered from their duty by one peevish
man.' Oliver's bullying had its intended effect: the weaker commissioners
pulled themselves together, while Downes, isolated and in disgrace, withdrew to the Speaker's chamber to 'ease my mind and heart with tears'.[224]

Upon the court's reassembling Bradshaw called upon the clerk to pro-
nounce the sentence. This done, the sixty-seven commissioners present

stood up, according to their prior agreement, to affirm their assent.[225] The king was shattered, not so much by the sentence of death, for which he had been long prepared, as by the characterization of himself as 'tyrant, traitor and murderer'. He asked to be heard, but Bradshaw refused, and ordered the guards to remove him. His exit was punctuated by Lieutenant-Colonel Axtell's men crying 'Execution! Justice! Execution!'[226] As he descended the stairs the soldiers blew smoke into his face and rolled their pipes in his way so that he might trip.[227] The commissioners now dealt with their last item of business: the time, place and details of the execution. Five officers – Sir Hardress Waller, Thomas Harrison, Henry Ireton, Richard Deane and John Okey – were charged with settling these matters.[228]

Sunday provided a brief hiatus in the hastening tragedy. It was kept as a fast day by soldiers, clergy and the pious on both sides. At St James's the soldiers were treated to a homiletic extravaganza by Hugh Peters on a grisly text from Isaiah: 'thou art cast out of thy grave like an abominable branch, and as the raiment of those that are slain, thrust through with a sword.... Thou shalt not be joined to them in burial, because thou hast destroyed thy land and slain thy people.'[229] The officers, who evidently did not need the stiffening of Peters' oratory, were absorbed with a last-minute appeal from the Dutch ambassadors to save the king's life. The meeting, which took place at Fairfax's house, brought no satisfaction, since the ambassadors were only treated to the individual opinions of each officer. Fairfax meanwhile had not given up. Early on Monday the 29th he summoned a council of war, at which he strove to persuade his fellow officers to postpone the execution. They were unyielding.[230]

Only a day or two earlier the commissioners had finally approved the time and place of the execution. It was to be outside the Banqueting House designed by Inigo Jones for Charles at the beginning of his reign. The commissioners had also formally ordered the death warrant to be drawn up. As S. R. Gardiner has shown, this had already been done, probably on Friday the 26th, which had been the expected date of sentencing. Some commissioners had signed as early as the 26th or 27th, and, rather than court the risk that they would balk at signing a second time, the first copy was messily corrected to reflect the changed dates of sentencing and execution. The names of the officers first charged with carrying out the execution had also been erased, and replaced with those of Colonel Francis Hacker, Colonel Hercules Huncks and Lieutenant-Colonel Robert Phayre.[231] Cromwell had probably been collecting signatures over the weekend. On Monday morning he stood at the Commons door with the warrant in his hand, intending to add to the total. Some MPs slipped by him and took their seats, but he pursued them into the house, saying, 'those that are gone in shall set their hands, I will have their hands now.' On that same day, the warrant lay on a table in the Painted Chamber waiting for those who might yet be brought to sign. Reacting against the almost intolerable tension, Cromwell took the pen and marked up Henry Marten's face, and Marten did the same to Cromwell.[232]

Although heavy pressure was put on all commissioners who could be found, it is likely, as Lucy Hutchinson stated, that no one was subjected to outright coercion.[233] Colonel Tomlinson, the officer in charge of the king, had excused himself from most meetings on the grounds of his duties. Other officers who avoided signing were Fairfax, Major-General Skippon, Colonel Lambart, Colonel Fleetwood and Major John Disbrowe. There is no need to credit Richard Ingoldsby's claim in 1660 that Cromwell dragged him to the table, held his hand and forced him to sign. The firmness of his signature belies his story.[234] By the end of the day the number of signatures totalled fifty-nine, of which eighteen belonged to army officers in current service: Oliver Cromwell, Edward Whalley, John Okey, Henry Ireton, Sir Hardress Waller, William Goffe, Thomas Pride, Thomas Harrison, John Hewson, Richard Deane, Adrian Scrope, William Constable, Richard Ingoldsby, John Barkstead, Isaac Ewer, Valentine Wauton, Thomas Horton and Robert Lilburne. Former officers who signed were Michael Livesey, Thomas Mauleverer, John Hutchinson, Owen Rowe, Edmund Ludlowe, Henry Marten and John Jones.[235]

Although they numbered less than half the signatories, the army officers had played a pre-eminent role in bringing the king to the scaffold. But, on the day of the event for which they had striven so sedulously, they would be strangely absent.

Charles was escorted from St James's to Whitehall at half-past ten in the bitterly cold morning of Tuesday 30 January. His execution, however, did not occur till after two o'clock. What caused the delay? Was there trouble finding an executioner? The common hangman, Richard Brandon, may have had scruples about cutting off the king's head, but he was almost certainly one of the two masked executioners who assisted on the scaffold. The other was a sergeant in Colonel Hewson's regiment, William Hewlet. Subsequently he would be rewarded with a promotion to captain-lieutenant in Ireland.[236] A dispute among the officers charged with supervising the execution might have held up proceedings. No one wanted to sign the order for the actual beheading, so Huncks, Phayre and Hacker brought their dispute to Cromwell, whom they found in Ireton's chamber in Whitehall. It was still early enough in the morning for Ireton and Harrison to be lying in bed together. Cromwell instructed Huncks to write out and sign the order for the execution. Huncks demurred. Lieutenant-Colonel Axtell, who had come to the door, upbraided Huncks for his cowardice but Huncks stood his ground. Unwilling to tolerate further delay Oliver seized pen and paper and scribbled out the order, then handed the pen to Hacker, who stooped and signed it.[237]

There was another hold-up: a law had to be enacted making it illegal for anyone to proclaim a new king. The emergency bill was read twice, committed during the midday break, and then read a third time and passed.[238]

In the meantime the Dutch ambassadors had taken advantage of the delay to make a last-minute effort to prevail upon Fairfax to block the execution. By coming to his secretary's house in Whitehall they managed to gain access to him without Cromwell being present. Fairfax had already spent much of the night working for the same end as they. He promised to go directly to Westminster and prevail upon parliament to postpone the execution, but he drew back from an open confrontation with the Council of Officers. The only officers of high rank upon whom he might have counted were Philip Skippon, major-general of the infantry, and perhaps Colonel Nathaniel Rich.[239] Other opponents of the execution, such as Colonel John Lambart, Colonel Charles Fleetwood and Major John Disbrowe, were at that moment far away from London. Arrayed against Fairfax would have been the incomparably abler Cromwell and Ireton, who could count on the almost unanimous backing of the lower officers and probably most of the rank and file stationed in London. The private soldiers, angry at the king for dragging them through a second civil war, impatient at the lack of action on their arrears, stirred up by Peters' preaching, and bad-tempered because of the intense cold and lack of decent accommodation, were in no mood to support clemency for the 'grand author' of their misery.

While Fairfax did not attempt a coup against his officers on 30 January, he did go and talk to them. We know that he was in one of the rooms near the Banqueting House in the early afternoon. Thomas Herbert ran into him in the Long Gallery, coming from Colonel Thomas Harrison's apartment, where he had been in prayer or conversation with other officers.[240] The officers were willing enough to converse with their commander-in-chief so long as he did not interfere with the march of events in the street below. Knowing there was nothing effectual left for him to do, Fairfax permitted himself to be distracted.

Just before two o'clock Colonel Hacker knocked on the door to summon the king. Together they walked along the corridors and across the Banqueting Hall beneath Rubens' awe-inspiring portrayal of the last king's ascent into heaven. Through one of the windows Charles stepped onto the raised scaffold draped in black. Crowded into that small space were fourteen people: Colonels Tomlinson and Hacker, the two executioners, Richard Brandon and William Hewlet (masked and heavily disguised), Bishop William Juxon, Thomas Herbert, several guards and two or three scribes. One of the scribes was the army's secretary, William Clarke. Gifted with a canny intuition for memorable historical moments, he had already recorded the army's debates at Putney and Whitehall on the franchise, religious liberty and the Agreement of the People. His collection of civil-war pamphlets and newsbooks, now housed at Worcester College, Oxford, is second in magnitude only to the London bookseller George Thomason's. Twice on the scaffold Clarke attracted the king's attention. As he pressed closer to catch Charles's last words his cloak brushed against the 'bright execution axe'. Noticing this Charles turned and asked him to 'hurt not the axe that may hurt me.'[241]

Casting his eye across the sea of faces below him, Charles saw that he was separated from the populace by densely packed ranks of mounted troopers. The adjacent streets were also thick with soldiers. It was unlikely that his voice would reach the non-military audience. So he addressed his few words to the soldiers and scribes surrounding him on the platform. He proclaimed his innocence and affirmed that he was dying 'a Christian according to the profession of the Church of England.' The first executioner beheaded him with one stroke. The second picked up the severed head and displayed it with the traditional words, 'Behold the head of a traitor.' The throng were now hushed, but at the moment the axe had fallen they had involuntarily given out a deep heart-rending groan, expressive of their horror at the unprecedented act of parricide.

If any of them had formulated such a thought, however, they were not allowed to dwell on it. Almost immediately a troop of horse stationed at Charing Cross swept down Whitehall, while another approached from King Street in the opposite direction. Within minutes the people were scattered and the streets empty.[242]

There is one significant aspect of the execution that historians have not remarked on. Few if any of the officers or MPs directly responsible actually witnessed it. The Commons had been busy until a few minutes before the beheading, passing the law against proclaiming a new king, and dispatching Sergeant Dendy to proclaim it by sound of trumpet in Westminster and the City.[243] The army's higher officers congregated in Colonel Harrison's apartment at the end of the Long Gallery in Whitehall Palace, where they prayed and conversed. They had to make do without the eloquence of Hugh Peters, who spent the day sick in bed. Colonel Robert Lilburne also retired to his own chamber.[244] Likewise, Bulstrode Whitelocke, never a man to expose himself unnecessarily to danger, occupied the day in his study at prayer.[245] While the higher officers prayed and talked, less senior members of the High Court of Justice met in the Painted Chamber. About the time that the king's head was being chopped off, they were busy preparing warrants to Captain John Blackwell for the payment of the court's expenses.[246] The highest-ranking officer to witness the execution was apparently Colonel Tomlinson, who, though he had not signed the warrant, had stood up with the other commissioners to show his approval of the sentence.[247] At the Restoration he would successfully appeal for clemency on the grounds of his civil behaviour towards the king during his last days. Colonel Hacker and Lieutenant-Colonel Axtell, who could not make a similar claim, were not spared, although neither of them was a regicide.[248]

Bishop Juxon and Thomas Herbert had taken the king's body back into the palace. On their way they ran into Fairfax in the Long Gallery. To their amazement he inquired 'how the king did', and 'seemed much surprised' to learn that he was already dead. A few seconds later they encountered Cromwell, who knew what had just happened and drily informed the two men 'they should have orders for the king's burial speedily.'[249]

While the nation was still in shock at the king's death, the new rulers took resolute action to consolidate their power. On 1 February the remnant of the House of Commons, soon to be labelled the 'Rump' by its detractors, decided that no one who had voted on 5 December that the king's offers afforded a ground of settlement, or had been absent when the vote was given, should be allowed to sit until he had recorded his dissent from that motion. Five days later they voted to abolish the House of Lords as 'useless and dangerous'. On the 7th the office of king was also eliminated.[250] At the same time the chief executive agency of the previous two years, the Derby House Committee, was abolished, to be replaced by a larger Council of State with authority inferior only to parliament's in domestic and foreign affairs.[251] A small committee was asked to draw up a list of nominees for the Council of State. After a week they reported the results of their labour. Their slate included peers and army officers, as well as MPs. No objection was raised to the presence of friendly peers like Pembroke, Salisbury, Mulgrave and Grey of Warke, but some MPs took alarm at the number of active army officers. The principle of permitting the military to participate in the highest executive body was not accepted without debate, and at the end of the day two of the most prominent officers – Henry Ireton and Thomas Harrison – were rejected. Of the remaining thirty-nine nominees, seven were in active military service. They were Fairfax, Cromwell, Skippon, Hesilrige, Wauton, Constable and Jones. Another six had served during the war or would do so in the near future: Anthony Stapley, John Hutchinson, Henry Marten, Alexander Popham, William Purefoy and Edmund Ludlowe.[252] Fully a third of the new council had military associations, but the exclusion of Ireton and Harrison, two of the steersmen of recent events, was a stinging rebuke to their political aspirations. Only days before, Ireton had been the one to sketch the outline of the Engagement that would be required of all members of the Council of State. They were to declare their approval of the High Court of Justice, of the trial and execution of the king, and of the abolition of the monarchy and the House of Lords.[253] Many balked at giving retroactive approval to illegal acts; by the 19th twenty-two nominees were still holding out against the Engagement. They included Colonel Algernon Sidney, Sir Thomas Fairfax and the five peers.[254] Cromwell now intervened to effect a compromise. According to the revised draft, whose preparation he supervised, new members of the Council would only be expected to recognize the republican form of government 'for the future'. Over half the councillors, of whom Fairfax was one, continued to hold out against even this modified oath. In order to win his co-operation the revolutionaries had to let him write his own version of the Engagement in which he uttered no support for what had been done, but merely undertook to defend the present government 'without king and House of Peers'.[255]

By mid-February the ship of state appeared to be on a steady course. Officers and MPs accordingly began to ready themselves for the long-deferred invasion of Ireland. It was from that kingdom that the main threat to the republic was thought to emanate. A second cause of war, universally acknowledged, was the obligation of avenging the protestant massacres of 1641. But no invasion could take place unless the soldiers were willing to be part of it. After several months of seeing their own concerns ignored, the rank and file were again seething with dissatisfaction. In addition, John Lilburne had returned from the north, intent on stirring up more political discontent. The conjunction of Leveller agitation and rank-and-file unhappiness in the late winter and spring of 1649 would present the grandees with the most dangerous internal threat they had yet faced. How they handled this threat is the theme of the next chapter.

10

The Army and the Levellers,
February–September 1649

Once the great drama on the scaffold was over, the discontent that had been seething in the army since the end of the second civil war bubbled up to the surface. As in the spring of 1647, the principal source of discontent was arrears of pay. Although wages had been issued with reasonable regularity for several months, nothing had been done about money owing since as far back as 1642. The knowledge that many of them would soon be asked to embark for Ireland only deepened the soldiers' anxiety over back pay. Their mood was not improved by the recent experience of the animosity of the London populace, or of sleeping on bare boards in unheated rooms. A poor harvest, the third in as many years, added to a winter which had now turned bitterly cold, sharpened their discomfort.

In the autumn the soldiers' anger had been channelled against their parliamentary masters. But now the officers themselves partook of political power and so became an inevitable target of rank-and-file resentment. As an awareness of how well these officers seemed to be providing for themselves percolated down to the rank and file, the sense of grievance spread. The task of controlling the army was made doubly difficult by the swelling of its ranks since the outbreak of the second civil war. As in 1647 most of the newly enlisted men came from the metropolis, and there was a significant ratio of radicals among them.[1] Preserving military authority was not made easier by the Commons' ill-considered decision to allow Henry Marten and John Reynolds to fill up their regiments in Berkshire, Shropshire and Worcestershire.[2] Before the middle of February Reynolds' regiment had become unruly enough to warrant serious attention from army headquarters.[3]

Their political preoccupations from November to the end of January did not allow the higher officers to attend to the morale of their regiments. A pamphlet addressed to the private soldiers at the beginning of January, however, alerted them to the resentments that would soon erupt into open defiance. The pamphleteer, himself a soldier, wrote that, since parliament had declared the people to be the source of all power, the same principle should apply within the army. Existing commanders should be replaced with men who would show more consideration for the needs of the rank and file.[4]

The Agitation of John Lilburne and Richard Overton

The Leveller campaign against the grandees got seriously under way upon John Lilburne's return from Durham at the beginning of February. By the 8th of that month troopers were reported to be posting up his pamphlets and petitions in Hitchin, a few miles north of London. They also read them out in the market place, made speeches exhorting the people to refuse to pay the excise or give free quarter, and urged an alliance between people and soldiers. They apparently attracted some popular support.[5]

The grandees decided to meet the threat of mounting dissatisfaction with a programme combining reform and repression. At an important meeting of the Council of Officers on 22 February it was agreed to forward to parliament a moderate petition from Fairfax's own horse regiment.[6] At the same time the officers expressed concern over the radical petitions being circulated among the regiments by people who had nothing to do with the army. At the behest of Hewson, Whalley and Major Barton a new policy was laid down to curb outside agitators. 'Clandestine contrivances or private meetings' were to stop. Soldiers could still petition, but regiments were not to club together behind a single petition. All petitions were to be brought in the first instance to the regimental officers, who would then submit them to the general. He in turn would lay them before parliament.

It was decided also to ask parliament to make outside agitators who stirred up trouble in the army liable to the penalties of martial law. When a member of the council suggested that civilian agitators might better be prosecuted in the civil courts, Hewson allegedly fumed, 'we have had trial enough of civil courts; we can hang twenty before they will hang one.' Word of the council's request soon got out and caused great indignation among the civilian Levellers. But there is no evidence that parliament ever acted on it. Both Corporal William Thompson and Colonel Eyre were leading figures in the armed struggle between February and May 1649. Thompson, a former member of Whalley's regiment, had been cashiered in September 1647 for taking part in an ugly tavern brawl in Colnbrook, Buckinghamshire. Then, taking advantage of the unrest in the army at the time, he went to Fleetwood's regiment, where he tried to raise a mutiny.

For this he was court-martialled and imprisoned in Windsor Castle. During his sojourn there he managed to make friends with John Lilburne, and published *England's Freedom Souldiers Rights*, possibly with Lilburne's help. Allowed out on parole, he was soon found stirring up sedition in London, for which he was rearrested by Cromwell and sent back to prison, this time in Whitehall. He now found himself under sentence of death, but was reprieved by Fairfax.[7] While he was remarkably successful at attracting Leveller support for his activities, Thompson at bottom was one of those figures who is familiar in all revolutions: the man of violent or criminal propensities who for a time camouflages his lawlessness beneath the rhetoric of resistance to unjust authority. Eyre, who was perhaps one of Cromwell's original Ironsides, was styled a colonel by the autumn of 1647, though he had no command in Fairfax's army. He had already been arrested for inciting the soldiers to mutiny at Corkbush Field in November of that year.[8] Yet neither he nor Thompson was tried by a court martial for his offences, because neither was any longer a member of the army.[9]

According to John Lilburne it was the repressive policies adopted by the Council of Officers that prompted him to leap once more into action. Within four days of the officers' meeting he had framed, circulated, published and submitted to parliament a major statement taking the officers to task for their many sins. He first upbraided them for the compromises they had incorporated into their version of the Agreement of the People. In particular he was deeply suspicious of the provision that parliaments should meet for only six months in every two-year period, while the executive Council of State would carry on for the other eighteen.[10] What business, he asked, did the army have enforcing censorship of the press? Why did the hastily erected Council of State include among its members army officers, peers and Star Chamber judges, in violation of the principles of the Agreement? He reserved his harshest words for the higher officers, and their demand to execute martial law upon those who disturbed the army. Ever since the Engagement of 5 June 1647 the officers' conduct had been a sorry tale of broken promises and oppression of their own rank and file. What was needed was nothing less than a purge of the high command. Finally, parliament should set up a committee to settle all disputes between officers and soldiers, and should mitigate the martial law.

Late that day (26 February) Lilburne and several of his comrades presented *England's New Chains* to the Commons. Ushered in by the sergeant-at-arms, he was invited to introduce his petition at the bar of the house. It was the last time he would enjoy such respectful treatment.[11] His repeated, reckless and unrestrained attacks on the army leadership would drive an unhealable breach between him and them. Not only was his language intemperate, but his proposal for a committee to hear disputes between officers and men would have dangerously undermined discipline in the army.

On the same day as Lilburne launched his diatribe, the anonymous radicals within the army brought their own petition before the House. Besides rehearsing the familiar material grievances of the soldiers, they called for the abolition of tithes, liberty of conscience, the freeing of prisoners for debt, and the relaxing of the existing code of martial law 'as being too severe and tyrannous for any army of freeborn Englishmen.' Perhaps as part of their conscious strategy to forge an alliance with England's rural poor, they also urged 'that speedy provision be made for the continual supply of the necessities of the poor of this nation, whose miseries cry aloud in our ears for redress.' Along the same lines they suggested that regular pay for the army would enable it to avoid the oppressive practice of free quarter. To no one's surprise the House of Commons declined to endorse the petition, but it did not condemn it either.[12]

In the army the new rules for petitioning sparked immediate resentment. On 1 March at the regular weekly meeting of the Council of Officers, Fairfax produced a petition from eight troopers belonging to several regiments asserting the soldiers' right to petition without their officers' consent, and denouncing the Council of State and the High Court of Justice. Their root demand was for a democratization of the army. 'The strength of the officer doth consist in the arm of the soldier. Is it not the soldier that endureth the heat and burden of the day, and performeth that work whereof the officers beareth the glory and name?'[13] This wholesale challenge to the officers' authority was condemned as tending to disunite the army, and the troopers were ordered to be tried by a court martial.[14]

The trial was convened on 3 March. After a long debate all were found guilty under the fifth Article of War, 'that no man shall use reproachful nor provoking words or act to any, upon pain of imprisonment and further punishment.' They were sentenced to ride the wooden horse with their faces to the tail, to have their swords broken over their heads, and to be cashiered from the army. Richard Rumball was released after confessing that he had been misled. Two had already gone into hiding.[15]

The sentence was inflicted on the remaining five in the Palace Yard, Westminster, on 6 March. As they painfully rode the wooden horse, their swords, which had been nearly cut through by the blacksmith so as to snap easily asunder, were smashed over their heads. All of them were unrepentant, comparing their sufferings to those of Burton, Bastwick and Prynne at the hands of the bishops a decade before. When the ordeal was over they chatted with their friends, and then were driven away in coaches and feasted in a Leveller tavern. Their dress and stylish departure prompted one news editor to observe that they appeared like gentlemen of quality.[16]

A fortnight later the five cashiered men published their defiant answer to their tormentors. Entitled *The Hunting of the Foxes*, the pamphlet exposes the extreme animosity to the Levellers harboured by Colonels Hewson and Barkstead, the latter being the president of the court martial that had tried them. Just as the higher officers strongly suspected that the five troopers' earlier petition had been composed by someone outside the army, so we may reasonably suppose that someone helped with the publication of this tract. Its powerful eloquence points towards Overton's authorship.[17] With their denunciation of all the institutions of the new republic and their vitriolic attack on the officers, the Leveller leaders now effectively destroyed any possibility of a rapprochement with their erstwhile allies. In their eyes, the officers' original sin was the abolition of the General Council of the Army with its rank-and-file representatives in the autumn of 1647. Since then their behaviour had been that of 'apostates, ... jesuits and traitors to the people'. Even more repellent was their religious hypocrisy:

> Did ever men pretend an higher degree of holiness, religion, and zeal to God and their country than these? These preach, these fast, these pray, these have nothing more frequent than the sentences of sacred scripture, the name of God and of Christ in their mouths: You shall scarce speak to Cromwell about any thing, but he will lay his hand on his breast, elevate his eyes, and call God to record, he will weep, howl and repent, even while he doth smite you under the first rib.

What would satisfy the radicals? Nothing less than the immediate restitution of the General Council of 1647, with sovereign power over all the army's actions.[18] In addition the soldiers must have the uninhibited right to petition parliament, while the exercise of martial law must be sharply curtailed. Officers and men were to be on an equal footing. Indeed, it was the soldiers who were the essential part of the army, the officers being 'but the form or letter'. The soldiers therefore had the right to control and overthrow the officers if they threatened their life, liberty or freedom.[19] It was a quixotic and inherently anarchistic vision of the army. Such a vision had never been realized before, and would scarcely ever be tried by even the most revolutionary armies in the next three centuries. On an occasion when egalitarian principles were implemented – for example, in the popular militias of the republican army during the Spanish civil war – they were short-lived and of doubtful effectiveness.[20]

This unyielding animosity to the leaders of the republic was to prove a grave blunder on the Levellers' part. It is no accident that about this time several of their friends began to desert them. Major Francis White and Captain (now Colonel) John Reynolds, who had been their prominent advocates in 1647, decided to back the grandees. White remained a critical and independent-minded supporter, who was not afraid to publish several radical letters that he had written to Fairfax and Cromwell in early 1648 and 1649.[21] Having supported the resistance to parliament in 1647, endorsed the Leveller petition in September 1648, and opposed the execution of the king in January 1649, he obviously could not be counted on to back the grandees' every move. Yet he refused to align himself with the plot to overthrow them. In May he would be one of Fairfax's emissaries to the mutineers. Henry Marten, perhaps because of the handsome grant he was voted, perhaps because of the bullying of Oliver Cromwell, would also soon cease speaking and organizing on the Levellers' behalf.[22] Lord Grey of Groby and Alexander Rigby too were silent when the grandees decided to eradicate the Leveller influence in the army.[23] The haemorrhaging of Leveller support was remarkably sudden. In December and January a majority of the officers had compelled the grandees to adopt an Agreement of the People very similar to what the Levellers wanted. In April and May the only officer of note to maintain his radical allegiance was Major John Cobbett of Skippon's regiment.

Those few lesser officers who also continued to support the Levellers were either mavericks or had already left the army. There was William Bray, who had already compromised himself in the eyes of his fellow officers by his equivocal role in the mutiny of Lilburne's regiment before and during the Ware rendezvous. Now a captain-lieutenant in Colonel Reynolds' new regiment, he had spoken up for the five troopers' right to petition at the beginning of March. Soon afterwards he was thrown out of the Council of Officers. An apology would probably have got him back in, but instead he appealed to parliament in a long autobiographical pamphlet accusing Fairfax of being as greedy as William the Conqueror and as cruel as the Emperor Tiberius. To his surprise he got no sympathy, and was thrown into Windsor Castle for his pains.[24] Not to be silenced, he issued another tract, this time protesting against his imprisonment, and appealing to the Commons to assist him against 'my professed enemy the Lord General'. His popularity within his own troop was great enough to move them to issue a separate supporting petition and pamphlet on the same day. Bray cannot be dismissed as a voice crying in the wilderness, and it is almost certain that his troop was one of those which joined the armed resistance in May.[25]

Another maverick officer who continued to support the Levellers was John Jubbs, formerly lieutenant-colonel of Hewson's regiment. At the beginning of May – the worst possible time as far as the grandees were concerned – he published *An Apology unto ... the Lord Generals Army*.[26] Despite his almost complete sympathy for Leveller ideals, there is no evidence that he played a part in the violent uprisings within the army in May or September.

The vitriol of Richard Overton in *The Hunting of the Foxes* was matched by the wildness of John Lilburne's accusations in *The Second Part of Englands New-Chaines Discovered*.[27] The tract amounted to nothing less than a declaration of war against the grandees. Not only were they excoriated for betraying the Newmarket Engagement, but they were charged with responsibility for the outbreak of the second civil war. Furthermore, they had systematically blocked the promotions of Majors John Cobbett, John Reynolds and Francis White because of their radical convictions. They had deliberately sent Colonel Thomas Rainborowe on a perilous assignment to Pontefract, where he had met his death. Subsequently they had done everything in their power to cover up the facts surrounding his murder.[28] These 'monstrously wicked' men were guilty of 'vile apostasy' and bore direct responsibility for the bitterness, division and famine that presently stalked the land.

> Oh wretched England, that seeth, and yet suffereth such intolerable masters. What can be expected from such officers, who frequently manifest a thirst after the blood of such people, and soldiers, as are most active for the common freedom, peace and prosperity of the commonwealth? ... the intentions, and endeavours of these men, to enslave the Commonwealth, ... exceeds in the nature and measure of it all the wickedness of both the other parties put together.

What was the remedy for this sorry state of affairs? Nothing less than a new parliament, the restoration of the agitators to the Army Council, and the implementation of the complete Leveller programme of socio-economic reform, including the Agreement of the People.[29] The tract summed up all the helpless anger that Lilburne and his friends felt at the betrayal of their vision of the revolution. But, by allowing unbridled expression to his disappointment with the grandees, Lilburne wrote off any chance that he might wield effective political influence in the future. The uncompromising character of his demands signalled also his abandonment of political realism.

The Second Part of Englands New-Chaines came to the Commons' attention on 27 March, when it was debated for three hours. In the end the tract was voted 'highly seditious and ... tending to division and mutiny in the army', and its authors guilty of high treason.[30] The next morning the four Leveller leaders – Lilburne, Walwyn, Overton and Thomas Prince – were brought before the Council of State to answer for their alleged treason.[31]

After being kept waiting all day, they were called in singly for cross-examination, and then sequestered in an adjacent room. Lilburne crept up to the door in an attempt to overhear the Council's deliberations. According to his account he was able to identify Cromwell's shouting as he thumped the table,

> I tell you sir, you have no other way to deal with these men but to break them in pieces ... if you do not break them they will break you; yea, and bring all the guilt of the blood and treasure shed and spent in this kingdom upon your heads and shoulders; and frustrate and make void all that work that with so many years' industry, toil and pains you have done.... Sir I tell you again, you are necessitated to break them.

The Council then resolved to commit the four to the Tower to await trial. Lilburne maintained that Ludlowe's motion to have them released on bail was lost by only a single vote. However, there is no record in the minutes of the Council of State of such a motion; nor do they list Ludlowe as being present; nor is it likely that so conservative a body would have been nearly equally divided over whether to keep the Levellers in custody.[32] In any event they were sent to the Tower, but it happened that their custodian, John Jenkins, was a Durham man and 'an old and familiar acquaintance' of Lilburne. A captain in Cromwell's horse regiment, he was a minor gentleman and staunch Baptist who farmed near Stockton.[33] He greeted them all warmly, and then sent them home to their wives, in return for a promise to meet him the following morning at the Angel tavern near the Tower, which they did.

The kid-gloved treatment meted out by his gaoler did little to appease Lilburne's wrath at what he regarded as his illegal arrest. He warned the Council of State against putting him under the same military imprisonment as Captain Bray at Windsor Castle. Conceding that he was perhaps 'of an hasty choleric temper', he warned, 'I will fire it and burn it down to the ground, if possibly I can, although I be burnt to ashes with the flames thereof.' Turning his ire against the purged House of Commons, he dismissed it as a 'mock parliament', and called for an insurrection by people and soldiers against it.

In his honest moments Lilburne must have recognized that the chances of a general insurrection against the Rump and the army were remote. Nevertheless, throughout the month of April he and Overton strove with all their might to inspire the rank and file to overthrow their officers, take charge of the army and implement the Leveller agenda for England. The second prong of their insurrectionary strategy was the sending of agents into the countryside of southern England, Wales and Lancashire, to stir up the disaffected rural poor and align them with the soldiers. It was not an unreasonable plan but it came to grief for two reasons. First, the rural population saw no identity of interest between themselves, in a state of near-starvation at the end of a third nightmarish winter, and rebellious troops who could only survive by exacting free quarter. Second, the mutinous regiments were dispersed across several counties, and could not be brought together quickly enough to form the critical mass required to bring down the grandees. But the grandees could not know in advance that the planned insurrection was futile, and so they suffered many sleepless nights between the beginning of April and the middle of May 1649.

In April the Levellers attempted to shame the soldiers for their servility to their officers: 'He that takes one box on the ear invites another; and when soldiers that should be men in all things stand still and suffer their fellow soldiers to be thus abused by a pack of officers, no marvel if these officers turn tyrants and presume to do any thing to any man.'[34] What was to be done? The soldiers should insist on a new Council of the Army freely elected from every regiment. They should also see that the rights and liberties of the English people were established by an Agreement of the People. Until these things were accomplished they should refuse to go to Ireland.[35]

By accelerating their efforts in London, in the army and in the provinces, the radicals kept the pot bubbling ever more furiously. In late March the Council of State ordered Captain Smith to use his troop of Oxfordshire horse to break up meetings of disaffected people in the county.[36] From Lancashire came the disturbing news that Captain Bamber of Colonel Shuttleworth's regiment was not only refusing to disband his troop, but had almost tripled its size to about 220 men. Later in the month he announced that he was going to throw in his lot with the Levellers.[37] The news from Somerset was even more disturbing. Troops in those parts were said to be greatly discontented not only by lack of pay, but also by the imprisonment of the Leveller leaders. Their talk was of choosing a new parliament that would be bound by the principles laid down in the Agreement of the People.[38] In Oxfordshire, Colonel John Reynolds had decisively demonstrated his loyalty to the grandees by expelling from his regiment those who were 'contumacious and refractory'. These elements probably included, but were not limited to, the men of Captain Bray's troop. So pleased was the Council of State at Reynolds' success in imposing his authority on his men that they promised him regular pay for the remainder of the regiment until it was sent to Ireland. The promise was kept.[39]

Because of the mounting unrest in the army Fairfax reissued his January order commanding all officers to repair to their charges in the army. In future no officer was to leave his post for above twenty-four hours unless upon business at headquarters.[40]

In London, Leveller supporters continued to vent their rage against the Council of State, and stepped up their efforts to propagandize the regiments in the capital. Another petition was submitted to parliament calling for a jury trial for the prisoners in the Tower, and the implementation of the Agreement of the People. The Commons spared little time for the petition, merely appointing Ireton and two radicals, Lisle and Marten, to pen an answer to it. The moderation of the Commons' reply reflected the work of these two men. While it promised the petitioners that the four prisoners would be brought to a legal trial, it admonished them also for seeming to countenance the treason with which the four had been charged. They were warned not to expect such mild treatment in future.[41]

Parliament's rebuke produced a change in Leveller tactics. Less than a week later several hundred women trooped to the door of the Commons with a petition bearing 10,000 female signatures, making essentially the same demands, but speaking also of their distress that famine was now causing several deaths a week in London. The troops guarding the house showed them no gallantry, pointing loaded pistols at the women's breasts and throwing squibs into the crowd. One MP told them to go home and wash their dishes. Undaunted, they accosted Cromwell, who assured them that the prisoners would be treated lawfully. 'Sir,' replied a gentlewoman among them, 'if you take away their lives or the lives of any, contrary to law, nothing shall satisfy us, but the lives of them that do it, and Sir, we will have your life if you take away theirs.' Speaker Lenthall then emerged to tell them that the house had already given an answer to their husbands, and therefore 'you are desired to go home and look after your own business and meddle with your housewifery.'[42] This insult galvanized them to return to the attack the next day and the day after with similar petitions. Impatient at their importunity the MPs sent the sergeant-at-arms to tell them that 'the matter they petitioned about was of an higher concernment than they understood; that the House gave an answer to their husbands, and therefore desired them to go home.'[43]

This piece of male arrogance produced not quiescence, but a fourth demonstration. At the beginning of May the women brought yet another petition to the house, this time prefaced with a ringing statement of their equality with men:

> Since we are assured of our creation in the image of God, of an interest in Christ equal unto men, as also of a proportionate share in the freedoms of the commonwealth we cannot but wonder and grieve that we should appear so despicable in your eyes as to be thought unworthy to petition or represent our grievances to this honourable House.[44]

This was the last of the women's petitions. A day or two later the torch was taken up by yet another group – young men and apprentices from both City and suburbs. They too demanded that the prisoners should have the benefit of due process of law.[45]

Efforts to propagandize the army also intensified. Radicals distributed Leveller pamphlets among the troops. One trooper called Sawyer was arrested for this seditious activity, and was immediately added to the Leveller pantheon of martyr heroes.[46] On 23 April a broadsheet was scattered about the streets of London calling on men in the army to resist their officers and elect a council of agitators.[47] With the emasculation of the *Moderate* by the removal of its radical editor Gilbert Mabbott, a new and much more partisan newsbook appeared to take its place at the radical end of the political spectrum. Bearing the title *Mercurius Militaris*, its main focus of attention was the army, and it was evidently meant to be read by soldiers. Deeply hostile to the grandees, it bitterly accused them of attempting to manipulate the choice of regiments for the Irish expedition, and exposed their attempts to infiltrate and undermine the Leveller organization.[48]

The Diggers

Among the many disturbances that beset the new regime in the difficult spring of 1649 was one stirred up by a band of agrarian radicals a few miles south of the capital. In the middle of April the Council of State received word that a new group of 'Levellers' were digging up the common at St George's Hill near Oatlands, Surrey, and sowing it with parsnips, carrots and beans.[49] The activity there was the first of several practical experiments in voluntary agrarian communism. Jerrard Winstanley, the leader of this group of 'True Levellers' or Diggers, as they soon came to be known, produced a large and eloquent volume of writings denouncing the existing socio-economic system based on the 'cheating art of buying and selling', and calling for its replacement by a new system that would recognize the earth as the common treasury of mankind. Only the abolition of private property, he argued, could bring an end to the tyranny and bloodshed that had plagued Europe for centuries.[50]

The Council of State took no notice of the theoretical underpinnings of the Diggers' repudiation of traditional property relations. At another time the government might have regarded them as merely ridiculous and probably harmless, but it was Winstanley's misfortune to come to official attention when rural disturbances were seen as a danger to the security of the beleaguered republic. The Council of State was worried that other disaffected people might flock to their standard and cause political mischief. The Diggers numbered fewer than three dozen, but one of their leaders, William Everard, a soldier who had been cashiered from the New Model, boasted that they would shortly be 4000. The authorities accordingly instructed Fairfax to disperse them. Captain John Gladman, who was sent on this assignment, wrote back to Fairfax, clearly unhappy with his instructions. The Diggers were few in number, Everard was 'a mad man' and the whole business was 'not worth the writing nor yet taking notice of'.[51] The next day the two Digger leaders came in person to army head-quarters at Whitehall, where they were allowed to explain their actions to Fairfax himself. They assured him that they did not intend to meddle with private property, but only with what was common and untilled. Although their thinking was apocalyptic – 'the time of deliverance was at hand' – they would not take up arms or even defend themselves in the pursuit of their vision. This voluntaristic ideal of sharing land and wealth could boast ample historical precedent. Reminiscent of the Jewish year of Jubilee found in the Old Testament, and of More's *Utopia*, it had also formed part of the pro-gramme of the German Anabaptists under Thomas Munzer.[52]

Fairfax listened tolerantly to the two men, although his staff were offended by their refusal to remove their hats. For the time being he left them alone, but at the end of November, apparently yielding to pressure from local landowners, the Council of State again ordered a crackdown, and Fairfax sent a second party of soldiers to disperse the commune. The Diggers' poignant appeal to be allowed 'to conquer them with love' fell on deaf ears. Brought to court in Kingston, they were convicted of trespass and fined, while Winstanley's cows were beaten.[53]

Mutiny in Whalley's Regiment

In late April 1649 the army commanders were far more absorbed with London politics than with the activities of the Diggers in Surrey. Extreme instability in the capital prompted them to move some troops to new quarters in the outskirts where they would be less subject to Leveller pro-paganda. There was already considerable unrest in Whalley's regiment on account of parliament's refusal to release the four Leveller leaders from the Tower. It was not a complete surprise, therefore, that, when Savage's troop were assigned new quarters in Essex and told to report to Mile End Green for their marching orders, they balked.[54] Their defiance took the form of seizing the troop's colours and carrying them to the Bull Inn near Bishopsgate, a radical meeting place in the City[55] where several troopers also were quartered. Some of Captain Grove's men seized their troop's colours as well, but this second incipient mutiny seems to have fizzled out. Hearing what was happening, Captain John Savage, a yeoman or minor gentleman from Lockinge, Berkshire, who was later accused of graft, went to the Bull and demanded that his men bring out the colours.[56] When they refused he seized them, but they tore them from his hands, Robert Lockyer declaring that 'the colours belonged as well to them as to him, and that they had as well fought for them as he.' The other troopers cried, 'All, all.' Savage then went to report this insubordination to Colonel Whalley, who sent back strict orders to the troop to march to their rendezvous. They still refused to obey, so Whalley, Major Swallow and other officers of the regiment rode to the Bull. Before they would mount their horses the men demanded the fortnight's pay they claimed was due to them. Whalley answered that they had been well paid since their arrival in London the previous December. Yet, even though they had received a month's pay as recently as 23 April, he would order the clerk to give them an additional five days' pay.[57] They responded that they would still lack money to pay for their quarters. Whalley promised that they would receive enough for that purpose. They then tried to wring from him a promise to pay their arrears as well. At this impossible demand Whalley cut short the parley and ordered them once more to come down and mount their horses. He singled out Lockyer, ordering him personally to obey. Lockyer instead turned to his fellow troopers for their advice, and they shouted, 'No, no!' A crowd had now gathered in the courtyard and street. A conjunction between an unruly crowd and a group of mutinous soldiers could flare rapidly out of control. The army commanders' worst nightmare – an urban rising against the shaky regime – now seemed on the brink of being realized. In the event Whalley's horse were able to drive off the crowd and quell the mutiny.[58] Most of the sixty men slipped away, but fifteen were taken into custody. At that moment Fairfax and Cromwell arrived on the scene, 'furiously breathing forth nothing but death to them all.' The two generals refused the men's request to hear their grievances until they had been marched to Whitehall under guard. The following day all fifteen were tried by court martial; one was acquitted, three were left to Whalley's discretion, five were sentenced to ride the wooden horse with a carbine at each heel and cashiered, while the six judged to be the ringleaders were sentenced to death.

As intended, the death sentence terrified the condemned men into submission. They wrote to Fairfax professing that they were 'heartily sorry' for their 'unwise and unlawful action'. Cromwell accepted the sincerity of their apology and was for pardoning them. Fairfax, however, insisted that one must die. Because Lockyer was deemed the most guilty, he was denied the clemency granted the other five. The next day he was brought to St Paul's Churchyard to be executed by six musketeers from Hewson's regiment. That morning a hastily published letter from Lilburne and Overton protested against the court martial, accusing Fairfax and the Council of War of 'treason and murder', and threatening popular insurrection if they executed a soldier in peacetime.[59] The Leveller threats probably only stiffened Fairfax's resolve.

Lockyer's heroic behaviour at his execution won him the admiration of many, and must have swelled the crowd which attended his funeral on the Sunday afterwards. According to his friends he was 'honest, just and faithful', and 'beloved of many'. Indeed, Major John Carter of Hewson's regiment, who with Colonel Okey presided at the execution, was troubled at the thought that they were killing one of the saints. Lockyer also boasted a good war record, blemished only by his support for the Agreement of the People at Ware. His friends were convinced that it was his political radicalism that explained why he was singled out to pay the supreme price for disobedience. In his speech he regretted that he should lose his life for a dispute over pay rather than for the freedom and liberties of the nation which he had fought for since 1642. Disdaining the blindfold normally tied to the heads of men who were shot to death, he stared the six musketeers in the face, and entreated them to spare him. This appeal for disobedience infuriated Colonel Okey, who had already accused Lockyer of distorting his role in the mutiny. He strode over to the condemned man, pulled off his loose jacket, coat and belt, and distributed them among the soldiers. Lockyer now prayed, dressed only in his shirt and doublet. Then he gave the appointed signal by raising both arms, and seconds later crumpled beneath the bullets rained on him by all six musketeers.

The narrative outline of this well-reported mutiny is clear enough. What remain puzzling are its real causes. The man condemned to die said that it was a pity he should lose his life in a dispute over pay. The Levellers spoke darkly about ulterior motives. On the night of 24 April, they said, papers were scattered about the streets and there was an alarm about a plot to murder Fairfax and some other officers.[60] The reason for the attack on Savage's troop, they alleged, was to throw up a smokescreen for their illegal proceedings against some citizens the same night. It is true that the grandees were worried about the political situation in the capital. London was like tinder, and the loyalty of some troops was fragile. It was believed that John Lilburne was meeting with army radicals daily in the Tower, to see if they could force a revival of the council of agitators in the army.[61] At the very time the mutiny occurred several agents were being hired by the grandees to spy on the Levellers and uncover their conspiracy.[62] That Robert Lockyer had promoted the Agreement of the People during the Ware mutiny in November 1647[63] only deepened the grandees' fears when they learned that he was now leading a mutiny in one of their crack regiments in the heart of the City. Understandably, they jumped to the conclusion that the mutiny could easily set fire to the tinder and 'destroy [the City] in blood and ashes.'[64]

It was therefore the worry that the Levellers were finding a ready audience among the rank and file for their anti-establishment propaganda that made the grandees decide to move troops out of London. The resistance they encountered confirmed their worst fears, and convinced them that Savage's men might ignite a popular insurrection at any moment. This explains their sudden and ruthless action against the troopers. The debate between Cromwell and Fairfax about Lockyer's death sentence merely reflected a difference of opinion over whether the public shooting of a popular soldier who was also a native Londoner might screw the political tension even higher. Not for the first time Fairfax showed himself the stricter disciplinarian.

Lockyer's funeral proved that Cromwell's fears were well founded. Its contours are a reminder that the use of mourning for a martyred popular hero as a vehicle of political protest was invented long before its contemporary exploitation in South Africa and Northern Ireland. The burial procession on 27 April 1649 was one of the most impressive that people could remember. Starting from Smithfield in the afternoon, it trailed slowly through the heart of the City, and then back to Moorfields for the interment in the New Churchyard, which had been recently created to alleviate the overcrowding of parish graveyards. Led by six trumpeters, about 4000 people accompanied the corpse. Many wore ribbons, black for mourning and sea-green (Colonel Rainborowe's colour) for their political allegiance. Remarkably, there were more mourners for Trooper Lockyer than there had been for Rainborowe the previous autumn. Most alarming to the authorities was the fact that several hundred soldiers – some reformadoes, but also many troopers currently in the army – joined the procession. In addition to the mourners there were many thousand spectators, on the street and in overlooking windows. When the procession reached Moorfields it was joined by a large contingent 'of the highest sort' who had not wished to be seen walking through the City. In the churchyard there were eulogies, and then the crowd dispersed.[65]

A few onlookers had derided the mourners as Levellers, while others considered the procession itself a 'high affront' to parliament and the army, and were amazed that the City allowed it through its gates. The general reaction however, seems to have been sympathetic. Some commentators thought Lockyer had more mourners than King Charles.[66]

Resistance to the Irish Expedition

During and after the Lockyer affair radical agitation in the regiments and among the rural poor went on apace. Leveller agents are known to have been active in Northamptonshire, Hertfordshire, Berkshire, Oxfordshire, Essex, Suffolk, Hampshire, Gloucestershire, Worcestershire, Warwickshire and Wales. The two principal foci of their organizing efforts were the districts around Bristol and between Banbury and Oxford. Inside the army many regiments and garrisons were now overwhelmed by radical discontent. The unhappiness was particularly acute in the horse regiments designated for Ireland – Scrope's, Ireton's and Horton's – but it spilled over into Harrison's, Cromwell's, the new regiments of Reynolds and Marten,[67] and the regiments stationed in London. Few foot regiments from the field army were touched by discontent, but those that were included Skippon's in Bristol and Ingoldsby's in Oxford. Among the garrisons and local troops affected were Captain Bamber's in Lancaster, Portsmouth garrison, those in the region of Somerset, and Captain Smith's county troop in Oxfordshire. Potentially there were several thousand men ready to rise up against their commanding officers. The challenge facing the radicals was how to foster co-operation among these disparate groups of horse, foot, field-army, local and garrison troops, and, more difficult, how to bring them together into a critical mass large enough to outweigh the troops loyal to the grandees.

What converted the grumbling normal to any army into active mutiny was the project of Ireland. When the names of the regiments selected by lot were announced, there was deep resentment in those same regiments at the thought that they were being sent to their destruction. Labelling it the 'cut-throat expedition', they made it clear that the throats they objected to having cut were their own, not those of the Irish. The radicals also put it about that an ulterior motive for sending men to Ireland was to purge the army of dissident elements.[68] Substantial numbers of officers and men melted away from the designated regiments, and sought admittance to regiments that were staying in England. Fairfax quickly ordered that no one should be allowed to transfer in this fashion.[69]

Leveller political agents mixed humanitarianism and political interest in their appeal to the soldiers to resist the Irish service:

> and will you go on still to kill, slay and murther men, to make [your officers] absolute lords and masters over Ireland, as you have made them over England? Or is it your ambition to reduce the Irish to the happiness of tithes upon treble damages, to excise, customs and monopolies in trades? Or to fill their prisons with poor disabled prisoners, to fill their land with swarms of beggars ...?[70]

The soldiers were urged not to let their officers rush them out of the kingdom, but to stay until the rights and liberties of the English people were established by an Agreement of the People. Only then would it be appropriate for them to go as the missionaries of authentic social revolution.[71] Doubtless the Levellers were as sympathetic to the plight of the Irish as their enemies accused them of being.[72] The *Eighteen Queries* argued on both humanitarian and practical grounds that Ireland should be left to the Irish.[73] However, a more pressing concern of the Levellers was that their hopes for the revolution would be irrevocably lost if nearly half the army was sent to Ireland before fundamental social change had been effected in England.

A few soldiers were touched by Leveller idealism. An anonymous writer in Bristol, who I believe was Major John Cobbett of Skippon's regiment, published one of the most eloquent pamphlets of the revolutionary era. It opened with a confession of the army's bloodguilt:

> Fellow soldiers: it has pleased the Lord to open our eyes, and to let us see the wretched conditions we are brought under; and our crying sins which cry aloud in the ears of God. Oh! the ocean of blood that we are guilty of. Oh! the intolerable oppression that we have laid upon our brethren of England. Oh! how these deadly sins of ours do torment our consciences. Oh! how are we able to answer these pestilent acts of ours, at the dreadful bar of God's divine justice? Nay, this is the most sharpest conflict to them, that we never understood a true cause, or just reason for the shedding of so much innocent blood in our own nation, nor why we have done such horrid oppression to our own countrymen.

Then, after chastising the officers for their oppression of the rank and file, the writer launched upon a scathing indictment of the Irish project:

> What have we to do with Ireland, to fight and murther a people and nation ... which have done us no harm, only deeper to put our hands in blood with [the officers'] own? We have waded too far in that crimson stream (already) of innocent and Christian blood.[74]

The characterization of the Irish as innocent and Christian was extraordinary, challenging as it did the common belief that they were both followers of Antichrist and guilty of massacring innocent English settlers.

Far more representative of the views of the English soldiery was the statement of the rebellious soldiers of Colonel Scrope's regiment. Disclaiming any desire 'to hinder or retard the service of Ireland', they vowed that as soon as their material grievances were satisfied and liberty established in England 'we shall to the utmost of our abilities engage ourselves in the service of that land.'[75] While regiments in the west organized to resist the Irish expedition, discontent was also welling up in Oxfordshire and Northamptonshire. The leading figure in this region was the turbulent William Thompson.

The Mutinies at Banbury, Burford and Northampton

By the beginning of March 1649 Thompson had again got out of prison, thanks to John Lilburne, who paid his bail. Having promoted himself to the rank of captain, he rallied a number of men to form an unauthorized company of foot. Then, claiming the right to exact quarter and provisions, he and his band seized a gentleman's house in North Okenden, Essex, and terrorized its inhabitants. He was soon arrested and brought with five of his men to Whitehall for a second court martial. However, he pleaded that he was not in fact a member of the army, and this plea was upheld, with the result that he was sent back to the civil magistrates in Essex. A trial was appointed at the next assizes, but before the case could be heard he had returned to the gentleman's house, where he attacked and injured several of the occupants.[76]

Thompson then quit the county, turning up next in the region of Northamptonshire, Oxfordshire and Warwickshire. Employing his evident talent for demagoguery he was able to exploit both the economic misery of the countryside and the resentment of the soldiers. Besides the individuals he recruited by his own efforts he managed to weld together nearly 300 men, including at least half of Reynolds' regiment, and the county troop of Oxfordshire. Originally under the command of Captain Smith, this troop was now led by its rebellious Lieutenant Rowley. On 5 May Thompson's hybrid force issued a denunciation of parliament, the Council of State, the Council of Officers and the High Court of Justice.[77] The following day Thompson himself published a full-dress indictment of the regime. Casting his net widely, he attacked parliament and the army for suppressing the agitators in 1647, curbing the right of petition in 1649, abusing the law and levying unjust taxation while famine stalked the land. He went on to demand the release of the four Leveller leaders, and to endorse their 1 May version of the Agreement of the People. Finally he declared solidarity with the regiments of Scrope, Harrison and Skippon, and invited all men to join him 'for a new parliament by Agreement of the People'.[78]

Thompson and his force were stationed at Banbury, Dennington and Cirencester. To their numbers were added men from Henry Marten's fragmentary regiment and a trickle of recruits from London. Captain Hutchinson's troop from Ireton's regiment also joined them.[79] In spite of vague promises of money from wealthy radicals in London[80] they were penniless. Their only recourse, therefore, was to exact free quarter from the rural population whose support they were trying to woo. Thompson's intention was to march to Bristol and rendezvous with Scrope's and Skippon's men. He was blocked in this objective, however, by Colonel Reynolds, who, with a smaller force composed of his three remaining loyal troops of horse, marched to Banbury on Wednesday 9 May. There he succeeded in bottling up the main body of Thompson's force in a lane with no exit. Lacking the stomach for a fight, some of Thompson's soldiers began to slink off while he conferred with his advisers. Eventually the rebels capitulated but assisted Thompson to steal away with his lieutenant and a few guards. They were spotted, however, and Reynolds sent out a party to arrest them. Rather than submit, Thompson turned and shot Lieutenant Parry dead and unhorsed two other men. But no one imitated his conduct, and 120 surrendered themselves and their colours to Reynolds.

Thompson now retreated south of Banbury, meeting up with Lieutenant Rowley and the Oxfordshire troop. Alerted by his scouts to the presence of this second Leveller force, Reynolds dispatched Everard's troop in hot pursuit. The Oxfordshire men soon retreated in the face of their attack, but not before inflicting some casualties and taking a few prisoners. Reynolds then threw into the fray another detachment, which succeeded in capturing some of the rebels and chasing the others off. Thompson and the few men who still stuck with him then fled in the direction of Chipping Norton and Wiltshire.[81]

Given the size of his forces, Reynolds' achievement was impressive. At its peak, in late December, his regiment was perhaps 400–500 strong.[82] By May at least two thirds of it had deserted to join the Levellers.[83] He therefore confronted William Thompson's 300 men with a considerably smaller force which appears not to have exceeded 160 men. Had Lieutenant Rowley's Oxfordshire troop arrived on the scene earlier and been able to link up with Thompson's party *before* they clashed with Reynolds, the issue might easily have been different. At Banbury, as they would do again at Burford five days later, the army commanders overcame their foes by dividing them. If Thompson's and Rowley's united force had gone on to join the eleven mutinous troops from Scrope's, Ireton's and Harrison's regiments, the result at Burford might well have been in doubt. Small wonder then that the Levellers subsequently vilified Reynolds as a turncoat to their cause.[84]

By the beginning of May agitators were reported to be active again in every regiment.[85] Disaffection was most acute in Salisbury, where four troops of Scrope's cavalry regiment were stationed. On or before 1 May Scrope marshalled the Salisbury contingent and broke the news that they had been selected by army headquarters to go to Ireland. The news, now ten days old, must already have been circulating through the regiment, for the men had their answer prepared. Calmly they informed their officers that they chose not to go to Ireland. They were startled to be treated to angry threats and accusations of mutiny. Scrope also warned them that Fairfax and Cromwell were preparing a force to march against them.[86] At this provocation they engaged in their first overtly mutinous act. 'Civilly and with little or no opposition' they took hold of the regimental colours, and marched off in the direction of Bristol, having first declared their respect for General Fairfax. Only about eighty men, mainly officers, remained with Scrope. His other two troops, at Malmesbury, had already expelled their officers, rendezvoused with the rebellious men of Ireton's regiment, and also marched towards Bristol. We may suppose that they had heard of the discontent in Skippon's regiment over the death of Robert Lockyer and the imprisonment of the four Leveller leaders.[87]

The mutineers explained themselves in a document entitled *The Resolutions of the Private Souldiery of Colonel Scrope's Regiment of Horse*, which was published in London. Recalling their Engagement of 5 June 1647 not to disband or allow themselves to be disbanded, they called to mind their officers' oft-repeated promise that after the war the people should have 'freedom, peace and happiness', and the soldiers their arrears. Neither promise had been kept, 'and yet you would have us to engage, to give you power over another land.' The cavalry trooper's plight was particularly desperate. So great was the scarcity of provisions that no trooper could find lodgings and food for himself and his horse for less than 4s. or 5s. a night. This was more than double his daily pay. Denying that they were opposed in principle to the Irish service, the mutineers promised to engage for it as soon as liberty was established in England and their material demands met.[88]

This statement was soon taken up and endorsed by the men of Ireton's regiment in Sussex.[89] Four of his six troops held an unauthorized rendezvous on 9 May to discuss a letter and the *Resolutions* from Scrope's regiment. When they heard what was happening, Major Gibbon and Captain Prittie went and remonstrated with them.[90] Captain Morgan's men stuck with their officers. A quarrel broke out between this troop and the others, who seized the troop's colours until they promised to join the mutiny. As soon as they were given back their colours, however, Morgan's men marched off in the opposite direction. The mutineers let them go, and bent their own steps towards Bristol, planning to rendezvous with Scrope's men. Prittie had at first persuaded his own troop too to march away from the mutineers, but after they had gone 2 miles a letter from the regiment's agitators overtook them. A reading of its contents wrought a change of heart, so that they deserted Prittie and hurried back to the main part of the regiment, who welcomed them with rapture.[91] On the other hand, 150 men melted away before the regiment reached Bristol, and returned to obedience. This leaves the total number of mutineers who went to join Scrope's regiment at not more than ninety.[92] The two groups joined forces at Old Sarum, where they chose new officers and issued a declaration explaining their actions.

In London meanwhile the authorities scrambled to contain the mutiny. The Council of State sent Fairfax a frantic note ordering him, in view of the prevailing distemper, to stop payment of the money that was on its way to Reynolds' regiment.[93] Believing that the tumult in various regiments could be traced back to the imprisoned Leveller leaders, the authorities also changed and reinforced the guards in the Tower of London. 400 reliable infantry from Pride's and Hewson's regiments, well known for their anti-radical sentiments, were marched in on the night of 8 May. As they entered the gates they railed against Lilburne as the source of all their troubles 'and promised him fire and faggot for his pains if they live to see all quiet.'[94] That night the lieutenant of the Tower was instructed to keep Lilburne under strict surveillance, and to deny him pen, ink or paper.[95] Major-General Skippon was ordered to have his forces in a state of alert, while similar instructions were transmitted to the London and Westminster militia.[96] Care was also taken to ensure that the regiments based in London were punctually paid.[97] On 12 May the four Leveller leaders were placed in stricter confinement and separated one from another. A motion promoted by Henry Marten and Edmund Ludlowe to pay them an allowance during their close confinement was rejected.[98] In the mid-seventeenth century prisoners were still responsible for finding their own food. Usually friends, relatives or church members would see that they were fed, but close confinement meant no visitors. Denied an allowance as well, they faced the prospect of starvation. Finally a public outcry brought the Commons to its senses and three days later the prisoners were voted 'necessary provisions'.[99]

Fairfax and Cromwell knew that prompt action was essential if the revolt was not to become general throughout the cavalry. The infantry were as yet untouched, and indeed some regiments were openly hostile to the mutiny, but among the horse the discontent had spread even into Cromwell's own regiment.[100] Agitators travelled between regiments trying to convince them one by one that all the other regiments had thrown in their lot with the mutiny.[101] Other than in Bristol and Banbury, the fruit of Leveller organizing was seen in Portsmouth, the Isle of Wight, Somerset, Lancaster and Oxford garrison, whence reports of radical discontent emanated.[102]

Having ensured that London was under control, the grandees decided to move a large force to the locus of discontent around Bristol. On 9 May they mustered five of their best regiments in Hyde Park. Fairfax's and Cromwell's horse were joined by Fairfax's, Hewson's and Ewer's foot. While Fairfax listened, Cromwell assured the troops that parliament was looking out for the best interest of both nation and army. On the subject of martial law, those who found it a burden were at liberty to quit the army, collect certificates for their arrears, and be treated on the same basis as those who remained. One trooper bold enough to dispute with Cromwell was temporarily arrested. A few other troopers wearing the Leveller sea-green colours had them pulled from their hats.[103]

This force, under 4000 strong, then marched south to Bagshot, Surrey, where they spent the night. There had been murmurings of discontent with the army leadership all day, and several soldiers chose this moment to desert.[104]

Learning of Fairfax's approach, some of the mutineers in Scrope's regiment now had second thoughts about the venture they had embarked upon. On the 10th some of them rode to Bagshot to parley with the two generals, hoping for concessions. The fissures in the army had now become nakedly visible. While there was dissension in Cromwell's regiment, several troops not part of the expedition sent messages that they were ready to join Fairfax in suppressing the revolt.[105]

By Friday 11 May Fairfax and his force had reached Alton, Hampshire, where they were joined by Colonel Scrope with the eighty officers and men who had remained loyal. On the same day Scrope's regiment and the three half-troops from Ireton's held a rendezvous at Old Sarum, just outside Salisbury. Major Cobbett had been expected to bring two companies from Skippon's old regiment[106] at Bristol, but in the event he did not turn up. The mutiny was still restricted almost exclusively to the cavalry. At Old Sarum the soldiers vented their indignation against the treatment of those who had declined to enlist for Ireland, and voiced a by-now-familiar demand for the restoration of the Army Council with two rank-and-file agitators per regiment.[107] If this were done, 'we shall willingly show ourselves (many of us) in the van for Ireland.' To the people the mutineers offered an assurance that 'We seek not your disturbance but your ease; not the rifling of your houses, or seizing of your goods, or levelling of your estates (as may be suggested) but your freedom from the intolerable burthens lying upon your shoulders.' They concluded with an appeal for the people's forgiveness for temporarily having to extract free quarter.

Fairfax cannot have read this statement before he issued his own declaration the next day, but he answered its arguments directly. Accusing the mutineers of giving aid and comfort to the cavaliers, he rejected the allegation that there was any compulsion to join the Irish service. Far from neglecting the Agreement of the People, parliament was implementing it piecemeal, dealing with the most urgent matters first. It had begun by bringing the king to the scaffold, 'that great act of justice, which was by good men so called for, and was indeed so necessary a duty to take off the pollution of innocent blood, wherewith the land was defiled.' Next it had removed the House of Lords, which had been blocking everything that tended to the public good. In the space of three months it had also put to sea a great fleet to fend off invasion and revive trade. Now parliament was in the midst of preparations to relieve Ireland and provide for soldiers' arrears with the best security possible: the crown lands. Free quarter had been totally abolished unless (and this was a telling point) 'you now again begin it (and then I doubt the country will hardly judge you friends to their liberties or at all trust your fair pretences).' The rest of the Agreement's provisions were well in hand, said Fairfax, in particular the dissolution of the present parliament. Elections for a new, 'equal' parliament were high on the agenda. If the rebellious regiments returned at once to obedience they would be pardoned, but, if they persisted in their present course, 'I shall endeavour by force to reduce you.'[108]

The *Declaration* was a tough and shrewdly written piece of propaganda. It assured the mutineers that their grievances had been heard and were being attended to. It pointed out the folly of rebellion while offering them a way out of their predicament. It warned of dire consequences if they did not turn back. Although it bore Fairfax's name, the *Declaration* had probably been drafted by a committee, on which Cromwell would have played a leading part. The Cromwellian stamp is clear in the justification of the king's beheading. But the overall policy was Fairfax's, who at all times was keenly interested in the enforcement of army discipline. Fairfax's unvarnished threat to use force caused wavering among some of the mutineers, most of whom still cherished immense respect for their commander-in-chief.[109]

As the mutineers took stock they must also have been troubled by their limited success in mobilizing men. Their main force consisted of the bulk of Scrope's regiment (perhaps 450 men), and three half-troops from Ireton's regiment, numbering probably not more than 120 men. In spite of Major Cobbett's efforts at Bristol, not one soldier had materialized from Skippon's old regiment. By 12 May they would have time to digest the full significance of the disaster at Banbury. Thompson's miscellaneous army had now been eliminated as a military threat. Only Captain Robert Everard's small group of perhaps 200 men who had avoided the Banbury debacle was still at large roaming the countryside west of the town.[110] One crumb of hope was the news that on 8 May Everard had clashed with a party of Fairfax's, taken twenty prisoners and killed almost as many.[111] Otherwise the outlook was bleak. The money promised from London had not arrived; army pay had of course been stopped, and the necessity of taking free quarter from a hungry populace meant that the project of an insurrectionary union of rural poor and disenchanted soldiery was stillborn.

The mutineers' only hope now was to bolster their strength by joining first with Harrison's regiment stationed in Buckinghamshire, and then with Horton's in the west. They therefore headed north from Salisbury, reaching Marlborough, Wiltshire, on the 11th (see map 6).[112] In a last-ditch effort to win popular support they spread word through the countryside that their objective was only to restore 'magistracy, liberty and freedom ... under fair pretence for Charles the second.'[113]

The grandees had their own causes for anxiety. Although Reynolds had won a signal victory at Banbury, the main body of mutineers, now at Marlborough, was still attracting recruits.[114] There was no way of knowing on which side Harrison's regiment would come down, and there was cause for concern about the loyalty of Horton's regiment in the west. Equally worrying, the mettle of Fairfax's and Cromwell's horse regiments had not yet been tested. There had already been signs of discontent in Cromwell's regiment. If push came to shove, would they be willing to draw their swords against the comrades with whom they had fought so many battles?

On 12 May Fairfax and Cromwell arrived at Andover. The same morning, with the aim both of bolstering and testing their troops' morale, they summoned a rendezvous. Cromwell rode to the head of each regiment, where he addressed the soldiers with the message that he was resolved to live and die with them. Watching closely for their reaction, he said he had no doubt that they would all follow him to subdue the Levellers and bring the ringleaders to exemplary punishment. While many expressed their support for him, others were heard to mutter that they would not fight against their comrades.[115]

The mutineers were a scant 20 miles away at Marlborough. That evening Fairfax sent a delegation headed by Major Francis White of his own regiment, Captain Scotten, Captain Peverell and Lieutenant Bayley to negotiate with them. White's radical past was well known, while Scotten too had been closely identified with the original agitator movement. It was a brave risk that Fairfax took in entrusting them with this critical mission.[116] As they were leaving, Cromwell's parting words to White were 'that I should let them know that although they sent messengers to them they would not follow with force at their heels; which words my Lord General confirmed.'[117] The mutineers were already on the march from Marlborough, but agreed to meet with the delegation at Stanford-in-the-Vale, Berkshire, at ten o'clock on Sunday morning the 13th. Major White and his fellow officers arrived late for the meeting, and found themselves again obliged to follow the rebellious soldiers, who were on their way to Abingdon.

Both sides had sent delegations to each other. Shortly after White's had departed, Fairfax received a conciliatory letter from the eight agitators of Scrope's and Ireton's regiments. Pleased to have heard from Fairfax himself that the Irish service was not compulsory, even for the regiments that had been selected by lot, they assured him that many of them were 'very willing to put our lives in our hands for that service'. They asked the general now to hear their grievances, 'and to take us under your protection'. If he would honour the army's Solemn Engagement they would guarantee him perpetual obedience.[118] Both sides knew that this was the great stumbling block, since Levellers and grandees had radically different interpretations of

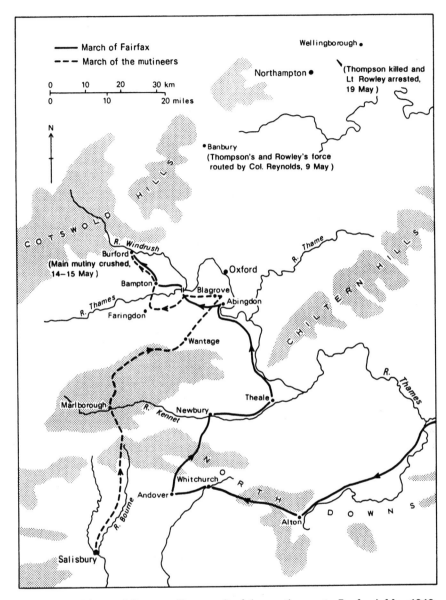

Map 6 Fairfax and Cromwell's pursuit of the mutineers to Burford, May 1649

the obligations entailed by the Engagement of 5 June 1647. At no time was Fairfax prepared to yield to the Leveller demand for the General Council to exercise sovereign power in the army.

However, in the soldiers' message Fairfax thought he saw an opening. Seizing upon their request to be taken under his protection, he now sent out a second mission headed by Colonel Scrope to test their seriousness. In an accompanying letter he reaffirmed his intention to subdue the mutineers, but added that he welcomed their request for his protection. Once Scrope had received their submission they could then discuss the June 1647 Engagement.[119] If Fairfax was guilty of misjudgement in any aspect of his handling of the May mutiny it was in his employment of Scrope as an envoy. The mutineers detested this colonel for his heavy-handed promotion of the Irish service a fortnight earlier. It was galling now to be asked to submit to his protection. Moreover, with their spirits momentarily buoyed by an infusion of recruits, the mutineers were emboldened to snub Scrope and press on to their rendezvous with Harrison's regiment. On the 13th they arrived at Wantage. To Fairfax this refusal to stand still while negotiations were being conducted was decisive proof of the Levellers' bad faith.[120] From their point of view, however, it was nothing less than self-preservation, while Fairfax's continued advance towards their quarters was evidence of *his* bad faith. On both sides mistrust escalated, a mistrust that Major White found impossible to break down. Unavailingly he wrote to Fairfax with details of the mutineers' grievances, underlining their indignation at the disbanding of Hewson's men, who had declined the Irish service, with only a fortnight's pay. Moderation, he urged, would avert an armed clash.[121]

For his part Fairfax would have been content to sit down at Andover and await the result of White's and Scrope's negotiations. But when he heard of the Levellers' advance to Wantage he decided that the time for talk had ended. The mutiny had to be suppressed before the conjunction with Harrison's and Horton's regiments made it twice as dangerous. Accordingly he left Andover on the 13th, and arrived at Theale, near Reading, the same day.[122]

Major White, however, stuck with the mutineers, and continued his efforts at reconciliation until shots were being fired. After setting out for rebel headquarters on 12 May Fairfax had sent two more officers ahead with a message for White to convey. But before their arrival the main force of Levellers had already left for Wantage, so that White was only able to read Fairfax's message to the 'trustees and officers'. Unmoved, these men threatened to dismiss White's delegation unless they were permitted to address Fairfax's troops directly. By now Captain Scotten was fed up, and quit the mutineers, apparently taking the other two officers with him. Only White, consistently the most sympathetic of all Fairfax's officers to the

Leveller position, stayed to continue trying to effect a reconciliation. In a remarkable display of confidence in him, the leaders of the revolt asked White to draft a document that might compose the differences between the two sides. He accepted their invitation with alacrity. The paper he drew up gained immediate approval from the leaders of the mutiny, who requested only a few revisions. Their positive reaction is not surprising, given that White had bent over backwards to accommodate their views and demonstrate his thoroughgoing sympathy to their demands. Through the medium of White's words they bluntly told the general that by failing to honour the Engagement of 5 June 1647 'you keep not covenant with us.' Only when the General Council of the Army had been reconvoked would the mutineers return to their obedience. As in the letter of 12 May, they acknowledged the necessity of the Irish expedition, but declared that if Fairfax rejected their principal demand for a revived General Council 'we must lay at your door all the misery, bloodshed and ruin that will fall upon this nation and army.' Such language was not calculated to effect a reconciliation with the senior officers. White's willingness to include it in the document he drafted demonstrates both the enduring emotional tug of his previous Leveller attachments, and the lengths to which he was still willing to go to conciliate them.[123]

The mutineers from Scrope's and Ireton's regiments had now encountered Captain Pecke's and Captain Winthrop's troops from Harrison's regiment at Blagrave, between Abingdon and Oxford. Their strength was now eleven troops, plus the Leveller Colonel William Eyre with a few soldiers and citizen volunteers from London.[124] Their confidence was bolstered by this fresh accession of strength, as well as by rumours that more troops would soon be on their way. But soberer heads wondered why only two of Harrison's troops had thrown in their lot with the mutiny. Realizing that there would be no more recruits from Buckinghamshire, they turned west in the hope of picking up Horton's regiment, now thought to be in Gloucestershire. Fairfax, however, had kept himself well informed of their intentions, and had already posted Colonel Reynolds and Major Abbott with over 200 horse and dragoons at Newbridge, where they had to cross the Thames. Before long the mutineers ran into an advance party from Reynolds' force. These men retreated to the main body at Newbridge, where they made a stand. Colonel Eyre, in charge of the forlorn hope, whipped his men into such a fury that they were ready to charge Reynolds' and Abbott's men and clear the bridge.[125] But Major White managed to interpose himself between the opposing forces, and persuaded them to listen while he read out his paper of reconciliation. It had the desired effect. Rather than fight their comrades, the Levellers marched a mile upstream and swam the river. Thence they made their way to Burford, arriving about nine o'clock. There and in the two nearby villages of Fulbrook and Shipton they settled for the night, having been assured by Major White that Fairfax would not attack them. Their quartermaster More accordingly posted a light guard and issued them no instructions.[126]

By the morning of the 14th Fairfax had concluded that the mutineers did not mean to negotiate seriously and that they had to be crushed before their numbers swelled any further. Scotten and his other emissaries had already told him of the mutineers' high temper. He dismissed from his mind White's appeal to preserve the peace with the thought that the precedent for violence had already been set the previous week when Reynolds and Thompson had clashed. Besides, had the generals not given the mutineers notice that if they failed to resume obedience they would be attacked? They could hardly claim that they had not been warned, while their refusal to stand still when negotiations were in progress proved their bad faith. The time for talk was over.

From Theale, Fairfax now advanced rapidly up the Thames valley, reaching Abingdon by the early afternoon of the 14th. There he learnt of the confrontation a few hours earlier at Newbridge, and proceeded to that crossing, where he conferred with Reynolds and Abbott. They revealed that the mutineers had headed off in a westerly direction, hoping to persuade the regiments in that region to make common cause with them. It troubled the generals to learn that the Levellers had managed to cross the Thames, since there was now no physical obstruction to their westward march.[127] Though the afternoon was now far spent, Fairfax pressed on to Bampton, where he heard that the mutineers had finally stopped at Burford. By now some of his troops had covered an astonishing 35 miles in one day, and it was almost dark. But Fairfax perceived that if they could cover another 10 miles they stood a good chance of pouncing upon the mutineers while they were in their beds. The twin advantages of surprise and superior numbers might furnish them a victory without bloodshed. It would also avoid the embarrassment of having men from the same army drawing swords against one another.[128] When Fairfax consulted his troops about their willingness to keep marching they evinced 'a great alacrity' and 'resolvedness to the service in hand'. The final stage of the operation he turned over to Cromwell. The two generals agreed that if the mutineers did not resist they would be offered mercy; otherwise they would be treated as enemies. Because speed was essential, and also because they wanted to avoid a pitched battle, Cromwell took only the cavalry regiments and a detachment of Okey's dragoons. They reached Burford after midnight.[129]

Suspecting nothing, Major White was at that moment working with Cornet Henry Denne on the final draft of their paper for Fairfax. Denne, a graduate of Sidney Sussex College, had been ordained priest in 1630. By

1643 he was a professed Baptist, openly preaching universal grace. He joined the New Model Army and was assigned the rank of cornet in Scrope's regiment.[130] Denne and White's labours were interrupted by the alarm that Fairfax and Cromwell were at the entrance to Burford with a large force of dragoons. What had happened was that Cromwell's forlorn hope had met the Levellers' scouts outside the town. Rather than wheel around they had stayed with the scouts as they raced back to raise the alarm. They thus achieved complete surprise by riding into Burford at the same moment as the scouts. They then charged down the main street lined with the handsome stone houses of the town's wool merchants, not stopping until they reached the outlying village of Fulbrook. There they discovered a whole troop of mutineers crammed into one house. Feeling safety in numbers these men held out for over an hour, but at last accepted the offer of quarter and emerged without casualties having been sustained on either side.

Following close behind the forlorn hope was the main party of cavalry led by Colonel Reynolds, and the dragoons under Colonel Okey and Major Shelburne, along with another cavalry regiment from Buckinghamshire. Fairfax held back with a party in reserve, while Colonel Scrope commanded another detachment in the rear.[131] Captain Fisher led a smaller party that circled west to enter the town from the opposite end.[132] There he ran into two enemy troops already mounted, with swords drawn and pistols cocked, ready to charge. Fortunately they too accepted his offer of quarter, and bloodshed was averted a second time.

At the first alarm, White, dismayed at appearing a liar in the eyes of the mutineers, ran into the street in his slippers, seeking Fairfax to beg him to call off the attack. It was a futile quest. Colonel Okey, Major Barton and the other officers accompanying the main body had shouted offers of mercy to the sleeping men if they surrendered at once. In their dazed condition most had accepted the offer, but in one house the desperate occupants had fired out the windows, wounding a few of their attackers. Colonel Okey, who was in the thick of this confused scene, narrowly escaped with his life. After these men had been subdued, another party led by Colonel Eyre barricaded themselves in the Crown Inn, where with muskets blazing they held off Captain Packer's troops for several minutes.[133] One man was killed on each side, and several wounded in the most serious exchange of the night.[134] This violent resistance was the signal for Fairfax's men to relieve their prisoners of all their horses, weapons and, in some instances, clothing. Yet nearly two thirds of the mutineers escaped on foot into the night: probably three of the five troops in Fulbrook and Shipton, as well as a sizable number from the seven troops in Burford itself. Of the roughly 900 mutineers, 340 were taken prisoner and locked in the parish church.

As the darkness grew more impenetrable on account of the smoke and roar of discharging firearms, and as men on horseback swirled dizzily about him, Major White kept up his search for General Fairfax. At length, utterly discouraged, he went back to his quarters until the fighting had died down. Later he found his way to Fairfax's headquarters, and handed in the papers that he and Denne had been working on. Fairfax quizzed him on the mutineers' state of mind, and whether he thought a rapprochement might have been achieved. White answered, 'that they generally spoke well of his Excellency, and that I thought the business might have been taken up without that breach.'[135] This irritated Cromwell, who rebuked White for what he regarded as a ridiculous suggestion.

Having collected the names of all prisoners, the officers now pondered what to do with them. On the 15th Fairfax's Council of War concluded that by the Articles of War they could not discriminate among the mutineers, and that they were all therefore equally liable to the penalty of death. When this awful finding was relayed to the prisoners its impact was devastating. The men who until that moment had been behaving insolently towards their captors were reduced to terror and remorse. A few hours later, when money was sent to them to buy provisions, they refused it, 'saying that they must take care to provide for the soul and not for the body.' Copious tears were shed, 'and indeed', noted Fairfax, 'it is hardly to be believed how many of them did melt into a noble and Christian sorrow.' In this mood they framed 'The humble petition of the sad and heavy-hearted prisoners remaining in the church of Burford'. All 340 confessed that they now realized 'the odious wickedness' of what they had done, and that they therefore deserved to die. Nevertheless, they beseeched Fairfax 'to extend the bowels of your tender compassion' towards them. This was just what the officers wanted to hear. Reviewing the petition, the Council of War decided to limit punishment to the ringleaders, who were identified as Colonel Eyre, Cornets Thomson and Denne and Corporals Perkins and Church. With scrupulous regard for the limits of their authority, they remanded Eyre, who was not a member of the army, to the Oxfordshire authorities for a civil trial. The other four were sentenced to be shot to death.[136]

The two cornets manifested remorse over what they had done, while the corporals remained defiant till the last. Henry Denne's submission was the most extravagant. Professing no further desire to live, he bought himself a winding sheet for his burial, and began to compose a tract acknowledging the error of his ways.[137] On 17 May the four condemned men were brought to the churchyard for execution.[138] The other prisoners watched from the church, some of them standing on the leads. Cornet Thompson died first, contrite and in 'great terror'. Corporals Perkins and Church both carried themselves with courage, Church staring the soldiers in the face as they fired upon him.[139] The last to die should have been Cornet Denne. He had no way of knowing that Fairfax, impressed by his contrition, had resolved to lift the sentence of death. This news was delivered by Cromwell moments before he was to be shot. 'I am not worthy of such a mercy', he answered, and wept bitterly.[140] Oliver then escorted him into the church and mounted the pulpit. He informed the tightly packed throng that it was not the officers but providence that had spared their lives. Many of their grievances, he conceded, were justified, and they would eventually be remedied. Then he yielded the pulpit to Denne, who, 'howling and weeping like a crocodile', confessed the unlawfulness of everything that he and the mutineers had done.[141]

Now that the mutineers had purged their guilt the officers had to decide what to do with these horseless men. Orders were issued to sheriffs, JPs and constables to pursue the 500 or so who had escaped and to notify army headquarters when they had been rounded up.[142] The prisoners in Burford were released with 10s. each and a debenture for their arrears.[143] In half a year the debentures would be good for crown land, but for the present, as the Levellers were dismayed to discover, they fetched only 15–20 per cent of their face value in cash.[144]

The Burford mutiny was the most serious internal challenge faced by the regime until 1659. While the number of men routed on the night of 14–15 May was less than a thousand, there were several times that many disaffected soldiers in the area bounded by Portsmouth in the south, Lancaster in the north, London in the east and Bristol in the west. It was geographic dispersion and the incapacity to stage simultaneous uprisings in different centres that condemned the Levellers to military failure. Yet the number who actually took up arms against their commanders was impressive. William Thompson wooed four troops away from Reynolds' regiment, augmented them with recruits from London as well as men he picked up along the way, and ended up with a force of 300 or 400. Lieutenant Rowley expanded his Oxfordshire troop to over 300 men, and narrowly missed linking up with Thompson. Watching the troop movements around Banbury with the keenest interest were the 1000 men of Ingoldsby's radical regiment, a mere 22 miles away in Oxford. Had they not waited until September to stage their own uprising, but acted in union with Thompson and Rowley, they could have created a major headache for Fairfax and Cromwell. Meanwhile in Burford, less than 18 miles from Oxford, there were three New Model cavalry regiments involved in the mutiny: Scrope's, with about 450 men; Ireton's, with three half-troops totalling only 120; and Harrison's with two troops numbering perhaps 150. They were reinforced by a motley band of 200 drawn mainly from Henry Marten's regiment and led by Colonel William Eyre. Significantly it was Eyre's irregular troops who were responsible for the only serious casualties at Burford.

The total number of men involved in Leveller-inspired mutinies against the republic between the spring and autumn of 1649 was thus over 2500. The expeditionary force dispatched from London on 8 May was not twice that size. Starting out with just under 4000 men, Fairfax picked up about another 800 along the way: eighty (mostly officers) from Scrope's regiment; 160 (two troops) from Reynolds' regiment; about 300 (four troops) from Harrison's regiment in Buckinghamshire; and at least 200 dragoons (Okey's and Abbott's troops). On the night of 14–15 May, having left his three infantry regiments several miles to the rear, Fairfax must still have outnumbered his foes by two to one. Besides the weight of numbers and the advantage of surprise, another factor working for him was the absence of any serving officer above the rank of cornet on the mutineers' side. A final consideration that told in Fairfax's favour was the reluctance of New Model cavalry troopers to sheathe their swords in one another's bowels.

After Burford, all that remained was for the officers to snuff out the last embers of radical disaffection, and then to receive the accolades of the intellectual and business communities for a job well done. William Thompson was still at large, with an ever-diminishing band of followers. When Scrope's and Ireton's regiments had rendezvoused at Old Sarum the previous week, Thompson had approached with an offer of help.[145] They had chased him off, however, since they did not wish their cause to be contaminated by association with a man of his evil reputation.[146] He was now wandering through the Northamptonshire countryside. On the morning of Sunday the 20th, as Fairfax was on his way to church, Captain Moody brought news that Colonel Reynolds had finally hunted Thompson down. Reynolds, formerly considered a friend by the Levellers, had already done more frontline work in suppressing their revolt than any other officer. He had militarily neutralized Thompson at Banbury, blocked the mutineers at Newbridge, and dominated the assault on Burford. Eliminating Thompson was his final accomplishment in this sphere. His scouts informed him that Thompson had recently been in Northampton. There he had seized the magazine, released three men in gaol for dispersing Leveller pamphlets, seized the excise money and thrown it to the poor in the street.[147] Forty-eight hours later, upon hearing of the army's approach, he fled in the direction of Wellingborough. Reynolds caught up with him on the 19th. Keeping back from the fray this time, the colonel sent a party under Major Butler to fall into Thompson's quarters. Thompson's men were captured, but their leader got away and hid in the woods. Butler's men rode in hot pursuit and soon came upon him. Knowing he was doomed, Thompson determined to take as many to the grave with him as he could. An eyewitness of that day's events recounted them in these words:

> [he], well mounted ... being alone, yet rid up to our party and desperately shot a cornet and wounded another, and retreated to his bush. [He] received two shots when they began again to advance near him. He charged again with his pistol and took and received another shot and retreated. The third time he came up, for he said he scorne[d] to take quarter. Major Butler's corporal had Colonel Reynolds his carbine. It being charged with seven bullets, gave Thompson his death wounds.[148]

Lieutenant Rowley of the Oxfordshire troop was captured during the same skirmish.[149]

Nothing more was heard from Bristol, where earlier Sydenham's (formerly Skippon's) regiment was thought to be on the brink of mutiny. Fairfax, however, took the precaution of cashiering its Leveller major, John Cobbett, and his comrade Captain John Rogers. On the south coast Leveller agents sought support in Portsmouth and Devon, but were turned away empty-handed. A few stirrings of disaffection on the Isle of Wight were soon put down. By now these fitful and unco-ordinated attempts at mutiny no longer required the attention of the higher officers. What had earlier seemed like a dangerous situation in Lancaster Castle was tamed before the end of May. In Somerset, Colonel John Pyne and Sir Thomas Wroth were vigilant against known radicals, and took ruthless counter-measures at the first sign of discontent.[150]

By now there remained only one centre of discontent, the garrison of Oxford. At the time of Burford, Colonel Ingoldsby's officers had written to Fairfax assuring him that their regiment was tranquil and obedient. Yet they had also expressed their disquiet at the army's lack of unity. They feared that if the divisions were not healed a new war would soon break out. They offered two concrete suggestions for effecting a reconciliation: (1) a speedy dissolution of parliament; (2) the settlement of the Commonwealth by 'an Agreement made amongst the faithful people of this nation; in which Agreement we desire that provision may be made for the certain beginning and ending of all future Representatives, and for the removing of grievances.'[151] Though couched in moderate language, these suggestions amounted to an endorsement of the Leveller programme. The mutiny that finally broke out in Oxford garrison the following September came too late to inspire emulation elsewhere in the country, and was soon quelled.[152]

By the beginning of June, with the loose ends mostly tied up, the army commanders could savour the plaudits of the political nation. Within four days of Burford the clerks of Oxford University had concocted a special convocation to bestow honorary degrees on the officers. Nobly entertained at a feast in Magdalen College, they proceeded to the Schools to receive their degrees. Fairfax and Cromwell donned the scarlet gowns of Doctors of Civil Law, while Harrison, Hewson, Okey and other leading officers were clothed in the more sober garb of Masters of Arts. Engulfed by pageantry, jubilation and flattery, they momentarily forgot the royalist hostility of the city's inhabitants, and the Leveller sympathies of their own garrison there.[153]

The Lessons of Burford

Once back in London they were welcomed with unrestrained rejoicing. When the news of Burford had broken, MPs, monied men and magistrates heaved a huge sigh of relief, since they now knew that the limits of the revolution had been decisively set. Tithes would not be abolished, nor free trade introduced. Parliament would not be dissolved, nor would the Agreement of the People be imposed. The Irish expedition would go ahead as planned, and the Irish adventurers could look forward, they thought, to an early return on their investment. Social and religious conservatives could now sleep peacefully, secure in the knowledge that Fairfax and Cromwell exercised unchallenged control over the army.[154] There was much to rejoice about, and so the House of Commons appointed Thursday 7 June as a day of national thanksgiving for the Levellers' defeat. To show its satisfaction at the army's victory the City of London extended a cordial invitation to the House of Commons and the leading officers to dine with them on that day.[155]

The day of thanksgiving was an appropriately puritan occasion, commencing with prayer and preaching, and finishing with a banquet that was both sumptuous and sober. After hearing a sermon from Cromwell's favourite preacher, John Owen, the assembled MPs, magistrates, judges, peers and army officers processed in pomp to Grocers' Hall. There the City presented Fairfax with a bason and ewer of beaten gold, while Cromwell was honoured with 'a fair cupboard of silver'. When the banquet was over, £400 was distributed to the poor.[156]

What lessons had been learned from the Leveller insurrection and its suppression? In the City, little. It was now safer to express antagonism towards radicals, with the result that those rash enough to continue sporting sea-green ribbon had them torn from their hats. Radicalism suddenly lost its chic. A number of gentlewomen who had earlier donned sea-green silk or satin gowns and petticoats to publicize their political sympathies now found it prudent to retire them to their wardrobe cupboards.[157]

To Oliver Cromwell the victory at Burford was like waking from a bad dream. Had the nightmare continued, he feared, England might soon have witnessed a general rising of 'discontented persons, servants, reformadoes [and] beggars'. This motley rabble would have 'cast off all government and chose[n] some amongst themselves to have made new laws.' They would have indiscriminately murdered all lawyers as well as presbyterian and episcopalian ministers. Finally, they would have abolished private property and instituted communal ownership of the land.[158]

The lessons that Fairfax drew from recent events were quite different. Although he had been if anything more incensed than Cromwell by the soldiers' insubordination, he understood their frustration and recognized the justice of many of their demands. To him the victory at Burford was another of God's mercies towards parliament, but he desired that, instead of lapsing into complacency, the politicians should use the opportunity that had been won for them to get back on track with the unfinished agenda of reform. Only by 'settl[ing] this poor nation upon foundations of justice and righteousness' would they rally the poor to their side.[159]

Now that England was once again politically quiescent, its rulers could at last address the troublesome and long-deferred business of Ireland.

11

The Conquest of Ireland, 1649–52

The conquest of Ireland was high on the Commonwealth's agenda. Less than a month after the king's execution a powerful committee composed of Cromwell, Vane, Marten, Colonel Jones and Thomas Scot was directed to organize the expedition. It was soon agreed that an army of 12,000 horse and foot would be required to subdue the kingdom.[1] Why Ireland ought to be conquered was not a subject for debate. In the first place it was assumed to belong to England, as it had under Charles I. Secondly, there existed a consensus that vengeance was required for the slaughter of thousands of English settlers in the revolt of 1641. Thirdly, all understood that unless Ireland were speedily brought under control it would become a dangerous base of operations against the fragile republican regime. Even the Levellers, who exploited rank-and-file disaffection with the 'cut-throat expedition', did not for the most part question this assumption.[2]

Recruitment

As early as mid-February the army had assigned seven regiments of foot and eight of horse for Ireland.[3] The question of who should lead them was harder to answer. Everyone looked to Cromwell, but he put off committing himself for as long as he could. Aware that Ireland was the graveyard of English military reputations, and now approaching his fiftieth birthday, he may have shrunk from so dangerous a challenge. He was also conscious that while he was absent he would have little influence on political events in England. He resolved that if he was to lead the expedition stringent conditions would have to be met. His army must be well equipped, well provisioned and well financed. The terms of enlistment must be generous enough to make recruitment attractive. As commander-in-chief he must

The Religious successfull and truly Valliant Lieutenant Generall Cromwell

Plate 11 Oliver Cromwell, Lieutenant-General of the Cavalry

(The Bodleian Library, Oxford)

have plenary powers, civil as well as military. In addition he must have a substantial personal treasury to spend as he saw fit. He must also be assured that the Irish project would continue to have top priority in Westminster.

It took time before all these conditions were satisfied; meanwhile Cromwell's fellow officers did their part. On 22 and 23 March they met to discuss the Irish business, and exhorted him to accept the Council of State's invitation to lead the expedition.[4] In response Cromwell launched into a long speech reviewing the perils facing the republic. There were the Scots, for example, who harboured 'a very angry hateful spirit' against them. But in the end he had to concede that the greatest threat came from the Irish. 'I had rather be overrun with a Cavalierish interest [than] of a Scotch interest; I had rather be overrun with a Scotch interest than an Irish interest; and I think of all, this is most dangerous.'[5] Still he refused to commit himself. The officers screwed up the pressure by appointing a large committee to meet the following morning to seek God.

On the 24th, after fasting and praying all day, the committee heard and approved Colonel Whalley's proposal that the commander-in-chief must have full power to treat with the enemy and not have his hands tied by harsh terms 'as either to eradicate the natives, or to divest them of their estates.'[6] It is a pity that the conquerors would not see fit to carry out this humanitarian mandate from their fellow officers. There followed a vehement debate on the selection of regiments. Evidently there had been dissatisfaction with the fifteen regiments named the previous month. The majority decided that instead of entrusting this delicate task to a committee they should cast lots, on the model of the New Testament when an apostle to replace Judas Iscariot was chosen. Casting lots, it was believed, had the double merit of handing the decision to God and short-circuiting the political infighting over who should go and who should stay.[7]

A month later, on 20 April, the selections were made. 'After a solemn seeking God by prayer' the lots were cast for the four horse and four foot regiments. Fourteen pieces of paper, ten blank and four bearing the word Ireland, were put into a hat and shuffled. Then the papers were drawn out by a child and handed to an officer from each regiment in turn. The four horse regiments on which the lot fell were those of Ireton, Scrope, Lambart and Horton. The foot were those of Ewer, Deane, Cooke and Hewson. Half the troops in Okey's dragoon regiment were also selected by the same procedure. Outwardly at least, the officers 'expressed much cheerfulness at the selections.'[8] The grandees' enemies immediately suspected that the selection had been cooked.[9] From the north there were also dark mutterings that the choice of Lambart's regiment was a design of Cromwell to advance the interests of Sir Arthur Hesilrige.[10] Apart from the fact that such manipulation would have caused an uproar in the Council, the result of the process contradicts Walker's supposition. The regiments selected by lot were almost entirely different from those designated by headquarters in February. Moreover, they included several of the grandees or their closest colleagues – men such as Ireton, Scrope, Horton and Hewson. On the other side of the coin, Henry Marten's notably radical regiment was no longer earmarked for Ireland. Fleetwood's, Harrison's and Fairfax's horse regiments, as well as Fairfax's, Ingoldsby's and Robert Overton's foot regiments, all of which were known for their radical militancy, were passed over.[11] The Levellers in the army were said to be 'sensible that themselves are destined to destruction in Ireland.'[12] In reality the regiments represented a broad political spectrum, and at least one notably radical regiment – Marten's – had been dropped.[13]

It was said that the news of Cromwell's acceptance of the command of the Irish expedition gave a fillip to recruitment, yet the newsbooks were also forced to admit that many in the designated regiments refused to go.[14] On 28 April the officers held another all-day session on Ireland.[15] There were many problems. Sir Michael Livesey's disorderly regiment, which had been given to Colonel Robert Phayre, was causing annoyance by the slowness of its progress across England.[16] A few days later the mutinous parts of Scrope's and Ireton's horse regiments were crushed and disbanded at Burford, and substitutes had to be found. Colonel Tuthill's regiment, which preceded the main contingent to Dublin, mutinied there because it was not paid promptly enough, and was still not trusted with arms.[17] Later in the summer, when it was decided to send a whole rather than half a regiment of dragoons, Colonel Abbott experienced considerable difficulty recruiting the extra men in Hereford.[18] Around the same time Colonel Cooke's foot regiment mutinied before reaching its port of embarkation. It cost the colonel a blow to the head before he was able to force his men aboard.[19] Attempted desertion continued to be a problem until the moment of embarkation. As a consequence, the pressing of men had to go on unabated.[20]

Financing and Outfitting the Expedition

Manning the expedition was hard enough. Paying for it posed an even greater challenge. If soldiers could be pressed, monied men had to be coaxed. The record shows that Cromwell devoted more attention to money and *matériel* than he did to manpower. In April he participated in a high-level delegation that approached the City for a loan. By July London had advanced £150,000 towards the cause.[21] In May he hectored parliament about the need for money. The result was an act charging £400,000 on the future receipts of the excise.[22] In an extraordinary act of high-handedness Cromwell had a consignment of £10,000 which was on its way to Bristol for the navy's use seized and locked up at army headquarters at Windsor. At first the Council of State expostulated with him, but a day later backed down and agreed that he could use the money to finance the brigade then on its march to the west. For practical purposes he had established that Ireland was to be the government's top financial priority.[23]

On 9 July, confident that the money would soon be forthcoming, Cromwell left London for the west coast. His departure was attended with great pomp – blaring trumpets, six Flanders mares drawing his coach, and eighty gentlemen forming his personal lifeguard.[24] Five days later he was in Bristol, where he spent the next month mustering his regiments, waiting for a favourable wind, and writing to the Irish governors of the ports on the Munster coast offering money if they would open the gates of their towns to him.[25]

No matter how favourable the wind, Cromwell was determined not to depart until he had enough money in his pocket to pay his troops for several months. His minimum requirement was £100,000. It is noteworthy that a significant proportion of this fortune would go towards Cromwell's salary as commander-in-chief and lord-lieutenant of Ireland, which had been set at £13,000 a year.[26] Another sizable chunk would be used to bribe the forces in the Munster ports to desert to parliament.[27] When the Council of State realized that Cromwell would not be budged from his £100,000 demand, it scrambled to raise the cash from the excise and the sales of dean and chapter lands, even though it meant robbing the navy again to do so.[28]

Despite having to play second fiddle to the land force, the navy was nevertheless crucial to Cromwell's success. Colonel Blake was sent with a squadron to block up Kinsale and neutralize the small royalist navy under Prince Rupert. Sir George Askew patrolled the area near Dublin, while another small squadron kept an eye on the seas to the north. Colonels Deane and Popham had the vital task of keeping the supply lanes clear between the south coast and the Irish sea.[29] In addition, some 130 ships were enlisted to transport the 12,000 men, their arms, ammunition and supplies. During the summer vast quantities of biscuit, salt, wheat and beer were loaded onto ships in Milford Haven, Chester and Bristol. Lesser quantities of rye, oats, peas, barley, and cheese were also taken aboard. Two surprising items were 274 barrels of raisins and 230 bags of rice. Rice pudding was apparently part of the military diet.[30] An even greater logistical challenge was the shipping of the artillery train. There was a total of fifty-six great guns, which included four whole cannon and five demi-cannon. To make these weapons operational there were 600 barrels of powder and large quantities of iron, timbers, steel and tools, as well as 900 carriage and draft horses. Each whole cannon was said to need eighteen 'oxen' to move it overland, so wherever possible the artillery train would be transported by sea or river.[31]

Initially it had been thought that Ireland could be conquered on a budget of £20,000 a month for a limited period.[32] Less than a year later it was found to have cost twice that much, and final conquest still lay far in the future.[33] Indeed, over the seven-year period 1649–56 the cost of subjugating Ireland came to £6.8 million. Until the second half of 1650 the money for the expedition was raised exclusively in England, but, as soon as a territorial foothold had been established, assessments, customs and fines began to be levied in Ireland, in order to make the country pay for its own conquest. By 1656 close to half the £3.8 million spent in Ireland had been raised there. But as early as 1653 there was an additional £3 million owing to the troops and creditors of the state just for the previous three years. The Commonwealth had fallen behind in its financial obligations because of other commitments: the invasion of Scotland and the Dutch war.[34] The impossibility of meeting these debts from existing sources of revenue was what led the republic in 1652 to adopt the fateful policy of paying its military and civilian creditors in Irish land, and transplanting most of the native population to the province of Connacht.

There was another dimension to Cromwell's preparation of the Irish project: that of diplomacy. During the spring and summer of 1649 he directed much of his considerable political talent to sabotaging the royalist coalition that was being erected against him. On paper at least the coalition was formidable. The Marquess of Ormonde had arrived in Ireland the previous autumn.[53] In January he had reached an agreement with the Catholics of the Kilkenny Confederation to support his own protestant royalist force, and that of the the Munster protestants led by Lord Inchiquin. Sir George Monro's Scottish protestant army in the north of Ireland, enraged by the execution of Charles I, also threw in its lot with Ormonde. By the end of May Ormonde boasted that his army had grown to almost 13,000, although he had to concede that owing to lack of money 'I have the greatest difficulty in the world to keep those Irish together.' Believing that the inspiration of the royal presence would weld these diverse elements into a unified fighting force, Ormonde invited Charles to come to Ireland. The new king held back, but sent his cousin Prince Rupert with a small fleet to Kinsale on the Munster coast.[36]

Fortunately for the republic, three of its key commanders – Lieutenant-General Michael Jones in Dublin, Sir Charles Coote at Londonderry and Colonel George Monk at Dundalk – resisted the blandishments of the Scots presbyterians and remained loyal to the regime.[37] Moreover, Monk was able to achieve a diplomatic breakthrough of potentially momentous proportions. On 1 May he embarked upon a three-month cessation of hostilities with Owen Roe O'Neill, leader of the Catholics in Ulster and Connacht. In return for O'Neill's promise to uphold the interests of parliament, Monk agreed to support liberty of conscience for O'Neill's followers, oblivion for all acts committed since 1641, and a suitable commission for O'Neill in the parliamentary army.[38] Monk wrote to Cromwell that because of the cessation O'Neill and Ormonde were now pitted against each other. He also indicated that O'Neill was ready for serious talks with parliament and would undoubtedly come down from his high demands. When Cromwell informed the Council of State of the cessation it neither ratified nor condemned the arrangement, but kept it secret until the maximum advantage had been extracted from it.[39]

If parliament had made a permanent rapprochement with O'Neill it might well have crushed the royalist coalition in the egg. But the price was high. It involved abandoning the quest for revenge of the 1641 massacre, accepting some form of toleration for Catholicism, and compromising on the land question. Unfortunately the Rump would have none of it. Once Monk's cessation had expired and its tactical advantages been exploited to the full, parliament hypocritically repudiated it. More than strategic considerations lay behind the invasion of Ireland. The desire for vengeance, the zeal to destroy Antichrist, and greed for plunder, all played their part.[40] After parliament had delivered its judgement Monk himself was called in and assured he would not be held blameworthy for his error. According to Whitelocke, the majority of MPs believed they were being clever 'thus to beat him, and afterwards to stroke him'. But Monk long remembered his humiliation.[41]

Cromwell's rapprochement with Roger Boyle, Lord Broghill, bore fruit that was more enduring than the cessation with Owen Roe O'Neill. In June, Broghill had set off for France to seek a commission from Charles II to serve the royalist cause in Ireland. But when he came through London he was waylaid by Cromwell, who simultaneously threatened him with imprisonment and offered him a commission if he would fight for parliament. Once again Cromwell's talent for friendship paid off. Broghill accepted the offer and became master of the ordnance in Ireland. His support would be invaluable to Cromwell in the months to come.[42] Finally, Cromwell prevailed on a number of officers to postpone their desertions from Inchiquin's army, in effect keeping them as money in the bank to be drawn when he needed them most.[43]

Rathmines

Now that everything possible had been done to ensure his success, Cromwell at last quit England. On 13 August he set sail from Milford Haven with 4000 horse and foot in thirty-five ships, intending for Dublin. Two days later Ireton and Deane sailed with about the same number in seventy-seven vessels. A third squadron of eighteen ships commanded by Colonel Horton left shortly afterwards, and finally Hugh Peters brought over the remnant when the first ships returned to collect them. In all some 130 English and Flemish ships bore down on Ireland with 10,000 men, nearly 4000 horses, and ammunition, supplies and artillery.[44] On the two-day voyage Cromwell was violently seasick,[45] but his spirits were buoyed by the knowledge of a sensational victory won by Michael Jones against Ormonde's main army at Rathmines, outside Dublin, just ten days before.

Rathmines was a stupendous reversal of royalist fortunes, which had incalculable psychological and strategic consequences. As Ormonde wrote to Clanricarde, 'No thing in the defeat [is] so terrible to me as the dejection it brings upon the best inclined, and the advantage it gives to others to work upon the fears of the people.'[46] From the parliamentary perspective, as Whitelocke put it, 'There was never any day in Ireland like this.'[47] The Irish royalists would not confront the English in a battle of this magnitude again. News of the victory was a spur to recruitment in England.[48] Conversely, had Dublin been lost Cromwell would have had nowhere to land, and the invasion of Ireland might have been postponed indefinitely.

Ormonde salvaged what he could from the disaster. The day after Rathmines he rode with a remnant of his horse to Ballyshannon and obtained the garrison's surrender by deluding its governor into thinking he had just won Dublin.[49] He then decided to reinforce Drogheda with the aim of holding out against the enemy at all costs.

Drogheda

One of Cromwell's first acts upon his arrival in Dublin was to issue strict orders to his soldiers against taking free quarter or plunder. He also published a statement promising the peasantry that if they brought goods or provisions to his army they would be paid in ready money.[50] As it happened, this policy did not last long after the end of 1649, but at the beginning of Cromwell's sojurn in Ireland it served the valuable purpose of winning much of the populace in Leinster and Munster to his side.

The records tell us little about the other steps Cromwell took to prepare his programme of conquest. His plan was evidently to take as many ports on the east coast as possible, starting with Drogheda in the north and ending with Cork in the south, before moving inland. Everything he needed to execute this conquest – men, money, arms and supplies – he had to hand.

Ormonde by contrast was desperately short in every category, and he also faced the daunting challenge of somehow repairing the shattered morale of his troops. In the six weeks after Rathmines his correspondence is full of orders to send money and provisions to Drogheda, since the town was in a sorry state. Without money, low on food and lacking shovels and pickaxes to build up its defensive works, it seemed pathetically vulnerable.[51]

The one resource in which Ormonde was theoretically rich was man-power, but unless his scattered forces could be concentrated at Drogheda they were useless. He sent despatches to Sir Thomas Armstrong and Lord Montgomery of Ards in Ulster, the Marquess of Clanricarde in Connacht, and Lord Inchiquin in Munster urging them to set out as rapidly as possible.[52] He took advantage of parliament's denunciation of Monk's cessation with O'Neill to woo the Catholic general and his army back to the royalist fold.[53] Every commander except Colonel Mark Trevor in Dundalk seemed to have a good reason why he could not help.[54] Ormonde's money-raising efforts among the towns and counties were even less fruitful than his attempts to mass troops at Drogheda. The garrison continued to be short of match and shot.[55]

Despite these overwhelming problems of money and *matériel* Ormonde was determined to make a stand at Drogheda. He replaced the ineffectual governor Lord Moore with a man of impeccable royalist credentials, Sir Arthur Aston.[56] He then installed the four regiments which were the cream of his infantry.[57] By contrast the 200 cavalry he assigned there were, by Aston's account, a dispirited lot.[58] Ormonde held a council of war at the town on 23 August. By a vote of ten to three it was decided 'that Drogheda was to be maintained'. Ominously, all three of the garrison's colonels present voted against the motion. Of the ten in favour of holding out, only one, the governor, Sir Arthur Aston, would be physically present for its defence.[59]

Aston can have had few illusions about his chances of repelling Cromwell. His troops were in arrears; the cattle promised by Colonel Warren had not materialized; and he was still short of shot, match and other materials.[60] He was thus sharply circumscribed in his ability to ride out and sally against Cromwell's forces, which at the end of August had begun their approach to the town.[61] Aston's urgent requests for money and supplies continued until the day of the parliamentary assault.[62]

Cromwell set out from Dublin towards the end of August. Ormonde, with 3000 men, lay at Tecroghan, out of sight of Drogheda, and too far away to be of any material use to Aston. In justification of his apparently timid behaviour he afterwards explained that his troops were in such low spirits that he did not dare bring them close to the enemy.[63] He seems to have had ample reason for being afraid. As Cromwell approached Drogheda a small party of Inchiquin's horse detached itself from Ormonde's camp and rode over to join him.[64] It was the first of many accessions to Cromwell's strength.

Yet even with 12,000 men Cromwell could not hope to command all the approaches to the town. Straddling the deep channel of the Boyne, Drogheda possessed only a single bridge between its two parts (see map 7). Cromwell chose to besiege it from the south, where its ancient wall was 20 feet high and 4–6 feet thick.[65] Below the south-east portion of the wall stood a steep ravine which was a formidable obstacle to a storming operation. Its advantage was that on the far side Cromwell was able to station

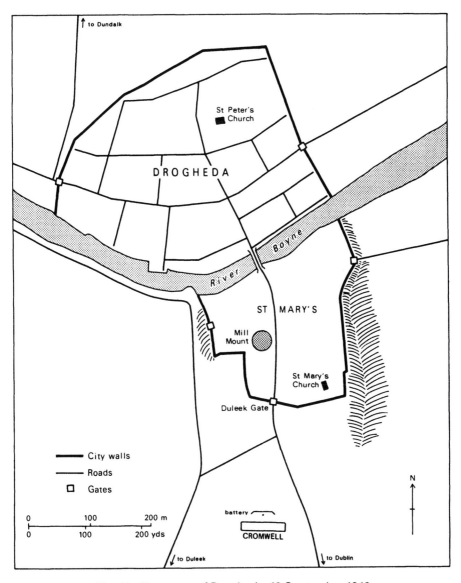

Map 7 The storm of Drogheda, 10 September 1649

his heavy guns exactly on a level with the wall. It took six days before his artillery arrived by sea, and he was not ready until 9 September. Altogether he had eleven siege guns and twelve field pieces. His heaviest guns were two 8-inch and two 7-inch cannon, firing 48- and 42-pound shot respectively.[66]

While Cromwell's artillery was being put in place Aston tried to keep him off balance with a number of spirited sallies. Although he inflicted several casualties, the cost in powder was too high, and after 8 September he had to halt these activities. That same day, not daring to approach himself, Ormonde had ordered Colonel Mark Trevor to use his party of horse 'to distress the enemy about Drogheda'. On the 9th nothing had been heard of Trevor, and Lieutenant-Colonel Edmund Verney, the scion of an ancient English Catholic family, wrote a poignant appeal to Ormonde to bring his troops closer to the town, on the north side of the Boyne.[67]

Early the following morning Aston received and contemptuously rebuffed a summons to surrender. Cromwell then began his bombardment in earnest, and by the evening had blasted a large hole in the southern wall at its eastern extremity, just outside St Mary's Church. In his last letter Aston wrote Ormonde that there was still no sign of Colonel Trevor and his party of horse, while his ammunition was decaying apace: 'Your Excellency's speedy help is much desired.... Living I am, and dying I will end, my Lord, your Excellency's most faithful and most obliged humble servant.'[68] Cromwell resumed the bombardment on Tuesday the 11th and kept it up most of the day. By the late afternoon there were two breaches in the south and east wall. They were not low enough to permit cavalry to enter, so Cromwell assigned three infantry regiments – Castle's, Hewson's and Ewer's – to be the shock troops. Castle's 700 or 800 men, who were the first to enter the breach, ran into unexpectedly bitter resistance. The defenders had not been idle during the bombardment, but had dug three lines of earthworks arching back from St Mary's Church to Duleek Gate, and from the church to the eastern wall. After quarter of an hour of furious fighting Colonel Castle was killed by a shot to the head, and his men fell back in fear and confusion, tumbling over the breach and down the steep ravine below.

Cromwell then unleashed a cannonade of half-pound shot to clear the royalist horse from the breaches. Augmenting the three regiments with reserves from Venables' and Farre's, he and Hewson accompanied the men on foot for the second assault. As the last daylight ebbed away they overran the enemy's entrenchments, took possession of St Mary's Church, and opened the nearby gate to their own cavalry. Some of Aston's soldiers fled down the narrow street to the bridge hoping to find safety in the northern part of the town. Others, including Aston himself, made a stand on a high mound of earth known as Mill Mount. Still others, hearing the shouted offer of quarter from Cromwell's men, surrendered and were taken prisoner. Spying the royalists still resisting on Mill Mount, Cromwell ordered them all put to the sword, 'and indeed, being in the heat of action, I forbade them to spare any that were in arms in the town.'[69] Some soldiers and officers, dismayed by Cromwell's order, defied it and let their prisoners escape,[70] but their isolated acts of humanity scarcely redeemed the night of terror. As the soldiers clattered over the bridge in pursuit of Aston's panic-stricken men, they trapped many of them inside the steeple of another church – St Peter's – and two towers in the northern and western walls. The steeple was set on fire and the men butchered as they tried to escape. Thirty refugees from the towers were spared and later shipped to the Barbados.[71]

In mitigation of the slaughter of Drogheda, we may reflect that it was mostly perpetrated during the heat of battle. Some of it, however, continued during the following day when resistance was all but at an end. The majority of the royalist officers had been taken prisoner, and were alive twenty-four hours after the battle was over, but they too were massacred in cold blood.[72] The noble Verney was removed from Cromwell's presence and stabbed to death. Legend has it that Aston was clubbed to death with his own wooden leg by Castle's soldiers, enraged by the loss of their commander.[73] According to official estimates there were 3100 soldiers in the town, of whom 2800 were killed, as well as many inhabitants, including every friar who could be found. The final toll may thus have been in the neighbourhood of 3500 soldiers, civilians and clergy.[74] Parliamentary losses were about 150.[75]

After he had recovered from the shock of this second disaster, Ormonde mournfully attributed it to God's punishment for royalist sins.[76] His foes interpreted it in the same fashion. Hewson, not a sensitive man at the best of times, trumpeted,

> Let them then behold the face of God against them, and the hand of God lifted up, for if they will not see, they shall see and be ashamed for their envy at the people, when the lord by his power shall break them in pieces like a potter's vessel.[77]

Cromwell too was convinced that God had been involved, not just in the result, but in the moment-by-moment fluctuations of the battle:

> That which caused your men to storm so courageously, it was the spirit of God, who gave your men courage and took it away again, and gave the enemy courage and took it away again, and gave your men courage again, and therewith this happy success.

But he was more ambivalent about the slaughter he had authorized:

> I am persuaded that this is a righteous judgment of God upon these barbarous wretches, who have imbrued their hands in so much innocent blood, and that

it will tend to prevent the effusion of blood for the future, which are satisfactory grounds to such actions, which otherwise cannot but work remorse and regret.[78]

It was a startling doctrine which held a town that had at no time been in the hands of the Confederate Catholics responsible for the massacre which they had unleashed in 1641. Among Drogheda's defenders, moreover, were many English officers, one of whom (Colonel Byrne) commanded a whole regiment of protestants.[79] As a practical man, Cromwell hoped that the terrible example of Drogheda would bring Irish resistance to a speedy end, and produce a net saving of lives. Events were to prove him wrong.

Could the royalists have averted the catastrophe of Drogheda? Given Cromwell's overwhelming superiority in numbers, firepower and money, as well as his decisive speed and able generalship, it is hard to see how the result could have been different. Ormonde's forces were widely dispersed, but he could not have supported them for a day even if they had come when he beckoned. Yet, though he personally commanded only 3000 men, he did his cause no good by timidly keeping them in the background at Tecroghan. Apart from his mediocrity as a military leader, most of Ormonde's problems stemmed from the fact that he was trying to hold together an uneasy coalition of protestant royalists, Old English Catholics and Gaelic Irish, who fundamentally distrusted one another. The only factor that might have tipped the balance in the royalists' favour at Drogheda was Owen Roe O'Neill and his Ulster Catholic army. But he was tardy like all the other generals, and was in any case already a dying man.[80]

The shock of Drogheda has continued to reverberate to the present day. At the time it was merely experienced as a second hammerblow to royalist morale. Ormonde told the king that 'it is not to be imagined how great the terror is that those successes and the power of the rebels have struck into this people.' Even though they knew that Cromwell's victory, if unchecked, would mean 'irrecoverable slavery', and even though their overall numbers were superior to his, they were 'so stupefied that it is with great difficulty I can persuade them to act anything like men towards their own preservation.'[81] Royalist strength continued to be sapped by desertions. Cromwell, with the magnetism of success, the power of money and the promise of protection, drew soldiers and civilians to him. He also injected ideological content into his appeal, as Sir Edmund Butler reported to Ormonde:

> so slyly the rogues allure [the countryfolk] by speaking that they are for the liberty of the commoners and that they will have no contribution of them if they serve the market at the camp, and by hanging troopers for taking three herrings.[82]

Like will to Like, else why should HEWSON be
Still among Knaves, Knaves love his Company. —

Plate 12 Colonel John Hewson

(Source: *Cromwelliana*)

Wexford

Without these accessions of strength Cromwell would have found himself uncomfortably stretched. Directly after conquering Drogheda he sent Colonels Robert Venables and Theophilus Jones with 5000 troops to subdue the region north of the town. By the end of November Carrickfergus was the only coastal town in Ulster still in royalist hands.[83] After allowing his main army to rest a few days, Cromwell left Dublin for Wexford, collecting garrisons as he went. These conquests drank up men, for, as he explained to parliament, each new garrison required anything from a few dozen to a few hundred soldiers to defend it. The shrinkage of his field army was accelerated by the ravages of dysentery, the 'country sickness' or 'bloody flux' as it was variously known. English soldiers had begun to succumb almost the moment they stepped off the boats in August. By the end of September 4000 men had fallen ill. Many died, while others were so weakened that they were good for little else than garrison duty. By its nature dysentery attacks violently and without warning. On 3 November, for example, a large part of the army, under attack by Inchiquin's army at Glascarrig, were forced to fight with their breeches down because of the 'flux'.[84] It was not only private soldiers who were felled by disease. Cromwell lost two of his most valued officers to it: Colonel Thomas Horton in October and Lieutenant-General Michael Jones in December.[85]

Speaker Lenthall responded to Cromwell's appeal with an assurance that 5000 fresh recruits would soon be on their way. Even though several of the grandees were paid in advance to raise this contingent, they either defaulted on their obligation or were very late in fulfilling it. By the following February recruitment was still far short of its target of 5000.[86] After the destruction at Drogheda Ormonde's efforts to recruit new men for his army ran into a blank wall of non-co-operation. Many Catholic Irish, taking the measure of English implacability, began leaving the country for Spain. The exodus continued and gathered momentum until the conquest was complete in 1652.[87]

Wexford had no desire to share the fate of Drogheda, and initially Ormonde too wanted it abandoned.[88] Long a base for privateering raids against English commerce, the town also stood out in English minds for its fervent Catholicism. But it was riven with faction, and its divisions were to prove advantageous to Cromwell. The party which adhered to the papal nuncio Rinuccini wanted to open the gates of the town to the besiegers, while the party of the Catholic Confederacy, which was regarded as primarily responsible for the massacre of 1641, wanted to hold out. The Confederates carried the day, and stipulated to Ormonde that he send only

Catholic troops to reinforce the garrison. Ormonde complied, and furnished two regiments of Castlehaven's Ulster foot, numbering 1500 men.[89]

On 29 September, in advance of the army, Colonel Deane arrived in Wexford harbour with a squadron of twenty ships bearing food, siege guns and ammunition. Violent storms prevented him from landing them for a week. Aside from the weather however, he met with no resistance. There was a fort at Rosslare guarding the entrance to the harbour (see map 8), but at the approach of Lieutenant-General Michael Jones with a detachment from the army it was hurriedly abandoned.[90]

On 2 October Cromwell, having overrun five garrisons in his ten-day march from Dublin, appeared before the town with his forces, less than 8000 strong.[91] His summons to surrender was met with a delaying answer from the governor, David Sinnott, who hoped that Ormonde would be able to relieve him. Ormonde did indeed approach, but his way was blocked by Lieutenant-General Michael Jones.[92] The parliamentary effort was also helped by the news that two of Lord Inchiquin's regiments had cast off their officers and seized the nearby garrison of Youghal for parliament. Cromwell was none the less anxious. The heavy winds and rain, food shortages and relentless attacks of dysentery had in a matter of days reduced his effective numbers to 6000 men. Sinnott's demands for liberty of worship and the maintenance of clerical privileges only added to Cromwell's impatience, and on the 11th he started his bombardment with eight heavy guns and two mortar pieces.[93] Under normal circumstances the town would have been a hard nut to crack. Its defenders had swelled to 4800 men. Protected by the sea on the east, it boasted heavy stone walls lined with earth on the west. Its southern end was protected by a strong castle on high ground. As it turned out, this castle was to be the town's undoing. Its walls had evidently not been reinforced with earth, so that Cromwell was soon able to blast a large hole through them. Again his tremendous firepower demoralized the enemy. The townsfolk began to flee by boat, the defenders quailed, and the magistrates sent out a message that they wished to negotiate a surrender.

While negotiations were going on, however, the Catholic governor of the castle, Captain Stafford, perhaps uninformed about what was taking place in the town, unilaterally yielded up the castle. Cromwell accordingly delayed his answer to the town's request for articles of surrender so that they could take account of his capture of the castle. The parliamentary soldiers lost no time, but immediately exploited their taking of the castle by training their guns on the town. Appreciating the disaster that had just taken place, the defenders at once gave up. Some threw themselves over the wall into the midst of the parliamentary horse, but most retreated within the town.

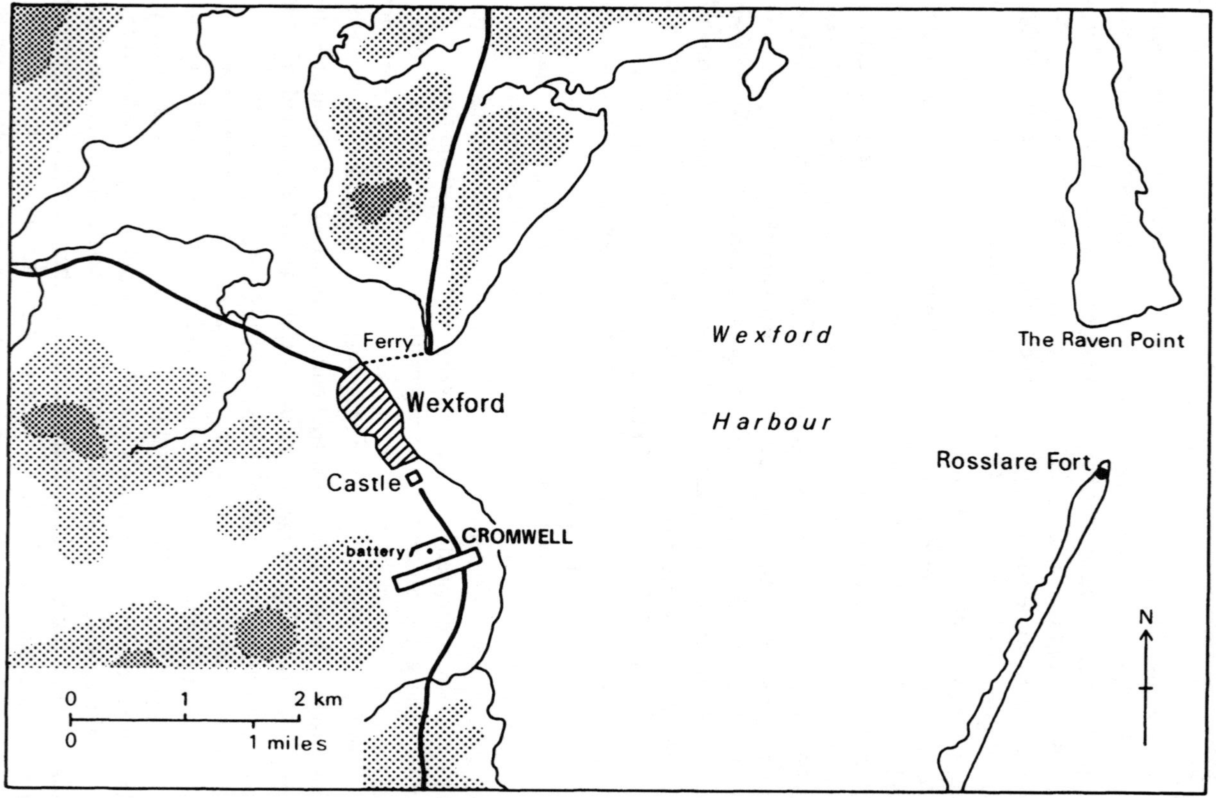

Map 8 The storm of Wexford, 11 October 1649

Seeing the collapse of the town's defences, the men occupying the castle did not wait for orders, but at once launched an assault. Hoisting themselves up with pikes and scaling ladders, they took possession of the town within half an hour.[94] Some of the enemy made a stand in the market place, but were soon overcome and slain on the spot. Another 300 who tried to escape across the harbour drowned when their boats sank. Any priests or friars unfortunate enough to cross the attackers' path were butchered without mercy. A parliamentary account illustrates the total incomprehension that existed between Irish Catholics and English protestants at this time:

> Some [priests] came holding forth crucifixes before them, and conjuring our soldiers (for his sake that saved us all) to save their lives; yet our soldiers would not own their dead images for our living saviour; but struck them dead with their idols; many of their priests (being got together in a church of the town, where 'tis said many poor protestants were kept and killed together in the beginning of the Rebellion) were slain together by our soldiers about their altar.[95]

Cromwell estimated the death toll at Wexford at around 2000 on the royalist side and less than twenty on his own.[96] What is dismaying is that the slaughter was more or less accidental. The garrison had been on the point of surrender, and there was no order from Cromwell to put defenders, townsfolk and priests to the sword. On the other hand his men carried out what they believed from previous practice to be his policy, and he did not rebuke them for it. In his orthodox Calvinist way he handed the entire responsibility to God. His own hope had been that they could take the town peacefully and preserve it from harm,

> yet God would not have it so; but by an unexpected providence, in His righteous justice, brought a just judgment upon them, causing them to become a prey to the soldier, who in their piracies had made preys of so many families.... Thus it hath pleased God to give into your hands this other mercy, for which, as for all, we pray God may have all the glory. Indeed your instruments are poor and weak, and can do nothing, but through believing, and that is the gift of God also.[97]

Writing at the beginning of the twentieth century, Gardiner found the slaughter at Wexford more justifiable than that at Drogheda. He ignored the fact that the Wexford slaughter occurred in the midst of negotiations for the town's surrender. For this, as Corish has pointed out, there could be no appeal to the recognized laws of war.[98]

After Wexford Cromwell's effective force was reportedly down to 5600 men, of which some would be left behind to garrison the town.[99] With men, money and supplies arriving very slowly from England, and with his soldiers now on half pay, the standard of conduct in his army deteriorated sharply.[100] His situation would have been desperate had it not been for the near-collapse of his foes.

Ormonde's shaky coalition was now on the point of dissolution. Thanks to the growing number of desertions by protestant English to the parliamentary forces, protestant and Catholic royalists were now separated by a wall of suspicion and hostility.[101]

Faction was not Ormonde's only problem. As he lamented to Lord Jermyn, lack of money meant that he could not keep his army together for a week at a time. Moreover, his soldiers' plundering of the countryside had driven most of the populace into the arms of the enemy.[102] Finally, the death of Owen Roe O'Neill in November paralysed the best force that Ormonde could call upon, because of the power struggle that ensued over the choice of O'Neill's successor as commander-in-chief.[103]

Ormonde's immediate problem after the loss of Wexford was the betrayal, within the space of a month, of five Munster towns. These betrayals could be traced back to Cromwell's negotiations with Lord Broghill in London the previous spring. With Cromwell's commission as master of ordnance in his pocket, he sailed from Bristol to Wexford in October. Quickly raising 1500 foot and a troop of horse on his own family's estates, he linked up with Colonel Richard Townsend of Inchiquin's army in Cork. On the night of 16 October Townsend and two other colonels, with the aid of the English part of the garrison and the English inhabitants of the city, seized power from the commanding officer, expelled him and his Irish followers from the town, and declared for parliament. Cromwell acted promptly by sending Colonels Blake and Phayre to assist Broghill and Townsend, and by reassuring the city's inhabitants that they would suffer no reprisals.[104] After the betrayal of Cork other Munster towns – Youghal, Kinsale, Bandon and Timoleague – were not long in following. The winning of Kinsale meant that Prince Rupert with his royalist fleet had to make a quick getaway.[105] By the middle of November Inchiquin had lost virtually all his army and Ormonde was in disgrace in the eyes of Irish Catholics.[106]

Waterford

Cromwell's next major target after Wexford was Waterford, another 35 miles down the coast. On 17 October he was before New Ross, which guarded the approaches to Waterford, and summoned the governor, Major Lucas Taaffe. He expected little trouble, since several townsmen had already let him know that they welcomed his arrival.[107] When Taaffe asked for liberty of conscience as one of the conditions of surrender Cromwell set him straight on the English understanding of this concept:

For that which you mention concerning liberty of conscience, I meddle not with any man's conscience. But if by liberty of conscience you mean a liberty to exercise the mass, I judge it best to use plain dealing, and to let you know, [that] where the parliament of England have power, that will not be allowed of.

He then underlined the futility of further talk by opening fire with his cannon, and Taaffe immediately yielded. As he withdrew from the town 500 of his soldiers crossed over to the parliamentary side.[108]

Cromwell spent the next several weeks at New Ross building a bridge over the river Barrow to improve access to Waterford. For much of the time he and his soldiers were sick and unable to stir from their beds. As he told Speaker Lenthall, 'a considerable part of your army is fitter for an hospital than the field.'[109] By the time he arrived before Waterford at the end of the month his troops again numbered no more than 6500, this despite large accessions of strength from Inchiquin's army.[110]

Waterford was the last port on the south and east coasts still in royalist hands. The second city in Ireland, its fervently Catholic citizenry had made of it a thriving commercial centre that ranked next to Dublin in both population and wealth.[111] Defensively it was well situated on the river Suir, its ample harbour guarded by two forts: Duncannon on the east, and the smaller decayed fort of Passage on the west. The harbour had to be held if the enemy was to be stopped from bringing in heavy artillery by sea. Ormonde therefore decided to invest all three points as strongly as possible. Castlehaven was put in charge of Passage with instructions to repair it. The defeatist Captain David Roche, most of whose soldiers had run away, was replaced by Colonel Edward Wogan, the turncoat captain of dragoons who had quit the New Model Army in 1647.[112] The whole operation was the most skilful that Ormonde mounted during the 1649–50 campaign, and it was crowned with success.

Most remarkable was the mauling given to Lieutenant-General Michael Jones's forces by Wogan at Duncannon. A brilliant tactician, as well as a man of extraordinary personal magnetism, Wogan possessed the qualities of a born fighter. The sight of Jones's 2000 men investing his garrison made him decide that his only hope lay in a ruse. He arranged with Castlehaven to ferry eighty cavalry from across the harbour at Passage. When he used these troops in the course of his next sortie, Jones, believing that Wogan had no cavalry, jumped to the conclusion that Ormonde must have suddenly arrived with the field army. As a result he withdrew in disorder, leaving behind two brass cannon.[113]

This setback was most unwelcome to Cromwell. 'Crazy in my health', as he reported to parliament, and with his army demanding to retire to winter quarters, he paused before launching his planned assault against Waterford itself.[114] He also hoped that in time the garrison would destroy itself from within and yield without a struggle. On 21 November Castlehaven appeared before Waterford with a relieving force to strengthen the garrison. Despite his Catholic credentials, the town refused him admission because he was an Englishman. The recent betrayal of the other Munster towns had made them incorrigibly suspicious of all but their own countrymen.[115] On the same day Cromwell summoned Waterford to surrender, reminding them of the fate of Wexford if they did not obey. The mayor, however, delayed, having already appealed to Ormonde to send a a strong force of Ulster Catholics from O'Neill's army. Swallowing his anger at the rebuff given to Castlehaven, Ormonde did just that. The 1300 troops he despatched under Lieutenant-General Farrell arrived on the 24th, the same day as Ireton took Passage.[116]

In preparation for the storm Cromwell had ordered 1200 horse and foot to come from Cork to assist him. With ten men being carried off every night by disease, and many more disabled, his own numbers were down to barely 3000 troops fit for action. In addition, the unaccustomed prospect of having to do battle with some of the finest soldiers in Ireland, on ground that the rain had converted into a quagmire, gave him no alternative but to abandon the siege. And so on 2 December he left Waterford, under pelting rain, 'it being as terrible a day as ever I marched in, all my life.' The cost of defeat was high. Not only were his men demoralized, but he had lost two valued officers – his kinsman Major Cromwell and Lieutenant-General Jones – to disease.[117]

Waterford is notable for being the only Irish city that successfully resisted a siege by Oliver Cromwell. The explanation for this unique setback lies partly in the determination of Ormonde, Castlehaven, Ferrall and Wogan to hold the town,[118] but also in the shrewdness of the mayor and inhabitants for their insistence on having only Ulster Catholics to man their defences. Sickness and poor morale in the parliamentary army also played their part. Finally, we must remember that at Waterford alone Cromwell was deprived of his artillery. The wretched weather made the ground 'so moist and rotten' that he could not haul the heavy guns overland.[119] Wogan's brilliant defence of Duncannon meant that he could not bring them by sea either. The resistance at Waterford showed that the terror of Drogheda and Wexford had already worn off. Far from preventing further bloodshed, these atrocities had sharpened the resolve of royalists and Catholics alike to resist the invader with every resource at their command.

Apart from this one setback, Cromwell at the end of 1649 could contemplate with satisfaction what he had accomplished during his short sojourn in Ireland. With the fall of Carrickfergus to Sir Charles Coote on 6 December, his control of the entire Irish eastern and southern coastline was broken only at Waterford. The betrayal of five Munster towns by Inchiquin's soldiers gave him comfortable winter quarters for his field army, whose numbers were reported now to be hovering around 6500.[120] In comparison with his enemy Cromwell was still richly endowed with arms, ammunition and money, and he knew that Sir Hardress Waller would soon be on his way from England with an infusion of 3000 recruits. More important for the moment were the seasoned troops he detached from Inchiquin and other commanders. Their familiarity with the country made them much less susceptible to disease.[121] Cromwell knew there was a lot more to be accomplished before he could announce that Ireland was conquered. Had he been aware that at that moment parliament was planning to recall him to England he would have been profoundly dissatisfied at leaving a job half done.

Ormonde's position, both military and political, was far more precarious than Cromwell's. The town of Kilkenny allowed him to establish his head-quarters there, but his troops soon provoked 'an universal exclamation of the people' because of their exactions. Waterford and Limerick would admit none of his troops to quarter for the winter. All too often it seemed that the population was readier to co-operate with Cromwell than with Ormonde. Even royalist soldiers found the parliamentary service more attractive.[122] The only bright spot on this gloomy canvas was Clonmel, which permitted Major-General Hugh Dubh O'Neill to occupy it with 1600 Ulster Catholic troops. A few months later Clonmel would be the site of Cromwell's second setback in Ireland.[123]

The aura of defeat had fatally undermined Catholic Irish confidence in Ormonde. Increasingly the Irish were heard to say they could trust no one who did not go to Mass.[124] In a bid to arrest the corrosion of trust within the royalist alliance, the bishops met at Clonmacnoise and issued a call for Irish unity. Cromwell was a mortal enemy, they reminded their people, for they could expect from him neither toleration nor mercy.[125]

The bishops' appeal for unity drew from Cromwell a ferocious counter-blast which revealed the depth of his anti- Catholicism. His 'Declaration ... for the Undeceiving of Deluded and Seduced People' indicted the clergy for greed, pride, cruelty and ambition. They had kept the people ignorant and plunged the country into a horrid rebellion:

Your covenant is with death and hell.... Is God, will God be, with you? I am confident he will not! ... You are a part of Antichrist, whose kingdom the Scripture so expressly speaks should be laid in blood; yea in the blood of the Saints. You have shed great store of it already, and ere it be long, you must all of you have blood to drink; even the dregs of the cup of the fury and the wrath of God, which will be poured out unto you!

In a gross distortion of history he lectured the bishops that their country had prospered under English rule.[126] He denied any intention to 'massacre, banish and destroy the Catholic inhabitants' of Ireland, unless they took up arms against him. The purpose of the parliamentary army was 'to ask an account of the innocent blood that hath been shed', and also 'to hold forth and maintain the lustre and glory of English liberty in a nation where we have an undoubted right to do it.' Nevertheless,

> if this people shall headily run on after the counsels of their prelates and clergy and other leaders, I hope to be free from the misery and desolation, blood and ruin, that shall befall them, and shall rejoice to exercise utmost severity against them.[127]

It may be true that Cromwell had the mind of England as well as its sword at his disposal. It is strange nevertheless for Gardiner to conclude that, because Cromwell was sincere in this bloodthirsty tirade, he was guilty of nothing worse than ignorance in ordering the slaughter of Drogheda.[128] Cromwell had been in parliament in 1641 during Strafford's impeachment. He had heard Pym build up the elaborate web of charges against Strafford's misgovernment of Ireland.[129] He should therefore have had an inkling of the grievances of the native population against their English overlords.

Kilkenny

The Irish were not given long to digest the significance of Cromwell's Declaration. On 29 January the mild winter permitted him to resume military operations. He was determined to make quick work of it. By mid-March, apart from the province of Connacht, only Limerick, Waterford, Kilkenny and Clonmel still held out.[130] But time was now all too plainly running out. In March and again in April parliament sent him urgent instructions to return home.[131] Absorbed in his sieges, he attempted to block out the unwelcome messages from England. In March he was engaged with Hewson and Ireton in a pincer movement against Kilkenny. Under Cromwell's instructions, Hewson had marched from Dublin through Kildare, to rendezvous with his commanders at Gowran Castle. Once the threat of artillery fire had brought the defenders to their knees, all but one of the officers were shot and a priest was hanged, while the soldiers who were English crossed to the other side.[132]

On 22 March they were before Kilkenny. The handsome headquarters of the Committee of Estates, it was also the chief inland town of Ireland. Standing on the banks of the river Nore, it was divided into two parts, Kilkenny proper and Irishtown, and would not be easily overrun.[133] However, it was now experiencing its own tribulation. The plague, which had commenced at Galway the previous summer, had spread rapidly inland, and now was raging within Kilkenny's walls. Castlehaven, with his roving army of 4000 men, was powerless to offer any assistance, owing to the preparatory work of Cromwell, Ireton and Hewson. Despite the hopelessness of his situation the governor of the town, Sir Walter Butler, refused to surrender. Cromwell began his artillery attack at 9 a.m. on 25 March, and by noon, after firing nearly a hundred shot, had made a breach in the town wall. The counter-measures taken by the defenders revealed that the Irish were now becoming adept at neutralizing Cromwell's heavy guns. Around the area where the hole was blasted they had thrown up two counterworks of earth, strongly palisaded. To create a diversion Cromwell sent Colonel Ewer across the river with 1000 foot to possess Irishtown. When Cromwell flung his men into the breach under the leadership of Axtell and Hewson, the Irish were more than ready, and poured withering fire on them from the safety of their palisades. Cromwell did not acknowledge the ingeniousness of the defence, but blamed his men for not performing 'with usual courage nor success'. They were beaten off with the loss of a captain and twenty or thirty men killed or wounded.

A second attempt was also abortive, and after each assault the defences were repaired. A third order to attack was disobeyed. There were other losses. An officer who had led a detachment across the bridge into the town with the objective of setting fire to the gate was killed, and forty or fifty of his men lost or wounded as well. By now, however, Ewer had taken Irishtown, and Butler could see that the end was in sight. The townsfolk wished to avoid the fate of Drogheda, so he reopened negotiations. Cromwell, in a hurry to get to Clonmel, granted generous terms, leaving Lieutenant-Colonel Axtell behind as governor.[134]

Clonmel

The siege of Clonmel a month later demonstrated afresh the maturing Irish ability to withstand the shock of parliamentary heavy guns. So skilful were the defenders that they inflicted upon Cromwell the severest check of his military career. In response to an appeal from the mayor of Clonmel, Ormonde had in December sent Major-General Hugh O'Neill with 1300 of his Ulster Catholic troops to defend the town.[135] A month later, however, the mayor complained because Ormonde had sent no money to support the soldiers, and their exactions were driving the citizens away. In the end Ormonde's inability to supply the garrison made its surrender inevitable. Clonmel was a populous, well-fortified town, about 25 miles upstream from

Waterford on the river Suir. By April the size of the garrison had grown to over 2000. Cromwell encamped before the town for three weeks before he unleashed his heavy artillery. At the point where the breach was being opened, O'Neill enlisted every available person within to build a twin set of makeshift walls out of rubbish, stones, timber and mortar, running back 80 yards from either side of the breach. At the end of the lane thus created he dug a deep ditch, and then planted his own guns behind it. As fortune would have it there was a row of houses running just behind one of the walls where the breach was appearing. The upper storeys of these houses he filled with soldiers so that they could fire on the invaders when they poured through the breach.

Not suspecting any of these preparations, Cromwell ordered the storm to begin at eight o'clock on the morning of 16 May.[136] The town was eerily quiet, and there was no opposition as Colonel Culme led the men into the breach, singing a hymn. In contrast to most assaults on city walls, this one included a sizable contingent of horse, because the foot had demanded that cavalry should run the same hazards as they. By the time those at the front realized they were in a trap, the whole lane was crammed with troops. Vainly they cried to those behind them to halt. The men entering the breach, hearing them shout, thought the defenders of the garrison were on the run, and jubilantly cried, 'Advance! Advance!' In the confusion no one could budge. At that instant a party of O'Neill's pikemen and musketeers ran to the breach and sealed it off. His main force then fell on those trapped in the lane with muskets, pikes, scythes and stones. They also cast long timber posts amongst the helpless invaders, and let loose with their two artillery pieces from the end of the lane, cutting the invaders between the knees and the stomach with chained bullets. In the space of an hour a thousand men were piled dead on top of one another.

In the meantime Cromwell had ridden with his guard to the town gate, expecting it to be opened for him. His first hint that something had gone wrong was the sight of men retreating from the breach, and the sound of cannon going off within the town. Unaccustomed to defeat, Cromwell determined that they must attack again. For four hours he poured men through the deadly breach, but they were continually mowed down. At the end of the day he had lost 1500 men and still failed to break the town's resistance.[137]

Later that night, however, O'Neill and his Ulster regiment slipped out of the town in the direction of Waterford. Their ammunition had run out and they knew that they could expect no relief from Ormonde or Castlehaven. At midnight the townsmen sent a message asking to treat for surrender. Cromwell, ignorant of the fact that the soldiers had stolen away, quickly granted the town easy terms. Only after he had made the agreement did he discover the deception. Angry as he was he stuck to his terms, and when his men entered the town they did no damage. He vented his frustration by sending out some troops after the stragglers in O'Neill's party. They overtook and slew 200 of the women and wounded.[138]

A week later Cromwell left Ireland after a stay of barely nine months. He had come intending a sharp, quick conquest. His deliberate policy had been to shed blood in order to save it later. But as his campaign wore on he found the Irish unexpectedly stubborn. Despite notable diplomatic successes in winning over the Munster towns under Inchiquin's control, and despite very able support from Sir Charles Coote in Ulster, Lieutenant-General Michael Jones around Dublin and Lord Broghill in Munster, his victories became ever more costly. His initially well-paid and well-supplied army shrank alarmingly, from the dysentery that tore through its ranks, and from the necessity to leave behind defenders in every garrison that was conquered. Recruits were slow to arrive from England. Had it not been for substantial defections from the enemy, he would have had almost no men left to put in the field by the end of 1649. By the following spring it was reported that virtually none of the soldiers he had brought with him in August were still in service.[139] When he left Ireland Cromwell had bent many towns to his will, but he had never met an army in the field. That honour was reserved to Colonel Michael Jones, Sir Charles Coote and, later, Henry Ireton.

In principle the war should now have been largely a mopping-up operation, for the Irish resistance appeared to be in an advanced state of disintegration. The provinces of Ulster and Leinster were firmly under parliamentary control, while in Munster the Irish held only Waterford, Duncannon, Limerick and the fastnesses of Kerry. The only province they could still call their own was the poorest, Connacht.

Bubonic plague was now raging across the breadth of the country. Neither side was spared its devastation, and in Dublin in June it was reported that 200 a week were dying from it. By August the death toll had reached 797 a week, while in Wexford almost the entire remaining population had been wiped out.[140]

The royalist coalition had for practical purposes flown apart under the strain of Irish Catholic mistrust towards anyone who was Scottish, English or protestant. Upon the death of Owen Roe O'Neill in November 1649, for example, the provincial assembly of Ulster had insisted that it, not Ormonde, would nominate O'Neill's successor. After a lengthy political wrangle it commissioned Emer McMahon, Bishop of Clogher, as its general. A man of no military experience, he was chosen in the hope that he could unite the various Catholic factions in the province.[141] In June 1650 he led his 6000-strong[142] army a few miles west of Londonderry with the object of dividing the forces of Sir Charles Coote and Colonel Venables. Defying the advice of Major-General Henry Roe O'Neill to avoid battle, save lives and wear out the English by delay, McMahon impatiently sought an encounter. At Letterkenny he did battle with Coote's forces. The consequence was that the precious army he had inherited from Owen Roe was wiped out. Lieutenant-General Farrell, Major-General O'Neill, five colonels, a host of lower officers and 3000 common soldiers lost their lives. Bishop McMahon was captured the next day and taken to Enniskillen, where on Sir Charles Coote's orders he was hanged and quartered, and his head set on the gate at Londonderry.[143]

Thanks to the impetuosity and inexperience of its clerical leader, the main Catholic army in Ireland had been lost. Not surprisingly, most of the remaining garrisons in Leinster and Munster tumbled into parliament's lap that summer: Tecroghan, Killmallock, Athy, Carlow, Waterford, Duncannon. Those still bent on resistance withdrew to Connacht and to the fastnesses of Kerry in western Munster.[144] In December Ormonde left Ireland. The Irish bishops had disowned him at the end of the summer and threatened with excommunication anyone who still adhered to him. The news of Cromwell's sensational triumph at Dunbar, and Charles II's treaty with the Scots presbyterians, completed the discrediting of the royalist cause in Ireland.[145]

In reality the Irish would have been happy to bring to an end the killing and the physical destruction of their country but for one stumbling block: England's refusal to let them practise the Catholic religion.[146] Cromwell's Declaration of January 1650 had made it brutally clear that the price of maintaining their religion would be a struggle to the death. The instructions issued to the parliamentary commissioners for Ireland in December of the same year demonstrated that Cromwell's policy was still in force.[147] The eighteen instructions, heavily religious and anti-Catholic in content, must have been congenial to the commissioners – Lord Deputy Ireton, Lieutenant-General Edmund Ludlowe, Colonel John Jones, Miles Corbet and John Weaver – deeply committed puritans all. According to the first instruction, their mandate in Ireland was 'the advancement of religion and propagation of the gospel ..., and ... suppression of idolatry, popery, superstition and prophaneness.'[148] Yet a few months after their arrival in January 1651 the parliamentary commissioners, backed by the Lord Deputy Henry Ireton, wrote to the Council of State proposing a more tolerant and compassionate approach than their instructions permitted. They had apparently been moved by several petitions from inhabitants expressing loyalty to parliament, but wishing to know what assurance they could expect for the enjoyment of their religion, lives, liberties and estates. The commissioners recommended giving the Irish the assurances they sought; otherwise the soil would go untilled, flocks untended, the war would be lengthened indefinitely, and the financial burden to England would be incalculable. The Council of State and the Rump referred the letter back and forth to each other without taking action on its statesmanlike proposal, and Ireland descended deeper into the maelstrom of violence.[149]

When Cromwell left Ireland at the end of May 1650, Henry Ireton took charge, with the title lord deputy. Other soldiers had demonstrated greater military flair: Sir Charles Coote, Commissary-General Reynolds, Lord Broghill, even Colonel John Hewson, but none matched Cromwell's political and religious outlook as closely as his own son-in-law. A month later Edmund Ludlowe joined Ireton as lieutenant-general of horse.[150] For the remainder of the summer they had little trouble in their sweep of Munster garrisons, their main obstacle being the pestilence which ravaged Irish and parliamentary troops alike. Resolving to combat this foe with the weapons of divinity, Ireton proclaimed the first of eight fast days on 6 August.[151]

Limerick

In spite of a nearly uninterrupted chain of parliamentary victories, the Irish refused to give in. For every unit that was decapitated another seemed to sprout in its place. Lord Inchiquin raised 3000 recruits in Kerry during July, while Lord Clanricarde in Connacht was able to get 4500 men into the field in October.[152] Hugh O'Neill was in charge of the garrison at Limerick, while Lord Dillon governed Athlone. Limerick was the town of greater importance. A large and well-defended city, it boasted a position of great natural strength. Sitting athwart the river Shannon where it divides, its sturdy walls were shaped like an hourglass or figure-of-eight. These geographical advantages were vitiated by the bitter factionalism that seethed within the town walls. It was with great difficulty that even Hugh O'Neill, the defender of Waterford and Clonmel, was admitted as military commander of the city.[153]

Aware of the divisions within the city, Ireton was confident he could exploit them and accomplish the surrender of both Limerick and Athlone before another winter set in. He therefore divided his army, leaving Sir Hardress Waller in charge of the siege of Limerick, while he went to join Sir Charles Coote at Athlone.[154] By the beginning of October, however, Ireton had given up Athlone as a bad job and rejoined Waller before Limerick. Ten days later he decided that it was too late in the year to recommence active siege operations, and so withdrew to winter quarters. Yet if he had made a vigorous attack on Limerick any time during the preceding months he would almost certainly have toppled it. As O'Neill had told Ormonde, there was no ammunition in the city.[155]

In May, Ireton took his army on a sweep through county Clare on the north side of the Shannon. After several victories against Clanricarde's forces, victories which Ireton attributed to their having first set aside a day for seeking the Lord, he led his army again towards Limerick.[156] This time his preparation for the siege had been thorough. By the time he arrived opposite Limerick there was already a flotilla of parliamentary ships in the mouth of the Shannon. The ships blocked the estuary, kept the army supplied with provisions, and later brought up the heavy guns for siege operations.

On 14 June, Ireton summoned the town to surrender and at the same time started a bombardment of the castle with twenty-eight guns and two mortars. A number of soldiers fleeing in boats from the castle were shot and killed by the besiegers, while others who fell into the hands of Colonel Ingoldsby's men were spared and well treated. Fourteen men who surrendered to Colonel Robert Tothill's men on the promise of free quarter were put to the sword on the colonel's orders when they reached the shore. This wanton act of cruelty shocked enough officers, including Ireton himself, to have Tuthill brought before a court martial and stripped of his command.[157]

On the third day of the bombardment the defenders asked to treat, but the talks foundered on Ireton's refusal to countenance any security for the practice of the Catholic religion. O'Neill therefore prepared for a long siege and the ordeal of starvation. On 18 June he began expelling people who were of no use to the town's defence. In order to squeeze the town and possibly break its morale, Ireton ordered the people driven back, warning O'Neill that in future any civilians who fell into their hands would be more harshly dealt with. O'Neill refused to admit them and expelled even more. Ireton then ordered four of them killed as an example to the others, but the order was misunderstood, and to his horror all forty of them were put to the sword. Even this bloodbath did not stop O'Neill from continuing to drive civilians out of the town. Inconclusively the siege dragged on through the summer and into the autumn, with the daunting prospect that the besiegers might witness a third year before Limerick surrendered. Ireton was kept supplied with food, munitions and money in quantities that the Irish could only dream of, yet he seemed incapable of bringing the town to its knees. During the spring and summer of 1651 parliament sent an additional 9000 troops to Ireland, but disease, cold, hard marching, and enemy attack 'considerably wasted' them. By the end of October, 2000 had been lost at Limerick alone. Minor triumphs were offset by minor setbacks, and Ireton's main effort seems to have gone into building a great fort to shelter his men.[158] Throughout the siege he had to contend with dedicated efforts to relieve the town by forces under the command of Lord Muskerry and Colonel David Roche.[159] Moreover, the concentration of parliamentary forces at Limerick and in Connacht gave roving enemy bands the opportunity to make trouble in Leinster. In August, 2400 hostile troops were reported within 6 miles of Dublin itself.[160]

It is difficult to avoid the impression that had Cromwell been in charge of the siege it would have been over much sooner. The lord lieutenant would surely have found a way of exploiting the fact that two thirds of the town wanted to sue for peace, that the plague continued to rage within its walls, and that the people were starving. Ireton, however, lacked Cromwell's military decisiveness. For almost four months he relied on starvation to win the victory for him. Not until 27 October did he locate a sector of the town wall which lacked an earthen backing. Once he unleashed his battery against it, the masonry collapsed forthwith. As the storming party was about to enter, the defenders gave up their insistence on religious freedom, and surrendered under the articles that Ireton had offered them several months earlier. The soldiers were allowed to march out unarmed. The townsfolk lost their lands and houses. Twenty-two notables were excluded from mercy, including two bishops, a priest, Major-General Purcell and Governor O'Neill. Of these, seven were executed, including Purcell and one of the bishops, but the council of war found itself divided over the fate of the governor.[161] He had impressed all the parliamentary officers by his courteous and co-operative behaviour after the surrender. When Ireton asked him what he had to say in his own defence, he cogently argued that he had prevailed on the garrison to offer a timely capitulation. Ireton's mind, however, was fixed on the chastisement that O'Neill had administered to the parliamentary troops at Clonmel. Twice he compelled the council of war to vote for O'Neill's death, although some officers, like Ludlowe, reminded him that O'Neill's actions at Clonmel were not pertinent to the present trial. After the second vote Ireton's conscience bothered him, so he referred the case a third time, and did not obstruct his fellow officers when they followed their inclination to save O'Neill's life. The incident sheds interesting light on the officers' sense of honour, and their admiration for O'Neill. Ireton's attitude was harsher than his colleagues', but his ability to listen to them and to change his mind points to a saving flexibility.[162]

The five-month siege of Limerick cost Ireton his life. A few days after he wrote his despatch to the Speaker narrating the siege and its successful conclusion he came down with a bad cold. The weather had turned nasty, and Ireton was run down. He may have caught the infection from Lieutenant-

General Ludlowe, who had contracted his own heavy cold several days earlier. Whatever the cause, Ireton refused to relax his tempo of work. He rode through a storm to Clare, where his cold turned to fever, but he insisted on carrying on. By 26 November he was dead.

Guerrilla Warfare, 1651–2

At the time of Ireton's death the war had already entered a new phase. The capture of Clare Castle by Ludlowe on 5 November and of Galway by Coote the following April meant that virtually all the 350–400 forts and garrisons in the country were in parliamentary hands.[163] Control of the garrisons paradoxically weakened parliament's grip on the country. Pinned down by their responsibilities, the soldiers found it less and less safe to venture outside the walls of their fortresses. The enemy, whose numbers never seemed to diminish, were by contrast free to roam at large wreaking havoc when and where they chose.[164] Defeated in the field and deprived of their urban strongholds, the Irish adopted a classic pattern of guerrilla warfare against the occupying power.

Dispossessed native outlaws known as tories were reported driving away cattle on the outskirts of Dublin as early as June 1650, the month when the Ulster army under the Bishop of Clogher was destroyed. Three months later the three provinces of Munster, Leinster and Ulster were 'much infested with tories'. They were particularly strong in the Wicklow mountains, immediately south of Dublin. Characteristically they conducted lightning raids that were over before the parliamentary foot could be engaged. They then retreated to bogs, woods or mountains where the cavalry could not pursue them. Lacking their own supply lines, except for the occasional shipment from the Duke of Lorraine, they captured the arms and munitions they needed from their enemy. The problem of violence and disorder seemed endless. Every garrison that was reduced inflated the number of tories in the woods, bogs and fastnesses of Ireland. In Leinster and Munster parliament's supporters could not travel 2 miles outside a garrison without an armed convoy. The root of the problem, as the commissioners acknowledged, was parliament's refusal to give the Irish guarantees for the security of their estates. The result was the economic near-collapse of the country. The stock of cattle almost disappeared, while four fifths of the fertile land lay waste and uninhabited.[165]

Between the summer of 1651, when the parliamentary commissioners wrote their doleful report on the condition of Ireland, and the passage of the Act for the Settlement of Ireland thirteen months later, the situation only worsened. As the commissioners appealed for still more recruits 'to attend the motions of a restless, desperate enemy', the army grew to over 33,000 – nearly three times the number Cromwell had brought over in 1649. Moreover, a third of the recruits parliament had sent over the previous year were now dead.[166] Yet in February 1652 the commissioners had to confess that great stretches of the country were still under enemy control in all four provinces. Two and a half years after Cromwell's arrival in Ireland, parliament was still engaged in an unremitting war against the native population. At the end of 1651, 'besides the people generally ready to join with them upon any occasion,' there were said to be 30,000 men in arms against parliament. 5000 rebels fought under Clanricarde against Coote and Venables in Ulster and Connacht, while in Munster Ludlowe confronted a similar number under Lord Muskerry, and in Leinster Colonel Grace led 3000 men against Colonels Ingoldsby and Abbott. At all times there were countless minor skirmishes, sometimes involving up to 2000 of the enemy. As late as the summer of 1652 the parliamentary commissioners reported that they were still engaging enemy armies larger than their own. Yet by that time many of the 34,000 Irish soldiers who would enlist in continental armies during the early 1650s had already departed.[167]

In this guerrilla phase the parliamentary commanders strove to imitate the tactics of their enemies, by denying the tories food and rendering them hateful to the rural population. In county Wicklow, Hewson systematically destroyed the corn and cattle on which they survived during the winter. Because it had been unco-operative in paying its taxes, Sir Hardress Waller laid waste the barony of Burren.[168] Obstructed in his attempts to scour the enemy from the woods and bogs around Enniscorthy, Colonel Cooke also resorted to material destruction:

> In searching the woods and bogs, we found great store of corn, which we burnt, also all the houses and cabins we could find: in all which we found great plenty of corn. We continued burning and destroying for four days: in which time we wanted no provision for horse or man, finding also housing enough to lie in; though we burnt our quarters every morning, and continued burning all day after. He was an idle soldier that had not either a fat lamb, veal, pig, poultry, or all of them, every night to his supper.... I believe we destroyed as much as would have served some thousands of them until next harvest.... Doubtless this is the only way to make a speedy end of these wars.[169]

By 1652 every vestige of the earlier enlightened attitudes espoused by Whalley, Ireton and Ludlowe had vanished. Just before his death Ireton had denounced the Irish clergy as 'these incendiaries of blood and mischief'. In March 1652 Ludlowe opposed any communication with those 'guilty of a bloody and cruel massacre' who had still not 'delivered up those Achans to justice for whom the land mourns.' Colonel Jones too opposed easy terms for 'bloody men'.[170] In April the parliamentary commissioners rejected the articles of surrender negotiated by Sir Charles Coote for Galway because they seemed to ignore the massacre of 1641.[171] In the same month a joint meeting of army officers and parliamentary commissioners at Kilkenny held their own lenity and weakness responsible for encouraging the obstinate resistance of the Irish. Indicting the whole nation for 'blood-guiltiness', they professed to be 'deeply ... affected with the barbarous wickedness of ... these cruel murthers and massacres.' The commissioners' loathing for the Irish was reinforced in May by reading Scoutmaster-General Henry Jones's lengthy abstract of several thousand depositions concerning barbarous cruelty to protestants in 1641 and after. To loathing was added bafflement at the Irish refusal to give up fighting, which they could only ascribe to the 'wickedness and malice of the generality of this people'. Colonel Jones believed that because the Irish were a 'cursed people' Christ had had to fetch instruments farther off to save the country. As one of these instruments he was engaged in nothing less than a holy mission.[172]

Formally speaking, resistance had come to an end in May 1652 with the signing of the Kilkenny articles between the parliamentarians and the Irish in Leinster. The forces in that province agreed to lay down their arms by 1 June. In Munster the Irish forces were expected to deliver up their weapons on 4 June, while those in Connacht and Ulster were asked to follow suit two days later. Prisoners of war were to be exchanged, and a general pardon was issued, except to those implicated in the 1641 massacre, and to 'priests, jesuits, or others in popish orders'. Yet at the end of the year the royalist agent William Heald asserted that 11,000 men still kept up the resistance against parliament.[173]

The Land Settlement

If the Irish were a cursed people, then it was justifiable to clear them out and replace them with a new population. In a report drafted at the beginning of 1652 the commissioners called for the creation of four allotments out of sixteen Irish counties, in addition to a pale between the Boyne and Barrow rivers. Even though the war was not ended, the adventurers for Irish land should be invited to come and settle. They should be joined by soldiers, to whom land would be given in lieu of their arrears of pay. Peasants willing to lay down arms and accept parliament's protection should be allowed to pursue agriculture, but not, apparently, within the pale. To enforce the segregation of the two populations any soldier who married an Irishwoman would lose his place in the army and his arrears, and be made incapable of inheriting lands in Ireland.[174] It soon became evident that total exclusion of the native population from the pale was impractical, so the policy was modified to permit peasants willing to accept parliament's protection to live in areas under parliamentary control. This exemption did not apply to the gentry, who were to be completely dispossessed of their lands.[175] The adventurers for Irish land, however, took a jaundiced view of the invitation to come and settle the country. Perfectly aware of 'the multitude of tories that yet swarm', in the spring of 1652 they demanded a guarantee of protection against tories and rebels, and they strenuously objected to being obliged to occupy their property within three years.[176]

Overriding the misgivings of the adventurers, parliament passed the Act for the Settlement of Ireland on 12 August 1652.[177] The act's preamble announced that it was 'not the intention of parliament to extirpate that whole nation, but that mercy and pardon, both as to life and estate may be extended to all husbandmen, plowmen, labourers, artificers and others of the inferior sort.' None the less the body of the act was given over to defining categories of people who were excepted from pardon as to life and estate. They included everyone who had participated in the rebellion of 1641, all jesuits and priests who had abetted the rebellion or war, 105 notables listed by name, and all those in arms against parliament who did not lay down their arms within twenty-eight days. Gardiner estimated that under these provisions no fewer than 80,000 people were liable to the death penalty.[178] In addition, all papists who had not 'manifested their constant good affection to the interest of the Commonwealth of England' were to forfeit a third of their estates, the other two thirds to be assigned in whatever part of Ireland parliament deemed fit. The hard reality was that parliament needed every acre of Irish land it could lay its hand on. To honour the longstanding pledge to the Irish adventurers alone would require about a million acres. By 1652 not less than £1.75 million was owed to the soldiers for their service there. Thus, while little attempt was made to hound the people liable to the death penalty, all Catholic landowners, with very rare exceptions, were transplanted to Clare and the western counties of Connacht. More than half the landmass of Ireland was transferred to adventurers and soldiers.[179] In parliament's view, Ireland was by the summer of 1652 conquered and open for colonization. To the officers it was a blank sheet 'ready to have anything writ in it that the state shall think fit.' In the event this was too rosy a view, for violent resistance continued long after the Act of Settlement. An apter metaphor than a blank sheet, given 'the miserableness of this place', was, in John Percivall's view, 'the first chaos'.[180]

From 1651 onward Ireland had been afflicted by great hunger.[181] It is worth noting that this was a recent development. As late as 1650 the plenitude of Ireland was such that provisions were cheaper there than in England.[182] By the end of 1651 that situation had reversed itself, and the price of bread was much higher than in England.[183] Major Benjamin Smyth discovered in county Clare that 'the people die under every hedge ... and [it] is the saddest place ... as ever was seen.' From Kilkenny it was reported in May 1652 that many inhabitants were reduced to eating their plough horses to stay alive. Elsewhere the inhabitants ate grass and green corn. A year later widespread starvation was reported in Wexford. The effects of starvation were compounded by the plague which swept across the country in 1652.[184] The new settlers were dismayed to discover the drawbacks of occupying a graveyard. Destroying the population had reduced the value of the land almost to zero.[185]

Sir William Petty estimated that Ireland's population fell from almost 1.5 million in 1641 to 850,000 in 1652, a loss of over 600,000.[186] Given what we know about the low price of food until 1650, it is likely that most of the depopulation occurred between 1650 and 1652. As we have already seen, this nightmare could have been largely avoided had the parliamentarians been willing to grant the Irish their land and the practice of their religion. In a dignified statement dated 4 August 1652 Sir Phelim O'Neill and sixteen other Irish leaders declared their willingness even to give up their lands,

> but since you, the ministers of so powerful a state deny us those favours, and concessions which are usually given by the swaying hand to a people inclining to submission, we do invoke the Lord of hosts to be the judge of what innocent blood may be spilt hereafter, and we beseech the omnipotent God to protect us from the violence of such as thirst after Catholic blood and our extirpation.[187]

Three years later the guerrilla war continued almost unabated, and the three provinces reserved to the English still swarmed with tories.[188]

Much as the parliamentarian authorities dreamt of eradicating Roman Catholicism in Ireland, that goal was beyond their reach. Two thirds of the soldiers sold their arrears to their officers, and no more than 12,000 settled in Ireland.[189] The reluctance of the majority of the rank and file to sink roots in a foreign land effectively sabotaged the vision of a protestant yeomanry tilling the soil of Ireland.

12

The Conquest of Scotland,
July 1650 to September 1651

By 1650 the parliamentary regime had accumulated a great many grudges against its erstwhile allies in Scotland. Seven years earlier, the Scots had sent an army south of the Tweed to help parliament defeat the king. In return parliament had promised to adopt the presbyterian system of church government in England. Within a short time each side had disappointed the other. Except at Marston Moor the Scots' military contribution was lacklustre. For its part, parliament was less than punctual in meeting the payments it had promised to keep the Scots army in the field. Nor did it hasten to impose presbyterianism upon England. The system that was eventually voted was, as Robert Baillie sniffed, but a 'lame erastian presbytery'.[1] In 1645 the founding of the New Model Army had led to the departure of several high-ranking Scottish officers from the parliamentary army. Over the next two years the Scots grew more and more distressed by what they heard of the religious and social radicalism within the army. Led by the Duke of Hamilton, Engagers signed an agreement with Charles I, and invaded England in his support during the summer of 1648. The invasion, however, was doomed by the fierce opposition of the Covenanters under the Marquess of Argyle. When after his triumph at Preston Cromwell took the army into Scotland he was cordially received by the Covenanters. Upon his departure a month later Cromwell left about 1500 troops at Argyle's request to help the Covenanters maintain their ascendancy over the Engagers.[2]

The execution of Charles I extinguished this Independent–Covenanter entente. Revolution in England provoked a counter-revolutionary realignment of forces in Scotland, whereby a majority of the Covenanters or Kirk party joined with the Engagers to resist the English. By January 1650, thanks in part to the failure of Charles II's cause in Ireland, the Kirk party was able to extract a high price for its support of the royalists. In his politically weakened condition Charles II had no choice but to swallow a bitter pill by swearing allegiance to the Covenant, 'which', Alexander Jaffray wrote, 'we knew from clear and demonstrable reasons, that he hated in his heart.'[3]

Fairfax's Resignation

It was this alarming metamorphosis, by which first English and then Scottish presbyterians turned into militant defenders of the monarchy, that prompted the Rump to recall Cromwell from Ireland early in 1650. When he finally consented to come home at the end of May, it was to a heartfelt welcome from the republican establishment.[4] The political crisis he had to face had already blown into major proportions. With Charles II proclaimed King of Scotland, and now about to land there and be greeted with 'all signs of joy' from the people, members of the Rump were in no doubt that war was around the corner.[5] On 20 June the Council of State grasped the nettle by resolving on an invasion of Scotland in order to protect England itself from being invaded.[6]

Parliament hoped that Fairfax and Cromwell would together lead the expedition northward, but there were grounds for anxiety about how far Fairfax could be relied upon. Not only had he conspicuously refused to associate himself with the king's trial and execution; in the autumn of 1649 he had avoided taking the Engagement to be loyal to the Commonwealth without king or House of Lords. By the beginning of 1650 rumours were already in the air that the leaders of the Rump foresaw the need to replace Fairfax as commander-in-chief.[7] It was widely known that he had scruples about declaring war against their old ally, so no one was surprised when in June 1650 he demurred. To satisfy themselves that he really was immovable, the Council of State sent Cromwell, St John, Whitelocke, Lambart and Harrison in an unavailing attempt to talk him around. Cromwell appears to have made a sincere effort to prevail upon his commander, but Whitelocke believed that he and the others 'did not overmuch desire' to dissuade Fairfax, and there is reason to believe that he was right.[8] Undeniably Fairfax's resignation was a grave blow to the regime; on the other hand the prospect of becoming commander-in-chief must have appealed to Cromwell. His main concern, therefore, was not to change Fairfax's mind, but to control the political damage caused by his retirement. This goal was achieved by having Fairfax attribute his demurral to health reasons rather than a difference of principle.[9]

Preparations for Invasion: Propaganda and Logistical Support

Having been named commander, Cromwell set out almost at once for the north. In early July he was in Newcastle, organizing the expedition, holding a fast with his officers, and hearing sermons by five preachers.[10] As he waited for men, money and *matériel*, Cromwell wasted no time preparing the political ground for his advance. Just as he had done in Ireland the previous year, he worked to build a party for himself by writing to key political figures and striving to undermine their allegiance to the king.[11] Much of this work was carried on in secret, but for public consumption he penned two army declarations: one 'to the people of Scotland'; the other 'to all that are saints, and partakers of the faith of God's elect in Scotland.' The address to the people merely assured them that they had nothing to fear from the army. The one to the saints expressed 'tenderness' towards them as 'our brethren', but taxed them for their alliance with a completely untrustworthy king. On the religious issue he implored them to soften their rigidity. 'Are we to be dealt with as enemies because we come not to your way? Is all religion wrapped up in that or any one form? ... We think not so.'[12] Developments over the next few months would demonstrate Cromwell's effectiveness in planting doubts in sincere minds, and weaning Scots from their allegiance to Charles.

Important as the work of political subversion was, the primary task in the summer of 1650 was military. Collecting the soldiers was apparently easy: by mid-July there were eight cavalry and eight infantry regiments at Newcastle, numbering over 16,000 men. Confident of the quality of his men, Cromwell was none the less disquieted by reports that the Scottish general David Leslie disposed of at least twice as many. He therefore pressed for more recruits to bring the invading force up to 25,000. Over the next year a further 8500 men were raised and sent, but, owing to a punishing attrition rate, it was not until 1651 that Cromwell's force reached 20,000 effectives.[13] One of the new foot regiments that he took across the border with him on 22 July had been leaderless because Colonel Bright suddenly threw up his commission over a difference of opinion with his general. The manner in which Bright was replaced was an interesting exercise in army democracy. Instead of merely imposing the commander he wanted – George Monk – Cromwell took the precaution of consulting the regiment first. When they heard Cromwell's nominee their reaction was vehement. '*Colonel Monk*! ... What! to betray us? We took him not long since, at Nantwich prisoner: We'll have none of him.' The next day Cromwell sent his agents back with a fresh name – Lambart – at which the men threw up their hats in the air and shouted, 'A Lambart! a Lambart!' Monk was consoled with a new infantry regiment drawn half from Newcastle and half from Berwick garrisons.[14]

Logistical support was the key to the formidable effectiveness of Cromwell's inferior numbers during their twelve-month campaign. A fleet initially of fifteen but in the end 140 ships ranging between 100 and 500 tons' displacement was employed to transport arms, ammunition, food and supplies from London, Harwich, Lynn and Newcastle. Flatboats were also built in Lynn and Newcastle and shipped to Scotland to transport troops and supplies on the Forth. Once Leith was captured, the English were able to exploit their superiority in firepower. Their heavy guns numbered over fifty pieces. At least 1300 draught horses were required to pull the gun carriages and wagons that made up the artillery train.[15]

In the face of Leslie's systematic policy of evacuating population and live-stock and destroying the food supply in the path of the invading army, virtually all food had to be imported from England or Holland. On the march each soldier was required to carry several days' ration on his back. In principle one day's ration consisted of just under a pound of biscuit, half a pound of cheese and a pint of small beer. Abundant quantities of wheat and beer were sent to the army, but no meat. We hear of Scottish women being hired to brew beer and bake bread in Edinburgh and Leith after capture of these cities in September 1650. Most of the food was supplied by London merchants, of whom the biggest was John Gauden, but at least some cheese was shipped from Holland or Hamburg. Food also included animal prov-ender, since for several months the Scots succeeded in denying the English access to grazing land. During the Scottish expedition 2800 tons of oats and about 10,700 tons of hay, mostly from East Anglia, Surrey and Kent, were shipped to the northern kingdom.[16]

In view of these vast quantities it is no surprise that the system of logistical support did not always run smoothly. Especially before the cap-ture of Leith in September there were blockages and bottlenecks in the supply lines. That summer the soldiers were frequently short of food and drink, and for a time had to do without tents. Bad food ('corrupt bread') and short measure were chronic complaints.[17] Overall, however, the provisioning and equipping of the army were an impressive achievement, which reflected the quality of Cromwell's generalship. As he had done at the time of the Irish expedition, Cromwell kept in touch with the highest authorities in the government to ensure that the needs of his army were diligently attended to.[18] It was this support that made victory with fewer numbers in a foreign country possible. By enabling Cromwell to keep his forces concentrated, it denied the Scots the opportunity to weaken them by picking off small parties of foraging and looting soldiers.[19]

Less important than food, arms and supplies was pay, since there was

Table 12.1 Pay of the parliamentary forces in Scotland, July 1650 to
September 1651

No. of weeks paid	Horse and dragoons	Foot and artillery
July 1650	4	4
September	4	4
December	6	6
January 1651	1	1
February	2	8
April	5	10
June	6	6
September	7	11
Total	35	50

Source: SP28/69–80, *passim*.

often nothing for the soldiers to spend their money on. Nevertheless, the
treasurers at war doled out £1,210,000 to the Scottish expedition between
May 1650 and December 1651.[20] Impressive as this sum was, the expeditionary army was paid much less faithfully than the forces stationed
in England during the same period. At home the soldiers were paid month
by month with almost clockwork regularity. In Scotland, during the sixty-
four weeks of active service, the foot and artillery were paid just over
three-quarters of the time, while the horse and dragoons only got just over
half what was due to them.

Table 12.1 does not show how erratic pay really was. Although
warrants were issued, the soldiers actually received nothing between the
time they entered Scotland and the battle of Dunbar. From the end of
December until 13 February they got only a week's pay. From mid-June
until 1 September 1651 they again got nothing. On occasion officers
borrowed money to pay their men.[21] There was only one exception to this
pattern of haphazard remuneration: Oliver Cromwell received his £10 a day
as commander-in-chief punctually, and usually in advance. For the rest of
the army the consequence of being erratically paid was a lot of grumbling in
the ranks, and in the spring of 1651 a good deal of desertion.[22]

Preliminary Engagements: Musselburgh and the Pentland Hills

When the English army crossed the border into Scotland on 22 July it
surveyed a deserted country. The Scots general David Leslie had stripped
the border region between the river Tweed and Edinburgh of its food and

population. He had also entrenched his immense army behind a fortified line running from Edinburgh to Leith. If he remained behind his defences his position was nearly impregnable. Any attempt by the English to outflank Leslie by marching west of Edinburgh ran the risk that they would be attacked in the flank or have their supply lines cut.[23]

The problems that the Scottish army did face were largely ideological. All year long there had been a protracted struggle over whether to allow 'malignants', as Charles's non-presbyterian supporters were called, into the army. In June the hardline Covenanters had triumphed when a commission was set up for purging the army, while at the end of July the king was told to depart from the army following a disturbing display of his popularity when he appeared at Leith. Several days in August were devoted to expelling 4000 unrepentant cavaliers. These measures sapped the morale of the officer corps, while eliminating many seasoned fighters from the rank and file.[24]

By the end of July the English army had occupied Dunbar, Musselburgh and Haddington, the vanguard taking up positions just 6 miles from Scottish outposts. Provisions were unloaded at Dunbar, but fewer ships arrived from Newcastle than expected. Hardship increased when armed country people suddenly appeared and cut off the supplies coming by road from Northumberland.[25]

Ignoring these setbacks, Cromwell pushed his army to the outskirts of Leith on 29 July. With the support of four men-of-war he subjected the port to intense bombardment. Torrential rain prevented the soldiers from pressing home the offensive, however, and the Scots refused to be drawn outside the walls. All night long the soldiers stood in battle order. By the morning of the 30th, having subsisted on bread and water for six days, they were in a sorry state, and Cromwell decided to withdraw.[26] While they trudged towards Musselburgh they had to fend off persistent attacks on their rear, during one of which Lambart was wounded and briefly taken prisoner.[27] They arrived dirty and tired at their camp, but were able to take little rest. That night, between three and four o'clock, the Scots sent 800 troopers, the cream of their cavalry, to fall upon the sleeping enemy. They succeeded in breaking past the guards and four bodies of horse before Fleetwood's and Lambart's regiments finally drove them off, killing Major-General Montgomery and wounding Colonel Strachan.[28]

After this bruising encounter Cromwell decided to suspend military activity for a while and resume the battle for his adversaries' hearts and minds. As a goodwill gesture he sent back sixty wounded prisoners, lending his own coach to ferry them. Then he wrote to the General Assembly of the Kirk, taxing them with censorship and intolerance, and rating them for their alliance with Charles II: 'a covenant made with death and hell'. 'Is it therefore infallibly agreeable to the Word of God, all that you say? I beseech you, in the bowels of Christ, think it possible you may be mistaken.' He wrote to David Leslie in the same vein, professing also his great affection 'to the honest people of Scotland'. The Covenanters were unimpressed. To Oliver's appeal to re-examine their position they caustically replied, 'Would you have us to be sceptics in our religion?'[29]

Cromwell's next step as he awaited the arrival of the tardy supply ships was to stir up his men spiritually. Much time was spent during the early August days in 'preaching, praying and heavenly communion with God'.[30] At last the desperately needed supplies arrived, and with morale restored Cromwell embarked on another foray. Leaving Dunbar, he took his army to the Pentland Hills south of Edinburgh. Word had reached him that Leslie was running short of food. This inspired Cromwell to think that he might be able to provoke a battle by outflanking the Scots army and cutting it off from its rich hinterland. Leslie responded by stationing the right wing of his army at Coltbrig. As the English edged westward in the direction of South Queensferry, so did the Scots. On 20 August Leslie stationed a strong force on Corstorphine Hill to protect the Stirling road and block English access to the sea. Hunger was beginning to make many in his camp eager for a fight, and he came under intense pressure from the ministers of the Kirk to engage the army, but he refused to let himself be drawn out. The price was the loss of Red Castle and its garrison of eighty defenders.[31]

The last steps in this *pas de deux* were Cromwell's attempt to take control of the road to Stirling, which in turn was countered by Leslie's prompt move westward to block his way. The two armies met at Gogar, and the English drew up in battle order. In anticipation of a decisive battle the English soldiers threw away their tents and knapsacks, but Leslie had chosen his ground so as to frustrate that objective. Between the two armies lay an expanse of bog, a ditch and sheepfolds divided by sod walls.[32]

Cromwell had hoped that he could force Leslie to fight by cutting his supply route. But, now that his own supplies were again running short, he was in real danger of being isolated from his base. His only recourse was to hurry back to Musselburgh. The Scots were only prevented from mauling the English on their retreat by the terribly stormy weather: 'trees ... were blown down, and the rain fell with that force it made my face smart, and so dark we could scarce see our way.'[33]

And so the English fell back to Dunbar, 'the provisions of our army being once more near exhausted and gone, the nights cold, the ground wet, the bloody flux and other diseases prevailing in the army, and the Scots hitherto refusing to fight.'[34] At the beginning of September it looked as if Cromwell had been out-generalled. Not only had he failed to tempt Leslie into a decisive engagement, but he had suffered heavy losses – at first from disease, now increasingly from desertion. By 1 September his 'poor, shattered, hungry, discouraged army' numbered only 11,000 'sound men'. Within a month his expeditionary force had been reduced by a third. Small wonder that a despairing Council of War concluded that there was nothing to be gained by playing cat and mouse with Leslie any longer. The invasion was over; the only question was, could they get back to England alive?[35]

The Battle of Dunbar

The English army now busied itself putting 500 of the sickest men into waiting ships, fortifying the town and establishing a storage depot. This superficial busyness did not conceal the fact that Cromwell was trapped, and, as he later admitted to Hesilrige, at a loss what to do.[36] He had brought his army back to Dunbar with the Scots snapping at its heels. Encamped in the midst of swamps and bogs, and with their back to the sea, it seemed that the invaders were about to be encircled and devoured by a force more than twice their size. Yet Cromwell had one consolation: unlike Leslie he did not have to cope with bitter quarrelling among his officers. They were as bewildered as he,[37] yet they continued to display 'unparalleled unity'. The officers strove to keep morale high by a unleashing a torrent of prayer, and God-seeking. In the midst of these spiritual activities they were also conscious of being borne up by the prayers of the faithful in England.[38]

On 1 September the Scots army occupied the high ground known as Doon Hill overlooking the town. The clergy kept up their unremitting pressure for an engagement with the enemy, and it was at their behest that Leslie sent a detachment to cut off the pass at Cockburnspath, 6 miles south-east of Dunbar (see map 9). In this manner the road to Berwick was blocked against an English retreat, leaving their only mode of escape an evacuation by sea.[39]

In reality the English position was less precarious and the Scottish more vulnerable than first appeared. On each side of the town of Dunbar flowed a little stream. Spott Burn (known then as Brock's Burn) on the south-east descended through a narrow glen about 40 feet deep, which protected the English from a surprise attack by the Scots on the other side. The English camp was also out of the range of the Scots artillery.[40] The only way Leslie could attack was to come down the hill to the plain south-east of the town on the other side of Spott Burn. In contrast to Cromwell, he could boast no unified counsel within his camp. The Committee of Estates never let up in its campaign to throw caution to the winds and pounce on a weakened enemy. He was doubtless more conscious than they of the Scots' own weakness after the summer purges of seasoned officers and men. Moreover, his

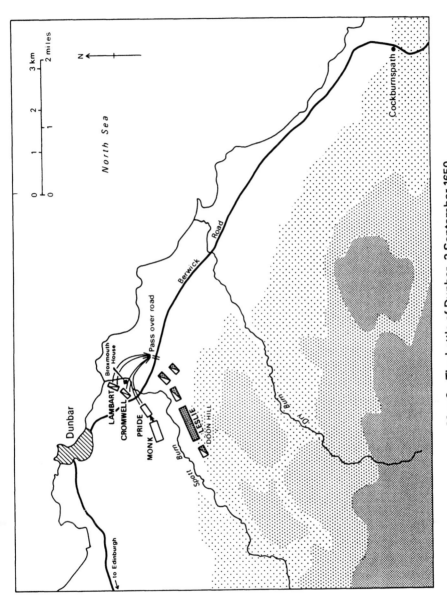

Map 9 The battle of Dunbar, 3 September 1650

army's situation on Doon Hill was far from pleasant. The high ground overlooking the sea exposed the Scots much more than the English to wind, cold and wet.

When Cromwell evacuated the men with dysentery, Leslie thought that he was trying to effect a wholesale retreat.[41] The foot and artillery, he surmised, were being shipped by sea, while the horse would try to force their way past the Scots and get to Berwick. Confident that Cromwell had abandoned any thought of an offensive, Leslie brought his army down the hill on the morning of Monday 2 September.[42] In the course of this manoeuvre he transferred two thirds of the left wing of his cavalry – about 2000 men – to the right. This caused the right wing to edge down towards the sea. His army was now strung along a front 1 mile in length. At four in the afternoon he completed his troop placements by moving the artillery train down the hill.[43] His intention was to fall upon the flank or rear of the the English cavalry as they tried to make good their escape along the coast road. According to Baillie and other sources Leslie would rather have waited until the English were on the march before descending the hill to attack them, but he was browbeaten by the Committee of the Kirk into coming down before the enemy started their march.[44] However, Leslie himself never sought to excuse the disaster on these grounds. Nor was the move down Doon Hill as foolish as it is often said to have been. By preparing to attack the English before they had time to fortify their position he retained the initiative. Equally, he saved his own army from further attrition through sickness and desertion, which would have been inevitable had he stayed on the bleak hilltop. With his crushing numerical superiority he could be forgiven for believing he had Cromwell on the run. He can hardly have thought when he moved off the hill that the English would turn and attack.[45]

That they did attack was thanks to the intense reconnoitring work of the commanders, most notably Lambart. The major-general spent most of 2 September on horseback observing the Scots' troop movements and noting the new posture in which they were drawn up. Through their experienced eyes Cromwell and Lambart both spotted the same weakness in the situation of the Scottish army, and their perception was corroborated by Colonel George Monk. They saw how the Scots' left wing was crowded against the steep slope of Spott Burn glen. Given the superior quality of the English soldiers, they agreed that an assault on Leslie's right wing would not permit the left to rally to its assistance.[46]

In order to concentrate his forces against the right wing, Cromwell had to get the bulk of his army past the front of the enemy's line. At five o'clock in the afternoon on the 2nd he held a council of war on horseback in the fields, so that the officers could all scrutinize the Scottish position.[47] After sundown the discussion continued indoors. Captain Hodgson tells us that many of the colonels wanted to ship the foot – as Leslie assumed they already had – and leave the cavalry to cut their way through the Scots army. But with Cromwell's encouragement Lambart urged the impracticality of such a scheme, and presented the case for going on the offensive. Time did not permit the evacuation of the foot, he pointed out, but in any event there was not room in the ships for more than a fraction of them. If they were able to get the better of the Scottish right wing Leslie's whole army would be imperilled. Because of the hill and the ravine, the Scots would not be able to wheel around quickly enough to meet an attack on their flank. The English could also discharge their heavy guns at the left wing while attacking the right. The discussion in the council of war appears to have been uninhibited and wide-ranging, but in the end Lambart's arguments carried the day, as Cromwell doubtless intended they should. When one officer stepped forward to propose that Lambart should lead the attack next morning, Cromwell freely granted the request.[48]

Both generals ordered their armies to stand in battle order throughout the night. Discipline, however, was slack in the Scots army. The night was so wet and windy that the officers refused to believe in the likelihood of an English attack. Many of them, who were strangers to their men, took shelter in the farmhouses or tents behind the lines. Leslie later pointed to this failing by the officers as the key to his defeat. In the absence of their commanders the soldiers lay down to snatch a few hours of sleep, covering themselves with newly reaped corn against the rain. Horses were unsaddled and allowed to forage. Around two in the morning Major-General Holborne, making his rounds among the foot, gave permission for most musketeers to extinguish their matches.[49]

The English by contrast were on the move all night long. The main part of the army was drawn up, with a field gun in each regiment, opposite the Scots. Cromwell personally supervised the arrangements, riding all night from one regiment to another by torchlight, 'upon a little Scots nag, biting his lips till the blood had run down his chin without his perceiving it, his thoughts being busily employed to be ready for the action now at hand.'[50] For a time the hail and stormy weather screened the English movements from Scottish eyes.[51] Inevitably, however, the reforming of the regiments was not conducted with clockwork precision. During their march Captain Hodgson heard a cornet praying aloud. Exalted by what he had heard, he returned to his own company and encouraged them with an impromptu sermon of his own.[52] In their miserable condition the men needed encouragement from whatever quarter they could get it: 'our bodies enfeebled with fluxes, our strength wasted with watchings, want of drink, wet and cold being our continual companions.'[53] Yet the prospect of battle itself did much to renew their spirits after six weeks of being stymied.

By 4 a.m. the troops movements were nearly complete, and Cromwell was impatient to be on the move. Already the Scots had caught wind of what the English were up to and were sounding the trumpets to rouse their men. Suddenly Lambart was nowhere to be found. As it happened, he was preoccupied in the rear with the ordering of the heavy guns. At last he took up his position at the head of the vanguard that was to spearhead the attack.[54] This brigade, consisting of three regiments of horse – Lambart's, Whalley's and Robert Lilburne's – and two of foot, was drawn back and taken across lower Spott Burn near where it empties into the sea. Lambart now led it along low ground out of sight of the Scots army to the pass over the Berwick road guarded by an enemy detachment. Capturing the pass was necessary in order to protect the passage of the main body of the English army across Spott Burn ford, preparatory to falling on the Scottish right flank.[55]

As Lambart and his brigade neared the pass they were discovered by a party of Scots on their way to make a surprise attack on the English camp. There ensued a fierce clash under moonlight, during which both sides discharged their artillery. After an hour Lambart wrested control of the pass from its defenders, and passed over to confront the main body of the Scottish army.[56]

Lambart's brigade was met with a resolute charge down the hill by Scottish cavalry armed with lances. The English troops recoiled a little under the shock, but quickly rallied. With the help of Cromwell's own horse regiment led by Major Packer they fell on the Scottish flank, and the foot behind them charged the enemy home. Cromwell himself came up behind Lambart's foot regiment and ordered it to incline more to the left in order to have a clear run at the Scottish infantry. It was now daybreak, just before 6 a.m. At that moment the full sun appeared over the sea; Oliver, echoing the psalmist, shouted, 'Now let God arise, and his enemies shall be scattered.' The horse and foot were quickly engaged all over the field. Soon panic gripped the Scottish ranks, and Captain Hodgson heard Cromwell exult, 'I profess they run!' After a second combined charge by the cavalry regiments of Lambart, Fleetwood, Whalley and Twisleton, and the foot regiments of Cromwell and Pride, the Scots' right wing collapsed. Like the horse, the foot had at first been repulsed, but after regrouping they had engaged the Scots' crack infantry regiments 'at push of pike' and overwhelmed them. This main action lasted barely an hour, meaning that the battle was over by 7 a.m. As Hodgson observed, 'they routed one another after we had done their work on their right wing.'[57]

Seeing the cavalry and the cream of the infantry bested, the artillery deserted their station. The rest of the foot then flung down their weapons, and scattered terrified in all directions, unwilling to stand against the remorseless advance of their English counterparts. The English cavalry then rode amongst these panic-stricken men, who became, in Cromwell's words, 'stubble to their swords'.[58] Rushworth, observing the battle from the valley near Broxmouth House, testified, 'I never beheld a more terrible charge of foot than was given by our army, our foot alone making the Scots foot give ground for three quarters of a mile together.'[59]

Meanwhile, having crossed the full breadth of the battlefield, trampling the commanders' tents as they went, the cavalry encircled the left wing of the Scots cavalry, which until now had not struck a blow in the battle. Leslie may have intended to use them as a reserve, but the success of the English advance was so sudden and so devastating that this plan was pre-empted.[60] It was short work for the triumphant Ironsides to cut through these demoralized men. Finally the English came to Leslie's own lifeguard, who bravely stood their ground for a time but were at length sent packing. One correspondent singled out Whalley's regiment for its gallantry during this action.[61] The cavalry then wheeled about and returned the way they had come, charging and mowing down fleeing bodies of the enemy as they went. The experience of many Scots that day is mirrored in Alexander Jaffray's account of how he narrowly escaped death,

> my horse being shot under me, and I having received two wounds in my head, one in my right hand, and another in my back.... While the fourth stroke was coming to have made an end of me, the hand that drew it was diverted, before he could bring his sword from his shoulder, which he was drawing with great passion, to my throat, who was then lying on the ground, not recovered since my horse fell with me, he being lying on my left leg.... Thereafter, I, having gotten quarter, and rendered my arms, was wounded by a thrust in the back, which made me to be in more danger than ever; being thereby unable to walk, I was like to have fallen among the common soldiers. But the Lord provided a gentleman, who took care of me, and having mounted me on horseback, carried me to Major-General Lambart, and by his order to Broxmouth, where my wounds were very carefully [stanched].[62]

The English could scarcely believe their good fortune at having an enemy more than twice as large crumble before their eyes. Of Cromwell Aubrey records that he 'was carried on with a divine impulse; he did laugh so excessively as if he had been drunk; his eyes sparkled with spirits.'[63] According to his familiar practice Cromwell pursued the fleeing soldiers for many miles, but not before giving thanks for the victory. He halted his pursuing horsemen for a few moments to sing Psalm 117.[64]

Tactically the key to the victory was Cromwell and Lambart's perception of the weakness of Leslie's position once his troops had descended Doon Hill. Their brilliance lay in their willingness to act on this perception by attacking with much smaller numbers, rather than waiting for Leslie to attack them. Cromwell again demonstrated his ability as a field commander by massing overwhelming force against a single point. His daring stroke was made possible by the superior quality of the English troops.[65] In a larger sense the victory was the product of England's superior economic might. Mastery of the sea enabled Cromwell to keep his army relatively well fed and supplied. He therefore never had to disperse them to search for food and shelter.

Dunbar was Cromwell's most one-sided victory. The Scottish dead numbered 3000, while almost 10,000 were taken prisoner.[66] On the English side the slain did not exceed twenty men, all of whom had perished in the struggle for the pass. Not a single English soldier was killed during the main part of the battle.

Many of the Scottish prisoners were either wounded or so feeble from lack of food that they posed no menace to the English army. Cromwell released over half of them at once. The others he sent to Hesilrige in Newcastle, intending that they should serve the Commonwealth, perhaps in Ireland. This was not to be. The men endured a rough march to Newcastle. Arriving at Morpeth in a famished condition, they descended upon a garden of cabbages, which they devoured in their entirety. Some of them fell violently ill and died. Hesilrige sent the 3000 who remained to Durham Cathedral, where they continued to die at a great rate from dysentery. By 30 October, when the Council of State asked him to select 2300 men for Irish service, Hesilrige had to confess that he had only 600 healthy men left, most of them Catholic Highlanders, 'they being hardier than the rest'.[68]

Dunbar had far-reaching strategic and political consequences. Having lost almost half his soldiers, Leslie no longer had the manpower to hold his heavily fortified line from Edinburgh to Leith. Both the capital and the port town fell to Cromwell, although Edinburgh Castle held out until late December. Leslie withdrew to Stirling to try to repair his shattered force. The defeat was also a blow to the prestige of the Kirk party, for informed opinion in Scotland blamed it for its purging and interference in military matters.[69] Not surprisingly, the Covenanters refused to hold themselves at fault. Instead they blamed the Committee of Estates for trying to compromise with the royalists. Colonels Archibald Strachan and Gilbert Ker and Sir John Chiesley now attempted to create their own power base by recruiting a new army of godly men in the west. But they could not prevent the rapprochement between Charles and the Committee of Estates, which was consummated with Charles's coronation on 1 January 1651.[70]

Religious Warfare

Immediately after Dunbar, knowing that the war was far from over, Cromwell requested reinforcements from England. The energetic response of the Council of State produced 6000 fresh soldiers over the next several weeks.[71] While he awaited the arrival of these new regiments, Cromwell launched anew his theological offensive. Bolstered by three ministers sent from London,[72] he talked to whoever would listen. One of his converts was Alexander Jaffray, member of the Committee of Estates, who had been wounded and imprisoned at Dunbar. It took Cromwell, Fleetwood and Owen several conversations to persuade Jaffray of God's quarrel with Charles II, and of the correctness of religious toleration. After his conversion Jaffray travelled up and down the country trying to win others to the same opinion.[73] English preaching seems occasionally to have struck an emotional chord. A newswriter records that one congregation responded to a sermon by Colonel Stapleton 'in their usual way of groans.'[74]

While Cromwell did not get very far in his effort to unyoke the Committee of Estates in Stirling from their alliance with the king, he met with an altogether different reception from the Kirk party in Glasgow. In mid-October he visited the western city, accompanied by 9000 soldiers. Patiently he attended a presbyterian sermon in the high church, submitting to long-winded raillery from Zachary Boyd. Cromwell, however, had the last word. He sought out Boyd and overwhelmed the hapless minister with a prayer of two to three hours' duration. Cromwell also took advantage of the opportunity to cultivate Colonel Strachan, who was increasingly disenchanted with presbyterian rigidity.[75] One fruit of the theological offensive was the promulgation by Strachan and Ker of a Remonstrance against fighting for Charles when he had not repented his ways and abandoned the 'malignants'. While still pledging to expel the English from Scotland, they implicitly recognized the triumph of the Independents in England. A number of western army officers went farther than Ker and Strachan, and were not ashamed to call themselves Independents.[76] For his part Cromwell demonstrated his goodwill towards the presbyterians by purging Captain Covell from his own regiment because he denied the divinity of Christ, and holding a day of humiliation for the sins of the army.[77] Showing less subtlety than his commanding officer, Commissary-General Whalley penned an exhortation to Colonel Ker to understand 'the great work [the Lord] is now in these latter days carrying on.... Those that are acquainted with the secrets of God', he went on, 'do clearly see the quarrel is betwixt Christ and the Devil.'[78]

By late November, Cromwell had grown impatient at the slowness of negotiations with the western Covenanters, irritated by the attacks of moss troopers (the Scottish equivalent of the Irish tories) and frustrated at the refusal of Edinburgh Castle to capitulate. Feeling the need of a fresh military victory to refurbish his prestige, he ordered Whalley and Lambart to rendezvous with him at Hamilton for the purpose of bringing the western army to heel. When the other two commanders failed to appear on the appointed day, Cromwell marched his eight regiments back to Edinburgh. Lambart and Whalley turned up two days later, however, clashed with Ker, and on the night of 30 November destroyed the western army.[79] This second military disaster revived the fears of the extreme Covenanters that in resisting Cromwell they were opposing the will of God.[80]

One of their number was Sir Walter Dundas, governor of Edinburgh Castle. Cromwell knew that Dundas was susceptible to the appeal of Independency, and had since September been proselytizing him ardently. In his second letter to Dundas he scolded the presbyterians for their denial of Christian liberty, their reception of Charles II 'like fire into your bosoms', and their prohibition of lay preaching. 'Are you troubled that Christ is preached? Is preaching so inclusive in your function?.... Your pretended fear lest error should step in, is like the man that would keep all the wine out the country lest men should be drunk.'[81] For all his efforts to bludgeon Dundas with doctrine, and to undermine the walls of Edinburgh Castle with gunpowder, Cromwell made little headway before the beginning of December, when great siege guns and mortar pieces arrived at Leith from England. Four days of bombardment from land and sea were enough to bring Dundas to sue for surrender; on Christmas Eve he yielded up the castle on honourable terms.[82] It may be that Dundas's will to resist had been weakened by Cromwell's propaganda, but the English were faintly contemptuous of him for giving up so easily. In defence of Dundas, who had many detractors, it should be remembered that no fortress in the British Isles successfully withstood the full force of Cromwellian artillery.[83]

Cromwell's Illnesses, February–May 1651

By the end of 1650, through a combination of military action, ideological warfare and espionage, Cromwell had reduced the Covenanting party to ruins. Royalists and Engagers were by no means displeased with this turn of affairs. At the same time as Cromwell was undermining the Covenanters, Charles was directing his energies towards becoming the dominant political force in Scotland. Willingly he underwent the self-abasement necessary to get himself crowned at Scone on new year's day 1651. Before and after his coronation he conducted a vigorous recruitment campaign to rebuild Leslie's army and shape it into an instrument loyal to himself. The overriding purpose of this refashioned army was to invade England and restore monarchy there. To this end royalist agents were sent to organize risings in Chester, Liverpool, Hull, Norwich and other centres. Owing to its effective intelligence service, directed by Captain George Bishop and Thomas Scot, the Council of State was able to neutralize the work of these agents many weeks before Charles was ready to launch his invasion. In addition to the recruits sent to Scotland, 4000 new soldiers were raised for the defence of England. Fleetwood was placed in charge of the London region, while Harrison was given responsibility for Lancashire and the north. After an abortive and premature royalist rising in Norwich in December 1650, little more was heard of royalist subversion within England.[84]

Following the capitulation of Edinburgh Castle, the English war effort in Scotland was stalled for over half a year. In part this was due to the winter, which made campaigning impractical for at least three months. But more important was the fragile health of the commander-in-chief. On the day after Dunbar, Cromwell had confided to his wife that he was feeling his fifty-one years: 'I assure thee, I grow an old man, and feel infirmities of age marvellously stealing upon me.'[85] At the beginning of February 1651 he set out on an ill-advised expedition to overrun Fife, the breadbasket of Scotland, but was forced to turn back at Kilsyth because of wind, hail, snow and rain. As he retraced his steps to Edinburgh he fell ill from exposure. Upon his return he also suffered an attack of dysentery. By his own report a few days later, he was recovering from an attack of the intermittent fever or ague, which had so troubled him in his youth. Perhaps more truthfully, towards the end of March he acknowledged, 'I thought I should have died of this fit of sickness.' Other sources confirm that he had been 'desperately sick', and that his afflictions included a bad stomach.[86]

So alarming was this news to the authorities in England that they sent an agent, Jenkin Lloyd, to visit Cromwell and find out how sick he really was, and what could be done to assist his recovery. Lloyd allowed himself to be persuaded that Cromwell's health was 'as good as it hath been at any time in his life.' Taken in by his own optimism, Cromwell began riding in his coach and receiving visitors at the beginning of April. Around the end of the month he had a relapse, and was reported to be ill of the stone. On 16 May he succumbed to his most serious attack, suffering five fits of ague in three days.[87] Those about him were now seriously worried for his life. The Council of State and parliament ordered him to retire to England, where, it was supposed, the air was more salubrious, and his two personal physicians were dispatched to attend him. Cromwell did not obey the order to leave Scotland, and by 9 June his physicians were able to report that he was restored to health.[88]

These prolonged illnesses and relapses, with the idleness they enforced on the army, dampened the soldiers' morale. There was grumbling over lack of pay, while desertion and drunkenness increased. The Scots in turn exploited English discouragement to improve their position, particularly in the west. While they waited for Cromwell to get better, and for the grass to grow and provide fresh fodder for their horses, the English officers could think of only one method of keeping up their spirits: religious exercises. On 3 March they kept a day of humiliation for the army's sins; in April they spent another whole day in prayer; in May there was a fast, and in June another fast. Between relapses Cromwell continued trying to win his enemies 'by love', attending presbyterian sermons in Glasgow and Edinburgh, then arguing scripture verses with clerical and lay opponents.[89]

One of the apparently debilitating effects of illness was that Cromwell became indecisive about military strategy. In May he dithered over whether to invade corn-rich Fife in order to cut off the food supplies upon which Charles depended for his army, or to besiege Leslie in his stronghold at Stirling. His indecision evidently lasted until late July, when he summoned Harrison from the north of England to confer. A new strategy emerged from this parley. Harrison took his 3000 men south to guard against a royalist invasion, and Cromwell began to concentrate his forces at Queensferry.[90]

Inverkeithing

By July the size of the English army in Scotland was over 21,000. It was now the Scots who were outnumbered. News of the shortages of food, boots and saddles in Charles's army, and the downcast spirit of his soldiers, bolstered Cromwell's confidence. While conducting a number of skirmishing and reconnoitring moves towards the west, he proceeded to implement the contingency plan that had been held in reserve since the previous autumn. On the flatboats constructed for the purpose he transported 4000 men across the Firth of Forth under Overton and Lambart's leadership. Cromwell himself remained at Torwood with the remainder of the army. Leslie was now presented with an opportunity and a dilemma. He could attack the smaller force on the north side of the Forth, but he would find it stationed on a narrow, easily fortified peninsula. Alternatively, he could pursue Cromwell's weakened main force on the south side of the Forth. However, Cromwell might just as easily fall back to his stronghold at Edinburgh, and summon reinforcements from Harrison.[91]

In effect Cromwell's forays into the west during July were a blind, designed to divert attention from the east while Lambart and Overton crossed the Firth of Forth. The scheme worked, and the Scots were taken by surprise, which gave the English three days before Major-General Holborne and Sir John Brown hastened towards North Queensferry. Learning that a large force had left Stirling for North Queensferry, Cromwell advanced with his forces on Stirling. This in turn caused the major part of the Scottish army to turn back to that town. Those who had reached Queensferry decided to withdraw. Seeing his opportunity, Lambart went out to attack their rear at Inverkeithing. Although the two sides were about equal in numbers, Lambart inflicted a devastating defeat, slaughtering 2000 Scots and taking a further 1400 prisoner. He lost only eight of his own men in the battle. Once again Lambart covered himself with glory, but it was Cromwell who provided the protection that made the victory possible.[92]

Cromwell now hastened back to Edinburgh to reinforce Lambart. By the end of July he was in Fife with two thirds of the English army, leaving only eight regiments south of the Forth. On 1 August he appeared before Perth, and obtained a bloodless victory the next day. Thus, within the space of two weeks Cromwell and Lambart had transformed the military situation. They had fooled the Scots as to their intentions, and by establishing themselves in Perth, had cut them off from all hope of reinforcements and supplies from the north. The results of Inverkeithing were therefore more decisive than those of Dunbar.[93] The risk that the Scots at Stirling would profit from the opportunity to invade England was one they had taken with their eyes open. Cromwell's paramount objective had been to force the Scots into the field; hence, when they quit Stirling they were fulfilling his plan. If Oliver was to be believed, this extraordinary turn of events had come about because he had waited upon the Lord, 'not knowing what course to take.' In view of his commissioning of the flatboats the previous winter, we may take his avowal of indecision with a pinch of scepticism.[94]

Worcester

Knowing that their annihilation was imminent, we may wonder why Charles and the Scots imagined there was anything to be gained from invading England. There were in fact several reasons why they could legitimately hope for success. The Commonwealth's ablest troops and officers were behind them, unable to oppose their advance southward. In England they would be confronted for the most part by militia units and untried recruits. As they marched through southern Scotland and northern England, the royalists might expect to gather strength, and to exploit the disillusionment of much of the population with republican rule. Charles, furthermore, was weary of Scotland and bullying presbyterians, both lay and clerical. Now that Cromwell had cut him off from his supplies, invasion seemed to offer the only escape from an untenable situation. As the Duke of Hamilton candidly admitted to a friend, 'I cannot tell you whether our hopes or fears are greatest: but we have one stout argument, despair.'[95]

The intuition of Hamilton and others was correct: the invasion was doomed from the start. Once they left the safety of Stirling, their soldiers deserted by the thousand. Upon their entry into England many of the highlanders fell victim to dysentery. The invasion force was ill provided and ill armed. So rudimentary were their weapons that fifty to sixty archers had to make up the numbers in each infantry regiment. This ill-starred expedition attracted the promise of foreign support but not the substance. In England its many potential supporters were discouraged by the laughable ease with which the Norfolk rising had been quashed in December 1650. The arrest the following March of royalist agents who revealed all to save their skins shattered the conspiracy beyond repair. Hardly anyone reported to Charles's standard after he crossed the border at the beginning of August.[96]

Before it penetrated far into England, Charles's army had shrunk to about 12,000.[97] None the less, at the news that they had crossed the border, the Council of State was swept into a whirlwind of activity. Volleys of letters were unleashed against county officials up and down the country, stressing the urgency of the situation, exhorting them to do their duty, and hectoring them at any hint of sluggishness. Almost hourly, according to Whitelocke, messengers fanned out from Westminster with advice and directions for those mustering forces in different regions. The price of defending England while substantial forces were being maintained in Scotland and Ireland meant that by August the monthly assessment had risen to the 'monstrous sum' of £157,096.[98]

Cromwell, Lambart, Fleetwood, Harrison and the Council of State concerted a three-pronged strategy to break the invasion. First, troops were raised in every region to guard against royalist insurrection. Second, Harrison and Lambart, each with 3000 or 4000 horse and dragoons, were assigned to harass Charles's army, Harrison in the vanguard and Lambart in the rear. If possible they were to shepherd the king towards the west and away from London. Third, Cromwell was to bring his mounted regiments of horse and foot, together with a light artillery train – 10,000 troops in all – swiftly south in forced marches to rendezvous with Lambart and

Harrison. Once the three commanders had combined their forces, and augmented them with county militias, they were to hunt down and destroy Charles's army before it could get close to the capital.[99]

In the north-east Thomas Fairfax accepted responsibility for organizing Yorkshire, taking control of Hull in Overton's absence. The Yorkshire Committee set about recruiting 2400 foot. To the west, infantry from the Cheshire and Staffordshire militias were sent to assist Harrison. In late August four great military rendezvous were held in southern England: at Northampton for the Midlands; at Gloucester for Wales and the west Midlands; at St Albans for East Anglia and the south; and at Barnet for the defence of the London region. On 25 August, 14,000 men belonging to trained bands from London, Westminster and the environs were reviewed by the Speaker and members of parliament in Tothill Fields, outside the City walls. As Gardiner rightly observed, the rallying of so many men to the Commonwealth's defence, whether conscripted or not, showed that, however unpopular parliament was, the Scottish invaders were more unpopular still.[100]

While Fleetwood was assigned to London, Colonels Rich and Wauton were sent north with their regiments to swell Harrison's force. On 13 August, Harrison and Lambart met on Haslemoor in Lancashire, and two days later rendezvoused with the Cheshire and Staffordshire infantry at Warrington Bridge on the road to Worcester. Their united forces numbered between 12,000 and 13,000. The soldiers now began breaking down the bridge to block Charles's southward progress. Before they could finish their work the Scots were on the scene. Showing great valour, the king personally led his troops to attack the bridge. Even though he outnumbered the royalists, Lambart at length decided to abandon his position. The dense hedges enclosing the pastures in that region made it impossible to employ cavalry horse effectively. The chronicler of the skirmish paid tribute to the Cheshire foot for standing up to the royalist assault on the bridge for over an hour and a half.[101]

Meanwhile, Cromwell had entered Yorkshire, where he was joined by Thomas Fairfax, who rode with him for 3 miles in his coach. By 22 August he was in Nottinghamshire, and on the 24th he rendezvoused with Lambart and Harrison at Warwick. With Colonel Lilburne standing guard in Lancashire and Fleetwood's brigade stationed at Upton bridge on the river Severn, Charles was hemmed in on every side. On the 27th Cromwell stopped at Evesham. By the time the Essex and Suffolk militia arrived a few days later, his army had swollen to 31,000, in addition to several thousand local levies. The king no longer had the remotest chance of reaching London.[102]

On 25 August Charles's fortunes were dealt another hammerblow.

The Earl of Derby's contingent of 1500 men was annihilated by Robert Lilburne's cavalry regiment and three companies of Cheshire infantry at Wigan.[103]

By now Charles had halted at Worcester. Despite the cordial welcome he received from the citizens, it had not been his idea to make a stand there. He would have much preferred to head straight for London, but his infantry rebelled. After twenty-three days on the road with only one stop for refreshment, and with their shoes worn out, they were ready to give up. The cavalry were scarcely in better shape, not having changed horses since they left Scotland. Demoralized by their failure to attract soldiers to their cause, they began to drown their sorrows in drink. Charles therefore made the best of a bad lot by turning the city into his headquarters and fortifying it. He repaired the fort on the south-east side of the city near Sidbury Gate, and reinforced the city's walls, which had been dismantled only a couple of months earlier, with elaborate earthworks. To make the job of besiegers more difficult he fired the suburbs up to the walls. Finally, he broke down several bridges leading to the city – Upton, Bewdley, Powick and Branceford. His army numbered 12,000 men, barely a third the size of the one he would soon face.[104]

When on 26 August the Earl of Derby and his tiny band limped into Worcester, Charles was so disheartened that he resolved to break out of the city with his horse, leaving the foot to fend for themselves. But the latter caught wind of the king's intentions and threatened instant mutiny if he did not promise to stand by them. When Lambart and Fleetwood recaptured the bridge at Upton a couple of days later, in the process wounding Major-General Massey in the hand and arms, the demoralization of the king's army seemed to be complete.[105]

Cromwell arrived outside Worcester on 28 August, choosing for his headquarters Spetchley, 2 miles south-east of the city. His army, already two and a half times bigger than Charles's, continued to grow until the day of the battle, as county militia regiments streamed in from many parts of the country. By 30 August about one quarter of the army was composed of these militias. The proportion rose the next day with the arrival of the Essex and Suffolk forces, under Sir Thomas Honywood and Colonel Cook.[106]

The abundance of manpower at his disposal made it unnecessary for Cromwell to waste time on a siege. The city of Worcester, lying in the level fields on the east bank of the Severn, was connected to the west bank by a bridge to the suburb of St Johns (see map 10).

On the land side it was encircled with walls fortified by an outwork, Fort Royal, which was connected to the south-east wall. Now in possession of the bridges across the Severn, both at Bewdley, 15 miles to the north, and at

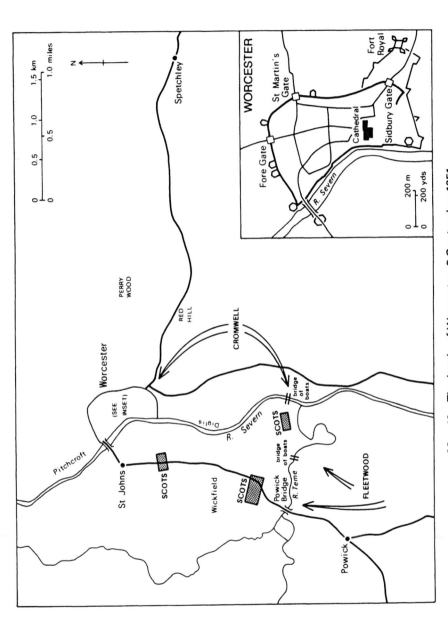

Map 10 The battle of Worcester, 3 September 1651

Upton, 9 miles to the south, the English could cross the river at will. A mile and a half south of St Johns the river Teme flowed into the Severn and was spanned by Powick Bridge, which had been dismantled by the Scots. Cromwell's numerical superiority enabled him to divide his army, thereby threatening a pincer movement against his enemy. As soon as Lambart had captured and restored Upton bridge, Oliver transferred 11,000 men to the west bank of the Severn, under Fleetwood's command. The main body of his army he kept at Perry Wood in a low range of hills near Spetchley.[107]

By the morning of Tuesday 2 September the English arrangements were complete. Boats had been collected to make bridges across the rivers Severn and Teme at their junction, and Major-General Deane with two regiments of foot and two of horse had joined Fleetwood at Upton. Cromwell's plan was not to storm Worcester's fortifications, which had been strengthened 'beyond imagination', but to force the Scots to come out and meet him in the fields west of the Severn, or wait to be attacked on the weaker west side of the city. The battle could have begun that day, but Oliver chose to put it off until Wednesday the 3rd, the anniversary of Dunbar.[108]

Between five and six o'clock on the morning of 3 September, Fleetwood's brigade set out from Upton along the west bank of the Severn. The speed of his advance was limited by his need to stay abreast of the boats that were being brought slowly up the Severn to form the two bridges over which the soldiers would cross the Severn and the Teme. The 8-mile trip to the River Teme took him until one o'clock in the afternoon. When he arrived there, Fleetwood split his regiments, sending the left wing to cross the broken bridge at Powick, and the right wing to run over the bridge of boats next to the Severn. Cromwell simultaneously brought about a third of his remaining forces across the bridge of boats to link up with Fleetwood. Over the bridge they poured, the first to set foot on the battleground being Cromwell himself, leading his men in their battle cry, 'The Lord of hosts', as they engaged the defenders.[109]

From atop the cathedral steeple, where they were holding a council of war, Charles and his officers had witnessed these manoeuvres. They quickly dropped their planned attack on the regiments at Perry Wood. Instead the king took part of his army across the bridge to St Johns, and in person led the charge against Fleetwood's left wing where they were trying to cross at Powick bridge. At first he was successful, but when he returned to the main body, who were struggling with Fleetwood's right wing and Cromwell's reinforcements, he found them in disorder. The Scots foot had fought manfully at first, using the thick hedges for cover, and fighting from field to field. But, when the parliamentary musketeers fired a second salvo, they 'gave back violently and forced the king to retreat into the town.'[110]

Thus defeated on the west side of the Severn, the royalists regrouped on the east side, and late in the afternoon the second phase of the battle commenced. While Cromwell and Fleetwood were still preoccupied on the west side, Charles seized the opportunity to attack the force which Cromwell had left near Perry Wood. The king could still call upon Leslie's cavalry at Pitch Croft, which so far had taken no part in the fighting.[111] Accordingly, the royalist horse and most of the foot thundered out of St Martin's and Sidbury gates for an attack on Red Hill, where Lambart and Harrison were stationed with the regiments of Whalley, Disbrowe, Pride, Cooper, Tomlinson, Cobbett and the militias. Leslie himself was of little help, but Charles, with his own and the Duke of Hamilton's regiments of horse, broke a regiment of foot and forced back a considerable body of parliamentary horse. But his success was short-lived, for Cromwell was able to lead his troops back and turn the tide of battle. There were three more hours of close fighting in which the Surrey, Essex and Cheshire militias played a notable part. Most memorable was their gallantry as they pursued their foe right up to the mouth of cannon planted upon the mount and works of Fort Royal. Cromwell himself tried to halt the butchery by riding up and down the ranks of the royalist infantry offering them quarter, 'whereto they returned no answer but shot.'[112] He then poured reserve upon reserve into the battle until the royalists were pushed back into Fort Royal and then behind the city walls.[113]

Now, after sundown, began the third phase of the battle, the struggle for Worcester itself. Cromwell hurled all his troops against the city, keeping none in reserve. The Essex militia took Fort Royal, and at once turned its guns against the royalists. Within the walls there was bitter and bloody fighting from street to street. Before long the foot had thrown down their arms and sought safety in flight. The cavalry under the king's own command still disputed the streets after everyone else had given up. Afterwards the royalist witnesses were unanimous in their paeans to the king's suicidal courage. Time and again he had led his troops in person against the enemy, evidently preferring death in the hopeless struggle to imprisonment.[114] Massey roused himself from his sickbed to make a stand, but because of his weakness could not prevail. Eventually the Duke of Hamilton and Major-General Middleton were wounded, and many of the other cavalry officers were either dismounted or slain, while David Leslie 'rode up and down as one amazed, or seeking to fly he knew not whither.' Later there would be recriminations on account of 'the cowardice of the Scottish horse, who hardly stood one charge.' Many of them evidently escaped through Fore Gate and made for Bewdley. In the end even Charles could find no one to obey him, and so after a hurried conference he fled with an improvised lifeguard of 600 mounted men. The battle was over by 8 p.m.[115]

The only task that remained for Cromwell's troops was to herd the last bodies of royalist resisters down to the quay, where they were taken prisoner and locked in the cathedral. One of these prisoners was Colonel Edward Wogan, against whom Cromwell nursed a longstanding grudge on account of his desertion to the royalists in 1647, and his success in eluding capture at Duncannon in 1649. Ever resourceful, he broke out with fifty of his comrades-in-arms after midnight and galloped northward in pursuit of the king. According to one account, Wogan and his men were responsible for saving Charles from capture that night.[116]

On Thursday morning Worcester and its environs were a scene of carnage and desolation. Dead bodies strewed the ground from Powick to the bridge at St Johns and from Sidbury Gate to Perry Wood. Within the walls, streets and buildings were choked with corpses. Soldiers, according to Major-General Harrison, 'plucked lords, knights and gentlemen out of holes.' Everywhere was the stench of death. The tally of the slain was estimated at between 2000 and 3000 royalists and fewer than 200 parliamentarians. Prisoners were said to number between 6000 and 7000, while perhaps 3000 cavalry escaped northward.[117]

For several days remnants of the Scots cavalry were hounded from town to town as they attempted to regain their native country. Charles himself was no longer with his troops. On the night of the battle he had broken away with sixty of his closest followers and, after sheltering at Boscobel, near Shrewsbury, had turned southward again. Six weeks later, following a series of fabulous adventures, he reached the south coast, where he boarded a ship for France.[118] The men he left behind did not fare so well. Constantly harassed on their journey northward, they had to contend with army and garrison forces by day and 'the clamorous country' by night. When they stuck together they were relatively safe, but if they straggled, or fell asleep from exhaustion on their horses, 'we might hear by their cry what the bloody country people were doing with them.'[119]

This popular antagonism to the Scots invaders is further evidence of how little support Charles had garnered for the project of reclaiming his kingdom. Loudly as they may have groaned under the financial burdens of the republic, and keenly as they may have resented the dominance of new men in local government, the English people in 1651 had no wish to see their country overrun by a foreign army. The contrast with 1639 is striking. In that year people had reacted either passively or with enthusiasm when a Scottish army had humiliated Charles I by invading and occupying the northern counties. The anger shown in 1651 to the alien soldiers, together with the massive outpouring of militia support at the battle of Worcester, testifies to the widespread if temporary favour enjoyed by the Commonwealth. Parliament shortly attempted to consolidate its unaccustomed popularity by reducing the size of the military establishment and thereby cutting its outlay by over £420,000 a year.[120]

On 12 September, Cromwell arrived in London to a hero's welcome. As he rode into Westminster by way of Acton and Kensington, the Council of State, members of parliament, the London magistrates and the City militia escorted him in pomp. Throughout his progress the streets were lined with shouting crowds, while cannon and musketry saluted his arrival in Whitehall. The following day 4000 of the prisoners taken at Worcester were paraded through the capital and encamped in the New Artillery Ground. The government then meted out varied punishments to them. The Earl of Derby and four others were executed. Leading Scots such as Lauderdale and David Leslie were kept in confinement till the Restoration, though Massey and Middleton effected their escape. Some of the common prisoners were sent to Ireland and Bermuda, while the rest, if they had not already died in England, were eventually sent home.[121]

The Political Settlement

It remained to complete the political settlement of Scotland. When Cromwell quit that country in August he left behind one of his ablest lieutenants, George Monk, with 5000–6000 troops to complete the country's subjugation. This task Monk accomplished with his usual adroitness. On 14 August Stirling Castle fell to him. The key to its surrender was artillery: mortars and heavy cannon transported by water. In the meantime he had sent Colonel Matthew Alured to take Alyth, where the remnant of the Committee of Estates made its headquarters. This done, Monk turned his attention to the last major Scottish stronghold, Dundee. Bad weather frustrated the artillery barrage at the end of August, so, to overcome the garrison's obstinacy, Monk decided on a storm. After half an hour of fierce fighting on 1 September the town was overrun and between 400 and 800 soldiers and townsmen put to the sword. The surviving population were plundered for a fortnight by the victorious soldiers.[122] Scottish political independence was now at an end. So many high-ranking prisoners had been taken at Alyth and Worcester that, as Marchamont Needham scoffingly observed, 'the nobility of Scotland that are at liberty may all sit about a joint-stool.'[123] Late in October eight commissioners were named to administer Scotland under the terms of the *Declaration ... concerning the Settlement of Scotland* adopted by Parliament on 24 December. The *Declaration* stipulated that there would be (1) religious toleration; (2) political union with England; (3) reparations to be paid out of the estates of the crown and leading Scottish royalist landowners; and (4) amnesty for most tenants and vassals. It also included a 'war-guilt' clause, which placed the onus, not on the Scottish nation as a whole, but on its social and political leaders. In contrast to the Irish policy of repression and punishment, the *Declaration* extended the hand of friendship to the mass of the people. It was indeed an attempt, by exporting the revolution to Scotland, to safeguard it in England.[124]

13

The Army and the Expulsion of the Rump Parliament, September 1651 to April 1653

The Reform Agenda, from Burford to Worcester

The conquest of Ireland and Scotland served to distract the army from political affairs until the autumn of 1651. Their remoteness from London together with the hazards of waging war in alien territories left the officers little time for active engagement with the parliamentary infighting and the popular campaigns that were being waged at home. After the crushing of the Leveller mutinies in May and September 1649 the army's rank and file never found its political voice again. Not only had radicalism been checked, but the private soldiers to whom it had been expected to appeal seemed on average to spend significantly less time in military service than before. During the 1650s the continuity of the army's political consciousness rested almost entirely on the permanence of its officer corps.

There is ample evidence that after the establishment of the Commonwealth the officers lost neither their religious ardour nor their critical attitude towards the ills and injustices of English society. Five officers from the field army were elected to the Commonwealth's first Council of State in February 1649: Fairfax, Cromwell, Skippon, Constable and John Jones, though Harrison and Ireton, both strongly identified with Pride's Purge and the revolution, were excluded.[1]

The officers were not backward in making their wishes known to the purged parliament, but at least until 1652 their tone was respectful and loyal. The officers' petition of March 1649, for example, confined itself to the army's material needs.[2] Before embarking for Ireland the officers disseminated two more political manifestoes which proved that they were

Plate 13 Oliver Cromwell, Lord Protector of England, Robert Walker, *c*.1649

(National Portrait Gallery, London)

still zealous for godly reformation. Their Humble Petition in July incorporated the demand that was then the litmus-paper test of radicalism, the abolition of tithes. Couched in exalted diction, the Representation of the Army in August argued pre-eminently for religious toleration.[3]

In spite of its military preoccupations, the army's disillusionment with parliament set in remarkably early. Cromwell's offhand comment to Lord Wharton at the beginning of 1650 was that the good MPs had been kept out at Pride's Purge, while most of the bad remained. Around the same time Captain William Siddall condemned parliament for being slow to act for the welfare of the kingdom.[4] It was an accusation that would be made with rising impatience over the next three years. In the meantime Cromwell, just as he cultivated moderates such as Wharton, St John and Whitelocke, also strove to keep fences mended with the Commonwealth's radical critics. In June 1650, for example, right after his return from Ireland, he delivered a petition to parliament for John Lilburne. The following month, while on his way to Scotland, he invited Lilburne and a party of his comrades to ride and sup with him. At their parting on the road north of Ware, Cromwell embraced them all and promised when he returned from Scotland 'to make the people of England the most absolute free nation on the earth.' He also reassured Ludlowe of his commitment to 'thorough reformation', but cautioned him that 'the sons of Zeruiah are yet too strong for us.'[5]

Cromwell took advantage of his glittering triumph at Dunbar to recommend to parliament a broad programme of social and legal reform. Writing a month or so later, Colonel Pride expressed his contempt for lawyers, and bluntly declared that it was time for the law to be reformed and the present parliament repurged.[6] During the winter of 1650–1, as economic hardship worsened, the army became more acutely conscious of its unpopularity, particularly in London. Embarrassed by the immiseration of the populace, it was tempted to recover some of its lost ground by taking up radical demands for the abolition of the excise and tithes, and by supporting the separatists during their tribulations.[7] In the summer of 1651 Cromwell again used a military victory – this time Lambart's at Inverkeithing – as an opportunity to press his argument for social justice. Quoting Psalm 119 he reminded the MPs of their duty to deliver the people from oppression. Robert Lilburne exploited his victory at Wigan to deliver a similar message.[8] After the delirium of Worcester – 'for aught I know a crowning mercy' – Cromwell exhorted the Rump 'that justice, righteousness, mercy and truth may flow from you, as a thankful return to our gracious God.' Major-General Thomas Harrison lectured his political masters in the same vein, though with chiliastic overtones. The Rump, he held, should open 'a wider door to the publishing the everlasting Gospel of our only Lord and Saviour, ... [so that] all his enemies shall be made his footstool.'[9]

From the Aftermath of Worcester to the Petition of August 1652

For all the religious exaltation that he felt in the autumn of 1651, Cromwell's political agenda was a moderate one. He had three objectives:

1 the dissolution of the Rump and the election of a new parliament;
2 an act of oblivion for most royalists in order to broaden the Commonwealth's base of support; and
3 systematic law reform that would give the people impartial justice.[10]

The problem with this agenda was that it was too radical for the Rump, and too insipid for most of the officers. As Woolrych points out, their long, hard and hazardous campaigns had radicalized them, while their victories had made them surer than ever that the Lord was with them and that they were the humble instruments of some tremendous divine purpose for which England had been singled out.[11] Men who had experienced fire and the sword were estranged from the arts of backroom politics, power-broking, compromise and deals, which now only aroused their disgust. Cromwell's effort, therefore, to bring the Rump to embrace a moderate programme of reform and defuse the appeal of radicalism was eminently sensible. On his way to London after the battle of Worcester he met and conferred with MPs Lisle, Whitelocke, Sir Gilbert Pickering and Oliver St John, the advocate of mixed monarchy. Throughout the autumn of 1651 he and St John would work closely together. Cromwell aimed to win support from across the political spectrum through a generous act of oblivion, fresh elections and some form of monarchy.[12] Understandably he believed that the regime should profit from its unaccustomed popularity to stage the long-overdue national elections. It was a tribute to his sway over parliament that on the day he resumed his Commons seat the bill for new elections was 'briskly revived.'[13]

Euphoria over their recent battlefield successes did not blind Cromwell and the officers to the reality that, if a new parliament was to continue on the path they had mapped out for it, its selection would have to be carefully guided. Since the time of the second Agreement of the People, in December 1648, the officers had known perfectly well that, if godly reformation was to be achieved, the 'ungodly' (i.e. the opponents of the revolution) would have to be excluded from the electoral process.[14] This is what Cromwell had in mind when he secured the Rump's reluctant assent to a motion for a new Representative with 'fit rules, qualifications, [and] proportions'. The same motion also stipulated that a date should be set for parliament's dissolution.[15] Perhaps to mollify the army, parliament debated the bill repeatedly for nearly two months before deciding by a paper-thin margin to fix a time for its dissolution. But the date chosen – 3 November 1654 – allowed the members a further three years to contemplate their demise.[16] Parliament had effectively undermined Cromwell's initiative. Its next rebuff to the army occurred at the elections to the Council of State. Cromwell as usual stood at the top of the poll, and was joined by military colleagues Fleetwood, Constable and Wauton. But two key men, Skippon and Thomas Harrison, were defeated.[17]

Undaunted by these setbacks, Cromwell pushed ahead with his strategy of radicalism in public and conservatism behind the scenes. While imprisoned debtors and the widows of slain officers implored parliament for relief, and while radicals in Yorkshire added their voices to the chorus demanding law reform and reduced taxes, Cromwell canvassed support for his idea of mixed monarchy. In December he brought together leading army officers and MPs at the Speaker's house to discuss what political system would suit England best. In the course of the discussion the divergence between military and parliamentary thinking was starkly exposed. The MPs leaned towards making room for monarchy in the constitution; the officers were adamantly opposed to monarchy in any form. According to Whitelocke, Cromwell got what he wanted from the meeting, which was an accurate sounding of opinion. Before the meeting broke up, however, he tipped his hand. Constitutional change was 'a business of more than ordinary difficulty', he allowed, but 'if it may be done with safety and preservation of our rights, both as Englishmen and as Christians, [then] a settlement of somewhat with monarchical power in it would be very effectual.'[18]

By the end of 1651 all reform initiatives were being stymied by the Rump's reactionary temper. Colonel Pride's appearance at the door of the house on 26 December was a none-too-subtle reminder to the MPs of what might happen to them if they continued to frustrate the army's programme. It was also a dramatic sign of the deterioration in relations between parliament and army since Worcester. Yet the MPs seemed unable to break the grip of their collective death wish. On the one hand, they assented to the establishment of the famous Hale Commission on law reform and nominated several officers and associates of the army to it. The commission met intensively during the first half of 1652. On the other hand, the Rump refused to implement a single one of the commissions's reasoned and practical proposals.[19]

More provoking in the short run than its deafness to the cry for law reform, was the Rump's vindictive treatment of John Lilburne early in 1652. With his familiar knack for turning a private cause into a burning public issue, Lilburne had once again claimed the spotlight of national attention, this time over a property dispute in Durham. It did not help his cause that his adversary was a leading member of parliament, Sir Arthur Hesilrige. In its rage against this gadfly, parliament decided to silence him once for all with a crushing fine of £7000. Called before the bar of the House to hear his sentence, Lilburne refused to kneel because in his view that would have implied acknowledgment of guilt. The house then ordered his banishment from England. Many in the army were said to be troubled at this excessive punishment, but the Rump was implacable, and within the month Lilburne had boarded a ship for Holland. Around the same time Hesilrige was made president of the Council of State. On 27 January Commissary-General Whalley laid a petition before parliament, apparently appealing the sentence against Lilburne. Several times the house deferred consideration of the petition and in the end referred it to the Committee for the Army, after which it was never heard of again.[20]

In February one of the key items on Cromwell's agenda of reconciliation was advanced with the introduction of a bill of oblivion for all except the regime's worst enemies. Fierce debates ensued day after day until the bill passed its third reading on the 24th. Among the bill's supporters were Lambart, Disbrowe, Rich, John Jones and Marten. But by the time it finally reached the statute book the act was so hobbled with provisoes, which filled page after page, that the objective of reconciling royalists was nullified. Cromwell had prominently opposed several provisoes, sometimes successfully, but he could not stop the most damaging one of all, which excluded anyone who had not taken the Engagement. Not just royalists, but the greater part of the inhabitants of the British Isles were thereby prevented from enjoying the benefits of the act. Whatever good the Act of Oblivion might have accomplished was further vitiated by parliament's attempt to prop up its tottering finances with more and more far-reaching confiscations of royalist land in 1651 and 1652.[21]

In the spring of 1652 the beginning of a major naval war with the Dutch signalled the permanent end of the Long Parliament's reforming activity. In the course of its final year it did next to nothing about tithes, law reform or the propagation of the gospel, all issues close to the officers' hearts. The occasional gesture in the direction of army sensibilities, such as the expulsion of Gregory Clement for adultery, hardly made up for the lack of accomplishment on substantive questions.[22]

Besides turning its back on reform, the Rump succeeded at the same time in permanently alienating one of the most powerful men in the army, Major-General John Lambart. A tolerant and enlightened man, Lambart was next to Cromwell the ablest general in the army. Having shown early promise in the Northern Army at the beginning of the war, he had recently covered himself with glory in the Scottish campaign at Dunbar, Hamilton and Inverkeithing. Nor were his talents confined to the battlefield. Trained at the Inns of Court, he was, as Whitelocke observed, a man 'of a subtle and working brain': he had helped Ireton draft the army's manifestoes in 1647. Now that the army's leading theoretician was dead, Lambart was probably the most intelligent man left on the Council of Officers.[23] Fourteen years younger than Cromwell, he had plenty of ambition, and doubtless considered it just recognition of his talents when the Council of State recommended him to succeed Ireton as deputy lieutenant of Ireland. With this appointment he was set to become the effective political as well as military governor of that country. He therefore left Scotland and went to considerable expense outfitting himself for his new post. Lucy Hutchinson recorded that he treated the MPs to whom he owed his advancement as 'underlings, and such as were scarce worth the great man's nod.' In May, perhaps to save money, perhaps as a slap against Cromwell, parliament abolished the post. The motion passed by a majority of only two, with Whitelocke and Harrison acting as tellers for the noes, and Marten and Hesilrige (who was emerging more and more as the army's *bête noire*) as tellers for the yeas. As a result Cromwell was reduced from lord lieutenant to commander-in-chief in Ireland. The loss of prestige applied equally to the second-in-command. Lambart was so offended that he turned down the lesser commission, which was then given to Cromwell's new son-in-law, Charles Fleetwood, who had just married Bridget Ireton. Lambart was further antagonized when the Council of State attempted (without success) to send him to Scotland in April 1653.[24]

The lack of progress on reform, mounting concern about the Dutch war and impatience over the Rump's refusal to dissolve itself all played a part in spurring the officers to launch a second major offensive against parliament, in August 1652. On the 2nd they held an all-day meeting which issued in a petition to Cromwell. Only an unofficial report of this document survives, but it evidently asked that the Gospel might be propagated and its ministers supported otherwise than by tithes; that the recommendations of the Hale Commission be implemented; that profane and scandalous persons be supplanted in places of authority by 'men of truth, fearing God and hating covetousness'; that soldiers be paid their arrears; that promises to royalists by articles of war be fulfilled; and, finally, 'that a new representative be forthwith elected.' According to the Venetian envoy Cromwell refused to lend his name to the petition, 'though it is supposed that he consented to its being drawn up.' However, when a revised version of it was submitted to parliament on 13 August it did carry the weight of his authority, since it was published in the name of the Council of War, over which he presided. Moreover, the officers who took it to parliament were for the most part loyal Cromwellians: Whalley, Hacker, Barkstead, Okey, Goffe and Worsley. In this official version the officers prefaced their demands with a reference to the several meetings they had held 'to seek the Lord, and to speak of the great things God hath done for this Commonwealth.' The wording of the demand for a new parliament was revised to bring it in line with the second Agreement of the People:

> That for public satisfaction of the good people of this nation, speedy consideration may be had of such qualifications for future and successive parliaments, as tend to the election only of such as are pious and faithful to the interest of the Commonwealth, to sit and serve as members in the said parliament.[25]

For a moment the Rump was shaken out of its complacency. It referred the petition to a high-powered thirty-four member committee which included five officers in active service: Cromwell, Harrison, Rich, Ingoldsby and Bennett. Significantly, neither Vane nor Hesilrige, who were regarded as obstructors of reform or enemies of the army, was appointed. In public the petitioners were thanked for their concern, but in private there was much resentment among the MPs, who saw it as 'improper, if not arrogant' for the officers so brazenly to engage in political lobbying. Whitelocke admonished Cromwell 'to stop this way of petitioning by the officers of the army with their swords in their hands, lest in time it might come too home to himself', but the general brushed aside the criticism. For all their misgivings the MPs continued to defer to the army by ordering the committee report on the petition within a month. Accordingly, on 14 September the chairman, Mr Carew, informed the house that the bill 'for setting a certain time for the sitting of this present parliament, and providing for successive parliaments' would pass more speedily if it were put in the hands of a select committee instead of the present grand committee. The house took his advice, and handed responsibility for the bill to Carew's committee, stipulating that a blank was to be left in the draft bill for the date of dissolution. Parliament had silently abandoned its previous dissolution date of 3 November 1654.[26]

From Petition to Prayer Meeting, August 1652 to January 1653

For the next two months parliament continued to throw conciliatory crumbs in the army's direction. To handle the many petitions with which it was inundated it set up a committee, and included Cromwell, Harrison, Fleetwood and Rich as members. Vane and Hesilrige again were excluded. As a sop to millenarian sentiment it appointed the Fifth Monarchist

Christopher Feake to preach at its September fast. Such largely symbolic acts did little to narrow the gulf of distrust that had grown up between the Rump and the officers. Captain Edmund Chillenden hinted broadly to his friend William Clarke in Scotland that the day was not far off when the army would get rid of parliament. More ominously, as the financial burdens imposed by the Dutch war accelerated the decline of the regime's popularity, fifty officers were reported meeting at Syon House to find a way to rid the commonwealth of the abuse of arbitrary power and 'the shadow of oppression.'[27]

Another nail was driven into the coffin of the Long Parliament by the protracted debate on the Act of Articles. Historians have paid little attention to this legislation, yet it was of fundamental and longstanding importance to the army. Since the beginning of the civil wars parliamentary commanders had negotiated many treaties of surrender with their counterparts in the royalist field armies and garrisons. Normally but not invariably, articles of surrender were submitted to parliament for ratification. To every commander from Fairfax downward it was of the utmost importance that the terms which they granted to their defeated foes should be upheld by parliament and the courts. Anything less would be highly destructive of military self-respect. On the question of surrender articles the parliamentarian and royalist armies shared the same chivalric sense of honour. Keeping faith was the crux; it can be summed up in the apophthegm of the sixteenth-century Catholic nobleman Lord Darcy: 'for what is a man but his promise?'[28] This ethic had very little to do with puritan principles and a great deal to do with the code of the feudal warrior, as mediated by medieval theology and sixteenth-century humanism.

Parliament had yielded to insistent pressure from the army when it passed the first Act of Articles in June 1649. A prestigious commission comprising the chief justices and other high officials, several London aldermen and two senior officers, Colonel Whalley and Lieutenant-General Thomas Hammond, was empowered to hear and redress the complaints of any who had been 'sued or molested contrary to any articles made in time of war.' The text of the act declared that its purpose was to protect the army's good name, recognizing 'how much it concerneth them in justice and honour that the [articles] may be made good.' Yet the act only lasted for a year, lapsing on 20 June 1650.[29]

Not until the spring of 1652 did parliament get round to hearing a motion to renew the Act of Articles. The motion was at once referred to the Indemnity Committee, and Colonel Rich instructed to take care of it. For the next half-year the bill meandered through committee hearings and suffered repeated amendment. Parliament spoilt the goodwill it might have garnered from the army by vetoing the nomination of Colonel Pride as one of the commissioners for articles. The name of Colonel Barkstead was more palatable to the MPs, so he was permitted to stand as Pride's surrogate. Before the bill was read a third time it was mutilated by a number of last-minute provisoes. Most drastic would have been a stipulation that any resolution of parliament could override any articles negotiated by the army. On first reading it gained a one-vote majority in a thin house, with Cromwell and Rich acting as tellers for the noes. The officers must have beat the bushes to rouse their supporters, for the amendment was defeated on the next reading. Another proviso, somewhat more diplomatically worded, achieved the same goal of checking the autonomy of military commanders. Claims arising from articles which had not been confirmed by parliament would have to be submitted to it for approval before the commissioners could proceed to hear them. With these qualifications, the new act, which finally reached the statute book on 28 September 1652, was voted to continue until September 1655. It did almost nothing to assuage the army's offended sense of honour. The cup was made more bitter still in November 1652 by the inclusion of a rider stipulating that the act did not apply to the additional bill for sale of lands forfeited for treason. Many royalist soldiers who had surrendered on the understanding that they could keep their estates were now stripped of the protection that Fairfax, Cromwell and their deputies had promised them. A postscript to this story exemplifies the vehemence with which the officers resented parliament's emasculation of the act. In June 1653, as soon as the Rump was out of the way, a committee of officers took over the administration of the act and restored several royalists to their estates.[30]

The mood of the officers had by now taken on an ugly cast. Recognizing the danger that could result from a state of intractable animosity towards parliament, a friendly newsbook, the *Faithful Scout*, besought the soldiers, 'though the sword is a prevailing argument, act fairly ... do violence to no man.'[31] According to Ludlowe, Cromwell worked to stir up hatred of the Rump during this time, excusing himself on the grounds that he was pushed on by Lambart and Harrison's factions 'to do that, the consideration of the issue whereof made his hair to stand on end.' Over a period of several weeks from October 1652 he held ten or twelve meetings with MPs, arguing that parliament was no longer capable of undertaking a programme of reform and must therefore be pulled down.[32]

Ludlowe's account tallies with Whitelocke's record of a conversation he had with Cromwell around the same time. On a fine autumn evening as he was walking in St James's Park, the general saluted him and began to unburden himself of his worries about the 'jarrings and animosities' that currently plagued the government. The root of the problem, he was convinced, was that the MPs were accountable to no superior power. He then asked abruptly, 'What if a man should take upon him to be king?' Alarmed, Whitelocke tried to puncture the general's ambition with the terse rejoinder, 'I think that remedy would be worse than the disease.' To drive the point home he reminded Cromwell that there was no shortage of officers plotting with MPs at that very moment 'to dismount your excellency.'[33]

Meanwhile, the Rump appeared oblivious to the danger it was now in. On 18 November it turned aside a resolution to compensate Lieutenant-General Thomas Hammond for the fact that he had been thwarted in his purchase of the Hare Warren in Hampton, Middlesex, for which he had contracted in 1650. This crown property worth £3500 had been taken back by parliament in order to raise cash for the navy. Though a regicide, Hammond boasted distinguished lineage, and was now also a political moderate. As a highly respected senior officer, he was the sort of man whose friendship parliament should have been cultivating.[34]

Of similar import was the Rump's move to subvert Cromwell's personal power by selling off Hampton Court, where he had resided since his triumphal return from Worcester. Their theory, as Ludlowe wrote, was that, if such a desirable property were no longer available, ambitious men might be less tempted to ascend the throne. The capital was rife with rumours that Cromwell was soon to be removed from his command.[35]

The Council of State elections later the same month produced a mixed result for the military. Among the twenty-two councillors whose mandate was renewed were only two serving officers: Cromwell and Wauton. Fleetwood was defeated. On the other hand, two officers who had been defeated the previous year, Skippon and Harrison, were returned, as was Colonel Richard Ingoldsby. Harrison, however, was tied with Colonel George Fenwick, governor of Berwick, at the bottom of the poll, and only scraped in after lots had been drawn.[36] The slightly improved military representation in government did little to dampen the molten rhetoric that was now pouring from radical City pulpits and Fifth Monarchist strongholds such as All Hallows the Great and Blackfriars. Harrison, along with 'many precious ones', was confident, as he wrote to his friend John Jones, that 'our blessed Lord will shortly work with eminence.' At the end of November he suggested that Jones should come to London with his troop, but the colonel prudently ignored the advice. While preachers began to 'pray for a new representative, and to preach somewhat against the old', the millenarian Baptist editor of the *Faithful Scout*, Daniel Border, began to criticize parliament openly, and was rewarded by having his newsbook suppressed.[37]

Other contributing factors to the army's conviction of the Rump's deadly hostility in this period were troop reductions, pay cuts and arrears. At the time of Worcester there had been 45,000 troops on the payroll in England,

and a further 8000 in Scotland. By December 1652 the army had been contracted to 31,500 in the two nations, at a monthly cost of £111,000. During the autumn Cromwell, Lambart, Ingoldsby and Goffe had all seen their regiments diminished, although Cromwell's was restored to its original size only a week later. On 4 December parliament voted to raise the monthly assessment from £90,000 to £120,000. A third of this sum, however, was earmarked for the navy. Thus, even assuming 100 per cent success in collecting the tax, the army would continue to fall into arrears at the rate of £31,000 a month. One instrument the Rump considered to narrow the gap between receipts and expenses was a decrease in the pay of troopers and foot soldiers by a fifth or a quarter. Not surprisingly, the prospect of lower pay angered the rank and file. On 1 January 1652 the Committee for the Army tried another tack: minor troop reductions in Scotland, the elimination of a few garrisons in England and the pruning of auxiliary personnel from the field army. This yielded a further reduction of 4000 men, but shaved less than £10,000 from the monthly bill.[38]

The Rump's repeated efforts to whittle away the army's numbers continued almost until the time it was dissolved. By early 1653 it had decided on the secondment of entire regiments for service in the navy. Most alarming to Cromwell must have been the order in April to send half the men from his and his close ally Barkstead's regiments to serve in the navy. As a consequence of this measure the officers became unshakably convinced that parliament was bent on their destruction.[39]

Counterpointing the army's discontent was the mounting agitation among the civilian population during the winter of 1652-3. There was widespread exasperation at the Commonwealth's chronic inability to satisfy its public-faith creditors. Heavier and heavier taxation to meet the costs of the war against Holland caused a conservative backlash, which led to the discomfiture of the 'honest party' in London politics. Several of the army's radical friends lost their seats on the Common Council in the December 1652 elections. The Dutch naval blockade interrupted English shipping in the North Sea and sent the price of coal in London soaring to astronomical heights. A more potent source of bitterness, however, were the naval press gangs which roamed through the streets of the capital, dragging men from their beds late at night and sending many to a watery grave.[40]

Preparations for the Suppression of the Rump, January–April 1653

In this atmosphere of swelling panic characteristic of a city under siege, the officers met at the end of December 1652 in St James's to launch a protracted series of prayer meetings. Every day during the first week of January they waited on God, confessing their sins to one another, and hearing sermons. 2 miles to the east soldiers were gathering at All Hallows the Great in Thames Street, to pray for a new Representative. Having fortified themselves with spiritual exercises, the officers convened a formal council meeting on 8 January to consider what stand the army should take on the great questions before the nation. After long debate it named a committee to frame a document embodying their thinking about 'the civil authority by successive parliaments', religion, and the dispensation of justice. In doing this, as Woolrych states, the Council of Officers showed that it was not prepared to let the clamorous millenarians who looked to Harrison for inspiration set the pace. Cromwell took steps to keep his heedless major-general politically at arm's length. Significantly, the Council refused to receive a paper addressed to it by several radical congregations.[41]

Almost no public notice was paid to the officers' prayer meetings in early January, but inside the army they had generated much turbulence. Flowing from this unsettledness was a letter which headquarters circulated to all the regiments in England, Scotland and Ireland, and also made available to the public in London. They informed their far-flung comrades that Satan had recently been very active. The army had shared in the general sinfulness and must repent. But the corruption in parliament could not be healed. The present MPs must therefore be replaced by successive parliaments consisting of 'men of truth, fearing God and hating covetousness'. There must also be law reform, liberty of worship, and publicly supported evangelization. The officers' letter signalled an escalation of political pressure. Whereas the petition of the previous August had come only from the officers in Whitehall, support was now being mobilized from officers in all segments of the army throughout the three nations. Few responses to the call from headquarters survive, perhaps because most of them were never published. One of those which was came from the artillery officers in Edinburgh, who reflected back with almost equal intensity the fervour of the Whitehall commanders. Reproaching themselves for their coldness 'in promoting the glorious things of Jesus Christ, and his precious people', they pronounced their dismay that 'floods of ungodly men are ready to break over the banks which the Lord hath raised for the defence of his own inheritance.' In these phrases we hear the familiar accents of perfervid chiliasm. Interestingly they came from the lips not of men who were marginalized or oppressed, but from the self-confident colleagues of the leaders of an undefeated army, impatient for the new age to begin.[42]

The issue of a new Representative had now moved to the forefront of the army's concerns. Ever since Worcester if not before, the soldiers' impatience at the longevity of the Long Parliament had been simmering away. Cromwell had wished to take advantage of the general euphoria consequent upon that 'crowning mercy' to dissolve parliament and hold immediate elections. But MPs fearful of defeat, or of their creditors or their enemies, threw roadblocks in his way. Cromwell did, however, prevail on parliament to resolve on 25 September 1651 to set a date for calling a new parliament, and to frame appropriate qualifications for voters and candidates.[43] This question became a major bone of contention between the officers and the republican MPs for the next year and a half. Yet to argue that the army's desire to be rid of the Rump 'came ... to overshadow the most elementary political calculation' is to misunderstand its position. At no time did the officers overlook the necessity of winnowing and sifting the electorate and new MPs in order to make sure that 'neuters' and 'malignants' were eliminated.[44]

A turning point was reached when parliament yielded to military pressure and dropped its scheme to hold recruiter elections. A second turning point was passed when it agreed by a narrow margin to set a date for its own dissolution. The apparent victory was rendered nugatory, however, when the chosen date turned out to be three years in the future.[45] Having been outfoxed, the officers temporarily retired from the political battlefield to lick their wounds. For the time being the debate on parliament's dissolution fizzled out. Then in April 1652 parliament proved, by spending a day reconsidering it, that it had not forgotten the old recruiter scheme to fill vacant seats with new members while allowing the existing ones to stay put. Even so, it was August by the time the officers returned to the fray with a repeated demand for a completely new Representative. Again they manifested a lively awareness of the pitfalls attendant upon unrestricted elections.

By January 1653, evidently alarmed at the intensity of the army's anger, the house turned over responsibility for the bill for a new Representative to Major-General Harrison with instructions to him to bring it before the house 'with speed'.[46] Implicit in this move was an acknowledgement that parliament's very continued existence had become one of the officers' core grievances. The Fifth Monarchist major-general had been handed an extraordinary opportunity to influence the shape of his country's political future, but, as we shall see, he fumbled it. Whether through political incompetence, or lack of interest, or perhaps because he was just not equal to the challenge of crafting legislation that would ensure the election of a godly parliament, he did nothing. Perhaps he already thought parliaments useless and preferred the simpler scheme of a hand-picked sanhedrin. Whatever the explanation for Harrison's failure to act, on 23 February 1653 it was Hesilrige, the army's arch foe, who reported the amendments to the bill for a new Representative. The text of Hesilrige's amendments has not survived.

All we know about them is that they were unacceptable to the officers, for instead of suspending their agitation while the debate was going on they stepped it up.[47]

Cromwell laboured to avoid an open breach, but the officers assembled on 4 March to consider how a new Representative might be achieved, 'either by petition or otherwise'. A week later, meeting at St James's, they resolved to turn out the Rump.[48] For the moment Cromwell tried to cool their ardour. Seconded by Disbrowe he challenged them to think,

> if they destroyed that parliament, what they should call themselves. A state they could not be. They answered that they would call a new parliament. Then, says the general, the parliament is not the supreme power, but that is the supreme power that calls it.... This seemed to satisfy them at present but they have met since and are framing a petition to the House which we hear is very high.[49]

Parliament was not ignorant of this deadly threat. Whitelocke writes that he warned the officers against laying violent hands upon the Rump, while plans were hatched to dismiss Cromwell and reappoint Fairfax. Meanwhile, more and more senior officers, including some from Ireland and Scotland, congregated in London. Not all of them supported a forcible dissolution. Scoutmaster-General George Downing from Scotland and Colonel Robert Venables from Ireland were initially opposed, but were won over by the others. Captain John Streater from Ireland, however, remained adamant in his civilian republicanism. When Harrison told Streater that Cromwell had no ambition for himself, 'but that King Jesus might take the sceptre', Streater shot back, 'Christ must come before Christmas, or else he would come too late.' Okey and Tomlinson were apparently equally troubled, at least retrospectively, by the dissolution.[50]

But the doubters comprised a small minority. Overwhelmingly the officers saw eye to eye on the necessity of sweeping away what they regarded as a hopelessly reactionary and corrupt regime. Cromwell was by now well positioned to repel any attempt by parliament to dislodge him. Surrounded by his leading officers and their trustworthy troops, his base of operations was the Cockpit, a few steps away from the House of Commons. He had seen to it that his own regiment of foot was appointed to guard the house. Contemporary reports of division within the Council of Officers make it appear that Cromwell experienced the greatest difficulty curbing the faction of Harrison, Pride, Rich and others who sought to usher in the reign of Jesus Christ. There is good reason for believing, however, that there existed a fundamental harmony of purpose between the Cromwellians, who included Fleetwood, Whalley, Disbrowe, Barkstead and Goffe, and the militant radicals under Harrison. Lambart, who at this time led no faction, was a moderate constitutionalist, more or less in the mould of Ireton. What conflict there was stemmed from a disagreement over timing. Like Harrison, Cromwell absented himself from the Council of State and the House of Commons for most of March and April. If he had not already written off these institutions he would surely have paid them more attention.

Cromwell manifested his alienation from parliament in other ways. Apart from boycotting its meetings and taking steps to defend himself militarily, he seems to have sanctioned the new petition hammered out by the officers in mid-March, insisting that the Rump convert into a statute its promise to dissolve not later than November 1654. More portentous still is the report of a conference held by Cromwell near the end of the month with leading City divines, at which he proposed the forcible dissolution of parliament. One of the divines, Edmund Calamy, denounced the scheme as unlawful and impracticable. 'Why impracticable?' asked Cromwell. 'Oh,' replied Calamy, ''tis against the voice of the nation; there will be nine in ten against you.' 'Very well,' said Cromwell, 'but what if I should disarm the nine, and put a sword into the tenth man's hand; would not that do the business?' Six days later, when parliament cancelled its usual Wednesday debate on the bill for a new Representative, Whitelocke ascertained that Cromwell was fed up with the MPs and chafing to have them gone.[51]

The seemingly contradictory evidence, which shows Cromwell striving with might and main to keep the radicals in check, is less authoritative and in the end unpersuasive. Its chief source is the pen of Hyde's newswriter. On 1 April, for example, he wrote that Cromwell was 'daily railed upon by the preaching party.' He added that the general had recently put Disbrowe at the head of four of the most violent regiments and dispatched them to Scotland in an endeavour to relieve the pressure for a sudden coup against parliament. Such a large troop movement would have attracted public attention, not to mention comment by Scottish correspondents. But newsbooks, pamphlets and the Baynes letters are all silent on the matter. A second royalist newswriter was more perceptive when he observed that, although Cromwell had distanced himself publicly from the militants, in private he was known to be very thick with them.[52]

It is worth emphasizing that the issue of a new Representative was but one of many irritants in army – parliament relations. The officers, for example, had made known a number of times their solicitude for the poor. In mid-February, however, the Rump gratuitously insulted military sensibilities by refusing to hear a bill for poor relief.[53] Law reform was another question on which the officers had repeatedly sought action. On 10 March the Commons resolved to dedicate every Thursday to this subject. Perhaps because of their complacency after Blake's great victory in the Channel, they forgot their good intentions, and law reform was never heard of again before the next parliament.[54] Religion loomed much larger than poor relief or law reform on the officers' mental landscape. First, they had several times pronounced themselves in favour of replacing tithes with a more equitable system of ecclesiastical taxation. However, tithes had by the mid-seventeenth century turned into a species of lay property no less than a source of church revenue. It is therefore not surprising that parliament always refused to contemplate their abolition. Second, the officers were noticeably more avid for the promotion of Christianity than the MPs were. Early in 1652 Whalley, Okey and Goffe had affixed their names to a petition for a religious settlement. Apparently authored by Cromwell's clerical friend John Owen, the scheme resembled the officers' Agreement of the People in that it provided for an established church surrounded by self-supporting, officially tolerated nonconformist churches. Recognizing the officers' zeal for evangelization, the Rump appointed six of their number – Whalley, Harrison, Okey, Goffe, Francis White and John Blackwell – to a twenty-seven man committee for the propagation of the Gospel. Other members included such leading lights of the London Independent clergy as John Owen, Philip Nye, John Goodwin and Shadrach Simpson.[55]

It took a full year before parliament got around to hearing their report. Wisely the committee had decided to respect army convictions by deleting from Owen's scheme two recommendations that would have fettered religious liberty. However, the Rump characteristically overrode the committee's advice and insisted on including the deleted clauses in its deliberations. In its dilatory way it never actually got to them, for it only managed to debate the first three. But in that short time it succeeded once again in treading on army sensibilities. The issue was lay preaching, a practice dear to the army's heart. Since 1645 the officers had stoutly defended the right to preach, regardless of his external qualifications, of anyone who believed he had received spiritual gifts. In its first clause the Owenite scheme sanctioned this practice. But the MPs could not stomach so much religious liberty. They therefore hedged the clause in with a qualification. When amended it read, 'that persons of godliness and gifts, of the universities and others, though not ordained, *that shall be approved* shall receive the public maintenance for preaching the gospel.'[56] This narrowing of the grounds for lay preaching was a further affront to the army.

Another major clash occurred over the propagation of the Gospel in Wales. The principality had long been regarded by puritans as one of the 'dark corners of the land'. Therefore in 1650 when the commission was established to promote the Gospel there it came as no surprise that a large number of serving army officers were nominated to it. Thomas Harrison was joined by Philip and John Jones, William Packer, William Boteler, Rowland Dawkins, Wroth Rogers, Stephen Winthrop, Robert Duckenfield,

Humphrey Mackworth, and several other commanders of local garrisons.[57]

In company with the fiery preacher Vavasour Powell, Harrison had set about energetically to root out malignant and scandalous clergy and plant a preaching ministry in their place. The propagation of the Gospel meant also the extension of English law, order and civilization. It is interesting too that Wales, the former recruiting ground of royalist infantry, supplied almost no soldiers to Charles II when he was on his way to Worcester in August 1651. None the less, for their pains Harrison and his associates earned themselves much enmity. Before long, charges of corruption were being bandied about. When in early 1653 the time came to consider renewal of the act, it was alleged that the Welsh commissioners wanted to prolong their mandate merely to avoid having to part with the money they had accumulated.

The commissioners were not idle in the face of these insinuations. In late 1652 they orchestrated a shower of letters describing their good steward-ship of the revenues and enthusing over the flourishing state of preaching and education throughout the thirteen counties. Wales had in fact benefited from the inspiring piety and tireless evangelism of true pastors such as Walter Cradock, as well as undergoing the proselytization of extremists such as Powell and Morgan Llwyd. After a lengthy investigation of the complaints by the Rump's Committee for Plundered Ministers, Colonel Robert Bennett exonerated the commissioners. Accordingly on 25 March the house voted that the original act of 1650 should be brought forward for renewal on 1 April. But on that day it declined to proceed with the act, and according to one source 'ordered a moderate clergy to be put in their places.' The MPs' frame of mind was further revealed by their cancellation of Walter Cradock's engagement to preach before the house later that month. It was a disastrously ill-timed decision. More than any other issue save the question of a new Representative, it sealed the Rump's fate.[58]

Parliament's waiving of the scheduled debate on a new Representative on 6 April was virtually the last straw. Privately Cromwell told Whitelocke that the time had come to be done with parliament.[59] On 7 April the army sub-mitted a fresh petition demanding that the house proceed with the bill, but emphasizing that it should first take care to define the qualifications that would exclude improper persons from future parliaments. In its previous debate on 30 March the house had ignored the army's other anxiety about sifting the electorate by passing a motion that 'all persons' possessing pro-perty worth £200 should have the vote.[60] As it stood this motion would have practically guaranteed the election of a royalist parliament.[61] A week later, at its next scheduled debate, the house complied with the army's request by adding a requirement that members of the new representative would only be allowed to take their seats if they were 'such as are persons of known integrity, fearing God, and not scandalous in their conversation.'[62]

The question now was, who was to judge? It was perhaps to resolve that very question that Cromwell broke his month-long boycott and attended the house on 14 April.[63] To his surprise he ran into a wall of hostility. It is high time, shouted one of the parliamentary leaders, to choose a new general. Cromwell traded angry words with his attacker, and the house had to intervene to restore order.

The chances of avoiding a violent breach with parliament were plainly evaporating. To prepare for the expected showdown Cromwell consolidated his political control of the army. Summoning the Council of Officers, he offered to resign as general. It is doubtful if the vote of confidence he received was less than unanimous.[64] At the same meeting the officers apparently 'resolved very speedily to pull ... down' the parliament.[65]

In the absence of any surviving copy of the Rump's bill for a new Representative, we can only infer the precise reasons for the army's irrepressible antagonism towards it. A crucial one seems to have been its dissatisfaction over who was to judge the qualifications of the MPs elected to the next parliament. According to Ludlowe the bill stipulated that during the interval between parliaments the country was to be governed by a Council of State chosen by parliament. The existing council was dominated by anti-army republicans such as Hesilrige and Scot who could be counted upon to keep the officers away from the levers of political power. Indeed, Bordeaux reported that the Rump was framing such conditions for the new Representative that army officers would have no place in it.[66]

Extra-parliamentary developments contributed to the gathering sense of crisis. For many weeks the coal fleet had been bottled up by the Dutch at Scarborough. Most Londoners shivered in unheated houses, while cooks and brewers closed up shop since they could not afford to fire their ovens. So desperate was the regime for manpower to bolster the navy that it now resorted to pressing gentlemen. Members of the Council of State walked in fear of their lives, two of them having been recently assaulted in Smithfield. The inhabitants of the metropolis had reached the end of their tether and yearned for a political upheaval to relieve their misery. While people murmured and preachers ranted against parliament, a petition made the rounds of the City condemning corruption in high places and implicitly calling upon the army to end the Rump's sitting. By mid-April the air was heavy with the odour of panic.[67]

In this charged atmosphere Oliver summoned his officers and several MPs to his lodgings in Whitehall for a marathon meeting that lasted well into the night of 19 April. On the table was a proposal that a committee of forty MPs and officers, to be nominated by the present parliament, should run the country until the next parliament met. All the officers and some of the MPs, notably Oliver St John, lined up behind the general. The majority of the MPs – among them Whitelocke and Widdrington – were strongly opposed. After all opinions had been aired, the meeting trailed on inconclusively until the early hours of the morning. Finally, collapsing with fatigue, the remaining participants agreed to go home and reconvene the following afternoon. The MPs who had not already left said they would endeavour to postpone the scheduled parliamentary debate until Cromwell's *ad hoc* committee had exhausted all possible avenues to a compromise.[68]

The Violence against Parliament and its Aftermath, 20 April to 4 July

On the morning of Wednesday 20 April about 100 members of the Long Parliament assembled, double their usual numbers. It was odd of Cromwell to believe that this institution would do his bidding without even his presence to explain why the debate should be delayed, when previously he had been so anxious to have the bill passed. Confident perhaps in their large numbers, the MPs refused to countenance the general's request, and called for the bill. Unaware of this development, Oliver was at that moment conversing with Ingoldsby, and a few other officers and MPs in his lodgings. Their conversation was interrupted by the arrival of a messenger with the news that parliament was in the final stages of its debate on the controversial bill. The MPs present immediately left for the house, where they found their colleagues debating 'an act, the which would occasion other meetings of them again and prolong their sitting.'[69]

Seeing the urgency of the situation, Colonel Ingoldsby rushed back to tell Cromwell what was happening in parliament. Enraged by what he presumed was a betrayal of trust, Cromwell prepared to go to the house in person. Having previously judged that his presence would be unnecessary that day, he had not dressed for the occasion. His garb consisted of plain black clothes, with grey worsted stockings. During the time it took his junior officers to marshal a party of soldiers to accompany him, he addressed the others at the Cockpit. According to Captain John Streater, an eyewitness, Cromwell told them

> that Reformation could not be expected from the present parliament, and that if they should put the people to elect a new parliament, it would but tempt God. Therefore his opinion was that God did intend to save and deliver this nation by few; and that five or six men, or few more, setting themselves to the work, might do more in one day than the parliament had or would do in one hundred days, for ought he could perceive: for (saith he) the burdens are continued still on the people, injustice aboundeth, the law is not regulated; they intend nothing but to seek themselves, and to perpetuate themselves to the great hurt and danger of the nation: therefore he thought that the nation

might be better settled by a certain number of unbiased men who should give more content to the nation and people of God than the present parliament.[70]

Cromwell then marched with soldiers to the house. Most of them he placed at the door and in the lobby. He also took in with him a file of thirty musketeers, leaving them at the entrance to the chamber. Harrison, who had preceded his commander to the house, had been 'most sweetly and humbly' exhorting them to lay the bill aside.[71] Oliver slipped into his usual place, where he sat quietly for a time. Then, just as the question was about to be put on the bill, he leaned over to Harrison and whispered, 'This is the time I must do it.'[72] Then he stood up and spoke. The time was about mid-day.[73] At first he commended parliament for all it had done for the public good. But shortly his tone changed and he began to upbraid the MPs for their delaying of justice, and other faults. Suddenly his language became barbed and personal. Leaving his usual place, he put his hat on his head and walked over to the open floor in the middle of the chamber. From this vantage point he berated them collectively, also singling out individuals on whom to vent his spleen. Among those who felt the blast of his wrath were Bulstrode Whitelocke, Sir Henry Vane junior and Alderman Francis Allein, all of whom had grown rich under the Commonwealth. 'You are no parliament, I say you are no parliament, I will put an end to your sitting,' he cried. Then he stamped his feet to give the prearranged signal for the musketeers to enter the house.[74] The soldiers seem to have missed their cue, for he had to shout to Harrison, 'Call them in.' As Lieutenant-Colonel Worsley brought in the thirty armed men of his own regiment, Oliver informed the MPs that 'the Lord had done with them, and had chosen other instruments for the carrying on his work that were more worthy.' Then, pointing to Speaker Lenthall, he ordered Harrison to fetch him down from his seat. Lenthall at first resisted until Harrison gently said, 'Sir, I will lend you my hand.' Most of the MPs beat a quick retreat, and as they streamed past him Cromwell reproached them in injured tones, 'It's you that have forced me to this, for I have sought the Lord night and day, that he would rather slay me than put me upon the doing of this work.' But, when a few attempted to protest against their expulsion, he turned vengeful again. Some of them were whoremasters, he fulminated, looking straight at Henry Marten and Peter Wentworth. 'Others of them [like Chaloner] were drunkards, and some corrupt and unjust men, and scandalous to the profession of the gospel.' Sir Henry Vane senior was a 'juggler' and his son a 'cheat'. Henry Marten was both atheist and adulterer. Sir Henry Mildmay, Francis Allein and Thomas Scot were embezzlers of public money. As if these gibes were not enough, the MPs also had to endure the jeering of the musketeers as they left the chamber. It was too much for Vane the younger, who expostulated, 'This is not honest, yea it is against morality and common honesty.' At which Oliver lashed out in a loud voice, 'O Sir Henry Vane, Sir Henry Vane, the Lord deliver me from Sir Henry Vane.' Then his eye lighted upon the mace, symbol of the Commons' authority. 'Take away that fool's bauble', he barked to one of the soldiers. Not until every other MP was out did Cromwell leave the house. Then he saw to it that the door was locked, and gave Colonel Okey custody of the key and Lieutenant-Colonel Worsley the mace.

Now, in the early afternoon, Cromwell returned to the Cockpit, where he met his officers again. He asserted to them that his act had been unpremeditated,

> that when he went into the House he intended not to do it; but the spirit was so upon him, that he was over-ruled by it: and he consulted not with flesh and blood at all, nor did premeditate the doing thereof; he seeing the parliament designing to spin an everlasting thread.[75]

In Streater's narration we can hear the authentic Cromwellian diction. It is quite believable that by his own lights Cromwell had not consciously planned what he would do on 20 April, even though he had been determined for several months that the Rump should go.

Public reaction to the disappearance of the Long Parliament was subdued. By the end of the day a wag had hung a sign on the door which read, 'This house is to be let, now unfurnished.' Within days there were expressions of popular relief and rejoicing that a new dispensation had begun. Soon two new ballads were heard in the streets of London celebrating Cromwell's action. The Venetian ambassador confirmed that the people were happy at parliament's demise. In tacit recognition of their unpopularity, the MPs had voiced no protest; some of them went into hiding. Even Whitelocke had to concede that the nation acquiesced in the army's action. Warm expressions of support came from the navy, as well as from officers in Scotland and the north. *The Humble Petition of the Church of Christ* hailed Cromwell as 'our Moses', while others urged him to put the crown on his own head. Almost the only discordant note came from several aldermen and Sheriff Stephen Estwick, who, at the instigation of some Rumpers, petitioned for the recall of the Long Parliament. When Cromwell retaliated by stripping them and their associates of all offices of profit no one rallied to their support.[76]

What happened on 20 April 1653, and the popular reaction to it, are both tolerably clear. Less clear is why the army chose to act the way it did, and, more precisely, what it was about the Rump's bill for a new Representative that was so unacceptable to it. Blair Worden has established beyond reasonable doubt that the bill reintroduced by Hesilrige in February 1653 did not, as the officers charged immediately afterwards, provide for the Long Parliament to perpetuate itself indefinitely by recruiting new members to vacant seats. The army's objection to the bill 'was not that it provided for recruiter elections. It was that it provided for elections at all.'[77] Woolrych, while accepting Worden's conclusion, has also analysed the problem from the army's perspective. His argument is that on 20 April the officers *believed* that the bill contained a recruiting clause. Otherwise they were guilty of deliberate lying in their statements over the subsequent week when they accused the Rump of intending merely to recruit itself. Woolrych's plausible suggestion is that the bill had previously provided for recruitment, but was changed at the last minute.[78]

But there was more to the army's objections than that. Ever since the autumn of 1648 it had known that, if the revolution was not to be reversed, the godly would have to govern for the foreseeable future. This implied that the rules for electoral eligibility would have to be as carefully drafted as they had been for the London election of 1648. Even when on 13 April parliament allayed the army's worries on this score there remained the question, who was to judge whether the future elected representatives truly met the requirement that they be 'persons of known integrity, fearing God, and not scandalous in their conversation'? Cromwell later charged that the Rump had made no provision for enforcing its qualifications for election, and, as Woolrych points out, no one ever contradicted this charge.[79]

The chasm of suspicion dividing the officers and the parliamentary majority was so wide that the former could not contemplate leaving the business of judging qualifications in the hands of the latter. That is why at the last moment the Council of Officers launched an intensive round of negotiations with the parliamentary leaders designed to put off the elections for a time and set up an interim government composed of about forty godly men – half officers and half MPs. Exercising supreme authority, the proposed executive would provide the nation with good and decisive government. This, the officers were confident, would be

> the most hopeful way to encourage and countenance all God's people, reform the law, and administer justice impartially; hoping thereby the people might forget monarchy, and, understanding their true interest in the election of successive parliaments, may have the government settled upon a true basis, without hazard to this glorious cause, or necessitating to keep up armies for the defence of the same.[80]

On the morning of 20 April, however, the MPs rejected Cromwell's plan and proceeded with a scheme that would have barred the officers from any participation in running the country. Even worse, according to Streater and

Hutchinson the Rump's bill would have fired Cromwell as commander-in-chief. Apparently it would have put the army command into commission, just as the Rump was to do in 1659. Equally disastrous in the army's eyes, it appears that it would have excluded serving officers from being elected to parliament.[81]

An officer-inspired report explaining the dissolution affirmed that, had the Rump's bill passed, the nation would have been 'in a sad condition, and involved in a labyrinth of new troubles.' The 'several things ... of dangerous consequence' in the bill included a reduction in the army's budget to £31,000 a month. This sum would not have paid the wages of more than 14,000 men. With the army both emasculated and excluded from the new Representative, a power vacuum would have existed, which would have furnished a tempting opportunity for the royalists to stage a *coup d'état*. Fears of a royalist or royalist–presbyterian seizure of power were widespread at the time, and were not confined to the army officers.[82]

Thus the officers' expulsion of the Rump was not only a last-ditch measure to forestall the accession to power of the ungodly; it was also an act of self-preservation against parliament's clear intention to destroy them. But it was something more as well. The officers' *Declaration of the Grounds and Reasons for Dissolving the Parliament*, issued on 22 April, opened with an indictment of the Rump for failing to provide good government, and for being dilatory about reform. That this was not empty rhetoric is shown by the officers' tireless twenty-month exhortation of the Rump to act on law reform, financial probity, religious toleration and the spreading of the Gospel. Cromwell summed up the matter tersely when he told the London aldermen that the MPs had been dismissed 'because they did not perform their trust.' Or, as the officers wrote to their comrades in Ireland in May, they took action because of 'the ill management of affairs by the late parliament.'[83]

A further reason why the Rump was dissolved was Cromwell's own drive for power. It may well be that on 20 April his goal was nothing more than to save himself from destruction by his opponents.[84] But it is also quite clear from his interview with Whitelocke the previous autumn, and his exchange with Edmund Calamy the previous month, that he had been meditating a seizure of power for his own purposes. That he should have such thoughts was entirely natural. He was an undefeated general with a secure power base among his troops. By risking their lives repeatedly for almost a decade, he and his officers had surely won the moral right to be listened to on political affairs. Yet ever since returning from Worcester they had been blocked at every turn. As Cromwell contemplated the men who thwarted him, the thought must have crossed his mind that he could do a better job at the helm of government than any of them. No one in parliament could boast his military prowess, and when it came to political subtlety and effectiveness he was a match for the best of them. The only individual who rivalled his military and political virtuosity was another soldier, John Lambart, and for the time being this much younger man backed his commander-in-chief. It was galling for Oliver to see his dreams for godly reformation and political settlement frustrated week after week by men of such blinkered vision as Hesilrige, Vane, St John, Marten and Whitelocke. It exasperated him that they were more troubled by the threat of usurpation by soldiers and militant sectarians than by a resurgent presbyterianism, and its potential ally, the House of Stuart. He therefore decided that 'the Lord had done' with these men, and that he, Cromwell, would wipe the slate clean of them. While he did not conceive of himself as a military dictator,[85] he indubitably wanted to be at the centre of political decision-making in the country.

As we have seen, he did not have to worry about popular support for the Rump. The fortuitous arrival of the long-awaited colliers in London within days of the dissolution brought a sudden drop in the price of fuel, which also redounded to the benefit of the new dispensation. Cromwell's pardoning of a band of condemned prisoners on their way to Tyburn, and his order that there should be no further hanging in London except for murder were an earnest of his commitment to law reform, which would have delighted Samuel Chidley and the other campaigners against hanging for theft.[86] His order to the commissioners for propagating the Gospel in Wales to continue their work would have similarly contented Harrison and his friends.[87] At the beginning of June the new regime further benefited from a major victory at sea, in the engagement off Gabbard Sands. Ironically the victory had been made possible by the activity of Vane and his committee, now extinct.[88]

The army quickly consolidated its power. The House of Lords, the Painted Chamber, the Court of Requests and adjacent rooms were garrisoned with soldiers 'lest the old parliament should steal together again and bring forth some monstrous votes.' Because the City was regarded as untrustworthy, a number of regiments were drawn closer to London.[89] The Council of Officers met daily in Whitehall to draw up plans for a self-perpetuating godly oligarchy until the people should be 'capable of their former government by parliaments.' Lambart leaned towards a small executive of no more than twelve, while Harrison favoured a larger council of seventy modelled on the Jewish sanhedrin. In the meantime Lambart was made president of the interim Council of State for a week, a move which demonstrated both his support for the regime, and Cromwell's confidence in him. With Cromwell, Harrison, Disbrowe, Bennett, Tomlinson, Colonel Sydenham (governor of Weymouth) and Colonel Philip Jones (governor of Swansea) also on the thirteen-man council, the domination of officers was plain enough. Emulating Cromwell, they speedily adopted a number of progressive measures, including an inquiry into the state of the post office, an investigation of the debtors' prison of the Court of Upper Bench, a scheme for the better management of the treasuries, and the suppression of bear- and bull-baiting. Nevertheless the new arrangements sparked resentment among many officers, when they realized that the small Council of State, and not the Council of Officers, was the effective locus of decision-making. The sense of alienation felt by many officers found a parallel in the umbrage taken by the rank and file at being 'cozened out of their debentures by the insinuation of the superior officers.' According to one report there was also a momentary rekindling of democratic aspirations among the soldiery. Military agitators were said to have presented a remonstrance to the Council of Officers claiming for every soldier 'an equal voice in electing the members of the forthcoming new representative.' With the aim of quelling this restlessness the senior officers placed the forces in and about London on a diet of two or three hours of daily prayer and preaching.[90]

After some discussion it was resolved to summon an assembly drawn from the three nations. The next question was whether Cromwell alone should choose the nominees with the help of his officers, or whether the various congregations of saints should choose them. 'Very much sweetly said both ways', as Harrison reported to Colonel John Jones.[91] For all his prestige among the sects, Harrison could not persuade fellow officers to give up the power of choosing the new representatives. Though they did impose upon themselves the principle of self-denial, they did not observe it unbendingly. No one from headquarters in Whitehall was nominated, but the names put forward did include three colonels from Ireland – Hewson, Henry Cromwell and John Clarke; the commander of the lifeguards, Charles Howard; the two generals at sea, Blake and Monk; and several garrison commanders – Robert Bennett, William Sydenham, John Bingham, Henry Danvers and Philip Jones. When the new assembly sat it also co-opted five officers from headquarters: Cromwell, Disbrowe, Harrison, Lambart and Tomlinson.[92]

At the end of May the officers sat with Cromwell for several days going over the names; it took almost two weeks to get the letters of nomination signed and sent out to 140 persons 'fearing God, and of approved fidelity and honesty'. Reflecting a spectrum of religious allegiance at least as broad as that found among the officers, the nominees included presbyterians (for example, Francis Rous), orthodox congregationalists (Samuel Moyer, Robert Tichborne and Sir Gilbert Pickering), to Baptists (Robert Bennett) and Fifth Monarchists (Hugh Courtney).[93]

On 4 July, 120 of the nominated representatives pressed into the cramped chamber of the Council of State to hear Cromwell's welcoming address and charge. The crush of bodies on this hot day was made worse by the addition of several higher officers who clustered around the general when he entered. Those present were treated to a 'grave[,] ... reasonable' and 'Christian-like speech' accompanied by frequent shedding of tears. After apologizing for the overcrowding and promising to abbreviate his remarks on account of the heat, he launched upon a two-hour oration ornamented with the full panoply of Cromwellian rhetoric. He began soberly enough with a history of the civil war and a defence of the recent dissolution. Warming to his theme, he then laboured to inspire his hearers with the thought that 'truly God hath called you to this work.' Promising to pray for rather than counsel them, he none the less uttered an impassioned plea for religious toleration for all who wished 'to lead a life of godliness and honesty.... Therefore I beseech you ... have a care of the whole flock. Love the sheep, love the lambs, love all, tender all, cherish and countenance all, in all things that are good.' Following these overtly Christian and Pauline echoes he next delivered his most exalted charge: 'Jesus Christ is owned this day by your call; and you own Him by your willingness to appear for Him; and you manifest this, as far as poor creatures can, to be a day of the power of Christ.'[94]

After these visionary flights, garnished with copious quotations from scripture, Oliver reminded his audience of the extraordinary thing that he and the army were doing: voluntarily relinquishing complete authority into their hands. Apologizing for speaking at inordinate length on so hot a day, he ended by having the 'Instrument' under which they were to govern read out. By its terms they were to exercise supreme power until November 1654, and then cede power to a new assembly nominated by themselves. Their successors were to govern for only a year. The unspoken assumption was that by that time the people would be ready again to elect their parliaments.

Regarding the prospect of a free election, Cromwell exclaimed, 'none can desire it more than I!' He thereby confirmed the essentially conservative character of his political vision. Though sharing the millenarian excitement of Harrison and the Fifth Monarchists, and possessing a genuine tenderness for the 'saints' in their variegated congregations, he was also animated by a profound respect for England's laws and political institutions. For the remaining five years of his life Cromwell would engage in a frustrating quest for the godly reformation that the army so ardently desired, at the same time trying to eschew the temptations of military tyranny, and struggling vainly to return the country to the normality of parliamentary elections. But on that sweltering July day, borne aloft by his soaring rhetoric, few men perceived how narrow were the lineaments of the Cromwellian political landscape.

Epilogue

From inauspicious beginnings in the spring of 1645, the New Model Army rapidly transformed parliament's military position. Within scarcely a year royalist forces had surrendered in all parts of the kingdom. Renewed uprisings in 1648 were quickly put down, and the Scottish invaders decisively smashed. Under Cromwell's leadership the army extended its record of battlefield invincibility, rolling over the Scots at Dunbar, Inverkeithing and Worcester. The Irish foe proved more stubborn, but, after three years of debilitating warfare which reduced their country to a wasteland, they too were brought to acknowledge the English army's dominance.

Reflecting on this unbroken chain of victories, Ambrose Barnes was confident that all rational unbiased witnesses 'will allow this army to be *fulmina belli*, the thundering army by the best judges thought to have been sufficient to march all the world over.'[1]

The political changes wrought by Fairfax and Cromwell's army were hardly less stupendous than its feats on the battlefield. In 1647 and 1648 the army blocked the peace party in its efforts to reach a compromise peace with the king. It twice invaded London, twice expelled peace-party members from parliament, and caused an unprecedented, illegal tribunal to be erected to try the king for crimes against the English people. In union with a radical minority in the Commons and the Lords, the army was the engine that powered the revolutionary momentum of 1648–9. During the time when the king's trial and execution were being prepared, the officers of the army were immersed in debate about a future constitution for England. Their version of the Agreement of the People, promulgated ten days before Charles went to the scaffold, was not markedly dissimilar from the earlier draft approved by the Leveller leadership. The failure of the army's proposed constitution is traceable to the Rump's hostility to that constitution, to the breakdown of the army–Leveller alliance, and to the army's renewed preoccupation with military affairs between 1649 and 1651.

In all their doings the army's leaders believed they were the instruments of providence. The failure of every enemy, military and political, seemed irrefutable proof that the rays of divine favour shone upon the New Model. Yet by 1660 their triumphs had turned to ashes, and the monarch had resumed his throne without a drop of blood being shed. What could explain this drastic reversal of the army's fortunes? To some officers it was God's punishment for their and the nation's sins. 'The Lord had ... spit in their faces', lamented General Fleetwood. Others, like General Ludlowe, were sure that the Restoration was only a temporary detour into the wilderness, and that England would eventually find its way again to the promised land.

If like many intellectuals one regards Christianity simply as a variety of religious myth, there is nothing troubling about the officers' convictions: they were merely a delusion, even if a powerfully effective one. But for the theist – and, surprisingly, opinion polls in various countries indicate that even in the late twentieth century the great majority continue to believe in God – the phenomenon of a group of warrior leaders claiming direct communication with the Almighty raises a difficult question. The adversaries of these warriors were also certain that they knew and were following God's will. Was either side right?

One approach to this conundrum is to ask if the officers' communication with God could have been impeded by their very reliance on what they themselves frequently referred to as 'the arm of flesh', meaning physical might. At times the officers showed flashes of insight into the unresolvable tension between their continual dependence upon violence to achieve their ends, and their quest for divine guidance. The officer who wrote *Vox Militaris* articulated this tension when he wrote at the beginning of August 1647,

> for the government of the Church, our judgement is this, that Sion's walls are not to be laid in blood, but that the God of peace, the prince of peace, the spirit of peace, the word of peace; truth and love will create temples of living stones, for the Lord of glory to dwell therein.[2]

A second example of some officers' awareness of the obligation to seek peace occurred during the emotional binge of the Windsor prayer meeting in April 1648. Before Lieutenant-General Goffe swayed them all with his rhetoric, a number of officers were inclined to lay down their arms rather than plunge the nation into renewed civil war. They pointed to the example of Christ, who, at the end of his earthly ministry, willingly sacrificed his own life.[3] The most forceful statement of the impossibility of combining obedience to God with a vocation to violence was made on the eve of the Irish expedition in 1649, by a writer who I believe was Major John Cobbett:

Oh! the ocean of blood that we are guilty of. Oh! the intolerable oppression that we have laid upon our brethren of England. Oh! how these deadly sins of ours do torment our consciences. Oh! how are we able to answer these pestilent acts of ours, at the dreadful bar of God's divine justice?

... What have we to do with Ireland, to fight and murther a people and nation ... which have done us no harm, only deeper to put our hands in blood with their [the officers'] own? We have waded too far in that crimson stream (already) of innocent and Christian blood.[4]

For his cry of anguish Cobbett was rewarded with dismissal from the army.[5]

In the last decade of the twentieth century, as we witness simultaneously the crumbling of repressive regimes and the spreading conviction that war is too terrible an instrument any longer to be used for the settling of humanity's quarrels, we may salute the prophetic witness of Major Cobbett. Did he in 1649 hear God's voice more clearly than the majority of his fellow officers?

Notes

Abbreviations

AA	Clement Walker, *Anarchia Anglicana, or the History of Independency Second part* (no publisher, London, 1649)
A & O	C. H. Firth and R. S. Rait (eds), *The Acts and Ordinances of the Interregnum, 1642–1660* (3 vols, HMSO, London, 1911)
Abbott	Wilbur Cortez Abbott (ed.), *The Writings and Speeches of Oliver Cromwell* (4 vols, Harvard University Press, Cambridge, Mass., 1937–47)
Add. MS	Additional Manuscript, British Library
AS	Archaeological Society
Baillie, I–III	Robert Baillie, *Letters and Journals*, ed. David Laing, Bannatyne Club, 72, 73, 77 (3 vols, 1841)
Battles	Austin Woolrych, *Battles of the English Civil War* (Batsford, London, 1961)
Bell	Robert Bell (ed.), *Memorials of the Civil War* (2 vols, Richard Bentley, London, 1849)
BIHR	*Bulletin of the Institute of Historical Research*
BL	British Library
Bodl. Lib.	Bodleian Library
Burns and Young	A. H. Burns and P. Young, *The Great Civil War* (Eyre and Spottiswoode, London, 1959)
C & P	S. R. Gardiner, *History of the Commonwealth and Protectorate 1649–1656* (4 vols, Longmans, Green, London, 1903)
Carte	(With MS no.:) Correspondence of the Marquess of Ormonde, Bodleian Library
	(With vol. and page nos:) Thomas Carte, *A Collection of Original Letters and Papers ... 1641–1660. Found among the Duke of Ormonde's Papers* (2 vols, A. Millar, London, 1739)
Cary	Henry Cary (ed.), *Memorials of the Great Civil War in*

	England from 1646 to 1652 (2 vols, Henry Colburn, London, 1842)
CCJ	Journal of the Common Council of London, Corporation of London Records Office
CJ	*Journal of the House of Commons*
Clar.	Clarendon Manuscripts, Bodleian Library
Clarendon, *History*	Edward Earl of Clarendon, *The History of the Rebellion and Civil Wars in England*, ed. W. D. Macray (6 vols, Clarendon Press, Oxford, 1888)
Clarke Papers	*Clarke Papers*, ed. C. H. Firth, Camden Society, new ser., XLIX, LIV, LX, LXII (4 vols, London, 1891–1901)
CLRO	Corporation of London Records Office
Codr. Lib.	Codrington Library, All Souls' College
Const. Docs	S. R. Gardiner (ed.), *The Constitutional Documents of the Puritan Revolution, 1625–1660*, 3rd edn (Clarendon Press, Oxford, 1906)
Crom. Army	C. H. Firth, *Cromwell's Army*, 4th edn (Methuen, London, 1962)
Crom. Navy	B. S. Capp, *Cromwell's Navy: the fleet and the English Revolution, 1648–1660* (Clarendon Press, Oxford, 1989)
CSPD	*Calendar of State Papers, Domestic Series*. For publication details see Bibliography.
CSPI	*Calendar of State Papers, Irish Series*. For publication details see Bibliography.
CSPV	*Calendar of State Papers, Venetian Series*. For publication details see Bibliography.
C to P	Austin Woolrych, *Commonwealth to Protectorate* (Clarendon Press, Oxford, 1982)
DNB	*Dictionary of National Biography*
Duffy	Christopher Duffy, *Siege Warfare* (Routledge and Kegan Paul, London, 1979)
Dyve	*The Tower of London Letterbook of Sir Lewis Dyve, 1646–47*, ed. H. G. Tibbutt, Bedfordshire Historical Record Society, XXXVIII (1958)
E	Thomason Tracts, British Library; *or* (in references prefixed PRO) Exchequer
EcHR	*Economic History Review*
EHR	*English Historical Review*
Evelyn, *Diary*	John Evelyn, *Diary*, ed. E. S. de Beer (6 vols, Clarendon Press, 1955)
Evelyn, *D & C*	John Evelyn, *Diary and Correspondence*, ed. William Bray (4 vols, G. Bell, London, 1887–9)
Gang.	Thomas Edwardes, *Gangraena* (3 vols, Ralph Smith, London, 1646)

GCW	S. R. Gardiner, *History of the Great Civil War, 1642–1649* (4 vols, Longmans, Green, London, 1893)
GLCRO	Greater London Record Office
Greaves and Zaller	Richard Greaves and Robert Zaller (eds), *Biographical Dictionary of British Radicals in the Seventeenth Century* (3 vols, Harvester, Brighton, 1982–4)
Haller and Davies	William Haller and Godfrey Davies (eds), *The Leveller Tracts, 1647–1653* (Columbia University Press, New York, 1944)
Harl.	Harley Manuscripts, British Library
HJ	*Historical Journal*
HLRO	House of Lords Record Office
HMC	Royal Commission on Historical Manuscripts. References by MS series; for details see Bibliography.
HMSO	His/Her Majesty's Stationery Office
Hodgson	*Original Memoirs Written during the Great Civil War; Being the Life of Sir Henry Slingsby and Memoirs of Capt. Hodgson* (Constable, Edinburgh, 1806)
Holles	Denzil Holles, *Memoirs* (T. Goodwin, London, 1699)
HRS	Historical Record Society
HS	Historical Society
Hughes	Ann Hughes, *Politics, Society and Civil War in Warwickshire* (Cambridge University Press, Cambridge, 1987)
Hutchinson	Lucy Hutchinson, *Memoirs of the Life of Colonel Hutchinson*, ed. James Sutherland (Oxford University Press, London, 1973)
Intell.	*Intelligencer* (in newsbook titles)
JEH	*Journal of Ecclesiastical History*
Juxon	Diary of Thomas Juxon, Dr Williams's Library, MS 24.50
Kishlansky, *Rise*	Mark Kishlansky, *The Rise of the New Model Army* (Cambridge University Press, Cambridge and New York, 1979)
Lanc. Tracts	*Tracts relating to Military Proceedings in Lancashire during the Great Civil War*, Chetham Society, II (Manchester, 1844)
Laurence	Anne Laurence, *Parliamentary Army Chaplains, 1642–1651*, Royal Historical Society Studies in History, 59 (1990)
LJ	*Journal of the House of Lords*
Ludlow[e]	Edmund Ludlow[e], *Memoirs*, ed. C. H. Firth (2 vols, Clarendon Press, Oxford, 1894)
Maseres	Francis Baron Maseres, *Select Tracts relating to the Civil Wars in England* (2 vols, R. Bickerstaffe, London, 1815–26)
Massarella	Derek Massarella, 'The Politics of the Army, 1647–1660' (unpublished PhD thesis, University of York, 1979)
McMichael and Taft	Jack R. McMichael and Barbara Taft (eds), *The Writings of William Walwyn* (University of Georgia Press, Athens, Ga., and London, 1989)

Merc.	*Mercurius* (in newsbook titles)
Montereul	*Diplomatic Correspondence of Jean de Montereul ... 1645–48*, ed. J. G. Fotheringham, Scottish Historical Society, XXIX–XXX (Edinburgh, 1898–9)
Nickolls	John Nickolls (ed.), *Originall Letters and Papers of State Addressed to Oliver Cromwell ... MDCXLIX to MDCLVIII, found among the political collections of Mr. John Milton* (John Whiston, London, 1743)
Nicoll	John Nicoll, *A Diary of Public Transactions and Other Occurrences, chiefly in Scotland, from January 1650 to June 1667*, ed. David Laing, Bannatyne Club (1836)
NLS	National Library of Scotland
NLW	National Library of Wales
OPH	*The Parliamentary or Constitutional History of England* (commonly known as *Old Parliamentary History*), 2nd edn (24 vols, J. & R. Tonson, London, 1762–3)
P & P	*Past and Present*
Perf.	*Perfect* (in newsbook titles)
PP	D. E. Underdown, *Pride's Purge* (Clarendon Press, Oxford, 1971)
PRO	Public Record Office, London
Procs	*Proceedings* (in newsbook and journal titles)
Quarrel	*The Quarrel between the Earl of Manchester and Oliver Cromwell*, ed. David Masson, Camden Society, new ser., XII (1875)
Reece	Henry Reece, 'The Military Presence in England, 1649–1660' (unpublished DPhil. thesis, University of Oxford, 1981)
Reg. Hist.	Sir Charles Firth and Godfrey Davies, *The Regimental History of Cromwell's Army* (2 vols, Clarendon Press, Oxford, 1940)
RHS	Royal Historical Society
RO	Record Office
Roy	Ian Roy (ed.), *The Royalist Ordnance Papers, 1642–1646*, Oxfordshire Record Society (2 pts, 1963–4, 1971–3)
RS	Record Society
Rushworth	John Rushworth, *Historical Collections* (8 vols, D. Browne, London, 1721–2)
S & S	Austin Woolrych, *Soldiers and Statesmen: the General Council of the Army and its debates, 1647–1648* (Clarendon Press, Oxford, 1987)
SHS	Scottish History Society
Sloane	Sloane Manuscripts, British Library
SP	State Papers, Public Record Office
Sprigge	Ioshua Sprigge, *Anglia Rediviva, England's Recovery* (John Partridge, London, 1647)

Stevenson	David Stevenson, *Revolution and Counter-Revolution in Scotland, 1644–1651*, Royal Historical Society (1977)
Sydney Papers	*Sydney Papers*, ed. R. W. Blencowe (John Murray, London, 1825)
Tanner	Tanner Manuscripts, Bodleian Library
TRHS	*Transactions of the Royal Historical Society*
VCH	*The Victoria History of the Counties of England*
Wallington, MS Diary	Diary of Nehemiah Wallington, Tatton Park, MS 104
Wheeler	'English Army Finance and Logistics, 1642–1660' (unpublished PhD thesis, University of California, Berkeley, 1980)
Whitelocke	Bulstrode Whitelocke, *Memorials of English Affairs* (4 vols, Oxford University Press, Oxford, 1853)
Wkly	*Weekly* (in newsbook titles)
Wolfe	Don M. Wolfe (ed.), *Leveller Manifestoes of the Puritan Revolution* (Thomas Nelson, New York, 1944; repr. London: Frank Cass, 1967)
Woodhouse	A. S. P. Woodhouse, *Puritanism and Liberty* (Dent, London, 1938)
Worc.	Worcester College Library
Worden	Blair Worden, *The Rump Parliament, 1648–1653* (Cambridge University Press, Cambridge, 1974)

Chapter 1   The Founding of the New Model Army

1   Add. MS 25465 (Collectanea Hunteriana Journal of Occurrences 1643–6), fo. 20.
2   Sprigge, pp. 120–1; Abbott, I, 377.
3   Clarendon, *History*, IV, 2–3.
4   Ibid., III, 451–60.
5   Thomas Carlyle (ed.), *The Letters and Speeches of Oliver Cromwell*, notes by S. C. Lomas (3 vols, Methuen, London, 1904), I, 188.
6   *GCW*, II, 251, 328–30; III, 82.
7   *Crom. Army*, pp. 35–6, 316–17.
8   Abbott, I, 358.
9   Christopher Hill, *The World Turned Upside Down* (Temple Smith, London, 1972), p. 46.
10 Kishlansky, *Rise*, pp. 50, 66–7, 73, 291.
11 See reviews by G. E. Aylmer in *History*, 65 (1980), 486–7; Blair Worden, in *EHR*, 97 (1982), 637; Clive Holmes in *HJ*, XXIV (1981), 505–8; and Ian Gentles in *Canadian Journal of History*, XV (1980), 412–15.
12 Baillie, II, 140, 146, 153.
13 Brian Manning, *The English People and the English Revolution, 1640–1649*

(Heinemann, London, 1976), pp. 128–31; Keith Lindley, *Fenland Riots and the English Revolution* (Heinemann, London, 1982), pp. 118–19.

14 *Quarrel* p. 60. These were wild and unconvincing allegations; their importance lies in demonstrating the strength of hostility against Cromwell.

15 Ibid., pp. xx, xxii, xxiv, xxv, xi; Baillie, ıı, 229–30.

16 Baillie, ıı, 208–9, 211, 218.

17 *Battles*, p. 88.

18 *Quarrel*, p. 93.

19 *Battles*, p. 82.

20 Clive Holmes, *The Eastern Association in the English Civil War* (Cambridge University Press, Cambridge, 1974), pp. 199, 204.

21 Baschet's Transcripts of the Correspondence of the French Ambassador, PRO31/3/75, fos 195, 199, 201; Defence of the Earl of Manchester, BL Loan 29/123/Misc. 31, unpag.; Add. MS 25465, fo. 22; *Quarrel*, p. 69; untitled broadside, [9 Dec.] 1644, E21/9.

22 Rushworth, v, 732; *Perf. Passages*, 20–7 Nov. 1644, E19/3, p. 48; *Quarrel*, 78–95; ııı (1803), 704.

23 BL Loan 29/123/Misc. 31, unpag.; *LJ*, vıı (n.d.), 79; Rushworth, v, 733–6; Simeon Ashe, *A True Relation of the Most Chiefe Occurrences, at, and since the Late Battell at Newbery* (n.d.), E22/10, p. 6.

24 Tanner MS 61, fos 205ᵛ–6. The same allegations were reported in similar words by the French envoy Sabran (PRO31/3/75, fos 204–5). Although J. S. A. Adamson has convincingly established Cromwell's links with radical members of the upper house, I do not share his conviction that, in a careless moment, he could not have condemned the institution of nobility. See 'Oliver Cromwell and the Long Parliament', in John Morrill (ed.), *Oliver Cromwell* (Longman, London, 1990), p. 61.

25 *Perf. Diurnall*, 2–9 Dec. 1644, E256/45, p. 563.

26 Cf. *Perf. Occurrences*, 22–9 Nov. 1644, E256/42, unpag., 25 Nov.; *Quarrel*, p. 69. One of the strengths of A. N. B. Cotton's article 'Cromwell and the Self-Denying Ordinance', *History*, 62, no. 205 (1977), is that it gives due weight to religious differences in the enmity between the Cromwellian and Essex-Manchester factions (see pp. 218–19). However, I think that Cotton exaggerates Cromwell's political weakness (pp. 220, 223–4). Apart from the comment by *Merc. Civicus*, 21–8 Nov. 1644, E19/4, p. 731, that Cromwell was most 'exclaimed against', all sources show that Manchester bore the brunt of criticism in London for the Newbury-Donnington fiasco. The earl himself admitted that public opinion blamed him before anyone else (PRO31/3/75, fo. 201). Whitelocke and the Scots commissioners, no friends of Cromwell, also had a healthy respect for his political strength and adroitness during these months (see above, p. 6). See also Adamson, 'Oliver Cromwell and the Long Parliament', p. 62 n. 48.

27 *Parliament Scout*, 21–8 Nov. 1644, E19/5, p. 602.

28 I cannot accept Kishlansky's contention that there was little party conflict in parliament at this time. Cf. Adamson, 'Oliver Cromwell and the Long Parlia-

ment', pp. 60–3, and Robert Ashton, *The English Civil War: conservatism and revolution, 1603–1649* (Weidenfeld and Nicolson, London, 1978), ch. 9, which draws on the work of Valerie Pearl, David Underdown, Clive Holmes and others.

29 Whitelocke, I, 343–8.

30 Ibid., p. 346.

31 Baillie, II, 244–5.

32 *Quarrel*, pp. 96–9.

33 Baillie, II, 246.

34 Rushworth, VI, 1–3; Add. MS 25465, fo. 28.

35 Add. MS 31116 (Lawrence Whitacre's diary), fo. 1ƒ8; Rushworth, VI, 3; Abbott, I, 314.

36 *CJ*, III, 718.

37 Unfortunately the record does not indicate whether the preachers promoted the self-denying resolution in their sermons (Whitelocke, I, 351; Kishlansky, *Rise*, pp. 32–3).

38 *CJ*, III, 718; *PP*, appendix A. Essex or peace-party adherents were Maynard and Reynolds.

39 L. Kaplan, *Politics and Religion during the English Revolution* (New York University Press, New York, 1976), pp. 86–7; Violet A. Rowe, *Sir Henry Vane the Younger* (Athlone Press, London, 1970), p. 57.

40 Sloane MS 1519, fo. 37, John Lambart to Sir Thomas Fairfax. I am grateful to Dr Ian Roy for this reference.

41 Baillie, II, 247.

42 *Perf. Occurrences*, 6–13 Dec. 1644, E258/1, unpag.; *Parliament Scout*, 5–12 Dec. 1644, E21/15, pp. 617–18; *Merc. Britanicus*, 9–16 Dec. 1644, E21/23, pp. 482–3.

43 Untitled broadside, [9 Dec.] 1644, E21/9.

44 *Perf. Occurrences*, 6–13 Dec. 1644, unpag., E258/1.

45 *Kingdomes Wkly Intell.*, 10–17 Dec. 1644, E21/25, pp. 681–2.

46 *LJ*, VII, 277. The fourteen moderate or peace-party commanders to be dismissed were Essex, Warwick, Manchester, Denbigh, Grey and Robartes from the Lords, and Sir Thomas Middleton, William Jephson, Sir Philip Stapleton, Sir Edward Boys, Sir Samuel Luke, Sir Gilbert Gerrard, Sir John Meyrick and Sir Walter Erle (*Wkly Account*, 4–11 Dec. 1644, E21/12, unpag.). For the political allegiances of the MPs see *PP*, appendix A; and M. F. Keeler, *The Long Parliament*, American Philosophical Society (Philadelphia, 1954), *passim*. For information on Warwick and Robartes I am indebted to John Adamson.

47 *Reg. Hist.*, pp. 87, 632–3, xxiv, 459–60; HLRO, Main Papers, 12 May 1645, fo. 110. I owe this reference to John Adamson.

48 *CJ*, III, 723, 726; *Perf. Passages*, 11–18 Dec. 1644, E21/26, p. 68; *Perf. Diurnall* 16–23 Dec. 1644, p. 579, E258/5; Sloane MS 1519, fo 39–9ᵛ; Whitelocke, I, 349.

49 Whitelocke, I, 355.

50   Sloane MS 1519, fo. 39.
51   *LJ*, vii, 109, 112–13.
52   *CJ*, iv, 4.
53   *Perf. Occurrences*, 27 Dec. 1644–3 Jan. 1645, E258/9, unpag.; *CJ*, iv, 11.
54   *LJ*, vii, 117, 122; HLRO, House of Lords Minute Book, unfol. (3 Jan. 1645).
55   *LJ*, vii, 129.
56   *CJ*, iv, 13, 14.
57   Rushworth, vi, 7.
58   *LJ*, vii, 134.
59   *CJ*, iv, 16.
60   Ibid., p. 18; Lotte Mulligan, 'Peace negotiations, politics and the Committee of Both Kingdoms, 1644–1646', *HJ*, xii (1969), 3–22.
61   *CSPD, 1644–5*, p. 63.
62   The members were John Maynard, Thomas Lane and Lawrence Whitacre. (*CJ*, iv, 18). With the substance of the ordinance having been decided, the appointment of moderates to draft it may have been a kind of window-dressing, designed to impress the upper house.
63   *Kingdomes Wkly Intell.*, 7–14 Jan. 1645, E24/18, p. 706.
64   The quarrel soon petered out as the Commons found themselves increasingly preoccupied with the more constructive task of creating a new army (*Quarrel*, pp. xc–xci, xciii; *LJ*, vii, 141).
65   *Merc. Civicus*, 16–23 Jan. 1645, E25/21, p. 795.
66   Bell, i, 142.
67   Ibid., p. 155.
68   *CJ*, iv, 26.
69   Bell, i, 142, 156, 162, *et passim*; Sloane MS 1519, fos 37, 39; J. S. A. Adamson, 'The baronial context of the English Civil War', *TRHS*, 5th ser., 40 (1990), 116.
70   *CJ*, iv 26.
71   *CJ*, iv, 28, 30, 31; *Perf. Diurnall*, 20–7 Jan. 1645, E258/17, pp. 621–2.
72   *LJ*, vii, 159.
73   *CJ*, iv, 36, 37; *LJ*, vii, 166, 169; *PP*, appendix A.
74   *LJ*, vii, 164.
75   Add. MS 25465, fos 31^v–2; *LJ*, vii, 166.
76   *LJ*, vii, 164–5; A. N. B. Cotton, 'John Dillingham, journalist of the Middle Group', *EHR*, 93 (1978), 821, 824.
77   *LJ*, vii, 175; HLRO, Main Papers, 4 Feb. 1645, fo. 87–7^v.
78   *CJ*, iv, 37; *Perf. Diurnall*, 27 Jan.–3 Feb. 1645, E258/19, p. 628.
79   *LJ*, vii, 178, 180.
80   This expectation of great changes attendant upon the new modelling of the armies is also mirrored in the comments of newsbook writers. See the *London Post*, 4 Feb. 1645, E27/10, p. 2; and the *Scotish Dove*, 31 Jan.–7 Feb. 1645, E269/3, p. 529.
81   *True Informer*, 1–8 Feb. 1645, E269/4, p. 495; *CJ*, iv, 43; *PP*, appendix A.

82 *Perf. Diurnall*, 3–10 Feb. 1645, E258/22, p. 638; *CJ*, IV, 44; *LJ*, VII, 190 (mispag. as 192), 192.

83 *Wkly Account*, 5–12 Feb. 1645, E269/12, unpag.; *LJ*, VII, 187.

84 *LJ*, VII, 187.

85 Ibid., pp. 166, 169.

86 *CJ*, IV, 46–7; Whitelocke, I, 372.

87 See above, p. 12.

88 *CJ*, IV, 47; *LJ*, VII, 192.

89 *CJ*, IV, 48; Harl. MS 166 (diary of Sir Simonds D'Ewes), fo. 177ᵛ. Sir John Evelyn and Cromwell were the tellers for the noes; Sir Christopher Wray and Sir William Lewes for the yeas.

90 The three were John Lisle, Sir Thomas Widdrington and the Recorder of London, John Glyn. While Glyn would emerge as a strong presbyterian in 1647, he appears to have been associated with the war party at the end of 1644. See J. R. MacCormack, *Revolutionary Politics in the Long Parliament* (Harvard University Press, Cambridge, Mass., 1973), p. 334.

91 *LJ*, VII, 193. Lisle and his colleagues were being somewhat disingenuous. In fact the majority in the Commons had wanted the whole proviso regarding the covenant eliminated, but as a compromise settled for the deletion of the phrase rendering refusers forever incapable of serving (*Perf. Diurnall*, 10–17 Feb. 1645, E258/25, p. 646).

92 Harl. MS 166, fo. 177ᵛ; *CSPD*, 1644–5, pp. 304–5, 307; *Perf. Diurnall*, 10–17 Feb. 1645, E258/25, p. 645.

93 Kaplan, *Politics and Religion*, p. 110.

94 *CJ*, IV, 48. On the day the amended ordinance finally passed, the 'violent party', according to Simonds D'Ewes, 'began to speak very highly' against the Covenant, but in the end they swallowed their pride (Harl. MS 166, fo. 178).

95 *LJ*, VII, 204–9.

96 *CJ*, IV, 51–2.

97 Ibid., 53–4; *Perf. Diurnall*, 17–24 Feb. 1645, E258/27, p. 649; Bell, I, 161.

98 Hull RO, BRL333, Pelham to Denman; PRO31/3/76, fos 98, 99, 102.

99 *LJ*, VII, 221, 224.

100 *CJ*, IV, 60; Holmes, *Eastern Association*, p. 199.

101 Harl. MS 166, fo. 179ᵛ.

102 Space does not permit a detailed analysis of the parliamentary struggles over Fairfax's officer list. I plan to publish such an analysis elsewhere.

103 *CJ*, IV, 64.

104 *CJ*, IV, 69, 71; HLRO, Main Papers, 10 Mar. 1645, fos 145, 146, 148.

105 Fairfax's nominations and the Lords' proposed amendments are in HLRO, Main Papers, 10 Mar. 1645, fos 145–8. The document has been printed in Robert K. G. Temple, 'The original officer list of the New Model Army', *BIHR*, LIX (1986), 54–77.

106 Mark Kishlansky, 'The case of the army truly stated: the creation of the New Model Army', *P & P*, 81 (1978), 68.

107   Harl. MS 166, fo. 183.
108   Kishlansky, 'The creation of the New Model Army', pp. 67–8.
109   Temple, 'The original officer list', p. 53. Emphasis in the original.
110   Hull RO, BRL342.
111   Add. MS 25465, fos 32ᵛ–3.
112   PRO31/3/76, fo. 119ᵛ.
113   *CJ*, IV, 77.
114   *LJ*, VII, 273.
115   Ibid., p. 274.
116   *CJ*, IV, 81.
117   The source for this interpretation is Juxon's journal, Add. MS 25465, fo. 33.
       Whitacre gives the 'official' if less political interpretation of the Lords' capitu-
       lation: namely, that altering the list would be a time-consuming infringement
       of Fairfax's prerogatives as commander-in-chief (Add. MS 31116, fo. 198ᵛ;
       CJ, IV, 81). D'Ewes, however, agreed essentially with Juxon about the Com-
       mons' application of coercion when he confided to his journal that the Com-
       mons threatened the Lords that if they did not concur 'Fairfax will recede
       from nomination and we from approbation' (Harl. MS 166, fo. 184ᵛ).
118   *LJ*, VII, 274.
119   Ibid., p. 277.
120   PRO31/3/76, fo. 142ᵛ; Vernon F. Snow, *Essex the Rebel* (University of
       Nebraska Press, Lincoln, Nebr., 1970), p. 476.
121   *LJ*, VII, 274.
122   Ibid., p. 277. John Adamson informs me that the one lord who opposed
       Fairfax's list but did not enter his dissent must have been Warwick.
123   *Fairfax Correspondence*, ed. George W. Johnson (2 vols, Richard Bentley,
       London, 1848), I, 166n.; Snow, *Essex*, p. 477; Whitelocke, I, 408; *CJ*, IV, 83.
124   *CJ*, IV, 82, 88–91; *LJ*, VII, 289.
125   PRO31/3/76, fo. 141ᵛ; Kaplan, *Politics and Religion*, pp. 111–12. The figure
       of 300 is Sabran's, and may have been exaggerated. Certainly it must have
       included non-commissioned as well as commissioned officers.
126   Tanner MS 60, fo. 93; *Reg. Hist.*, pp. xv, 82, 430, 442. In the Main Papers
       (HLRO) Ennis is referred to as lieutenant-colonel (10 Mar. 1645, fo. 145ᵛ).
127   *CJ*, IV, 94; *LJ*, VII, 293.
128   *CJ*, IV, 91, 93.
129   *LJ*, VII, 292. They were Northumberland, Kent, Nottingham, Salisbury, Saye
       and Sele, Wharton, Howard and Pembroke.
130   *CJ*, IV, 94; *LJ*, VII, 293.
131   Twenty lords were listed at the beginning of the afternoon sitting. Only sev-
       enteen had been listed in the morning, but their numbers had risen to nine-
       teen by the time of the vote. The late arrivals were Manchester and Berkeley,
       supporting the peace party, and Wharton supporting the war party.
132   *LJ*, VII, 297. *LJ* does not record the numbers of yeas and noes on divisions.
       Nevertheless, the margin of 11 to 9 can be inferred by the fact that twenty
       lords were present at the beginning of the afternoon sitting. Nine entered

their dissents, but Saye and Sele did not attempt to use Mulgrave's proxy as he had done previously. Therefore the majority for the motion must have been greater than one. It is possible that more lords took their places in the chamber during the course of the afternoon. Thomas Juxon, who is usually quite accurate in his reporting of parliamentary affairs, said that the margin was 13 to 9, although he erroneously assigned the vote to Monday instead of Tuesday (Add. MS 25465, fo. 33^v).

133 Add. MS 25465, fo. 33^v; *LJ*, vii, 298–9.
134 PRO31/3/76, fo. 150^v.
135 *LJ*, vii, 298.
136 Ibid., p. 300; *CJ*, iv, 97.
137 *LJ*, vii, 295.
138 Bell, i, 142, 156; Sloane MS 1519, fo. 39.
139 *LJ*, vii, 303.
140 Ibid., p. 310. The five were Northumberland, Kent, Pembroke, North and Howard.
141 Tanner MS 60, fo. 73.
142 *CSPD, 1644–5*, pp. 425, 423.
143 Ibid., p. 445.
144 *CJ*, iv, 138; *LJ*, vii, 365; Whitelocke, i, 432.
145 *CSPD, 1644–5*, pp. 275–325 *passim*.
146 Abbott, i, 339.
147 *Perf. Occurrences*, 2–9 May 1645, E260/33, unpag. Oliver Cromwell was not the only parliamentarian who was reappointed after being discharged under the Self-Denying Ordinance. Forty-day extensions were granted to three other MPs: Sir William Brereton, Sir Thomas Middleton and Sir John Price; however, in contrast to Cromwell's reappointment, theirs also named the men who would replace them once the extension had elapsed (*CJ*, iv, 138–9, 147; Whitelocke, i, 433). On 6 June Sir Samuel Luke was continued as governor of Newport Pagnell for twenty more days (*CJ*, iv, 166).
148 *CSPD, 1644–5*, pp. 526, 553, 558.
149 *LJ*, vii, 408, 411–12, 414–15, 419, 420, 424.
150 Ibid., p. 421.
151 Rushworth, vi, 39.
152 *CJ*, iv, 176; *LJ*, vii, 433.

Chapter 2   Recruitment, Provisioning and Pay

1 Wheeler, pp. 80, 174.
2 PRO, Treasurers at War Accounts, 28 Mar. 1645–25 Dec. 1651, E351/302, fos 1–6, printed in Ian Gentles, 'The arrears of pay of the parliamentary army at the end of the first civil war', *BIHR*, xlviii (1975), 62–3.
3 *LJ*, vii, 204ff.
4 Ibid., p. 78.

5 *LJ*, vii, 537–8; viii, 275; *CJ*, iv, 692.
6 PRO, E351/302, fo. 1.
7 *CJ*, iv, 78, 90.
8 *LJ*, vii, 381.
9 *CJ*, iv, 265; HMC *Portland*, i, 267; *Moderate Intell.*, 25 Sept.–2 Oct. 1645, E303/31, p. 147.
10 Tanner MS 59, fos 551, 585, 353, 345.
11 Sprigge, p. 127.
12 *LJ*, vii, 563.
13 *CJ*, iv, 298; *LJ*, vii, 635–6.
14 PRO, Treasurers at Warre, Accounts Various, Leger of Assessments for the Armie, E101/67/11A, fos 14–21, 89, 112; Gentles, 'Arrears of pay', pp. 60–1.
15 *CJ*, iv, 388, 484; *LJ*, viii, 244.
16 *CJ*, iv, 314.
17 By 1651 over 31 per cent of the army's revenue had come from sources other than the monthly assessment. Treasurers at War Accounts, 28 Mar. 1645–25 Dec. 1651, printed in Gentles, 'Arrears of pay', pp. 62–3.
18 Add. MS 31116 (Lawrence Whitacre's diary), fo. 304; *CJ*, v, 396; PRO, E101/67/11A, fos 68–85, 112–13. Thanks to protracted resistance from the Lords, the ordinance for the new twelve-month assessment, scheduled to begin on 25 March 1647, was not actually passed until 23 June. Its controversial nature, as well as parliament's oversight in neglecting to name the treasurers at war to receive the assessment until 23 September, doubtless had much to do with the its failure to generate revenue for the first nine months (*CJ*, v, 114, 119, 130; *LJ*, ix, 288; *A & O*, i, 958, 1015).
19 PRO, E351/302, fo. 2.
20 Commonwealth Exchequer Papers, SP28/41, fos 359, 234.
21 *CJ*, iv, 51, 56.
22 *LJ*, vii, 256.
23 *CJ*, iv, 75, 76; *LJ* vii, 269; Harl. MS 166, fo. 183.
24 *CJ*, iv, 76; Rushworth, vi, 17–18; Whitelocke, i, 418; *Merc. Civicus*, 3–10 Apr. 1645, E277/12, pp. 882–3; Tanner MS 60, fo. 73; 'An Historicall Diarie of the Militarie Proceedings of ... Sir Thomas Fairfax ... by John Rushworth', Harl. MS 252, fo. 33.
25 Tanner MS 60, fo. 73; *Scotish Dove*, 25 Apr.–2 May 1645, E281/10, p. 632.
26 HMC, *Portland*, i, 215; John Adair, *Roundhead General: a military biography of Sir William Waller* (Macdonald, London, 1969), p. 185.
27 Hull RO, BRL340, Peregrine Pelham to Nicholas Denman; *CSPD, 1644–5*, p. 358.
28 *CJ*, iv, 85.
29 Ibid., p. 90.
30 *CSPD, 1644–5*, pp. 381, 444.
31 *CSPD, 1644–5*, pp. 411, 420, 426, 437; *Perf. Occurrences*, 11–18 Apr. 1645, E260/17, unpag.
32 Tanner MS 60, fos 101, 138; *LJ*, vii, 334–5.

33 *LJ*, vii, 457; *CJ*, iv, 383, 418.
34 *LJ*, vii, 461.
35 *Perf. Diurnall*, 23–30 June 1645, E262/14, p. 795; *Perf. Occurrences*, 18–25 July 1645, E262/29, unpag.
36 *CJ*, iv, 192.
37 *Perf. Passages*, 3–10 Dec. 1645, E266/26, p. 468.
38 *Moderate Intell.*, 16–23 Apr. 1646, E334/2, p. 402.
39 Ibid., 16 June–3 July 1645, E292/3, p. 139.
40 *LJ*, vii, 268.
41 *Moderate Intell.*, 16–23 Apr. 1646, E334/2, p. 404.
42 Ibid., 23–30 Apr. 1646, E334/18, p. 410.
43 SP28/34, fo. 464ᵛ.
44 Sprigge, pp. 192, 195, 196.
45 *Citties Wkly Post*, 24 Feb.–3 Mar. 1646, E325/19, p. 5; *LJ*, viii, 230; John Rushworth, *A More Full and Exact Relation … of the Several Treaties between Sir Thomas Fairfax and Sir Ralph Hopton* (1646), E328/15, pp. 4–5.
46 *CSPD, 1645–7*, p. 128; Bell, i, 249; Sprigge, p. 99; *Perf. Occurrences*, 12–19 Sept. 1645, E264/17, unpag.
47 Tanner MS 60, fos 128, 132ᵛ.
48 *LJ*, vii, 565, 570; *CJ*, iv, 262.
49 SP28/43, fos 528, 536; vol. 246, unfol. Another account, for Warwickshire, shows only £29 15s. 10d. being spent to impress and pay 250 soldiers, but the list of expenses may be incomplete (SP28/42, fo. 678).
50 SP28/246, unfol.
51 SP28/34, fo. 365.
52 Ibid., fos 463–4.
53 *LJ*, viii, 170. A report in February 1646 of drums beating up in the suburbs to raise foot recruits adds plausibility to this claim (*Moderate Intell.*, 12–18 Feb. 1646, E322/35, p. 304).
54 London's early disenchantment with the New Model is shown both in its almost complete failure to produce the 1469 men demanded of it in September 1645, and in the sharply reduced quota which it was assigned the following January (*CJ*, iv, 299; *CSPD, 1645–7*, p. 319). For the extra responsibility laid upon the Eastern Association see Tanner MS 60, fo. 244.
55 *CJ*, iv, 418; *CSPD, 1645–7*, p. 319.
56 HMC, *Portland*, i, 215. An exact figure for the cavalry is nowhere given. However, since no impressment of cavalry later took place, and since service in the cavalry was so attractive that former officers volunteered to serve as troopers, there is little doubt that the target was reached or nearly reached. At the beginning of June the cavalry regiments appear to have been at nearly full strength (*CSPD, 1644–5*, p. 563).
57 *CSPD, 1644–5*, pp. 358–9.
58 *Kingdomes Wkly Intell.*, 22–9 Apr. 1645, E279/11, p. 778; *Wkly Account*, 23–9 Apr. 1645, E279/12, unpag.; *A Diary or an Exact Journal*, 24 Apr.–1 May 1645, E281/3, unpag. The last figure includes the four regiments already

dispatched to relieve Taunton. Their numbers, conservatively estimated, would have been around 3000. The figures drawn from the newsbooks are probably only accurate to the nearest 100. That the newsbooks did not merely copy one another is suggested by minor discrepancies in their figures.

59 *Merc. Civicus*, 24 Apr.–1 May 1645, E281/4, p. 910.

60 *Perf. Occurrences*, 2–9 May 1645, E260/33, unpag.; *Kingdomes Wkly Intell.*, 6–13 May 1645, E284/2, p. 792.

61 *Parliaments Post*, 6–13 May 1645, E284/1, p. 3; *Wkly Account*, 21–7 May 1645, E285/19, unpag.

62 *Parliaments Post*, 3–10 June 1645, E287/5, p. 6; *Perf. Passages*, 4–11 June 1645, E262/6, p. 264.

63 Sprigge, p. 29; *Exchange Intell.*, 4–11 June 1645, E288/3, p. 29; *Moderate Intell.*, 29 May–5 June 1645, E286/26, p. 112. Robert Baillie (II, 276) reported to one of his correspondents that the army's total strength was only 14,000 on the eve of Naseby. However, Baillie had a political motivation for underestimating the army's strength: he wished to establish that the exclusion of the Scots had been a disastrous mistake which had irreparably damaged parliament's military effort in 1645. His estimate is also belied by the very precise figures supplied by the *Scotish Dove* for the 5 June muster before the arrival of Cromwell's and Vermuyden's forces: 7031 foot and 3014 horse (*Scotish Dove*, 6–13 June 1645, E288/11, p. 678).

64 Whitelocke, I, 444; Sprigge, illustration of Naseby battlefield, opp. p. 32. It is possible that the 500 from the Eastern Association were part of Cromwell's 3000.

65 Burne and Young, p. 210; *Battles*, p.125.

66 *CSPD, 1644–5*, pp. 600, 603. A week before Naseby the Eastern Association had been 1515 below its quota (*LJ*, VII, 414).

67 *CSPD, 1644–5*, pp. 625–6.

68 *Scotish Dove*, 27 June–4 July 1645, E292/5, p. 702.

69 Troops were required to garrison Leicester, captured a few days later, and also to escort the royalist prisoners to London. The latter task was performed by Colonel Fiennes's regiment, while Leicester seems to have been garrisoned by local forces under Colonel Needham (Whitelocke, I, 451, 454).

70 *Scotish Dove*, 27 June–4 July 1645, E292/5, p. 702; *Perf. Diurnall*, 23–30 June 1645, E262/14, p. 795; *LJ*, VII, 463.

71 *Perf. Occurrences*, 8–15 Aug. 1645, E262/44, unpag.; *Perf. Passages*, 13–20 Aug. 1645, E262/46, p. 341.

72 *CJ*, IV, 267–8.

73 *CJ*, IV, 264, 266, 299; *LJ*, VII, 571–2.

74 *CSPD, 1645–7*, pp. 118, 121, 130, 152, 170.

75 *CJ*, IV, 299.

76 Bell, I, 249.

77 *Perf. Passages*, 3–10 Dec. 1645, E266/26, p. 468.

78 *CJ*, IV, 383.

79 *LJ*, VIII, 102.

80 *CSPD, 1645–7*, p. 319.

81 *CJ*, IV, 418.

82 *Moderate Intell.*, 26 Feb.–5 Mar. 1646, E327/2, p. 319; 12–19 Mar. 1646, E328/21, p. 341; 16–23 Apr. 1646, E334/2, p. 402; *LJ*, VIII, 230, 268; *Scotish Dove*, 11–18 Mar. 1646, E328/18, p. 599. The 3000 foot and horse mentioned in this source include Ireton's regiment of 700 horse, who were not recruits, but armed escorts. See *Moderate Intell.*, 12–19 Mar. 1646, E328/21, p. 341.

83 The wastage rate discovered by Hughes for the Warwickshire forces was similarly high, except that the losses were greater in the horse than the foot, evidently because it was the horse who did the actual fighting (Hughes, pp. 199–202).

84 In *Caesar's Due*, (1983), ch. 4, Joyce Lee Malcolm vividly portrays the king's difficulties in raising troops. However, her less thorough knowledge of parliament's difficulties in mobilizing the New Model leads her to exaggerate the contrast between the two.

85 *CJ*, IV, 78 (14 Mar. 1645). The six contractors were Sir Walter Erle, Anthony Nicoll, Thomas Hodges, Robert Scawen, Sir John Evelyn senior and Thomas Pury senior.

86 Tanner MS 60, fo. 171; *Scotish Dove*, 27 Nov.–3 Dec. 1645, E311/4, p. 877.

87 The address of most of the suppliers has not been determined, but it is known that the gunmakers occupied workshops mostly in the Minories or East Smithfield, the streets adjoining the Tower of London, to which they made their deliveries. It was only from 1645 that parliament ordered on a regular basis from London gunmakers. See Walter M. Stern, 'Gunmaking in seventeenth-century London', *Journal of the Arms and Armour Society*, I (1954), 61, 80. Joan Thirsk points out that provision merchants placed their orders in specialist farming regions: Suffolk for butter and Cheshire for cheese, for example. Army provisioning thus enhanced the specialization of regions. See Joan Thirsk, *Agrarian History of England and Wales*, V, pt ii (Cambridge University Press, Cambridge, 1985), pp. 302–3.

88 'The New Model Army Contract Book, 1645–6', London Museum, 46–78/709, fo. 114 [source printed in G. I. Mungeam, 'Contracts for the supply of equipment to the "New Model" Army in 1645', *Journal of the Arms and Armour Society*, VI (1968–70), 60–115]; SP28/29, fos 207–8, 226.

89 'New Model Army Contract Book', 46–78/709, fo. 58; SP28/33, fos 168, 208.

90 'New Model Army Contract Book', 46–78/709, fo. 36; SP28/37, fos 355–7.

91 Valerie Pearl, *London and the Outbreak of the Puritan Revolution* (Oxford University Press, London, 1961), pp. 144, 315, 323–4; Roy, pt i, 8, 14. Andrewes: SP28/33, fo. 164. Estwick et al.: SP28/36, fos 188–9; vol. 37, fos 407, 413. Rowe: SP28/352, fos 55–8. Normington: SP28/36, fo. 181. Prince: SP28/30, fos 363, 375. Hammond: SP28/352, fos 180–1. Mercer: SP28/36, fo. 658. Bromfield: SP28/30, fo. 374; vol. 37, fo. 345. Browne: SP28/29, fo. 137; vol. 30, fo. 294; vol. 32, fo. 376; vol. 33, fo. 165; *CSPD, 1644–5*, pp. 606–8, 619.

92 In contrast to the hapless Northamptonshire shoemakers, obliged to wait six

years for reimbursement for the shoes they had furnished to Essex's army (SP28/305, unfol).

93   *CJ*, IV, 386, 388. The supply warrants for the first year of the New Model's operations may be found in SP28/29–33, 36–7 and 352. Testimony to the fullness and accuracy of this archive is provided in the account book of horses delivered to Sir Thomas Fairfax's army, 3 Apr. 1645–25 Aug. 1646. For the twelve-month period ending 2 April, 1646 the account book shows 4739 horses being delivered to the army (SP28/140, pt 7). For the twelve months ending 31 March 1646 the supply warrants show that 4660 horses were paid for. The slight discrepancy may be entirely due to the two extra days covered by the account book.

94   SP28/31, fo. 547.

95   *Perf. Passages*, 30 Apr.–7 May 1645, E260/32, p. 218.

96   *CJ*, IV, 85.

97   *Perf. Diurnall*, 31 Mar.–7 Apr. 1645, E260/10, p. 702.

98   SP28/29, 30, *passim*.

99   *CSPD, 1644–5*, p. 594; *Colonel Weldon's Taking of Inch House* (1646), E330/5, p. 6.

100 'New Model Army Contract Book', 46–78/709, fo. 27ᵛ. Red coats faced with blue were worn throughout the army, except that the firelocks who guarded the artillery train were clad in tawny coats (*Perf. Passages*, 30 Apr.–7 May 1645, E260/32, p. 218). Moreover, once a campaign was under way, coats were not always replaced in the same colour. See Geoffrey Parker, *The Military Revolution* (Cambridge University Press, Cambridge, 1988), pp. 71–2.

101 Martin L. Van Creveld, *Supplying War* (Cambridge University Press, Cambridge, 1977), pp. 6, 24, 29. According to C. S. L. Davies, Henry VIII's government took a rather larger role in supplying its soldiers with victuals. See Davies, 'Provisions for armies, 1509–50; a study in the effectiveness of early Tudor government', *EcHR*, 2nd ser., XVII (1964–5), 234–5.

102 *Merc. Civicus*, 28 Aug.–4 Sept. 1645, E299/7, p. 1049; ibid., 7–14 May 1646, E337/21, p. 2241; *A Continuation of Certain Speciall and Remarkable Passages*, 23–30 Jan. 1646, E319/21, p. 7; *Wkly Account*, 27 May–3 June 1646, E339/14, unpag.; *Kingdomes Wkly Intell.*, 23–30 June 1646, E342/6, p. 151.

103 *A Diary, or an Exact Journal*, 12–18 Feb. 1646, E322/36, p. 7.

104 SP28/29–31, *passim*.

105 SP28/136, fo. 51; vols 171–3 (Northants), 182–6 (Warwickshire), *passim*. For Kineton, see vol. 182, unfol.; for Stretton under Fosse, vol. 185, unfol.

106 *Moderate Intell.*, 6–13 Nov. 1645, E309/11, p. 195.

107 *Wkly Account*, 27 May–3 June 1646, E339/14, unpag.; *Perf. Occurrences*, 22–9 May 1646, E339/5, unpag.

108 Whitelocke, I, 446; Malcolm, *Caesar's Due*, pp. 170, 172, 175, 184, 188; R. Hutton, *Royalist War Effort, 1642–1646* (Longman, London, 1982), pp. 96, 98, 181.

109 *LJ*, IX, 66–71. This pay scale, approved on 3 November 1647, had in fact prevailed in the New Model since the beginning.

110 SP28/301, fo. 757; vol. 303, fo. 465.

111 *A Diary, or an Exact Iournall*, 2–9 Oct. 1645, E304/13, unpag.

112 *CSPD, 1645–7*, p. 196. See also p. 110, for the Committee of Both Kingdoms' order to Sir Thomas Fairfax in September 1645 to send his own troops to collect money waiting for the army at Reading.

113 The only officer I know of who was accused of withholding pay from his men was Captain John Savage of Whalley's regiment in April 1649 (see below, p. 326). Far from withholding money from the rank and file, officers reached into their own pockets when money was delayed in order to help their men pay for food and lodging, and not unduly oppress the region where they were stationed. *Perf. Occurrences*, 10–17 Oct. 1645, E266/3, unpag.; Reece, p. 41.

114 According to a report to the Commons, on 1 February 1647 the foot were in arrears by eighteen weeks, and the horse by forty-three weeks (*CJ*, v, 126). Table 2.2, based on the pay warrants, shows them 19–20 weeks and 40–2 weeks behind respectively at that date. It may be that the discrepancy is due solely to the chaotic records for April 1646 (SP28/37).

115 On this point see also Kishlansky, *Rise*, pp. 184–5.

116 *Moderate Intell.*, 25 Sept.–2 Oct. 1645, E303/31, p. 142.

117 Ibid., 2–9 Oct. 1645, E304/11, p. 153.

118 *CJ*, IV, 307.

119 SP28/32, fos 18, 28, 29; vol. 33, fo. 156.

120 Bell, I, 235–318, *passim*.

121 *Continuation of Certain Speciall and Remarkable Passages*, 7–14 Nov. 1645, E309/15, p. 5; *Perf. Diurnall*, 10–17 Nov. 1645, E266/18, p. 958; *Kingdomes Wkly Intell.*, 11–18 Nov. 1645, E309/21, p. 1013; *Scotish Dove*, 12–19 Nov. 1645, E309/24, p. 860; *Merc. Civicus*, 13–20 Nov. 1645, E309/27, p. 1139; *Moderate Intell.*, 6–13 Nov. 1645, E309/11, pp. 189, 195; *Perf. Occurrences*, 10–17 Oct. 1645, E266/3, unpag.

122 *A Solemne Engagement of the Army under Sir Thomas Fairfax* (8 June 1647), E392/9, p. 13; Gentles, 'Arrears of pay', p. 55.

Chapter 3 Victory in Battle, 1645–6

1 Rushworth, VI, 17–18.

2 *CSPD, 1644–5*, 453, 461; *Moderate Intell.*, 8–15 May 1645, E284/6, p. 88.

3 *Perf. Diurnall*, 28 Apr. – 5 May 1645, E260/29, p. 729.

4 *Moderate Intell.*, 1–8 May 1645, E282/10, p. 74.

5 Bell, I, 228.

6 Rushworth, VI, 30, 34.

7 *GCW*, II, 213.

8 *LJ*, VII, 390.

9 Bell, I, 228.

10 For the Committee of Both Kingdoms' frequent chopping and changing in the latter part of May, see *CSPD, 1644–5*, pp. 502–54, *passim*.

11   Ibid., pp. 578–9.
12   *GCW*, ii, 200.
13   See above, p. 26.
14   *CJ*, iv, 169–70.
15   Sprigge, p. 32.
16   The messenger who carried this and other letters was either a renegade or a double agent, since he delivered them not to royalist headquarters but to Scoutmaster–General Watson, who brought them to Fairfax. The general at first refused to open the king's mail, but Cromwell and Ireton at length prevailed on him to conquer his scruples. What they read convinced them of the necessity of fighting the king at once and then moving quickly to smash Goring at Taunton. (Rushworth, vi, 49; Tanner MS 59, fo. 750).
17   Peter Young estimates the size of the royalist army as 9590–9690 men. He variously estimates the New Model's numbers as 13,500 or 14,600. See his *Naseby 1645* (Century Publishing, London, 1985), pp. 237, 133, 182, 245. In his *Briefe Relation*, Lord Belasyse estimated the New Model at 15,000 (See Young, *Naseby 1645*, p. 321).
18   A forlorn hope was a thin screen of skirmishers whose role was to throw an attacking enemy into confusion by a volley of shot, and then to fall back upon their main force. I am grateful to Austin Woolrych for help on this point.
19   Young, *Naseby 1645*, pp. 118, 245.
20   *A True Relation of a Victory ... [at] Naseby* (1645), E288/22, unpag.
21   George Bishop, *A More Particular and Exact Relation* (1645), E288/38, p. 2.
22   'The copie of a letter sent from a gentleman of publike employment in the late service neere Knaseby', in *An Ordinance ... for a Day of Thanksgiving ...* (1645), E288/26, p. 3.
23   Clarendon, Abbott, Gardiner, Firth, Woolrych and Young award the palm to Cromwell, but the eyewitness accounts place much more emphasis on Fairfax's role. See *A Glorious Victory* (1645), E288/21, p. 4; *A True Relation*, unpag.; *A Relation of a Victory* (1645), E288/25, pp. 33–4; *An Ordinance ... for a Day of Thanksgiving*, p. 2; *Three Letters* (1645), E288/27, p. 4.; *A More Exact and Perfect Relation of the Great Victory in Naisby Field* (1645), E288/28, pp. 2–4; *Parliaments Post*, 10–17 June 1645, E288/30, p. 7; George Bishop, *A More Particular and Exact Relation*, p. 2; Sprigge, pp. 33–45; Add. MS 5015*, fos 10, 14; Carte, i, 128–9. For modern accounts see *Battles*, ch. 6; Young, *Naseby 1645*, ch. 15; John Wilson, *Fairfax* (John Murray, London, 1985), ch. 7; Barry Denton, *Naseby Fight* (Partizan Press, Leigh-on-Sea, Essex, 1988).
24   *CSPD, 1644–5*, p. 594; Sprigge, p. 40.
25   *A True Relation*, unpag.; *A More Exact and Perfect Relation*, p. 5; 'The copie of a letter sent from a gentleman of publike Employment', p. 4.
26   *CJ*, iv, 182, 187.
27   *CSPD, 1644–5*, pp. 610, 617, 626.
28   I plan to write elsewhere in greater detail about the New Model's relations with the clubmen in 1645–6.
29   *LJ*, vii, 484–5.

30 John Lilburne, *A More Full Relation of the Great Battle Fought between Sir Thomas Fairfax and Goring* (1645), E293/3, p. 8; D. E. Underdown, *Somerset in the Civil War and Interregnum* (David and Charles, Newton Abbot, 1973), p. 104.

31 John Blackwell, *A More Exact Relation of the Great Defeat Given to Goring's Army by Sir Thomas Fairfax* (1645), E293/8, p. 7.

32 Whitelocke, I, 480.

33 *Sir Thomas Fairfax Entering Bridgwater by Storming* (1645), E293/27, p. 4; *A Letter concerning the Routing of Colonel Goring's Army near Bridgewater* (1645), E293/17, p. 8.

34 HLRO, Nalson MS, IV (13), fos 1241–2.

35 Underdown, *Somerset*, p. 106. I prefer Underdown's interpretation to Aylmer's 'more old-fashioned view' that the clubmen 'were against whichever army was on their backs at a particular time and place.' G. E. Aylmer, 'Collective mentalities in mid seventeenth-century England: IV. Cross currents: neutrals, trimmers and others', *TRHS*, 5th ser., 39 (1989), 8.

36 *Two Great Victories* (1645), E 296/6; *Two Letters* (1645), E296/7; *Procs of the Army*, 1–7 Aug. 1645, E296/14, pp. 3–5; Abbott, I, 368; *Moderate Intell.*, 7–15 Aug. 1645, E296/27, p. 187.

37 *Kingdomes Wkly Intell.*, 19–26 Aug. 1645, E298/11, p. 918. Another newsbook estimated the number of clubmen put to the sword at eighty (*Merc. Civicus*, 21–8 Aug. 1645, E298/15, p. 1045). For the importance of Sherborne Castle in promoting anti-parliamentary club activity see *Sir Thomas Fairfax's Letter concerning the Taking of Sherborne Castle* (1645), E297/3, p. 4.

38 *Mr Peters Report from Bristol* (1645), E301/4, pp. 1–2.

39 Sprigge, p. 91; Underdown, *Somerset*, p. 113.

40 Underdown, *Somerset*, p. 113; Sprigge, p. 99; *Mr Peters Report from Bristol*, p. 3. Peters thought his oratory had produced 3000 recruits, but other sources put the figure at 2000.

41 Bell, I, 250; *Merc. Civicus*, 4–11 Sept. 1645, E300/19, p. 1058.

42 *A True Relation of the Storming of Bristoll* (1645), E301/5, p. 20.

43 Whitelocke, I, 515, 529, 584.

44 *CSPD, 1644–5*, p. 602.

45 Sprigge, pp. 332–3; *Procs of the Army*, 1–6 July 1645, E292/16, p. 8.

46 *CJ*, IV, 182; Rushworth, VI, 51; *Procs of the Army*, 1–6 July 1645, E292/16, p. 3; *CSPD, 1644–5*, p. 617.

47 *CSPD, 1644–5*, p. 617.

48 Ibid., p. 626. See also above, pp. 35, 37, 46.

49 Burne and Young, pp. 209–15; Abbott, I, 364–6; Underdown, *Somerset*, pp. 100–4; *GCW*, II, 267–73; Sprigge, pp. 60–6; Whitelocke, I, 475; *LJ*, VII, 496; Rushworth, VI, 55; *The Coppie of a Letter … concerning the Great Battle … at Langport* (1645), E261/4; *Procs of the Army*, 6–11 July 1645, E292/28, pp. 5–6; *A True Relation of a Victory … neer Langport* (1645), E292/30; Lilburne, *A More Full Relation*, pp. 5–6; Blackwell, *A More Exact Relation*, pp. 2–3.

50 *Mr Peters Report from the Army* (26 July 1645), E261/7, p. 1.

51   The mixed indignation and embarrassment of the presbyterian bookseller
     George Thomason is revealed in his marginal comment on the published
     army letter: 'an Independent letter, for Massey took the town.' Thomason did
     not attempt to refute later newsbook accounts, because by then the fact
     of Fairfax's triumph was undeniable. See *A Fuller Relation from Bridg-
     water* (1645), E293/34, pp. 4–5; Sprigge, pp. 68–74; Whitelocke, I, 484–5
     (Whitelocke improbably estimated the treasure as worth £100,000); *III Great
     Victories* (1645), E292/28, p. 2; *Procs of the Army*, 19–23 July 1645, E294/9,
     pp. 2–3, 6; *Mr Peters Report from the Army*, p. 1; *LJ*, VII, 511; Bell, I, 239–40;
     Duffy, pp. 154–5.
52   Sprigge, p. 76; *A Full Relation of the Taking of Bath* (1645), E294/21; *A Fuller
     Relation of the Taking of Bath* (1645), E294/30.
53   *Perf. Diurnall*, 11–18 Aug. 1645, E262/45, p. 848.
54   HMC, *Portland*, I, 242.
55   Sprigge, pp. 84–5; *Procs of the Army*, 8–15 Aug. 1645, E 296/31, pp. 2–3; *A
     True Relation of the Taking of Sherborn-Castle* (1645), E296/32.
56   Sprigge, pp. 86–7.
57   Ibid., p. 92; *CSPD, 1645–7*, pp. 96, 104.
58   *Moderate Intell.*, 11–18 Sept. 1645, E302/2, unpag. (Montagu). For
     Rushworth's contribution see *A True Relation of the Storming of Bristol*
     (1645), E301/5, pp. 14ff. For Fairfax see *LJ*, VII, 584; Abbott, I, 374; *Mr Peters
     Report from Bristol*, p. 2.
59   Abbott, I, 377. Gardiner (*GCW*, II, 314) says 1500.
60   Sprigge, p. 91.
61   Whitelocke, I, 509; *CSPD, 1645–7*, p. 102. *Perf. Occurrences* (22–9 Aug.
     1645, E264/3, unpag.) estimated the parliamentary force at 15,000. This
     figure must have included 5000 countrymen, leaving a balance of 10,000
     belonging to the New Model. However, Fairfax's payments of 6s. to each of
     the rank and file as a bonus for storming Bridgewater totalled £1300, which
     suggests that no more than 4333 men were rewarded (SP28/32, fo. 392).
62   *CSPD, 1645–7*, p. 128; *Merc. Civicus*, 4–11 Sept. 1645, E300/19, p. 1058.
63   Sprigge, p. 89.
64   Ibid., p. 92.
65   *Merc. Civicus*, 11–18 Sept. 1645, E302/4, p. 1065.
66   Sprigge, p. 95; SP28/32, fo. 392. The fact that there was ready cash for such a
     gesture indicates that the army's financial condition was rather better than its
     friends and publicists made out.
67   Sprigge, pp. 98–100.
68   Ibid., p. 98.
69   Ibid., p. 100.
70   Ibid., pp. 106–8; Abbott, I, 375–7; HMC, *Portland*, I, 268–9; Carte, I, 133–
     4.
71   HMC, *Portland*, I, 269.
72   Edward Walker, *Historical Discourses Upon Several Occasions*, ed. H.
     Clopton (Samuel Keble, London, 1705), p. 137, quoted in Roy, pt I, 46.

73 Clarendon, *History*, IV, 93.
74 *CJ*, IV, 272.
75 Sprigge, p. 118. I prefer Sprigge's text, which is the same as that found in Rushworth, VI, 88, to Abbott's (I, 377-8). An identical letter went to the Lords over Fairfax's signature, but omitting the appeal for religious toleration (*LJ*, VII, 584-6).
76 HMC, *Portland*, I, 275; *Lieut: General Cromwells Letter ... of Taking the City of Bristoll* (1645), E301/18.
77 *The Conclusion of Lieut: General Cromwells Letter to the House of Commons concerning the Taking of Bristol* (1645), BL, 669.f.10/38. Thomason wrote on his copy: 'September 22. This was printed by the Independent Party and scattered up and down the streets last night, but expressly omitted by order of the House.'
78 *CJ*, IV, 312, 323, 320, 414.
79 Sprigge, p. 125.
80 Ibid., pp. 123-4.
81 Ibid., pp. 128-33; Abbott, I, 381.
82 *CSPD, 1645-7*, pp. 176, 180.
83 Sprigge, pp. 137-42; *GCW*, II, 362; Abbott, I, 385-7; *Kingdomes Wkly Post*, 15 Oct. 1645, E304/28, p. 8; P. Young and W. Emberton, *Sieges of the Great Civil War* (Bell and Hyman, London, 1978), pp. 89, 95.
84 Hugh Peters, *The Full and Last Relation of All Things Concerning Basing-House* (1645), E305/8, pp. 2-3.
85 Sprigge, pp. 135-7, 143-6; Rushworth, VI, 94; HMC, *Portland*, I, 292-3; *Moderate Intell.*, 16-23 Oct. 1645, E306/3, p. 171; *LJ*, VII, 657; *The Taking of Tiverton* (1645), E306/1.
86 *Kingdomes Wkly Post*, 11-17 Nov. 1645, E309/22, p. 45.
87 Sprigge, pp. 47-50, 155, 157-8, 161, 163; *Merc. Veridicus*, 11-18 Oct. 1645, E305/10, p. 181; *A Packet of Letters from Sir Thomas Fairfax His Quarter*, 30 Oct. 1645, E307/24; *Perf. Occurrences*, 31 Oct.-7 Nov. 1645, E266/14, unpag.; *Moderate Intell.*, 6-13 Nov. 1645, E309/11, p. 195; ibid., 13-20 Nov. 1645, E309/25, p. 203; ibid., 27 Nov.-4 Dec. 1645, E311/7, pp. 205, 209; *Perf. Occurrences*, 28 Nov.-5 Dec. 1645, E266/24, unpag.; Bell, I, 261, 263; *Perf. Passages*, 3-10 Dec. 1645, E266/26, p. 468; *Moderate Intell.*, 18-25 Dec. 1645, E313/21, p. 238.
88 Sprigge, p. 163.
89 *LJ*, VII, 713; Whitelocke, I, 538; *Kingdomes Wkly Post*, 11-17 Nov. 1645, E309/22, p. 48.
90 *CSPD, 1645-7*, pp. 221, 235, 244, 261, 263, 269-70, 281, 283-4, 341, 348; *LJ*, VII, 713; *CJ*, IV, 350-1, 355; Whitelocke, I, 538, 542, 543, *Perf. Passages*, 26 Nov.-3 Dec. 1645, E266/24, p. 462.
91 *Perf. Passages*, 26 Nov.-3 Dec. 1645, E266/24, p. 462.
92 Sprigge, pp. 158-60. The account of the action at Powderham Castle, with its vivid details absent from Rushworth's account, seems to confirm that Sprigge was present. Further evidence that *Anglia Rediviva*, while drawing copiously

upon Rushworth and other official army writers, was more than a compilation of other men's work, is the occasional use of the first personal pronoun – for example, in describing the fall of Winchester in September 1645 (p. 132). Finally, and surely decisively, a number of the published letters from the army were signed by a 'J. S.' who was attached to the Scoutmaster-General's quarters. (See E328/7 and E333/7 for example.) While we do not hear anything about Sprigge as a preacher, it appears that, like John Rushworth and William Clarke, he was part of the army secretariat. He also took part in the Whitehall debates in 1648–9.

93   Dell had just replaced Edward Bowles (Laurence, p. 101).
94   John Rushworth, *A Full and Exact Relation of the Storming and Taking of Dartmouth* (1646), E317/14; *LJ*, VIII, 117–18, 122; *CJ*, IV, 415; *Mr Peters Message to ... Parliament ... of the Taking of Dartmouth* (1646), E318/6, p. 5; Whitelocke, I, 568, Sprigge, pp. 166–76; *Kingdomes Wkly Intell.*, 3–10 Feb. 1646, E322/8, p. 10.
95   *CSPD, 1645–7*, p. 325; Bell, I, 282; *Sir Thomas Fairfax's Proceeding about the Storming of Exeter* (9 Feb. 1646), E322/3, p. 7; Tanner MS 60, fos 403–3ᵛ (printed in *LJ*, VIII, 153), 405.
96   Sprigge, p. 177.
97   *Sir Thomas Fairfax's Proceeding about the Storming of Exeter*, p. 5.
98   See Fairfax's letter to Lenthall printed in Sprigge, pp. 189–192, where it is made clear that each side numbered 5000–6000. It is worth remembering that Fairfax had just over half the regiments of the New Model at his disposal at Torrington. Gardiner's estimate that Fairfax commanded 10,000 men (*GCW*, III, 64) wrongly assumes the regiments were at nearly full strength.
99   John Rushworth, *A True Relation concerning the Late Fight at Torrington* (1646), E323/8, p. 8.
100   *A Fuller Relation of Sir Thomas Fairfax's Rovting all the Kings Armies in the West ... at Torrington* (1646), E324/6, p. 12.
101   Bell, I, 285.
102   Upon orders from the Commons, Fleetwood's, Whalley's and Ireton's regiments were told that their primary task was to prevent any royalist incursions from Oxford into the west (*CSPD, 1645–7*, p. 351; *LJ*, VIII, 189).
103   For Torrington and its aftermath see Sprigge, pp. 182–96; Bell, I, 283, 285; *A Famous Victorie ... at Torrington* (1646), E323/7; Rushworth, *A True Relation concerning the Late Fight at Torrington*; *A Fuller Relation of Sir Thomas Fairfax's Rovting all the Kings Armies in the West*; HMC, *House of Lords 1644–47*, p. 100; Whitelocke, I, 576; Rushworth, VI, 103; W. C., *A More Full Relation of the Continved Successes of His Excellency Sir Thomas Fairfax at and since the Routing of the Enemies Forces at Torrington* (1646), E325/2.
104   Sprigge, p. 197.
105   *Two Letters ... to ... William Lenthall* (1646), E325/17, p. 7.
106   *Master Peters Message from Sir Thomas Fairfax Delivered in Both Houses of ... Parliament* (1646), E329/2, pp. 1–9.
107   HMC, *House of Lords 1644–47*, p. 102; Whitelocke, I, 579.

108 *A Letter Sent to ... William Lenthall ... concerning Sir Thomas Fairfax's Gallant Proceeding in Cornwall* (1646), E327/7; *Western Informer*, no. 1 (7 Mar. 1646), E327/11; *The Late Victorious Proceeding of Sir Thomas Fairfax against the Enemy in the West* (1646), E327/12.
109 Sprigge, p. 201.
110 For the provisions of the treaty see Sprigge, pp. 220–8; *LJ*, VIII, 227–30; *A More Full and Exact Relation ... of the Several Treaties between Sir Thomas Fairfax and Sir Ralph Hopton* (1646), E328/15, p. 5.
111 R. Hutton, *Royalist War Effort, 1642–1646* (Longman, London, 1982) p. 196.
112 Hugh Peters, *Gods Doing and Mans Duty* (1646), E330/11, foreword, pp. 9, 44–5.
113 Sprigge, pp. 236–43. For Fairfax's remarkably generous conditions of surrender see *A True Copy of the Articles Agreed on at the Surrender of Exeter* (1646), E334/4, p. 6.
114 Bell, I, 291.
115 *CSPD, 1645–7*, p. 416.
116 *Merc. Civicus*, 23–30 Apr. 1646, E335/3, pp. 2219–20.
117 Whitelocke, II, 18–44.
118 *Kingdomes Wkly Intell.*, 28 Apr.–5 May 1646, E336/1, p. 89.
119 *CSPD, 1645–7*, p. 438.
120 Whitelocke, II, 23.
121 *LJ*, VIII, 374.
122 Sprigge, p. 273.
123 Ibid., p. 262.
124 Ibid., pp. 313–15.

Chapter 4   The Importance of Religion

1 Sprigge, from the Epistle Dedicatory (unpag.).
2 Ibid., p. 323.
3 See above, pp. 32–3.
4 *Moderate Intell.*, 13–20 Nov. 1645, E309/25, p. 203. This report is all the more trustworthy for appearing in a pro-army newspaper.
5 *Moderate Intell.*, 16–23 Apr. 1646, E334/2, p. 404.
6 Ibid., 23–30 Apr. 1646, E334/18, p. 410.
7 See above, p. 34.
8 *Gang.*, III, 18.
9 Ibid., I, 123; II, 6–7, 152–3, 154; III, 22, 107, 250–1, 260.
10 The debate on the worth of *Gangraena* as a historical source goes on. Christopher Hill considers that it stands up quite well to examination, while Colin Davis dismisses it as wholly unreliable. It must be kept in mind that much of *Gangraena* comprises letters from Edwardes' correspondents throughout England. As Murray Tolmie observes, '*Gangraena* must have car-

ried conviction because it dealt with phenomena within the personal experience of so many of its conservative readers', a view with which William Lamont concurs. See Christopher Hill, 'Irreligion in the "puritan" revolution', in J. F. McGregor and B. Reay (eds), *Radical Religion in the English Revolution* (Oxford University Press, Oxford, 1984), p. 206; J. C. Davis, *Fear, Myth and History: the Ranters and the historians* (Cambridge University Press, Cambridge, 1986), p. 126; Murray Tolmie, *Triumph of the Saints* (Cambridge University Press, Cambridge, 1977), p. 134; W. Lamont, review of Tolmie, *Times Literary Supplement*, 11 Aug. 1978.

11   W. Ca. ('a member of the army'), *A Sad and Serious Discourse* ... (1646), E540/3, unpag.

12   See *AA*, pp. 152–3, for a report of six soldiers who announced at Walton-on-Thames the abolition of the sabbath, tithes, the clergy, magistracy and the Bible.

13   Davis, *Fear, Myth and History*, pp. 76, 13 (citing McGregor). While I believe that Davis's argument is substantially correct, he has overlooked some manuscript evidence pointing to the ephemeral existence of Ranterism (e.g. NLW, MS 11439D, no. 34) about which I plan to write elsewhere.

14   Printed in *Crom. Army*, p. 400.

15   Whitelocke, III, 110.

16   *Perf. Diurnall ... of the Armies*, 17–24 June 1650, E777/14, pp. 318–19.

17   *Perf. Diurnall ... of the Armies*, 29 July–5 Aug. 1650, p. 394, quoted in Davis, *Fear, Myth and History*, p. 77.

18   HMC, *Leyborne-Popham*, p. 78.

19   *Merc. Politicus*, 7–14 Nov. 1650, E616/1, p. 375; *Crom. Army*, pp. 344–5; G. E. Aylmer, 'Unbelief in seventeenth century England', in D. H. Pennington and K. Thomas (eds), *Puritans and Revolutionaries* (Clarendon Press, Oxford, 1978), p. 40. Dr Aylmer points out that Bowen was in reality something between what we would call a deist and an agnostic.

20   *Perf. Diurnall ... of the Armies*, 7–14 Apr. 1651, E785/7, p. 960; ibid., 17–24 Mar. 1651, E784/30, p. 916.

21   Nickolls, pp. 81–2.

22   NLW, MS 11440D (letterbook of Col. John Jones), p. 151.

23   NLW, MS 11439D (leters and papers addressed to Morgan Llwyd), no. 34.

24   B. S. Capp, *The Fifth Monarchy Men* (Faber and Faber, London, 1972), p. 80; McGregor and Reay, *Radical Religion*, pp. 153–5.

25   In the Cromwellian navy too Bernard Capp has found a large core of strongly puritan officers, including five of the six generals at sea (Crom. Navy, pp. 293–4).

26   Sprigge, pp. 321, 322.

27   Bell, I, 279.

28   Sprigge, pp. 88, 112.

29   Bell, I, 285.

30   Ibid., pp. 284, 251.

31   Whitelocke, I, 191.

32 *Crom. Army*, 327; PRO, Wills, PROB11/300, fos 257–63ᵛ (21 Feb. 1660).
33 Abbott, ɪ, 416.
34 Ibid., p. 429.
35 Colin Davis, 'Cromwell's religion', in John Morrill (ed.), *Oliver Cromwell* (Longman, London, 1990), p. 207.
36 Abbott, ɪ, 385, 387.
37 Ibid., p. 360.
38 Ibid., p. 365.
39 Ibid., p. 377.
40 For further expressions of religious fervour on the part of individual officers see Nickolls, p. 10 (Harrison), 26 (Disbrowe); *OPH*, xɪx, 481–3 (Hewson); *Two Letters from Col. Robert Lilburne* ([30 Aug.] 1651), E640/26, pp. 2–3; *Perf. Diurnall*, 8–15 Sept. 1651, E787/19, p. 1295 (Fleetwood); Hodgson, p. 89; *The Rest of Faith* ([19 Feb.] 1649), E544/2, dedication, unpag. (Tichborne); Clar. MS 42, fos 195–238 (an anonymous officer with Reynolds and Ludlowe in Ireland).
41 *A Religious Retreat Sounded to a Religious Army* ([27 Aug.] 1647), E404/34, p. 9.
42 *The Building and Glory of the Truely Christian and Spiritual Church* (1646), E343/5, 'To the reader', unpag.
43 Hodgson, p. 146.
44 *England's Remembrancer*, [14 Jan.] 1646, E513/33, p. 7.
45 Quoted in Andrew Coleby, *Central Government and the Localities: Hampshire 1649–1689* (Cambridge University Press, Cambridge, 1987), p. 68.
46 *Memoirs of the Life of Mr Ambrose Barnes*, Surtees Society, 50 (1867), 107. The story, if true, points to the low velocity of seventeenth–century musket balls.
47 *Perf. Occurrences*, 22–9 May 1646, E339/5, unpag. For further evidence of the soldiers' appetite for sermons see Robert Bacon, *A Taste of the Spirit of God* ([6 July] 1652), E669/13, p. 27.
48 The most striking feature of the naval officers' faith was also the conviction that they were merely instruments of divine providence (*Crom. Navy*, p. 298).
49 Hugh Peters, *Narration of the Taking of Dartmouth* (1646), E318/6, pp. 3, 4; *Mr Peters Last Report of the English Wars* (1646), E351/12, pp. 4–5.
50 *The Building and Glory of the Truely Christian and Spiritual Church*, 'To the reader', unpag.
51 Kishlansky, *Rise*, pp. 70–5; Laurence, pp. 54, 78, 84, 86–7.
52 John Vicars, *Jehovah Jireh* (1644), quoted in Laurence, pp. 76–7.
53 R. P. Stearns, *Strenuous Puritan: Hugh Peter, 1598–1660* (University of Illinois Press, Urbana, 1954) p. 249.
54 *Moderate Intell.*, 27 Nov.–4 Dec. 1645, E311/7, p. 209.
55 *Perf. Passages*, 16–23 July 1645, E262/27, p. 307; *Moderate Intell.*, 3–10 July 1645, E292/21, p. 149; *A Bloody Plot Discovered against the Independents*

([21 Jan.] 1647), E371/18, unpag.; John Pounset, *Certaine Scruples from the Army* (1647), Bodl. Lib., Fairfax Deposit, pp. 1–2; *Perf. Diurnall ... of the Armies*, 19–26 May 1651, E785/31, p. 1046.

56 *The Humble Desires and Proposals of the Private Agitators of Colonel Hewsons Regiment* (1647), Codr. Lib., vx, 2.1/29, pp. 1–2.

57 Worc., 'The Devises, Mottos, &c. used by the Parliament Officers on Standards, Banners, &c. in the Late Civil Wars' (framed print, n.d.). There are forty-eight mottoes in all, mainly in Latin and mostly belonging to pre-New Model officers. I am grateful to Lawrence Weeks, who translated them for me.

58 *Perf. Passages*, 23 July 1651, E786/23, p. 383.

59 Sprigge, pp. 35, 167; *Perf. Occurrences*, 20 Feb. 1646, E323/9, unpag.; *Sydney Papers*, p. 117.

60 Sprigge, pp. 70, 92, 163. For the use of similar exercises in the navy see *Crom. Navy*, p. 297.

61 Worc. MS 18, fos 8–12^v; untitled broadside (1650), Worc., AA.8.3 (127); 'A letter from the general meeting of the officers of the army', untitled broadside (28 Jan. 1653), Worc., LR.8.58; Sir John T. Gilbert (ed.), *A Contemporary History of Affairs in Ireland, from 1641 to 1652*, Irish Archaeological and Celtic Society (3 vols, 1879–80), III, 219.

62 *Merc. Militaris*, 17–24 Apr. 1649, E551/13, p. 15.

63 *Perf. Diurnall ... of the Armies*, 4–11 Mar. 1650, E534/16, p. 110; ibid., 17–24 June 1650, E777/14, pp. 311–12, 313, 316; ibid., 23–30 Sept. 1650, E780/16, p. 553.

64 *Winthrop Letters*, Massachusetts HS, 5th ser., VIII (1882), 212 (6 Feb. 1651).

65 Derbyshire RO, correspondence of Major Thomas Saunders, 1232 M/065.

66 HMC, *Portland*, III, 190–1; Jacqueline Eales, *Puritans and Roundheads: the Harleys of Brampton Bryan* (Cambridge University Press, Cambridge, 1990), pp. 66, 193.

67 BL, Stowe MS 189, fo. 40. For an equally ardent letter from Thomas Margetts (secretary of the Northern Army) to Clarke see Worc. MS 114, fo. 163.

68 *Perf. Occurrences*, 28 Sept.–4 Oct. 1649, E533/15, p. 1276; Clar. MS 34, fo. 34; *Diary of Sir Archibald Johnston of Wariston*, ed. D. H. Fleming, SHS, 2nd ser., XVIII (1919), 59.

69 NLW, MS 11440D, p. 43.

70 Worc. MS 18, fos 8–8^v, 9^v.

71 Abbott, I, 365.

72 *Mr Peters Report from the Army to Parliament* [on Bridgwater] (26 July 1645), E261/7, pp. 11–12.

73 Sprigge, p. 323; Abbott, II, 378.

74 Sprigge, p. 212.

75 *Perf. Diurnall*, 25 Dec. 1648–1 Jan. 1649, E527/1, p. 2276.

76 Sprigge, p. 40. In fact the New Model outnumbered the king's forces by almost two to one. See above, p. 55.

77 *The Christian Soldiers Great Engine, or the Mysterious and Mighty Workings of Faith* (Oxford, 20 May 1649), E531/31, pp. 5, 7, 18–19, 27.

78 Untitled broadside (28 Jan. 1653), Worc., LR.8.58; Abbott, II, 153.

79 *GCW*, II, 192–3; *CJ*, IV, 123; *LJ*, VII, 337.

80 *The Letter Books of Sir Samuel Luke*, ed. H. G. Tibbutt, Bedfordshire HRS (1963), p. 324.

81 Ibid., pp. 322–8, 582–4. See Christopher Hill, *A Tinker and a Poor Man: John Bunyan and His Church, 1628–1688* (Knopf, New York, 1989), pp. 50–5, for a good account of Hobson's career.

82 *Gang.*, I, 121–4.

83 Ibid., pp. 215–16. See also II, 20, which may refer to the same incident, or to a different group of soldiers who invaded Northamptonshire pulpits from the west.

84 Ibid., III, 41, 95, 96, 107, 174, 250, 251–2.

85 *A Bloody Plot Discovered against the Independents*, unpag.; *Kingdomes Wkly Intell.*, 12–19 Jan. 1646, E371/12, pp. 394–5; *Moderate Intell.*, 31 Dec.–7 Jan. 1647, E370/19, p. 842; *Quarter Sessions Records for the County of Somerset*, III *Commonwealth 1646–1660*, ed. E. H. Bates Harbin, Somerset RS, 28 (1912), xxxix. Trooper Ives is very possibly the man who was commissioned chaplain of Whalley's regiment in 1649 (Laurence, p. 138).

86 *Severall Procs in Parliament*, 6–13 May 1652, E794/37, p. 2137. The officer in question may have been Lt-Col. Timothy Wilkes (*Reg. Hist.*, p. 389).

87 *Gang.*, III, 23, 252–3; *Moderate Intell.*, 17–24 Sept. 1646, E355/8, p. 655; *Merc. Civicus*, 16–23 July 1646, E345/17, p. 2319.

88 *A Publike Conference betwixt the Six Presbyterian Ministers and Some Independent Commanders Nov. 12 1646*, E363/4, pp. 2–5, 11–14; *A True Relation of the Late Conference Held at Oxford between the Presbyterians and the Independents* (1646), E363/6.

89 W. G., *A Just Apologie for an Abused Armie* ([29 Jan.] 1646), E372/22. The views advanced in this pamphlet are consonant with those expressed elsewhere by Goffe; therefore it seems not unlikely that he was the author. Edmund Chillenden, *Preaching without Ordination* ([2 Sept.] 1647), E405/10, p. 6.

90 Richard Laurence, *The Anti-Christian Presbyter: Or, Antichrist Transformed* ([9 Jan.] 1647), E370/22; Massarella, pp. 4–5. For other episodes of lay preaching see Harl. MS 7001, fo. 186 (Colchester); Nicoll, pp. 68–9 (Edinburgh).

91 *Moderate Intell.*, 3–10 July 1645, E292/21, p. 147; *Kingdomes Wkly Intell.*, 22–9 July 1645, E294/10, p. 878; *Perf. Occurrences*, 24–31 Oct. 1645, E266/10, unpag.; ibid., 22–9 May 1646, E339/5, unpag.

92 *Mr. Peters Message ... to ... Parliament ... of the Taking of Dartmouth* (1646), E318/6, p. 5.

93 Abbott, I, 377.

94 *Gang.*, III, 45; *Clarke Papers*, I, 256.

95 Sprigge, pp. 19–20.

96   Sprigge, pp. 65, 70, 80, 111, 106–7, 126.
97   Sprigge, p. 130; *Perf. Diurnall*, 3–10 Aug. 1646, E511/29, p. 1270.
98   *Perf. Occurrences*, 10–17 Oct. 1645, E266/3, unpag.; Reece, pp. 41, 271.
99   The phrase is Col. John Jones's (NLW, MS 11440D, p. 89).
100 Richard Baxter, *Reliquiae Baxterianae*, ed. Matthew Sylvester (T. Parkhurst et al., London, 1696), p. 51.
101 Sir William Brereton, *Cheshire's Success* (1643), Cambridge University Library, Syn. 7.64.236.63. I owe this reference to John Morrill.
102 Eric C. Walker, *William Dell: master puritan* (Heffer, Cambridge, 1970), p. 69.
103 *Perf. Diurnall ... of the Armies*, 8–15 Dec. 1651, E791/27, pp. 1506–8; ibid., 5–12 Jan. 1652, E793/9, pp. 1571–2 (corrected pag.).
104 Worc. MS 18, fos 7–11ᵛ; untitled broadside (1650), Worc., AA.8.3 (127).
105 NLW, MS 11440D, p. 145.
106 *Clarke Papers*, I, 254.
107 Nickolls, p. 74. Ten officers signed the letter, but to me it reads like the composition of its first signatory, Henry Ireton.
108 Untitled broadside (1650), Worc., AA.8.3 (127).
109 See below, p. 110.
110 Abbott, I, 387; John Goodwin, *Right and Might Well Met* (1649), E536/28, p. 44.
111 Sprigge, pp. 76, 84, 107, 144.
112 See above, pp. 70–83.
113 See below, p. 352.
114 Sprigge, p. 15; *Moderate Intell.*, 15–22 May 1645, E285/7, p. 93; *A Narration of the Expedition to Taunton* (1645), E285/10, p. 83; *Perf. Occurrences*, 4–11 July 1645, E262/20, unpag.
115 *Perf. Occurrences*, 16 Jan. 1646, E506/1, unpag. For other examples of blasphemy being punished in this way see *Merc. Civicus*, 15–22 May 1645, E285/3, p. 928; *True Informer*, 22 Nov. 1645, E309/31, p. 242. The punishment was revived during the Scottish campaign. See *True Intelligence*, 23–30 July 1650, E608/17; *Severall Procs in Parliament*, 6–13 Mar. 1651, E784/23, p. 1163; ibid., 24–31 July 1651, pp. 1475–6. While the navy did not resort to boring through the tongue, officers such as Penn and Blake imposed fines and whippings for blasphemy and drunkenness. The effect, as Capp observes, was to create a moral climate very different from that of the Stuart navy (*Crom. Navy*, p. 324).
116 *Perf. Occurrences*, 16 Jan. 1646, E506/1, unpag.; ibid., 22–9 May 1646, E339/5, unpag.; *Scotish Dove*, 18–26 Feb. 1646, E325/11, p. 572.
117 *Perf. Occurrences*, 30 May–6 June 1645, E262/3, unpag. The army chaplains of course concurred in this high estimate of the army's conduct, but so did neutral observers such as Ralph Josselin, who had no propagandistic motivation. See *The Diary of Ralph Josselin 1616–1683*, ed. Alan Macfarlane, British Academy, Records of Social and Economic History, new ser., III (1976), 91.

118 *Scotish Dove*, 18–26 Feb. 1646, E325/11, p. 572; *Perf. Occurrences*, 16 Jan. 1646, E506/1, unpag. No one seemed to notice that this line of reasoning was at odds with the Calvinistic and antinomian rejection of good works.

119 *Moderate Intell.*, 12–19 June 1645, E288/37, p. 125.

120 Blair Worden, 'Providence and politics in Cromwellian England', *P & P*, no. 109 (Nov. 1985), 90–1, 99.

121 Untitled broadside (20 May 1650), Worc., AA.8.3 (127).

122 *Gang.*, III, 23.

123 NLW, MS 11440D, pp. 53, 66, 62, 105, 75, 103.

124 See Lt-Col. Goffe's lengthy disquisition on Antichrist in *Clarke Papers*, I, 281–5; and for millenarianism see W. Lamont, *Godly Rule* (Macmillan, London, 1969), p. 97. For the importance of apocalyptic millenarianism in preparing the intellectual ground for the civil war see Paul Christianson, *Reformers and Babylon: English apocalyptic visions from the Reformation to the eve of the Civil War* (University of Toronto Press, Toronto, 1978), esp. chs 1 and 5.

125 Margaret Aston, *England's Iconoclasts*, I: *Laws against Images* (Clarendon Press, Oxford, 1988), pp. 66–7; John R. Phillips, *The Reformation of Images* (University of California Press, Berkeley, 1973), p. 195; G. E. Aylmer and R. Cant (eds), *A History of York Minster* (Clarendon Press, Oxford, 1977), p. 439.

126 V. Staley, *Hierurgia Anglicana*, rev. edn (3 vols, De La More Press, London, 1902–4), I, 100, 185–6; G. B. Tatham, *The Puritans in Power* (Cambridge University Press, Cambridge, 1913), pp. 259–61; J. G. Cheshire, 'William Dowsing's destructions in Cambridgeshire', *Transactions of the Cambridgeshire and Huntingdonshire AS*, III (1914), 78, 81; *The Journal of William Dowsing, A. D. 1643–44*, ed. J. Charles Wall (London, n.d.), p. 6.

127 *Merc. Aulicus*, 26 Oct. 1644, p. 1219; William Dugdale, *The Life, Diary and Correspondence of Sir William Dugdale*, ed. W. Hamper (no publisher, London, 1827), p. 559; Richard Symonds, *Diary of the Marches of the Royal Army during the Great Civil War*, ed. Charles Edward Long, Camden Society, LXXIV (1859), 67; *Gang.*, III, 17–18.

128 *Notes and Queries*, XII (1867), 490; Keith Thomas, *Man and the Natural World* (Allen Lane, London, 1983), p. 109; *Gang.*, III, 253; *Merc. Aulicus*, 10 May 1644, p. 977; ibid., 5 Oct. 1644, p. 1187; Dugdale, *Life*, p. 566.

129 Aston, *England's Iconoclasts*, pp. 63–5, 68–9, 71–3, 84–92; Bruno Ryves, *Mercurius Rusticus: Or, the Countries Complaint* (R. Royston, London, 1685 edn), pp. 136–7, 139, 154; *Merc. Aulicus*, 21 Sept. 1644, p. 1168; Dugdale, *Life*, pp. 557, 559, 566; *Notes and Queries*, XVIII (1873), 207; *CJ*, III, 583; HMC, *Lechmere*, pp. 46, 48; *VCH, Northants*, II, 446, 449, 454.

130 Aylmer and Cant, *York Minster*, pp. 439–40.

131 Tatham, *Puritans in Power*, pp. 257–8; CLRO, Repertories, 59, fos 322^v–3.

132 *CSPD, 1641–3*, p. 372; *VCH, Gloucestershire*, II, 37. From less reliable sources we learn of destruction at Sudeley, Glos; St Mary's, Warwick; Wedon Pinckney, Northants; Corfe, Dorset; Chichester (Ryves, *Merc. Rusticus*, pp. 67, 70, 107–9, 142), Taunton (*A True and Briefe Relation*, Oxford, 1643,

p. 41); Lambeth, Surrey; Romsey Abbey, Hants; St Margaret's, Westminster; Earl's Chapel, Warwick; St Mary Woolchurch, London; Odiham, Hants; Lydney, Glos; Abingdon, Berks; Lostwithiel, Cornwall; Alcester, Warwicks (*Merc. Aulicus*, pp. 98–9, 130, 228, 320, 560, 977, 1003, 1168, 1187); Elvaston, Derbys; Little Compton, Warwicks (Dugdale, *Life*, pp. 559, 68); Buckingham and Hillesden, Bucks: Newton St Cyres, Devon: South Petherton, Somerset; Tong, Salop; Tenbury, Worcs (Symonds, *Diary of the Marches of the Royal Army*, pp. 20, 25, 41, 102, 169, 273; in the last instance the damage was done by the Scots), Bishopston and Westbury, Wilts (John Aubrey, *Wiltshire. The Topographical Collections of John Aubrey, F. R. S., A. D. 1659–70*, ed. John Edward Jackson, Wiltshire Archaeological and Natural History Society, 1862, pp. 312, 402), East Sutton, Kent (Elizabeth Melling, ed., *Kentish Sources II: Kent and the Civil War*, Kent Archives Office, 1960, p. 19); Yaxley, Hunts; and Wallington, Herts (*Gang.*, III, 18, 253).

133   *Perf. Diurnall ... of the Armies*, 17–24 Dec. 1649, E533/31, p. 18; *Moderate Intell.*, 11–18 May 1648, E443/21, p. 1319; Hutchinson, p. 206; Roger Howell, 'The army and the English Revolution: the case of Robert Lilburne', *Archaeologia Aeliana*, 5th ser., IX (1981), 310, and *Newcastle upon Tyne and the Puritan Revolution* (Oxford University Press, London, 1967), pp. 232–3; Reece, pp. 183–4; *Reg. Hist.*, p. 459.

134   Worc. MS 114, fo. 19.

135   Reece, p. 184; Ian Gentles, 'London Levellers and the English Revolution: the Chidleys and their circle', *JEH*, 29 (1978), 287; *Perf. Occurrences*, 4–11 May 1649, E530/1, p. 1030.

136   *Perf. Occurrences* 1–8 June 1649, E530/32, p. 1088; *Merc. Politicus*, 20–7 June 1650, E604/6, pp. 39–40.

137   Howell, 'Robert Lilburne', p. 310.

138   *Gang.*, III, 44, 30.

139   *Perf. Diurnall*, 3–10 Sept. 1649, E532/39, p. 2766; *Merc. Elencticus*, 12–19 Nov. 1647, E416/13, p. 21.

140   *Merc. Politicus*, 20–7 June 1650, E604/6, pp. 39–40; *Perf. Diurnall ... of the Armies*, 4–11 Mar. 1650, E534/16, p. 108.

141   *Perf. Diurnall ... of the Armies*, 7–14 Oct. 1650, E780/21, p. 551.

142   Ibid., 14–21 Oct. 1650, E780/23, pp. 561, 565; Reece, p. 163.

143   *Perf. Diurnall ... of the Armies*, 14–21 Oct. 1650, E780/23, pp. 567–8.

144   John Musgrave, *A True and Exact Relation* (1650), E619/10, p. 22; Robert Bacon, *A Taste of the Spirit of God* (1652), E669/13, pp. 32–4.

145   *Perf. Diurnall*, 18–25 Apr. 1653, E211/22, p. 2660.

146   Reece, p. 164; *A Letter from His Excellency Sir Thomas Fairfax ... conceraing* [sic] *the Abuses and Injuries Done to Certain Godly Ministers* (26 Aug. 1647), E404/27; *Hinc Illae Lachrymae* ([23 Dec.] 1647), E421/6, pp. 11–13; *Man in the Moon*, 9–16 Jan. 1650, E589/15, p. 302; *The Kingdomes Faithfull and Impartiall Scout*, 2–9 Feb. 1649, E542/2, p. 12.

147   Reece, pp. 169–70.

148   Ibid., pp. 165–8.

149 Ralph Farmer, *Sathan Inthron'd* (1656), E897/2; George Bishop et al., *The Cry of Blood* (1656), E884/3; Reece, pp. 172–6.

150 George Fox et al., *The West Answering to the North* (1657), E900/3.

151 Howell, 'Robert Lilburne', p. 303.

152 *Moderate Intell.*, 6–13 Sept. 1649, E575/19, p. 2254.

153 *Severall Procs in Parliament*, 29 Apr.–6 May 1652, E794/33, pp. 2123–4.

154 Ibid., 15–21 May 1651, E785/28, p. 1308.

155 *Certain Passages*, 17–24 Aug. 1655, E852/11, p. 46.

156 *Perf. Diurnall ... of the Armies*, 8–15 Dec. 1651, E791/27, pp. 1506–8; ibid., 5–12 Jan. 1652, E793/9, pp. 1571–2.

157 Ralph Hopton to Thomas Fairfax, 8 Mar. 1646, printed in Sprigge, p. 210.

158 *A Serious and Faithfull Representation of the Judgement of Ministers of the Gospell within the Province of London* (1649), E538/25, p. 13.

159 Edmund Ludlow[e], *A Voyce from the Watch Tower: Part Five 1660–1662*, ed. A. B. Worden, RHS, Camden 4th ser., xxi (1978), 149–50.

160 NLW, MS 11440D, p. 22; T. Pape, *Newcastle-under-Lyme in Tudor and Early Stuart Times* (Manchester University Press, Manchester, 1938), p. 173; Bell, i, 251; Abbott, i, 429.

161 Abbot, i, 371. Both the tone and the diction of the letter point to Cromwell as its author.

162 Ibid., p. 421.

163 Nickolls, p. 72.

164 Untitled broadside (28 Jan. 1653), Worc., LR.8.58.

165 *Clarke Papers*, iv, 220.

166 I have profited enormously from Christopher Hill's *The Experience of Defeat: Milton and some contemporaries* (Faber and Faber, London, 1984), and especially from his treatment of the regicides, pp. 70–8.

167 Quoted in C. H. Firth, 'Memoir of Major-General Thomas Harrison', *Procs of the American Antiquarian Society*, new ser., viii (1893), 442.

168 Quoted in Hill, *Experience of Defeat*, p. 71.

169 Ludlow[e], *Watch Tower*, pp. 248, 149; Hill, *Experience of Defeat*, pp. 77–8.

Chapter 5   The Army and the People

1 *Kingdomes Wkly Intell.*, 31 Dec.–7 Jan. 1645, E23/19, p. 701.

2 *Moderate Intell.*, 20–7 Aug. 1646, E351/14, p. 611.

3 Ian Roy, 'England turned Germany? The aftermath of the civil war in its European context', *TRHS*, 5th ser., 28 (1978), 141; J. Broad, 'Gentry finances and the civil war: the case of the Buckinghamshire Verneys', *EcHR*, 2nd ser., xxxii (1979), 187.

4 Quoted by Lois Schwoerer in *No Standing Armies!* (Johns Hopkins University Press, Baltimore, 1974), p. 62. See also G. R. Quaife, 'The consenting spinster in a peasant society: aspects of premarital sex in "puritan" Somerset 1645–1660', *Journal of Social History*, 11 (1977), 233.

5   Worc. MS 41, fo. 113.
6   *A & O*, I, 936–8; Robert Ashton, 'The problem of indemnity, 1647–1648', in Colin Jones et al. (eds), *Politics and People in Revolutionary England* (Basil Blackwell, Oxford, 1986), p. 124.
7   *A & O*, I, 953–4, 1054–5, 1119–20.
8   Ibid., II, 235, 588–90, 830; *CJ*, VII, 124, 144. I am grateful to Dr Aylmer for letting me read and use his unpublished paper on the Indemnity Committee. See also his *The State's Servants*, (Routledge and Kegan Paul, London, 1973), pp. 299–302; John Morrill, 'The army revolt of 1647', in *Britain and the Netherlands*, VI (1977); Hughes, pp. 203–5, 302–4; Ann Hughes, 'Parliamentary tyranny? Indemnity proceedings and the impact of the civil war', *Midland History*, XI (1986).
9   Interregnum Committee and Commissioners for Indemnity, 1647–1656, SP24/1, fos 41ᵛ (King's Bench), 105ᵛ (Chancery), 151 (Exchequer); vol. 30, *Adderton* vs *Lea* (Common Pleas).
10 SP24/1, fos 6ᵛ (Wood Street Compter), 26 (Southwark Compter), 41ᵛ (Newgate), 133 (King's Bench); vol. 6, fos 110ᵛ–11 (Marshalsea); vol. 3, fo. 20 (Clerkenwell); vol. 4, fos 85ᵛ, 114ᵛ, 121 (Colchester); vol. 1, fo. 122 (Warwick).
11 See for example SP24/1, fos 121ᵛ–2.
12 SP24/3, fos 1ᵛ, 8ᵛ.
13 SP24/2, fo. 13.
14 The true total may be a few dozen higher than the 1116 shown, since SP24/9, covering the committee's proceedings between 29 April and 7 November 1651, is lost. By 1651 however, the number of new military cases had fallen off sharply.
15 SP24/1, fos 3, 13ᵛ, 26, 41ᵛ 76 (twice), 76ᵛ, 121ᵛ, 145ᵛ; vol., 2, fos 28, 56ᵛ, 174, 180; vol. 3, fo. 13ᵛ; vol. 4, fo. 85ᵛ; vol. 5, fos 39ᵛ, 43ᵛ, 160; 6, fo. 50.
16 SP24/5, fos 67, 78ᵛ; vol. 6, fo. 91.
17 SP24/6, fo. 40.
18 SP24/1, fo. 155; vol. 4, fo. 106ᵛ; vol. 5, fos 2ᵛ, 41ᵛ; vol. 8, fo. 100; vol. 13, fo. 112ᵛ.
19 SP24/1, fos 8ᵛ, 18ᵛ, 21; vol. 5, fo. 148; vol. 3, fo. 99; vol. 6, fo. 6; vol. 12, fo. 6ᵛ. The other colonels and notable officers who petitioned the committee were Cols Howell Gwyn (vol. 1, fo. 68ᵛ; vol. 2, fo. 86ᵛ), Daniel Souton (vol. 1, fo. 95), Robert Ireland (vol. 4, fo. 50ᵛ), John Fettiplace (vol. 5, fo. 94), Edward Ashenhurst (vol. 6, fo. 9), Thomas Rookby (vol. 6, fo. 55), Hastings Ingram (vol. 7, fo. 24ᵛ), Simon Rudgely, Sherriff of Staffordshire (vol. 7, fo. 24ᵛ), Sackville Moore (vol. 7, fos 71ᵛ, 86ᵛ), Robert Martin (vol. 7, fo. 71ᵛ, 86ᵛ, 170ᵛ, vol. 8, fo. 121), Waldive Willington (vol. 8, fo. 101ᵛ), Thomas Croxton (vol. 8, fo. 111), Edmund Jordon (vol. 57, *Jordon* vs *Sanders*), Hercules Hannay (vol. 51., *Hannay* vs *Williams*), Wm Herbert (vol. 10, fo. 22ᵛ), John White (vol. 10, fo. 46), Richard Aileworth (vol. 10, fo. 132ᵛ), Capt. Adam Baynes (vol. 33, *Baynes* vs *Dixon*), Lt-Col. Jeremy Baynes (vol. 2, fo. 145), Sir Edward Rhodes (vol. 3, fo. 35), William Cater, mayor of

Hereford (vol. 4 fo. 75^v), Sir John Seymour (vol. 5, fo. 94), Captain George (brother of Col. John) Hutchinson (vol. 5, fo. 135^v).

20 SP24/1, fos 8, 18^v; vol. 33, *Barkstead* vs *Stockwell*.

21 SP24/5, fos 148–8^v, 160, 178–8^v; vol. 6, fos 42^v, 108^v, 117^v.

22 SP24/8, fos 100, 113, 118, 120–20^v; vol. 10, fo. 90; vol. 70, *Pye* vs *Phipps*.

23 SP24/1, fos 68^v, 91^v, 99, 112, 167^v.

24 SP24/5, fo. 135^v. There is no evidence that the petitions of Colonels Jordon and Hannay were ever considered by the committee.

25 Cf. SP24/5, fo. 83.

26 SP24/15, fos 48^v, 138^v; vol. 16, fos 42, 51, 147^v, 217, 253^v–4.

27 A quarter (thirteen) of these cases have to do with money, while many contain vague allegations that the defendant was 'a person disaffected to the parliament' (for example SP24/75, *Sherrott* vs *Bostock*; vol. 63, *Mayer* vs *Ridgeley*; vol. 79, *Tasborowe* vs *Hider*).

28 The committee's conscientious regard for due process sometimes led to a case being thrown out on narrowly technical grounds. The most remarkable instance of this finely honed legalism concerned a group of soldiers who had instigated the arrest of Gerald Lord Angier of Ireland for his failure to settle a debt for 'meat and drink'. The unfortunate official who procured the writ was dismayed to find himself sued for trespass and false imprisonment because, following the soldiers' advice, he had had made out the writ in the name not of the king, but of the custodians of the liberty of England. Even though he could adduce an act of parliament in support of this wording, the committee dismissed his appeal, as the writ had been issued one day before the king was executed (SP24/5, fos 152^v, 170^v; vol. 46, *Elsyott* vs *Angier*).

29 SP24/44, *Day* vs *Underwood*. See also vol. 83, *Way* vs *Mansell*.

30 SP24/3, fos 1^v, 8^v. For other cases involving words see SP24/2, fos 102, 157–7^v; vol. 1, fo. 3; vol. 5, fos 5, 30^v, 81, 125; vol. 6, fos 39, 49^v; vol. 35, *Bligh* vs *Morrell*.

31 SP24/10, fos 157, 161–2, 167; vol. 11, fos 64^v–5, 80, 104^v, 114^v; vol. 12, fos 11, 56, 94^v; vol. 42, *Coxe* vs *Stephens*.

32 SP24/7, fo. 97; vol. 86, *Wray* vs *Abdey*.

33 SP24/1, fo. 170; vol. 65, *Moreton* vs *Wenman*. For the continuing conservatism of many JPs see A. Fletcher, *Reform in the Provinces* (Yale University Press, New Haven, Conn., and London, 1986), pp. 15–16.

34 SP24/3, fos 13^v–14; vol. 84, *Wheeler* vs *Edmead*.

35 SP24/1, fo. 76^v; vol. 39, *Cheeke* vs *Crosse*.

36 SP24/4, fo. 104^v; vol. 41, *Coppleston* vs *Edmonds*.

37 SP24/5, fos 75^v, 109^v; vol. 6, fo. 39^v; vol. 31, *Ash* vs *Hincksman*.

38 SP24/6, fo. 55.

39 SP24/2, fos 105^v, 175^v–6; vol. 3, fo. 35–5^v; vol. 34, *Beckwith* vs *Elsyott*. Stephen F. Black, 'The Judges of Westminster Hall during the Great Rebellion, 1640–1660' (unpublished BLitt. thesis, Oxford University, 1970), pp. 42, 95.

40 SP24/3, fos 35, 41^v.

41 SP24/2, fos 80^v–1; vol. 3, fos 9, 68^v–9.

42 SP24/4, fos 13^v–14, 124.

43 SP24/5, fo. 135; vol. 6, fo. 49.

44 SP24/6, fos 12, 93.

45 SP24/7, fo. 136; vol. 8, fos 15^v, 25–5^v, 33^v.

46 The royalist officer who tore up its order and 'uncivilly handled and abused' the messenger who carried it was only a dramatic example of the many people who spurned the committee's authority, and had to be ordered repeatedly to submit to its judgements (SP24/3, fos 67, 67^v).

47 John Morrill, 'Mutiny and discontent in English provincial armies 1645–1647', *P & P*, 56 (1972), 64–5.

48 Joan Thirsk, *Horses in Early Modern England: for service, for pleasure, for power* (University of Reading, Reading, 1978), p. 28; Peter Edwards, *The Horse Trade in Tudor and Stuart England* (Cambridge University Press, Cambridge, 1988), pp. 14–15.

49 SP24/8, fos 55, 110–10^v; /51, *Hall* vs *Short*.

50 SP24/2, fos 1^v, 98; vol. 3, fos 72, 75; vol. 70, *Price* vs *Longwell*.

51 SP24/2, fo. 44^v; vol. 3, fos 147^v–8.

52 SP24/2, fos 91^v, 167; vol. 86, *Wright* vs *Houghton*.

53 SP24/2, fos 1^v, 30; vol. 34, *Beale* vs *Fells*.

54 Add. MS 34326, fo. 54, cited in W. Urwick, *Nonconformity In Worcester* (Simpkin, London, 1897), pp. 51–2.

55 Cambridge County RO, R77/25, no. 24, letter of Phillip Barrow, 12 June 1647; SP24/2, fos 131, 146^v; vol. 83, *Wakefield* vs *Bitten*.

56 For example SP24/1, fos 13–13^v, 26, though later on they became wary of soldiers who used this excuse to avoid paying their private debts (e.g. SP24/11, fos 41, 55^v, 66–6^v; vol. 12, fo. 92; vol. 15, fos 3–3^v, 48^v, 138^v; vol. 16, fos 42, 51, 147^v, 217, 253^v–4).

57 SP24/3, fos 22^v, 58–8^v, 63; vol. 70, *Price* vs *Meakin*.

58 Cf. SP 24/3, fo. 118.

59 SP24/1, fo. 166^v; vol. 2, fo. 106; vol. 48, *French* vs *Wright*.

60 SP24/5, fo. 157^v; vol. 7, fos 119, 122, 129^v–30; vol. 45, *Downe* vs *Beare*.

61 Roy, 'England turned Germany', p. 142; *Lanc. Tracts*, pp. 277–8; Tanner MS 59, fo. 145; *Perf. Occurrences*, 7–14 Apr. 1648, E527/17, p. 476.

62 HLRO, Main Papers, July 1647, fo. 143.

63 See for example SP24/1, fos 6^v, 14^v (Capt. John Ash), 9^v, 12^v (Maj. Isaac Dobson); vol. 2, fo. 180; vol. 3, fos 30, 57; vol. 41, *Private Francis Cooper* vs *Poll*.

64 *Perf. Occurrences*, 23–30 Dec. 1648, E526/45, p. 775; ibid., 30 Mar.–6 Apr. 1649, E529/7, p. 933; *A Perf. Account ... from the Armies*, 22–9 Oct. 1651, E644/3, p. 342.

65 SP24/2, fo. 164.

66 SP24/3, fo. 153; vol. 4, fos 8^v, 25, 52^v.

67 SP24/5, fo. 179; vol. 6, fo. 24^v *et passim*; vol. 7, fos 60, 73^v, 76–6^v.

68 Bristol RO, Common Council Proceedings 04264(4), p. 122 (12 Nov. 1645).

69 SP24/5, fos 43ᵛ, 114–15ᵛ, 134; vol. 6, fos 9, 43, 48; vol. 70, *Prescott* vs *Lechmere* et al.
70 SP24/5, fos 67ᵛ, 147, 165ᵛ; vol. 6, fos 71ᵛ–2.
71 SP24/4, fos 27ᵛ, 33ᵛ, 47–7ᵛ, 116. See also John Morrill (ed.), *Reactions to the English Civil War* (Macmillan, London, 1982), pp. 111–12.
72 SP24/4, fos 49, 51ᵛ.
73 SP24/1, fos 37ᵛ, 39; vol. 48, *Frith* vs *Medcalfe*.
74 R. W. Ketton-Cremer, *Norfolk in the Civil War* (Faber and Faber, London, 1969), pp. 334–48.
75 For the preceding paragraphs I am indebted to Stephen Porter for permission to cite chapters ɪᴠ and ᴠ of his University of London PhD thesis, 'The Destruction of Urban Property in the English Civil Wars, 1642–1651' (1984). See also his articles 'Property destruction in the English civil war', *History Today*, 36 (Aug. 1986), 40, and 'The fire-raid in the English civil war', *War and Society*, 2 (1984), 35–7.

Chapter 6   The Political Wars, 1646–8 (I): From the King's, Surrender to the Assault on Parliament

1 *Perf. Passages*, 19–25 Nov. 1645, E366/22, p. 450; *Perf. Occurrences*, 31 Oct.– 7 Nov. 1645, E266/14, unpag.
2 *An Explanation of Some Truths* ([3 Jan.] 1646), E314/15, p. 53.
3 *LJ*, ᴠɪɪɪ, 95, 99. The Commons would not accept the Lords' requirement that there be at least one peer for a quorum at meetings of the treasurers at war.
4 *Gang.*, ɪ, 121–3; ɪɪ, 173–4.
5 *The Last Warning to All the Inhabitants of London* ([20 Mar.] 1646), E328/24, p. 4.
6 CCJ 40, fos 178ᵛ–182ᵛ.
7 *Londons New Colours Displaid* (13 July 1648), E452/21, p. 2.
8 *Conscience Caution'd* ([20 June] 1646), E341/7, p. 4.
9 *Gang.*, ɪɪɪ, 45, 24, 229.
10 Bodl. Lib., Fairfax Deposit, Tracts, 26/1.
11 *Plain English: Or, the Sectaries Anatomized* ([17 Aug.] 1646), E350/11, pp. 10–11. Peters was well aware that he was hated in the City (*Mr Peters Last Report of the English Wars*, [27 Aug.] 1646, E351/12).
12 J. S. A. Adamson, 'The Peerage in Politics 1645–49' (unpublished PhD thesis, Cambridge University, 1986), p. 144.
13 *LJ*, ᴠɪɪɪ, 425; Montereul, ɪ, 272; Kishlansky, *Rise*, p. 117.
14 *CJ*, ɪᴠ, 631–2; Ludlow[e], ɪ, 141.
15 See for example, Zachary Grey, *Impartial Examination* (Bettesworth and Hitch, London, 1737), appendix, pp. 26–46. Complaints of the behaviour of the Scots army in the north are also found in the papers of Speaker William Lenthall (e.g. Tanner MS 59, fo. 428).

16   *The True Mannor and Forme of the Proceeding to the Funerall of the Right Honourable Robert Earle of Essex* (22 Oct. 1646), E360/1, pp. 16–19.

17   Holles, p. 70; Rushworth, vii, 766. I am grateful to David Evans for permission to read the chapter on the Western Brigade from his forthcoming London PhD thesis on the career of Edward Massey. The thesis explores fully the antagonism between Massey and the New Model Army from as early as 1645. In the paragraphs that follow I have adhered to Evans' interpretation of the politics of the brigade's disbandment.

18   *A & O*, i, 812; *LJ*, viii, 17; *True Informer*, 6 Dec. 1645, E311/10, p. 260.

19   *LJ*, viii, 17.

20   Ibid., pp. 114–15.

21   Whitelocke, i, 583; *CJ*, iv, 467.

22   *CJ*, iv, 670; *GCW*, iii, 147; Ludlow[e], i, 141. The collapse of discipline in the brigade was traceable directly to the Committee of the Army's policy of starving it financially at the same time that it favoured the New Model (Cary, i, 101; *Scotish Dove*, 24 June–1 July 1645, E342/11, p. 711; *CJ*, iv, 581, 652).

23   Ludlow[e], i, 141–2; Sprigge, p. 310.

24   *LJ*, viii, 530–1.

25   Kishlansky, *Rise*, p. 117; *LJ*, viii, 563.

26   Holles, p. 45, Richard Baxter, *Reliquiae Baxterianae*, ed. Matthew Sylvester (T. Parkhurst, et al., London, 1696), p. 59; Juxon, Diary, fo. 87; Montereul, i, 251, 259, 267–8, 317.

27   Clar. MS 29, fo. 72ᵛ.

28   See for example their petition of July 1647, HLRO, Main Papers, fos 139–40.

29   Juxon, Diary, fo. 94; Ian Gentles, 'The sales of bishops' lands in the English Revolution, 1646–60', *EHR*, xcv (1980), 574–5, 591.

30   *Kingdomes Wkly Intell.*, 15–22 Dec. 1646, E367/3, p. 359; *Perf. Occurrences*, 1–8 Jan. 1647, E370/21, unpag.; *GCW*, iii, 188; Rushworth, vi, 389; Tanner MS 59, fos 694–5, 714.

31   Valerie Pearl, *London and the Outbreak of the Puritan Revolution* (Oxford University Press, London, 1961), p. 302; Juxon, Diary, fo. 91.

32   According to Nehemiah Wallington it rained every day from 18 August until 11 November. The rain resumed on the 18th, and continued intermittently until the end of December, when the frost began (Wallington, MS Diary, p. 507). I am extremely grateful to Dr G. E. Aylmer for letting me consult his notes on the Wallington Diary.

33   CCJ 40, fo. 200.

34   Ibid., fo. 204.

35   Whitelocke, ii, 91, 93.

36   *Plain English: Or, the Sectaries Anatomized* ([17 Aug.] 1646), E350/11, p. 10; *A Copy of a Letter Written from Northampton Containing a True Relation of the Souldier's Preaching and Murdering a Woman* (28 Jan. 1647), Worc., BB.8. 16/14; *Perf. Diurnall*, 11–18 Jan. 1647, E513/34, p.1453; *A Bloody Plot Discovered against the Independents* ([21 Jan.] 1647), E371/18.

37 *Englands Remembrancer* ([14 Jan.] 1647), E513/33, p. 3; Montereul, I, 372; Clar. MS 29, fo. 161ᵛ.
38 CCJ 40, fo. 204ᵛ.
39 *LJ*, VIII, 621.
40 Montereul, I, 272; GCW, III, 145; *LJ*, IX, 57. Despite the administrative limbo to which it had been consigned, the committee continued to perform its functions (SP28/49, fos 268, 383, *et passim*).
41 Clar. MS 29, fo. 161ᵛ; *CJ*, v, 25.
42 The imminent publication of *Anglia Rediviva* was announced in *Perf. Diurnall*, 11–18 Jan. 1647, E513/34, p. 1454. George Thomason, the book-seller who collected a copy of almost every book, pamphlet and newsbook published in London during the revolution, did not acquire Sprigge's volume. A payment by the army of £150 to a Mr Partridge in May 'for the losses he sustained by *Anglia Rediviva*' indicates that the book found few readers in London (Chequers, MS 782, fo. 42ᵛ). I am grateful to Ian Roy for drawing this entry to my attention.
43 *Kingdomes Wkly Intell.*, 15–22 Dec. 1646, E363/3, p. 364.
44 PRO31/3, fo. 82. Hyde's London correspondent also reported troop move-ments near the City, and hinted that some dark purpose lay behind them (Clar. MS 29, fos 67ᵛ, 68ᵛ).
45 *Moderate Intell.*, 7–14 Jan. 1647, E311/4, p. 854. It is true that all the reports are found in royalist sources, and may therefore be tainted, but there was probably something to them.
46 *The Petition of Many Well-affected Freemen of the City of London* ([29 Jan.] 1647), E372/23, p. 4; CCJ 40, fo. 204ᵛ.
47 Richard Laurance, *The Anti-Christian Presbyter: or, Antichrist Transformed* ([9 Jan.] 1647), E370/22.
48 Add. MS 37344 (Whitelocke's annals), fo. 78.
49 The presbyterians' new political dominance was seen symbolically in the appointment of Obadiah Sedgwick to deliver the February fast sermon. In November the fast sermon had been preached by the radical New Model chaplain William Dell (*Right Reformation*, 25 Nov. 1646, E363/2). On 12 December, the presbyterians had referred Dell's sermon to a committee because it contained a denial of the magistrate's right to interfere with Gospel reformation (GCW, III, 183). In January, when the presbyterian triumph was complete, Sedgwick likened the spread of Dell's brand of sectarianism to a gangrene on the body politic (*The Nature and Danger of Heresies*, 27 Jan. 1647, E372/13).
50 *Nicholas Papers*, I: *1641–1652*, ed. George F. Warner, Camden Society, new ser., XL (1886), 75; Clar. MS 29, fo. 97.
51 Ian Gentles, 'The arrears of pay of the parliamentary army at the end of the first civil war', *BIHR*, XLVIII (1975), 52–63.
52 HMC, *Portland*, I, 447.
53 *CJ*, v, 91; PRO31/3/82, fo. 124ᵛ; Tanner MS 59, fo. 786.
54 *CJ*, v, 90.
55 Add. MS 31116 (Whitacre's diary), fo. 302.

56 Juxon, *Diary*, fo. 102; *The Humble Petition of the Inhabitants of the County of Suffolk ... 16 February 1646[1647]*, E377/4, p. 4; *To the Lords, the Petition of the County of Essex* (11 Mar. 1647), BL, 669.f.10/119; Nathaniel Hardy, *The Arraignment of Licentious Libertie* (24 Feb. 1647), E377/25, p. 38; Richard Vines, *The Authours, Nature and Danger of Haeresie* (10 Mar. 1647), E378/29, p. 16; Thomas Hodges, *The Growth and Spreading of Haeresie* (10 Mar. 1647), E379/1.

57 Add. MS 19399 (original letters, 1646–1768), fo. 1. The horse regiments were those of Pye and Graves, while the dragoons were under the command of Major Nicholas Moore of Okey's regiment. All three men would support the Irish expedition in May and join the Holles-Stapleton party in attempting to subdue the New Model. (*Clarke Papers*, I, 58; *Reg. Hist.*, pp. 104, 129, 293.)

58 *CJ*, v, 106–7.

59 *CJ*, v, 90–1, 107–8. For the little-noticed abortive Cirencester election see *Perf. Occurrences*, 8–15 Jan. 1647, E371/5, p. 13.

60 *Perf. Diurnall*, 1–8 Mar. 1647, E515/2, p. 1505.

61 CCJ 40, fo. 207-ᵛ.

62 A royalist newswriter asserted that it had been signed by only 400, 'visibly against the rest' (Clar. MS 29, fo. 147).

63 Wolfe, p. 138.

64 *A Warning for All the Counties of England* ([24 Mar.] 1647), E381/13, p. 9.

65 *A Sectary Dissected* ([22 Apr.] 1647, E384/17), p. 16.

66 *An Apollogie of the Souldiers* (26 Mar. 1647), E381/18, pp. 1–2.

67 *The Petition of the Officers and Souldiers ... [of] Sir Thomas Fairfax* (2 Apr. 1647), E383/12. In the *Army Book of Declarations* published in September the word 'humble' is inserted into the title, and the petition is said to be directed to Fairfax, not parliament (E409/25, p. 1). The original version of the petition does not make it clear to whom it is directed.

68 See for example Robert Overton's view of the importance of pay arrears, Bell, I, 349.

69 *The Petition of the Officers and Souldiers*, unpag.

70 The work of Massarella, Kishlansky and Woolrych, as well as a rereading of the sources, have convinced me to revise the argument I originally presented in 'Arrears of pay and the army revolt of 1647', *War and Society*, I (1975), 44–5.

71 *Perf. Diurnall*, 15–22 Mar. 1647, E513/4, p. 1526; *Kingdomes Wkly Intell.*, 16–23 Mar. 1647, E381/9, p. 467.

72 *Kingdomes Wkly Intell.*, 23–30 Mar. 1647, E383/2, p. 475; *CJ*, v, 127.

73 Tanner MS 58, fo. 16; HMC, *Portland*, I, 418.

74 Tanner MS 58, fo. 18. The letter was signed 'H', but according to William Waller the writer was Rossiter's major, Philip Twisleton. See Waller's *Vindication* (J. Debrett, London, 1793), p. 58.

75 *Army Book of Declarations*, p. 5; Tanner MS 58, fo. 28.

76 *Clarke Papers*, I, 2.
77 *CJ*, v, 127; *OPH*, xv, 344–5; Ludlow[e], I, 149–50; Waller, *Vindication*, p. 62; *S & S*, pp. 37–8.
78 Clar. MS 29, fo. 165ᵛ.
79 *CJ*, v, 127; Rushworth, VI, 454.
80 The Derby House Committee named the Earls of Warwick, Lincoln and Suffolk, Lord Dacres, Sir William Waller, Edward Massey, John Clotworthy and Richard Salwey. Salwey was an Independent, but remained inactive on the committee. (*CSPI, 1647–1660*, pp. 738, 741; Waller, *Vindication*, pp. 77–8.)
81 HMC, *Egmont*, I, 384, 389.
82 *Perf. Diurnall*, 15 Apr.–3 May 1647, E515/10, pp. 1570–1.
83 The first three horse regiments designated to be kept up in England belonged to the Northern Association and were commanded by the well-known presbyterians Poynts, Copley and Bethell (*Perf. Diurnall*, 29 Mar.–5 Apr. 1647, E515/6, p. 1536). Five New Model regiments were to be kept up: Fairfax's, Cromwell's, Whalley's, Graves's and Rossiter's. Cromwell had been eliminated by the vote of 8 March, and his regiment was to be commanded by its presbyterian major, Robert Huntington (Waller, *Vindication*, p. 66). Although Whalley would be a staunch Cromwellian in the 1650s, he was at the time considered religiously moderate and orthodox (Baxter, *Reliquiae*, p. 53.) Rossiter was to be replaced by his major Philip Twisleton, who had recently acted as a presbyterian informer (Tanner MS 58, fo. 18; Waller, *Vindication*, pp. 58, 66). Graves had been entrusted with the guardianship of the king, and fled to parliament when Joyce wrested the king from him on 3 June. The ninth horse regiment to be kept up was to be composed of local forces led by Col. John Needham, former governor of Leicester, whose political views are unknown. Finally, the presbyterian major-generals Mitton and Laugharne were each to command 200 troopers in north and south Wales (*Perf. Diurnall*, 5–12 Apr. 1647, E515/7, p. 1549).
84 *Clarke papers*, I, 425.
85 *Letters from Saffron Walden, the Generalls Head Quarters, by Way of Apologie and Vindication of the Army under Sir Thomas Fairfax* (3 Apr. 1647), E383/24, pp. 4–5.
86 A second hostile petition had been launched from Essex at the beginning of April. This time it had the blessing of the county committee at Chelmsford (Tanner MS 58, fo. 50).
87 *A New Found Stratagem Framed in the Old Forge of Machivilisme ... to Destroy the Army* (4 Apr. 1647), E384/11, pp. 4, 11, 14. For Style see PRO, E307, Box 19/S4/1; SP26/1/142; BL, Loan 29/175, fos 53ᵛ–4; HMC, *House of Lords 1644–47*, p. 171.
88 *A New Found Stratagem*, p. 5.
89 *Moderate Intell.*, 23–30 Oct. 1645, E307/22, p. 175; Worc. MS 41, fo. 158. Although Tulidah's payment for his commission is dated 19 August 1648 it is

clear that he had been relieved of his post by November 1647 if not before (Worc. MS 67, fo. 27; SP28/48, fo. 402; Chequers MS 782, fo. 45). See also *CSPD, 1650*, p. 565, for his status as a foreigner.

90 *Perf. Diurnall*, 5–12 Apr. 1647, E515/7, p. 1543.

91 HMC, *Portland*, III, 156.

92 The minister of the parish of Colne, Ralph Josselin, commented several times on the civil behaviour of the soldiers quartered near him. See *The Diary of Ralph Josselin 1616–1683*, ed. Alan Macfarlane, British Academy, Records of Social and Economic History, new ser., III (1976), 91, 95.

93 *Clarke Papers*, I, 5n.

94 *CJ*, V, 134; CCJ 40, fos 212, 214. In the event the loan was secured on the remaining bishops' lands (Gentles, 'The sales of bishops' lands', pp. 577, 591–3).

95 Juxon, *Diary*, fo. 107. Other sources give Pembroke's figure as 4000, but Juxon, who says 7000, most probably heard the speech for himself. Cf. *S & S*, p. 70.

96 *Perf. Wkly Account*, 5–12 May 1647, E386/17, unpag.

97 See above, pp. 34, 38.

98 Tanner MS 58, fo. 46; Clar. MS 29, fo. 197.

99 HMC, *Portland*, III, 156. Rich's and Ireton's regiments were among those stationed in the two counties, but there were three unidentified horse regiments and some foot as well (ibid., p. 155; *Perf. Diurnall*, 26 Apr.–3 May 1647, E515/10, p. 1569).

100 Henny Foley (ed.), *Records of the English Province of the Society of Jesus*, II (Burnes and Oates, London, 1884), 561.

101 *Clarke Papers*, I, 25.

102 Clar. MS 29, fo. 235.

103 Ibid., fos 193, 203, 220.

104 Woolrych also discusses these royalist undercurrents in the army (*S & S*, pp. 69–71).

105 HMC *Portland*, I, 414; Holles, *Memoirs*, p. 73.

106 *The Petition of Officers and Souldiers*, unpag.

107 Thoresby Society Library, Leeds, MS SD ix (William Clarke's account book), unfol. (1 June 1649).

108 LJ, IX, 114.

109 *Perf. Diurnall*, 12–19 Apr. 1647, E515/8, p. 1558.

110 *Clarke Papers*, I, 6.

111 *Wkly Account*, 14–21 Apr. 1647, E384/16, unpag.

112 They were Cols Harley, Fortescue and Butler, Lt-Col. Jackson, Majors Fincher, Alford, Duckett and Gooday, Capt. Robotham, 'and divers others'. In addition Col. Butler had evidently put the names of two of his captains – Pennyfather and Burges – on the list of engaged officers without their knowledge (*Clarke Papers*, I, 12).

113 Cary I, 195–6.

114 Tanner MS 58, fos 62–7. The foot regiments were Fairfax's, Rainborowe's,

Hammond's, Sir Hardress Waller's, Fortescue's, Ingoldsby's, Harley's, Herbert's and Lilburne's; the horse, Sheffield's, Butler's, Rich's and Graves's.

115   Clarke Papers, I, 14.

116   BL, Loan 29/175 (Harl.), fos 49, 52ᵛ; Clarke Papers, I, 14.

117   Howard's sense of disappointment at attracting only six recruits must have been all the keener for having been recommended to a colonelcy in Ireland (LJ, IX, 135; Clarke Papers, I, 15).

118   BL, Loan 29/175, fo. 53–3ᵛ; Clarke Papers, I, 16.

119   Clarke Papers, I, 25.

120   Ibid., p. 28. It was a lame excuse that many of the horse officers were stationed too far away to attend the meeting (Worc. MS 41, fo. 28ᵛ).

121   Clarke Papers, I, 28–31.

122   Perf. Wkly Account, 5–12 May 1647, E386/17, unpag.

123   BL, Loan 29/175, fo. 50ᵛ.

124   Ibid., fos 50ᵛ–1; Juxon, Diary, fo. 107; Worc. MS 41, fo. 107ᵛ.

125   BL, Loan 29/175, fos 52ᵛ–3.

126   Wkly Account, 21–9 Apr. 1647, E385/10, unpag. The Kingdomes Wkly Intell. gave the number of officers as 111 (20–7 Apr. 1647, E385/6, p. 506).

127   Worc. MS 110, unfol., n.d. (c.28 Apr. 1647).

128   Clarke Papers, I, 15–17.

129   Worc. MS 41, fo. 117.

130   Cf. Tanner MS 58, fo. 61.

131   S & S, p. 54.

132   Lawson Nagel, 'The Militia of London, 1641–1649' (unpublished PhD thesis, University of London, 1982), pp. 241–5.

133   Juxon, Diary, fo. 104ᵛ.

134   Ibid., 107ᵛ–8.

135   CCJ 40, fos 200, 207ᵛ, 215ᵛ; A & O, I, 928. [25 June]

136   John Lilburne, Rash Oaths Unwarrantable (3 May 1647), E393/39, p. 45.

137   Army Book of Declarations, p. 91.

138   The Apologie of the Common Souldiers (3 May 1647), E385/18, pp. 2–4 (also printed in Army Book of Declarations, pp. 7–9). The Apologie was circulating in the army before 23 April (Clarke Papers, I, 15).

139   A Second Apologie of All the Private Souldiers (n.d., c.1 May 1647), E385/18, pp. 5, 7–8.

140   The Petition and Vindication of the Officers … to the House of Commons (27 Apr. 1647), E385/19, p. 1.

141   CJ, V, 154–5; S & S, pp. 56–7; HMC, House of Lords 1644–47, p. 171; LJ, IX, 152; HLRO, Main Papers, 27 April 1647, fo. 61. After summoning them to appear, both houses seem to have forgotten about Style and Saunders, who were never interrogated.

142   In the version of the Apologie published on 6 May, the representatives of the eight regiments were said to be 'agitating' on behalf of their several regiments (BL, 669.f.11/9).

143   Clarke Papers, I, 430–1.

144   Worc. MS 41 fos 31, 123, 127ᵛ. Woolrych argues that agitators were selected
        at troop level from the beginning *S & S*, pp. 61–3). As usual his reasoning is
        cogent; however, while the soldiers *talked* of electing two representatives per
        troop on 15 April (HMC, *Portland*, III, 155–6), on the 30th we hear of only
        two per regiment (*Clarke Papers*, I, 430–1). By mid-May, on the other hand,
        several regiments had one agitator or two per troop or company. See Worc.
        MS 41, fos 31 (Herbert's), 123 (Harley's), 127ᵛ (Fairfax's foot). Several other
        regiments listed only two to four agitators, and some showed only officer
        representatives (ibid., fos 108–26ᵛ, *passim*).
145   The definitive study of the General Council is *S & S*.
146   *Clarke Papers*, I, 431.
147   The date of his commission is not given, but it was probably some time in
        1649 (Worc. MS 67, p. 35).
148   Ibid., fo. 17 (the MS is partly paginated and partly foliated); *Clarke Papers*, I,
        432.
149   PRO, E121/3/3/31; Worc. MS 67 fo. 13.
150   *Reg. Hist.*, p. 606; James Berry and S. G. Lee, *A Cromwellian Major-General:
        the career of Colonel James Berry* (Clarendon Press, Oxford, 1938), p. 2.
        Berry became a major–general under the Protectorate.
151   Worc. MS 67, fos 11, 17, 19, 20, 22, 25.
152   *Clarke Papers*, I, 430–1; *Perf. Wkly Account*, 28 Apr.–5 May 1647, E386/31,
        unpag.
153   Holles, p. 89. Holles identified the MP as Warmworth, but no one of this
        name is known to have sat in the Long Parliament. The radical MP for
        Newcastle was John Blakiston.
154   *CJ*, v, 158; Worc. MS 41, fo. 17.
155   *Perf. Diurnall*, 26 Apr.–3 May 1647, E515/10, p. 1574.
156   *Holles*, pp. 84–5.
157   Other higher officers who were absent from their regiments during this criti-
        cal period included Cols Ingoldsby, Harley, Rossiter, Lilburne, Hammond
        and Rainborowe (Tanner MS 58, fos 16, 18, 62–3, 111, 121; Cary, I, 221;
        Perf. Diurnall, 19–26 Apr. 1647, E515/9, p. 1566).
158   *Perf. Diurnall*, 26 Apr.–3 May 1647, E515/10, p. 1569. Which were the four
        regiments? The reference to Maj. Huntington suggests that Cromwell's was
        one of them, though elsewhere we read that it was stationed at Walden, Essex
        (Worc. MS 41, fo. 108). The others may have been Ireton's, which was
        stationed in nearby Suffolk (HMC, *Portland*, III, 155), Rich's and Fairfax's, all
        of which had backed the *Apologie of the Common Souldiers*.
159   *Clarke Papers*, I, 21–2; Worc. MS 41, fo. 20ᵛ; Rushworth, VI, 481.
160   Worc. MS 41, fo. 19ᵛ.
161   *Clarke Papers*, I, 26.
162   Worc. MS 41, fo. 18–18ᵛ.
163   John Lilburne, *Ionah's Cry out of the Whale's Belly* (26 July 1647), E400/5,
        p. 9.
164   *Clarke Papers*, I, 24, 91. The author of the letter from London of 5 May

whose identity baffled Firth because of William Clarke's unintelligible cipher has been established by Frances McDonald as John Rushworth, the army's secretary. Clarke's shorthand notation reads '[letter from] Master Rushworth to me'. I am extremely grateful to Mrs McDonald for permission to make use of this vital piece of evidence from her forthcoming D Phil. thesis. See also *S & S*, p. 68 n. 32.

165 *Clarke Papers*, I, 22–4.
166 *CJ*, v, 156, 162, 166–7.
167 See above, p. 56.
168 *Perf. Occurrences*, 7–14 May 1647, E387/5, p. 152.
169 Worc. MS 41, fo. 127.
170 Ibid., fo. 113.
171 Ibid., fo. 120.
172 The pervasive pessimism was eloquently expressed by Lambart's regiment (ibid., fo. 124).
173 These were the lifeguard under Capt. Henry Hall; five troops of Okey's dragoons under Maj. Nicholas Moore, Capt. John Farmer, Harold Scrimsheire, Edward Wogan and Ralph Farr; Col. Thomas Fairfax's foot (under Lt-Col. Jackson). See Worc. MS 41, fos 125–7.
174 *Clarke Papers*, I, 36–8, 42–3.
175 Worc. MS 41, fo. 101ᵛ.
176 For Rich's regimental paper see *Divers Papers from the Army* (15 May 1647), E388/18, pp. 7–11. Woolrych advances an alternative hypothesis: that the committee drafted its text on the basis of a 'model version' drawn up by the meeting of agitators at Bury St Edmunds (*S & S*, pp. 75–7).
177 *Perf. Diurnall*, 10–17 May 1647, E515/12, p. 1588. The editor Samuel Pecke's phraseology shows that he was fed his information by Rushworth. See *Clarke Papers*, I, 24; and above, n. 164.
178 *Clarke Papers*, I, 97. Capt. William Rainborowe's anecdote about how the troopers at the meeting of Sheffield's regiment had shouted 'Imdempnity, Imdempnity' and later asked him what it meant is implausible. Indemnity had been a burning issue for months, and any soldiers who still did not understand what was at stake can only have been found in isolated pockets of the army (ibid., p. 66).
179 For a valuable discussion of the importance of honour to the army, see Kishlansky, *Rise*, pp. 212–15.
180 The committee's statement is found in *Divers Papers from the Army*, pp. 3–6; *A Perfect and True Copy of the Severall Grievances of the Army* (16 May 1647), E390/3; and *Army Book of Declarations*, pp. 17–21. *The Declaration of the Armie under His Excellency Sir Thomas Fairfax* ([4 June] 1647), E390/26, with its ominous title-page inscription 'the time is coming when God will execute justice and judgment on the earth' is, as Woolrych convincingly argues, spurious. It may have emanated from a circle of Leveller sympathizers comprising Capt. Francis White, Commissary Nicholas Cowling, and the printer John Harris among others (*S & S*, p. 93 n. 7).

181   *Clarke Papers*, ı, 76–7.
182   Ibid., p. 58.
183   Ibid., p. 72. I see no reason to doubt the sincerity of Cromwell's appeal for obedience, even though two weeks later he would vote with his feet and join the rebels.
184   Worc. MS 41, fo. 53–3ᵛ.
185   *Clarke Papers*, ı, 85; *Perf. Diurnall*, 17–24 May 1647, E515/14, p. 1596.
186   *Clarke Papers*, ı, 96–9; Juxon, Diary, fo. 108ᵛ.
187   Worc. MS 41, fo. 131ᵛ.
188   *Moderate Intell.*, 13–20 May 1647, E388/13, p. 1079.
189   On 30 August Lt Chillenden was paid £78 17s. 'for Mr Coe's printing press', though it had probably been acquired well before that date (Chequers, MS 782, fo. 43ᵛ).
190   *LJ*, ıx, 245–6.
191   Tanner MS 58, fo. 129.
192   In early 1645 the army's monthly pay was estimated at very nearly £45,000 (*CSPD, 1644–5*, p. 232).
193   CCJ 40, fo. 218ᵛ; Montereul, ıı, 129.
194   Montereul, ıı, 160.
195   *GCW*, ııı, 253.
196   *CJ*, v, 158, 181.
197   *LJ*, ıx, 246.
198   A motion to release him with £10 for his pains was narrowly defeated on the 17th, but it was hinted that he could secure his release by personally petitioning the House (Worc. MS 41, fo. 131ᵛ).
199   *Perf. Diurnall*, 17–24 May 1647, E515/14, p. 1598. Ashburnham was the treasurer and paymaster of the royalist army. He would later be vilified by royalists for allowing Charles to fall into Col. Robert Hammond's hands on the Isle of Wight in November 1648 (*DNB*).
200   Clar. MS 29, fo. 227. For the history of the three radical London petitions see *Gold Tried in the Fire* (1647), printed in McMichael and Taft, pp. 275–93.
201   HMC, *Portland*, ı, 421. The account is also printed in Zachary Grey's *Impartial Examination*, appendix, p. 138, where the witness is referred to as a clerk.
202   Worc. MS 41, fo. 132ᵛ.
203   SP21/26, fos 72–3; Worc. MS 41, fo. 132ᵛ.
204   *Perf. Diurnall*, 17–24 May 1647, E515/14, p. 1598.
205   Clar. MS 29, fo. 229.
206   *CJ*, v, 183, 188; *LJ*, ıx, 207–8.
207   Add. MS 10114 (Harington's diary), fo. 25; Waller, *Vindication*, pp. 64–5, 67; *CJ*, v, 207.
208   *Clarke Papers*, ı, 168–9.
209   Montereul, ıı, 164.
210   *Perf. Diurnall*, 7–14 June 1647, E515/19, p. 1622.
211   *CSPI, 1647–60*, p. 754.

212 SP28/124, fo. 337^v; Holles, p. 121.

213 *CSPD, Addenda, 1625–49*, pp. 709–11.

214 Add. MS 37344 (Whitelocke's annals), fos 92, 93^v.

215 *CSPI, 1647–60*, p. 753.

216 Add. MS 37344, fo. 93^v. Dalbeir's work evidently galvanized the reformadoes from Sir John Clotworthy's old regiment and Massey's Brigade to petition for their arrears. (SP21/26, fo. 78; HLRO, Main Papers, June 1647, fos 139–40). See also Valerie Pearl, 'London's counter-revolution', in G. E. Aylmer (ed.), *The Interregnum: the quest for settlement, 1646–1660* (Macmillan, London, 1972), pp. 44–56.

217 Tanner MS 58, fo. 129; *A Plea for the Late Agents of the Army* (1647), Worc., AA.1.19/147; *Clarke Papers*, I, 112; *Perf. Diurnall*, 31 May–7 June 1647, E515/17, pp. 1617–18.

218 In the eleven horse regiments there were seventy-seven officers, in the twelve foot regiments 132, in the dragoon regiment eleven and in the lifeguard two. However, Fairfax had two colonelcies, while Skippon, in addition to being colonel of a foot regiment, was captain of a troop in Scrope's horse regiment. On the other hand I have also included Lt-Gen. Thomas Hammond, who had no regiment. I have excluded the other officers attached to the general staff – adjutant-generals, quartermaster-generals and the like. Thus the total number of officers is 221. The figure for the number who were replaced is derived from the army pay warrants in SP28/46–9, and the lists of new commissions recorded in Worc. MS 67, fos 3–27. In *The Rise of the New Model Army*, Kishlansky states that 'almost a third' of the senior officers were replaced in the summer of 1647, even though his total is only fifty-one. Besides not including captain-lieutenants in his cohort, he has inexplicably counted only ten instead of twelve foot regiments. In addition he has counted Maj. George Sedascue, who had returned to the army as adjutant-general of horse by October 1648 (*Reg. Hist.*, p. 119; see also Chequers, MS 782, fo. 94^v), as well as Capts Richard Pooley and Arthur Young, who never left (PRO, E121/2/11/23; *Clarke Papers*, I, 176). On the other hand, apart from the three captain lieutenants – Charles Holcroft, Robert Fish and Goodhand – he has not counted the following captains who *did* leave: William Bland, Edward Foley, John Forgison and Samuel Gooday. See also *S & S*, p. 134.

219 *Clarke Papers*, I, 18–19.

220 *A Vindication of a Hundred Sixty Seven Officers that are Come off from the Army* ([26 June] 1647), E394/3.

221 There were 398 horse and dragoons and thirty-six gentlemen of the lifeguard (Tanner MS 58, fo. 153). The number of foot who came off was reported as no more than 400 (Juxon, Diary, fo. 112). The private soldiery in the army at that time amounted to 19,160 (Worc. MS 41, fo. 16; misprinted in *Clarke Papers*, I, 19).

222 *Perf. Diurnall*, 24–31 May 1647, E515/15, p. 1603.

223 *LJ*, IX, 227; BL, Egerton MS 1048, fo. 50; Rushworth, VI, 498; *Clarke Papers*, I, 108; Add. MS 34253, fo. 45.

224　Clar. MS 29, fo. 229; Holles, pp. 95–6; Clarke Papers, I, 112–13.

225　Clar. MS 29, fo. 229ᵛ.

226　*Perf. Diurnall*, 31 May–7 June 1647, E515/17, p. 1608. While the committee was dominated by militants, it is noteworthy that it included the moderate Rich and the presbyterian Jackson, who the next day was to be repudiated by the men of his regiment.

227　Add. MS 18979 (Fairfax letters, 1625–88), fo. 235.

228　*Clarke Papers*, I, 112.

229　John Harris, *The Grand Designe* (8 Dec. 1647), E419/15, p. 3; *Windsor Projects and Westminster Practices* ([15 May] 1648), E442/10, p. 2 (corrected pag.).

230　*Perf. Diurnall*, 31 May–7 June 1647, E515/17, p. 1617. There were also said to be men from Maj. Ralph Knight's troop in Col. Tomlinson's regiment.

231　See *S & S*, pp. 106–9, for a convincing account of the chronology of Joyce's movements.

232　The royalist colonel Bamfield later wrote that he had stationed horses near Holdenby for the king's escape. See *Colonel Joseph Bamfield's Apology* (The Hague, 1685), p. 25.

233　*Clarke Papers*, I, 118–19.

234　Add. MS 31116 (Whitacre's diary), fo. 312ᵛ.

235　The phrase is Harris's (*The Grand Designe*, p. 3).

236　Rushworth, VI, 516; OPH, xv, 416–19; HMC, *De L'Isle and Dudley*, VI, p. 567; *A True Impartiall Narration concerning the Armies Preservation of the King* ([4 June] 1647), E393/1.

237　Rushworth, VI, 516–17.

238　Charles was held at Childersley Hall during the rendezvous, and not permitted to proceed to Newmarket until Fairfax and other officers had conferred with him on 7 June (*S & S*, p. 114).

239　OPH, xv, 410–11.

240　*Clarke Papers*, I, 125.

241　*A Narrative of the Causes of the Late Lord General Cromwell's Anger against Lieutenant-Colonel Joyce* (1659), BL, 669.f.21/50.

242　Clarendon, *History*, IV, 223; Harris, *The Grand Designe*, p. 3; Holles, p. 246.

243　It is implicit in John Rushworth's letter of 9 June to Ferdinando Lord Fairfax that the seizure of the king was carried out with the full support of the army high command (Add. MS 18979, fo. 238).

244　T. Fairfax, *Short Memorials*, ed. Brian Fairfax (1699), repr. in Maseres, II, 444–51. As Woolrych points out, the *Short Memorials* may have suffered the same sort of editorial tampering as Ludlowe's memoirs (*S & S*, p. 103 n. 48).

245　OPH, xv, 390. See also his letter to the Derby House Committee (*Clarke Papers*, I, 116).

246　For Bellièvre's exasperated comment on presbyterian indecisiveness, see Montereul, II, 160.

247　Holles, p. 160; Add. MS 37344, fo. 88ᵛ.

248　Add. MS 34253 (Civil War papers, 1640–7), fo. 59.

249 Sir Robert Harley, for example, dreaded open conflict, and urged that the army be paid in full, then reformed into a smaller body under its existing officers (BL, Loan 29/122, fo. 16; I owe this reference to Dr Michael Mahoney).

250 CCJ 40, fo. 224; Worc. MS 41, fos 79–9ᵛ, 96ᵛ.

251 Nagel, 'The Militia of London', pp. 236–9.

252 Pearl, 'London's counter-revolution', pp. 44, 48.

253 Waller, *Vindication*, p. 162. The City's petition to the House of Commons on 1 July, supporting several of the army's demands and urging parliament to stop raising forces within the lines of communication, was probably inspired by its commissioners at headquarters (CCJ 40, fos 231ᵛ–2ᵛ).

254 Cary, I, 293; *Clarke Papers*, I, 168.

255 Add. MS 37344, fo. 105ᵛ.

256 'Colonel Wogan's Narrative,' in *Clarke Papers*, I, 428–9.

257 Nickolls, p. 52; Montereul, II. 168.

258 Add. MS 37344, fos 96, 98; *Perf. Diurnall*, 12–19 July 1647, E518/6, p. 1663; Stevenson, pp. 89–91.

259 *CJ*, V, 202; Juxon (who misdates it as 3–4 June), Diary, fo. 109ᵛ; *LJ*, IX, 247–8. The Lords at first rejected the motion to repeal the Declaration of Dislike (*LJ*, IX, 242).

260 *LJ*, IX, 246.

261 *A Plea for the Late Agents of the Army* (1647), Worc., AA1.19/147, p. 4.

262 *The Humble Representation* (4 June) and the *Solemne Engagement* (5 June) were published together (E392/9).

263 *Perf. Diurnall*, 31 May–7 June 1647, E515/17, p. 1616.

264 In addition, the record of the Reading and Putney debates shows that senior officers who were not members of the General Council attended and took part in its deliberations. The presence of men like Cols Rainborowe, Hewson, Rich, Waller and Tichborne suggests that Fairfax assumed that his council of war could also sit on the General Council. I am grateful to Austin Woolrych for discussion on this point.

265 For a lucid discussion of the make-up and functions of the General Council see *S & S*, p. 117ff.

266 I am indebted to John Morrill for raising this question with me.

267 Worc. MS 41, fo. 13ᵛ.

268 They were Herbert's, Harley's and Rich's regiments (Worc. MS 41 fos 31, 123; *Clarke Papers*, I, 140). In mid-May there were seven agitators in Fairfax's foot regiment (Worc. MS 41, fo. 126ᵛ).

269 Worc., AA1.19/129.

270 Lilburne, *Ionah's Cry*, p. 9.

271 *A Plea for the Late Agents of the Army*.

272 See also *S & S*, pp. 61–3.

273 Lists of the new agents, with the regiments they purported to represent, may be found in Thomason Tracts E411/9, E412/21, E413/18, and also in Worc., AA1.19/145.

274 *The Copy of a Letter Printed at New-Castle, July the 6, 1647*, E398/16, pp. 2–3. This letter came from the officer agitators. A similar letter was sent by the soldier agitators to the forces in Lancashire: see *A Copie of that Letter … to the Souldiery of Lancashire* ([13 July] 1647), E398/7. For more evidence about the activities of the officers and agitators in the north see Add. MS 18979, fos 242–4; Cary, I, 282–4; Bell, I, 363–4.

275 Clarke's account book may be consulted at the library of the Thoresby Society, Leeds, MS SD ix, unfol. I am grateful to the librarian, Mrs J. Mary D. Foster, for permission to cite the MS. It has also been printed, unfortunately with a number of errors, in Thoresby Society, XI (1902). I am indebted to Henry Reece for first drawing my attention to this source. A contemporary transcript of the account book also exists at Chequers, MS 782. Apart from a few errors, and the omission of several dates, the copy is less useful than the original because normally it does not reproduce the word 'agitator(s)', which has been crossed out in several entries in the original. The Chequers copy thus illuminates less strikingly the close links between agitators and army headquarters. The evidence for Rolphe as agitators' paymaster is found in the entry for 11 October, when he received £50 'for the use of the agitators' (in Thoresby Society, XI, 144 his name is misprinted as 'Roper').

276 *S & S*, p. 130.

277 Worc. MS 41, fos 56, 75ᵛ. The Eleven were Denzil Holles, Sir Philip Stapleton, Sir William Lewis, Sir John Clotworthy, Sir William Waller, Sir John Maynard, Maj.-Gen. Edward Massey, John Glyn, Col. Edward Harley, Walter Long and Anthony Nicholls (BL, Egerton MS 1048, fo. 51).

278 *A Charge Delivered in the Name of the Army* (14 June 1647), E393/5. Pending the delivery of the formal impeachment the army demanded that the Eleven be suspended from sitting in the house. In the *Humble Remonstrance* the following week the same demand was made more forcefully (Rushworth, VI, 572, 591). The Commons replied that it could not expel the members until it had heard the evidence against them (*CJ*, v, 223).

279 Montereul, II, 179; Juxon, Diary, fo. 112; Bell, I, 359; Clar. MS 29, fo. 249. In the latter part of June two lawyers, Solicitor John Cooke and Mr Norbury, were hired by headquarters to frame the impeachment in proper legal language. They shared the handsome sum of £45 for about half a month's work (Thoresby Society, XI, 141–2).

280 *Clarke Papers*, I, 151, where Firth misdates the submission of the impeachment; *CJ*, v, 236.

281 BL, Egerton MS 1048, fos 51–80. The MS breaks off at the beginning of article 25, but the full text is printed in *Army Book of Declarations*, E409/25, pp. 79–94, and also separately in Thomason E397/17.

282 *Perf. Diurnall*, 5–12 July 1647, E518/3, pp. 1640–1.

283 Ibid., 12–19 July 1647, E518/6, p. 1647.

284 *S & S*, p. 124.

285 Worc. MS 41, fo. 63.

286 Montereul, II, 164; *Severall Letters Sent from … Sir Thomas Fairfax … to …*

London ([26 June] 1647), E394/3, pp. 2–3; *Perf. Diurnall*, 7–14 June 1647, E515/19, unpag.; *CSPI, 1647–60*, pp. 753–4; Clar. MS 29, fo. 236.

287 Clar. MS 29, fo. 235; CCJ 40, fo. 218ᵛ.

288 CCJ 40, fo. 219.

289 *LJ*, ɪx, 275.

290 CCJ 40, fo. 224; Worc. MS 41, fos 79, 96ᵛ.

291 Worc. MS 41, fo. 75ᵛ.

292 *Army Book of Declarations*, p. 39.

293 Ibid., pp. 40–6. Woolrych argues convincingly that the body which ratified this document was not the General Council of the Army, which only began meeting on 16 July (*S & S*, pp. 126–30).

294 *CJ*, v, 214; SP28/46, fos 112ff.; Tanner MS 58, fo. 222.

295 Tanner MS 58, fo. 182.

296 Worc. MS 41, fos 81, 84.

297 Tanner MS 58, fo. 184.

298 Clar. MS 29, fo. 246.

299 Tanner MS 58, fo. 244.

300 Ibid., fos 235, 237; Bell, ɪ, 370.

301 Tanner MS 58, fos 241, 265; Cary, ɪ, 257; *A New Declaration Presented to the Commons of England* (c.25 June 1647), Worc., AA.1.19/65, pp. 6–8.

302 Tanner MS 58, fo. 269.

303 *Remonstrance of the Representations of the Army*, ([21 June] 1647), E393/17.

304 *An Humble Remonstrance from ... the Army* (23 June 1647), E393/36, pp. 11–15.

305 On 24 June, for example, the three-man committee earlier sent by the City to treat with the army was enlarged to twelve members, four of whom were aldermen, the others being militia officers and common councillors (CCJ 40, fos 227, 229).

306 Juxon, Diary, fo. 112; Bell, ɪ, 359; Clar. MS 29, fo. 249. Juxon was convinced that the Eleven Members nevertheless continued to plot resistance to the New Model in concert with their friends in the City.

307 *CJ*, v, 226.

308 *LJ*, ɪx, 306.

309 *A Manifesto from ... the Army* (27 June 1647), E409/25, p. 70.

310 *Army Book of Declarations*, p. 71. For other conciliatory gestures see *A Letter from ... a Councel of War at Uxbridge* (29 June 1647), E396/4; *LJ*, ɪx, 313.

311 *CJ*, v, 247. The soldiers in Worcester had been guilty of shockingly royalist behaviour. On Midsummer Day (24 June), St Peter's Eve and St Peter's Day (28–9 June) they had staged festivals of Morris dancing, drinking healths to the queen, Prince Rupert and Prince Maurice, and cursing the parliament's friends as 'roundheaded rogues, roundheaded whores, gospel whores, ... etc.' (Tanner MS 58, fo. 305).

312 *Army Book of Declarations*, pp. 94–5; *CJ*, v, 248. The Lords followed suit two days later (*LJ*, ɪx, 339).

313 John Rushworth reported that the French ambassador, Prince Maurice

(brother of Rupert and son of the elector palatine) and numerous cavaliers all paid him respectful court (Bell, I, 368). Although the *DNB* records Maurice's expulsion from England in July 1646, it does not note his presence in 1647.

314 *Clarke Papers*, I, 170–5.

315 While the attendance list for the first day's debate included only officers, the presence of the rank and file is proved by the minutes recording the interventions of three leading soldier agitators–William Allen, Nicholas Lockier and Edward Sexby.

316 Bell, I, 368.

317 J. S. A. Adamson, 'The English nobility and the projected settlement of 1647', *HJ*, 30 (1987), 571–9, 601. Dr Adamson has brilliantly illuminated the role of Lords Saye and Wharton and their faction in formulating and promoting the Heads of the Proposals, but I am not convinced by his argument that Saye was the guiding force behind the Proposals. For example, Adamson does not refer to John Rushworth's assertion on 13 July that the Heads of the Proposals were being prepared by the army (Bell, I, 368; see also *S & S*, p. 152).

318 *Clarke Papers*, I, 213, 216–17.

319 The most accessible text is that printed in *Const. Docs.*, pp. 316–26.

320 Ireton and Cromwell of course still favoured a national church supported out of the public treasury. Ireton made his position explicit in the Whitehall Debates (see below, p. 289).

321 *S & S*, p. 164 n. 81.

322 See *Walwyns Just Defence* (1649), printed in McMichael and Taft, pp. 423–4, 430.

323 *S & S*, p. 174 n. 20.

324 Ibid., p. 177.

325 Berkeley, '*Memoirs*', in Maseres, II, 369. Huntington corroborated Berkeley's recollection (ibid., pp. 403–4).

326 Ludlow[e], I, 151.

327 Adamson, 'The English nobility and the projected settlement of 1647', pp. 577–8; *S & S*, p. 179.

328 *Clarke Papers*, I, 152ff.

329 Worc. MS 41, fo. 176; Dyve, p. 68.

330 Dyve, p. 60; Worc. MS 41, fo. 165ᵛ.

331 Bell, I, 369; *Clarke Papers*, I, 215.

332 *CJ*, V, 254; Rushworth, VI, 634–5.

333 Nagel, 'The Militia of London', p. 279.

334 CCJ 40, fo. 238ᵛ; Dyve, p. 71.

335 Clar. MS 30, fo. 12.

336 Bell, I, 380.

337 Juxon, Diary, fo. 112ᵛ.

338 Ibid., fo. 113.

339 Nagel, 'The Militia of London', p. 314.

340 Juxon, Diary, fo. 113ᵛ; Hugh Peters, *A Word for the Armie* ([11 Oct.] 1647),

E410/16, p. 6; Add. MS 37344, fo. 100–100^v; HLRO, Main Papers, 25 Sept. 1647, fo. 21–1^v.

341 *Perf. Summary*, 26 July–2 Aug. 1647, p. 12.
342 Ludlow[e], I, 161.
343 Adamson, 'The English nobility and the projected settlement of 1647', p. 573; *Clarke Papers*, I, 218.
344 Bell, I, 381; Waller, *Vindication*, pp. 182–3; Add. MS 37344, fo. 100. Of the newsbooks only the *Perfect Summary* seems to have given the *coup* against parliament the coverage it deserved.
345 Holles, p. 152.
346 See Pearl, 'London's counter-revolution', p. 51; Kishlansky, Rise, pp. 267–8; Adamson, 'The English nobility and the projected settlement of 1647', pp. 567–8, 576; *S & S*, pp. 168–72.
347 *Sydney Papers*, pp. 15–16; Dyve, p. 72.
348 Patricia Crawford, *Denzil Holles*, 1598–1660, RHS (1979), p. 156.
349 HLRO, Main Papers, 25 Sept. 1647, fos 23^v–4.
350 Glyn had lodgings directly below the Commons chamber (*LJ*, X, 16–18).
351 HLRO, Braye MS 96 (photocopy of John Browne's commonplace book), pp. 237–9.
352 Holles, pp. 153–4.
353 Adamson, 'The English nobility and the projected settlement of 1647', p. 576 nn. 64–5.
354 *S & S*, p. 172.
355 Add. MS 37344, fo. 101.

Chapter 7   The Political Wars, 1646–8 (II):
From the Occupation of London to the Second Civil War

1 Ludlow[e], I, 161–2; *Clarke Papers*, I, 219n.
2 Zachary Grey, *Impartial Examination* (Bettesworth and Hitch, London, 1737), appendix, pp. 124–5.
3 *Perf. Diurnall*, 26 July–2 Aug. 1647, E518/12, p. 1681.
4 *CJ*, V, 260; Rushworth, VI, 647.
5 HLRO, Main Papers, 30 July 1647, fo. 130; Rushworth, VI, 652–3. *CJ*, V, 260; *LJ*, IX, 358. Though he would later be identified with Fifth Monarchism, Col. Rich was known as a political moderate and detested by the London radicals. At all times, however, he was loyal to the army. Although he was living in London in 1647, there is no evidence that he had anything to do with the Committee of Safety.
6 *CJ*, V, 262.
7 Juxon, Diary, fos 114^v–15; Worc. MS 110, unfol.; CCJ 40, fo. 244.
8 Holles, p. 159; Clar. MS 29, fo. 24.
9 *Perf. Diurnall*, 26 July–2 Aug. 1647, E518/12, p. 1683; *Colonel Joseph Bamfeild's Apology* (The Hague, 1685), p. 33; Juxon, Diary, fo. 116.

10 *Sydney Papers*, p. 26.

11 *By the Committee for the Militia of the City of London* (31 July 1647), Bodl. Lib., Fairfax Deposit.

12 Worc. MS 110, unfol.

13 Ibid.; CCJ 40, fo. 243ᵛ.

14 Clar. MS 30, fos 24, 26, 28; Rushworth, ᵥᴵᴵ, 753; *Perf. Wkly Account*, 29 July –4 Aug. 1647, E401/1, unpag. (3 Aug.); *S & S*, pp. 180–1.

15 CCJ 40, fo. 248–8ᵛ.

16 *Perf. Diurnall*, 7–14 June 1647, E515/19, p. 1625; ibid., 14–21 June, E515/21, pp. 1626–8; Rushworth, ᵥᴵ, 575, 577; Tanner MS 58, fo. 218.

17 Tanner MS 58, fo. 435; *Perf. Diurnall*, 2–9 Aug. 1647, E518/16, pp. 1686–7; *Perf. Occurrences*, 6–13 Aug. 1647, E518/17, p. 216.

18 Worc. MS 110, unfol. (31 July).

19 Juxon, Diary, fos 116, 117ᵛ; Clar. MS 30, fo. 24; *Perf. Diurnall*, 2–9 Aug. 1647, E518/6, p. 1685.

20 Even John Lilburne counselled his friends to hasten away before it was too late (Wallington, MS Diary, p. 536).

21 Holles, p. 159; Clar. MS 30, fo. 24.

22 Juxon, Diary, fo. 117ᵛ. See also *Perf. Diurnall.*, 2–9 Aug. 1647, E518/16, p. 1685.

23 Add. MS 37344 (Whitelocke's annals), fo. 103; CCJ 40, fo. 250ᵛ.

24 *Clarke Papers*, ᵢ, 220; *Perf. Diurnall*, 2–9 Aug. 1647, E518/16, pp. 1688–9. The figure of 20,000 troops given in this source, reproduced by Rushworth (ᵥᴵᴵ, 750) and cited by Gardiner (*GCW*, ᴵᴵᴵ, 344) is out of line. Skippon's regiment was at Newcastle; Horton's was in the west; some of Whalley's were with the king at Stoke House; Ingoldsby's was in Oxford; and 2000 troops were at that moment occupying Gravesend and Tilbury (MS Diary, Wallington, p. 539; see also *Perf. Summary*, 2–9 Aug. 1647, E518/15, p. 24, which lists the regiments that marched through London on 7 August). A number of detachments were also engaged in patrolling the perimeter of London. The estimate of 15,000, which was Bellièvre's, is if anything too high PRO31/3/84, fo. 72).

25 BL Microfilm 330 (Duke of Northumberland, Alnwick MS 548), fo. 1; Gloucestershire RO, Microfilm 285, Barwick MS 33b (I owe this reference to David Evans); *Perf. Diurnall*, 2–9 Aug. 1647, E518/16, p. 1691; *Moderne Intell.*, 19–26 Aug. 1647, E404/28, p. 10; *A Speedy Hue and Crie after Generall Massie, Col. Poyntz, Sir Robert Pye, William Pryn, and Many Other New-modelled Reformadoes* ([10 Aug.] 1647), E401/20.

26 Hardwick, a Southwark merchant with dealings in London, was later vilified for his pivotal role in facilitating the New Model's entry to the City. See *A Paire of Spectacles for the Cities* ([4 Dec.] 1647), E419/9, p. 8; HLRO, Main Papers, 21, 23 Aug. 1647, fos 86–8.

27 Juxon, Diary, fo. 117ᵛ; Clar. MS 30, fo. 30; PRO30/3/84, fo. 72; Wallington, MS Diary, pp. 538–9.

28 *Army Book of Declarations*, E409/25, p. 109.

29 Westminster Public Library, MS F4 (churchwardens' accounts, St Martin's), p. 39, cited in J. S. A. Adamson, 'The English nobility and the projected settlement of 1647', *HJ*, 30 (1987), 578.

30 Clar. MS 30, fo. 33.

31 All the newsbooks reported the army's procession through the City, and their observations about its conduct were uniformly favourable. See for example *Perf. Summary*, 2–9 Aug. 1647, E518/15, p. 24. Other eyewitness sources are Juxon's Diary, fo. 119; Wallington's MS Diary, pp. 539–40; and the royalist newswriter in Clar. MS 30, fo. 33.

32 Juxon, Diary, fo. 119. A royalist newswriter sneered that the New Model troops were poorly armed, ill horsed and ill clad (Clar. MS 30, fos 33^v–4). While other observers also thought the New Model was poorly armed, it may be that the soldiers deliberately piled their weapons into carts in order to be less frightening to the citizens.

33 *Seria Exercitus* ([4 Dec.] 1647), E419/6, p. 30. This testimony is the more impressive for having been penned by a royalist.

34 *Perf. Summary*, 2–9 Aug. 1647, E518/15, p. 24.

35 *Two Speeches Made by the Speakers of Both Houses of Parliament to His Excellency Sir Thomas Fairfax Generall* ([9 Aug.] 1647), E401/15, pp. 3–4.

36 Worc. MS 67, p. 13. Tichborne, a member of the Skinner's Company who practised as a linen-draper in Cheapside, had been first captain then colonel of the Yellow Regiment of trained bands. A writer of lengthy religious tracts, he would become alderman in 1649 and lord mayor in 1656. In the 1650s he would buy substantial crown properties in Kent. See Lawson Nagel, 'The Militia of London, 1641–1649' (unpublished PhD thesis, University of London), pp. 314–15; Society of Genealogists (London), Percival Lloyd, Index of Seventeenth–Century London Citizens, no. 15,594; Skinners' Hall, (London), Apprenticeships and Freedoms 1601–94, no. 104D; Ian Gentles, 'The Debentures Market and Military Purchases of Crown Land during the English Revolution, 1649–1660' (unpublished PhD thesis, University of London, 1969), p. 345. By his own testimony William Shambrooke had been put out of his command by the presbyterian London Militia Committee on 21 June 1647 because of his political Independency and religious sectarianism. He would die the following summer at the siege of Colchester (*Clarke Papers*, I, 153 and n.).

37 Juxon, Diary, fo. 119^v.

38 CCJ 40, fos 251, 252^v; *A Continuation of Certain Speciall and Remarkable Passages*, 14–21 Aug. 1647, E404/5, unpag. The newswriter states that the dinner was on Thursday 20 August, when 'The lords sat not, many of them purposing to dine with his Excellency at the Earl of Manchester's house at Chelsea.' However, the 20th was a Friday, and the Lords did sit on that day. I infer therefore that the dinner must have been on Thursday the 19th, and that the friendly peers must have been informed of the military show of force planned for the following day.

39 *Sydney Papers*, p. 28. The seven peers were the Earls of Lincoln, Suffolk and

Middlesex, and Lords Berkeley, Willoughby of Parham, Rochfort and Maynard.

40   Clar. MS 30, fo. 33ᵛ.

41   *LJ*, ɪx, 375.

42   Ibid., p. 379; Adamson, 'The English nobility and the projected settlement of 1647', pp. 579–80.

43   *CJ*, v, 269–70, 271, 273, 275, 279; HMC, *Egmont*, ɪ, 443–4; *S & S*, pp. 184–5; J. S. A. Adamson, (Politics and the nobility in Civil War England', *HJ*, 34 (1991), pp. 246–7. I am grateful to Dr Adamson for letting me read his article in advance of publication.

44   *The Humble Address of the Agitators ... on the 5 of this Instant August* (1647). Thomason's copy is dated 14 August (E402/8). In their *Remonstrance and Protestation* of 23 August (referred to in *The Resolution of the Agitators ... 2 Sept. 1647*, E405/22, title page and p. 7), the agitators would reiterate their complaint against the 'usurpers and incendiaries' who continued to sit. See also *S & S*, p. 193.

45   *Two Letters from his Excellency Sir Thomas Fairfax ... with ... a Remonstrance of ... the Army* (20 Aug. 1647), E402/28, pp. 23–4. The Remonstrance was sent to parliament on the 18th.

46   *The Machivilian Cromwellist and Hypocritical Perfidious New Statist* (1648), Bodl. Lib., Fairfax Deposit, Tracts, 38/21, p. 6. This anonymous tract, which carried no printer's name, appears from internal evidence to have been published in early 1648, before the disbandments of February, and the outbreak of the second civil war. The author had a detailed knowledge of parliamentary affairs, and was probably one of the excluded presbyterian MPs. That the purpose of the doubled guards at Westminster and mustering of cavalry in Hyde Park was to intimidate the MPs was also alleged by Mayor Thomas Adams in his anti-army tract *Plain Dealing* ([17 Nov.] 1647), E416/3, p. 6; by the anonymous author of *The Petition of Right of the Freeholders* ([8 Jan.] 1648), E422/9, p. 19; and by the authors of *The Petition of Right of the Freeholders and Freemen of the Kingdom of England ... to the Lords and Commons* ([8 Jan.] 1648), E422/9, p. 19. See also Holles, pp. 172–3. Cf. Woolrych (*S & S*, p. 188), who is sceptical of the hostile accounts of army intimidation.

47   *Kingdomes Wkly Intell.*, 17–24 Aug. 1647, E404/13, pp. 642–3; *CJ*, v, 280.

48   HMC, *Portland*, ɪ, 433. I take 'the prisoners in the Tower' to refer to these two.

49   Despite his bitter complaints 'Lilburne enjoyed much milder treatment after the army took control of London. On 7 August he was paid £10 out of the army's contingency fund (Chequers, MS 782, fo. 43ᵛ). Two days later we find him signing a receipt for £533 15s. for two weeks' pay for his brother Robert's foot regiment (SP28/47, fo. 298). His new gaoler, Robert Tichborne, evidently handled him with kid gloves, since in early November it was noted that 'he is seen often abroad', contrary to the Lords' order to keep him confined (*Perf. Occurrences*, 5–12 Nov. 1647, E520/4, p. 305). His situation

was regularized on 9 November, when he was given leave to go out of the Tower during the day without a keeper (*CJ*, VI, 353). The implication is that between August and November he had been free to wander about London at will.

50 Holles, p. 173.

51 *Perf. Occurrences*, 24 Sept.–1 Oct. 1647, E518/39, pp. 266–7; *A Charge and Impeachment of High Treason against Sir John Geyer, Lord Major of London, [et al.]* (1647), Bodl. Lib., Fairfax Deposit; *The Impeachment by the House of Commons against the Lord Major of the City of London and Divers Other [s]* ... (1647), Bodl. Lib., Fairfax Deposit, Tracts, 6/19.

52 This citizen regiment relieved Pride's men of their duties at the beginning of November (*Perf. Occurrences*, 29 Oct.–5 Nov. 1647, E520/2, p. 311).

53 Ian Gentles, 'The struggle for London during the Second Civil War', HJ, 26 (1983), 284.

54 Ibid.

55 Ibid.; CCJ 40, fos 254, 255–5ᵛ; PRO, E101/67/11A, fo. 112.

56 *Perf. Diurnall*, 16–23 Aug. 1647, E518/21, p. 1716; *Perf. Occurrences*, 27 Aug.–3 Sept. 1647, E518/26, p. 235.

57 See above, pp. 148–9.

58 *LJ*, IX, 244.

59 *A Second Letter from the Agitators* ([July] 1647), Codr. Lib., vx.2.3./26, p. 2.

60 See Richard Overton, *Eighteene Reasons Propounded to the Soldiers ... Why They Ought to Continue the Several Adjutators* (11 Aug. 1647), BL, 534.d.10; John Lilburne, *The Ivst Mans Ivstification* ([18 Sept.] 1647), E407/26; and *The Case of the Armie Truly Stated* (printed in Wolfe, pp. 196–222), which was in part the work of John Wildman.

61 *A Religious Retreat Sounded to a Religious Army* ([27 Aug.] 1647), E404/34, p. 12; *The Army Brought to the Barre* ([17 Sept.] 1647), E407/22, p. 8.

62 Worc. MS 66 (Minute Book of the Committee of General Officers), fo. 1. Skippon's and Lambart's omission from the committee is explained by their absence in the north.

63 Ibid., fo. 1–1ᵛ.

64 Ibid., fos 2ᵛ, 26, 28.

65 Ibid., fos 12, 18.

66 Ibid., fos 6, 12, 15ᵛ.

67 This is evidence again that Fairfax continued to play a strong leadership role in the army. After Joyce had been turned down for Fleetwood's regiment, he was renominated as governor of Southsea Castle and captain of a company in Portsmouth. This time Fairfax approved the recommendation (Ibid., fos 13ᵛ, 16ᵛ).

68 Dyve, pp. 84–5, 89.

69 John Lilburne, *The Ivst Mans Ivstification* ([27 Aug.] 1647), E407/26, pp. 24–8; *Army Book of Declarations*, pp. 149–50, 154–6; *Resolution of the Agitators* (2 Sept. 1647), E405/22, p. 4.

70 SP28/47, fos 281–480. Another month's pay was received in October (SP28/48, fos 90, 155, *et passim*).

71   'Advice to the Private Soldiers', *The Ivglers Discovered* (8 Sept. 1647),
      E409/22, pp. 10–11. Had Lilburne forgotten Allen's courageous answers to
      the House of Commons when they had grilled him on 30 April? Can he have
      been unaware of how Allen had stood up to Cromwell and Ireton at the
      Reading Debates in July? (*Clarke Papers*, I, 430–1; 189–90, 193, 199–201;
      see also *S & S*, p. 191).

72   Dyve, pp. 85–6.

73   Ibid., pp. 90–1.

74   *Clarke Papers*, I, 140, 161 (Dober, Symons); *Humble Address of the Agitators*
      (Wood). The evidence for Joseph Aleyn is his signature on a letter to Fairfax
      written from the north in July 1647. Firth prints the letter (*Clarke Papers*, I,
      164–5) but wrongly states that it was unsigned. See Worc. MS 110, unfol.
      (July 1647).

75   Rushworth, VII, 859–60. I have been able to identify fifty-eight new agents
      from twelve of the sixteen regiments. Besides the original five horse regiments
      there were the lifeguard, Fairfax's horse, Harrison's, Okey's, Waller's,
      Lilburne's, Twisleton's and an unidentified regiment. See *A Copy of a Letter
      Sent by the Agents of Severall Regiments … to all the Souldiers …* (11 Nov.
      1647), E413/18; *A Copy of a Letter from the Com. Gen. Regiment to the Con-
      vention of Agents Residing in London* (11 Nov. 1647), Worc., AA.1.19/145.

76   *Clarke Papers*, I, 367.

77   Dyve, p. 91.

78   For example, they got themselves mixed up in a murky dispute between John
      Morris, alias Poyntz, and his friends, and the clerk of the House of Lords,
      John Browne. Persuaded by Morris's version of the quarrel, and not
      bothering to find out Browne's, they wrote to Fairfax as 'fellow feelers' of
      Morris's oppression. In their eyes the case was merely another instance of the
      tyranny of the House of Lords over the common people of England. 'If these
      exorbitancies are not stopped,' they exclaimed, 'no man will have any secur-
      ity in his estate.' John Rushworth and Col. Edward Whalley were embar-
      rassed and exasperated that the soldiers had been duped by Morris, and
      Whalley assured Fairfax that the men of his regiment were ignorant of what
      the new agents had done on their behalf. Morris seems to have forged an act
      of parliament to prove his title to an estate in Essex, and to have accused
      Browne of having lost or destroyed the official copy of the act. When Morris
      was fined and imprisoned for his impudence he took his case to the new
      agents (HLRO, Main Papers, 13 Oct. 1647, fos 88–8^v, 90–90^v, 92; HMC,
      House of Lords 1644–47, pp. 184, 189, 200, 206, 211; *LJ*, IX, 521).

79   The original agitators had first thought about organizing such a convention in
      July, but only with representatives from friendly counties (Bodl. Lib., Nalson
      MS 12, fo. 358; Dyve, p. 65).

80   *A Copy of a Letter from the Com. Gen. Regiment.*

81   Ibid.

82   *Perf. Wkly Account*, 10–17 Nov. 1647, E416/2, unpag. (emphasis added).

83   As late as 22 September, Cromwell and Ireton were reported to have opposed
      in the Commons breaking off talks with the king (Clar. MS 30, fo. 73).

84 *S & S*, p. 200; *Perf. Diurnall*, 11–18 Oct. 1647, E518/45, p. 1768; *Proposalls from ... the Councell of the Army, by Way of Address to the Parliament* (17 Oct. 1647), E411/5.

85 *A Word for the Armie* ([11 Oct.] 1647), E410/16, pp. 8–9.

86 *The Case of the Armie Truly Stated*, printed in Wolfe, pp. 206–7. As Woolrych points out, the composite authorship of this document probably included John Wildman, Edward Sexby, and some of the other agents (*S & S*, pp. 207–8).

87 Wolfe, p. 220.

88 Ibid., pp. 199–218.

89 Ibid., pp. 214–15. The dean and chapter lands would only have reduced the army's arrears by about one third. See Ian Gentles, 'The arrears of pay of the parliamentary army at the end of the first civil war', *BIHR*, xlviii (1975), 55; H. J. Habakkuk, 'Public finance and the sale of confiscated property during the interregnum', *EcHR*, 2nd ser., xv (1962–3), 87.

90 The point about the anti-army subtext of the Leveller message was first made by John Morrill in a brilliant article, 'The army revolt of 1647', in *Britain and the Netherlands*, vi (1977), 67–9, 75–6.

91 *Propositions of the Adjutators of the Five Regiments* ([20 Oct.] 1647), E411/13.

92 *Perf. Diurnall*, 18–25 Oct. 1647, E518/47, p. 1779; Rushworth, vii, 849.

93 Rushworth, vii, 850.

94 *Papers from the Armie* (22 Oct. 1647), E411/19, p. 4.

95 D. E. Underdown, 'The parliamentary diary of John Boys, 1647–8', *BIHR*, xxxix (1966), 152.

96 *S & S*, p. 213.

97 Ibid., p. 215; McMichael and Taft, p. 31.

98 Rushworth, vii, 857.

99 *S & S*, p. 217 n. 10. The first three agents in Whalley's regiment are listed in *The Case of the Armie Truly Stated*, while the fourth is found in a petition to Fairfax signed by the new agents on 14 October (HLRO, Main Papers, 14 Oct. 1647, fo. 88ᵛ).

100 *Clarke Papers*, i, 227–8.

101 The Agreement is printed in Wolfe, pp. 226–8.

102 *Clarke Papers*, i, 236–7.

103 Clar. MS 30, fo. 60, cited in *S & S*, 196.

104 *Clarke Papers*, i, 244–7.

105 *S & S*, p. 224.

106 *Clarke Papers*, i, 254.

107 Ibid., pp. 263–4.

108 Ibid., pp. 277–8.

109 *S & S*, p. 226. I count Rich as a political conservative, even though he was to get into trouble during the 1650s for his Fifth Monarchist views. Between 1647 and 1649 he was repeatedly criticized by the Levellers for being anti-revolutionary. See below, n. 126.

110 There were two quartermaster-generals, of foot and horse respectively

(Worc. MS 66, fo. 1; SP28/48, fo. 10). Woolrych assumes that the meeting was held in the lodgings of the quartermaster-general of horse, Thomas Ireton (*S & S*, p. 224). However, Quartermaster-General Ireton is nowhere mentioned in the context of Putney. On the other hand in *Clarke Papers*, I, 415 there is a reference to 'Quartermaster General's quarters', and on the next page, to Quartermaster-General Grosvenor. It therefore seems more probable that Grosvenor, not Ireton, was the host of the prayer meeting.

111　*Clarke Papers*, I, 280, 287; Dyve, p. 95.

112　J. Richard Williams, 'County and municipal government in Cornwall, Devon, Dorset and Somerset 1649–1660' (unpublished PhD thesis, University of Bristol, 1981), pp. 322, 476.

113　Reece, p. 155.

114　This and other passages in the Putney record confirm Kishlansky's characterization of the debates as 'a sincere effort to achieve a peaceful settlement to the English civil war'. See Mark Kishlansky 'Consensus politics and the structure of debate at Putney,' *JBS*, 20 (1980–1), 53.

115　*Clarke Papers*, I, 281–5.

116　Printed by Matthew Simmons in September 1647 (E409/25).

117　*Clarke Papers*, I, 288.

118　Ibid., p. 297.

119　As John Morrill perceptively noted in 'The army revolt of 1647,' pp. 72–3.

120　*Clarke Papers*, I, 301.

121　Ibid., pp. 301–2.

122　See Derek Hirst, *The Representative of the People?* (Cambridge University Press, Cambridge, 1975), pp. 22, 63, 96.

123　*Clarke Papers*, I, 304, 305. For a man of substance Rainborowe was surprisingly radical. However, his consciousness had not been raised to the point of advocating that women too should participate in the electoral process. Very few people at the time did.

124　*Clarke Papers*, I, 309, 313.

125　Ibid., p. 320.

126　Ibid., p. 315. For Rich's biography see *DNB*. For the hostility of the Levellers to him see John Wildman, *Putney Proiects* ([30 Dec.] 1647), E421/19, p. 45; John Lilburne, *Ionah's Cry out of the Whales Belly* (26 July 1647), E400/5, p. 8.

127　*Clarke Papers*, I, 318.

128　Ibid., p. 320. William was if anything more radical than his elder brother, for whom Leveller ideas seem to have been a passing fancy. William had lived in New England before the civil war, and was related by marriage to Stephen Winthrop. By 1649 Cromwell had dismissed him from his command, and in September 1650 the House of Commons would disable him from being a JP on account of his share in the publication of a blasphemous pamphlet by Lawrence Clarkson entitled *A Single Eye, All Light, No Darkness* (1650). See James Savage, *A Genealogical Dictionary of the First Settlers of New England* (4 vols, Little, Brown, Boston, Mass., 1860–2), III, 502; Christopher Hill, *The*

World Turned Upside Down (Maurice Temple Smith, London, 1972), p. 174;
Reg. Hist., p. 184.

129 *Clarke Papers*, I, 323. I concur with Woolrych in italicizing 'were' to indicate
that Sexby was alluding to the famous assertion in the June *Declaration* that
'we were not a mere mercenary army' (*S & S*, p. 239n.).

130 I find Woodhouse's reading of this speech preferable to Firth's. Cf. Woodhouse, p. 71; and *Clarke Papers*, I, 325–6.

131 This class of tenant had almost as much security as the freeholder. Holding
his tenancy for life upon the payment of an entry fine, he was normally able
to bequeath his property to his heir, who in turn became tenant for life on
payment of a fine. Rents were usually unalterable, and the landlord's only
way of keeping up with inflation was to raise the entry fine.

132 Woodhouse, p. 74.

133 *Clarke Papers*, I, 333–4.

134 GLCRO, Finchley St Mary's Parish Register 1558–1701, DRO 32/A1/1, 21
Mar. 1619; Clothworkers' Hall (London), Register of Apprentices 1606–41,
unfol. (7 Dec. 1632). Rolfe did not complete his apprenticeship. Royalist
newsbooks later referred to him as a shoemaker (*Merc. Pragmaticus*, 1–8 Aug.
1648, E457/12, unpag.; *Merc. Elencticus*, 21–8 May 1649, E556/19, p. 37).
In late 1648 he would sign a radical petition from the Isle of Wight
demanding justice for grand delinquents (BL, 669.f.13/71).

135 The previous month he had published *Preaching without Ordination* (2 Sept.
1647), E405/10. For his occupation see John Lilburne, *The Legall Fundamentall Liberties of the People of England* (1649), E560/14, p. 21. See also
Reg. Hist., pp. 226–7. Chillenden was an active trader in crown lands in the
1650s (Gentles, 'The Debentures Market', p. 265).

136 Woodhouse (p. 80) makes better sense of Clarke's speech than Firth.

137 This is a collation of Waller's two short speeches (*Clarke Papers*, I, 339,
345).

138 Ibid., p. 341. Such phrases point to Ireton's sincerity and ought to clear him
of the suspicion of cynically prologing the debate so that it would eventually
fizzle out. The London Levellers, it is true, did warn Robert Everard that the
grandees would 'keep you in debate and dispute till you and we [shall] all
come to ruin' (ibid., p. 343). Cf. Ivan Roots, *The Great Rebellion* (Batsford,
London, 1965), pp. 119–20.

139 Even the moderate Petty had declared, 'I judge every man is naturally free'
(*Clarke Papers*, I, 312).

140 This was C. B. Macpherson's contention in *The Political Theory of Possessive
Individualism* (Clarendon Press, Oxford, 1962), ch. 4. Several authors have
contested his argument, but I believe Keith Thomas supplies the most convincing refutation in 'The Levellers and the franchise,' in G. E. Aylmer (ed.),
The Interregnum: the quest for settlement, 1646–1660 (Macmillan, London,
1972).

141 *S & S*, p. 242.

142 *Clarke Papers*, I, 349.

143 Ibid., pp. 359–61.
144 *Perf. Occurrences*, 29 Oct.–5 Nov. 1647, E520/2, p. 306; *A Copy of a Letter Sent by the Agents of Severall Regiments ... to all the Souldiers* (11 Nov. 1647), E413/18, pp. 1–2. See *S & S*, pp. 243–4, for a lucid discussion of this point. My nominees for the three officers who opposed this franchise are Rich (because of his expressed cynicism about democracy), Hewson (because of his future implacable hostility to the Levellers) and Ireton. Another plausible candidate is Sir Hardress Waller. Apart from the fact that he was in the chair, Cromwell would never have allowed himself to be part of a tiny minority on any vote in the General Council.
145 William Allen and Samuel Whiting were agents from Cromwell's regiment, while Edward Sexby represented Fairfax's, and Nicholas Andrewes, Pride's. See *Clarke Papers*, I, 363; *Apologie of the Common Souldiers* (3 May 1647), E385/18; Worc. MS 41, fo. 123. The two other men, Mr Walley and Mr Gayes, *may* have been Matthew Weale or Wealey, a new agent of Whalley's regiment (Wolfe, pp. 221, 231, 234), and William Gray, a new agent of Twisleton's (*A Copy of a Letter from the Com. Gen. Regiment*).
146 *Clarke Papers*, I, 363–7, 407–11; *S & S*, p. 247.
147 *Reg. Hist.*, p. 456; Rushworth, VII, 1226.
148 *Clarke Papers*, I, 370, 373; SP28/257, unfol.; *Apology unto the Officers of the Lord General's Army* ([4 May] 1649), E552/28.
149 *Clarke Papers*, I, 374, 377.
150 Ibid., p. 382.
151 G. E. Aylmer, *The State's Servants* (Routledge and Kegan Paul, London, 1973), p. 21.
152 *Clarke Papers*, I, 383.
153 Ibid., pp. 391–5.
154 Rushworth, VII, 861. These points are presented in an abbreviated and garbled form by Henry Walker in *Perf. Occurrences*, 29 Oct.–2 Nov. 1647, E520/2, p. 310.
155 *Perf. Occurrences*, 29 Oct.–2 Nov. 1647, E520/2, p. 312.
156 Rushworth, VII, 863; *Perf. Diurnall*, 1–8 Nov. 1647, E520/3, pp. 1774–5.
157 *Clarke Papers*, I, 414n; *S & S*, p. 260.
158 *A Cal to All the Souldiers of the Armie* ([29 Oct.] 1647), E412/10, p. 7. I accept C. H. Firth's attribution of this anonymous tract to Wildman (*DNB* sub Wildman).
159 *An Alarum to the Headquarters* ([9 Nov.] 1647), E413/10, p. 4. While Thomason did not acquire the tract until 9 November Woolrych argues persuasively that it must have dated from around 28 October (*S & S*, p. 228, n. 51).
160 Dyve, p. 95.
161 *Perf. Occurrences*, 5–12 Nov. 1647, E520/4, p. 305.
162 Wolfe, p. 225.
163 *The Humble Remonstrance and Desires of [Hewson's regiment]* (4 Nov. 1647), E413/6.

164 The evidence for this is not as strong as one would like. No copy of the petition survives, and the first reference to it was made a year-and-a-half later by Cornet Henry Denne in *The Levellers Designe* ([24 May] 1649), E556/11, p. 4. Yet the defeated Levellers did implicitly admit that the five horse regiments who had first chosen new agents petitioned to have them sent back. One reason apparently was that they no longer wanted to pay their living costs. See *Sea-Green and Blue* ([6 June] 1649), E559/1, p. 11.

165 *Clarke Papers*, I, 412–13.

166 *S & S*, pp. 262–3.

167 *Clarke Papers*, I, 413–14; *CJ*, v, 353.

168 *Clarke Papers*, I, 413.

169 *S & S*, pp. 266–7.

170 Ibid., p. 267; *Clarke Papers*, I, 414–15.

171 It may have been residing in Norfolk (*Perf. Diurnall*, 26 Apr.–3 May 1647, E515/10, p. 1569).

172 *Clarke Papers*, I, 417.

173 HMC, *Portland*, I, 441.

174 The writer, who signed his letter 'E. R.', may have been Lt-Col. Henry Lilburne, brother of John. He would turn royalist in the second civil war. See *OPH*, XVI, 328; Pauline Gregg, *Freeborn John* (Harrap, London, 1961), pp. 203–5.

175 *Kingdomes Wkly Intell.*, 9–16 Nov. 1647, E416/1, pp. 730–1.

176 Edward Whalley, *A More Full Relation of the Manner and Circumstances of His Majesties Departure from Hampton-Court* ([22 Nov.] 1647), E416/23, p. 6.

177 *S & S*, 268. Cf. Bamfield, *Apology*, p. 36.

178 *Perf. Occurrences*, 12–19 Nov. 1647, E520/6, p. 313.

179 Underdown, 'Parliamentary dairy of John Boys', p. 151.

180 *Perf. Wkly Account*, 10–17 Nov. 1647, E416/2, unpag.; *Merc. Pragmaticus*, 9–16 Nov. 1647, E414/16, pp. 69–70; *Merc. Elencticus*, 12–19 Nov. 1647, E416/13, p. 21; *The Character of an Agitator* ([11 Nov.] 1647), E414/3, p. 7; *A New Declaration from Eight Regiments in the Army* (22 Nov. 1647), E416/35, p. 2. Other radical meeting places at this time were in Southwark, and the Spittlehouse in the City (*Merc. Melancholicus*, 13–20 Nov. 1647, E416/17, p. 72).

181 Grey, *Impartial Examination*, appendix, p. 130; *A New Declaration from Eight Regiments*, p. 3.

182 *A Copy of a Letter Sent by the Agents*.

183 *A Copy of a Letter from the Com. Gen. Regiment*. Another possibility, suggested to me by Austin Woolrych, is that the letter did not emanate from Ireton's regiment at all, but was fabricated by the Levellers.

184 *S & S*, pp. 228–9.

185 *The Iustice of the Army Vindicated against Evildoers Vindicated* (5 June 1649), E558/14, pp. 1–3.

186 Ibid., p. 4. Bray's unauthorized appearance at the General Council (he was

not one of the officer representatives) on 8 November, when he tackled Cromwell on the franchise question, further demonstrates his deep involvement with the Leveller faction in the army (*Clarke Papers*, I, 411).

187   *The Iustice of the Army Vindicated*, pp. 1–3, 5–6; [John Canne], *The Discoverer ... the Second Part* ([13 July] 1649), pp. 52–4; *Perf. Occurrences*, 12–19 Nov. 1647, E520/6, p. 313; Mark Kishlansky, 'What happened at Ware?', *HJ*, 25 (1982), 833–4.

188   Gentles, 'The struggle for London', p. 285.

189   *A Full Relation of the Proceedings at the Rendezvous in Corkbush Field* (15 Nov. 1647), E414/13, pp. 4–5.

190   *LJ*, IX, 528.

191   *A Full Relation of ... Corkbush Field*, p. 6; Rushworth, VII, 876; *CJ*, v, 378.

192   *S & S*, p. 280, citing Firth, *Clarke Papers*, I, 407.

193   Worc. MS 41, fo. 167, and MS 110, unfol. (30 Nov. 1647); Ian Gentles, 'London Levellers and the English Revolution: the Chidleys and their circle', *JEH*, 29 (1978), 291; *Merc. Pragmaticus*, 16–22 Nov. 1647, E416/19, p. 73; *Perf. Occurrences*, 12–19 Nov. 1647, E520/6, p. 318.

194   *Merc. Anti-Pragmaticus*, 18–25 Nov. 1647, E416/383, p. 4.

195   *A Copy of a Letter Sent by the Agents*; *Moderate Intell.*, 11–18 Nov. 1647, E416/8 (pag. erratic). Like Professor Woolrych, I am sceptical of Lt Nathaniel Rockwell's reminiscence six years after the event, alleging that Col. Harrison had supported his mutinuous soldiers. Such flagrant conduct would surely have earned him punishment similar to William Bray's and Thomas Rainborowe's (*S & S*, p. 281 n. 14). The man who retailed Rockwell's story was an obscure officer who signed his name Ja:[mes] Reynuds, and is not to be confused with Capt. (later Col.) John Reynolds, one of Cromwell's most valued colleagues from 1647 until his death a decade later. See SP46/97, fo. 71–1ᵛ. Cf. Massarella, pp. 92–3.

196   *S & S*, 282; *A Full Relation of ... Corkbush Field*, p. 6.

197   *A Remonstrance from His Excellency Sir Thomas Fairfax and His Councell of Warre* (15 Nov. 1647), E414/14, unpag.

198   Wildman, *Putney Proiects*, p. 27.

199   *The Iustice of the Army Vindicated*, p. 6.

200   Rushworth, VII, 937.

201   *Clarendon State Papers*, ed. R. Scrope and T. Monkhouse (3 vols, Clarendon Printing House, Oxford, 1767–86), II, appendix, p. xlii. The story is corroborated by the eight officers of the regiment, although they did not mention Cromwell by name (*The Iustice of the Army Vindicated*, p. 6). These two quite separate sources seem to me sufficiently solid evidence. Cromwell's similar action towards Harrison's men was also referred to by Rockwell in 1653 (SP46/97, fo. 71). The fact that no newsbook at the time mentioned the incident does not vitiate the credibility of the other sources. The parliamentarian newswriters gave abbreviated accounts stressing the army's unity. Fairfax and Clarke also had their reasons for not dwelling on the violent conflict that occurred that day. Royalist newswriters such as Marchmont

Needham would not have ventured near Ware on 15 November. Cf. Kishlansky, 'What happened at Ware?', p. 839; *S & S*, pp. 283–4.

202 [Canne], *The Discoverer ... the Second Part*, p. 55; *LJ*, IX, 528. Woolrych is right to be baffled by Kishlansky's statement that 'there was no mutiny at Ware' (*S & S*, p. 285). Even if we disregard the activities of Lilburne's regiment before it arrived at Ware, there remains the stoning of Maj. Gregson on Corkbush Field. If breaking the head of a higher officer in the presence of one's commander-in-chief does not constitute mutiny, what does?

203 *Perf. Diurnall*, 15–22 Nov. 1647, E520/7, pp. 1788–90.

204 Ibid., p. 1789.

205 *A Full Relation of ... Corkbush Field*, p. 13.

206 *A New Declaration from Eight Regiments*, pp. 2–3, 5.

207 This figure counts the general's lifeguard as a regiment.

208 *A Remonstrance Sent from Colonell Lilburnes Regiment to His Excellency Sir Thomas Fairfax* ([29 Nov.] 1647), E417/15. Also printed in Rushworth, VII, 913–14, where the date is given as 23 November. Remarkably absent from the list of signatories was Col. Robert Lilburne himself. Did he perhaps refrain from putting his name to this condemnation of the Levellers out of regard for his brother John? The third brother, Lt-Col. Henry Lilburne, of course, had no such scruples, and may well have been the drafter of the Remonstrance.

209 *Perf. Occurrences*, 3–10 Dec. 1647, E520/12, p. 331.

210 Cf. Massarella, p. 88.

211 For Ingoldsby's regiment see *Clarke Papers*, I, 114n; for Scrope's *LJ*, IX, 528; for Twisleton's, *A Copy of a Letter from the Com. Gen. Regiment*.

212 *To the Supream Authority of England* (25 Nov. 1647), printed in Wolfe, pp. 237–41.

213 Underdown, 'Parliamentary diary of John Boys', pp. 152–3.

214 *A Letter from His Excellency Sir Thomas Fairfax to ... the City of London* (19 Nov. 1647), E416/18.

215 *Perf. Diurnall*, 15–22 Nov. 1647, E520/7, p. 1792; *Perf. Occurrences*, 19–26 Nov. 1647, E520/8, pp. 323–4; *Merc. Pragmaticus*, 23–30 Nov. 1647, E417/20, unpag.; *Kingdomes Wkly Intell.*, 16–22 Nov. 1647, E416/28, p. 740; CCJ 40, fo. 260; *A Letter from ... London to ... Fairfax* (25 Nov. 1647), E417/3; Rushworth, VII, 888.

216 The house also sat as a committee on 30 November and 2, 4 and 6 December wrestling with the monumental problem (*Perf. Diurnall*, 29 Nov.–6 Dec. 1647, E520/11, pp. 1828, 1830–1; *Kingdomes Wkly Intell.*, 30 Nov.–7 Dec., E419/3, p. 756).

217 The orders are printed in *A Letter from ... London ... to Fairfax*, pp. 9–11.

218 According to the *Perf. Wkly Account* (30 Nov.–8 Dec. 1647), E419/17, unpag. (4 Dec.), 3000 men had enlisted since the Newmarket Engagement. Army headquarters claimed that they numbered thirty or forty per company. For the twelve foot regiments of the New Model this would mean between 3600 and 4800 men (Rushworth, VII, 921).

219 Rushworth, vii, 921.
220 *LJ*, ix, 556–63.
221 Both MPs and army officers seemed unaware that most of the episcopal property had already been contracted for.
222 This legislation took the form of ten ordinances that were ratified by the Lords on 24 December 1647 (*A & O*, i, 1048–56; *LJ*, ix, 605–10).
223 SP28/50, fo. 16–vol. 54, fo. 793.
224 SP28/48, fo. 14.
225 Greaves and Zaller, iii, 136–7; Rushworth, vii, 913.
226 *Perf. Diurnall*, 29 Nov.–6 Dec. 1647, E520/11, p. 1832.
227 *Wonderfull Predictions ... by John Saltmarsh* ([29 Dec.] 1647), E421/16, p. 5; *Perf. Diurnall*, 20–7 Dec. 1647, E520/19, p. 1856; *S & S*, p. 296.
228 *Perf. Diurnall*, 13–20 Dec. 1647, E520/17, p. 1848; Massarella, p. 105.
229 Drapers' Company (London), Index of Apprentices, 1615–1750, unfol., 18 June 1628 (Ralph Cobbett); Guildhall Library, Merchant Taylors' Company, Apprenticeship Bindings (Microfilm 316), 11, p. 56 (Robert Cobbett); *Clarke Papers*, i, 407n.; PRO, Wills, PROB 11/274, fo. 329; GLCRO, Parish Register of Edmonton 1653–78, DRO 40/A1/2, unfol., 8 Jan. 1657; PRO, E121/2/3/40/3 (lieutenant in Essex's army), E121/4/9/95 (purchase of Pevensey manor).
230 *Perf. Occurrences*, 17–24 Dec. 1647, E520/18, p. 402.
231 *S & S*, pp. 300–4.
232 Rushworth, vii, 943.
233 *Perf. Diurnall*, 20–7 Dec. 1647, E520/19, p. 1855.
234 This was evidently his part of the bargain by which the officers campaigned for him to be made vice-admiral (*CJ*, v, 378; *LJ*, ix, 615).
235 Rushworth, vii, 943; *Clarendon State Papers*, ii, appendix, p. xliv.
236 *Kingdomes Wkly Intell.*, 21–8 Dec. 1647, E548/16, pp. 780, 782; Rushworth, vii, 943.
237 BL, Stowe MS 189, fo. 39ᵛ; *Heads of Chiefe Passages in Parliament* 16–23 Feb. 1648, E429/16, pp. 52, 55–6; *Kingdomes Wkly Post*, 22 Feb.–1 Mar. 1648, E430/6, p. 65; J[ohn] R[ushworth], *A True Relation of Disbanding the Supernumerary Forces in the Several Counties of this Kingdom and the Dominion of Wales, Amounting to Twenty Thousand Horse and Foot* (28 Feb. 1648), E429/10, p. 7. Payments to these disbanded troops are recorded in SP28/50, fos 81, 233, 266, 239, 250, 272, 274, 320 and 324, and vol. 51, fo. 171.
238 *Kingdomes Wkly Post*, 26 Jan.–2 Feb. 1648, E425/5, p. 36. The men actually received only £800, but by then it was too late to complain. (SP28/50, fo. 320–20ᵛ). Part of Constable's regiment also replaced Hopton's and Humphrey's forces in Hereford (Rushworth, *A True Relation of Disbanding*, pp. 4–5).
239 Clar. MS 29, fo. 134; *Merc. Elencticus*, 23 Feb.–1 Mar. 1648, E430/3, p. 106.
240 SP28/51, fos 134–6.

241 *Kingdomes Wkly Intell.*, 22–9 Feb. 1648, E429/11, pp. 853–4; Clar. MS 29, fo. 134–4ᵛ.

242 See SP28/50–1 for the two-month-pay warrants issued to these forces in February and March. The regiments of the Northern Army kept up were Col. Bright's, Mauleverer's and Charles Fairfax's foot and Maj.-Gen. Lambart's horse and Col. Robt. Lilburne's horse. See SP28/52, fos 217, 219, 288; Add. MS 21417 (Baynes correspondence), fos 127, 155. Rushworth gives an incomplete summary of the troops disbanded in *A True Relation of Disbanding.*

243 *Kingdomes Wkly Post*, 16–22 Feb. 1648, E429/16, p. 61; *Perf. Occurrences*, 18–25 Feb. 1648, E520/41, p. 421. After their uprising on 18 February the men of Plymouth garrison were hastily paid £4010 in two instalments, after which there was no further recorded incident. Indeed, mutiny seems to have been richly rewarded at Plymouth, as the garrison received a further payment of £7990 on 27 March. These men are the only supernumeraries known to have been paid their entire arrears in cash (SP28/50, fo. 315–15ᵛ; vol. 51, fo. 184–4ᵛ).

244 *LJ*, x, 66–71. Though not ratified by the Lords until 19 February 1648, the establishment was intended to take effect from 3 November 1647.

245 *CJ*, v, 459. There is no record of the Lords giving their approval to this change.

246 Worc. MS 110, unfol. (9 Feb. 1648); Rushworth, vii, 993–6.

247 Besides the five regiments from the Northern Army, these included Col. Francis Thornhaugh's horse in Nottinghamshire, Robert Duckenfield's in Cheshire, Robert Tichborne's in the Tower of London, Valentine Wauton's in East Anglia, and a number of companies belonging to Col. Robert Bennett in Cornwall, Col. Philip Jones in Swansea, Cols Thomas Mason and John Carter in Caernarvonshire, Lt-Col. George Twisleton in Denbigh Castle, Col. Edward Prichard in Cardiff, Col. Hugh Price in Red Castle, and Col. Thomas Bettesworth in Portsmouth. The evidence for the retention of these forces is found in the pay warrants (SP28/50, fos 70, 131, 144, 292; vol. 51, fos 20, 42, 46, 48, 50, 52, 355; vol. 52, fos 80, 219, 288).

248 SP28/52, fos 137–9.

249 Worc. MS 110, unfol. (28 Feb. 1648); *Kingdomes Wkly Post*, 22 Feb.–1 Mar. 1648, E430/6, p. 72. For evidence of Gittings' survival see PRO, E315/5/153.

250 SP28/52, fo. 135 – vol. 53, fo. 325.

251 SP28/53, fo. 349.

252 *Kingdomes Wkly Post*, 16–22 Feb. 1648, E428/13, p. 57.

Chapter 8 The Second Civil War

1 Gilbert Burnet (ed.), *The Memoires of the Lives and Actions of James and William Dukes of Hamilton and Castleherald ... 1625–1652* (R. Royston,

London, 1677), p. 324; J. S. A. Adamson, 'The English nobility and the projected settlement of 1647', *HJ*, 30 (1987), 600.

2 Firth conjectures that Berkeley's informant was Scoutmaster Leonard Watson, but I find it hard to believe that the army's chief of intelligence should have been acting in effect as a royalist double agent (Ludlow[e], I, 176n.).

3 'Major Huntington's reasons for laying down his commission', in Maseres, p. 404; John Berkeley, 'Memoirs', ibid., p. 385; Ludlow[e], I, 177; Abbott, I, 569.

4 Abbott, I, 564–5. Gardiner surprisingly accepts the so-called 'saddle letter' story (*GCW*, IV, 27). On 21 November, Ireton wrote to Col. Hammond that Cromwell was 'on scout, I know not where.' *Letters between Col. Robert Hammond ... and the Committee of Lords and Commons at Derby House, [et al.] relating to King Charles I* (Robert Horsfield, London, 1764), p. 22.

5 *Const. Docs*, pp. 335–41.

6 Burnet, *Memoires*, pp. 327, 329; *LJ*, IX, 567.

7 Ludlow[e], I, 178; *Const. Docs.*, pp. 347–52; Stevenson, p. 97.

8 *CJ*, V, 378, 403, 413; *LJ*, IX, 615–16.

9 CCJ 40, fo. 263; Clar. MS 30, fo. 211; *GCW*, IV, 35–6.

10 Montereul, II, 349; Sloane MS 1519, fo. 166.

11 *Reg. Hist.*, pp. 350–2.

12 *Perf. Occurrences*, 10–17 Dec. 1647, E520/16, p. 348; *CJ*, V, 391; Abbott, I, 574; Ludlow[e], I, 181; *LJ*, IX, 620.

13 Abbott, I, 575–6; *OPH*, XVI, 492–3; Clement Walker, *The Compleat History of Independency* (4 pts in 1 vol., R. Royston, London, 1661), pt i, 70–2. The 'quotation' is a paraphrase of Job 34:30.

14 *CJ*, V, 415.

15 Abbott, I, 576–7; *CJ*, V, 416; *CSPD, 1648–9*, p. 5ff.

16 *A Declaration from ... the Army* (12 Jan. 1648), E422/21, p. 7; *CJ*, V, 426.

17 *Perf. Occurrences*, 7–21 Jan. 1648, E520/27, pp. 401–2; *The Earnest and Passionate Petition* ([3 Feb.] 1648), E425/10, p. 5; Rushworth, VII, 965; *CJ*, V, 432–3; *LJ*, IX, 661–2; Walker, *Compleat History of Independency*, I, 72–3; Ian Gentles, 'The struggle for London during the Second Civil War', *HJ* 26 (1983), 287; *Kingdomes Wkly Post*, 19–26 Jan. 1648, E423/26, pp. 30–1; *Perf. Diurnall*, 24–31 Jan. 1648, E520/31, p. 1883. The story about the army being called in order to intimidate the Lords is dubious. I am grateful to John Adamson for discussion on this point. See his *The Nobility and the English Civil War* (Oxford University Press, Oxford, forthcoming).

18 Stevenson, p. 98.

19 Gentles, 'The struggle for London', p. 286.

20 Clar. MS 31, fo. 42.

21 Gentles, 'The struggle for London', pp. 287–9; SP28/54, fo. 350.

22 For John Morrill the Dorset petition of June 'provides the key to the second civil war.' Ignoring the army, the men of Dorset complained about taxes, committees and the loss of their liberties. Their first demand was that the king

should be restored so parliament would 'no longer be called master without a head.' 'The army's conflict with the county communities, otherwise known as the second civil war' is how David Underdown once interpreted these insurrections. See John Morrill, *The Revolt of the Provinces* (Allen and Unwin, London, 1976), pp. 126, 130; *PP*, p. 98. See also *Perf. Occurrences*, 7–14 Apr. 1648, E527/17, pp. 476–7; Alan Everitt, *The Community of Kent and the Great Rebellion 1640–60* (Leicester University Press, Leicester, 1966), pp. 252–5, 258; Anthony Fletcher, *A County Community in Peace and War: Sussex 1600–1660* (Longman, London, 1975), pp. 272–3, 276; Robert Ashton, *The English Civil War* (Weidenfeld and Nicolson, London, 1978), pp. 286–7, 321.

23   D. E. Underdown, *Revel, Riot and Rebellion* (Clarendon Press, Oxford, 1986), pp. 230–2, 260–1; Brian Lyndon, 'Essex and the king's cause in 1648', *HJ*, 29 (1986), 19; Hughes, pp. 220–1, 254.

24   Tanner MS 58, fo. 653; *CJ*, v, 410; *Perf. Wkly Account*, 28 Dec.–5 Jan. 1647–8, E421/33, unpag.; John Morrill (ed.), *Reactions to the English Civil War 1642–1649* (Macmillan, London, 1982), p. 114. The best modern account of the Canterbury Christmas Day riot is in Everitt, *Kent*, pp. 231–4.

25   For the draft of an anonymous protest against free quarter, dating from early 1648, see BL, Stowe MS 361, fo. 100.

26   This statement, and table 8.1, are based on an analysis of the warrants for army pay found in SP28/50–7.

27   Rushworth, vii, 1101; *CJ*, v, 551, 563; *LJ*, x, 244; Lyndon, 'Essex and the king's cause', p. 24.

28   Whitelocke, ii, 304; *CJ*, v, 553, and vi, 294; Cary, i, 399, 402; *PP*, p. 91.

29   Worc. MS 114, fo. 11ᵛ; *OPH*, xvii, 254; Rushworth, vii, 1112, 1119; *LJ*, x, 302.

30   *The Hamilton Papers*, ed. S. R. Gardiner, Camden Society, new ser., xxvii (1880), 182; *OPH*, xvii, 159–61; Worc. MS 114, fo. 26–67ᵛ; *CJ*, v, 569. Of Waller's assessment Underdown comments, 'it was easy to mistake localism for malignancy' (*PP*, p. 92). Yet Waller was one of Fairfax's most trusted and politically experienced senior officers. I think he knew what he was up against in Devon.

31   Hutchinson, p. 177, *CJ*, v, 585, 594, 614, 617; *CSPD, 1648–9*, 105–6, 108, 146, 148, 152; Whitelocke, ii, 330; *Clarke Papers*, ii, 28; Morrill, *Revolt of the Provinces*, p. 207; Rushworth, vii, 1175. For the student brawl in Cambridge see BL, Loan 29/176, fo. 24.

32   *Clarke Papers*, ii, 250.

33   Whitelocke, ii, 265; Worc. MS 110, unfol. (22 Feb. 1648); Tanner MS 58, fos 721, 724.

34   Morrill, *Revolt of the Provinces*, pp. 129–30.

35   Tanner MS 58, fos 733, 735.

36   SP28/50, fos 233–37ᵛ, 237, 266–67ᵛ. Those who carried through with their promise to disband received a further £790 15s. on 16 June (ibid., fo. 235–5ᵛ).

37 Whitelocke, II, 286–7; Rushworth, VII, 1036–7.
38 Whitelocke, II, 288–9; Worc. MS 114, fos 1, 8ᵛ; Morrill, *Revolt of the Provinces*, pp. 202–3.
39 Whitelocke, II, 298; Rushworth, VII, 1065.
40 Whitelocke, II, 306.
41 *CSPD, 1648–9*, p. 53; Rushworth, VII, 1098.
42 Abbott, I, 606.
43 Besides his own regiment Horton commanded half of Scrope's regiment under Maj. Barton, six troops of Okey's dragoons, and eight companies of Overton's foot (*Reg. Hist.*, pp. 85, 107, 295, 387). Once the van of the royalist foot had been overcome, those who were behind them – mostly green soldiers, half of them lacking weapons – began to shift for themselves. Many were slain, and 3000 taken prisoner. Horton had only one explanation for his stunning victory: 'with one heart [we] desire that the honour of this work may be wholly given to God' (Rushworth, VII, 1110; Whitelocke, II, 311; Ludlow[e], I, 192). Ludlowe estimated royalist strength at 7000; Horton put it at 8000. For his detailed accounts of the battle see Bell, II, 22–5; and *LJ*, X, 253–4.
44 Clar. MS 31, fo. 83; *Clarke Papers*, II, 6–7.
45 *Perf. Diurnall*, 31 Jan.–7 Feb. 1648, E520/34, pp. 1901, 1904; C. Walker, *History of Independency*, I, 83.
46 *A Declaration of the Commons of England* (11 Feb. 1648), E427/9; *GCW*, IV, 60–1.
47 Abbott, I, 583–4; Ludlow[e], I, 184–5. Clar. MS 29, fo. 134, may be a garbled account of the same meeting.
48 *Sir Philip Musgrave's Relation*, SHS, XLIV (1904), 303; *OPH*, XVII, 107; *CSPD, 1648–9*, p. 29; Abbott, I, 593–4; *Clarke Papers*, II, 23–4; Rushworth, VII, 1060; *Hamilton Papers*, p. 174.
49 CCJ 40, fo. 269; *The Humble Petition of the … City of London* ([27 Apr.]. 1648), E437/11, pp. 7–8; *The True Answer of the Parliament to the Petition of the Lord Major …* (27 Apr. 1648), E437/12; *LJ*, X, 234–5; *Hamilton Papers*, p. 191.
50 *Hamilton Papers*, pp. 178, 189.
51 *The Armies Petition* ([3 May] 1648), E438/1; *Windsor Projects* [15 May 1648], E442/10; *Perf. Wkly Account*, 26 Apr.–3 May 1648, E438/8, pp. 58–9; Massarella, p. 121.
52 I suspect that Goffe quoted extensively from the rest of Proverbs 1 in order to achieve his effect. Cf. *S & S*, p. 334 n. 35.
53 William Allen, *A Faithful Memorial of that Remarkable Meeting of Many Officers of the Army in England at Windsor Castle, in the Year 1648* ([27 Apr.] 1659), E979/3, pp. 2–5. Even though he put down his recollection of these events more than a decade later, and for a polemical purpose, I believe Allen's account is basically trustworthy. It was plainly one of the most vivid and meaningful experiences of his life, and he may well have jotted down some notes on it shortly after it occurred, (see *S & S*, pp. 332–5, for a some-

what more sceptical view). In his assessment of the Windsor prayer meeting, Underdown mistakes emotional intensity for 'scripture-laden hysteria'. Nor can I accept his conclusion that 'the army was out of hand; Cromwell and Ireton could no longer control it even if they wished' (*PP*, p. 96). Goffe was no hysteric. A man of sober piety, he never did anything of which Cromwell disapproved. The army was as united in the summer of 1648 as it had been in 1645.

54 *CSPD, 1648–9*, p. 53; Abbott, I, 599–601.
55 Tanner MS 57, fo. 27; D. E. Underdown, 'The parliamentary diary of John Boys, 1647–8', *BIHR*, XXXIX (1966), 164. Evelyn, *Diary*, III, 18; Ludlow[e], I, 188–9; Gentles, 'The struggle for London', pp. 289–90.
56 Tanner MS 57, fo. 27; *CJ*, v, 549, 574; SP 21/24, pp. 61, 75–8; Gentles, 'The struggle for London', p. 292.
57 Worc. MS 114, fo. 19; Cary, I, 421–2; Everitt, *Kent*, pp. 247–8; Matthew Carter, *A Most True and Exact Relation of That as Honourable as Unfortunate Expedition of Kent, Essex and Colchester* (London, 1650), pp. 76–7.
58 *Clarke Papers*, II, 15–18; *CJ*, v, 572; Everitt, *Kent*, p. 255.
59 *CSPD, 1648–9*, pp. 79–80.
60 SP21/24, pp. 75–8; Clar. MS 31, fo. 92; Whitelocke, II, 320; Gentles, 'The struggle for London', p. 292.
61 Everitt, *Kent*, pp. 252–3, 258–9; Carter, *A Most True and Exact Relation*, p. 81; *Clarke Papers*, II, 22; Rushworth, VII, 1133. Gardiner (*GCW*, IV, 137) follows Rushworth in numbering Fairfax's brigade at 8000 men. However, it comprised only four horse and three foot regiments, plus a few companies of Ingoldsby's. Moreover, Barkstead's regiment consisted of only six companies, two of which he left at Southwark. Three troops of horse were also left behind to guard the southern approach to London. (*Perf. Wkly Account*, 24–31 May 1648, E445/18, unpag.; SP21/24, pp. 75–8; *Clarke Papers*, II, 22.) If every troop and company was at full strength (eighty men), and if we allow an additional 100 for the train of artillery, the total force could not have exceeded 4180. As Everitt observes, some sources do indeed put Fairfax's force as low as 4000 (*Kent*, p. 261n.).
62 Cary, I, 437–8; Whitelocke, II, 322; Rushworth, VII, 1136; Everitt, *Kent*, p. 261.
63 For the battle of Maidstone see Carter, *A Most True and Exact Relation*, pp. 88–91; HMC, *De L'Isle and Dudley*, VI, 572; Rushworth, VII, 1137; *LJ*, x, 301, 304; *Perf. Occurrences*, 2–9 June 1648, E522/37, pp. 543, 546; R. Temple, 'Discovery of a manuscript eye-witness account of the battle of Maidstone', *Archaeologia Cantiana*, XCVII (1981), 210–11; Whitelocke, II, 323–4; Ludlow[e], I, 193–4; Everitt, *Kent*, 261–3.
64 *LJ*, x, 304; Whitelocke, II, 324.
65 *CSPD, 1648–9*, pp. 92–3; Rushworth, VII, 1138 (corrected pag.); *Perf. Occurrences*, 2–9 June 1648, E522/37, p. 543; Everitt, *Kent*, p. 265; *An Impartiall Narration of the Management of the Late Kentish Petition* ([21 July] 1648), E453/37, p. 3.

66　HMC, *Beaufort*, p. 21; Everitt, *Kent*, 265; Carter, *A True and Exact Relation*, p. 120.

67　Everitt, *Kent*, pp. 267–8; *LJ*, x, 320; Rushworth, vii, 1143 (corrected pag.).

68　Rushworth, vii, 1143–4 (corrected pag.), 1149–50; *CSPD, 1648–9*, pp. 105–6, 108–9, 111; Worc. MS 114, fo. 38ᵛ; *Hamilton Papers*, p. 211; Bell, ii, 8–9.

69　Lyndon, 'Essex and the king's cause', p. 35; Gentles, 'The struggle for London', pp. 293–9; *CSPD, 1648–9*, p. 185.

70　Cf. *CSPD, 1648–9*, pp. 105–6, 108–9, 111.

71　SP21/24, fos 182, 184; *CSPD, 1648–9*, pp. 167, 169; Whitelocke, ii, 351, 354–5; HMC, *De L'Isle and Dudley*, vi, 573; *Perf. Diurnall*, 3–10 July 1648, E525/4, p. 2079; Rushworth, vii, 1183.

72　Tanner MS 57, fo. 194; *Clarke Papers*, ii, 29–30; Worc. MS 114, fos 56, 67. I am indebted to John Adamson for a helpful discussion on this point.

73　HMC, *Beaufort*, p. 21; Lyndon, 'Essex and the king's cause', p. 26.

74　Lyndon, 'Essex and the king's cause', pp. 26–7; Matthew Carter, *A Most True and Exact Relation*, 119–20, 124; HMC, *Beaufort*, p. 22; *GCW*, iv, 149; *Clarke Papers*, ii, 26–7.

75　*GCW*, iv, 150–1; *CSPD, 1648–9*, pp. 120–1.

76　*GCW*, iv, 151.

77　HMC, *Beaufort*, pp. 23–5; *Hamilton Papers*, p. 215; Carter, *A True and Exact Relation*, pp. 131–3; Whitelocke, ii, 332; Rushworth, vii, 1155; *GCW*, iv, 151–3. Gardiner's generally clear account notes the royalist losses, but is silent about Fairfax's. He also refers to Barkstead's foot as 'the ever-victorious soldiers of the New Model', ignoring the high turnover of men in the infantry. It is doubtful if many of the foot who attacked Colchester had seen action three years before.

78　Carter, *A True and Exact Relation*, pp. 141, 146.

79　*Clarke Papers*, ii, 27; *OPH*, xvii, 152; Rushworth, vii, 1150, 1153; HMC, *Beaufort*, p. 22; Whitelocke, ii, 330; Brian Lyndon, 'The parliament's army in Essex, 1648', *Journal of the Society for Army Historical Research*, 59 (1981), 145; Whitelocke, ii, 339. When Needham was killed, the Tower regiment's six companies went to Lt-Col. William Shambroke. Upon the latter's death the command passed to Col. Thomas Rainborowe (SP28/54, fo. 168; Worc. MS 114, fo. 65). The numbers sent by Skippon are credible since they are given in a hostile royalist source (*Merc. Melancholicus*, 17–24 July 1648, E453/43, p. 127). Yet according to another royalist many of these volunteers were secret royalists who only awaited a pitched battle between besiegers and defenders to reveal their true colours. (Carter, *A True and Exact Relation*, p. 155).

80　Rushworth, vii, 1166–7, 1196–232; Whitelocke, ii, 365; Worc. MS 114, fo. 56ᵛ; Carter, *A True and Exact Relation*, p. 163.

81　Rushworth, vii, 1234; Carter, *A True and Exact Relation*, pp. 172, 181–3, 187; HMC, *Beaufort*, p. 30; HMC, *De L'Isle and Dudley*, vi, 575; Worc. MS 114, fo. 66.; Harl. MS 7001, fo. 189.

82   Rushworth, VII, 1242; Harl. MS 7001, fo. 189ᵛ; Whitelocke, II, 394 gives the
      fine as £14,000.
83   Harl. MS 7001, fo. 189ᵛ; Carter, *A True and Exact Relation*, pp. 203–4.
84   Abbott, I, 642–3; Sir James Turner, *Memoirs*, Bannatyne Club, 28 (1829), 70;
      Worc. MS 114, fo. 74ᵛ; *CJ*, v, 695; Bell, II, 56–7; John Wilson, *Fairfax* (John
      Murray, London, 1985), pp. 138–9.
85   *Clarke Papers*, II, 34–9; Ludlow[e], I, 95–6.
86   SP28/55, fo. 337.
87   Abbott, I, 606; *A Declaration of Lieut.-General Cromwell* (8 May 1648),
      E441/16, p. 3.
88   Whitelocke, II, 311; Abbott, I, 608, 611; *CJ*, v, 576; *CSPD, 1648–9*, p. 101.
      Before they could reach Coventry, Ewer's men were diverted to Colchester to
      assist Fairfax (Abbott, I, 612).
89   Abbott, I, 611, 613, 618–19; *CSPD, 1648–9*, p. 102; Rushworth, VII, 1146;
      Whitelocke, II, 334.
90   Abbott, I, 620–1.
91   Sir Philip Musgrave's Relation, pp. 304–5; *Clarke Papers*, II, 25–6.
92   Cary, I, 397, 407, 410–11, 419; Rushworth, VII, 1106, 1113, 1122, 1127;
      Clarke Papers, II, 9; *Moderate Intell.*, 11–18 May 1648, E443/21, p. 1327.
      Parliament initially ordered Fairfax to march to the north and tackle Langdale
      immediately, but by the end of May thought better of it (*LJ*, x, 250; *CJ*, v,
      554–5; Whitelocke, II, 318; *Sir Philip Musgrave's Relation*, p. 306. Rush-
      worth, VII, 1132, 1141 (corrected pag.) estimated royalist strength through-
      out the north at between 7000 and 8000, but this figure may be a product of
      alarmist exaggeration (*Clarke Papers*, II, 25–6).
93   Rushworth, VII, 1122, 1127, 1148, 1157, 1177; Whitelocke, II, 313, 334,
      337; *LJ*, x, 267; Sir Philip Musgrave's Relation, pp. 306, 308; *CSPD, 1648–9*,
      p. 130. Whitelocke, II, 339, reported Lambart's strength as 8000 at the end of
      June, but this figure is clearly too high.
94   The sources differ as to the exact numbers. Sir James Turner (*Memoirs*, p. 77)
      declared that the invading army never exceeded 14,000, but I take this figure
      to include Monro's 3300 from Ireland. Gilbert Burnet (*Memoires*, p. 356)
      also placed their numbers at 14,000. Rushworth (VII, 1188) estimated the
      Scots army at 9000, apparently not including Monro's Irish brigade. This esti-
      mate is corroborated in a letter from Lambart of 18 July in which he put
      Hamilton's and Langdale's combined forces at 12,000. On the other hand the
      author of *A Letter from Holland* ([12 Oct. 1648], E467/21, pp. 1–2) says
      Hamilton only brought 5500 with him, and that their numbers had reached
      7000 by 14 July. However, these figures, at variance with all the other
      sources, seem too low.
95   *Hamilton Papers*, pp. 233–4; Rushworth, VII, 1140–1 (corrected pag.); *Sir
      Philip Musgrave's Relation*, p. 292; Burnet, *Memoires*, pp. 354–5; Turner,
      Memoirs, p. 62; Stevenson, p. 113.
96   Turner, *Memoirs*, p. 78.
97   Burnet, *Memoires*, p. 358; Turner, *Memoirs*, p. 62.

98 Rushworth, vII, 1191, 1205, 1208, 1211, 1218.
99 *CSPD, 1648-9*, p. 210; Rushworth, vII, 1211; *GCW*, Iv, 178-80; Abbott, I,
    628, 634; *The Declaration of Lieut. Genll. Cromwell* ([18 Aug.] 1648),
    E459/24, pp. 1-2; *The Bloudy Battel at Preston* (22 Aug. 1648), E460/20,
    p. 3.
100 *GCW*, Iv, 180, 182.
101 Abbott, I, 638; Hodgson, p. 114; Rushworth, vII, 1211.
102 Abbott, I, 634; *Battles*, p. 166.
103 *Letter from Holland*, pp. 3-4; Abbott, I, 631; Burnet, *Memoires*, p. 358. On
    17 August, Cromwell and Lambart's army included five horse and five foot
    regiments, plus 'the remaining horse' and Ashton's Lancashire regiments –
    one horse and three foot. If these regiments were at full strength parliamen-
    tary strength at the battle of Preston was well over 11,000 (Abbott, I, 635,
    637).
104 *Battles*, p. 167.
105 Abbott, I, 635.
106 Hodgson, p. 116.
107 *Bloudy Battel at Preston*, pp. 4-5; Hodgson, pp. 116, 119; Abbott, I, 635-6;
    Burnet, *Memoires*, pp. 358-60; Turner, *Memoirs*, pp. 63-4; *Lanc. Tracts*,
    pp. 267-9 (Langdale's account); *Battles*, 168-71.
108 Burnet, *Memoires*, p. 360; Turner, *Memoirs*, pp. 63-4; Hodgson, p. 120;
    Letter from Holland, pp. 4-6.
109 Burnet, *Memoires*, pp. 360-1; Turner, *Memoirs*, pp. 64-5; Abbott, I, 636;
    Battles, pp. 172-3.
110 Hodgson, p. 122; Abbott, I, 637; Turner, *Memoirs*, pp. 66-7; Baillie, III, 457.
111 Abbott, I, 637.
112 Burnet, *Memoires*, pp. 362-3; *Letter from Holland*, pp. 8-10.
113 *AA*, p. 10; Sir William Dugdale, *A Short View of the Late Troubles in England*
    (Moses Pitt, London, 1681), p. 288; *Sir Philip Musgrave's Relation*, p. 309;
    Turner, *Memoirs*, p. 78.
114 *CSPD, 1648-9*, pp. 255-6; HMC, Braye, pp. 169-72; *Battles*, pp. 177-8;
    Stevenson, pp. 115-18.

Chapter 9   Revolution at Westminster, September 1648 to May 1649

1 Fairfax to Speaker Lenthall, 29 Nov. 1648, Worc. MS 114, fo. 115.
2 Ludlow[e], I, 203-4.
3 *To the Right Honourable the Commons of England ... The Humble Petition
   of Divers Wel Affected Persons ...* (1648), E464/5. Also printed in Wolfe,
   pp. 279-90. The Levellers were not all of one mind. John Lilburne, for
   example, opposed trying the king until the constitution of the commonwealth
   had been agreed upon and a new Representative of the People elected. See
   Legal Fundamental Liberties in Woodhouse, pp. 343, 354.
4 *Merc. Pragmaticus*, 12-19 Sept. 1648, E464/12, unpag.

5 Worc. MS 114, fo. 77^v.
6 *The Demands, Resolutions and Intentions of the Army* ([26 Sept.] 1648), E464/41.
7 *CSPD, 1648–9*, p. 290.
8 Worc. MS 114, fo. 80.
9 *Merc. Pragmaticus*, 26 Sept.–3 Oct. 1648, E465/19.
10 The regiments (with the Thomason numbers of their petitions) were Constable's (E467/34), Ireton's (E468/18), Fleetwood's (E468/32), Fleetwood's, Whalley's and Barkstead's (E470/32), Rainborowe's and Overton's (E473/1), Cromwell's and Harrison's (E474/5), Ingoldsby's (E526/25), the Northern Brigade (E472/6), and 'several regiments' in the west (E470/23). Marchamont Needham, who is not the most trustworthy source for army politics, reported that two of the radical letters to Fairfax 'had their frame from Ireton, and countenance from his father[-in-law] Cromwell, and that the prosecution of it among the soldiery is left to Sir Arthur Hesilrige, Harry Marten, Paul Hobson, and Major Cobbett' (*Merc. Pragmaticus*, 3–10 Oct. 1648, E466/11).
11 The twelve Leveller petitions were from Nottingham Castle (E475/24), the Northern Brigade (E475/4), Portsmouth and seven other south-coast garrisons (BL, 669.f.13/71), Bristol, Dover (E477/4), Mackworth's regiment and the garrisons of Shrewsbury and Ludlow (E527/1), Pride's regiment (E476/27), Lambart's brigade (E477/10), Boston garrison (E536/2), Col. Michael Livesey and the forces in Kent (E536/15) and Denbigh garrison (E536/30). The other petitions came from five northern garrisons (E473/23), Pride's and Deane's regiments (E474/5), Reynolds' regiment (Worc. MS 114, fos 119–20^v), Scrope's, Sanders's and Wauton's regiments, the Northumberland county troops (E475/13), the garrisons of Arundel, Rye and Chichester (E475/24), Hull garrison (E527/1) and Hurst Castle (E477/7).
12 *CJ*, vi, 43, 46.
13 See above table 8.1.
14 Rushworth, vii, 1297–8.
15 Ibid., p. 1309.
16 *CJ*, vi, 59, 76.
17 Rushworth, vii, 1320, 1324.
18 Worc. MS 16, fo. 1; Abbott, i, 324; J. S. A. Adamson, 'The English nobility and the projected settlement of 1647', *HJ*, 30 (1987), 572–4 n. 51; *True Informer*, 7 Oct.–8 Nov. 1648, E526/28, p. 8. A doctor of physic, Stane was the second son of a minor Essex gentleman (Essex RO, Wills D/DC q. E1; I owe this reference to Jeremy Ives).
19 *True Informer*, 7 Oct.–8 Nov. 1648, E526/28, p. 5. The editor of *Merc. Militaris* confused the judge advocate with Col. Edward Whalley, who if not a radical would soon emerge as one of the leaders of the revolution (10–17 Oct. 1648, E467/34, p. 6).
20 An anonymous pamphlet calling itself *The Declaration of the Armie* ([5 Oct.] 1648, E465/38) threatened on its title page that, if the royalist party in the City were not suppressed, the soldiers would 'put hundreds of them to the

sword, and hang their quarters upon the gates, and set their heads upon the spires of the steeples.' A friendlier letter from the army addressed its friends in the City, thanking them for their support and encouragement, and promising to return the compliment. See *His Majesties Gracious Message ... [and] A Letter from the Army, to the Citizens of London* (10 Oct. 1648), E467/6, pp. 5–6.

21 *The Declaration and Resolution of Many Thousand Citizens of London concerning the Army* ([12 Oct.] 1648), E467/18, p. 6.

22 *The Moderate*, 3–10 Oct. 1648, E467/1. Capt. Robert Hutton had joined Fairfax's army in the summer of 1647, having previously served under Robert Lilburne in Ferdinando Lord Fairfax's army (*Reg. Hist.*, p. 456; PRO, E121/5/7/52/481–2).

23 *The Declaration of the Armie ... to his Excellency the Lord Generall Fairfax* (9 Oct. 1648), E466/10.

24 'A joyfull message from the army to the citizens of London ...', in *The Independents Declaration and Remonstrance to the Parliament of England* ([18 Oct.] 1648), E468/13, p. 2.

25 *The Articles and Charge of the Officers and Souldiers in the Armie* (18 Oct. 1648), E468/23, p. 4.

26 We know of collaboration between agitators and officers in Fleetwood's and Ireton's regiment (E468/32, 18).

27 Cf. Thomason, E464/41; E465/38; E467/6; E468/13, 23, 28; E470/34.

28 *The Moderate*, 26 Sept.–3 Oct. 1648, E465/25.

29 *Fruitfull England Like to Become a Barren Wilderness through the Wickedness of the Inhabitants ...* ([17 Oct.] 1648), E467/36, pp. 7–8. See also the Devon petition in *Packets of Letters from Severall Parts of England ...* (10 Nov. 1648), E472/9, pp. 4–5.

30 *CJ*, VI, 66; *The Moderate*, 31 Oct.–7 Nov. 1648, E472/14, unpag.

31 *CJ*, VI, 54; *CSPD, 1648–9*, p. 307.

32 *CJ*, VI, 63, 67, 69. Cf. E472/9.

33 *Merc. Pragmaticus*, 24–31 Oct. 1648, E469/10.

34 *The Moderate*, 17–24 Oct. 1648, E468/24, p. 123.

35 *The True Copy of a Petition Promoted in the Army ... by the ... Regiment under the Command of Commissary General Ireton* (18 Oct. 1648), E468/18, p. 4.

36 Rushworth, VII, 1271.

37 Worc. MS 114, fo. 93; Rushworth, VII, 1314; Whitelocke, II, 426; Tanner MS 57, fo. 378–8ᵛ.

38 *CJ*, VI, 60.

39 *A Full and Exact Relation of the Horrid Murder Committed upon the Body of Col. Rainsborough* ([3 Nov.] 1648), E470/4; *The Moderate*, 31 Oct.–7 Nov. 1648, E472/4; *The Innocent Cleared: or the Vindication of Captaine John Smith* (13 Nov. 1648), E472/25; Clar. MS 34, fos 27ᵛ–8ᵛ; Nathan Drake, *A Journal of the First and Second Sieges of Pontefract Castle, 1644–5 ... with an Appendix of Evidence relating to the Third Siege*, Surtees Society, 37 (1861), 96–8.

40 Rushworth, VII, 1319.
41 *Merc. Militaris*, 14–21 Nov. 1648, E473/8, p. 37; *Merc. Melancholicus*, 14–21 Nov. 1648, E472/26; *Merc. Elencticus*, 15–22 Nov. 1648, E473/9, pp. 503–4.
42 *The Representations and Consultations of the Generall Councell of the Armie at St. Albans* ([14 Nov.] 1648), E472/3, p. 3. There is no attendance record for 10 November, but on the 7th there were only two colonels present (Whalley and Hewson) and four lieutenant-colonels (Axtell, Kelsey, Cooke and Goffe). See Worc. MS 16, fo. 1ᵛ; *A Declaration of the Armie* ([9 Nov.] 1648), E470/23, pp. 2–3.
43 *A Letter from the Head-quarters, at St Albanes* (10 Nov. 1648), E470/34.
44 *A Remonstrance from the Army to the Citizens of London* (15 Nov. 1648), E472/13, p. 3.
45 *Clarke Papers*, II, appendix D, pp. 270–81.
46 *CJ*, VI, 76–7; Whitelocke, II, 439; *Moderate Intell.*, 16–23 Nov. 1648, E473/15, p. 1742; Ian Gentles, 'The struggle for London during the Second Civil War', *HJ*, 26 (1983), 295–6, 300.
47 *PP*, p. 122. Underdown believes that the Commons' act of inviting the king to London was the only factor that transformed the Council of Officers. He neglects the fact that forty-eight members attended on 16 November, in comparison with twenty on the 7th. A rallying of the militants had obviously occurred between the two meetings.
48 John Lilburne, *The Legall Fundamentall Liberties of the People of England* (1649), E560/14, pp. 29–34. Like Barbara Taft I reject Lilburne's claim that the officers agreed not to alter the final version of the Agreement of the People drawn up by the committee of sixteen. See Taft, 'The Council of Officers' Agreement of the People, 1648/9', *HJ*, 28 (1985), 173. For Ireton's lengthy residence at Windsor see *A Complete Collection of State Trials and Proceedings for High Treason*, 4th edn, ed. Francis Hargrave, (11 vols, Bathurst, etc. London, 1776–81), II, 359.
49 *Merc. Militaris*, 14–21 Nov. 1648, E473/8, p. 40. For Cecil, who was at all times politically marginal in army affairs, see A. Collins, *Peerage of England*, ed. E. Brydges (9 vols, Rivington, London, 1812), II, 491. Unfortunately there is no record of his attendance at any meetings of the Council of Officers between November 1648 and February 1649 (*Clarke Papers*, II, 272–3). I am sceptical whether Rich in fact dissented from the Remonstrance. While he had opposed the Levellers over the franchise in 1647, he favoured liberty of conscience in 1648, was on good terms with Cromwell and Ireton, and showed Fifth Monarchist sympathies in 1649. As one of the more important of the higher officers, it seems unlikely that he would have stood out against the virtual unanimity of his colleagues. See *A Remonstrance of his Excellency, Thomas Lord Fairfax … and of the Generall Councell of Officers Held at St Albans the 16 of Nov., 1648*, E473/11, p. 71. Given what we know of Fairfax's honesty, I am more inclined to believe him than the editor of *Merc. Militaris* (*Clarke Papers*, I, 315, and II, 77–8; *Reg. Hist.*, p. 148).
50 Rushworth, VII, 1334.

51 *CJ*, vi, 81; *Merc. Elencticus*, 22–9 Nov. 1648, E473/39, p. 514.

52 *The Moderate*, 14–21 Nov. 1648, E473/1, p. 164; Whitelocke, ii, 457; *Merc. Pragmaticus*, 21–8 Nov. 1648, E473/35; *OPH*, xviii, 238–9.

53 The original printed version of the Remonstrance may be found in the Thomason Tracts, E473/11. In the discussion below, page references are to the version found in *OPH*, xviii, 161–238.

54 Charles of course had always maintained that his covenant was with God, not the people, and that they were therefore not competent to judge whether he had broken it.

55 For the development of the idea of the king's blood guilt during the 1640s see Patricia Crawford, ' "Charles Stuart, That Man of Blood" ', *Journal of British Studies*, xvi (1977), 41–61.

56 The Council of Officers would delete this requirement from the second Agreement of the People in December (Woodhouse, p. 357).

57 *Clarke Papers*, ii, 55.

58 Abbott, i, 677–8. The phrase 'an accursed thing' is a reference to the sin of Achan in Joshua 7. See Blair Worden, 'Oliver Cromwell and the sin of Achan', in Derek Beales and Geoffrey Best (eds), *History, Society and the Churches* (Cambridge University Press, Cambridge, 1985).

59 *Letters between Col. Robert Hammond and the Committee of Lords and Commons at Derby House [et al.] ... relating to King Charles I* (Robert Horsfield, London, 1764), pp. 87–8, 95–101.

60 Abbott, i, 696–9.

61 Tanner MS 57, fos 425, 428.

62 *LJ*, x, 614–15.

63 *A Most Horrid and Bloody Plot against the King's Majesty in the Isle of Wyght* (1648), E451/8; Tanner MS 57, fo. 450.

64 *CJ*, vi, 87, 88; *LJ*, x, 616; Worc. MS 114, fo. 110.

65 Lt-Col. Cobbett's brother John was the major of Skippon's foot regiment who was cashiered in 1647 and 1649 for his involvement with the Levellers (*Clarke Papers*, i, 407; *The Moderate*, 12–19 June 1649, E560/17, p. 564). In his will in 1656 John would refer to Ralph as his 'trusty and well-beloved brother' (PRO, Wills, PROB11/274, fo. 329). Merriman had been wounded in the suppression of the City's royalist insurrection the previous spring. See Add. MS 37344 (Whitelocke's Annals), fo. 144.

66 Sir Thomas Herbert, *Memoirs of the Two Last Years of the Reign of King Charles I* (G. & W. Nicol, London, 1813 edn), p. 117.

67 Worc. MS 114, fo. 115 (29 Nov. 1648).

68 Ludlow[e], i, 206.

69 *Merc. Pragmaticus*, 21–8 Nov. 1648, E473/35; Whitelocke, ii, 461.

70 Worc. MS. 114, fo. 104.

71 In addition to Ireton, they included Thomas Hammond, lieutenant-general of the ordnance, cavalry colonels Sir William Constable, Thomas Harrison, Edward Whalley and Matthew Tomlinson, and Col. Christopher Whichcote, governor of Windsor Castle (*Clarke Papers*, ii, 56).

The uncle of the erstwhile governor of the Isle of Wight, Hammond shared none of the anguish of his younger relative, and would be a signatory to the king's death warrant. See M. Noble, *The Lives of the English Regicides* (2 vols, J. Stockdale, London, 1798), I, 278; *DNB sub* Robert Hammond.

Constable was a baronet and the oldest officer in the New Model Army. An ancient gentleman of declining fortunes, he had fought the Irish under the Earl of Essex at the turn of the century, been imprisoned for his refusal to pay the forced loan in 1627, and attended the English church in Arnhem in 1640. Related by marriage to Lord Fairfax, he had given good military service in Yorkshire, and would also sign the king's death warrant. See *DNB*; J. T. Cliffe, *The Yorkshire Gentry from the Reformation to the Civil War* (Athlone Press, London, 1969), p. 351; Champlin Burrage, *The Early English Dissenters* (2 vols, Cambridge University Press, Cambridge, 1912), II, 291; Joseph Foster, *Pedigrees of the County Families of Yorkshire* (4 vols, W. Wilfred Head, London, 1874–5), II, unpag.; *Reg. Hist.*, p. 399.

Harrison had a lengthy record of religious piety and radicalism, and worked sedulously to bring about the execution of the king. See C. H. Firth, 'Memoir of Major-General Thomas Harrison', *Procs of the American Antiquarian Society*, new ser., VIII (1893), 391–2, 394–5, 398.

Whalley, though less flamboyant in his religiosity than Harrison, had been active in the army's political affairs since the spring of 1647. A university-educated gentleman of declining fortunes, he too would be a regicide. See *Reg. Hist.*, p. 214; G. Jaggar, 'The Fortunes of the Whalley Family of Screveton, Notts' (unpublished MPhil. thesis, University of Southampton, 1973), pp. 82–5.

Tomlinson was the second son of a lesser-gentry family in Yorkshire and a regicide (*DNB*; J. T. Cliffe, private communication).

Whichcote was the only non-New Model officer and non-regicide member of the committee. His political reliability and importance is implied, however, in the grant of £1500 voted him by the purged House of Commons in January 1649 (*CJ*, VI, 116).

72 Worc. MS 114, fo. 111; *Reg. Hist.*, p. 374.
73 For a second account of the 26 November prayer meeting, which places less emphasis on its religious character, see *Clarke Papers*, II, 58–9.
74 Ibid., II, 61.
75 Worc. MS 114, fo. 116ᵛ; *The Moderate*, 28 Nov.–5 Dec. 1648, E475/8, pp. 185, 187; Tanner MS 57, fo. 448.
76 Worc. MS 16, fo. 21.
77 Add. MS 37344, fo. 231; *His Majestie Going from the Isle of Wight* ([4 Dec.] 1648), E475/5, p. 5.
78 *The Declaration of his Excellency and the General Council of Officers* (30 Nov. 1648), in Rushworth, VII, 1341–3.
79 *CJ*, VI, 91; *The Moderate*, 28 Nov.–5 Dec. 1648, E475/8, p. 187; *Clarke Papers*, II, 65; *LJ*, X, 618. Less tactfully, an anonymous officer lectured the City that their hostility to the army was tantamount to defiance of God's will.

'O when will you see It's God [who] fights our battles for us and delivers enemies into our hands. Take heed how you are found fighters against God.' *A Warning, or a Word of Advice to the City of London* ... ([30 Nov.] 1648), E474/6, p. 5.

80 Worc. MS 114, fos 110, 112ᵛ, 115; *CJ*, vɪ, 91.

81 *LJ*, x, 611.

82 *Merc. Pragmaticus*, 5–12 Dec. 1648, E476/2.

83 *Kingdomes Wkly Intell.*, 28 Nov.–5 Dec. 1648, E475/14, p. 1176; *Perf. Wkly Account*, 29 Nov.–6 Dec. 1648, E475/20, p. 302 (corrected pag.); Whitelocke, ɪɪ, 466.

84 Their lodgings are noted in Harl. MS 4898 (Inventory of the effects of King Charles I), fos 9ᵛ, 12–12ᵛ, 14, 189, 193, 280 (I am indebted to Dr Ian Roy for this reference). See also J. S. A. Adamson, 'The Peerage in Politics 1645–49' (unpublished PhD thesis Cambridge University, 1986), pp. 17, 262.

85 *The Demands of His Excellency Thomas Lord Fairfax and the Generall Councell of the Army* ([5 Dec.] 1648), E475/10, pp. 4–6.

86 Rushworth, vɪɪ, 1345, 1348; Tanner MS 57, fo. 450; Capt. C. W. Firebrace, *Honest Harry, being a Biography of Sir Henry Firebrace, Knight (1619–1691)* (John Murray, London, 1932), pp. 165–81 (Col. Edward Cooke's narrative).

87 *CJ*, vɪ, 93.

88 *Merc. Pragmaticus*, 5–12 Dec. 1648, E476/2.

89 Ian Gentles, 'The sales of bishops' lands in the English Revolution, 1646–1660', *EHR*, 95 (1980), 589–90; *The Parliament under the Power of the Sword* ([11 Dec.] 1648), E476/1, pp. 6–7.

90 *CJ*, vɪ, 93; *Merc. Pragmaticus*, 5–12 Dec. 1648, E476/2; Evelyn, *Diary*, ɪɪ, 545. The Lords ratified their motion the same day (*LJ*, x, 624).

91 Rushworth, vɪɪ, 1353; *Perf. Occurrences*, 1–8 Dec. 1648, E526/38, p. 755; *CJ*, vɪ, 94. Cf. *Merc. Pragmaticus*, 5–12 Dec. 1648, E476/2.

92 Ludlow[e], ɪ, 209–10. I am sceptical of Underdown's assumption (*PP*, p. 140, esp. n. 89) that the meeting described by Lilburne in *Legall Fundamentall Liberties*, p. 34, is indeed the meeting that took place on 5 December. The context and phraseology of Lilburne's account suggest that he could well have been referring to a meeting that occurred after Pride's Purge.

93 Worc. MS 114, fo. 128; *CJ*, v, 666; *The Articles and Charge of the Armie against Fourscore and Odd of the Parliament Men Who Have Acted Contrary to the Trust Reposed in Them by the People* ... ([8 Dec.] 1648), E475/30.

94 Ludlow[e], ɪ, 209.

95 *Clarke Papers*, ɪ, 56. Col. Edward Whalley is another possible candidate. Thomas Pride, although he gave his name to the purge, was almost certainly not a member of the committee that planned it. Never a man of articulate opinions, he played no active role in the political deliberations of the army, was appointed to no important army committees, and held no important public office until his election to the 1656 parliament.

96 *PP*, pp. 141–2.

97   This account of the events of 6 December is based on *PP*, ch. 6, unless otherwise noted.
98   Hutchinson, p. 188.
99   Whitelocke, II, 472.
100 Adamson, 'The Peerage in Politics', pp. 260–1.
101 *CJ*, VI, 93–4; *The Humble Proposals and Desires of His Excellency Lord Fairfax and of the General Councel of Officers* ... (6 Dec. 1648), E475/25, pp. 4–8. Rushworth's version of this document is defective (VII, 1354–5).
102 Ludlow[e], I, 211–12.
103 Massarella, p. 149; Lilburne, *Legall Fundamentall Liberties*, p. 29; *Merc. Elencticus*, 14–21 Oct. 1648, E469/15, p. 400.
104 Whitelocke, II, 431.
105 Abbott, I, 676–8.
106 Lilburne, *Legall Fundamentall Liberties*, p. 29. The words are not explicitly attributed to Cromwell, but the linkage is apparent. Lilburne's account of these events must however be treated with caution.
107 *Severall Petitions Presented to his Excellency the Lord Fairfax* ... ([30 Nov.] 1648), E474/5, pp. 3–4.
108 Abbott, I, 690.
109 Ibid., pp. 698–9.
110 *Clarke Papers*, II, 63.
111 Abbott, I, 707; Worc. MS 114, fo. 124; *Moderate Intell.*, 30 Nov.–7 Dec. 1648, E475/26, p. 1776.
112 *Merc. Elencticus*, 5–12 Dec. 1648, E476/4, p. 528; *Kingdomes Wkly Intell.*, 5–12 Dec. 1648, E476/9, p. 1180.
113 For the view that Cromwell kept away from army headquarters because he could not make up his mind, and then played a moderating role in the month after the purge, see *GCW*, IV, 248–52; *PP*, pp. 119, 148–50; Worden, p. 67. For the view that Cromwell's position was not materially different from Ireton's see Abbott, I, 708; C. V. Wedgwood, *The Trial of Charles I* (World Books edn, London, 1968), pp. 25–7, 77–9.
114 *Merc. Militaris*, 31 Oct.–8 Nov. 1648, E470/13, p. 32. See also his implicit condemnation of Charles after the battle of Preston (Abbott, I, 638). For evidence that Cromwell 'hated the king as a man of blood' as early as the spring of 1647, see *A Cal to All the Souldiers* ([29 Oct.] 1647), E412/10, p. 6. For evidence suggesting that Cromwell approved of Pride's Purge in advance see Stevenson, p. 128.
115 *Packets of Letters* ([15 Nov.] 1648), E472/9, p. 4; *Perf. Diurnall*, 27 Nov.–4 Dec. 1648, E526/36, p. 2242.
116 *Perf. Diurnall*, 27 Nov.–4 Dec. 1648, E526/36, p. 2242.
117 *The Resolution of the Armie* ([28 Nov.] 1648), E473/36.
118 The last-minute character of the decision to purge parliament rather than dissolve it is confirmed by an internal army newsletter of 12 December (*Clarke Papers*, II, 67).

119 Whitelock, II, 477. Whitelocke seems to have been vaguely conscious of the symbolism of Cromwell's posture.

120 Abbott, I, 710; *Merc. Pragmaticus*, 12–19 Dec. 1648, E476/35.

121 The following June Lilburne maintained that the document produced by the sixteen commissioners was meant to be final and unalterable. (*Legall Fundamentall Liberties*, p. 35). If this was so he could have raised the point at the 24 December meeting, which he did not (*Clarke Papers* II, 78). Nor did he make the claim of unalterability in the pamphlet that he and fifteen other Levellers published on 28 December (*A Plea for Common-right and Freedom*, E536/22) criticizing the conduct of the Whitehall debates. The authoritative judgement on this point is made by Barbara Taft in 'The Council of Officers' Agreement of the People, 1648/9', *HJ*, 28 (1985), 169–85, esp. p. 173. For several aspects of my discussion of the Agreement of the People I am indebted to this article, and also to Barbara Taft, 'Voting lists of the Council of Officers, December 1648', *BIHR*, LII (1979), 138–54.

122 For the text of the Agreement see Rushworth, VII, 1358–61. It is interesting that the committee of sixteen turned down two of Lilburne and Overton's most radical schemes: annual popular election of JPs, sheriffs and other officials, and courts of justice in every hundred (*Foundations of Freedom*, in Wolfe, p. 303).

123 Worc. MS 16, fos 28ᵛ–9. The civilian Levellers were represented by John Lilburne and John Wildman. For the City there were two aldermen: Stephen Estwick and Sir John Wollaston. Army chaplains included Joshua Sprigge, Henry Denne, Hugh Peters, Mr Walford, Thomas Collier and Isaac Knight. Independent City clergy were represented by John Goodwin, Mr Seaman, William Nye, Dr Marty, Dr Parker and Dr French. In addition there was a Lt-Col. Wilton and five unidentified civilians: Mr Brooke, Mr Baker, Mr Gilbert, Mr Russell and Mr Hewett.

124 The debate is printed in *Clarke Papers*, II, 73–132. The page numbers in the following paragraphs refer to this source.

125 The Articles and Proposals appear in *The Articles and Charge of the Armie* ([8 Dec.] 1648), E475/30, pp. 3–4.

126 *The Resolution of the Army* ([13 Dec.] 1648), E476/16, pp. 1–3. The printer of this tract, Nehemiah Wilson, was not employed by the army for any of its official publications. See Paul G. Morrison, *Index of Printers, Publishers and Booksellers in Donald Wing's Short-Title Catalogue ... 1641–1700* (University of Virginia Press, Charlottesville, 1955), p. 213. Clearly then, the tract represents the view of a faction, not the army high command.

127 It is clear that Ireton, who adjourned the debate, was in the chair by the end of the day (*Clarke Papers*, II, 131). After p. 107 the speakers stop referring to the chairman as 'your lordship' and 'your excellency', and either call him 'sir' (p. 108) or address him by no title at all.

128 Lilburne, *Legall Fundamentall Liberties*, p. 35.

129 The names of the original committee members have not been preserved. Nevertheless the influence of Ireton can be detected in the names of those

who were later added to the committee: two moderates, Maj. John Carter and Capt. Richard Hodden on 16 December, and conservatives Hewson, Barton and Okey on the 18th. The radicals seem to have fought back on the 19th, however, when they secured the addition of radicals Maj. William Coleman and Capt. John Spencer (*Clarke Papers*, II, 135–6).

130 Printed in Wolfe, pp. 348–9.

131 Rushworth, VII, 1360.

132 *Clarke Papers*, II, 270–81; Taft, 'Voting lists of the Council of Officers', pp. 146–7.

133 *A Declaration to the City and Kingdome ... Likewise a New Covenant and Agreement from the Army, to be Tendered to All Free-born English-men ...* ([18 Dec.] 1648), E476/33, p. 6.

134 *Clarke Papers*, II, 271–81; Taft, 'Voting lists of the Council of Officers', p. 147.

135 John Evelyn, D & C, III, 34–5.

136 Wolfe, p. 348.

137 The fifth reserve would have abolished all privileges and exemptions from the laws (Wolfe, p. 300; Rushworth, VII, 1360).

138 Rushworth, VII, 1360.

139 Taft, 'Voting lists of the Council of Officers', p. 147. Col. Pride put in one of his rare appearances at the 18 December meeting, but, symptomatic of his political unimportance in the army, he abstained on this crucial vote.

140 Taft, 'Voting lists of the Council of Officers', p. 148. With Col. Richard Deane abstaining, the only colonel to vote with the majority was Nathaniel Rich. Although it must have been a galling defeat for Ireton, he respected the wishes of the majority in his revised version of the article when it was submitted to the House of Commons on 20 January. Things 'spiritual or evangelical' were explicitly excluded from the Representative's sovereign power (Wolfe, p. 347).

141 Taft, 'Voting lists of the Council of Officers', p. 149. In the officers' Agreement of 20 January this reserve appears as no. 5 (Wolfe, p. 348).

142 *Clarke Papers*, II, 155–6; Wolfe, pp. 301, 346.

143 *Clarke Papers*, II, 156; Wolfe, pp. 301, 349.

144 The conservatives were Ireton, Waller, Barton and Capt. Deane; the radicals, Col. Deane, Lt-Col. Edward Salmon, Capt. John Clarke and Capt. Richard Hodden; the moderates Cols Harrison and Rich (*Clarke papers*, II, 156). By 1653, of course, Harrison and Rich had become radicals, while Clarke no longer was one.

145 Wolfe, pp. 349–50.

146 *Clarke Papers*, II, 170–1.

147 Not the least ironical aspect of this situation was that, as Murray Tolmie points out, by early 1649 the Levellers had lost the support of most of the sects and the godly, well-affected people of the nation. See his *Triumph of the Saints* (Cambridge University Press, Cambridge, 1977) pp. 180–3. In fairness, it must be remembered that the Levellers were only a minority on the com-

mittee of sixteen, and therefore the second Agreement cannot be regarded as a strictly Leveller document. This did not, however, prevent Lilburne from endorsing it.

148 See for example John Vernon, *The Sword's Abuse Asserted* (1648), E477/3, p. 17; *AA*, pp. 22, 24, 41–2.

149 *The Moderate*, 14–21 Nov. 1648, E473/1, p. 154. See also *A Warning, or a Word of Advice to the City of London* ([30 Nov.] 1648), E474/6, p. 3, for an admission that 'the major party ... are not to have any vote.'

150 Gentles, 'The struggle for London', pp. 302–3. It was remarked at the time that so many soldiers were elected common–councillors 'that they may almost serve for a Council of War' (*Moderate Intell.*, 21–8 Dec. 1648, E536/18, p. 197). One of their first acts was to pass a resolution calling for justice 'against all grand and capital actors in the late war against the parliament' (Rushworth, VII, 1391).

151 *CJ*, VI, 122.

152 Taft, 'The Council of Officers' Agreement of the People, 1648/9', pp. 179–85.

153 Whitelocke, II, 467.

154 *A True and Ful Relation of the Officers and Armies Forcible Seising of Divers Eminent Members of the Commons House, ...* ([13 Dec.] 1648), E476/14, pp. 4–6; *The Parliament under the Power of the Sword*, p. 3.

155 *Merc. Pragmaticus*, 5–12 Dec. 1648, E476/2.

156 *CJ*, VI, 94.

157 The phrase is Whitelocke's (II, 480).

158 *CJ*, VI, 96–7.

159 Evelyn, *D & C*, III, 33.

160 *Merc. Pragmaticus*, 12–19 Dec. 1648, E476/35; ibid., 19–26 Dec., E477/30.

161 *CJ*, VI, 101.

162 *The Second Part of the Narrative concerning the Armies Force and Violence upon the Commons ...* ([23 Dec.] 1648), E477/19, p. 8; *Merc. Pragmaticus*, 19–26 Dec. 1648, E 477/30; Clar. MS 34, fo. 12.

163 Whitelocke, II, 477, 479.

164 Rushworth, VII, 1363; *Merc. Pragmaticus*, 12–19 Dec. 1648, E476/35; *Kingdomes Wkly Intell.*, 12–19 Dec. 1648, E476/39, p. 1192.

165 Adamson, 'The Peerage in Politics', pp. 260–1.

166 Worc. MS 114, fo. 129; *CJ*, VI, 100–1. The meeting of the four peers with Fairfax took place about 10 December. The king's real gaoler at Windsor was of course the governor of the castle, Col. Christopher Whichcote.

167 According to royalist reports of the encounter the lords appeared more respectful of the officers than the officers of the lords (Clar. MS 34, fo. 12). In *Merc. Pragmaticus*, 19–26 Dec. 1648, E477/30, Marchamont Needham embroidered John Lawrans' story with anecdotes about Pembroke removing his hat, knocking off his wig in the process, and Denbigh holding Fairfax's stirrup while he mounted his horse.

168 Adamson, 'The Peerage in Politics', p. 263.

169 *The Joynt Resolvtion, and Declaration of the Parliament and Counsell of the Army* ... ([11 Jan.] 1649), E538/1*, pp. 1–2; Adamson, 'The Peerage in Politics', pp. 265–6.

170 *Merc. Pragmaticus*, 5–12 Dec. 1648, E476/2.

171 *Merc. Pragmaticus*, 19–26 Dec. 1648, E477/30; Clar. MS 30, fo. 13; *Merc. Melancholicus*, 25 Dec.–1 Jan 1648/9, E536/27, p. 7; Gilbert Burnet, *History of My Own Time*, ed. Osmund Airy (2 vols, Clarendon Press, Oxford, 1897), I, 79.

172 *Clarke Papers*, II, 132. Since the terms of reference of this committe were purely administrative, and its membership all at or below the rank of colonel, there is no significance to the fact that Cromwell and Ireton were not appointed to it. They had more important things to do at the time. Cf. *PP*, p. 165.

173 *PP*, pp. 144–5; Worc. MS 16, fo. 61; Abbott, I, 713–15; *Clarke Papers*, II, 146n.

174 Gentles, 'The struggle for London', pp. 301–2; *The Moderate*, 5–12 Dec. 1648, E476/5, p. 199.

175 Abbott, I, 732–3.

176 Burnet, *History*, I, 79.

177 In his two-to-three-hour fast-day address at St Margaret's, Westminster, on 22 December he called for the rooting-out of monarchy both in England and throughout Christendom. The army leaders he likened to Moses leading the Israelites out of Egypt. The citizens of London he compared to the Jerusalem crowd crying for the release of Barabbas (Charles I) and the crucifixion of Christ (the soldiers). See *Merc. Pragmaticus*, 19–26 Dec. 1648, E477/30; *State Trials*, II, 362.

178 *The Declaration and Proposals of the Citizens of London* ([12 Dec.] 1648), E476/6, p. 4; *Perf. Occurrences*, 8–15 Dec. 1648, E526/40, p. 745; *The Unparalleld Arrest: or Maior Generall Browne ... Taken Prisoner ...* (1648), Worc., AA.8.3/104.

179 *The Joynt Resolvtion, and Declaration of the Parliament and Counsell of the Army*, pp. 2–5.

180 Gentles, 'The struggle for London', pp. 302–3.

181 *The Second Part of the Narrative*, p. 8; *Merc. Pragmaticus*, 19–26 Dec. 1648, E477/30; Clar. MS 34, fo. 12ᵛ; *CJ*, VI, 101.

182 *Heads of the Charge against the King ... by the Generall Councell of the Armie ...* ([24 Dec.] 1648), E477/25, pp. 4–6.

183 *CJ*, VI, 102–3. There is no need to interpret Cromwell's absence from this committee as an indication of his indecision about the wisdom of trying the king. His words and actions of the previous fortnight demonstrated that he was unequivocally committed to this course of action. I suspect that at this juncture Cromwell found that he was needed for more sensitive political work, and could not afford to spend his time debating the legal ins-and-outs of the king's trial.

184 *Clarke Papers*, I, 417 (11 Nov. 1647).

185 Herbert, *Memoirs*, pp. 134–6.
186 Ibid., pp. 141–2; *His Majesties Declaration ... Also the Declaration and Proposals of Colonel Harrison ...* (1 Jan. 1649), E536/25, p. 6.
187 Tanner MS 57, fo. 474.
188 Whitelocke, ii, 480.
189 *Clarke Papers*, ii, 150–4, 163–9. I assume that Poole did not simply barge into the Council of Officers, but that she was sponsored by one or more of its members who sought to deflect the majority from their determination to kill the king.
190 Clar. MS 34, fo. 72. This version of Cromwell's words is slightly different from that given in Abbott, i, 719.
191 Rushworth, vii, 1376.
192 *CJ*, vi, 107, 110–11; *LJ*, x, 641–2.
193 Massarella, pp. 192–3. This figure excludes officers who had served or would do so in the future – for example, Cols Robert Tichborne, Edmund Ludlowe, Robert Duckenfield and John Hutchinson.
194 Rushworth, vii, 1386.
195 Massarella, pp. 193–4; Wedgwood, *Trial of Charles I*, p. 99.
196 For a fuller treatment of the trial see the matchless account in Wedgwood's *Trial of Charles I*.
197 Rushworth, vii, 1390.
198 Evelyn, *Diary*, ii, 547; *State Trials*, ii, 364.
199 *The Moderate*, 9–16 Jan 1649, E538/5, p. 257.
200 *A Serious and Faithfull Representation of the Judgements of Ministers ... within the Province of London ... to the Generall and his Councell of Warre* (18 Jan. 1649), E538/25. For another denunciation of regicide see the anonymous *A Vindication of the Army* ([22 Jan.] 1649), E538/29.
201 *Right and Might Well Met* ([2 Jan.] 1649), E536/28, pp. 6–7, 20, 35, 43–4.
202 See above, pp. 297–8, 300; Abbott, i, 732–3; Burnet, i, 63.
203 Rushworth, vii, 1391.
204 See the petition from the south-coast garrisons to army and parliament (Rushworth, vii, 1388–9; *CJ*, vi, 120). See also Thomas Margetts' letter expressing puzzlement on behalf of the northern officers at the release of most of the imprisoned MPs. (Worc. MS 114, fo. 163).
205 Clar. MS 34, fo. 73ᵛ; *CJ*, vi, 132, 168.
206 *PP*, pp. 194–5.
207 *A New-years Gift* ([1 Jan.] 1649), E536/24; *A Declaration of the Lords and Commons ... [and the] Resolution of the Army ...* ([3 Jan.] 1649), E536/36.
208 *CJ*, vi, 102; *LJ*, x, 637; Wedgwood, *Trial of Charles I*, p. 74 n.28; Tolmie, *Triumph of the Saints*, pp. 180–1; Pauline Gregg, *Freeborn John* (Harrap, London, 1961), pp. 258–61.
209 *State Trials*, ii, 317, 359.
210 This incident was recounted rather melodramatically by Sir Purbeck Temple at Henry Marten's trial in 1660, but Marten did not deny the testimony (*State Trials*, ii, 392).

211 Evelyn, *Diary*, II, 547.
212 *The Kingdomes Faithfull and Impartiall Scout*, 26 Jan.–2 Feb. 1649, E541/5, p. 3; Clar. MS 34, fos 86, 88.
213 Clarendon, *History*, IV, 486; Rushworth, VII, 1395.
214 At his own trial in 1660 Axtell admitted ordering the soldiers to silence Lady Fairfax, but denied commanding them to shoot (*State Trials*, II, 371, 378).
215 Rushworth, VII, 1396–8.
216 *The King's Tryal ... on Saturday, January 20. 1648*, E538/26, p. 4.
217 *State Trials*, II, 371.
218 *The Moderate*, 16–23 Jan. 1649, E539/7, p. 271.
219 Wedgwood, *Trial of Charles I*, p. 145.
220 Clar. MS 34, fo. 88.
221 Worc. MS 66, fos 6, 13ᵛ, 26ᵛ.
222 *State Trials*, I, 1027, 1034; Rushworth, VII, 1411.
223 Wedgwood, *Trial of Charles I*, p. 155.
224 *State Trials*, II, 397–8.
225 Thus, while only fifty-nine signed the death warrant, the correct total for the number of regicides, including those who stood up, but did not sign, as well as those who signed but were not present when the sentence was pronounced, is sixty-nine. See A. W. McIntosh, 'The numbers of the English regicides', *History*, 67 (1982), p. 197.
226 *State Trials*, I, 1041.
227 Rushworth, VII, 1425.
228 *State Trials*, I, 1037.
229 Isaiah 14:19–20; John Winthrop, *Papers 1598–1649*, Massachusetts HS (5 vols, 1929–47), V, 348; Wedgwood, *Trial of Charles I*, p. 166.
230 *Moderate Intell.*, 25 Jan.–1 Feb. 1649, E541/4, p. 1869; *The Kingdomes Faithfull and Impartiall Scout*, 26 Jan.–2 Feb. 1649, E541/5, p. 3; François Guizot, *History of the English Revolution of 1640* (Bohn, London, 1856), appendix, pp. 460–1.
231 *GCW*, IV, 308–11.
232 *State Trials*, II, 392, 400.
233 Herbert, *Memoirs*, p. 190.
234 *DNB*, *sub* Richard Ingoldsby.
235 For a full list of the signers of the death warrant see *GCW*, IV, 309.
236 *State Trials*, II, 386, 389–90.
237 At his trial in 1660 Axtell denied Huncks' story, but a little later confessed, 'my memory is not very good' (*State Trials*, II, 370, 383–4).
238 *CJ*, VI, 125.
239 The evidence about Rich is ambiguous. In November he was said to have opposed the army Remonstrance, with its demand for justice upon the king. He was not named to the High Court of Justice, yet at the Restoration he was alleged to have been a close confidant of Cromwell, Ireton and Peters during the weeks leading up to the execution. However, the evidence for this last allegation is shaky (*State Trials*, II, 359; Guizot, *History*, p. 461).

240 Herbert, *Memoirs*, p. 194.
241 *Moderate Intell.*, 25 Jan.–1 Feb. 1649, E541/4, p. 1872; *King Charls his Speech Made upon the Scaffold* (30 Jan. 1649), p. 9. In the Worcester College copy of this pamphlet (AA.2.4/11), pp. 9, 12, the two incidents to do with the axe have been asterisked in ink, and a contemporary hand has written 'W. C.' in the margin. I am very grateful to the Worcester College librarian, Lesley Le Claire, for drawing this evidence for William Clarke's presence on the scaffold to my attention.
242 *State Trials*, I, 1044; *Diaries and Letters of Philip Henry, 1631–96*, ed. Matthew Henry Lee (Paul, London, 1882), p. 12.
243 *CJ*, VI, 125.
244 *State Trials*, II, 364, 395.
245 Whitelocke, II, 516.
246 'A journal of the proceedings of the High Court of Justice', in *CSPD, 1648–9*, pp. 351–2.
247 McIntosh, 'The numbers of the English regicides', p. 197.
248 *State Trials*, II, 374, 383–4.
249 Herbert, *Memoirs*, pp. 194–5.
250 *CJ*, VI, 129, 132–3.
251 *CSPD, 1648–9*, p. 340; *CJ*, VI, 133.
252 *CJ*, VI, 140–1.
253 *C & P*, I, 4.
254 Ibid., p. 6.
255 *C & P*, I, 6–7; Worden, pp. 180–1.

Chapter 10   The Army and the Levellers, February–September 1649

1 The army pay warrants issued after 2 December 1648 for regiments in or near the capital point to an increase of about 15 per cent over their previous strength (SP28/57, 58, fos 106, 136, 168, 278, 304, *et passim*). A number of the newly enlisted men drew pay without performing military duties (*Perf. Wkly Account.* 10–17 Jan. 1649, E538/20, pp. 345–6). For the comparable radicalism of the men who had flooded into the army after its invasion of London in August 1647 see *S & S*, p. 206.
2 *CJ*, VI, 129; *Armies Modest Intell.*, 1–8 Feb. 1649, E541/28, p. 9.
3 Worc. MS 69, unfol. (12 Feb. 1649).
4 Untitled MS ([4 Jan] 1649), E537/8.
5 *Moderate Intell.*, 8–15 Mar. 1649, E546/24, p. 1935.
6 This anodyne document proposed (1) that all people who had handled public money during the interregnum should be brought speedily to account; (2) that soldiers should have debentures for their arrears; (3) that these arrears should be secured on the dean and chapter lands; (4) that soldiers should be compensated for lost horses; and (5) that free quarter should be abolished. When Col. Whalley presented it to the Commons on behalf of the officers the

following week he was warmly thanked for 'these your discreet and serious representations.' See *The Petition of the General Councel of Officers* ... (3 Mar. 1649), E545/30, pp. 6–10; *Perf. Diurnall*, 26 Feb.–5 Mar. 1649, E527/29, p. 1346; *CJ*, VI, 153.

7 *Clarke Papers*, II, 200n; *The Justice of the Army against Evill-Doers Vindicated* ([5 June] 1649), E558/14, pp. 7–9; For a more sympathetic account of Thompson see Barry Denton, *William Thompson: Leveller, revolutionary or mutineer?* (Partizan Press, Leigh-on-Sea, Essex, 1988).

8 Greaves and Zaller, I, 262; *Reg. Hist.*, p. 9.

9 *Clarke Papers*, II, 190–2; *The Humble Petition of the Officers and Soldiers of his Excellency's Regiment of Horse* ([22 Feb.] 1649), E545/17, pp. 21–2; John Lilburne, *The Legall Fundamentall Liberties of the People of England* (1649), in Wolfe, p. 74; *The Hunting of the Foxes from New-Market and Triploe Heaths to Whitehall by Five Small Beagles, Late of the Armie*, in Wolfe, p. 368. It may well be true that Col. Whalley favoured hounding civilian disturbers of the army, but his attendance was not recorded at the 22 February meeting (*Clarke Papers*, II, 281). While William Thompson called himself a captain in 1649, his New Model rank had never been higher than corporal.

10 Lilburne was being inconsistent and unfair. The first Agreement (November 1647) had prescribed that parliament should sit for just under six months 'and no longer' (Woodhouse, p. 444). The Levellers had said nothing about how the country was to be governed during the eighteen months between parliaments. I am grateful to Prof. Woolrych for this point.

11 Haller and Davies, pp. 157–68.

12 *[To the] Svpreme Entrvsted Avthority of this Nation ... the Humble Petition of Divers of the Well-Affected Officers and Souldiers of the Army* ... (1649), Worc., BB.8.7/189, also printed in OPH, XIX, 50–1.

13 Printed in *The Hunting of the Foxes*, in Wolfe, pp. 373–4.

14 *Perf. Diurnall*, 26 Feb.–5 Mar. 1649, E527/29, p. 1345. The five troopers were Robert Ward, Thomas Watson, William Sawyer, Simon Graunt and George Jellis. The three signatories who were not court martialled were Richard Rumball, John Benger and Thomas Harbye (*Clarke Papers*, II, 193–4n.).

15 *Perf. Diurnall*, 26 Feb.–5 Mar. 1649, E527/29, p. 1347; *Perf. Occurrences*, 2–9 Mar. 1649, E527/31, p. 886.

16 *Certain Occurrences of Parliament*, 2–9 Mar. 1649, E527/32, p. 43; *Kingdomes Wkly Intell.*, 6–13 Mar. 1649, E546/19, pp. 1282–3; H. N. Brailsford, *The Levellers, and the English Revolution* (Cresset Press, London, 1961), p. 475.

17 Marie Gimelfarb-Brack, *Liberté, Egalité, Fraternité, Justice! La vie et l'oeuvre de Richard Overton* (P. Lang, Berne, 1979), pp. 379–80.

18 They ignored the fact that the General Council had at no time exercised sovereign power. The Council of War continued to control discipline, while the commander-in-chief's authority over promotions and other military affairs was never challenged.

19   Wolfe, pp. 360, 370, 380–1.
20   For a sympathetic account see George Orwell, *Homage to Catalonia* (Secker and Warburg edn, London, 1951), pp. 26–8, 57.
21   Francis White, *The Copies of Severall Letters Contrary to the Opinion of the Present Powers* ([20 Mar.] 1649), E548/6.
22   *Merc. Pragmaticus* reported that on 4 March in the House of Commons Cromwell drew his dagger, laid it on the seat beside him and 'expressed great anger against Harry [Marten] and his levelling crew' (27 Feb.–5 Mar. 1649, E546/4, unpag.). The report should perhaps be taken with more than a grain of salt. For Marten's financial rewards from the Rump, see Worden, p. 198.
23   Worden, pp. 198–9.
24   William Bray, *An Appeal in the Humble Claim of Justice against Thomas Lord Fairfax* ([19 Mar.] 1649), E546/30; *CJ*, vi, 167; *The Moderate*, 13–20 Mar. 1649, E548/2, pp. 371–2; Whitelocke, ii, 557. An anonymous commentator within the army wrote cynically of Bray, 'make him the parson of a church and you stop his mouth' (Worc. MS 114, fo. 172).
25   William Bray, *A Second Appeale* ([2 Apr.] 1649), E549/6; John Naylier et al., *The Foxes Craft Discovered* ([2 Apr.] 1649), E549/7.
26   John Jubbs, *An Apology unto ... the Lord Generals Army* (May 1649), E552/28, pp. 1, 2, 4–7, 16, 17ff.
27   Printed in Haller and Davies, pp. 171–89.
28   In fact two suspects in the Rainborowe murder case had already been arrested exactly a week before this allegation was published (Whitelocke, iii, 9).
29   Haller and Davies, pp. 174, 181–2, 184, 186–9.
30   *Merc. Pragmaticus*, 27 Mar.–3 Apr. 1649, E549/13; *CJ*, vi, 174; *OPH*, xix, 92–4.
31   The story of the arrest and questioning of the Leveller leaders is vividly told by John Lilburne in *The Picture of the Councel of State*, printed in Haller and Davies, pp. 191–246. The quotations below are taken from this source. See also William Walwyn, *The Fountain of Slaunder Discovered*, in McMichael and Taft, pp. 362–6.
32   Worden, p. 190.
33   PRO, C54/3636/4; University of Durham, Department of Paleography and Diplomatics, Wills, T295 (1661); D. H. Pennington and K. Thomas, *Puritans and Revolutionaries* (Clarendon Press, Oxford, 1978), p. 254.
34   *The English Souldiers Standard* ([5 Apr.] 1649), E550/1, p. 7. I cannot accept Brailsford's ascription of this pamphlet to Walwyn. The most fastidious and pacific of the Levellers never wrote so pugnaciously. By his own admission, moreover, he had been uninvolved in party activities for almost a year. The literary style points to Overton. Walwyn's hand is much more clearly evident in *A Manifestation*, issued from the Tower on 14 April. Devoid of Overton's bitterness and irony, and lacking Lilburne's egoism and tortuous style, this pamphlet is written in a clear, conciliatory tone. The central statement is 'Peace and freedom is our design; by war we were never gainers nor ever wish

to be' (McMichael and Taft, p. 343). I note that Barbara Taft has arrived at similar conclusions (ibid., pp. 38–9, 532).

35 *The English Souldiers Standard*, pp. 9–10. Without denying the breadth of vision expressed by the author of this pamphlet it should be noted that he was not unambiguously opposed to an English invasion of Ireland. His point was that the revolution in England would be irrevocably lost if the soldiers allowed themselves to be shipped to that country before they had first set England's house in order. Cf. Brailsford, *The Levellers*, pp. 498–9. For a thorough discussion of the Levellers' attitude to the conquest of Ireland, see the valuable article by Noah Carlin, 'The Levellers and the conquest of Ireland in 1649', *HJ*, 30 (1987), 269–88.

36 *CSPD*, 1649–50, p. 60.

37 *Perf. Occurrences*, 6–13 Apr. 1649, E529/10, p. 961; *England's Moderate Messenger*, 23–30 Apr. 1649, E529/25, p. 4.

38 *Moderate Intell.*, 19–26 Apr. 1649, E552/4, p. 2001. According to the army pay warrants, at this juncture the troops stationed in the region included Capt. Neale's company of dragoons, Col. Tomlinson's and Barton's regiments of horse (SP28/59, fos 287, 289; vol. 60, fo. 212).

39 *CSPD*, 1649–50, pp. 92, 94. Pay for fourteen weeks, totalling almost £4000, was issued to Reynolds' regiment in March, April and May (SP28/59, fos 95–5ᵛ, 97–9ᵛ).

40 *Perf. Occurrences*, 6–13 Apr. 1649, E529/10, pp. 966–7.

41 *CJ*, vi, 189; Whitelocke, iii, 17.

42 *Merc. Militaris*, 17–24 Apr. 1649, E551/13, pp. 13–14; Whitelocke, iii, 20.

43 Whitelocke, iii, 21, 22.

44 *The Humble Petition of Divers Well-affected Women* ([5 May] 1649), BL, 669.f.14/27; Patricia Higgins, 'The reactions of women', in B. Manning (ed.), *Politics, Religion and the English Civil War* (E. J. Arnold, London, 1973), pp. 200–5.

45 *The Humble Petition of Divers Young Men and Apprentices* (May 1649), BL, 669.f.14/31.

46 *Perf. Occurrences*, 13–20 Apr. 1649, E529/15, p. 950. On 18 April, the day after his arrest, he was included in the list of Levellers whose release was demanded in a London petition to parliament (*The Man in the Moon*, 16–23 Apr. 1649, E551/10, p. 11).

47 Untitled, E551/21. Thomason gives the date as 25 April, but *Merc. Militaris*, which appeared on 24 April, reported the incident as having occurred on the 23rd (E551/13, p. 14).

48 The first issue appeared on Tuesday 24 April 1649 (*Merc. Militaris*, 17–24 Apr. 1649, E551/13).

49 *CSPD*, 1649–50, p. 95; Whitelocke, iii, 17; *Clarke Papers*, ii, 210.

50 See *The Collected Writings of Gerrard Winstanley*, ed. George H. Sabine (Cornell University Press, Ithaca, NY, 1941, pp. 188, 197, 529–34).

51 *Clarke Papers*, ii, 211–12.

52 *Perf. Wkly Account*, 18–25 Apr. 1649, E552, pp. 454–5. The vision continues to have its adherents in the late twentieth century. In western Canada the Hutterites, descendants of the German Anabaptists, still practise a communal agriculture. In India during the 1950s and 1960s the prophet Bhave Vinobe persuaded landlords to surrender several hundred thousands of acres to peasant communes.

53 William Everard, *The Declaration and Standard of the Levellers of England* (23 April 1649), E551/11; Jerrard Winstanley, *A Letter to the Lord Fairfax and his Councell of War* ([13 June] 1649), E560/1; BL, Egerton MS 2618, fo. 38; *Clarke Papers*, II, 215–20.

54 Besides the reports in various newsbooks there are two detailed accounts of the mutiny in Whalley's regiment. The official version is *A True Narrative of the Late Mutiny Made by Several Troopers of Captain Savage's Troop in Col: Whaley's Regiment* ... (1 May 1649), E552/18. The mutineers' version is found in *The Army's Martyr* ([7 May] 1649), E554/6. See also *The Copie of a Letter, from Lieut. Col. Iohn Lilburn, M. Richard Overton, April 27, 1649. In behalf of M. Robert Lockwer [sic]* ..., BL, 669.f.14/23; *A Modest Narrative of Intelligence*, 21–8 Apr. 1649, E552/7, pp. 31–2; *England's Moderate Messenger*, 23–30 Apr. 1649, E529/25, p. 7; *Perf. Occurrences*, 27 Apr.–3 May 1649, E529/32, pp. 1003–4.

55 *A Salva Libertate Sent to Collonell Francis West ... by Lieutenant Collonell John Lilburne* ... (14 Sept. 1649), BL, 669.f.14/76.

56 PRO, C54/3589/26; PRO, Wills, PROB6/26, fo. 100; Berkshire RO, East Lockinge Parish Register, 1546–1663, D/P 82/1/1, unfol.; *The Army's Martyr*, p. 7.

57 The army pay warrants bear out most of Whalley's statement. On 28 December 1648 the regiment received three weeks' pay, on 30 January four weeks', on 24 February four weeks', and on 8 March six weeks'. In sum, the regiment had received pay for seventeen weeks since its arrival in London nineteen weeks earlier. Another warrant for six weeks' pay was signed on 10 April but the money was not received until 16 May. (SP28/57, fo. 458–8^v; vol. 58, fos 346–8^v, 614–14^v; vol. 59, fo. 281–1^v.) While there is no surviving pay warrant for four weeks' pay received on 23 April, the pro-mutineer pamphlet acknowledged that it had been received (*The Army's Martyr*, p. 3). Of course the pay record of these four months has no bearing on the question of arrears, which in some cases went as far back as 1642.

58 As an army writer would later reflect, had Whalley and his loyal troops not managed to bring the 'discontented popular multitude' under control, 'it might have proved as bloody day to that great City, and more fatal to the kingdom's interest, than ever yet England saw or thought of' (*The Justice of the Army against Evill-Doers Vindicated*, p. 13).

59 See above, n. 54.

60 The higher officers had been worried about a plot against their lives for at least a month. NLS, Advocates' MS 35.5.11 (Clarke Papers), fo. 15^v.

61 *Merc. Pragmaticus*, 24 Apr.–1 May 1649, E552/15, p. 15. A few days later three soldiers from Hewson's regiment would be punished for having falsely accused two Londoners of uttering dangerous words against Cromwell (*The Kingdomes Faithfull and Impartiall Scout*, 27 Apr.–4 May 1649, E529/31, pp. 111–12).

62 John Lilburne, *A Preparative to a Hue and Cry* ([13 Sept.] 1649), E573/16, pp. 7–14. Infiltration of the Levellers' councils by the grandees is also hinted at in NLS, Advocates' MS 35.5.11, fo. 20.

63 *The Army's Martyr*, p. 5.

64 *Perf. Occurrences*, 27 Apr.–3 May 1649, E529/32, p. 1003.

65 The funeral received detailed coverage in most newsbooks of the day. See especially *The Moderate*, 24 Apr.–1 May 1649, E552/20, p. 483; *Moderate Intell.*, 26 Apr.–2 May 1649, E552/26, p. 2013; *Merc. Pragmaticus*, 24 Apr.–1 May 1649, E552/15, p. 15; *Perf. Occurrences*, 27 Apr.–3 May 1649, E529/32, p. 1006; *Kingdomes Wkly Intell.*, 24 Apr.–1 May 1649, E552/21, p. 1344; *Impartiall Intell.*, 25 Apr.–2 May 1649, E529/29 p. 72.

66 *Perf. Diurnall*, 30 Apr.–7 May, E529/34, p. 2469.

67 In the immediate aftermath of the king's execution Marten had been authorized to recruit his horse to a full regiment (*CJ*, vi, 129). In May many of them would join the Leveller mutiny (*Perf. Occurrences*, 4–11 May 1649, E530/1, p. 1031).

68 *Merc. Pragmaticus*, 24 Apr.–1 May 1649, E552/15, p. 14.

69 *Perf. Diurnall*, 30 Apr.–7 May 1649, E529/34, p. 2469.

70 *The English Souldiers Standard*, p. 9.

71 Ibid., pp. 9–10, 12.

72 *Walwins Wiles*, in Haller and Davies, pp. 288–9.

73 See Brailsford, *The Levellers*, ch. 25, for a humanitarian interpretation of the Levellers' motivation. *The Eighteen Queries* do not survive, but were reproduced in the five issues of the *Moderate Intelligencer* for May 1649, and are printed in Brailsford, *The Levellers*, pp. 501–2. The best discussion of them is in Carlin, 'The Levellers and the conquest of Ireland in 1649', pp. 271–2.

74 *The Souldiers Demand* (Bristol, [18 May] 1649), E555/29, pp. 1, 4–7, 9, 12–13. The fact that the pamphlet was published in Bristol points to a member of Skippon's or Reynolds' regiments, which were stationed there at that time. Maj. Cobbett had already been cashiered for his involvement in the Ware mutiny, but was evidently reinstated. He was again dismissed on 18 June 1649, and it seems reasonable to conjecture that his dismissal was connected with the publication of *The Souldiers Demand*. See also above, pp. 229–30.

75 *The Moderate*, 1–8 May 1649, E554/15, unpag.

76 *Perf. Occurrences*, 2–9 March 1649, E527/31, p. 895; *Impartiall Intell.*, 7–14 Mar. 1649, E546/23, p. 10; Worc. MS 16, fo. 85.

77 *CSPD, 1649–50*, pp. 124–6; *Modest Narrative of Intelligence*, 5–12 May 1649, E555/8, p. 47.

78 *Englands Standard Advanced* (6 May 1649), E553/2. A few days later Thompson put forth an enlarged edition of this pamphlet, printing the entire text of the 1 May Agreement of the People E555/7).

79 *Perf. Summary*, 4–12 May 1649, E530/3, p. 152.

80 *A Declaration of the Proceedings of His Excellency the Lord General Fairfax in the Reducing of the Revolted Troops* (23 May 1649), E556/1, p. 8.

81 *Kingdomes Wkly Intell.*, 8–15 May 1649, E555/18; *The Moderate*, 8–15 May 1649, E555/16, pp. 503–4; *The Kingdomes Faithfull and Impartiall Scout*, 4–11 May 1649, E530/2, p. 120.

82 Worc. MS 72 (Proceedings of the Committee of Officers on Garrisons), unfol.

83 *Moderate Intell.*, 2–10 May 1649, E555/3, p. 2034. Three troops–Owen's, Strelley's and Wildman's, were stationed at Chester apparently awaiting their passage to Ireland. The other three – Bray's, Chaplin's and Reynolds's own – were stationed in Hampshire (Worc. MS 72, unfol.). Bray's troop was known to be mutinous. I conjecture that the three troops at Chester may also have mutinied. Was Capt. Wildman related in any way to the Leveller spokesman at the Putney debates?

84 *The Levellers (Falsly So Called) Vindicated* (20 Aug. 1649), E571/11, p. 4.

85 *Modest Narrative*, 5–12 May 1649, E555/8, p. 45.

86 *The Levellers (Falsly So Called) Vindicated*, pp. 2–3.

87 *Impartiall Intell.*, 9–16 May 1649, E530/8, p. 187; *Perf. Occurrences*, 4–11 May 1649, E530/1, p. 1029 (corrected pag.); *Kingdomes Wkly Intell.*, 8–15 May 1649, E555/18, p. 1353.

88 *The Moderate*, 1–8 May 1649, E554/15, unpag.

89 *Modest Narrative*, 5–12 May 1649, E555/8, p. 45.

90 *Perf. Occurrences*, 4–11 May 1649, E530/1, p. 1029 (corrected pag.); *Moderate Intell.*, 2–10 May 1649, E555/3, p. 2034. Maj. Gibbon's troop was at Rye and did not join the mutiny. Hutchinson's troop was already with Thompson at Banbury. Thus only three troops (not four, as most historians have written) can have marched to the rendezvous with Scrope's men near Bristol.

91 *The Moderate*, 8–15 May 1649, E555/16, p. 497.

92 *Moderate Intell.*, 2–10 May 1649, E555/3, p. 2034; *Perf. Diurnall* 7–14 May 1649, E530/6, pp. 2498–9; Worc. MS 16, fos 103–9.

93 *CSPD, 1649–50*, p. 130 (8 May). Their instruction referred to £1000, but in fact just over £2000 had been authorized by three warrants of 7 May. The money was eventually paid out several weeks later (SP 28/60, fos 92, 96, 176).

94 Evelyn, *D & C*, III, 51; *Merc. Elencticus*, 7–14 May 1649, E555/9, p. 22; *The Kingdomes Faithfull and Impartiall Scout*, 4–11 May 1649, E530/2, p. 118; *Perf. Wkly Account*, 9–16 May 1649, E530/7, p. 478.

95 *Perf. Wkly Account*, 9–16 May 1649, E530/7, p. 478.

96 *OPH*, XIX, 120.

97 *CSPD, 1649–50*, p. 139.

98 *CJ*, VI, 208.

99 *CJ*, VI, 208, 210; *The Moderate*, 7–15 May 1649 E555/16, p. 503. Can it be only a coincidence that the policy of starving the Levellers to death was only reversed after the mutiny in the army had been vanquished?

100 *The Moderate*, 7–15 May 1649, E555/16, p. 498.

101 *Declaration of the Proceedings*, p. 6. The mutineers themselves indignantly denied employing this tactic, and hurled the same accusation back at their foes. The grandees, they alleged, had tried to increase recruitment by telling each troop separately that all the others had signed on for the Irish service (*The Levellers (Falsly So Called) Vindicated*, p. 3).

102 *Impartiall Intell.*, 16–23 May 1649, E530/15, p. 96; *A Moderate Intelligence*, 17–24 May 1649, E556/13, unpag.; Whitelocke, III, 38, 43; *Moderate*, 22–9 May 1649, E556/31, p. 529; *Perf. Occurrences*, 4–11 May 1649, E530/1, p. 1032.

103 *Perf. Occurrences*, 4–11 May 1649, E530/1, pp. 1030–1 (corrected pag.); Worc. MS 16, fo. 93. Two companies of Fairfax's foot regiment were left behind to guard Whitehall.

104 *The Moderate*, 8–15 May 1649, E555/16, p. 498.

105 *Perf. Diurnall*, 7–14 May 1649, E530/6, pp. 2507–8.

106 The regiment was now commanded by Col. William Sydenham (*Reg. Hist.*, p. 433).

107 In Hewson's regiment, it was reported, men had been cashiered with 14s. 9d. – not enough to get them home. Col. Scrope had told his men that he had nothing to give those who would not go to Ireland. Those who objected were threatened with immediate disbandment, in contravention of the army's Solemn Engagement of 5 June 1647. See *The Unanimous Declaration of Colonel Scrope's and Commissary General Ireton's Regiments* (11 May 1649), E555/4.

108 *A Declaration from his Excellencie ... Aulton, Hamshire* (12 May 1649), E555/6.

109 See for example the respect accorded to Fairfax's messenger at the mutineers' rendezvous of 1 May (*The Moderate*, 7–15 May 1649, E555/16, p. 504).

110 According to *The Kingdomes Faithfull and Impartiall Scout*, 4–11 May 1649, E530/2, p. 120, Everard had 400 or 500 followers, but this estimate seems far too high.

111 *The Declaration of the Levellers concerning Prince Charles* (17 May 1649), E555/26, p. 3. One's confidence in the accuracy of this report is strengthened by the fact that it appeared in an anti-Leveller pamphlet.

112 R. H. Gretton, *The Burford Records* (Clarendon Press, Oxford, 1920), p. 241.

113 *Declaration of the Levellers concerning Prince Charles*, p. 3. This hostile source must be treated with caution; however, there are enough independent indications that the Levellers were tempted by the royalist option at this juncture to make the allegation credible. (Cf. Carte, I, 273; Whitelocke, III, 100).

114 *Impartiall Intell.*, 9–16 May 1649, E530/8, p. 188.

115 Abbott, II, 68; *The Declaration of Lieutenant-Generall Cromwell concerning the Levellers* (14 May 1649), E555/12, pp. 1–2.

116 I owe this point to Prof. Woolrych.

117 Francis White, *A True Relation of the Proceedings in the Businesse of Burford* (17 Sept. 1649), E574/26, p. 1.

118 Worc. MS 181, unfol. (12 May 1649).

119 *A Full Narrative of All the Proceedings between His Excellency the Lord Fairfax and the Mutineers...* ([18 May] 1649), E555/27, p. 7.

120 I use the term 'Levellers' advisedly. Although there is no positive proof that the London Levellers organized the mutiny by Scrope's, Ireton's and Harrison's men, and while the mutineers made no public reference to the Agreement of People of 1 May 1649, their programme was clearly Leveller-inspired, and their suppression at Burford was bitterly denounced in Leveller circles. The Burford mutiny, moreover, was commonly referred to as 'the Leveller rising' (SP24/25, fo. 12–12ᵛ; Add. MS 21417, fo. 134; *Perf. Occurrences*, 4–11 May 1649, E530/1, p. 1031; Massarella, p. 221).

121 *A Full Narrative of All the Proceedings*, pp. 10–11.

122 *Declaration of the Proceedings*, pp. 7–8.

123 *The Levellers (Falsly So Called) Vindicated*, p. 6; *England's Moderate Messenger*, 14–21 May 1649, E530/13, pp. 27–8. See also White, *Businesse of Burford*, p. 6; A. L. Morton, (ed.), *Freedom in Arms*, (Seven Seas, Berlin, 1975), pp. 304–6.

124 *Declaration of the Proceedings*, p. 8. The sources generally refer to twelve troops, because they erroneously include Hutchinson's troop, which had earlier joined Thompson's force at Banbury. See above, p. 332.

125 *The Declaration and Speeches of Cornet Thompson and the Rest of the Levellers* (22 May 1649), E556/7, p. 4.

126 *White Businesse of Burford*, p. 7; *The Levellers (Falsly So Called) Vindicated*, p. 6. In the bitterness of defeat the Levellers would later accuse More of being an agent of the two generals (*The Levellers (Falsly So Called) Vindicated*, p. 7).

127 *Perf. Summary*, 14–21 May 1649, E530/12, p. 151.

128 *Moderate Intell.*, 10–17 May 1649; E555/25, p. 2048.

129 *Declaration of the Proceedings*, p. 9.

130 Anne Laurence, 'The Parliamentary Army Chaplains, 1642–1651' (Oxford D. Phil. thesis, 1982), pp. 326–7.

131 *A Full Narrative of all the Proceedings*, p. 3.

132 Gretton, *Burford Records*, p. 243; *Perf. Summary*, 14–21 May 1649, E530/12, pp. 150–1 (Capt. Samuel Bridger's account to the House of Commons).

133 *Full Narrative of All the Proceedings*, p. 3.

134 Gretton, *Burford Records*, p. 255. Gretton provides a good account of the clash at Burford, but his dating is inaccurate.

135 *White, Businesse of Burford*, p. 8.

136 *Declaration of the Proceedings*, pp. 10–11, 14; *Declaration and Speeches of Cornet Thompson*, p. 4.

137 *Kingdoms Wkly Intell.*, 15–22 May 1649, E556/6, p. 1363.

138 The newsbooks say that the executions occurred on Saturday 19 May, but the officers were in Oxford that day for their honorary degrees. A contemporary pamphlet states that they were executed on 18 May (*Declaration and Speeches of Cornet Thompson*, title page). But Gretton points out that the three soldiers' burial is entered in the Burford parish register under Thursday the 17th (*Burford Records*, p. 155).

139 *The Moderate*, 15–22 May 1649, E556/3, pp. 516–17.

140 *Declaration of the Proceedings*, p. 12.

141 *The Levellers (Falsly So Called) Vindicated*, pp. 7–8.

142 *A Full Narrative of All the Proceedings*, p. 14.

143 *Declaration of the Proceedings*, p. 12.

144 *The Levellers (Falsly So Called) Vindicated*, p. 7.

145 *Moderate Intell.*, 10–17 May 1649, E555/25, p. 2048.

146 *England's Moderate Messenger*, 14–21 May 1649, E530/13, p. 32.

147 *Moderate Intell.*, 17–24 May 1649, E556/12, p. 2057.

148 Worc. MS 16, fo. 100–100ᵛ.

149 *Impartiall Intell.*, 16–23 May 1649, E530/15, p. 96.

150 Whitelocke, iii, 38, 41, 43, 55; *Impartiall Intell.*, 16–23 May 1649, E530/15, p. 96; *A Moderate Intelligence*, 17–24 May 1649, E556/13, unpag.; *The Moderate*, 22–9 May 1649, E556/31, p. 529.

151 *A Full Narrative of All the Proceedings*, pp. 12–13.

152 See C. H. Firth's account of the Oxford mutiny in *Procs of the Oxford Architectural and HS*, new ser., iv (1884), pp. 235–46.

153 *C & P*, i, 54; Anthony à Wood, *The History and Antiquities of the University of Oxford [Annals]*, ed. John Gutch (2 vols, printed for the editor, Oxford, 1792–6), ii, 619–21; Worc. MS 16, fo. 101.

154 Brailsford, *The Levellers*, p. 520.

155 *CJ*, vi, 218.

156 Whitelocke, iii, 46–7; Evelyn, *D & C*, iii, 55.

157 *Merc. Militaris*, 8 May 1649, E554/13, p. 32; *Perf. Occurrences*, 25 May–1 June 1649, E530/25, p. 1054.

158 *Perf. Occurrences*, 25 May–1 June 1649, E530/25, p. 1054 (Cromwell's report to the House of Commons, 26 May).

159 *A Full Narrative of All the Proceedings*, p. 2. Fairfax is sometimes thought to have written no important public letters of his own after the spring of 1647. However, the contrast with Cromwell's interpretation of Burford is sharp enough to leave little doubt of Fairfax's authorship. Also, as an MP Fairfax had every right to deliver a political message to his parliamentary colleagues.

Chapter 11   The Conquest of Ireland, 1649–52

1 *CSPD, 1649–50*, pp. 22, 28.

2 See above, pp. 330–1.

3 Worc. MS 72, unfol. (16 Feb. 1649).

4 *Perf. Diurnall*, 19–26 Mar. 1649, E529/1, p. 2380; *Clarke Papers*, ii, 200–6.
5 *Clarke Papers*, ii, 205.
6 Ibid., p. 208.
7 Ibid., p. 209.
8 Worc. MS 16, fo. 91–1ᵛ.
9 Clement Walker (*AA*, p. 151) accused them of forcing the lots to be drawn again and again until they fell on the regiments they wanted to get rid of.
10 Add. MS 21417 (Baynes correspondence), fo. 129. By July, Lambart had managed to extricate himself and most of his regiment from the expedition (*Reg. Hist.*, p. 255).
11 The editor of *Merc. Militaris* (17–24 Apr. 1649, E551/13, p. 12) said that the grandees tried to overthrow the selection but were prevented from doing so by the lower officers. I see no reason not to accept the version found in the Clarke Papers (Worc. MS 16, fo. 91–1ᵛ).
12 *Merc. Pragmaticus*, 24 Apr.–1 May 1649, E552/15, p. 14.
13 Marten had raised his own regiment without authorization in August 1648 (Whitelocke, ii, 382). However by early 1649 it had evidently been incorporated into the establishment. Cf. Worc. MS 72, unfol. (16 Feb. 1649); *Clarke Papers*, ii, 209n.
14 *Perf. Passages*, 22 Apr.–4 May 1649, E529/30, p. 19.
15 *England's Moderate Messenger*, 23–30 Apr. 1649, E529/25, p. 8.
16 *Moderate Intell.*, 2–10 May 1649, E555/3, p. 2025.
17 *England's Moderate Messenger*, 14–21 May 1649, E530/13, p. 29.
18 *Perf. Diurnall*, 6–13 Aug. 1649, E532/15, p. 2694.
19 *The Moderate'*, 7–14 Aug. 1649, E569/9, p. 666.
20 *Great Britaines Paine-Full Messenger*, 9–16 Aug. 1649, p. 4; Clar. MS 38, fo. 7ᵛ; Whitelocke, iii, 87; *Moderate Intell.*, 9–16 Aug. 1649, E569/19, p. 2212.
21 *Moderate Intell.*, 12–18 Apr. 1649, E551/1, p. 1989; Abbott, ii, 93.
22 *CJ*, vi, 245.
23 *CSPD, 1649–50*, pp. 132, 134. The pretext for seizing the money was to prevent it from falling into the hands of the Burford mutineers, but this does not alter the fact that it was transferred from the navy to the Irish expeditionary force. Cf. Abbott, ii, 67.
24 *Sydney Papers*, p. 76.
25 *C & P*, i, 97.
26 *CSPD, 1649–50*, pp. xlv, 229. A significant proportion of this salary would be consumed by Cromwell's personal staff.
27 Sir John T. Gilbert (ed.), *A Contemporary History of Affairs in Ireland, from 1641 to 1652*, Irish Archaeological and Celtic Society (3 vols, 1879–80), ii, 223.
28 *CSPD, 1649–50*, pp. 239, 245–6, 257, 581–3.
29 Whitelocke, iii, 67; *Crom. Navy*, pp. 61–4.
30 Council of State, Charges for the War in Ireland, 1 Mar. 1649–16 Feb. 1650, SP25/118, pp. 55–65.

31 Wheeler, pp. 220–1 (I am indebted to Dr Ian Roy for this reference); J. G. Simms, *War and Politics in Ireland 1649–1730* (Hambledon Press, London, 1986), p. 2; Carte MS 25, fo. 624.

32 *CSPD, 1649–50*, p. 28.

33 From 1 March 1649 to 16 February 1650 the invasion cost £535,590. Of this sum just over £100,000 represented the payment of two months' arrears to all the old soldiers who agreed to enlist. This left the real cost of the war in Ireland at £435,562 (SP25/118, unpag. abstract at beginning of volume). Of this sum £45,000 per month went to pay the troops (Wheeler, p. 211).

34 Ibid., pp. 205, 211–12.

35 Carte, I, 188.

36 Ibid., II, 369, 379, 382; Simms, *War and Politics in Ireland*, p. 1.

37 *C & P*, I, 73–5.

38 *CSPI, 1647–60*, p. 365. The parliamentary commander in Londonderry, Sir Charles Coote, also endorsed O'Neill's demands later the same summer (Gilbert, *Contemporary History*, II, 217–18, 446).

39 The benefits of the cessation were extensive. Later in May O'Neill signed a similar agreement with Sir Charles Coote, the parliamentary commander of Londonderry. Until that moment Coote had been under severe threat from Sir George Monro, who had been sent by Ormonde to besiege him. In June, O'Neill and Col. Jones came to an understanding not to disturb one another's quarters, while later that summer O'Neill actually relieved Coote in Londonderry. This act halted the royalist sweep through Ulster. See Gilbert, *Contemporary History*, II, 221–2; *C & P*, I, 78, 83; Whitelocke, III, 56; Edward Earl of Clarendon, *A History of the Rebellion and Civil Wars in Ireland* (Patrick Dugan, Dublin, 1719–20), p. 98.

40 *CJ*, VI, 277.

41 Whitelocke, III, 84.

42 *OPH*, XIX, 486; Abbott, II, 83–4.

43 Abbott, II, 88.

44 HMC, *Leyborne-Popham*, p. 35; *The Moderate*, 14–21 Aug. 1649, E571/7, p. 675; Abbott, II, 104. An additional 2600 men had already sailed in July to bolster Col. Michael Jones's defence of Dublin.

45 *C & P*, I, 105.

46 Carte MS 25, fo. 193. Clarendon gloomily reflected that on that day Ormonde's troops contracted a great fear of the enemy, a fear which they never overcame (*Rebellion in Ireland*, p. 93).

47 Whitelocke, III, 85.

48 *Merc. Elencticus*, 13–20 Aug. 1649, E471/1, p. 129; Abbott, II, 102 (citing Leicester's journal).

49 Edmund Borlase, *The History of the Irish Rebellion* (Oli Nelson and Charles Connor, Dublin, 1743), p. 281.

50 Abbott, II, 111–12.

51 Carte MS 25, fos 144, 171.

52 Ibid., fos 148, 214, 235, 251–3; MS 162, p. 15.

53 Carte MS 25, fo. 325.
54 Ibid., fos 212, 274, 362, 471, 486.
55 Ibid., fos 319, 353, 367.
56 Carte MS 162, p. 46; *C & P*, I, 110.
57 The regiments were those of Cols Warren, Walle, Berne and Lt-Col. Edmund Verney. Like Aston, Verney was an English Catholic, while Berne and most of his men were protestants.
58 Carte MS 25, fo. 452.
59 Ibid., fo. 341.
60 Ibid., fo. 397.
61 Ibid., fo. 438.
62 Ibid., fos 450, 473, 483.
63 Carte, II, 398.
64 Abbott, II, 117.
65 Ibid., p. 119.
66 Simms, *War and Politics*, p. 5; *Perf. Occurrences*, 28 Sept.–4 Oct. 1649, E533/15, p. 1275 (Hewson's account).
67 Carte MS 25, fos 483, 501; MS 162, p. 80.
68 Carte MS 25, fo. 505.
69 Abbott, II, 126. When he gave this order Cromwell may still have been gripped by the fear that must have assailed him as he personally led the second charge up to the breach. His exposure to the immediate risk of death may have further justified in his mind the command to deny quarter.
70 Clar. MS 38, fo. 24ᵛ (Inchiquin to Ormonde). This startling royalist testimony to the compassion of some of Cromwell's troops at Drogheda has until now gone unnoticed by historians. Cf. Carte, II, 412.
71 Because nearly all men of the garrison were slaughtered, the eyewitness accounts of Drogheda emanate exclusively from the parliamentary side. They consist of Cromwell's letters to parliament and the Council of State (Abbott, II, 124–8), Hewson's letter (*Perf. Occurrences*, 28 Sept.–4 Oct. 1649, E535/15, pp. 1275–6) and four anonymous letters: in *Perf. Diurnall*, 1–8 Oct. 1649, E533/17, pp. 2811–13; *Cromwelliana*, ed. Machell Stace (George Smeeton, London, 1810), p. 64; and *The Kingdomes Faithfull and Impartiall Scout*, 28 Sept.–5 Oct. 1649, E533/16, pp. 258–9. Edmund Ludlowe's account (I, 233–4) is also useful. All the eyewitness accounts agree that the parliamentary soldiers were repulsed once from the breach, so there seems little point in accepting, as Gardiner does (*C & P*, I, 116–17) the royalist assertions that they were hurled back twice. See Carte, II, 412; *A Letter from Sir Lewis Dyve* (The Hague, 1650), E616/7, p. 24; Gilbert, *Contemporary History*, II, 49; Clarendon, *Rebellion in Ireland*, p. 94; Borlase, *Irish Rebellion*, p. 282. What could explain the discrepancy is that the royalists may have counted the throwing–back of Castle's regiment and the holding of Hewson's and Ewer's at bay as two repulses, while the parliamentarians thought of it as one.
72 J. G. Simms, 'Cromwell at Drogheda, 1649', *Irish Sword*, 11 (1973–4), 220.

73 C & P, ɪ, 119.
74 *Letters from Ireland, relating ... the Taking of Drogheda* ... (2 Oct. 1649), E575/7, pp. 12, 14 (corrected pag.).
75 *Perf. Occurrences*, 28 Sept.–4 Oct. 1649, E533/15, p. 1276.
76 Carte, ɪɪ, 412.
77 *Perf. Occurrences*, 28 Sept.–4 Oct. 1649, E533/15, p. 1276. (Hewson's letter).
78 Abbott, ɪɪ, 127.
79 Simms, *War and Politics*, p. 4; T. W. Moody et al. (eds), *New History of Ireland* (Clarendon Press, Oxford, 1976), ɪɪɪ, 340.
80 Simms, *War and Politics*, p. 10.
81 Carte, ɪɪ, 398.
82 Carte MS 25, fo. 624. See also *Letter from Sir Lewis Dyve*, p. 41.
83 *Letters from Ireland*, E575/7, p. 15; *A Very Full and Particular Relation of the Great Progress ... toward the Reducing of Ireland* ([31 Oct.] 1649), E576/6, p. 50; Moody et al., *New History*, ɪɪɪ, 340.
84 *AA*, p. 255; Abbott, ɪɪ, 128, 130; Ludlow[e], ɪ, 239.
85 *Perf. Diurnall*, 5–12 Nov. 1649, E533/23, p. 2834; Ludlow[e], ɪ, 235.
86 Abbott, ɪɪ, 133. The grandees in question were Pride, Whalley, Disbrowe, Harrison and Sir Hardress Waller (SP25/118, pp. 138–40, 143–4; *CSPD, 1649–50*, p. 50).
87 Carte MS 25, fos 553, 585, 689, 712; HMC, *Leyborne-Popham*, p. 45.
88 Carte MS 25, fos 632, 637.
89 C & P, ɪ, 126, 128; *A Very Full and Particular Relation*, p. 50; Clarendon, *Rebellion in Ireland*, p. 96; Carte MS 25, fo. 676.
90 HMC, *Leyborne-Popham*, p. 47; *A Very Full and Particular Relation*, p. 51; Abbott, ɪɪ, 141.
91 Gardiner gives a figure of 9000, but does not take sufficient account of the losses at Drogheda (160), deaths from disease, and the fact that a third of Cromwell's original 12,000 had been assigned to garrison duty (C & P, ɪ, 127).
92 Gilbert, *Contemporary History*, ɪɪ, 288; Abbott, ɪɪ, 143.
93 *A Very Full and Particular Relation*, pp. 50–1; Gilbert, *Contemporary History*, ɪɪ, 289–90.
94 Apart from Cromwell's letters, the best accounts of the taking of Wexford are Col. Deane's narration in HMC, *Leyborne-Popham*, p. 47, and the two anonymous reports in *A Very Full and Particular Relation*, pp. 50–2.
95 *A Very Full and Particular Relation*, p. 56.
96 Abbott, ɪɪ, 141.
97 Ibid., pp. 142–3.
98 C & P, ɪ, 133; Moody et al., *New History*, ɪɪɪ, 341.
99 Carte MS 25, fo. 757.
100 Abbott, ɪɪ, 154–5.
101 Carte MS 26, fos 45, 300ᵛ; Gilbert, *Contemporary History*, ɪɪ, 56.
102 Carte, ɪɪ, 415; Carte MS 26, fo. 300ᵛ.

103   Carte MS 26, fo. 300ᵛ.
104   Cary, ii, 185–6; Abbott, ii, 150–1, 157.
105   Gilbert, *Contemporary History*, ii, 322; Moody et al., *New History*, iii, 342.
106   Cary, ii, 186; Carte MS 26, fo. 23.
107   Carte MS 25, fo. 738.
108   Abbott, ii, 146, 153.
109   Ibid., ii, 163, 173.
110   Clar. MS 38, fo. 146ᵛ.
111   Simms, *War and Politics*, p. 11.
112   Carte MS 26, fos 7, 14, 21.
113   Diarmuid Murtagh, 'Colonel Edward Wogan', *Irish Sword*, 2 (1954–6), p. 47; Simms, *War and Politics*, pp. 13–14.
114   Abbott, ii, 160.
115   *C & P*, i, 141; Simms, *War and Politics*, 14.
116   Simms, *War and Politics*, pp. 15–17. There is some uncertainty about the size of the Ulster force that Farrell took into Waterford. Cromwell estimated them at 2000, but he was excusing his abandonment of the siege, and almost certainly exaggerated (Abbott, ii, 176; *C & P*, i, 142). The mayor asked Ormonde for only 300 'picked and choice men' out of the Ulster army, but he seems to have got more than he bargained for. Borlase, Clarendon and the author of the *Aphorismicall Discovery* say Farrell's force numbered between 1300 and 1500, while a muster of Ulster horse and foot in Waterford on 24 January 1650 revealed 694 men besides officers (Simms, *War and Politics*, p. 15; Borlase, *Irish Rebellion*, p. 289; Clarendon, *Rebellion in Ireland*, p. 103; Gilbert, *Contemporary History*, ii, 57, 506–7).
117   Abbott, ii, 176.
118   Carte MS 26, fo. 312ᵛ.
119   Whitelocke, iii, 136.
120   Clar. MS 39, fo. 22.
121   SP25/118, pp. 143, 145; Clar. MS 39, fo. 40ᵛ.
122   Carte MS 142, p. 103.
123   Carte MS 26, fo. 363; Abbott, ii, 181; Carte, ii, 420.
124   Clar. MS 38, fos 155, 282.
125   *Calendar of the Clarendon State Papers*, ed. O. Ogle et al. (4 vols, Clarendon Press, Oxford, 1869–1932), ii, 33.
126   He seems to have derived this and other convictions about the Irish from a reading of Sir John Temple's *The Irish Rebellion*, published in 1646. See T. C. Barnard, 'Crisis of identity among Irish Protestants, 1641–1685', *P & P*, 127 (May 1990), 52–9.
127   Abbott, ii, 197–9, 201, 203–5.
128   *C & P*, i, 148.
129   Moody, et al., *New History*, iii, 344.
130   Abbott, ii, 208–11, 220; *C & P*, i, 150.
131   Abbott, ii, 221; *CSPD, 1650*, p. 90.
132   Tanner MS 56, fo. 182; Carte MS 67, fo. 195.

133 Gilbert, *Contemporary History*, II, 388.
134 Abbott gives an excellent account of the siege of Kilkenny, based on the diary of Dr Jones, Hewson's scoutmaster-general, which corrects Cromwell on one or two vital points (Abbott, II, 223–40). See also Whitelocke, III, 176–7; Carte MS 67, fo. 195; Gilbert, *Contemporary History*, II, 388. The accounts given by Borlase and the author of *Aphorismicall Discovery* (printed in Gilbert's *Contemporary History*) are unreliable.
135 Carte MS 26, fos 170, 238, 534; Gilbert, *Contemporary History*, II, 504.
136 Abbott is correct that the action could not have taken place on the 10th, but it is clear that the error in *Severall Procs in Parliament*, 23–30 May 1650, is a misprint for 16 May, not 17, as Abbott would have it. This is shown in a source which he apparently did not consult, *Perf. Diurnall*, 20–7 May 1650, E777/5, p. 278 (corrected pag.), where a report dated 14 May declares that the storm should occur in two days. That it did occur on the 16th is suggested by the fact that it was known in Dublin on the 17th that Clonmel had been taken (ibid., 27 May–3 June 1650, E777/8, p. 272 [*sic*]). Cf. Abbott, II, 250.
137 Gardiner mentions an estimate of 2500 as the parliamentary death toll (*C & P*, I, 156). Yet a sensible royalist account puts it at no more than 1500 (Gilbert, *Contemporary History*, II, 417).
138 For the siege see the various accounts in Gilbert, *Contemporary History*, II, 408–17; *Severall Procs in Parliament*, 23–30 May 1650, E777/6, pp. 504–5; *Perf. Diurnall*, 27 May–3 June 1650, E777/8, p. 272; Whitelocke, III, 196; *Cromwelliana*, p. 81.
139 *Letter from Sir Lewis Dyve*, p. 50.
140 Whitelocke, III, 200, 212, 231–2.
141 Gilbert, *Contemporary History*, II, 70, 390.
142 This was the figure that Clogher gave in a letter to Ormonde on 1 June (Carte MS 27, fo. 602).
143 Gilbert, *Contemporary History*, II, 84–8, and III, 148–9; Whitelocke, *Memorials*, III, 203, 215–17; Clarendon, *Rebellion in Ireland*, pp. 133–4; Ludlow[e], I, 255.
144 Borlase, *Irish Rebellion*, p. 314; Ludlow[e], I, 251.
145 Gilbert, *Contemporary History*, II, 100, 179; Carte MS 28, fo. 584; Carte, II, 453–5, 460; Clarendon, *Rebellion in Ireland*, 146, 163–4, 183; HMC, *Leyborne-Popham*, p. 75.
146 Whitelocke, III, 174.
147 The commissioners were appointed at different times over a six-month period beginning at the end of June 1650 (*CSPD, 1650*, pp. 219, 376, 442, 461). Their appointment was confirmed by act of parliament on 25 December 1650 (*A & O*, II, 494).
148 BL, Egerton MS 1048, fos 192–3. The BL catalogue misdates the MS as 1649.
149 Tanner MS 56, fo. 253; *CSPD, 1651*, pp. 147, 175.
150 Ludlow[e], I, 249.
151 Ludlow[e], I, 250; Whitelocke, III, 233; Clar. MS 41, fo. 55.

152 Whitelocke, III, 223; Carte MS 67, fo. 203ᵛ.
153 Carte, II, 426; Carte MS 28, fos 432, 459; Clarendon, *Rebellion in Ireland*, p. 130; Simms, *War and Politics*, p. 22.
154 Simms, *War and Politics*, pp. 22–3; Clar. MS 40, fo. 191.
155 Simms, *War and Politics*, p. 23.
156 Clar. MS. 42, fos 198–204, 208.
157 *Reg. Hist.* p. 664; Ludlow[e], *Memoirs*, I, 274; Clar. MS 42, fo. 215–15ᵛ; *Severall Procs in Parliament*, 31 July–7 Aug. 1651, E786/29, pp. 1486–7.
158 Clar. MS 42, fos 217–218, 221; Ludlow[e], I, 275, 278 n. 1; *CSPD, 1651*, p. 171; *Perf. Diurnall*, 23–30 June 1651, E786/11, pp. 1121–2; Robert Dunlop, *Ireland under the Commonwealth* (2 vols, Manchester University Press, 1913), I, 69, 74; PRO, E101/67/11B, fo. 141ᵛ.
159 Ludlow[e], I, 276–7. Ludlowe estimated Muskerry's force at 5000 and Roche's at between 2000 and 3000. Another officer estimated Muskerry's force at no more than 2500 (Clar. MS 42, fo. 212).
160 Dunlop, *Ireland under the Commonwealth*, I, 27–8.
161 Clar. MS 42, fos 226, 228; Dunlop, *Ireland under the Commonwealth*, I, 69; Gilbert, *Contemporary History*, III, 264, 266; Ludlow[e], I, 286; Duffy, p. 162; Tanner MS 55, fo. 97.
162 The story is told in detail in Ludlow[e], I, 287–8. See also Clar. MS 42, fos 233–4.
163 Ludlow[e], I, 290–1, 308; Carte MS 67, fo. 238; Tanner MS 53, fo. 4; HMC, *Egmont*, I, 508. The parliamentary commissioners estimated that their troops occupied 350 garrisons on 8 January 1652, but that 100 more would have to be planted to make the country completely safe (Carte MS 67, fos 223–4). The following August, Col. Jones said that parliament's troops were distributed among 400 garrisons. See NLW, MS 11440D (Jones's letterbook), p. 62. In May 1653 the figure he gave was 400 or more. See J. Mayer, 'Inedited Letters of Cromwell, Colonel Jones, Bradshaw and other regicides', *Transactions of the Historic Society of Lancashire and Cheshire*, new ser., I (1860–1), 234. In October 1652 Whitelocke (III, 461) gave a figure of 500.
164 Tanner MS 53, fo. 31.
165 Whitelocke, III, 205; Carte MS 67, fos 202, 223ᵛ; Ludlow[e], I, 491; Tanner MS 55, fo. 73; Cary, II, 280–1; *CSPD, 1650*, p. 427; W. McCarthy, 'The Royalist collapse in Munster 1650–1652', *Irish Sword*, 6 (1963–4), 171–2, 176; Dunlop, *Ireland under the Commonwealth*, I, 6–7.
166 Tanner MS 55, fos 99, 133; Dunlop, *Ireland under the Commonwealth*, I, 130, 133. By August 1652 the army's numbers had reached 34,128, exclusive of officers (*Dunlop, Ireland under the Commonwealth*, I, 248–9).
167 Dunlop, *Ireland under the Commonwealth*, I, 113; Tanner MS 53, fos 24–5, 69, 74; Carte MS 67, fos 248, 266; Ludlow[e], I, 317–18, 320–2; D. Bryan, 'Colonel Richard Grace, 1651–1652', *Irish Sword*, 4 (1959–60), 47; Moody et al., *New History*, III, 362.
168 Cary, II, 281; Ludlow[e], I, 302.

169 Cary, II, 419–20.

170 Clar. MS 42, fo. 241ᵛ; Ludlow[e], I, 509; NLW, MS 11440D, p. 42.

171 Carte MS 67, fo. 238; NLW, MS 11440D, pp. 47–8; HMC, *Egmont*, I, 508.

172 Tanner MS 53, fo. 20; Karl S. Bottigheimer, *English Money and Irish Land* (Clarendon Press, Oxford, 1971), p. 127; Tanner MS 53, fo. 31; NLW, MS 11440D, pp. 54, 75, 105.

173 *Severall Procs in Parliament*, 20–7 May 1652, E795/8, pp. 2171–4; Dunlop, *Ireland under the Commonwealth*, I, 236; Gilbert, *Contemporary History*, III, 348; Clar. MS 44, fo. 137–7ᵛ.

174 Carte MS 67, fos 224–5ᵛ; Ludlow[e], I, 500.

175 Ludlow[e], I, 301; NLW, MS11440D, p. 85.

176 Carte MS 67, fos 232ᵛ–3ᵛ, 258.

177 *A & O*, II, 598–603.

178 S. R. Gardiner, 'The transplantation to Connaught', *EHR*, 14 (1899), 703.

179 Bottigheimer, *English Money and Irish Land*, pp. 117, 139–40; Moody et al., *New History*, III, 359–61, 369.

180 HMC, *Egmont*, I, 514, 517, 520.

181 Dunlop, *Ireland under the Commonwealth*, I, 8; Tanner MS 53, fo. 24.

182 Gilbert, *Contemporary History*, III, 167; *CSPD, 1650*, p. 60.

183 Dunlop, *Ireland under the Commonwealth*, I, 113. Cf. Whitelocke, III, 317, who reported the price of wheat at Limerick as £7 a barrel in July 1651. For the high prices in Waterford see *Severall Procs in Parliament*, 8–15 Jan. 1652, E793/11, p. 1856.

184 Tanner MS 53, fo. 71ᵛ; Dunlop, *Ireland under the Commonwealth*, I, 189, 239–41, 329.

185 John Percivall found it impossible to draw any income from his vast estates in Munster. Sir Hardress Waller had the same experience in Leinster. (HMC, *Egmont*, I, li–lii; Tanner MS 53, fo. 139).

186 According to Corish, Petty's estimate of population loss may be too low by as much as 40 per cent (Moody et al., *New History*, III, 357).

187 Tanner MS 53, fo. 101.

188 Gardiner, 'The transplantation to Connaught', pp. 723, 725.

189 Moody et al., *New History*, III, 373.

Chapter 12 The conquest of Scotland, July 1650 to 6 September 1651

1 Baillie, II, 362.

2 F. D. Dow, *Cromwellian Scotland, 1651–1660* (John Donald, Edinburgh, 1979), p. 6.

3 Stevenson, p. 314; Carte, I, 373–4; *Diary of Alexander Jaffray* 3rd edn, ed. John Barclay (George and Robert King, Aberdeen, 1856), p. 55.

4 For the joyful reception accorded to Cromwell at Hounslow Heath and Hyde Park on Sunday 30 May see *Perf. Diurnall*, 27 May–3 June 1650, E777/8, p. 280.

5   Nicoll, p. 16.
6   *CSPD, 1650*, p. 210.
7   PRO31/3/90, fo. 31, cited in Massarella, p. 257.
8   Whitelocke, III, 211. See also Hutchinson, p. 195; Ludlow[e], I, 242–3; J. Wilson, *Fairfax* (John Murray, London, 1985), pp. 158–62.
9   Both Gardiner and Abbott accept the sincerity of Cromwell's attempt to change Fairfax's mind, but I am more persuaded by the interpretation of Whitelocke, not only because he was a shrewd political observer, but because at various times he demonstrated considerable insight into Cromwell's motivation (*C & P*, I, 259–60; Abbott, II, 268).
10 *Cromwelliana*, ed. Machell Stace (George Smeeton, London, 1810), p. 82.
11 *CSPD, 1650*, p. 267; Stevenson, p. 175.
12 *OPH*, XIX, 298–312; Abbott, II, 285.
13 *Perf. Diurnall*, 22–9 July 1650, E778/7, p. 390 (corrected pag.); Abbott, II, 291; Wheeler, pp. 248–9.
14 Hodgson, pp. 139–40; *CJ*, IV, 454.
15 *Perf. Diurnall*, 5–12 Aug. 1651, E778/18, p. 409; Wheeler, pp. 246–7; Nickolls, p. 41.
16 Wheeler, pp. 236, 243, 247–8; *A Brief Relation*, 13–20 Aug. 1651, E609/17, p. 802. For information about the size of daily rations see *CSPD, 1650*, p. 464; Wheeler, p. 243; *Perf. Diurnall*, 8–15 Dec. 1651, E791/27, p. 1502. The ration of 1 pint of beer per day seems very low. Beer was brewed in Newcastle for the expeditionary, force just after its departure at the end of July 1650 (Nickolls, pp. 11–12; see also Nicoll, p. 55). For information about suppliers see Wheeler, p. 245; *CSPD, 1650*, p. 464; *Merc. Politicus*, 20–7 Feb. 1651, E625/6, pp. 614, 622.
17 *Perf. Diurnall*, 22–9 July 1650, E778/7, p. 391; *CSPD, 1650*, p. 478; *CJ*, VI, 483.
18 See for example the letter from Sir Henry Vane on 28 December 1650 (Nickolls, p. 41).
19 Wheeler, pp. 233, 250.
20 PRO, Treasurers at War Accounts, 28 Mar. 1645–25 Dec. 1651, E351/302, fo. 5ᵛ.
21 Add. MS 21419, fo. 271; Reece, p. 41.
22 Add. MS 21420, fos 131, 157; *Perf. Diurnall*, 19–26 May 1651, E785/31, p. 1058.
23 Stevenson, p. 173.
24 *Diary of Sir Archibald Johnston of Wariston*, ed. David Hay Fleming, SHS, 2nd ser., XVIII (1919), II, 3, 5, 8–9, 19; *Correspondence of Sir Robert Kerr, First Earl of Ancram and his son William*, ed. David Laing (2 vols, R. & R. Clark, Edinburgh, 1875), II, 287–8; Stevenson, p. 174; Abbott, II, 301; *Perf. Diurnall*, 29 July–5 Aug. 1650, E778/12, p. 408; Sir Edward Walker, *Historical Discourses upon Several Occasions*, ed. H. Clopton (Samuel Keble, London, 1705), p. 162; Sir James Balfour, *Historical Works*, IV (W. Aitchison, Edinburgh, 1825) p. 86.

25 *Perf. Diurnall*, 5–12 Aug. 1650, E778/18, p. 409; Abbott, II, 297.

26 *Perf. Diurnall*, 5–12 Aug. 1650, E778/18, p. 410; Abbott, II, 300.

27 Hodgson, pp. 132, 214.

28 The sources differ as to whether the engagement at Musselburgh occurred on 30 or 31 July, but I think the weight of evidence supports the later date. This means that Cromwell's letter of 30 July describing the engagement should be corrected to 31 July. See Hodgson, pp. 215–20, 236–40; *Merc. Politicus*, 1–8 Aug. 1650, E609/5, p. 142; *Perf. Diurnall*, 5–12 Aug. 1650, E778/18, p. 411; Wariston, *Diary*, II, 6; *Cromwelliana*, p. 87; Nicoll, p. 22; Balfour, *Historical Works*, IV, 87; Abbott, II, 300.

29 *C & P*, I, 275; Abbott, II, 303, 305–6.

30 *Merc. Politicus*, 15–22 Aug. 1650, E610/3, p. 165; *Perf. Diurnall*, 12–19 Aug. 1650, E778/20, p. 440; *Severall Procs in Parliament*, 15–22 Aug. 1650, E778/21, p. 692.

31 Abbott, II, 305, 309. This action is misdated as 2 August in Ancram, *Correspondence*, II, 276; cf. Wariston, *Diary*, II, 21; *Perf. Diurnall*, 26 Aug.–2 Sept. 1650, E780/1, p. 472; *Severall Procs in Parliament*, 29 Aug.–5 Sept. 1650, E780/2, pp. 725–6.

32 *Perf. Diurnall*, 2–9 Sept. 1650, E780/4, p. 485 (corrected pag.); Hodgson, pp. 140–1.

33 Anon. correspondent, *Perf. Diurnall*, 2–9 Sept. 1650, E780/4, p. 486 (corrected pag.); W. S. Douglas, *Cromwell's Scotch Campaigns: 1650–51* (E. Stock, London, 1898), pp. 89–90.

34 *Perf. Passages*, 9–13 Sept. 1650, E780/6, p. 71.

35 CSPD, 1650, p. 321; Hodgson, pp. 143, 267; Abbott, II, 323; *Severall Letters from Scotland* ([7 Sept.] 1650), E612/8, p. 4; Douglas, *Cromwell's Scotch Campaigns*, p. 92.

36 Abbott, II, 314, 322.

37 See for example C[harles] F[leetwood]'s letter in Hodgson, p. 267. (It is possible that the letter's author is Col. Charles Fairfax, who was also on the expedition.)

38 *Severall Procs in Parliament*, 15–22 Aug. 1650, E778/21, p. 692; *Perf. Diurnall*, 26 Aug.–2 Sept. 1650, E780/1, p. 470; Nickolls, p. 18.

39 *Perf. Passages*, 9–13 Sept. 1650, E780/6, p. 77; *A True Relation of the Routing of the Scotish Army, near Dunbar* (9 Sept. 1650), E612/9, p. 4; Abbott, II, 322.

40 Abbott, II, 314.

41 OPH, XIX, 341; Abbott, II, 316.

42 Not the evening, as Abbott has it (II, 323). See *Merc. Politicus*, 5–12 Sept 1650, E612/14, p. 218.

43 C. H. Firth, 'The battle of Dunbar', *TRHS*, new ser., XIV (1900), 36n.; Abbott, II, 323; Hodgson, p. 323; Carte, I, 381.

44 Baillie, III, 111; *Perf. Passages*, 9–13 Sept. 1650, E780/6, p. 77; Gilbert Burnet, *History of My Own Time*, ed. Osmund Airy (2 vols, Clarendon Press, Oxford, 1897), I, 96; Douglas, *Cromwell's Scotch Campaigns*, p. 107; CJ, VI, 464.

45 Stevenson, p. 178.
46 Abbott, II, 316.
47 Cadwell's account in Carte, I, 382.
48 Hodgson, pp. 144–5.
49 Rushworth's report in *OPH*, XIX, 341. For Leslie's statement see Ancram, *Correspondence*, II, 298; Firth, 'Dunbar', p. 41; Walker, *Historical Discourses*, p. 180.
50 *Memoirs of the Life of Ambrose Barnes*, Surtees Society, 50 (1867), 111.
51 *Merc. Politicus*, 12–19 Sept. 1650, E613/1, p. 228.
52 Hodgson, p. 146.
53 An anonymous correspondent in *Merc. Politicus*, 12–19 Sept. 1650, E613/1, pp. 227–8.
54 Hodgson, pp. 146–7; Abbott, II, 317, 323.
55 *A Brief Narrative of the Great Victorie … near Dunbar* (7 Sept. 1650), E612/7, p. 2; *Merc. Politicus*, 5–12 Sept. 1650, E612/14, p. 218; *A True Relation of the Routing of the Scotish Army*, p. 4; James Heath, *Flagellum: or the life and death, birth and burial of Oliver Cromwell, the late usurper* (L. R., London, 1663), pp. 98–9. Except for Heath, our sources do not identify by name the pass where Lambart fought the first engagement of the battle. Heath states that it was at Cockburnspath, but that would have placed it 6 miles from the English camp, and would hardly have allowed Lambart to get back in time for the main battle, in which we know he participated. Douglas (*Cromwell's Scotch Campaigns*, p. 109) interprets the pass to mean the ford over Spott Burn, but this does not agree with the primary sources cited above.
56 *Perf. Passages*, 9–13 Sept. 1650, E780/6, p. 72; *A Brief Narrative*, p. 2.
57 Cadwell in Carte, I, 383; Hodgson, pp. 147–8, 279; *C & P*, I, 292 n.3; *A Brief Narrative*, pp. 2–3; Abbott, II, 324.
58 Abbott, II, 324.
59 *OPH*, XIX, 341.
60 Douglas, *Cromwell's Scotch Campaigns*, p. 112.
61 *Perf. Passages*, 9–13 Sept. 1650, E780/6, p. 74.
62 Jaffray, *Diary*, pp. 57–8.
63 John Aubrey, *Miscellanies upon Various Subjects* (W. Ottridge, London, 1784), pp. 160–1.
64 Hodgson, p. 147.
65 Abbott, II, 334.
66 *Cromwelliana*, p. 91.
67 Carte, I, 384.
68 *Perf. Diurnall*, 9–16 Sept. 1650, E780/7, p. 503; Abbott, II, 331; *OPH*, XIX, 417–20.
69 Stevenson, p. 181.
70 Clarendon, *History*, V, 149; *Merc. Politicus*, 12–19 Sept. 1650, E613/1, p. 259; Hodgson, p. 147; Dow, *Cromwellian Scotland*, pp. 8–9; Nickolls, p. 24.
71 Abbott, II, 327, 331–2; *CSPD, 1650*, pp. 333, 339, 348–50, 352, 363, 394; Nickolls, p. 19.

72 They were John Owen, Joseph Caryl and Edward Bowles (Abbott, II, 346).
73 Jaffray, *Diary*, pp. 58–60.
74 *Cromwelliana*, p. 92.
75 Abbott, II, 354; Baillie, III, 119.
76 Abbott, II, 355; Dow, *Cromwellian Scotland*, p. 9; Ancram, *Correspondence*, II, 335n.; Stevenson, p. 195; Baillie, III, 125.
77 *Merc. Politicus*, 24–31 Oct. 1650, E615/10, p. 337; *Cromwelliana*, p. 92; Abbott, II, 357; Hodgson, p. 336.
78 Clar. MS 41, fo. 34.
79 Abbott, II, 363; *Merc. Politicus*, 12–19 Dec. 1650, E620/8, p. 467.
80 *Merc. Politicus*, 19–26 Dec. 1650, E620/12, p. 483.
81 Abbott, II, 335–6, 338–9.
82 *Merc. Politicus*, 19–26 Dec. 1650, E620/12, pp. 473, 477; Abbott, II, 369–72.
83 *Merc. Politicus*, 26 Dec. 1650.–1 Jan. 1651, E621/4, pp. 494, 497; Duffy, p. 156. For Dundas's detractors see Baillie, III, 125; Nicoll, p. 37; Heath, *Flagellum*, p. 107; Abbott, II, 373; Douglas, *Cromwell's Scotch Campaigns*, pp. 203n, 206.
84 Nicoll, p. 48; Nickolls, pp. 48–50; Stevenson, pp. 196–7; *C & P*, I, 346; Baillie, III, 107; *OPH*, XIX, 456; *CJ*, VI, 551, 557; *CSPD, 1651*, pp. 102–3, 177.
85 Abbott, II, 329.
86 Ibid., pp. 329, 393–5, 400; *Faithful Scout*, 14–21 Feb. 1651, E784/12, p. 72; *Cromwelliana*, 100; Add. MS 21419, fo. 333; Carte, I, 426; John Yonge Akerman (ed.), *Letters from Roundhead Officers, Written from Scotland and Chiefly Addressed to Captain Adam Baynes July MDCL –June MDCLX*, Bannatyne Club, 108 (1823), pp. 10, 12, 24.
87 *Faithful Scout*, 23–30 May 1651, E785/34, p. 183.
88 *CSPD, 1651*, pp. 91, 218; Abbott, II, 400, 403, 419; *Cromwelliana*, p. 102; Wariston, *Diary*, II, 54–5; *CJ*, VI, 579; Whitelocke, III, 308.
89 Whitelocke, III, 293, 300–1, 306, 310, 313; Add. MS 21420, fos 114, 122; Akerman, *Letters from Roundhead Officers*, p. 31; Abbott, II, 408, 415, 420, 424; *CSPD, 1651*, pp. 84, 98–9; *Perf. Diurnall*, 19–26 May 1651, E785/31, p. 1046; Wariston, *Diary*, II, 59; Nicoll, p. 50.
90 Wariston, *Diary*, II, 53; *OPH*, XIX, 480; *C & P*, II, 29; Abbott, II, 434–5. For the agricultural richness of Fife see *Merc. Politicus*, 24–31 July 1651, E638/10, p. 957.
91 Whitelocke, III, 310, 318; Ancram, *Correspondence*, II, 360; *CSPD, 1651*, pp. 555–66; Abbott, II, 430; Nicoll, p. 53.
92 Stevenson, p. 205; Abbott, II, 430; Wariston, *Diary*, II, 85; *Merc. Politicus*, 24–31 July 1651, E638/10, p. 953; Whitelocke, III, 321–3; Akerman, *Letters from Roundhead Officers*, pp. 34–5. Lambart's casualties may have been higher than he allowed, though Balfour's allegation (*Historical Works*, IV, 313) that both sides suffered equally is implausible.
93 Douglas, *Cromwell's Scotch Campaigns*, p. 277.
94 Stevenson, p. 206; Abbott, II, 431–2.
95 Abbott, II, 441; *C & P*, II, 34; Cary II, 305.

96 Stevenson pp. 206–7; Cary, ɪɪ, 305; *Merc. Politicus*, 14–21 Aug. 1651, E640/14, p. 1012; ibid., 21–8 Aug. 1651, E640/23, p. 1024; D. E. Underdown, *Royalist Conspiracy in England, 1649–1660* (Yale University Press, New Haven, Conn., 1960), pp. 42–7.

97 *OPH*, xx, 19. Thomas Wentworth had boasted that the army numbered over 20,000 at the beginning of August. This figure took no account of the drastic attrition that had occurred as soon as Charles left Stirling (ibid., pp. 4, 11).

98 *OPH*, xɪx, 498, 510; *CSPD, 1651*, pp. 301ff.; Whitelocke, ɪɪɪ, 332–3.

99 Nickolls, pp. 78–9; Cary, ɪɪ, 295, 297–81, 301–2; *CSPD, 1651*, pp. 307–8; Abbott, ɪɪ, 446–8; HMC, *De L'Isle and Dudley*, vɪ, 603.

100 Tanner MS 55, fo. 8; *CSPD, 1651*, pp. 327–8, 340, 344, 346; Whitelocke, ɪɪɪ, 335; *C & P*, ɪɪ, 35.

101 *CSPD, 1651*, p. 307; Cary, ɪɪ, 301; Whitelocke, ɪɪɪ, 331–2; Clar. MS 42, fo. 151; *Merc. Politicus*, 14–21 Aug. 1651, E640/14, pp. 1010–11.

102 Abbott, ɪɪ, 450–2; *Merc. Politicus*, 21–8 Aug. 1651, E640/23, p. 1019; Cary, ɪɪ, 327; *C & P*, ɪɪ, 41, 43.

103 Tanner MS 55, fos 2, 4; Hodgson, p. 152; *Merc. Politicus*, 28 Aug.–4 Sept. 1651, E641/4, p. 1038; Whitelocke, ɪɪɪ, 338, 343; *Two Letters from Col. Robert Lilburne* ([30 Aug.] 1651), E640/26 (printed in Cary, ɪɪ, 339–41, 343–4); *A Great Victory … near Wigon* ([29 Aug.] 1651), E640/27.

104 Clar. MS 42, fo. 151ᵛ; Tanner MS 55, fo. 50; *Merc. Politicus*, 21–8 Aug. 1651, E640/23, p. 1019; Ibid., 28 Aug.–4 Sept. 1651, E641/4, p. 1041; Whitelocke, ɪɪɪ, 335–6, 340; *Several Procs in Parliament* (28 Aug.–4 Sept. 1651, E787/12, pp. 1557–8, 1564; HMC, *Lechmere*, p. 299; Abbott, ɪɪ, 455; Duffy, p. 157; P. Styles, *Studies in Seventeenth Century West Midland History* (Roundwood Press, Kineton, Warwicks, 1978), p. 249.

105 *Faithful Scout*, 29 Aug.–5 Sept. 1651, E787/13, p. 256; *Perf. Passages*, 29 Aug.–5 Sept. 1651, E787/14, p. 370; *Severall Procs in Parliament*, 28 Aug.–4 Sept. 1651, E787/12, p. 1558; *Merc. Politicus*, 28 Aug.–4 Sept. 1651, E641/4, p. 1042; *Wkly Intell.*, 26 Aug.–2 Sept. 1651, E641/2, p. 272; Whitelocke, ɪɪɪ, 344; Clar. MS 42, fo. 151ᵛ.

106 Abbott, ɪɪ, 455; Tanner MS 55, fo. 23; *Merc. Politicus*, 28 Aug.–4 Sept. 1651, E641/4, pp. 1042–4; Whitelocke, ɪɪɪ, 337–8. There were other militia regiments on their way to Worcester, which did not arrive in time for the battle.

107 Abbott, ɪɪ, 456.

108 Ibid., p. 458; Styles, *Studies*, p. 249.

109 *Perf. Diurnall*, 8–15 Sept. 1651, E787/19, p. 1293; *Severall Procs in Parliament*, 4–11 Sept. 1651, E787/16, p. 1566; HMC, *Lechmere*, p. 299; *Merc. Politicus*, 4–11 Sept. 1651, E641/12, p. 1052.

110 Clar. MS 42, fos 151ᵛ–2; Tanner MS 55, fo. 37–7ᵛ; Abbott, ɪɪ, 459; Cary, ɪɪ, 363.

111 The royalist colonel Raynes would later accuse Leslie of having done nothing during the whole battle (Clar. MS 42, fo. 167).

112 Tanner MS 55, fo. 37ᵛ. Whitelocke (ɪɪɪ, 346), following the newsbooks,

mistranscribes 'mount and works' as 'mountain works'. For Cromwell's bravery see *Merc. Politicus*, 4–11 Sept. 1651, E641/12, p. 1054.

113 Clar. MS 42, fos 149ᵛ, 167; *Merc. Politicus*, 4–11 Sept. 1651, E641/12, p. 1053; Cary, ii, 363; Tanner MS 55, fos 37ᵛ–8.

114 From the letter of an anonymous royalist prisoner, Clar. MS 42, fo. 152ᵛ.

115 HLRO, Braye MS 3, fo. 34 (printed in HMC, *Braye*, p. 175); Clar. MS 42, fo. 149ᵛ; *Wkly Intell.*, 2–9 Sept. 1651, E641/11, p. 278.

116 D. Murtagh, 'Col. Edward Wogan', *Irish Sword*, 2 (1954–6), p. 49. Other accounts of the third phase of the battle are in Abbott, ii, 461, Tanner MS 55, fo. 50; *Faithful Scout*, 5–12 Sept. 1651, E787/18, p. 258; Cary, ii, 354; Ronald Hutton, *Charles II* (Clarendon Press, Oxford, 1989), pp. 64–7.

117 These figures are a trifle high if we agree that the royalist army at Worcester was no more than 11,000 strong (Abbott, ii, 464; Whitelocke, iii, 348–9; Clar. MS 42, fo. 151). Cromwell, it is true, estimated the royalist army at 16,000 (Abbott, ii, 462), but in order to accept this figure we must discount the reports of the army's attrition from disease and desertion. For the carnage see also HLRO, Braye MS 3, fo. 34.

118 For a reliable account of the king's escape see Hutton, *Charles ii*, pp. 67–70.

119 Gardiner, *C & P*, ii, 52–6; Clar. MS 42, fo. 150; Whitelocke, iii, 349; *Merc. Politicus*, 4–11 Sept. 1651, E641/12, pp. 1057–8.

120 *CJ*, vii, 24–5.

121 Whitelocke, iii, 352; Abbott, ii, 472, 474, 476; *CJ*, vii, 46; *C & P*, ii, 62–5.

122 C. H. Firth (ed.), *Scotland and the Commonwealth …. August 1651 to December 1653*, SHS, xviii (1895), 2–3, 11–12, 14–16, 325; Cary, ii, 327–30; Whitelocke, iii, 334; Stevenson, pp. 207–8; Dow, *Cromwellian Scotland*, pp. 11, 14; Tanner MS 55, fo. 19; Nicoll, p. 58. Gardiner states that 'it seems likely that the Scottish authorities exaggerated the slaughter' at Dundee (*C & P*, ii, 68 n.). However, the army secretary William Clarke acknowledged a toll of 800 (Cary, ii, 366), so on balance it seems that the higher estimate is correct.

123 *Merc. Politicus*, 11–18 Sept. 1651, E641/20, p. 1076.

124 The commissioners were Oliver St John, Sir Henry Vane junior, Maj. Richard Salwey, Col. George Fenwick, Maj.-Gen. John Lambart, Maj.-Gen. Richard Deane, Alderman Tichborne and Lt-Gen. George Monk (Dow, *Cromwellian Scotland*, pp. 31–2; *CJ*, vii, 30). For the revolutionary quality of the new regime in Scotland, see Nicoll, pp. 69–70, 73.

Chapter 13   The Army and the Expulsion of the Rump Parliament

1 *CJ*, vi, 141.

2 *CJ*, vi, 153; *The Petition of the General Council of Officers … to … the Commons of England* (3 Mar. 1649), E545/30.

3 Whitelocke, iii, 66–7; Tanner MS 56, fos 91–2ᵛ; *CJ*, vi, 280; *The Petition of Thomas Lord Fairfax and his Councel of Officers for the Recalling of All Penal*

Laws Made against Private Meetings, the Punishing of Prophaneness, &c. (16 Aug. 1649), E569/22.

4   Abbott, II, 189; Add. MS 21418, fo. 286.

5   John Lilburne, *Apologetical Narration* (L. I., Amsterdam, Apr. 1652), E659/30, pp. 12–13; Ludlow[e], I, 244–6. The quotation is from 2 Samuel 3:39.

6   Abbott, II, 325; Worc. MS 181, unfol., 29 Oct. 1650, cited in Massarella, p. 269.

7   See the letters addressed to Cromwell by Peter Chamberlen and Samuel Chidley in Nickolls, pp. 50–1, 58–64.

8   Abbott, II, 433; Cary, II, 344.

9   Abbott, II, 463; Cary, II, 375–6.

10 Worden, p. 265.

11 *C to P*, p. 9.

12 Worden, pp. 275, 278.

13 *OPH*, xx, 57.

14 It will be remembered that the second Agreement would have excluded well over half the adult males from the franchise. See above, pp. 292–3.

15 *CJ*, VII, 20.

16 Ibid., pp. 36–7.

17 HMC, *De L'Isle and Dudley*, VI, 609; Abbott, II, 501.

18 Worden, pp. 276, 278; *C to P*, pp. 29–30; Abbott, II, 499; *CJ*, VII, 38–9; Massarella, p. 278; Whitelocke, III, 372–5.

19 M. Cotterell, 'Interregnum law reform: the Hale Commission of 1652', *EHR*, LXXXIII (1968), 694, 703; Worden, pp. 271, 280. Massarella, p. 281. The army's representatives on the Hale Commission included Disbrowe, Tomlinson, Packer, Hugh Peters, and John Rushworth (*CJ*, VII, 74).

20 Worden, p. 282; *CJ*, VII, 55, 71–5, 77, 80, 101, 104; Lilburne, *Apologetical Narration*, pp. 19–20; *Faithful Scout*, 23–30 Jan. 1652, E793/20, pp. 418–21. According to the *Faithful Scout*, the officers were divided over Lilburne; moreover the content of the 27 Jan. petition is unknown. The fact that it was submitted at the height of the Lilburne-Hesilrige conflict, however, strongly suggests that it dealt in part with that issue.

21 Worden, pp. 269–70; Abbott, II, 515; *CJ*, VII, 84–7 *et passim*; Whitelocke, III, 392. For a jaundiced and to my mind unwarranted view of Cromwell's motivation on this issue, see Ludlow[e], I, 345. For the more and more extensive confiscations of royalist land see *CJ*, VII, 147–51 *et passim*.

22 Worden, p. 298; *CJ*, VII, 131.

23 Add. MS 37344 (Whitelocke's annals), fo. 93ᵛ. For Lambart's early military career see the forthcoming York University (Toronto) PhD thesis on the Northern Army by Jennifer Jones.

24 *CJ*, VII, 77, 79, 133–4, 142; Abbott, II, 517; Hutchinson, p. 204; Whitelocke, III, 438; *CSPD, 1652–3*, pp. 242, 260, 263. I am not persuaded by Whitelocke's assertion (III, 431) that Lambart blamed Cromwell for the fiasco

of the Irish command. The confidence in him that Cromwell displayed in 1653 indicates that their falling-out must have occurred later.

25 *A Declaration of the Armie to his Excellency the Lord General Cromwel* ([10 Aug.] 1652), E673/13; *The Humble Petition of the Officers of the Army* ([14 Aug.] 1652), BL, 669.f.16/62; *Wkly Intell.*, 10–17 Aug. 1652, E674/3, p. 561; *CJ*, VII, 164. Gardiner and Abbott's misleading statement that Cromwell did not sign the petition, when in fact it was submitted in the name of all the officers, seems to arise from a misreading of the Venetian envoy's comment, dated 5/15 August, which clearly referred to the 2 August draft of the petition. Abbott overlooked the fact that the envoy's letter was dated new style and therefore could not possibly have referred to the 13 August version. (Cf. Gardiner, *C & P*, II, 223–4; *CSPV, 1647–52*, p. 270; Abbott, II, 573.) I am dubious of Ludlowe's second-hand account, according to which Cromwell pretended to oppose the petition and put Disbrowe up to speaking against it. Apart from the fact that he was in Ireland at the time, Ludlowe's rooted hostility to Cromwell makes him untrustworthy on this point (Ludlow[e], I, 348).

26 *CJ*, VII, 175, 178; Whitelocke, III, 446; Worden, p. 309; *C to P*, p. 41n. 36.

27 *CJ*, VII, 171; Worden, p. 309; HMC, *Leyborne-Popham*, 104; *Nicholas Papers*, I, ed. G. F. Warner, Camden Society, new ser., XL (1886), 310; *Wkly Intell.*, 21–8 Sept. 1652, E675/23, p. 603.

28 Quoted by M. E. James in his illuminating essay 'English politics and the concept of honour', in his *Society, Politics and Culture* (Cambridge University Press, Cambridge, 1986), p. 341. See also pp. 345, 389; and Maurice Keen, *Chivalry* (Yale University Press, New Haven, Conn., 1984), p. 177.

29 *A & O*, II, 148–51.

30 *CJ*, VII, 110, 130, 140, 186–7, 217; Worden, p. 284; *C to P*, p. 38; *A & O*, II, 618–20; Clar. MS 45, fos 356, 485.

31 *Faithful Scout*, 1–8 Oct. 1652, E799/10, p. 708. It is true, as Worden points out (p. 310), that some of the officers appeared to extend an olive branch to parliament in a pamphlet entitled *The Beacons Quenched* (8 Oct. 1652), E678/3, which bore the names of Pride, Goffe and several others. However, the object of the pamphlet was to blacken the London presbyterians. The positive reference to MPs as 'the happy instruments of our freedom, and painful labourers in the work of Christ' (p. 9) appears to have been a tactical attempt to drive a wedge between the MPs and the City presbyterians. I doubt the sincerity of the officers' apparent benevolence towards parliament in the light of the hostility that was expressed in several other documents at the time.

32 Ludlow[e], I, 345–6, 350–1. Firth points out that Ludlowe's version of events is confirmed by Daniel O'Neill's letter to Hyde (ibid., p. 347 n.). See also Abbott, III, 55.

33 Whitelocke, III, 468–73.

34 *CJ*, VII, 217; M. Noble, *The Lives of the English Regicides* (2 vols, J. Stockdale, London, 1798), I, 277; Clives Holmes, *The Eastern Association in the English Civil War* (Cambridge University Press, Cambridge, 1974), p. 176. The *DNB*

(*sub* Robert Hammond) errs in stating that Thomas Hammond died before 1652. In July 1653 he bought crown land in Surrey (PRO, E121/4/8/58).

35 Ludlow[e], I, 347; *C to P*, p. 47.

36 *CJ*, VII, 220–1.

37 J. Mayer, 'Inedited Letters of Cromwell, Colonel Jones, Bradshaw and Other regicides', *Transactions of the Historic Society of Lancashire and Cheshire*, new ser., I, (1860–1), 214, 218; Woolrych, *C to P*, 47; B. S. Capp, *The Fifth Monarchy Men* (Faber and Faber, London, 1972), pp. 57, 59. See also William Erbury, *The Bishop of London* ([8 Jan.] 1653), E684/26, pp. 1–2; Worden, pp. 315–16.

38 Reece, p. 287; *CJ*, VII, 128, 224, 241–2; *CSPD, 1651–2*, pp. 424, 432, and *1652–3*, p. 95; *CSPV, 1653–4*, p. 9.

39 *CSPD, 1652–3*, pp. 261, 266, 291, 297. In the end, thanks to the dissolution, only 100 soldiers from Barkstead's regiment were sent to sea.

40 Ian Gentles, 'London Levellers in the English Revolution: the Chidleys and their circle', *JEH*, 29 (1978), 303–7; J. E. Farnell, 'The usurpation of honest London householders: Barebone's parliament', *EHR*, LXXXII (1967), 41; *Moderate Intell.*, 22–9 Dec. 1652, E684/14, p. 2630; *Flying Eagle*, 25 Dec. 1652 – 1 Jan. 1653, E684/18, p. 40; Clar. MS 45, fos 205^v, 222, 223, 270, 292. The price of coal continued to rise to above £6 a chaldron by early April. It was also around this time that the press gangs were at their most active. However, the newsbooks indicate that both matters caused serious hardship earlier in the winter as well.

41 Erbury, *Bishop of London*, pp. 1–2, 7; C. H. Firth, 'Cromwell and the expulsion of the Long Parliament in 1653', *EHR*, VIII (1893), 527; Worden, pp. 317–18; *C to P*, pp. 48–9.

42 Cf. Norman Cohn, *The Pursuit of the Millennium* (Secker & Warburg, London, 1957), pp. 31–2. For a specimen of the circular letter from headquarters bearing the actual signature of Thomas Margetts, see the Bodleian Library's untitled broadside in the Fairfax Deposit, Smith. newsb.a.3/5. It is also reproduced in *Merc. Politicus*, 3–10 Feb. 1653, E686/12, pp. 2113–16. For the answer of the Edinburgh artillery officers see *Perf. Diurnall*, 28 Mar.–4 Apr. 1653, E211/11, pp. 2605–7. Similarly chiliastic responses were recorded from Robert Lilburne's and Anthony Morgan's regiments in Scotland (Massarella, pp. 295–6).

43 Abbott, II, 484–5, 487; *CJ*, VII, 20.

44 Both Worden (pp. 287–8) and Woolrych (*C to P*, pp. 11, 19) discern a lack of political realism in the officers' desire for new elections. However, as we have seen above (pp. 292–3) the Levellers and the Council of Officers were quite prepared in 1648–9 to exclude more than half the adult male population from the franchise. From 1651 to 1653 the officers, while not ready to go as far as the Fifth Monarchists, who would have excluded all but the 'Saints', nevertheless appreciated the need to eliminate the commonwealth's enemies from the electoral process.

45 Worden, p. 266; *CJ*, vii, 36–7.
46 *CJ*, vii, 244.
47 *C to P*, pp. 54–5.
48 Worden, p. 331; *EHR*, viii (1893), 527.
49 Clar. MS 45, fo. 204, printed in *EHR*, viii (1893), 527.
50 *EHR*, viii (1893), p. 530; James Heath, *Flagellum,: or the life and death, birth and burial of of Oliver Cromwell* the late usurper (L. R., London, 1663), pp. 133–4; Ludlow[e], i, 356; HMC, *Portland*, iii, 201.
51 Ludlow[e], i, 348–9; *C to P*, pp. 56–7; Abbott, ii, 626; Whitelocke, iv, 2.
52 Clar. MS 45, fos 222, 223, 270ᵛ. Cf. Dow, who, stresses how short of troops Robert Lilburne was in this period when he was striving to combat the highland rising. F. D. Dow, *Cromwellian Scotland, 1651–1660* (John Donald, Edinburgh, 1979), pp. 79–80.
53 *CJ*, vii, 258–9.
54 Ibid., pp. 266, 268–9; Abbott, ii, 624.
55 *C & P*, ii, 98–100; Abbott, ii, 520; *CJ*, vii, 258–9.
56 *CJ*, vii, 258–9 (emphasis added); *OPH*, xx, 125; *C to P*, pp. 53–4.
57 See Christopher Hill's essay 'Puritans and "the dark corners of the land"', repr. in his *Change and Continuity in Seventeenth-Century England* (Weidenfeld and Nicolson, London, 1974), pp. 32–8; *A & O*, ii, 342–8; Massarella, p. 263.
58 *C & P*, ii, 249, 251–2; Whitelocke, ii, 252–3; Clar. MS 45, fo. 269; *C to P*, pp. 58, 60–1; Thomas Richards, *History of the Puritan Movement in Wales* (National Eisteddfod Association, London, 1920), pp. 271–2; Abbott, iii, 57; Worden, p. 328.
59 *EHR*, viii (1893), 529; Whitelocke, iv, 2.
60 *CJ*, vii, 273. The army's petition has not survived, but its contents were reported by the French ambassador, Bordeaux (PRO30/3/90, fo. 653). See also *C & P*, ii, 252–3; and *C to P*, p. 61.
61 The Instrument of Government would have retained the £200 qualification, but, unlike the Rump, the officers who framed the Instrument were careful to exclude from the franchise Roman Catholics and anyone who had aided any of the wars against parliament, including the Irish rebellion (*Const. Docs*, p. 410).
62 *CJ*, vii, 277–8.
63 Clar. MS 45, fo. 293.
64 *C & P*, ii, 255. I am sceptical of the Venetian ambassador's speculation that Harrison would have liked to step into Cromwell's shoes but lacked the boldness to confront him (*CSPV, 1653–4*, p. 60).
65 Clar. MS 45, fo. 292ᵛ. Woolrych points out that on the 18th or 19th the Council of Officers again agreed to dissolve the Rump (*C to P*, p. 80); however, the references which he cites may refer to the same meeting as Hyde's correspondent reported as occurring on the 15th.
66 Ludlow[e], i, 351; *C to P*, p. 80.

67 *CSPD, 1652–3*, pp. 205, 274; Clar. MS 45, fos 292, 270, 223; *Humble Remonstrance of Many Thousands* ([21 Apr.] 1653), E692/4, pp. 6–7 (corrected pag.).

68 Whitelocke, iv, 4–5; *EHR*, viii (1893), 531–2; *C & P*, ii, 258; *C to P*, pp. 63–4; Abbott, iii, 59.

69 Whitelocke, iv, 5.

70 John Streater, *Secret Reasons of State* ([23 May] 1659), E983/24, pp. 2–3. The best accounts of the dissolution of parliament on 20 April 1653 are Whitelocke's (iv, 4–6), and Algernon Sidney's as told to his father the Earl of Leicester (HMC, *De L'Isle and Dudley*, vi, 615–16). I have supplemented them with the account of the Genoese ambassador, which is printed in Firth, 'The expulsion of the Long Parliament', *History*, new ser., ii (1917–18), 135–6. Ludlowe's account (i, 351–5), which was evidently derived from Maj.-Gen. Harrison three years later, is not wholly to be trusted.

71 *OPH*, xx, 130.

72 Ludlow[e], i, 352. I am dubious of the impression conveyed by Ludlowe that Harrison tried at first to restrain Cromwell from going through with the dissolution. If anyone wanted more fervently than Cromwell to be rid of the Rump it was Harrison. The account in the *Moderate Publisher*, 15–22 Apr. 1653, E211/21, p. 813, gives the impression that Harrison and Cromwell were hand in glove at this moment.

73 Worden, p. 336.

74 Firth, 'The expulsion of the Long Parliament', p. 194.

75 Streater, *Secret Reasons of State*, p. 3.

76 *Several Procs in Parliament*, 21–8 Apr. 1653, E211/24, p. 2945; ibid., 28 Apr.–5 May 1653, E213/2, p. 2959; *Rump Songs* (H. Brome & H. Marsh, London, 1662), pt i, 305, 320; *CSPV, 1653–4*, pp. 64–5; Clar. MS 45, fos 326ᵛ, 358; Whitelocke, iv, 9; *OPH*, xx, 145–7; Massarella, pp. 309–10; Tanner MS 52, fo. 13.

77 Worden, pp. 345, 363.

78 *C to P*, pp. 80–1.

79 Abbott, iii, 60; *C to P*, p. 89.

80 *Declaration of the Grounds and Reasons for Dissolving the Parliament* (22 Apr. 1653), in *OPH*, xx, 140.

81 Worden, p. 348; Streater, *Secret Reasons of State*, p. 4; Hutchinson, p. 205; *C to P*, pp. 69–71, 85–90; Abbott, iii, 56.

82 *Another Declaration … by the Lord Generall and his Council of Officers* (26 Apr. 1653), E693/17, pp. 4, 6; *A Letter to a Gentleman in the Country* (3 May 1653), E697/2, pp. 10–11; John Spittlehouse, *The Army Vindicated* ([24 Apr.] 1653), E693/1. Thomason acquired his copy of *Another Declaration* on 3 May; however *Several Procs in Parliament*, 21–8 Apr. 1653, E211/24, pp. 2957–9, prints the text under 26 April. Although the pamphlet is probably spurious (the printer, T. Brewen, was not employed for any of the official army publications so far as I am aware), it seems to contain accurate information about army affairs, and is therefore a valuable source. It has, as Woolrych says,

'the kind of authority attaching to a press release' issued by the officers or one of their agents. Cf. Austin Woolrych, 'The calling of Barebone's parliament', *EHR*, LXXX (1965), 495n; Worden, 353; *C to P*, p. 52 n. 62).

83 The Army's *Declaration* is printed in *OPH*, xx, 137–43. For Cromwell's statement see Tanner MS 52, fo. 13. The officers' letter to Ireland is printed in *The Fifth Monarchy ... Asserted* ([28 Aug.] 1659), E993/31, p. 22.

84 I do not think there is any substance to the speculation that Cromwell acted to save himself from the threat of being pre-empted by Harrison or Lambart. *Pace* the royalist commentator, his enemies in the spring of 1653 were in parliament, not the army. See *Nicholas Papers*, II, Camden Society, new ser., L (1892), 13. Cf. Abbott, II, 650–1.

85 *C to P*, pp. 101–2.

86 Whitelocke, IV, 9; Abbott, III, 13; *Clarke Papers*, III, 2; Gentles, 'London Levellers in the English Revolution', pp. 295–7; D. Veall, *The Popular Movement for Law Reform 1640–1660* (Oxford University Press, London, 1970), pp. 128–31.

87 *CSPD, 1652–3*, p. 293; Abbott, III, 13.

88 Abbott, III, 32.

89 Clar. MS 45, fos 335, 486ᵛ; D. A. Johnson and D. G. Vaisey, *Staffordshire and the Great Rebellion* (Staffordshire County Council, Stafford, 1965), pp. 76–7.

90 *CSPD, 1652–3*, pp. 299–301, 339; *C & P*, II, 284; HMC, *Portland*, III, 200; *Several Procs in Parliament*, 21–8 Apr. 1653, E211/24, p. 2952; Johnson and Vaisey, *Staffordshire and the Great Rebellion*, pp. 73–4; *Clarke Papers*, III, 4; Ludlow[e], I, 358; Massarella, p. 312; *C to P*, p. 141; Clar. MS 45, fos 381ᵛ, 439.

91 Mayer, 'Inedited Letters,' p. 226; *Clarke Papers*, III, 8; Whitelocke, IV, 15.

92 Massarella, p. 323; *C to P*, pp. 132, 431–2.

93 *C to P*, pp. 128–9, appendix B.

94 Abbott, III, 51–66. As Woolrych points out (*C to P*, pp. 148–9) Abbott mistranscribed 'a day' as 'the day', which had the effect of making Cromwell sound like a Fifth Monarchist.

Epilogue

1 *Memoirs of the Life of Mr. Ambrose Barnes*, Surtees Society, 50 (1867), 109.

2 *Vox Militaris* [11 Aug. 1647], E401/24, p. 4.

3 William Allen, *A Faithful Memorial of that Remarkable Meeting ... at Windsor Castle in ... 1648* [27 Apr.] 1659), E979/3, p. 3.

4 *The Souldiers Demand* (Bristol, [18 May] 1649), E555/29, pp. 1, 12.

5 See above, p. 347.

Bibliography

This bibliography includes all sources listed in the notes, apart from the pamphlets and newsbooks in the British Library's Thomason Collection which are too numerous to itemize separately. Unless otherwise noted, contemporary printed sources may be found in the British Library. Items from the Thomason collection are recognizable by call numbers preceded by the letter E *or* (for broadsides) by the initial digits 669. The letter E in manuscript references stands for Exchequer in the Public Record Office.

A   Primary Sources

1   Manuscripts

Bodleian Library

Thomas Carte MSS, vols 25–9 (correspondence of the Marquess of Ormond, June 1649–Jan. 1652).
Clarendon MSS, vols 24–45 (Jan. 1645–June 1653).
Nalson MSS, vols 12 (1641–59), 15 (1647–9), 22 (various dates, Interregnum).
Rawlinson MS B239 (conveyances for bishops' lands).
Tanner MSS, (parliamentary letters and papers), vols 52–61 (1644–58).
MS Top. Bucks. C 11 (Cuddington MSS, 1623–1713).

Bristol Record Office

Common Council Proceedings, 04624 (4): 1642–9; 04624 (5): 1649–85.

British Library

Add. MS 4929 (Thoresby Papers vol. IV: sermon notes by Thomas, 3rd Baron Fairfax and his wife Anne).
Add. MS 5015* (royal letters, warrants, etc. 1620–1722).

Add. MSS 18777–80 (Diary of Walter Yonge, 19 Sept. 1642–10 Dec. 1645).

Add. MS 18979 (original letters addressed to Thomas, Ferdinando and Thomas, 1st, 2nd, and 3rd Lord Fairfax ... 1625–88).

Add. MSS 19398–9 (original letters ... of royal and noble persons, vol. ɪ, 1399–1646; vol. ɪɪ, 1646–1768).

Add. MS 25465 (Collectanea Hunteriana Journal of Occurrences 1643–46 [a copy of Thomas Juxon's diary]).

Add. MS 31116 (Parliamentary Diary of Lawrence Whitacre, 1642–7).

Add. MS 34253 (Civil War Papers 1640–7, mainly addressed to Edward Montagu, 2nd Earl of Manchester).

Add. MS 37344 (Bulstrode Whitelocke's Annals, 1645–9).

Egerton MSS, vol. 1048 (parliamentary documents, 1624–59).

——vol. 2126 (papers of Sir William Sydenham, governor of the Isle of Wight, 1618–56).

——vol. 2518 (historical letters and papers 1556–1753).

Harley MSS, vol. 166 (Parliamentary Diary of Sir Simonds D'Ewes 1643–45).

——vol. 252, fo. 33–3ᵛ (An Historicall Diarie of the Militarie Proceedings of ... Sir Thomas Fairfax ... by John Rushworth ... April 1st [to 14th] 1645).

——vol. 986 (R. Symonds, The Kings Army 1643).

——vol. 1236 (letters, etc. by royal, noble and eminent persons. Temp. Henry VI to George III).

——vol. 4808 (royal and other letters, Henry VII–1645).

——vol. 4898 (Inventory of the Effects of King Charles I).

——vol. 7001 (original letters 1633–1711).

Loan 29/123/Misc. 31 (Defence of the Earl of Manchester after the Second Newberry Battle 1644).

Loan 29/175–6 (Harley Papers 1644–47, 1647–52).

Microfilm 330 (Duke of Northumberland MSS at Alnwick Castle: vols 547 [Letterbook of John Fitzjames, 20 Oct. 1645–23 June 1647], 548 [continuation, 30 Aug. 1647–10 Nov. 1649]).

Sloane MSS vol. 1519 (original letters 1574–1667).

——vol. 5247 ('Cornetes', or Flags and Arms in Colors, of the several Companies of the Earl of Essex's Army ... in the time of the Commonwealth).

Stowe MSS, vol. 143 (historical collections, fifteenth to eighteenth century).

——vol. 184 (historical papers 1628–51).

——vol. 189 (historical letters and papers 1641–60).

Chequers Court, Bucks

MS 782 (William Clarke's account book 1649–59: Harvester microfilm, reel 17, 4/8).

Derbyshire Record Office

1232 M (correspondence and other papers relating to the career of Thomas Sanders of Little Ireton in the Civil War and Commonwealth Period).

Dr Williams's Library

Baxter Letters (6 vols).
MS 24.50 (Thomas Juxon, A Contemporary Chronicle, Nov. 1643–Aug. 1647).

Drapers' Company, London

Index of Apprentices 1615–1750.

Gloucestershire Record Office

Corporation Minute Book 1652–6, GBR B3/2.

Guildhall Library, London

MS 11592A (Grocers' Company Admissions 1345 – c.1670 [photostat]).
MS 15860/4 (Haberdashers' Company, Apprenticeship Bindings 1610–30).
MS 15857/1, unfol. (Haberdashers' Company, Freedom Admissions 1526–1641).

House of Lords Record Office

Books of Orders, Ordinances, etc. (of both Houses), 4 Nov. 1644–1 Nov. 1645, B5.
A Book of Orders, 1644–5, B14.
Braye MS 96 (John Browne's Commonplace Book [photocopy of the original in Yale University Library]).
Main Papers (Feb.–Jan. 1649).
Manuscript House of Commons Journal, vol. xxxiii (2 Sept. 1648–13 June 1649).
Nalson MSS, vol. iv (photocopy).

Huntington Library, San Marino, California

Ellesmere MS 7778 (anonymous protest against the Self-Denying Ordinance, 1645).

Inner Temple, London

Admissions (typescript), vols i (1505–1659), ii (1660–1750).

Institute of Historical Research London

T.C.C. Dale, 'The Members of the City Companies in 1641' (typescript, 1935).

City of Kingston upon Hull Record Office

Bench Books 5 (1609–50), 6 (1650–64).

Leathersellers' Company, London

Index of Apprentices 1629–77.
Register of Apprentices 1629–77.
Index to Names of Apprentices and early members of Yeomanry, Livery and Court, 1444–1630.
Index to Freemen 1630–1694.
Register of Freemen 1630–1694.

National Library of Scotland

Advocates' MS 35.5.11 (Clarke Papers).

National Library of Wales

Brogyntyn MSS: Clenennau Letters and Papers.
MS 11434B (A Vindication of the Army and Parliament [probably by Morgan Llwyd, *c.*1649]).
MS 11439D (letters and papers addressed to Morgan Llwyd).
MS 11440D (Letterbook of Colonel John Jones 1651–60).
MS 14441D (correspondence of Colonel John Jones).

Public Record Office

Chancery
C54 (Close Rolls).
Computerized list of JPs for 1643–1700, based on C231/6–8, C181/6–7.

Exchequer
E101/67/11A (Treasurers at Warre, Accounts Various, Leger of Assessments for the Armie 1645–9).
E101/67/11B (Second Accompt of the Treasures at Warr, 1649–52).
E121 (crown lands, certificates as to the sale of).
E307 (deeds of sale, fee-farm rents, Interregnum).
E315/5 (sums due to troops in the employment of the Parliament, 1647–52).
E351/301 (Pipe Office Declared Accounts: the account of Justinian Peard, treasurer of Plymouth garrison, 8 Feb. 1646–12 June 1649).

E351/302 (Pipe Office Declared Accounts: treasurers at war's accounts, 28 Mar. 1645–25 Dec. 1651).

E351/303 (Colonel R. Hammond, governor of the Isle of Wight, 1647 and 1648).

E351/304 (W. Leman and J. Blackwell, treasurers at war 25 Dec. 1651–24 July 1653).

E351/305 (continuation, 24 June 1653–2 Feb. 1660).

PRO31/3 (Paris Archives, Baschet's Transcripts), vols 75–89 (Sept. 1644–Dec. 1649).

State Papers

SP21 (State Papers Domestic, Interregnum: Committee of Both Kingdoms or Derby House Committee, 1644–50).

SP23 (Committee for Compounding with Delinquents, 1643–60).

SP24 (Committee and Commissioners for Indemnity, 1647–56).

SP25/118 (Council of State charges for the war in Ireland, 1 Mar. 1649–16 Feb. 1650).

SP26/1–4 (trustees for fee farms, contracts or agreements for purchase).

SP28 (Commonwealth Exchequer Papers).

SP46 (State Papers Domestic: Supplementary, 1653–5).

Society of Genealogists, London

Percival Lloyd, 'Index of Seventeenth Century London Citizens' (typescript).

Tatton Park, Cheshire

MS 104 (Diary of Nehemiah Wallington 1644–8).

Thoresby Society, Leeds

MS SD ix (An Acompt of Contingencies Disbursed since December 1646 by Warrants from his Excy the Lord General Fairfax).

Worcester College: Clarke Papers

Note: the Clarke Papers at Worcester College have been microfilmed and edited by G. E. Aylmer for Harvester Press, Brighton, 1977.

MS 16 (copies of letters and papers relating to the army and parliament, Nov. 1648–Nov. 1649).

MS 17 (copies of letters and papers relating to the army and parliament, Nov. 1649–Nov. 1650).

MS 18 (copies of letters between army members, and of letters and declarations between the officers in London and those of various garrisons, mainly 1649–50).

MS 41 (copies of letters and papers relating to the army and parliament 1646–7).

MS 65 (Proceedings of the General Council of the Army and its committees Oct.–Nov. 1647).

MS 66 (Minutes of the Committee of General Officers, Aug.–Nov. 1647).

MS 67 (military commissions granted during 1647–50, etc.).

MS 69 (Sir Tho. Fairfax's order book 1648–9 [actually begins 1 Feb. 1649 and ends 24 June 1650]).

MS 72 (Proceedings of the Committee of Officers for Garrisons and Supernumeraries Dec. 1648).

MS 110 (copies of letters and papers relating to the army and parliament, 1647–8).

MS 114 (copies of letters and papers relating to the army and parliament, 1648–9; from the back: Proceedings of the General Council of Officers, July 1647, Dec. 1648–Jan. 1649).

York City Archives

MS E63 (City of York Association Committee Proceedings, 1645–52).

2   Printed Sources

Abbott, Wilbur Cortez (ed.), *The Writings and Speeches of Oliver Cromwell*, 4 vols (Harvard University Press, Cambridge, Mass., 1937–47).

Akerman, John Yonge (ed.), *Letters from Roundhead Officers, Written from Scotland and Chiefly Addressed to Captain Adam Baynes July MDCL – June MDCLX*, Bannatyne Club, 108 (1823).

Ancram, *Correspondence of Sir Robert Kerr, First Earl of Ancram, and his son William*, ed. David Laing, 2 vols (R. & R. Clark, Edinburgh, 1875).

Aubrey, John, *Miscellanies upon Various Subjects* (W. Ottridge, London, 1784).

—— *Wiltshire, The Topographical Collections of John Aubrey, F. R. S., A. D. 1659–70*, ed. John Edward Jackson, Wiltshire Archaeological and Natural History Society (1862).

Baillie, Robert, *Letters and Journals*, ed. David Laing, 3 vols, Bannatyne Club, 72, 73, 77 (1841).

Balfour, Sir James, *Historical Works*, iv (W. Aitchison, Edinburgh, 1825).

Bamfeild, Col. Joseph, *Colonel Joseph Bamfeild's Apologie* (The Hague, 1685).

Bates, Frederic Alan, *Graves Memoirs of the Civil War* (William Blackwood and Sons, London, 1927).

Baxter, Richard, *Reliquiae Baxterianae*, ed. Matthew Silvester (T. Parkhurst et al., London, 1696).

Bedfordshire Historical Record Society, xxxv: H. G. Tibbutt, *Colonel John Okey* (1955).

—— xxxviii: *The Tower of London Letterbook of Sir Lewis Dyve, 1646–47*, ed. H. G. Tibbutt (1958).

Bell, Robert (ed.), *Memorials of the Civil War*, 2 vols (Richard Bentley, London, 1849).

Borlase, Edmund, *The History of the Irish Rebellion* (Oli Nelson and Charles Connor, Dublin, 1743).

Boys, John, MP, 'The parliamentary diary of John Boys, 1647–8', ed. D. E. Underdown, *BIHR*, xxxix (1966).

Burke, John, *A Genealogical and Heraldic History of the Commoners of Great Britain and Ireland*, 4 vols (Henry Colborn, London, 1833–8).

Burke, John and John Bernard, *A Genealogical and Heraldic Dictionary of the Landed Gentry of Great Britain and Ireland*, 3 vols (Henry Colborn, London, 1849).

Burnet, Gilbert, *History of My Own Time*, ed. Osmund Airy, 2 vols (Clarendon Press, Oxford, 1897).

—— (ed.), *The Memoires of the Lives and Actions of James and William Dukes of Hamilton and Castleherald ... 1625–1652*, (R. Royston, London, 1677).

Burton, Thomas, *Diary*, ed. J. T. Rutt, 4 vols (Henry Colburn, London, 1828).

Calendar of the Clarendon State Papers, 4 vols (Clarendon Press, Oxford, 1869–1932).

Calendar of the Manuscripts in the William Salt Library, Stafford, ed. M. E. Cornford and E. B. Miller, William Salt Archaeological Society (London, 1921).

Calendar of the Proceedings of the Committee for Compounding, 1643–1660, ed. M. A. E. Green, 5 vols (HMSO, London, 1889–92).

Calendar of State Papers, Domestic Series, Addenda: March 1625 to 1649, ed. W. D. Hamilton and S. C. Lomas (HMSO, London, 1897).

Calendar of State Papers, Domestic Series [1644–54] (HMSO, London, 1875–93).

Calendar of State Papers, Ireland, 1647–1660, ed. Robert P. Mahaffy (HMSO, London, 1903).

Calendar of State Papers ... Venice, 1647–1652, 1653–1654, ed. Allen B. Hinds (HMSO, London, 1927–9).

Camden Society, lxxiv: Richard Symonds, *Diary of the Marches of the Royal Army during the Great Civil War*, ed. Charles Edward Long (1859).

—— new ser., xii: *The Quarrel between the Earl of Manchester and Oliver Cromwell*, ed. David Masson (1875).

—— new ser., xxvii: *The Hamilton Papers, 1638–1650*, ed. S.R. Gardiner (1880).

—— new ser., xl: *The Nicholas Papers, i: 1641–1652*, ed. George F. Warner (1886).

—— new ser., l: *The Nicholas Papers, ii: 1653–1655*, ed. George F. Warner (1892).

—— new ser., xlix, liv, lx, lxii: *Clarke Papers*, 4 vols, ed. C. H. Firth (1891–1901).

—— 4th ser., xxi: Edmund Ludlow[e], *A Voyce from the Watch Tower: Part Five 1660–1662*, ed. A. B. Worden (1978).

Carte, Thomas, *A Collection of Original Letters and Papers ... 1641 to 1660. Found among the Duke of Ormonde's Papers*, 2 vols (A. Millar, London, 1739).

The Carte Manuscripts in the Bodleian Library, Oxford, ed. C. W. Russell and J. P. Prendergast (HMSO, London, 1871).

Carter, Matthew, *A Most True and Exact Relation of That as Honourable as Unfortunate Expedition of Kent, Essex and Colchester ... 1648*, (no publisher, London, 1650).

Cary, Henry (ed.), *Memorials of the Great Civil War in England from 1646 to 1652*, 2 vols (Henry Colburn, London, 1842).

Chetham Society, II: *Tracts relating to Military Proceedings in Lancashire during the Great Civil War* (1884).

City and County of Kingston upon Hull, *Calendar of the Ancient Deeds, Letters, Miscellaneous Old Documents, &c. in the Archives of the Corporation*, ed. L. M. Stanewell (Hull, 1951).

Clarendon State Papers, ed. R. Scrope and T. Monkhouse, 3 vols (Clarendon Printing House, Oxford, 1767–86).

Clarendon, Edward Hyde, 1st Earl of, *The History of the Rebellion and Civil Wars in England*, ed. W. D. Macray, 6 vols (Clarendon Press, Oxford, 1888).

——*A History of the Rebellion and Civil Wars in Ireland* (Patrick Dugan, Dublin, 1719–20).

Cokayne, George Edward [G. E. C.], *The Complete Peerage of England, Scotland, Ireland, Great Britain and the United Kingdoms*, 2nd edn, 13 vols (St Catherine's, London, 1910–59).

Collins, Arthur, *Peerage of England, Genealogical, Biographical and Historical*, 9 vols (Rivington, London, 1812).

A Complete Collection of State Trials and Proceedings for High Treason, 4th edn, ed. Francis Hargrave, 11 vols (Bathurst, etc., London, 1776–81).

Cromwelliana, ed. Machell Stace (George Smeeton, London, 1810).

Dowsing, William, *The Journal of William Dowsing, A. D. 1643–44*, ed. J. Charles Wall (London, n.d.).

Dugdale, Sir William, *The Life, Diary and Correspondence of Sir William Dugdale*, ed. W. Hamper (Harding, Lepard and Co., London, 1827).

——*A Short View of the Late Troubles in England* (Moses Pitt, London, 1681).

Dunlop, Robert, *Ireland under the Commonwealth*, 2 vols (Manchester University Press, Manchester, 1913).

Edwardes, Thomas, *Gangraena*, 3 vols (Ralph Smith, London, 1646).

Evelyn, John, *Diary*, ed. E. S. de Beer, 6 vols (Clarendon Press, Oxford, 1955).

——*Diary and Correspondence*, ed. William Bray, 4 vols (G. Bell, London, 1887–9).

Fairfax, Brian, *A Catalogue of the Curious Collection of Pictures of George Villiers, Duke of Buckingham ... with the Life of George Villiers, Duke of Buckingham* (W. Bathoe, London, 1758).

Fairfax Deposit, Bodleian Library. A deposit of several hundred pamphlets, mostly pertaining to the 1640s, some with shorthand notes by John Rushworth. Some of these pamphlets are not listed in Donald Wing's *Short-Title Catalogue, 1641–1700*.

Fairfax, Thomas, *The Fairfax Correspondence*, ed. George W. Johnson, 2 vols (Richard Bentley, London, 1848).

Firebrace, Capt. C. W. *Honest Harry, being a Biography of Sir Henry Firebrace, Knight (1619–1691)* (John Murray, London, 1932).

Firebrace, Henry, *Memoirs of the Two Last Years of the Reign of ... King Charles I,* By Sir Tho. Herbert, Major [Rob.] Huntington, Col. Edw. Coke and Mr Hen. Firebrace (Robert Clavell, London, 1702).

Firth, C. H. and Rait, R. S. (eds), *The Acts and Ordinances of the Interregnum, 1642–1660,* 3 vols (HMSO, London, 1911).

Foster, Joseph, *Alumni Oxonienses: the members of the University of Oxford, 1500–1714,* 4 vols (Parker, Oxford, 1891–2).

—— (ed.) *London Marriage Licences 1521–1869* (Bernard Quaritch, London, 1887).

——*Pedigrees of the County Families of Yorkshire,* 4 vols (W. Wilfred Head, London, 1874–5).

——*Pedigrees Recorded at the Visitation of the County Palatine of Durham* [1575, 1615, 1656] (Joseph Foster, London, 1887).

——*The Register of Admissions to Gray's Inn 1521–1889* (privately printed, London, 1889).

Gardiner, S. R. (ed.), *The Constitutional Documents of the Puritan Revolution, 1625–1660,* 3rd edn (Clarendon Press, Oxford, 1906).

Gilbert, Sir John T. (ed.), *A Contemporary History of Affairs in Ireland from 1641 to 1652,* Irish Archaeological and Celtic Society, 3 vols (1879–80).

Gretton, R. H., *The Burford Records* (Clarendon Press, Oxford, 1920).

Grey, Zachary, *An Impartial Examination of the Third Volume of Mr. Daniel Neal's History of the Puritans ... with a large appendix of letters and papers copied from original manuscripts of the late John Nalson, LL.D.* (A. Bettesworth and C. Hitch, London, 1737).

Gwynne, John, *Military Memoires of the Great Civil War* (Archibald Constable, Edinburgh, 1822).

Haller, William and Davies, Godfrey (eds), *The Leveller Tracts 1647–1653* (Columbia University Press, New York, 1944).

Hammond, Robert, *Letters between Colonel Robert Hammond Governor of the Isle of Wight and the Committee of Lords and Commons at Derby House, General Fairfax, Lieut. General Cromwell, Commissary General Ireton, &c. relating to King Charles I while he was Confined in Carisbrooke Castle in that Island* (Robert Horsfield, London, 1764).

Harleian Miscellany, ed. W. Oldys, 10 vols (London 1808–13).

Heath, James, *Flagellum: or the life and death, birth and burial of Oliver Cromwell the late usurper* (L. R., London, 1663).

Henry, Philip, *Diaries and Letters of Philip Henry, 1631–1696,* ed. Matthew Henry Lee (Paul, London, 1882).

Herbert, Sir Thomas, *Memoirs of the Two Last Years of the Reign of King Charles I* (G. & W. Nicol, London, 1813).

Heywood, Oliver, and T. Dickenson, *The Nonconformist Register of Baptisms, Marriages and Deaths* (Brighouse, London, 1881).

Hodgson, Capt. John, *Original Memoirs Written during the Great Civil War; Being the Life of Sir Henry Slingsby and Memoirs of Capt. Hodgson* (Constable, Edinburgh, 1806).

——*Autobiography of Captain John Hodgson,* ed. J. Horsfall Turner, (A. B. Boyes, Brighouse, 1882).

Holles, Denzil, *Memoirs* (T. Goodwin, London, 1699).

Hutchinson, Lucy, *Memoirs of the Life of Colonel Hutchinson*, ed. James Sutherland (Oxford University Press, London, 1973).

Inner Temple, *Students Admitted to the Inner Temple 1547–1660*, ed. Joseph Foster (privately printed, London, 1877).

Jaffray, Alexander, *Diary of Alexander Jaffray*, ed. John Barclay, 3rd edn (George and Robert King, Aberdeen, 1856).

Johnson, D. A. and Vaisey, D. G., *Staffordshire and the Great Rebellion* (Staffordshire County Council, Stafford, 1965).

Josselin, Ralph, *The Diary of Ralph Josselin 1616–1683*, ed. Alan Macfarlane, British Academy, Records of Social and Economc History, new ser., III (1976).

Journal of the House of Commons, III–VII [1642–59] (London, 1803–13).

Journal of the House of Lords, VII–X [1644–9] (London, n.d.).

Kentish Sources II: Kent and the Civil War, ed. Elizabeth Melling Kent Archives Office (1960).

Ludlow[e], Edmund, *Memoirs*, ed. C. H. Firth, 2 vols (Clarendon Press, Oxford, 1894).

Luke, Sir Samuel, *The Letter Books of Sir Samuel Luke 1644–45*, ed. H. G. Tibbutt (HMSO, London, 1963).

Maseres, Francis (ed.), *Select Tracts relating to the Civil Wars in England*, 2 vols (R. Bickerstaffe, London, 1815–26).

Massachusetts Historical Society, 5th ser., VIII (1882): *Winthrop Letters*.

Mayer, J. (ed.), 'Inedited Letters of Cromwell, Colonel Jones, Bradshaw and other Regicides', *Transactions of the Historic Society of Lancashire and Cheshire*, new ser., I (1860–1).

Meikle, H. W. (ed.) *Correspondence of the Scots Commissioners in London, 1644–1646*, Roxburghe Club (1917).

Middle Temple, *Register of Admissions to the Honourable Society of the Middle Temple, I: Fifteenth Century to 1781* (Butterworth, London, 1949).

The Minute Books of the Dorset Standing Committee, 23rd Sept. 1646, to 8th May 1650, ed. Charles H. Mayo (Wm Pollard, Exeter, 1902).

Morrison, Paul G., Index of Printers, Publishers and Booksellers in Donald Wing's Short-Title Catalogue.

Morton, Arthur Leslie (ed.), *Freedom in Arms: a selection of Leveller writings* (Seven Seas, Berlin, 1975).

Nickolls, John (ed.), *Original Letters and Papers of State Addressed to Oliver Cromwell ... MDCXLIX to MDCLVIII, Found among the Political Collections of Mr. John Milton* (John Whiston, London, 1743).

Nicoll, John, *A Diary of Public Transactions and Other Occurrences, Chiefly in Scotland, from January 1650 to June 1667*, ed. David Laing, Bannatyne Club (1836).

Noble, M., *The Lives of the English Regicides*, 2 vols (J. Stockdale, London, 1798).

Nuttall, G. F. (ed.), *Early Quaker Letters, from the Swarthmore MSS, to 1660* (privately printed, London, 1952).

Oxfordshire Record Society, *The Royalist Ordnance Papers, 1642–1646*, ed. Ian Roy, 2 pts (1963–4, 1971–3).

The Parliamentary or Constitutional History of England [Old Parliamentary History], 2nd edn, 24 vols (J. & R. Tonson, London, 1762–3).

Peacock, Edward (ed.), The Army Lists of the Roundheads and Cavaliers, 2nd edn (Chatto and Windus, London, 1874).

Peck, Francis, Desiderata Curiosa, 2 vols (London, 1732–5).

Records of the Borough of Nottingham, v: 1625–1702, ed. John Henry Brown (Bernard Quaritch, London, 1900).

Records of the County of Wiltshire, being Extracts from the Quarter Sessions Great Rolls of the Seventeenth Century, ed. Edward B. H. Cunnington (G. Simpson, Devizes, 1931).

Records of the English Province of the Society of Jesus, ii, ed. Henry Foley, SJ (Burns and Oates, London, 1884).

Royal Commission on Historical Manuscripts, Reports (HMSO, London):

   4 Fifth Report, Lechmere MSS (1876)
   5 Sixth Report, House of Lords MSS, 1644–47 (1877)
   6 Seventh Report, House of Lords MSS, 1648–65 (1879)
   15 Tenth Report, Appendix vi, Braye MSS (1887)
   27 Twelfth Report, Appendix ix, Beaufort MSS, Gloucester MSS (1891)
   29 Thirteenth Report, Appendix i, Portland MSS, i (1891)
      Thirteenth Report, Appendix ii, Portland MSS, ii (1893)
      Fourteenth Report, Appendix ii, Portland MSS, iii (1894)
   51 Mr. F. W. Leyborne-Popham (1899)
   63 Earl of Egmont, i (1905)
   77 Lord De L'Isle and Dudley, vi (Sidney Papers) (1966)

Rump Songs (H. Brome and H. Marsh, London, 1662).

Rushworth, John, Historical Collections, 8 vols (D. Browne, London, 1721–2).

Ryves, Bruno, Mercurius Rusticus: or, the countries complaint (R. Green, Cambridge, 1685).

Scottish History Society, xviii: Scotland and the Commonwealth ... August 1651 to December 1653, ed. C. H. Firth (1895).

—— xxix–xxx: The Diplomatic Correspondence of Jean de Montereul ... 1645–48, ed. J. G. Fotheringham (1898–9).

—— xliv: Miscellany, ii: Sir Philip Musgrave's Relation (1904).

—— 2nd ser., xviii: Diary of Sir Archibald Johnston of Wariston, ii, 1650–1654, ed. David Hay Fleming (1919).

Somers, John (ed.), A Second Collection of Scarce and Valuable Tracts, 4 vols (F. Cogan, London, 1750).

Somerset Record Society, 28: Quarter Sessions Records for the County of Somerset, iii: Commonwealth 1646–1660, ed. E. H. Bates Harbin (1912).

Sprigge, Ioshua, Anglia Rediviva, England's Recovery (John Partridge, London, 1647).

Suffolk Records Society, 3: Suffolk and the Great Rebellion 1640–1660, ed. A. Everitt (1961).

—— 13: Suffolk Committee for Scandalous Ministers, ed. Clive Holmes (1970).

—— 17: The Field Book of Walsham-Le-Willows 1577, ed. K. M. Dodd (1974).

Surtees Society, 37: Nathan Drake, *A Journal of the First and Second Sieges of Pontefract Castle, 1644–5 ... with an Appendix of Evidence relating to the Third Siege* (1961).

—— 50: *Memoirs of the Life of Mr Ambrose Barnes* (1867).

Sydney Papers, ed. R. W. Blencowe (John Murray, London, 1825).

Thoresby Society, xi: *Some Civil War Accounts 1647–50*, ed. Ethel Kitson and E. Kitson Clark (1902).

Turner, Sir James, *Memoirs of his own Life and Times*, Bannatyne Club (Edinburgh, 1829).

Venn, John and J. A., *Alumni Cantabrigienses, part i: From the earliest times to 1751*, 4 vols (Cambridge University Press, Cambridge, 1922–7).

Walker, Clement, *Anarchia Anglicana, or the History of Independency Second Part* (no publisher, London, 1649).

—— *The Compleat History of Independency* (R. Royston, London, 1661).

Walker, Sir Edward, *Historical Discourses upon Several Occasions*, ed. H. Clopton (Samuel Keble, London, 1705).

Waller, William, *Vindication* (J. Debrett, London, 1793).

Walwyn, William, *The Writings of William Walwyn*, ed. Jack R. McMichael and Barbara Taft (University of Georgia Press, Athens, Ga., and London, 1989).

Whitelocke, Bulstrode, *Memorials of the English Affairs*, 4 vols (Oxford University Press, Oxford, 1853).

Winstanley, [J]errard, *The Works of Gerrard Winstanley*, ed. George H. Sabine (Cornell University Press, Ithaca, NY, 1941).

Winthrop, John, *Papers 1598–1649*, Massachusetts Historical Society, 5 vols (1929–47).

Wolfe, Don M. (ed.), *Leveller Manifestoes of the Puritan Revolution* (Thomas Nelson, New York, 1944; repr. London: Frank Cass, 1967).

Wood, Anthony à, *Athenae Oxonienses ... to which are added the Fasti*, 2 vols in 1 (Thomas Bennet, London, 1691–2).

—— *Fasti Oxonienses*, ed. Philip Bliss, 2 vols (Rivington, London, 1815–20).

—— *Athenae Oxonienses ... to which are added the Fasti*, ed. P. Bliss, 4 vols (Rivington, London, 1813–20).

—— *Fasti Oxonienses or Annals of the University of Oxford*, ed. P. Bliss, 2 vols (Rivington, London, 1815–20).

—— *The History and Antiquities of the University of Oxford* [*Annals*], ed. John Gutch, 2 vols (printed for the editor, Oxford, 1792–6).

Yorkshire Pedigrees, ed. J. W. Walker, 3 vols, Harleian Society, 94 (1942).

Young, Alexander, *Chronicles of the First Planters of the Colony of Massachusetts Bay from 1623 to 1636* (Little, Brown, Boston, Mass., 1846).

B Secondary Sources

Since this book was written a number of important secondary sources have been published, including Charles Carlton's *Going to the Wars: the experience of the British Civil Wars 1638–1651* (Routledge, London & New York, 1992); Barry Coward, *Cromwell* (Longman, London & New York, 1991); Jane Ohlmeyer, *Civil*

War and Restoration in the Three Stuart Kingdoms: the career of Randal MacDonnell, marquis of Antrim, 1609–1683 (Cambridge University Press, Cambridge, 1993); R. C. Richardson, (ed.), *Town and Countryside in the English Revolution* (Manchester University Press, Manchester & New York, 1992); John Morrill, *The Nature of the English Revolution* (Longman, Harlow, 1993). Those with a taste for the historiographical civil wars may wish to consult Mark Kishlansky, 'Saye what?', *HJ*, 33 (1990) and his 'Saye no more', *JBS*, 30 (1991); John Adamson, 'Politics and the nobility in civil-war England', *HJ*, 34 (1991), and the subsequent correspondence in the *Times Literary Supplement*, from January to April 1992.

1 Books

Adair, John, *Roundhead General: a military biography of Sir William Waller* (Macdonald, London, 1969).

Ashton, Robert, *The English Civil War: conservatism and revolution, 1603–1649* (Weidenfeld and Nicolson, London, 1978).

Aston, Margaret, *England's Iconoclasts, I: Laws against Images* (Clarendon Press, Oxford, 1988).

Aylmer, G. E., *The State's Servants* (Routledge and Kegan Paul, London, 1973).

——(ed.), *The Interregnum: the quest for settlement, 1646–1660* (Macmillan, London, 1972).

—— and R. Cant (eds), *A History of York Minster* (Clarendon Press, Oxford, 1977).

Beales, Derek and Geoffrey Best (eds), *History, Society and the Churches* (Cambridge University Press, Cambridge, 1985).

Berry, James and S. G. Lee, *A Cromwellian Major-General: the career of Colonel James Berry* (Clarendon Press, Oxford, 1938).

Bottigheimer, Karl S., *English Money and Irish Land* (Clarendon Press, Oxford, 1971).

Brailsford, H. N. *The Levellers and the English Revolution* (Cresset Press, London, 1961).

Burns, A. H. and P. Young, *The Great Civil War* (Eyre and Spottiswoode, London, 1959).

Burrage, Chaplin, *The Early English Dissenters*, 2 vols (Cambridge University Press, Cambridge, 1912).

Capp, B. S., *Cromwell's Navy: the fleet and the English Revolution, 1648–1660* (Clarendon Press, Oxford, 1989).

——*The Fifth Monarchy Men* (Faber and Faber, London, 1972).

Christianson, Paul, *Reformers and Babylon: English apocalyptic visions from the Reformation to the eve of the Civil War* (University of Toronto Press, Toronto, 1978).

Cliffe, J. T., *The Yorkshire Gentry from the Reformation to the Civil War* (Athlone Press, London, 1969).

Cohn, Norman, *The Pursuit of the Millenium* (Secker and Warburg, London, 1957).

Coleby, Andrew, *Central Government and the Localities: Hampshire, 1649–1689* (Cambridge University Press, Cambridge, 1987).

Crawford, Patricia, *Denzil Holles, 1598–1660* (RHS, London, 1979).

Davis, J. C., *Fear, Myth and History: the Ranters and the historians* (Cambridge University Press, Cambridge, 1986).

Denton, Barry, *Naseby Fight* (Partizan Press, Leigh-on-Sea, Essex, 1988).

— *William Thompson: Leveller, revolutionary or mutineer?* (Partizan Press, Leigh-on-Sea, Essex, 1988).

Douglas, W. S., *Cromwell's Scotch Campaigns: 1650–51* (E. Stock, London, 1898).

Dow, F. D., *Cromwellian Scotland, 1651–1660* (John Donald, Edinburgh, 1979).

Duffy, Christopher, *Siege Warfare* (Routledge and Kegan Paul, London, 1979).

Eales, Jacqueline, *Puritans and Roundheads: the Harleys of Brampton Bryan* (Cambridge University Press, Cambridge, 1990).

Edwards, Peter, *The Horse Trade in Tudor and Stuart England* (Cambridge University Press, Cambridge, 1988).

Everitt, Alan, *The Community of Kent and the Great Rebellion, 1640–60* (Leicester University Press, Leicester, 1966).

Firth, C. H., *Cromwell's Army*, 4th edn (Methuen, London, 1962).

— and Godfrey Davies, *The Regimental History of Cromwell's Army*, 2 vols (Clarendon Press, Oxford, 1940).

Fletcher, Anthony, *Reform in the Provinces* (Yale University Press, New Haven, Conn. and London, 1986).

— *A County Community in Peace and War: Sussex 1600–1660* (Longman, London, 1975).

Gardiner, S. R., *History of the Commonwealth and Protectorate, 1649–1656*, 4 vols (Longmans, Green, London, 1903).

— *History of the Great Civil War, 1642–1649*, 4 vols (Longmans, Green, London, 1893).

Gilbert, John T. (ed.), *A Contemporary History of Affairs in Ireland from 1641 to 1652*, 3 vols (Irish Archeological and Celtic Society, 1879–80).

Gimmelfarb-Brack, Marie, *Liberté, Égalité, Fraternité, Justice! La vie et l'oeuvre de Richard Overton* (P. Lang, Berne, 1979).

Greaves, Richard and Robert Zaller (eds), *Biographical Dictionary of British Radicals in the Seventeenth Century*, 3 vols (Harvester, Brighton, 1982–4).

Gregg, Pauline, *Freeborn John* (Harrap, London, 1961).

Guizot, François, *History of the English Revolution of 1640* (Bohn, London, 1856).

Hill, Christopher, *Continuity and Change in Seventeenth-Century England* (Weidenfeld and Nicolson, London, 1974).

— *The Experience of Defeat: Milton and some contemporaries* (Faber and Faber, London, 1984).

— *A Tinker and a Poor Man: John Bunyan and his Church, 1628–1688* (Knopf, New York, 1989).

— *The World Turned Upside Down* (Temple Smith, London, 1972).

Holmes, Clive, *The Eastern Association in the English Civil War* (Cambridge University Press, Cambridge, 1974).

Howell, Roger, *Newcastle upon Tyne and the Puritan Revolution* (Oxford University Press, London, 1967).

Hughes, Anne, *Politics, Society and Civil War in Warwickshire* (Cambridge University Press, Cambridge, 1987).

Hutton, Ronald, *Charles II* (Clarendon Press, Oxford, 1989).

—— *The Royalist War Effort, 1642–1646* (Longman, London, 1982).

James, M. E., *Society, Politics and Culture* (Cambridge University Press, Cambridge, 1986).

Jones, Colin, et al. (eds), *Politics and People in Revolutionary England* (Basil Blackwell, Oxford, 1986).

Kaplan, L., *Politics and Religion during the English Revolution* (New York University Press, New York, 1976).

Keeler, M. F., *The Long Parliament* (American Philosophical Society, Philadelphia, 1954).

Keen, Maurice, *Chivalry* (Yale University Press, New Haven, Conn., 1984).

Ketton-Cremer, R. W., *Norfolk in the Civil War* (Faber and Faber, London, 1969).

Kishlansky, Mark, *The Rise of the New Model Army* (Cambridge University Press, Cambridge and New York, 1979).

Lamont, William, *Godly Rule* (Macmillan, London, 1969).

Laurence, Anne, *Parliamentary Army Chaplains, 1642–1651* (RHS, London, 1990).

Lindley, Keith, *Fenland Riots, and the English Revolution* (Heinemann, London, 1982).

MacCormack, J. R., *Revolutionary Politics in the Long Parliament* (Harvard University Press, Cambridge, Mass., 1973).

MacGregor, J. F. and B. Reay (eds), *Radical Religion in the English Revolution* (Oxford University Press, Oxford, 1984).

Macpherson, C. B., *The Political Theory of Possessive Individualism* (Clarendon Press, Oxford, 1962).

Malcolm, Joyce Lee, *Caesar's Due* (RHS, London, 1983).

Manning, Brian, *The English People and the English Revolution, 1640–1649* (Heinemann, London, 1976).

—— (ed.), *Politics, Religion and the English Civil War* (E. J. Arnold, London, 1973).

Moody, T. W., et al. (eds), *New History of Ireland*, vol. III (Clarendon Press, Oxford, 1976).

Morrill, John (ed.), *Oliver Cromwell* (Longman, London, 1990).

—— (ed.), *Reactions to the English Civil War* (Macmillan, London, 1982).

—— *The Revolt of the Provinces* (Allen and Unwin, London, 1976).

Morton, A. L. (ed.), *Freedom in Arms* (Seven Seas, Berlin, 1975).

Orwell, George, *Homage to Catalonia* (Secker and Warburg, London, 1951).

Pape, T., *Newcastle-under-Lyme in Tudor and Early Stuart Times* (Manchester University Press, Manchester, 1938).

Parker, Geoffrey, *The Military Revolution* (Cambridge University Press, Cambridge, 1988).

Pearl, Valerie, *London and the Outbreak of the Puritan Revolution* (Oxford University Press, London, 1961).

Pennington, D. H. and Keith Thomas (eds), *Puritans and Revolutionaries* (Clarendon Press, Oxford, 1978).

Phillips, John R., *The Reformation of Images* (University of California Press, Berkeley, 1973).

Richards, Thomas, *History of the Puritan Movement in Wales* (National Eisteddford Association, London, 1920).

Root, Ivan, *The Great Rebellion* (Batsford, London, 1965).

Rowe, Violet, *Sir Henry Vane the Younger* (Athlone Press, London, 1970).

Savage, James, *A Genealogical Dictionary of the First Settlers of New England*, 4 vols (Little, Brown, Boston, Mass., 1860–2).

Schwoerer, Lois, *No Standing Armies!* (Johns Hopkins University Press, Baltimore, 1974).

Simms, J. G., *War and Politics in Ireland, 1649–1730* (Hambledon Press, London, 1986).

Snow, Vernon F., *Essex the Rebel* (University of Nebraska Press, Lincoln, Nebr., 1970).

Staley, V., *Hierurgia Anglicana*, rev. edn, 3 vols (De La Mare Press, London, 1902–4).

Stearns, R. P., *The Strenuous Puritan: Hugh Peter, 1598–1660* (University of Illinois Press, Urbana, 1954).

Stevenson, David, *Revolution and Counter-Revolution in Scotland, 1644–1651* (RHS, London, 1977).

Styles, P., *Studies in Seventeenth Century West Midland History* (Roundwood Press, Kineton, Warwicks, 1978).

Tatham, G. B., *The Puritans in Power* (Cambridge University Press, Cambridge, 1913).

Thirsk, Joan, *Horses in Early Modern England: for service, for pleasure, for power* (University of Reading, Reading, 1978).

—— (ed.), *The Agrarian History of England and Wales*, V, pt. ii (Cambridge University Press, Cambridge, 1985).

Thomas, Keith, *Man and the Natural World* (Allan Lane, London, 1983).

Tolmie, Murray, *The Triumph of the Saints* (Cambridge University Press, Cambridge, 1977).

Underdown, D. E., *Pride's Purge* (Clarendon Press, Oxford, 1971).

—— *Revel, Riot and Rebellion* (Clarendon Press, Oxford, 1986).

—— *Royalist Conspiracy in England, 1649–1660* (Yale University Press, New Haven, Conn., 1960).

—— *Somerset during the Civil War and Interregnum* (David and Charles, Newton Abbot, 1973).

Van Creveld, Martin L., *Supplying War* (Cambridge University Press, Cambridge, 1977).

Veall, D., *The Popular Movement for Law Reform 1640–1660* (Oxford University Press, London, 1970).

Walker, Eric C., *William Dell: master puritan* (Heffer, Cambridge, 1970).

Wedgwood, C. V., *The Trial of Charles I* (World Books edn, London, 1968).

Wilson, John, *Fairfax* (John Murray, London, 1985).

Woolrych, Austin, *Battles of the English Civil War* (Batsford, London, 1961).

——*Commonwealth to Protectorate* (Clarendon Press, Oxford, 1982).
——*Soldiers and Statesmen: the General Council of the Army and its debates, 1647–1648* (Clarendon Press, Oxford, 1987).
Worden, Blair, *The Rump Parliament, 1648–1653* (Cambridge University Press, Cambridge, 1974).
Young, Peter, *Naseby 1645* (Century Publishing, London, 1985).
——and W. Emberton, *Sieges of the Great Civil War* (Bell and Hyman, London, 1978).

2 Articles

Adamson, J. S. A., 'The baronial context of the English Civil War', *TRHS*, 5th ser., 40 (1990).
——'The English nobility and the projected settlement of 1647', *HJ*, 30 (1987).
——'Politics and the nobility in Civil War England', *HJ*, 34 (1991).
Aylmer, G. E., 'Collective mentalities in mid seventeenth-century England: IV. Cross currents: neutrals, trimmers and others', *TRHS*, 5th ser., 39 (1989).
Barnard, 'Crisis of identity among Irish protestants, 1641–1685', *P & P*, 127 (May 1990).
Broad, J., 'Gentry finances and the civil war: the case of the Buckinghamshire Verneys', *EcHR*, 2nd ser., xxxii (1979).
Bryan, D., 'Colonel Richard Grace 1651–1652', *Irish Sword*, 4 (1959–60).
Carlin, Noah, 'The Levellers and the conquest of Ireland in 1649', *HJ*, 30 (1987).
Cheshire, J. G., 'William Dowsing's destructions in Cambridgeshire', *Transactions of the Cambridgeshire and Huntingdonshire AS*, iii (1914).
Cotterell, M., 'Interregnum law reform: the Hale Commission of 1652', *EHR*, 83 (1968).
Cotton, A. N. B., 'Cromwell and the Self-Denying Ordinance', *History*, 62, n. 205 (1977).
——'John Dillingham, journalist of the Middle Group', *EHR*, 93 (1978).
Crawford, Patricia, ' "Charles Stuart, That Man of Blood" ', *JBS*, xvi (1977).
Davies, C. S. L., 'Provisions for armies, 1509–50, a study in the effectiveness of early Tudor government', *EcHR*, 2nd ser., xvii (1964–5).
Farnell, J. E., 'The usurpation of honest London householders: Barebone's parliament', *EHR*, 82 (1967).
Firth, C. H., 'The battle of Dunbar', *TRHS*, new ser., xiv (1900).
——'The expulsion of the Long Parliament', *History*, new ser., ii (1917–18).
——'Memoir of Major-General Thomas Harrison', *Procs of the American Antiquarian Society*, new ser., viii (1893).
Gardiner, S. R., 'The transplantation to Connaught', *EHR*, 14 (1899).
Gentles, Ian, 'The arrears of pay of the parliamentary army at the end of the first civil war', *BIHR*, xlvii (1975).
——'London Levellers and the English Revolution: the Chidleys and their circle', *JEH*, xxix (1978).
——'The sales of bishops' lands in the English Revolution, 1646–60', *EHR*, xcv (1980).

—— 'The struggle for London during the Second Civil War', *HJ*, 26 (1983).

Habakkuk, H. J., 'Public Finance and the sale of confiscated property during the interregnum', *EcHR*, 2nd ser., xv (1962–3).

Howell, Roger, 'The army and the English Revolution: the case of Robert Lilburne', *Archaeologia Aeliana*, 5th ser., ix (1981).

Hughes, Anne, 'Parliamentary tyranny? Indemnity proceedings and the impact of the civil war', *Midland History*, xi (1986).

Kishlansky, Mark, 'The case of the army truly stated: the creation of the New Model Army', *P & P*, 81 (1978).

—— 'Consensus politics and the structure of debate at Putney', *JBS*, 20 (1980–1).

—— 'What happened at Ware?', *HJ*, 25 (1982).

Lyndon, Brian, 'Essex and the king's cause in 1648', *HJ*, 29 (1986).

—— 'The parliament's army in Essex in 1648' *Journal of the Society for Army Historical Research*, 59 (1981).

McCarthy, W., 'The royalist collapse in Munster 1650–1652', *Irish Sword*, 6 (1963–4).

Morrill, John, 'The army revolt of 1647', *Britain and the Netherlands*, vi (1977).

—— 'Mutiny and discontent in English provincial armies 1645–1647', *P & P*, 56 (1972).

Mulligan, Lotte, 'Peace negotiations, politics and the Committee of Both Kingdoms, 1644–1646', *HJ*, xii (1969).

Mungeam, G. I., 'Contracts for the supply of equipment to the "New Model" Army in 1645', *Journal of the Arms and Armour Society*, vi (1968–70).

Murtagh, Diarmuid, 'Colonel Edward Wogan', *Irish Sword*, 2 (1954–6).

Porter, Stephen, 'The fire-raid in the English civil war', *War and Society*, 2 (1984).

—— 'Property destruction in the English civil war', *History Today*, 36 (Aug. 1986).

Quaife, G. R., 'The consenting spinster in a peasant society: aspects of premarital sex in "puritan" Somerset 1645–1660', *Journal of Social History*, 11 (1977).

Roy, Ian, 'England turned Germany? The aftermath of the civil war in its European context', *TRHS*, 5th ser., 28 (1978).

Simms, J. G., 'Cromwell at Drogheda, 1649', *Irish Sword*, 11 (1973–4).

Stern, Walter M., 'Gunmaking in seventeenth-century London', *Journal of the Arms and Armour Society*, i (1954).

Taft, Barbara, 'The Council of Officers' Agreement of the People, 1648/9' *HJ*, 28 (1985).

—— 'Voting lists of the Council of Officers, December 1648', *BIHR*, lii (1979).

Temple, Robert K. G., 'Discovery of a manuscript eye-witness account of the battle of Maidstone', *Archaeologia Cantiana*, xcvii (1981).

—— 'The original officer list of the New Model Army', *BIHR*, lix (1986).

Woolrych, Austin, 'The calling of Barebone's parliament' *EHR*, 80 (1966).

Worden, Blair, 'Providence and politics in Cromwellian England', *P & P*, n. 109 (1985).

Theses

Adamson, J. S. A., 'The Peerage in Politics 1645–1649', PhD thesis, Cambridge University, 1986.

Beats, Lynn, 'Politics and Government in Derbyshire 1640–1660', PhD thesis, University of Sheffield, 1978.

Black, Stephen F., 'The Judges of Westminster Hall during the Great Rebellion, 1640–1660', B Litt. thesis, Oxford University, 1979.

Jaggar, G., 'The Fortunes of the Whalley Family of Screveton, Notts', M. Phil. thesis, University of Southampton, 1973.

Lynch, G. J., 'The Risings of the Clubmen in the English Civil War', MA thesis, University of Manchester, 1973.

McParlin, Geoffrey E., 'The Herefordshire Gentry in County Government, 1625–1661', PhD thesis, University of Wales, Aberystwyth, 1981.

Massarella, Derek, 'The Politics of the Army, 1647–1660', PhD thesis, University of York, 1978.

Nagel, Lawson Chase, 'The Militia of London 1641–1649', PhD thesis, University of London, 1982.

Porter, Stephen, 'The Destruction of Urban Property in the English Civil War, 1642–1651', PhD thesis, University of London, 1984.

Reay, Barry G., 'Early Quaker Activity and Reactions to it 1652–1664', DPhil. thesis, Oxford University, 1979.

Reece, H. M. 'The Military Presence in England, 1649–1660', DPhil. thesis, Oxford University, 1981.

Wheeler, James Scott, 'English Army Finance and Logistics 1642–1660', PhD thesis, University of California, Berkeley, 1980.

Williams, James Richard, 'County and Municipal Government in Cornwall, Devon, Dorset and Somerset 1649–1660', PhD thesis, University of Bristol, 1981.

Wrightson, K. E., 'The Puritan Reformation of Manners with Special Reference to the counties of Lancashire and Essex 1640–1660', PhD thesis, University of Cambridge, 1973.

Index

Index

Lightning Source UK Ltd.
Milton Keynes UK
28 November 2009

146832UK00001B/99/P